Jürgen Straub, Doris W
Carlos Kölbl, Barbara Z
Pursuit of Meaning

JÜRGEN STRAUB, DORIS WEIDEMANN,
CARLOS KÖLBL, BARBARA ZIELKE (EDS.)
Pursuit of Meaning.
Advances in Cultural and
Cross-Cultural Psychology

[transcript]

Printing kindly supported by
Alfred-Anger-Fonds im Verein zur Förderung des
Kulturwissenschaftlichen Instituts in Essen

Bibliographic information published by Die Deutsche Bibliothek
Die Deutsche Bibliothek lists this publication in the Deutsche
Nationalbibliografie; detailed bibliographic data are available on the
Internet at http://dnb.ddb.de

© 2006 transcript Verlag, Bielefeld

Cover layout: Kordula Röckenhaus, Bielefeld
Cover illustration: Errata 1998, Aquarell auf Bütten, 29 x 41 cm,
© Romain Finke, www.romainfinke.com
Typeset by: Doris Weidemann, Chemnitz
Printed by: Majuskel Medienproduktion, Wetzlar
ISBN 3-89942-234-1

Distributed in North America by:

Transaction Publishers
New Brunswick (U.S.A.) and London (U.K.)

Transaction Publishers	Tel.: (732) 445-2280
Rutgers University	Fax: (732) 445-3138
35 Berrue Circle	for orders (U.S. only):
Piscataway, NJ 08854	toll free 888-999-6778

CONTENTS

Methodology and Comparison

Methods and Instruments

Self and Development in Culture

ACKNOWLEDGEMENTS

The book at hand is a result of several preparatory steps: A first initiation was marked by an international symposium *Cultural and Cross-Cultural Psychology. Theoretical and Methodological Alternatives and Controversies* held at the Institute for Advanced Studies in the Humanities (*Kulturwissenschaftliches Institut*), Essen, Germany, from May 17th to 19th 2001. Once again, the institute has constituted an ideal surrounding for this purpose. Not only have we been granted generous financial support, which we owe to the institute's chairman, Prof. Jörn Rüsen; furthermore, we have benefited greatly from the competent and highly professional support, particularly rendered by the office of Gabriele Schäfers and Monika Wühle. I would like to thank all those who have assisted in the preparation, implementation, and evaluation of the symposium, as well as all the scholars, who, following the ideals of the institute, have made their valuable contributions, and encouraged inspiring discussions. It was their productive suggestions which created the idea for this book.

The primary purpose of this book is to display and reflect theoretical and methodological advances in cultural and cross-cultural psychology, with due regard to examples of empirical research practice. Thus, the thematically suitable presentations given at the above-mentioned symposium have been revised and integrated, and some additional contributions have been collected, too. I would like to express my gratitude to all the authors who have made this project possible—which, as I would like to emphasize, applies to those colleagues, too, whose presentations could not be included in this book. Many of the imprinted contributions reflect what has been discussed then, during the symposium. The scope of the book encompasses both the complementary perspectives brought up during our debates, as well as the controversial view points, ways of thinking, and empirical approaches. This productive "diversity in unity" of, as is commonly stated, the contemporary *culture inclusive psychology* has long become an integral part of current discussions and researches into this field.

Complex, joint projects such as this book require creative authors—and their patience with the editors. The same can be said about the numerous persons who have generously lent their hands 'in the background'. In our case, a spate of student assistants have taken their share by designing lay-out sketches, and revising (or proof-reading) manuscripts: Jacqueline Alter, Frances Blüml, Qingying Jiang, Manon Karls, Eva Lösch, Cordula Sonder, and, taking the lion's share of the workload, Levke Heitmann, have proven their great dedication and reliability. Furthermore, Nancy Kluth has provided accurate linguistic revisions and translations, which Paula Ross has linguistically standardized, and finalized. Maik Arnold and Angela Lehmann have provided graphic solutions. Corina Markert has handled correspondence and organizational tasks. I would like to thank them all for their support, which has been funded by the Philosophical Faculty of Chemnitz University of Technology.

My co-editors and colleagues have constantly supported and accompanied the work process from the initial symposium until this very moment. My special appreciation goes to Doris Weidemann, who has, as always, shown greatest decisiveness, energy, and professionalism, and who has held this "bunch of diligent helpers" together.

Chemnitz, November 2005

Jürgen Straub

Psychology, Culture, and the Pursuit of Meaning: An Introduction

Jürgen Straub & Doris Weidemann

Culture and Psychology

Contemporary psychology offers countless theoretical and methodological studies in which the concept of culture is central. This could be seen as the belated confirmation of an insight Stuart Chase had more than half a century ago, when he wrote that the cultural concept of anthropology and sociology "is coming to be regarded as the foundation stone of the social sciences" (Chase 1948: 59). Alfred Kroeber and Clyde Kluckhohn cited Stuart at the very beginning of their famous analysis of the concept of culture, first published in 1952. Though more guarded, they nonetheless left no doubt that "the idea of culture, in the technical anthropological sense, is one of the key notions of contemporary American thought" (1967: 3). They saw Bronislaw Malinowski's dictum confirmed, and along with him, regarded culture "as the most central problem of all social [and cultural] sciences" (3). They expressly included psychology among the disciplines in which this problem had appeared.

However, it took quite some time before academic psychology studied cultural realities in any notable way, and even today, it seems no more certain that the now widespread talk of 'culture' is more than lip service to a mode of research that barely touches the 'deep grammar' of psychological investigation. The fear that cultural and cross-cultural psychology will remain marginal in a discipline that again sees its future in an alliance with biology and other natural sciences is not far-fetched (Laucken 2001).

Certainly in many countries there are serious and ongoing attempts to relate psychology to cultural and especially comparative perspectives. The *cross-cultural psychology* that has been built up over the last half century, foremost in the United States, has certainly attained critical mass. Yet, the *cultural psychology* that has departed more or less deliberately from the domain of nomological thought, and is attempting to install a predominantly interpretive approach similar to that of Cultural Studies, has likewise taken shape and gained some attention. It has meanwhile clearly left its former position as a threshold phenomenon, as the work of Jerome Bruner, Ernst Boesch, and numerous other colleagues, including many present here, emphatically demonstrate (Miller 1997; Boesch and Straub 2006). The integration of culture into psychological thought is further propelled by the search for *indigenous psychologies* that aim to develop psychological theories, constructs, and methodologies that are appropriate to cultural and societal realities of the countries that have only during recent decades imported the (Euro-American) academic discipline of psychology. Despite their different background and motives, cultural, cross-cultural, and indigenous psychology contribute to the development of a culture-inclusive approach that is increasingly being acknowledged by the discipline's mainstream.

Now, neither nomological cross-cultural psychology, interpretive cultural psychology, nor indigenous psychology is homogenous. These summary designations suggest a unity that does not really exist. They also suggest a competition, which is somewhat problematic. This now common distinction not only obscures commonalities, but also could discourage cooperative and complementary relations from the outset. This would be professionally regrettable. We should keep this in mind, even though we should not overlook the real differences between the aforementioned tendencies (Straub 2001, Straub and Thomas 2003). This is especially true if one has an interest in integrative efforts. A successful integration of 'the different' preserves its particularity. This presumes that the individuality of the 'elements' to be integrated has actually been precisely identified and named. Integration does not eliminate difference, but rather unifies it into a larger form in order to conceive this as the unity of oppositions.

Despite considerable debates between representatives of the nomological cross-cultural psychology and interpretive cultural psychology, we should recall that the participants display important commonalities, which even in contemporary psychology should not go unremarked.

Thus, the attempt to avoid the errors of ethnocentric or nostrocentric thought constitutes a shared central objective of *both* approaches. Criticism of ethnocentric representation of 'the other' has unanimously been directed at two points. First, the investigation and representation of the other with conceptual and methodological instruments that are clearly designed for one's own culture, for its practices and symbolic contents, fails to appropriately describe, understand, and explain different cultural realities. Research that uncritically views 'the other' in terms of its own perspectives, notions, and cognitive schemata is bound to miss scientific epistemic objectives and is prone to succumbing to own projections. It is precisely this insight that has stimulated the search for indigenous methods, concepts, and theories. Yet, cognitive-epistemic assumptions of similarity that level empirical differences from the outset are not only intellectually dubious, but, second, also violate the practical imperatives of justice that hold the recognition of and respect for difference to be indispensable, not least of all in terms of cultural difference. The term 'culture' not only implies problems of epistemic representation, in other words problems of knowledge, but problems of justice, which require the empirically tenable representation of others and their life practices. Ethnology and cultural anthropology have most intensively taken up this question, for obvious reasons. If these disciplines did not simply follow in the wake of 'imperialist' adventures, their constitutive 'curiosity about the other' was not always harmless either since this other was of course very often conceived in the image of the self, and by 'own' descriptive and normative standards.

Such debates are well underway in cultural, cross-cultural, and indigenous psychology. Basically, and in general, all areas of psychological research are supposed to increasingly respect culturally determined differences—even when, as in large areas of nomological cross-cultural psychology, the ultimate objective is not only the identification of such differences, but also, and perhaps primarily, the search for empirically valid psychological universals. It seems to us pointless to argue over which represents the more noble or 'scientific' objective. Both are possible, both are legitimate, and in certain cases, either may be more interesting or relevant. On the other hand, a further aspect of the concept of culture demands the greatest attention and the greatest effort. Here we proceed to one of the central themes of this volume.

Culture as Construction and Structure of Meaning

The concept of 'culture' has not only the aforementioned function of bringing scholarly attention to psychologically significant cultural differences and their practical construction and significance. It does not simply make us more aware that potential differences must be accounted for and reflected on, where similarity, along with a corresponding methodological and conceptual consistency, could once have been assumed. For the methods of the empirical disciplines, there is another, at least equally exciting and very basic aspect of the concept of culture. In cross-cultural and cultural psychology today, when we speak of 'culture,' it requires a

basic hermeneutic concept—for better or for worse; completely deliberate, or completely unconscious. 'Culture' unavoidably comprises a specific way of conceiving the psychologically relevant facts. Psychological
facts are thus *basically meaning-structured.* Meaning here is not something added to a (constructed) psychological 'entity'—whether phenomenon, structure, process, or function—by discrete mental acts. It does
not first appear ex post facto, in acts of interpretation. For the psyche, as
cross-cultural and cultural psychology see it, it is actually constitutive.
This has been shown paradigmatically for action, a concept now indispensable to psychology, and which was quite strategically conceived
against the behaviorist concept of 'mere' reactive behavior. The point is
not that we cannot differently grasp some 'something,' and thereby understand and treat it differently. Without meaning, however, psychological entities would have no ontological basis as far as cross-cultural and
cultural psychology are concerned. Countless passages from the literature
could be cited here in support of this point—including authors representing cross-cultural psychology.

Every writer starts from the assumption that the concept of culture is
necessary because it represents very particular—not egological, individualistic, or in the narrower sense intentionalist—aspects of the mean-
ing-structure of psychological 'entities,' and helps disclose them. Segall
expresses this much in a lapidary way when he says, "human behavior is
meaningful only when viewed in the socio-cultural context in which it
occurs" (Segall 1979: 3). This passage, though chosen at random, is perfectly representative. The concept of culture has, even for representatives
of nomological psychology, the status of a basic hermeneutic concept,
which is functionally related to the interpretive analysis of psychological
realities. For how else but through interpretation, i.e., through a hermeneutic praxis, could meaning be explicated? This basic insight is unavoidable, even if one has not yet confronted the detailed theoretical
bases of specific interpretive perspectives or of methodologically controlled interpretation, and even if the prospect might make one uneasy.

The point is this: 'culture' means meaning, as a rule expressis verbis,
and the study of culture is (or, consequently, should be), openly or sur-
reptitiously, a hermeneutic practice. The concept of culture opens the
door to efforts of interpretation. Cultural or cross-cultural research without a focus on structures of meaning would be difficult. On this basic,
general point, there is surprisingly broad agreement. This is true even
with respect to the basic methodological consequences.

Some of the theoretical and methodological *commonalities* are, for
example, expressed in the *consistent usage of the same concepts.*

Thus, Kenneth Pike's (1954, 1967) methodologically and practically important distinction between the emic and the etic standpoint in the description of behavior are important in a nomologically oriented cross-cultural psychology *as well as* in cultural psychology. John Berry (1969, 1980, 1999) soon took up Pike's distinction, in his influential categorization of the different approaches in the domain of cross-cultural psychology, where he at the same time argued for a certain integration of the emic and the etic perspectives (see Berry et al. 1992). The discussion continues, as for example a 1999 article by Hede Helfrich in *Culture & Psychology*, and the subsequent commentaries by Chaudhary, Berry, and Lonner, as well as Baerveldt and Verheggen, show (also see Helfrich and Jahoda, in this volume).

An Outline of this Volume

These commonalities constitute the shared ground of all contributions to this volume. While authors explore the interplay of psyche and culture from different angles and toward different ends (including, e.g., theoretical, historical, methodological, and empirical perspectives) several reoccurring themes and concerns can be identified that appear as indicative of current trends and developments in the larger fields of cross-cultural and cultural psychology. These thematic orientations also serve to structure contributions to this volume.

The concept of culture and its integration into psychological theory still constitutes a topic of crucial *theoretical* concern. Traditional notions of 'culture' as discretely identifiable, integral, homogeneous, and static entities have increasingly been abandoned in favor of relational approaches, thus acknowledging the criticism of overly simple and often dichotomous concepts of culture, which was, for example, voiced by Hermans and Kempen. In their influential article (that appeared alongside a contribution by Marshall Segall, Walter Lonner, and John Berry "On the Flowering of Culture in Behavioral Research" in the October 1998 *American Psychologist*), they point to three developments of globalization that theories of culture must take into account: "(a) cultural connections leading to hybridization, (b) the emergence of a heterogeneous global system, and (c) the increasing cultural complexity" (1111). The resulting challenges for cultural and cross-cultural psychological research and theory building have become central topics of theory-oriented as well as of methodological strands of discourse. In the present volume, the first section addresses conceptual and theoretical issues when exploring 'glimpses of the past and current perspectives'.

Anyone interested in the meaning-structures of cultural realities and culturally mediated actions (cognitions, emotions, motives, etc.), will have to reassess psychology not only with respect to its object, but also to its *methodology*. Following the insight that culture is more than objective or reifiable cultural facts, the search for a different (mostly qualitative) methodology is another prominent issue (Ratner 1997; for a discussion of Ratner's approach see Kölbl and Straub 2001). Acts of description and comparison of cultural realities require alternative, yet precisely defined scientific operations that ensure, for example, appropriate sampling procedures, controlled cross-cultural comparisons, and adequate data interpretation. Psychological-hermeneutic approaches have progressed and increasingly provide an exact methodology that explicates the nature and validation of its their core activity: interpretation. The second section of this book is thus devoted to issues of 'methodology and comparison'.

Building on a general interpretive research framework, section three focuses on different 'methods and instruments' in the field of cultural and cross-cultural psychology. Heterogeneity of approaches indicates a high level of methodical creativity that draws equally on historical traditions, interdisciplinary cooperation, and mainstream psychological methods. The presentation of empirical research designs and results is not restricted to this section but also extends to other contributions that have been grouped under different headings.

Neither cross-cultural nor cultural psychology relies on or may be defined by the choice of distinct topics, concepts and methods. Both have approached a broad range of topics and thus proven the potentials of a culture-inclusive psychology, not as a subdiscipline, but as an alternative approach of psychological research and analysis. They have significantly contributed to an understanding of 'self and development' (see section four), yet have also taken up topics that are usually ignored by the mainstream, such as music or religion.

The meaning of a behavior depends not only on its cultural context, but also on what we, in our hermeneutic exertions, deduce to be and finally identify as culture. Such work is in principle never conclusive. Particular persons start this work, in concrete situations, and may interrupt it for various pragmatic reasons. All this means that meaning is always provisional, and can never be completely purified of traces of contingent interpretations. There is, therefore, never an unequivocal meaning to some behavior, nor for any other object of study.

Outlook

It is evident that 'culture' in this sense can no longer be conceptualized as a structure of causality, but as a frame, a medium (Cole) or field (Boesch) of human action.

"Culture is a field of action, whose contents range from objects made and used by human beings to institutions, ideas and myths. Being an action field, culture offers possibilities of, but by the same token stipulates conditions for, action; it circumscribes the goals that can be reached by certain means, but establishes limits, too, for correct, possible and deviant action. The relationship between the different material as well as ideational contents of the cultural field of action is a systemic one; i.e., transformations in one part of the system can have an impact in any other part. As an action field, culture not only includes and controls action, but is also continuously transformed by it; therefore, culture is as much a process as a structure" (Boesch 1991: 29).

Boesch's social constructivist and formal definition of culture can serve as a point of departure; however, here we extend on it. Like many other suggestions, it is a meaning-oriented definition in that 'technical anthropological sense' that Alfred Kroeber and Clyde Kluckhohn (and some others) brought into play. Such a concept of culture is, incidentally, not reserved for cultures that, like so-called high cultures, have extremely strong claims of continuity and coherence, and are often geographically extensive; it serves equally well for the analysis of partial, local, regional, and ephemeral cultural and subcultural forms. It can also be said of it that it directs our attention to the ceremonies as well as the everyday of a life world, to the deliberate, memorial, monumentalized, and ritualized specificities as well as the normal and conventional ones. It is distinctive and not normative; it does not distinguish between worthy and worthless cultures, nor between what is valuable and what is worthless within culture, between the refined and the popular, the high and the low (Straub 2003).

We may believe that psychology can in the future profitably work with such a concept of culture, but we should guard against excessive illusions or optimism. We do not mean simply that we should resist making larger claims than the current state of the art can hardly fulfill. The question we have been leading up to is more than just obstinate: Will this concept of culture be more than just a palliative against the stifling pressure of an overall biologization of psychology (Laucken 2001)? Why should culture not necessarily end up in the same role as the concept of society, which remained a guest in the territory of academic psychology, an unwelcome guest or interloper, as a rule, rather than one welcome for its challenges and contributions? (The relationship between these concepts, as it has been most often in the historical sciences, but certainly in psychology as well, ought to be analyzed far more precisely than it has been for culture). It might here and there have found a niche, but one from which it could of course cause little provocation, let alone change. Perhaps the present volume will contribute to theoretical, methodological, and practical advances in cultural and cross-cultural psychology; perhaps we will not find ourselves already in such a niche tomorrow. The future of cultural and cross-cultural psychology has just begun—it is, as every future, dependent on what we are willing and able to do today.

References

Baerveldt, C./Verheggen, T. (1999). Enactivism and the Experiential Reality of Culture: Rethinking the Epistemological Basis of Cultural Psychology. Culture & Psychology, 5, 183-206.

Berry, J.W. (1969). On Cross-Cultural Comparability. In: International Journal of Behavior, 4, 119-128.

Berry, J.W. (1980). Introduction to Methodology. In : H. Triandis/J.W. Berry (Eds.). Handbook of Cross-Cultural Psychology, Vol. 2: Methodology (pp. 1-28). Boston: Allyn & Bacon.

Berry, J.W. (1999). Emics and Etics: A Symbiotic Conception. In: Culture & Psychology, 2, 165-171.

Berry, J.W./Poortinga, Y.H./Segall, M.H./Dasen, P.R. (1992). Cross-Cultural Psychology. Cambridge: Cambridge University Press.

Boesch, E.E. (1991). Symbolic Action Theory and Cultural Psychology. Berlin: Springer.

Boesch, E.E./Straub, J. (2006). Kulturpsychologie—Prinzipien, Orientierungen, Konzeptionen. In: G. Trommsdorff/H.-J. Kornadt (Eds.). Kulturvergleichende Psychologie. Band 1: Theorien und Methoden in der kulturvergleichenden und kulturpsychologischen Forschung. Göttingen: Hogrefe. (In Press)

Bruner, J.S. (1990). Acts of Meaning. Cambridge/ MA: Harvard University Press.

Chase, S. (1948). The Proper Study of Mankind: An Inquiry into the Science of Human Relations. New York, NY u.a.: Harper and Row.

Chaudhary, N. (1999). Diversity, Definitions and Dilemmas: A Commentary on Helfrich's Principle of Triarchic Resonance. In: Culture & Psychology, 2, 155-163.

Helfrich, H. (1999). Beyond the Dilemma of Cross-Cultural Psychology: Resolving the Tension between Etic and Emic Approaches. In: Culture & Psychology, 2, 131-153.

Hermans, H.J.M./Kempen, H.J.G. (1998). Moving Cultures. The Perilous Problems of Cultural Dichotomies in a Globalizing Society. In: American Psychologist, 10, 1111-1120.

Kölbl, C./Straub, J. (2001). Qualitative Kulturpsychologie als Wissenschaft. Rezensionsaufsatz zu: Carl Ratner (1997). Cultural Psychology and Quantitative Methodology: Theoretical and Empirical Considerations. Forum Qualitative Sozialforschung / Forum Qualitative Social Research [Online Journal], 2 (2).

Kroeber, A.L./Kluckhohn, C. (1967 [1952]). Culture. A Critical Review of Concepts and Definitions (With the Assistence fo Wayne Untereiner and appendices by Alfred G. Meyer). New York: Vintage.

Laucken, U. (2001). Wissenschaftliche Denkformen, Sozialpraxen und der Kampf um Ressourcen—demonstriert am Beispiel der Psychologie. Handlung Kultur Interpretation, 10, 292-334.

Lonner, W.J. (1999). Helfrich's 'Principle of Triarchic Resonance': A Commentary on yet Another Perspective on the Ongoing and Tenacious Etic-Emic Debate, 2, 173-181.

Miller, J.G. (1997). Theoretical Issues in Cultural Psychology. In: J.W. Berry/Y.H. Poortinga/J. Pandey (Eds.). Handbook of Cross-Cultural Psychology: Vol. 1. Theory and Method (pp. 85-128). Boston: Allyn & Bacon.

Pike, K.L. (1954). Emic and Etic Standpoints for the Description of Behavior. In: K.L. Pike (Ed.): Language in Relation to a Unified Theory of the Structure of Human Behavior (pp. 8-28). Glendale, IL: Summer Institute of Linguistics.

Pike, K.L. (1967). Language in Relation to a Unified Theory of the Structure of Human Behavior. The Hague: Mouton.

Ratner, C. (1997). Cultural Psychology and Qualitative Methodology. Theoretical and Empirical Considerations. New York, London: Plenum Press.

Segall, M.H. (1979). Cross-Cultural Psychology: Human Behavior in Global Perspective. Monterey, CA: Brooks/Cole.

Segall, M.H./Lonner, W.J./Berry, J.W. (1998). Cross-Cultural Psychology as a Scholarly Discipline: On the Flowering of Culture in Behavioral Research. American Psychologist, 53, 1101-1110.

Straub, J. (2001). Psychologie und Kultur: Psychologie als Kulturwissenschaft. In: H. Appelsmeyer/E. Billmann-Mahecha (Eds.). Kulturwissenschaft: Felder einer prozeßorientierten wissenschaftlichen Praxis (pp. 125-167). Weilerswist: Velbrück.

Straub, J. (2003). Psychologie und die Kulturen in einer globalisierten Welt. In: A. Thomas (Ed.). Kulturvergleichende Psychologie. Ein Lehrbuch (pp. 543-566). Göttingen u.a.: Hogrefe.

Straub, Jürgen und Thomas, Alexander (2003). Positionen, Ziele und Entwicklungslinien der kulturvergleichenden Psychologie. In: A. Thomas (Ed.). Kulturvergleichende Psychologie (pp. 29-80). Göttingen: Hogrefe.

FROM COGNITION TO CULTURE: CULTURAL PSYCHOLOGY AND SOCIAL CONSTRUCTIONISM AS POST-COGNITIVIST MOVEMENTS IN PSYCHOLOGY

BARBARA ZIELKE

The Cognitive Revolution and the Concept of Meaning

In a certain sense, cognitivism has rendered psychology meaningful again: the insight that people's lives, the world around them, and their selves are shaped and strongly influenced, if not completely determined by their cognitive interpretation made it desirable for psychologists to investigate what people know and feel about what they do. As it is understood that we make judgements, plan actions, solve problems, construct our selves, thus master our everyday lives on the basis of cognitive activities, cognition is what psychology should study. And according to Jerome Bruner, even for the leading figures of the "cognitive revolution", the study of cognitive activities in the first place meant (re-)establishing "meaning as the central concept of psychology" (Bruner 1990: 2).[1]

Notably, Bruner continues, the concept of cognition at the time did not have the informational reading it has today. The word "cognition" then referred quite self-evidently to the kind of everyday and practical knowledge that a short while later would be excluded from cognitive psychology's field of interest. Back then, in contrast to contemporary

---

1 Some examples demonstrate this early interest in the construct of meaning: the 'New Look'-account in the psychology of perception searched for people's "meaningful interpretations of the environment" (Bruner and Postman 1949, Bruner and Tagiuri 1954) and concentrated on how "initially meaningless" stimuli "acquired meaning" in the process of being perceived (Osgood 1957: 95). Consequently, the methodological interest was in how to manage the "measurement of meaning" (Osgood, Suci and Tannenbaum 1957). In a similar vein, early attribution theory overtly asked how behavior data were construed as meaningful entities by their reference to personal dispositions (e.g., Heider 1957).

cognitivist experiments, the interest of academic research was not exclusively to understand the structure and function of human cognition—it went beyond this to face questions of how our thoughts and feelings and actions are shaped by culture and history and to investigate the "symbolic activities that human beings employed in construing and in making sense not only of the world, but of themselves"—at least this his how Bruner, one of the first protagonists of that cognitive revolution, recalls the genuine spirit of this scholarly movement (1990: 2).

Quite different from that first period, contemporary cognitive psychology clearly defines the individual mind as its core subject matter. And since the rise of cognitivism in psychology has from the beginning been connected with the rise of the computer and information theory, mind is quite self-evidently conceptualized as a system that encodes or transforms information into processable form and is able to retrieve stored information by use of a coded address (Anderson 2000; Thagard 1999). Due to this computational concept of mind, Bruner again resumes, "very early on, emphasis began shifting from 'meaning' to 'information'" (1990: 4); and so it is that just this computational model of cognition severely reduced psychology's pursuit of meaning.[2] What was captured by the expression "information processing" is surprisingly remote from the processes cultural psychology associates with "meaning and the processes that create it" (Bruner 1990: 5).

Bruner's own idea of what cognitive psychology should define as its subject matter concentrated on a species of "folk-psychology", which he describes as "a culture's account of what makes human beings tick": theories of mind, of motivation, of the self, and "all the rest" (Bruner 1990: 5-13). The more psychology realizes how closely human cognitive powers are related to culture and thus determined and shaped by the individual's participation in culture, the more it will have to refrain from treating the world as an indifferent flow of information. For Bruner—and for most representatives of culturally informed psychologies today—folk psychology is more than the sum of the naïve or subjective theories of all participants in a specific culture. It is a quasitheoretical pool of knowledge that is of great importance for scientific psychology and should be taken seriously by the academic discipline. Importantly, folk psychology in Bruner's sense is tied to communicative social processes and cannot be studied exclusively by analyzing the mental functions of individuals. As long as cognitivist concepts of semantic or everyday knowledge (e.g., Abelson 1981) mainly focus on how the individual mind manages its rep-

---

2   In their formulation of the symbol system hypothesis, computer scientists Allen Newell and Herbert A. Simon clearly stated that information is to be seen as indifferent with respect to meaning (Newell and Simon 1972).

resentation, they will fail to grasp important dimensions of that folk psychology.

Both the idea that cognition is the transformation of information and the question of whether folk psychology can provide cognitive science with acceptable knowledge about the functioning of cognition have important roots in the philosophy of mind. It is not new that Jerry Fodor's computationalist theory of a "Language of Thought" (Fodor 1975) can be understood as the metatheory of cognitivism (Gardner 1985, Thagard 1999). In his philosophy, Fodor supplied a "logical" explanation of how folk psychology could and would probably function: everything we can know must be traceable in our heads in the form of representations; there are causal relations between those different representations, and all representations are structure-sensitive and processed by means of their formal features (Fodor 1975, 1987). Fodor's idea of folk psychology is obviously in sharp contrast to that of Bruner. Raising the argument that mental representations must have the form of linguistic sentences on the one hand and reducing the concept of "language" to a representationalist, syntactic and strictly logical "language system" on the other, Fodor's "Language of Thought" provoked substantial critique within the area of philosophy of mind (Searle 1980; Putnam 1981; Dreyfus 1994).

I will now outline some aspects of that philosophical critique of Fodor's cognitivism, as they might be of help in fully understanding Bruner's critical analysis. What were the critical arguments against the philosophical metatheory of cognitivism, and how were they taken up by cognitive psychology?

Philosophical Critiques of Cognitivism: From Ryle to Putnam

Against Cognitivism

Gilbert Ryle had already developed an anticognitivist theory of mind prior to Fodor's model and prior to the rise of functionalism or cognitivism itself. Separating the kind of knowledge inherent in practical competences ("knowing-how") from the theoretical and propositional knowledge of facts and rules ("knowing-that"), Ryle attacked the general "intellectualist" bias attached to philosophical theories of mind in the 1940s. Especially in his essay "Knowing-that and knowing-how" (1949)—referring, by the way, to the kind of knowledge that Bruner captures as folk psychology—, he argues that many of our everyday descriptions of "cognitive" phenomena refer to dispositions and skills, thus to practices rather than to mental states or strictly intellectual capacities. We say someone is a good talker or listener; that he knows how to deal with people, or she is good at finding creative solutions to problems. Although we talk about doing, we are still referring to a special kind of knowledge. It must be knowledge because what all these activities (arguing, talking, listening) have in common is that they are subject to standards of correctness, propriety, or some other kind of evaluation, otherwise we couldn't find that one person argues better than another. Ryle, therefore, emphasizes that knowing-how as opposed to knowing-that must be a nonintellectual, practical competence, or even a technical skill, which cannot be made explicit without distortion.[3]

Of course, cognitive psychology has taken up some aspects of Ryle's original division by establishing the division between declarative and procedural knowledge (e.g., Anderson 1976). A closer look at the attempts to model procedural knowledge via "production systems" (e.g., Dörner, Kreuzig, Reither and Stäudel 1983; Opwis and Plötzner 1996), however, reveals that most psychological theories of procedural knowledge refer to programmable—and thus, explicable—rule-knowledge, stored in production systems. In those models, the implicit or practical character of procedural knowledge is realized in internal algorithmic canons of rules, be they in the heads of people or in the programs of computers. But somewhere and sometime, concrete hypotheses regarding the algorithms must have been generated by the programmer: therefore, it must in principle be possible to make those rules explicit and to formalize procedural knowledge without distortion—which is one way Ryle's intentions are thwarted here. More importantly, the social basis of implicit or practical knowledge does not play any role in cognitive models of the representation of procedural knowledge (Thagard 1999; Dörner et al. 1983). Ryle, in contrast, by using our everyday language as evidence, pointed to the fact that folk psychology is retrievable from the social language of a culture and that in this case a theory of mind is also a theory of meaning. Practical knowledge or "knowing-how", as he described it, is an essential part of a person's linguistic competence.

---

3 Similarly, from Wittgenstein's Philosophical Investigations we can learn that it is a different thing to know how and when a rule is applied and to know how the rule exactly reads. Even if we know the rule by heart, we can never be sure exactly how and when to apply it before we have done so (1956, § 201). Both philosophers' concepts imply that knowing-how (Ryle) or rule-application knowledge (Wittgenstein) necessarily remains vague or even uncertain, and this is one feature that makes practical knowledge different from theoretical, declarative, or propositional knowledge. Wittgenstein also tells us that it is this kind of "knowledge about rule-application" we have to accumulate when learning how to speak a social language or how to participate in a socio-cultural practice.

Presupposing this very connection—between theories of knowledge and theories of meaning—, John Searle criticized Fodor's computational model and began an at first quite startling critical debate. He argued that the representation of semantic meaning in the human mind cannot be fully explained by studying or understanding formal rules of storage, by discovering a specific "syntactic" or "logical" language. In his famous "Chinese room argument" Searle makes clear that even the perfect knowledge of the syntax of the Chinese language will not enable the knower to give a meaningful answer to a meaningful question in Chinese. The Chinese speaker in Searle's Chinese room makes use of some mysterious "intrinsic" or "genuine" intentionality in order to understand what the other Chinese speaker has said. Intrinsic intentionality, according to Searle, requires a first person perspective and is different from the kind of intentionality that can be described from the perspective of an outside observer (or computer programmer) who makes out and describes intentional states with reference to explicit criteria. Intentionality in the sense of Searle, thus, is an essential part of linguistic competences: it is what enables people to understand semantics, and semantics are more than syntax (Searle 1980).

Hilary Putnam, himself an early advocate of functionalism in the philosophy of mind, and teacher of Jerry Fodor himself, later became one of the most intelligent critics of computationalism. In his critique, Putnam gradually developed a pragmatist perspective, defending for any theory of knowledge or meaning the priority of the actor's perspective (Putnam 1987). Unlike Searle, Putnam did not strive to supply a concept of the speaker's intentionality, but a theory of knowledge and meaning in the broader sense. His interest in the actor's perspective was directed against the concept of neutral "information" serving as cognitive input and as the basis for symbol processing. Perception and thinking, Putnam argues, are not to be equated with the production and processing of symbolic mental representations, but represent a more direct access to their "content". This direct access is realized in our everyday *experience with things*. Putnam's famous claim that there are no "uncontaminated inputs" can be interpreted in two ways: stating that there are no uncontaminated inputs means on the one hand that there is no direct access to the "referent", uncontaminated by concepts, vocabularies, and social rules.[4] On the other hand, there is no "pure" theoretical concept—uncontaminated by traces of the practical contexts wherein it was construed. This is what can be understood as the essence of his "internal" or "pragmatic" realism (Putnam 1981, 1987). Investigating the manifold interpretations and cultural language games, Putnam argues, philosophy can regain the certainty

---

4   See also Quine 1953, 1960.

of everyday orientation in-the-world, namely, the certainty of the ordinariness of our everyday experience.[5]

This short overview indicates that each of these three philosophers from, different directions, criticizes cognitivism's fixation on and contention with the analysis of explicit, formal, and propositional knowledge and the narrow theory of meaning resulting from this fixation. Meaning is not captured by the syntax of a system, it is not "*computability*". The competence to produce or understand meaning—we called it linguistic competence—is not explained by describing the structure of some abstract knowledge "in the head" of individual speakers. Linguistic competence requires not only theoretical but practical knowledge, and this *practical knowledge*, as it is understood here, is a fundamentally social matter.

Connectionism as an Alternative?

There is one further critical position towards cognitivism to be discussed which became prominent in the philosophical debate on artificial intelligence and influential, in a different way, in psychology. Participating in the AI-debate, philosophers Hubert L. Dreyfus and Francisco Varela both pointed to the problem that the embodied and "lived" aspects of everyday knowledge can hardly be conceptualized within the framework of the symbol system hypothesis. Both theorists, however, thought the neoconnectionist findings and the new architecture of neural networks were promising alternatives (Dreyfus 1994; Varela 1988) and they seriously pursued the question of whether connectionism, and some of the characteristics of neural networks, provided a suitable model for representing culturally relevant "background knowledge" (Hintergrundwissen).

After all, there are some very challenging changes that came along with parallel processing: in neural networks the processing of information and intelligent action is no longer subject to a hierarchical, logic-based structure. Processing is distributed over innumerable units, some of them so-called "hidden" units. It is not always possible to say according to which exact rules intelligent behavior is caused. Connectionist systems, at first sight, seemed to promise an alternative to cognitivism—and this supplied good arguments against Fodor's dictum which suggested that intelligent behavior is subject to a hierarchically structured, logical system of rules. On the contrary: because of their "learning ability", neural networks seem to come much closer to the flexibility and situatedness

---

5   Ordinariness in this sense is similar to what Wittgenstein meant by "pragmatically founded certainty"; with Heidegger we can point to "prepredicative" or "ready-at-hand" aspects of the object of knowledge.

that characterize commonsense knowledge. This flexibility and learning ability is due to the fact that the coordination of the local activities in neoconnectionist neural networks is somehow "guided", but never completely determined by rules (Varela 1988; Dreyfus 1994; Münch 1998). Yet, after thorough scrutiny, Dreyfus as well as Varela—though with different connotation—denied connectionism the potential to supply an adequate model of a folk psychology. The kind of flexibility that is characteristic for a neural network, they would argue, is quite different from that of human semantic cultural knowledge. The fact that cognition as conceptualized by connectionism is tightly connected with the activity of local units, or that some configurations of knowledge emerge with discontinuity from rather randomly coordinated elements, is not the same kind of irregularity we associate with the specific, meaningful, social, situated, and action oriented knowledge that is essential for our everyday life: while cultural, everyday knowledge enables us to deal with the contingency of experience and the normativity of intentional states, the (partial) randomness of neural networks' processing results refers to some nonpredictable causal relations, to the unpredictability of technical and material connections. But contingency is not the same as randomness. The fact that the "cognition" represented by neural networks is determined by rules which we cannot explicitly reconstruct, cannot cover the difference between random neural activity and meaningful social interaction (Dreyfus 1994; Varela 1988).

Let us sum up what we have gathered so far: In the philosophical critiques of the cognitivist (and connectionist) concept of knowledge, we find a general tendency to challenge the syntactic or the neural modeling of cognition and to strengthen the pragmatic foundation of semantic, cultural, everyday knowledge. The semantic content of folk psychology not only points to the connection between everyday knowledge and action disposition (Ryle) or to a specific form of first-person intentionality (Searle), but also to the pragmatics of meaning, if we understand linguistic competence as a basis for cultural knowledge and language as a collective practice, the participation in which requires practical experience with others and with things (Putnam, Dreyfus). Francisco J. Varela himself concludes his critical review of the development of the concept of cognition with the statement that the claim of cognitive science to explain human knowledge was bound to fail because of the unsystematic, uncoordinated quality of cultural background knowledge (Hintergrundwissen). Because of the lack of computability and predictability, the cultural Hintergrundwissen, which includes Bruner's folk psychology, has been neglected by cognitive science. But this must not draw our attention away from the fact, Varela says in closing, that human cognition cannot

27

be understood without folk psychological background knowledge and that this background knowledge is inseparable from our embodied presence and social history (Varela 1988).

Advances Toward a
Post-Cognitivist Psychology

While not ignoring those theoretical flaws of cognitivist theory and metatheory, cognitive psychologists do not really think such debate should endanger their paradigmatic way of conceptualizing human action, mind, and psychology as a whole. There are some neuropsychologists, like Gerhard Roth and Antonio Damasio, who claim to supply new insights about genuinely "cultural" questions from a genuinely "scientific" perspective. At first glance, some of them seem to be prepared to at least doubt some aspects of the rationalist, "strong subject", which still is behind most psychological theories (Roth 2001). But after further reading, some things seem not so different anymore. Neuroscience, gradually inscribing itself into all psychological cognitive theories, may claim revolutionary new insights—yet it challenges neither the positivist ideal of (scientific) knowledge nor the individualist and universalist model of human cognition. Neuropsychologists self-evidently speak of the functions of one brain being in charge of influencing or bringing about the actions, thoughts, and feelings of one person, thus affirming the individualist premise of cognitivism. Only after the exact understanding of the individual brain's capacities and processes are understood can social interaction and communication be explained. As neuropsychological assumptions are to a large extent in accord with the premises of cognitivism, they are included as unchallenged givens, and since neuropsychological findings serve as a nice supplement and additional "positive" proof for well-known and neatly modeled aspects of cognition (e.g., Gazzaniga 2002), cognitivism is still the leading paradigm of modern psychology. Despite GOFAI being gradually drowned in neuro-cognitive-experimental scientific effort, as far as higher cognitive process is concerned, cognitive-scientific research is still dominated by primarily computational concepts since the systematicity and productivity of our thinking is best explained via symbol processing models (see Gold and Engel 1998: 13).[6]

---

6   The half-hearted way in which philosophical reflections have been taken up is again illustrated nicely in the way psychology deals with the connectionist "alternative": even among the advocates of neural networks, the potentials Dreyfus and Varela saw (and then denied) for psychological theories of knowledge representation were not taken seriously for long.

In fact, those who seek a truly "post-cognitivist psychology" (Potter 2000, Zielke 2004) must search for more radical alternatives. The pursuit of a psychology based on cultural folk psychologies in Bruner's sense must reach far beyond the striving for a gradual neuropsychological enrichment of computationalist models of the mind. It requires investigation into the social nature of knowledge, the constitutive role of language and cultural meaning, and the pragmatic process in which meaning is created, and in doing so it will have to challenge the cognitivist ideal that there is a prior cognitive schema involved in all human activities.[7] Recent post-cognitivist accounts, originating from the fields of cultural and constructionist psychology, start from this fundamental point: individual "knowers", it is argued, are always participants in a culture and realize their psychological states in the language of a culture. This makes it impossible for psychology to content itself with understanding the capacities and competences of the individual mind. On the contrary, all cognitive activities that make up the core subject matter of modern cognitive psychology—thinking, judging, planning, estimating, problem-solving, etc.—are described, communicated, defined, and discussed by people in their everyday lives, and when doing so people use a vocabulary which is characteristic for their particular cultural background or, more precisely, for their particular form of life. And it is within this interactive process that cognitive activities and mental states acquire their meaning. Thus, even if psychology wants to study meaning via the explication of cognitive process, the analysis must focus on the cognitive vocabulary and the conditions of its use in everyday life (see also Harré 2000).

Besides Bruner's influential book, there have been various works from the fields of action-theoretical cultural psychology that sketched the features of a post-cognitivist psychology (Boesch 1991; Straub 1999, Cole 1996). Another direction from which psychological critics of cognitivism emerged was the critical movement of constructionist and discursive psychologies (Gergen 1987, 1994, Edwards and Potter 1992, Potter 1996).

Thus, cultural psychology and social constructionism, each a broad and itself heterogenous field, represent the two main directions in which the critique of the cognitivist paradigm in psychology has been formu-

---

In the end, the important and unresolved questions of cognitivist psychology, e.g., questions of sociality, embodiment, common sense intentionality, and reference remain unchallenged despite the growing interest in the function of neural networks (e.g., Cohen 2002).

7 For different reasons, cognitivist theories of "semantic knowledge representation" (e.g., Abelson 1981) failed to supply an adequate conceptualization of cultural knowledge (for a more thorough critique see Zielke 2004, Ch. I).

lated, and both also supply a positive alternative. What do those post-cognitivist psychologies hold against cognitivism and what does their alternative look like?

First, for many advocates of a post-cognitivist psychology the most important step is to overcome the individualist and subject-centered bias of the discipline and to invite psychology to investigate the socio-pragmatic basis of all psychological process. To do so, it is important, among other things, to reclaim a specific notion of everyday knowledge, in the sense of Dewey's "reconstruction" (1938) or of Schütz and Luckmann's "Alltagswissen" (1979). This kind of knowledge, it is argued, is subject to contingently and spontaneously occurring variables, to the unsystematic stream of interactions in everyday situations. It is significantly different from the kind of cognitive performance produced and provoked in the psychology laboratory. Second, it is also generally accepted that the interactionist program in sociology, ranging from George H. Mead to Harold Garfinkel, offers promising potentials for the psychological understanding of how the self and our knowledge are embedded in culture (Gergen 1994; Potter 1996). And last but not least, psychology as a cultural science has to take into account (post-)structuralist, semiotics (from Saussure to Derrida) as well as pragmatist theories of language and linguistic meaning (from Wittgenstein to Austin), as they were in the center of what was to become the linguistic, later the cultural turn in the social and cultural sciences.

With the help of these incentives from the neighbor disciplines, it is argued, even psychology will finally become aware that "language not only includes reference, but also action and the constitution of reality" and that this is of fundamental importance for the subject matter of psychology (Miller 1997). Of course, even in cognitivism, the "meaningfulness" of psychological constructs is based on a constructivist concept of thought and remembering, as our cognitive processes do not mirror, but rather construe the reality we live in. But for the cultural and constructionist alternatives the constructions that make words, objects, or gestures meaningful are inseparably tied to social or intersubjective constructions and to cultural conventions of how to execute and understand those constructions. Furthermore, meaning is tightly bound to action and practice, which draws attention to the sometimes vague aspects of word meaning (Bruner 1990), the polyvalent character of meaningful action (Boesch 1991), and the implicit or "tacit" nature of cultural, everyday knowledge. All those features suggest an interpretive access to psychology's subject matter and the corresponding methods (Straub 1999).

Having listed some of the theoretical and methodological premises shared by many advocates of post-cognitivist psychologies, how are they applied? How do cultural and constructionist psychologists, after establishing criticism of the cognitivist mainstream's fundamental impasse, speak positively about the new subject-matter, about a post-cognitivist psychology? How are the assumptions that psychological constructs are meaning-laden, that they are construed and constructive at the same time, and that their meaning depends on a fundamentally social construction process applied in a post-cognitivist effort, be it research or theory? In order to outline this, it will first be necessary to take a look at the main differences between and similarities of cultural psychology and social constructionism.

Cultural Psychology:
Culture and the Individual

For the action-theoretical branches of cultural psychology, the insight into the culture-bound and culture-shaped quality of psychological constructs necessarily means leaving the nomological, experimental paradigm (Boesch 1991; Eckensberger 1990; Krewer 1992; Miller 1997; Straub 1999). As all psychological phenomena are fundamentally construed and built in a common cultural language, it is impossible to understand their meaning without access to the culture's collective symbolic practice. Of course, culture is also "objectified" in "language, discourse, norms, attitudes, values and knowledge" and even in material objects, like places or institutions (Schütz and Luckmann 1979; Straub 1999: 83). Those objectifications, however, as objectifications, are themselves products of meaning-constitutive and meaning-constituted processes and cannot be analyzed without interpretive access to the perspective of the participant in the cultural form of life.

The emphasis on culture as the product as well as the limiting field of the participants' symbolic practice (Boesch 1991) has different implications. One is that it draws attention to the inseparable connectedness of culture and self—not only in the sense of the social negotiation of meaning, but also in the sense of the embodied dealing with things (Hermans and Kempen 1993). It provides the basis for an alternative to the cognitivist ideal of the rationalist, self-contained, and disembodied "knower" who is independent from cultural meaning systems, at best influenced by external cultural factors. Here, many cultural psychologists overtly distance themselves from the individualist impasse of mainstream psychology: throughout the heterogenous field of writings labeled as "cultural psychological" it is understood that culture and the content of psychological constructs are "mutually constitutive phenomena" which should never be located completely "under the skin of the individual" (Miller

1997: 92). Rather, psychological functions and states are conceptualized as an "emergent quality of permanent interaction between subject, cultural artefacts and the world of objects" (Cole and Engestrom 1995: 21). The twofold claim here is an ontological and a methodological one, maintaining that the individual and the culture are inseparable and that it is impossible to conceptualize the individual's capacities and functions without placing them within a cultural context or frame. This does make it impossible, as Jerome Bruner states, "to construct a human psychology on the basis of the individual alone" (Bruner 1990: 12). Yet, this definition does not strive to exclude the individual and his/her capacities from psychological discourse, nor completely abandon the concept of (individual) knowledge, intentionality, or agency.

On the contrary, for many cultural psychologists, the idea of culture and self being inseparably connected directly points to the question of individual participation: by which means or on the basis of what kind of knowledge is culture represented, acquired, appropriated? On the basis of which "competences" is it possible for individuals to participate in a cultural language game or form of life (Wittgenstein)? Referring to the hermeneutic account of Clifford Geertz and his notion of "thick description" (which itself was taken over from Ryle), cultural psychologists Richard Shweder and Maria Sullivan, for example, have argued that to avoid ethnocentric generalizations when inquiring into what makes up the "other" culture (more exactly, a "radically different" culture), we must search for its participants' "experience-near concepts", concepts that are acquired rapidly, subliminally, and without deliberate reflection (1993: 508). German cultural psychologist Jürgen Straub employs what Giddens has conceptualized as "practical awareness" in exploring the status of "cultural knowledge" (1999: 96). It is understood that both "experience-near concepts", as well as "practical awareness", can never be fully explained or made completely explicit, not even by the most integrated members of that culture: "It is possible," Shweder and Sullivan argue, "to 'know more than we can tell,'" a point also made earlier by Michal Polanyi in his work on implicit knowledge (Polanyi 1967). Going beyond this, Shweder and Sullivan conclude that the relation of a psychological theory of culture and its content "will be something analogous to the status of a grammarian's representations of speech performance" (1993: 510). With reference to Wittgenstein, again we can generalize that this is true not only for the study of different cultures, but whenever people act in coordination with each other—building up or participating in what we call social-cultural practices or forms of life. Cultural psychology gives us an idea of the interconnectedness of self and culture, of the methodological significance of implicit (cultural) knowledge—folk psychology—and of the problematic role of the investigator who wants to make a theory of the cultural practice.

However, in many cases the presupposition of the interdependence of culture and self does not prevent cultural psychologists from researching and investigating cultural variation of self-related capacities and functions. This is the point where inconsistencies within cultural psychology arise and where there is disagreement among representatives of the heterogeneous field of cultural psychologies (see Straub 2001). Many empirical investigations, for example, tend to search for the point where the cultural "construction" ends and the universal "entity" starts—reinstalling, perhaps unwillingly, a universalist perspective and the separation of culture and self. There are various contributions on emotion (e.g., Shweder 1994), self (e.g., Markus and Kitayama 1991), and related constructs that lead in this direction: one example Miller describes in her overview on research in cultural psychology (Miller 1997) is the understanding of emotions as "complex intentional states" that can be decomposed into distinct components (e.g., antecedents, somatic phenomenology, affective phenomenology, implications for self and self-management, and so forth). This general (universal) assumption serves as an implicit or explicit hypothesis for further comparative research aimed at filling in and combining the components or slots of this complex mixture of states and functions in culturally different ways (Miller 1997: 95). Obviously, this perspective presupposes many premises of the cognitivist concept of the person, such as the division of mind and body, the concept of "self-managing", and so forth. Despite the positive effects of such comparative research, many of its findings fail to include a differentiated view of culture, thus falling behind the methodological reflections mentioned above. Furthermore, in cultural psychological research cultural meanings are often portrayed along with the individualism/collectivism distinction (as for example in Markus' and Kitayama's notion of independent vs. interdependent selves) and fail to take into account questions of intracultural heterogeneity, questions of power and politics, as well as the principal indeterminacy and relational quality of cultural meanings (Hermans and Kempen 1993; Straub and Shimada 1999).

Thus, however promising the methodological reflections we may adopt from cultural psychology and its "forerunners", cultural anthropology and ethnology, they will lead only so far on the course toward a postcognitivist, anti-universalist, truly "cultural" psychology. Social constructionist efforts have produced a similar, but more radical position on the place of culture in psychology.

Social Constructionist Psychology:
Discourse and Social Pragmatics

From a social constructionist point of view, cultural psychology has been criticized as an account still oriented toward "traditional" psychological accounts, too much focussed on the capacities of the "individual mind" and on the possibility of achieving positive knowledge about universal human capacities (e.g., Edwards 1995; Gergen 1999). According to Gergen, a stronger and more consequential position than that of cultural psychology is needed to truly escape the impasse of the contemporary psychology of the individual. The constructionist alternative suggests, for example, conceptualizing psychological states not as results of individual perception or information processing, not even as individual interpretations of the world. Rather, those psychological states that we hold to be exclusively "individual" are themselves constitutive (sometimes: functional) elements of social and cultural practices. They are, in Gergen's words, not more and not less than "by-products" of networks of social relationships (Gergen 1982, 1994; Shotter 1993, 2003). Consequently, psychological phenomena are not of interest "per se" in terms of their social construction and transformation in the course of everyday practice (see Gergen 1985, 1994, Edwards and Potter 1992, Potter 1996).

A core assumption of constructionism is the view that discourse is prior to and constitutive of the world we can have knowledge about. This makes scientific enterprise no less a product of discourse than psychological functioning. For example, it is only because of the modernist tradition of individualism and rationalism that psychology could come to understand internal cognitive process as an anchoring point of all psychological explanations in the first place (Gergen 1994). In order to provide a "full-blown successor project" of cognitivism, constructionist authors have explicitly sought to establish an "alternative theory of knowledge", understanding scholarly and everyday knowledge as a product of cultural practice and discourse, and thus as a communal possession (Gergen 1994: 24p., 44). Furthermore, this concept of knowledge bids farewell to the possibility of knowledge picturing reality. Referring to psychological discourse, Gergen goes as far as saying that all scholarly and everyday concepts about psychological constructs are "semantically free floating" (1987: 118).

However, "discourse", according to most constructionist authors, is not to be understood exclusively in the sense of broad, anonymous *dispositives* of power and knowledge in the sense of Foucault's influential works (Foucault 1976); the micro-social realm of "lived" and everyday social interaction is emphasized as the primary locus where meaningful activity is generated and where psychological inquiry should begin (Gergen 1999: 76pp., Potter 1996). All those processes that "traditional" cognitive psychology would study with reference to underlying "internal conditions of the mind"—cognition, emotion, volition, and other psychological states or functions—in constructionism are to be explained via the analysis of (micro-)social process. Simply everything psychologists may be interested in is constructed in the course of everyday social activity: actions, internal states, and cognitive activities, as well as scientific "facts", and last not least, the "individuals" as alleged bearers of knowledge themselves (Gergen 1994, 1999; Potter 1996). Consequently, all psychological phenomena must be explained and analyzed in the context of the public performances in which they come up, in which they are discussed, negotiated, and judged in the language of a culture.

Similar to Gergen's version of constructionism, discursive psychologists like Michael Billig, John Shotter, Jonathan Potter, and Derek Edwards work to deconstruct the dominant tradition of studying the inner dynamics of the individual psyche and strive to rebuild psychology "in discursive terms". Again, in doing so "the aim is certainly not to replace one psychology of the individual with another" (Edwards and Potter 1992: 384). The intention is rather to show that not only seemingly neutral, "factual" external reality, but also the psychologically relevant "internal" reality of cognitive or affective states are constituted in interactions and conversations (Edwards and Potter 1992: 386). Mind is no longer to be viewed as an "objective developmental outcome", but as a category of participants in conversations (Edwards 1995: 64).

Emphasizing that social constructionism is "ontologically mute" (Gergen 1994, Edwards, Ashmore and Potter 1995), constructionism is neutral as to the existence of an observer-independent world: whatever there is may simply be, but for us it must be accessed through language or another symbolic practice in order to acquire meaning. Again, it is important to note that the constructionist theory of language is a pragmatic one—this is true for Gergen's version as well as for that of discursive psychology. The positive embracing of theories of discourse and postmodern semiotics in many constructionist writings (Gergen 1994: 36-39, Potter 1996; Hepburn 2006) must not be misunderstood in the sense of a strictly (post-)structuralist view of language and discourse. There must be more than the swirl of signification, constructionists argue: language is not only a system of signs, but a lived communal practice (in the sense of Wittgenstein or Austin): there are actions and supplementary actions, but only "joint action" can account for what is referred to as the "communal origins of meaning" (Gergen 1994, 1999, see also: Shotter 1993; Potter 1996). And even though the impression may be given at times that discursive psychologists analyse social interaction as if it was (linguistic) discourse, the emphasis of discursive work is never on discourse as a finished social "product", but on the practice-laden and ongoing process of discursive activity—we are, after all, talking "discourse in action" (Potter, Edwards and Wetherell 1993).

One Step Further than Cultural Psychology and Another Step too far

Due to its more radical position on the place of culture in psychology, constructionism is able to produce a more fundamental and thorough critique of the cognitivist and individualist impasse inherent in most traditional psychological accounts: First, the emphasis on the social and cultural grounds of all psychological constructs is most plausible, as constructionism understands individual psychological functioning as a derivative of social interaction and cultural convention. Second, constructionist psychologists do not force their accounts into coherence with "traditional" psychological approaches—instead, they draw substantially from neighboring disciplines, for example, literary-rhetorical critique. Many constructionist psychologists even predict that the incentive for a post-cognitivst psychology will eventually come "from the outside" (Potter 2000). This allows constructionist proposals to save a lot of creative energy and concentrate on exploring culture in manifold ways, employing various techniques of discourse and conversation analysis. Third, constructionism is more decidedly anti-universalist than cultural psychology: For constructionism, there are no "brute facts"—at least probably not. But even if there were, the constructionist metatheory of epistemic relativism, which de-establishes all correspondence theories of truth and all claims to descriptive validity, allows excluding them from theorizing and research (Zielke 2005). Finally, the deconstruction of psychological knowledge forces constructionist writings into a radical form of self-reflexivity, understanding their own insights and constructs as "mere" (cultural) constructions. For these reasons, I think it is fair to say that in a certain sense, constructionism has furnished a more consequential realization of psychology's "embeddedness" in a culture's folk psychology. Social constructionist psychologies have, with impressive clarity, shown what it means for psychology to presuppose the existence of a socio-cultural practice as the basis of scientific knowledge, psychological states, and of meaningful human action as such.

Having mentioned its advantages, I now want to draw attention to the disadvantages of the constructionist version of a post-cognitivist psychology. While it may at first seem suitable for a truly cultural view of psychology, the evasion of all questions concerning individual functions,

36

capacities, or representations causes serious problems. Emphasizing the importance of lived cultural practice over "anonymous" discourse, whenever asked about the role of the participants in a cultural language game, constructionism provides no answer.

Furthermore, the view of the meaning-making process as completely detached from the material world (or from the alleged "referent") and from the participant's personal interests, agency, and intentionality, results in a rather "anonymous" view of social or cultural practice, cultural meaning, or folk psychology, which does not do justice to the constructionist claim of an action-oriented or pragmatic account of cultural meaning (Zielke 2004, Ch. 4). Rather, while dedicated to the ideal of dialogical, "joint action", (Shotter 1993; Gergen 2001), constructionism fails to supply a conceptualization of the dialogue partners' active participation and of their ability to critique (and maybe convince) others in case of conflict. In fact, those who act within pragmatic contexts, those who actively participate in the collective production of any culture's reservoir of meanings are excluded from the field of scholarly interest in constructionism

For many psychologists, this is too high a price to pay, and it is the point where the constructionist program fails to explain what Gergen himself called the "place of the psyche in a constructed world" (Gergen 1997). Last but not least, although the complete detachment from "traditional" psychological accounts may be helpful, it is not always necessary for overcoming the cognitivist impasse and sometimes results in the binary construction of "traditional" vs. "constructionist" accounts.

From Individual Constructs to the Participant's Stake in Cultural Meaning

As we have seen, philosophical positions against the narrow cognitivist concept of meaning suggest the turn from syntax via semantics to the pragmatic grounds of cultural meaning (Putnam, Wittgenstein). This goes together well with the pragmatist and action-oriented stance of many cultural and constructionist psychologists: where cultural psychology refers to "symbolic action theory" (Boesch 1991; Straub 1999) or relates closely to "activity theory" (Cole 1996), social constructionism and discursive psychology want to be understood as "action-oriented" accounts (Potter 1996) and favor a "pragmatic" standpoint (Gergen 2001).

But why should this pragmatic stance keep us from theorizing the participant's stake in social construction or from reflecting on the status of psychological phenomena from a cultural psychological viewpoint?

Isn't the new emphasis on cultural practice rather a reason to once again reflect on the complex relation between psychological functions and cultural grounds, hopefully in a new way? Perhaps many constructionist authors think it a risk to unwillingly invite the autonomous, self-sufficient subject in through the back door when attributing to the psychological subject any kind of individual intentionality and agency. Indeed, the failure to see this risk is what can be held against many cultural psychological accounts. But the radical exclusion of the psychological subject from psychological discourse means going one step too far. If a post-cognitivist psychology is to be based on the communal constructions of the participants in a cultural life-form it must supply a theory of meaning where the semantics of cultural meaning are linked to those participants' intentional interpretation. It must supply a theory of cultural practice together with a theory of the social actor. What is needed is a non-cognitivist, non-individualist account of the participant.

To conceptualize this, we may refer—as Jonathan Potter or Kenneth Gergen might recommend—to proposals from "outside" psychology: social theories of practice, for example, locate knowledge in the social and in the individually incorporated, implicit "Habitus" (Bourdieu 1998). Philosophical, (neo-) pragmatist theories of meaning, which are constructionist and anti-skepticist at the same time (see Putnam 1995), may also be of interest here. It is not always necessary, however, to completely desert psychology since even some early versions of psychological constructivism may be worth investigating. For example, influenced by classical pragmatist philosophers such as Dewey and Mead, George A. Kelly's constructivist theory stressed the difference between "anticipation" and "construction", referring to the fact that seemingly "individual" constructions of a person's self must rely on the expectations and constructs of other participants (Kelly 1955: 51). Being unaware of the cultural turn or postmodern, semiotic theories of meaning, Kelly at least roughly suggested a vision of what constructionist authors might understand by the notion of meaning-constitutive "dialogical" or "joint action" (Gergen 1997, Shotter 1993). Similarly, the writings of Lew Vygotskij or Frederic C. Bartlett might be searched for instructive concepts of the individual's socially mediated appropriation of the world and the self via cultural knowledge (Vygotskij 1934; Bartlett 1933). Those psychological accounts can and must be re-read through post-cognitivist lenses, of course, but in many cases this re-reading should be worth the effort.

If a post-cognitivist psychology is to be psychology rather than a version of cultural studies, philosophy, discourse theory, or linguistic theory, it needs a non-cognitivist account of the participant and of his/her individual competences and functions. Psychology can avoid ethnocentric and universalist constructions by creating a more thorough awareness of the relational status of all psychological (and other scientific) knowledge. It can and will take into account developments in the field of the nonpsychological cultural sciences and build psychology on their fruitful concepts. But even a constructionist psychology that draws from postmodern semiotics needs a "place of the psyche in a constructed world" (Gergen 1997), and it needs a concept of the participant's stake in cultural practice. And sometimes, the step towards a future, post-cognitivist psychology might even point to the past of psychological theories.

References

Abelson, P. (1981). Psychological Status of the Script Concept. In: American Psychologist, 36, 715-729.

Anderson, J.R. (1976). Language, Memory and Thought. New York. Hillsdale.

Anderson, J.R. (2000). Cognitive Psychology and its Implications, 5th ed. New York: W.H. Freeman & Company.

Bartlett, F.C. (1932). Remembering: A Study in Experimental and Social Psychology. Cambridge: Cambridge University Press.

Boesch, E.E. (1991). Symbolic Action Theory and Cultural Psychology. Berlin, Heidelberg, New York, Tokyo. Springer.

Bourdieu, P. (1998). Practical Reason. On the Theory of Action. Polity Press. In: J. Bruner/L. Postman (Eds.). On the Perception of Incongruity: A Paradigm. In: Journal of Personality 18 (1949-1950), 206-223.

Bruner, J.S. (1990). Acts of Meaning. Cambridge: Harvard University Press.

Bruner, J./Tagiure, R. (1954). The Perception of People. In: G. Lindzey (Ed.). Handbook of Social Psychology, Vol 2 (pp. 634-654). Reading, Mass: Addison-Wesley.

Cohen, J. (2002). The Brain and the Computer: Is the Marriage Working? In: M.S. Gazzaniga/R.B. Ivry/G.R. Mangun (Eds.). Cognitive Neuroscience. The Biology of the Mind (pp. 532-533). New York: Norton and Company.

Cole, M. (1996). Cultural Psychology. A Once and Future Discipline. Cambridge, London: Harvard University Press.

Cole, M./Engestrom, Y. (1995). Mind, Culture, Person: Elements in a Cultural Psychology. Comment. In: Human Development, 38, 19-24.

Damasio, A.R. (1994). Descartes' Error. Emotion, Reason and the Human Brain. London: Picador.

Derrida, J. (1976). Of Grammatology. Baltimore: John Hopkins University Press.

Dewey, W. (1938). Logic: The Theory of Inquiry. New York: Henry Holt & Co.

Dörner, D./Kreuzig, H.W./Reither, F./Stäudel, T. (1983). Lohhausen. Vom Umgang mit Unbestimmtheit und Komplexität. Bern, Stuttgart, Wien: Huber.

Dreyfus, H.L. (1994). What Computers Still Can't Do. A Critique of Artificial Reason. Cambridge: MIT.

Eckensberger, L. (1990). On the Necessity of the Cultural Concept in Psychology: A View from Cross-Cultural Psychology. In: F.J.R. van de Vijver/G. Hutschemaekers (Eds.). The Investigation of Culture. Current Issues in Cultural Psychology (pp. 153-184). Tilburg: University Press.

Edwards, D. (1995). A Commentary on Discursive and Cultural Psychology. In: Culture and Psychology, 1, 55-66.

Edwards, D./ Ashmore, M./Potter, J. (1995). Death and Furniture. The Rhetoric, Politics and Theology of Bottom Line Arguments Against Relativism. In: History of Human Sciences, 8, 25-49.

Fodor, J.F. (1975). The Language of Thought, Cambridge: MIT.

Fodor, J.F. (1987). Psychosemantics. The Problem of Meaning in the Philosophy of Mind. Cambridge: MIT.

Foucault, M. (1976). The History of Sexuality, Vol. I. New York: Pantheon.

Gardner, H. (1985). The Mind's New Science. New York: Basic Books Inc.

Geertz, C. (1973). The Interpretation of Cultures. New York: Basic Books.

Gergen, K.J. (1982). Toward Transformation in Social Knowledge. Berlin, New York, Tokyo: Springer.

Gergen, K.J. (1985). The Social Constructionist Movement in Modern Psychology. In: American Psychologist, 40, 266-275.

Gergen, K.J. (1987). The Language of Psychological Understanding. In: H.J. Stam/T.B. Rogers/K.J. Gergen (Eds.). Metapsychology and the Analysis of Psychological Theory (pp. 115-129). New York: Hemisphere.

Gergen, K.J. (1991). The Saturated Self. Dilemmas of Identity in Contemporary Life. Basic Books.

Gergen, K.J. (1994). Realities and Relationships. Soundings in Social Construction. London, Thousand Oaks, New Delhi: Sage.

Gergen, K.J. (1997). The Place of the Psyche in a Constructed World. In: Theory and Psychology, 7, 723-746.

Gergen, K.J. (1999). An Invitation to Social Construction. New York, London, Thousand Oaks, New Delhi: Sage.

Gergen, K.J. (2001). Construction in Contention. Toward Consequential Resolutions. In: Theory and Psychology, 11 (3), 419-432.

Harré, R. (2000). Varieties of Theorizing and the Project of Psychology. In: Theory and Psychology, 19 (1), 57-62.

Heider, F. (1957). Trends in Cognitive Theory. In: H.E. Gruber/K.R. Hammond/R. Jessor (Eds.). Contemporary Approaches to Cognition (pp. 201-210). Cambridge: Harvard University Press.

Hepburn, A. (2006). Getting Closer at a Distance. Theory and the Contingencies of Practice. In: Theory and Psychology, 16 (in press).

Hermans, H.J.M./Kempen, H.J.G. (1993). The Dialogical Self. Meaning as Movement. San Diego, CA: Academic Press.

Kelly, G.A. (1955). The Psychology of Personal Constructs, 2 Volumes. New York: Norton.

Krewer, B. (1992). Kulturelle Identität und menschliche Selbsterforschung. Die Rolle von Kultur in der positiven und reflexiven Bestimmung des Menschseins, Saarbrücken, Fort Lauderdale: Breitenbach.

Markus, H.R./Kitayama, S. (1991). Culture and the Self: Implications for Cognition, Emotion and Motivation. In: Psychological Review, 98, 224-253.

Miller, J.G. (1997). Theoretical Issues in Cultural Psychology. In: J.W. Berry/Y.H. Poortinga/J. Pandey (Eds.). Handbook of Cross-Cultural Psychology, Vol. I, Theory and Method (pp. 85-128). Boston: Allyn and Bacon.

Münch, D. (1998). Kognitivismus in anthropologischer Perspektive. In: P. Gold/A.K. Engel (Eds.). Der Mensch in der Perspektive der Kognitionswissenschaften (pp. 17-48). Frankfurt am Main: Suhrkamp.

Newell, A./Simon, H.A. (1972). Human Problem Solving. Eaglewood Cliffs, NJ: Prentice Hall.

Opwis, K./Plötzner, R. (1996). Kognitive Psychologie mit dem Computer. Ein Einführungskurs zur Simulation geistiger Leistungen mit Prolog. Heidelberg, Berlin, Oxford: Spektrum Akademischer Verlag.

Osgood, C. (1957). A Behavioristic Analysis of Perception and Language as Cognitiv Phenomena. In: H.E. Gruber/K.R. Hammond/R. Jessor (Eds.). Contemporary Approaches to Cognition (pp. 75-118). Cambridge: Harvard University Press.

Polanyi, M. (1967). Tacit Knowledge. New York: Anchor books.

Potter, J. (1996). Representing Reality. Discourse, Rhetoric and Social Construction. London, Thousand Oaks, New Delhi: Sage.

Potter, J. (2000). Post-Cognitive Psychology. In: Theory and Psychology 10 (1), 31-37.

Potter, J./Edwards, D./Wetherell, M. (1993). A Model of Discourse in Action. In: American Behavioral Scientist 36, 383-401.

Putnam, H. (1987). The Many Faces of Realism. LaSalle, Ill.: Open Court.

Putnam, H. (1981). Reason, Truth and History. Cambridge University Press.

Putnam, H. (1995). Pragmatism: An Open Question. Cambridge University Press.

Quine, W.V.O. (1953). From a Logical Point of View. Cambridge: Harvard University Press.

Quine, W.V.O. (1960). Word and Object. Cambridge: MIT.

Roth, G. (1994). Das Gehirn und seine Wirklichkeit. Frankfurt am Main: Suhrkamp.

Ryle, G. (1949). The Concept of Mind. New York: Barnes and Noble.

Schütz, A./Luckmann, T. (1979). Strukturen der Lebenswelt. Frankfurt am Main: Suhrkamp.

Searle, J.R. (1980). Mind, Brains, and Programs. In: Behavioral and Brain Sciences 3, 417-424.

Shotter, J. (1993). Conversational Realities. Constructing Life through Language. London, Thousand Oaks, New Delhi: Sage.

Shotter, J. (2003). Real Presences. Meaning as Living Movement in a Participatory World. In: Theory and Psychology, 13 (4), 435-468.

Shweder, R.A./Sullivan, M.A. (1993). "Cultural Psychology: Who Needs It?" In: Annual Review of Psychology, 44, 479-523.

Shweder R.A. (1994). "You're not Sick, You're Just in Love": Emotion as an Interpretive System. In: P. Ekman/R.J. Davidson (Eds.). The Nature of Emotion. Fundamental Questions (pp. 32-44). New York, Oxford: University Press.

Straub, J. (1989). Historisch-psychologische Biographieforschung. Theoretische, methodologische und methodische Argumentationen in systematischer Absicht. Heidelberg: Asanger.

Straub, J. (1999). Handlung, Interpretation, Kritik. Grundzüge einer textwissenschaftlichen Handlungs- und Kulturpsychologie. Berlin, New York: de Gruyter.

Straub, J. (2001). Psychologie und Kultur, Psychologie als Kulturwissenschaft. In: H. Appelsmeyer/E. Billmann-Mahecha (Eds.). Kulturwissenschaften. Felder einer prozessorientierten wissenschaftlichen Praxis (pp. 125-167). Weilerswist: Velbrück.

Straub, J./Shimada, S. (1999). Relationale Hermeneutik im Kontext interkulturellen Verstehens. Probleme universalistischer Begriffsbildung in den Sozial- und Kulturwissenschaften—erörtert am Beispiel "Religion". In: Deutsche Zeitschrift für Philosophie, 47 (3), 449-477.

Osgood, C.E./Suci, G./Tannenbaum, P. (1957). The Measurement of Meaning. New York: Urbana.

Thagard, P. (1988). Computational Philosophy of Science. Cambridge: MIT.

Thagard, P. (1999). Kognitionswissenschaft. Ein Lehrbuch. Stuttgart: Klett-Cotta.

Varela, F.J. (1988). Cognitive Science. A Cartography of Current Ideas. Cambridge: Harvard University Press.

Vygotskij, Lew S. (1962 [1934]). Thought and Language. Cambridge: MIT Press.

Wittgenstein, L. (1956). Philosophical Investigations. New York: Mc-Millan.

Zielke, B. (2004). Kognition und soziale Praxis. Der soziale Konstruktionismus und die Perspektiven einer postkognitivistischen Psychologie. Bielefeld: transcript.

Zielke, B. (2005). The Case for Dialogue. Reply to "Social Constructionism as Cultism" by Carl Ratner (December 2004) [12 paragraphs]. Forum: Qualitative Social Research [On-line Journal], 6 (2), Parag. 13. Available at: http://www.qualitative-research.net/fqs-texte/2-05/05-2-13-e.htm.

Zielke, B. (2006). Sozialer Konstruktionismus. Göttingen: Vandenhoek & Ruprecht.

WHITHER CROSS-CULTURAL PSYCHOLOGY?[1]

GUSTAV JAHODA

"Now, of all the terms of comparison we can choose, there is none more fascinating, more fruitful in useful trains of thought than that offered by savage peoples. Here we can first remove the variations pertaining to climate, the organism, and the habits of physical life, and we shall notice that among nations much less developed by the effect of moral institutions, these natural variations are bound to emerge much more prominently: being less distinguished by secondary circumstances, they must chiefly be so by the first and fundamental circumstances belonging to the very principle of existence."

This was the beginning of an essay on methods of what we would call cross-cultural studies. It was written almost exactly two centuries ago by Joseph-Marie Degérando (1772-1842), and intended for the leaders of two French expeditions, to Africa and Australia respectively. It is remarkably sophisticated and many of its guidelines are just as relevant today as they were then; I will convey some his points in our current idiom. Degérando discussed the dangers of drawing inferences on the basis of small and unrepresentative samples; he warned against ethnocentrism; he drew attention to the need to be aware of the effect of the observer's presence on those being observed; he recommended a detailed list of psychological characteristics that ought to be studied by participant observers.

Degérando was a member of the Société des Observateurs de l'Homme founded in 1799 by Louis-François Jauffret. He proposed a considerable number of research topics, including ethnic and regional differences in customs, languages, and gestures, and observations of child development. Few of these could be put into practice, though all of you will have heard of one famous study, namely that of Victor, the "Wild boy of Aveyron". It is therefore fitting that we should pay tribute to these early ancestors of ours (cf. Copans and Jamin 1978).

---

1   Preparation of this paper has been supported by a grant from the Nuffield Foundation.

The first true cross-cultural studies were those of the Cambridge Expedition to the Torres Straits at the turn of the 19th century. Although well known, they are seldom read, though here again Rivers' (1901) treatment of methodological problems is exemplary. For instance, he considered representativeness, the best ways of 'selling' research, and dealing with declining attention of the subjects; he also arranged group discussions to obtain information about preferences. A major weakness was his belief (which he abandoned later) in Hebert Spencer's "energy theory", which postulated that savages devote too much energy to purely sensory activities and therefore are unable to achieve "the higher intellectual life" (Spencer 1876). Hence Rivers confined himself to investigating sensory functioning, especially vision.

Mention should also be made of the contribution of Richard Thurnwald (1869-1954). An anthropologist with deep interest in psychological issues, he consulted Carl Stumpf, one of the most prominent German psychologists at the time, before leaving for fieldwork in New Guinea and the Solomon Islands. Untroubled by the 'energy' theory, he explored the cognitive processes of the inhabitants.

After Thurnwald, little happened for a further half-century until the 1950s, when a few people, including myself, went into the field. The first large-scale study, inspired by Rivers' work on illusions, was that of Segall, Campbell, and Herskovits (1966). They used a hypothesis-testing design, postulating a relationship between ecology and illusion susceptibility. But most of the researches that began to multiply from the 1960s onward, were initially driven by a curiosity to find out how *they* are different from *us*. Hence they were confined to the description of differences—some interesting and valuable, others rather trivial. Almost invariably it was possible to find differences of various kinds, but the problem was to discover what, if anything, they meant. This has proved an elusive goal, and one that usually results only in post-hoc interpretations.

Over the years there has been a fairly radical change in the predominant *style of* research, which may be compared to the contrast between medieval artisans and modern mass production. Most of the old guard, like Berry, Dasen, Poortinga, and myself (I hope they don't object this label—all are younger than I am!) used to work mostly, though not exclusively, face-to-face with individuals. With the exception of some areas like child development, there has since been a shift towards large-scale use of tests, questionnaires, or other measures designed for group administration, with the investigator sometimes only in remote control. Such approaches obviously presuppose at least functional literacy on the part of the participants, a point to which I will return.

46

Methods and approaches have to be considered in relation to objectives, and I will briefly review some earlier ones before discussing the most recent ones in greater detail. One aim that has remained central is that of overcoming the limitations of allegedly universal psychological laws, based on a limited and biased sample of humanity (cf. Jahoda 1970; Serpell 1976; Triandis 1980). A little later, Poortinga and Malpass (1986) proposed that "Cross-cultural psychology is about the *explanation* [my emphasis] of differences—and sometimes similarities—in the behavior of people belonging to different cultures" (17). Although, as already noted, satisfactory explanations have seldom been forthcoming, the concern with *similarities* was a significant change, as pointed out by Berry (1997) in his preface to the new edition of the *Handbook*.

A wide-ranging and in many ways admirable text was published in 1992, and a revised edition in 2002 (Berry, Poortinga, Segall and Dasen 2002). There one can find an authoritative (in the sense of being formulated by outstanding practitioners) statement of the goals of cross-cultural psychology. Since these constitute important sign-posts for the future, I propose to discuss them in some detail; and I want to argue that they are less straightforward than might appear on the surface.

1. *Transport and test*: "... psychologists seek to transport their present hypotheses and findings to other cultural settings in order to test their applicability in other (and eventually in all) groups of human beings" (Berry et al. 1992: 3).

This is a goal to which I myself subscribed in the past, and continue to do so at least in principle. As far back as the 1950s a number of anthropologists noted the potential value for psychology of research in non-Western cultures. The points they were making have been summarized by Campbell and Naroll (1972: 436):

"[...] anthropological evidence has been, and can continue to be, of invaluable service as a crucible in which to put to more rigorous test psychology's tentative theories, enabling one to edit them and select among alternatives in ways which laboratory experiments and correlational studies within our own culture might never make possible."

Although the methods of cross-cultural psychology resemble those of the psychological mainstream more than those of anthropologists, they still wish to make a contribution of the same kind. It is an important aim to which I myself have long subscribed and continue to do so, at least in principle. Unfortunately the pursuit of this goal encounters some formidable practical obstacles. One is the sheer size of the task: which of the vast number of psychological generalizations should be tested?

Supposing one selects a particular sub-field such as experimental social psychology, based overwhelmingly on research with American college students. Given that social behavior is likely to vary quite widely across cultures, such a restriction to a single sub-population in a single country is likely to lead to parochial results. Faced with this objection, experimental social psychologists argue that this does not matter, "given the abiding faith in basic universals of humankind" (Gerard and Conolley 1972: 242). In fact, some of our mainstream colleagues respond to cross-cultural findings much as Titchener (1916) did to those of Rivers. Titchener's argument was, in essence, that cross-cultural research presents so many difficulties that it cannot lead to any firm conclusions. One can find more recent statements along the same lines: "The outcome of a cross-cultural replication is likely either to show that culture is unimportant for the phenomenon or to produce an uninterpretable result" (Messick 1988: 43). According to Kuhnian principles one could predict a reluctance to abandon seemingly solid findings based on numerous Western student samples, simply because of a few disconfirming results in other cultures. For instance, disconfirmation by Amir and Sharon (1987) caused barely a ripple in the complacent world of experimental social psychology. Nonetheless, it would be wrong to end on a negative note. There are encouraging signs in some parts of the mainstream, notably among developmental psychologists, who are now more willing to take cross-cultural findings on board.

2. "*Explore* other cultures in order to discover psychological variations that are not present in one's own limited cultural experience" (Berry et al. 1992: 3).

The authors maintain, rightly, that one should not be content to report the absence of, say, a primacy effect in memory, but rather explore the reasons for the failure to find it. This is certainly an important goal, but the direction taken by cross-cultural psychology decreases the likelihood of it being frequently achieved. I am referring here to the tendency, noted earlier, to administer tests and questionnaires of various kinds. With rare exceptions, such methods have ethnocentric assumptions built in; and since response alternatives are restricted, there is no room for *qualitative* as distinct from *quantitative* differences to manifest themselves. It may be suggested that it is mainly in *direct observation of behavior, and/or personal interaction*, that one comes across such qualitative aspects. I will illustrate this with a simple example from my own past research.

Before starting on my little story, let me remind you that until about half a century ago it was generally believed that non-verbal IQ tests were 'culture-free'. Hence such tests were administered to non-European populations who generally obtained much lower scores, leading to the conclusion that their IQ was much inferior. When I first went to Africa in the 1950s, I used the Kohs Blocks Test and obtained much the same results. However, I had spent quite a lot of time with African children, and they did not seem duller than European ones to me, so it became a puzzle why they did so poorly on the test. One possibility was a specific deficiency in spatial ability, but I also noted that those from a literate family background did better than those from an illiterate one. This seemed to make a specific deficiency less likely. It is worth mentioned in passing that I later did find that African children and students did have a problem with mental rotation, but only when that rotation was in three dimensions (Jahoda 1979). Anyway, in order to solve this puzzle, I carefully observed their behavior in the course of dealing with the task. This led me to formulate the hypothesis that their perception of the task differed from that assumed to be self-evident by psychological testers.

The task as prescribed by the test constructor was that of faithfully copying not only the patterns as such but also their *orientation in space*, which differed, as can be seen in Figure 1. The children, however, took it for granted that only *the internal structure* mattered. This was demonstrated by devising a task whereby the children had to judge the sameness or difference between pairs of stimuli, as shown in Figure 2.

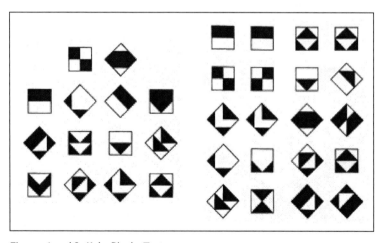

Figures 1 and 2: Kohs Blocks Test

It might be thought that this was a special case, but this is not the case— similar problems can arise in relation to personality tests, attitude scales, questionnaires, etc. For instance, if you ask a mother "how many children do you have?", there are multiple possibilities of ambiguity. Children who have died may or may not be included; similarly, children of co-wives will be included if the question is understood as "how many children are there in the family?" If the respondent thinks that the question is asked for a head tax, she may minimize the number, or if for welfare payments maximize it.

The general point I am trying to make is that cross-cultural research should never be treated as a merely mechanical procedure, as I fear it sometimes is. One should make every effort to understand at least the relevant aspects of the culture studied, so that ideally every cross-cultural psychologist should also be a cultural psychologist. It might be objected that this is not necessary in cases where, as often happens, a colleague from the culture to be studied is also involved. There are, I believe, at least two answers to this: (1.) It is a mistake to believe that any member of a culture knows all about that culture, e.g., the orientation to the task just described. (2.) In any culture there are things that are so much taken for granted that they are never articulated. An example would be the hot-cold dimension studied by Wassmann and Dasen (1994) in New Guinea; indirect methods had to be used since direct questioning would have been useless.

Let me now turn to the third and last goal:

3. "[...] *integrate* the results obtained by [1. and 2.] and [...] *generate* a more nearly universal psychology [...] It is [our] working assumption that [seeking] 'universal laws' of human behavior is [a realistic goal] [...] we believe that we will eventually discover the underlying psychological processes that are characteristic of our species [...] as a whole." (Berry et al. 1992: 3/4).

This is a very big and highly controversial issue, and I will concentrate on just two aspects. There is first of all the revealing phrase 'underlying psychological processes'—underlying what? Presumably culture is meant here, an interpretation strengthened by another passage dealing with methods, of which I will cite just one sentence: "More and more of this variance is 'peeled off', until ideally no difference between the cultures is left to be explained" (Berry et al. 1992: 231). It seems that culture is conceived as a kind of outer tegument, and the notion is reminiscent of that of 19th-century writers who believed that educated natives have only a 'veneer of civilization', and when that is stripped away the true savage stands revealed.

In my view this is a fundamentally misconceived image. Culture is not something superficial, but much of it becomes an integral part of the person in the course of development. There are no doubt underlying biological commonalities shared by the species (a point to which I will return), but as Geertz (1975: 49) rightly stated "there is no such thing as a human nature independent of culture".

The other general issue related to universality is that of comparability of psychological concepts across cultures. Westerners, it is said, operate with their own conceptual toolkit, and such an 'imposed etic' rides rough shot over cultural emics. Here I would like to critically examine a possible solution put forward by John Berry a generation ago and widely accepted. As is well known, this proposes a 'derived etic' that would make universal comparisons possible. John Berry is an old friend and comrade-in-arms, but on this issue we have often crossed swords. The discussion will focus on his example of 'intelligence' in a recent version of his famous paper (Berry 1990). It is suggested here that the seemingly simple moves to the derived etic are in fact illusory. In the passages below Berry's own words are in italics, and refer to Figure 3.

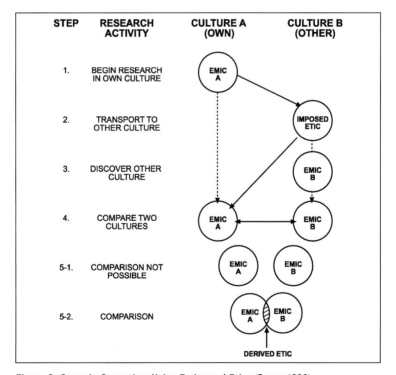

Figure 3: Steps in Operationalizing Emics and Etics (Berry 1990)

It should be explained that the first two steps relate to traditional procedures, which Berry wants to supersede.

Step 1: "[...] *a concept of intelligence is made explicit and tests are developed to assess it. Step 2 is then taken, with the same tests in another culture; at most, there is linguistic translation ... However, 'unexamined' is the very concept of intelligence being used, and 'unexplored' is the possibility that there exists an alternative idea about what constitutes the cognitively competent individual."* This is what Berry calls an 'imposed etic'.

"[...] *in Step 3, there is a deliberate attempt to come to know and assess another culture as reliably and as validly as one knows one's own in Step 1".* This is rather a tall order, since it implies not only that one has to become a cultural psychologist or even anthropologist, but that one has to become bi-cultural! In practice that is very rare, and certainly well beyond the reach of most cross-cultural psychologists.

"In Step 4, the two emic understandings are related to each other. If no communalities exist ... . then comparison of the intelligence of people in Culture A and Culture B is simply not possible (Step 5.1)."

Then follows a rather curious passage apparently suggesting that under certain circumstances even incompatible concepts can be validly compared:

"For example, if one concept includes being quick in responding, but the other does not mention it, then speed of responding cannot be a dimension on which the two groups can be compared; further, if the second group mentions being slow and deliberate as an element of intelligence, then speed of responding could be a valid dimension for comparison, but scoring would have to be in opposite directions in the two cultures." (Berry 1990: 95-96)

Unless I have totally misunderstood, the propositions put forward in this passage are logically flawed. One asks first, what is being compared here? The answer is, presumably, the conceptions of intelligence in two different cultures. Secondly, are the two conceptions compatible? The answer must be 'no', since they use opposite criteria: what is intelligent in one is stupid in the other and vice versa. The third question is, how could scoring in opposite directions make this a valid dimension for comparison? I think the answer is that it is not possible. If a person is slow and deliberate he will be regarded as intelligent in one culture and stupid in the other, and there is no way scoring procedures can alter that. So one is forced to the conclusion that this example does not make sense.

Let us now look at Figure 5.2 and assume that the derived etic, shown as the overlap in the Venn diagram, refers to something that is regarded as indicative of intelligence and positively valued in both cultures A and B, an example of which would be, say, social skills. Now if one looks again at 5.2 it will be seen that the overlap, indicating the shared component, is rather slight. It will thus be evident that while they agree that social skills are part of intelligence, the meaning of intelligence is still very different in cultures A and B. Hence the *derived etic* is not much use for devising a test of intelligence that would be acceptable in both A and B.

In the text (Berry et al. 1992: 233) it is suggested that "This [procedure] should lead eventually to the formulation of 'derived' etics that are valid cross-culturally". Now even if the procedure worked, the mind boggles at the thought of having to apply it to all major human cultures! All this is of course not to question John Berry's numerous and very substantial contributions, which I admired from the very first one (Berry 1966) onward, but the 'derived etic' is one the few issues on which we radically disagree.

Let me say once again that I do not wish to decry the first two of these goals, even if the path toward them is rockier than might appear. As regards a 'universal psychology', its advocates do not seem to have sufficiently thought through what its shape could possibly be—I will make a brief remark on this later.

Some Tentative Suggestions For the Future

In the latter part of the 19th century, the study of so-called 'primitives' or 'savages' was in part prompted by the view that there was little time left, as they were bound to soon disappear from the face of the earth. In a sense this forecast has become true in the 21st century, since the last isolated New Guinea Stone Age cultures have been invaded by the outside world. Yet it is still the case that a considerable part of the world population is either semi- or totally illiterate, and retains significant parts of their traditional cultures. Hence, in order to gain an adequate picture of cultural variations, the increasing tendency in cross-cultural psychology to take the more convenient way of concentrating on high school or even university students, ought to be reversed.

Moreover, unlike *cultural* psychologists, cross-cultural ones frequently display a lack of concern for cultural boundaries. This is a particularly tricky issue in large multicultural societies, and the problem is by-passed by the common practice of equating 'cultures' with 'nations'. It is an issue that deserves more discussion than it receives.

Perhaps even more important is the widely neglected topic of *cultural change*, including social, cognitive, and other aspects. There was a time when anthropologists regarded cultures as static, dubbed the 'pickle-pot' stance after the pots in which jam or marmalade is preserved. But while anthropologists have long abandoned this assumption, cross-cultural psychologists often report their data as though they had discovered eternal verities. Indeed, one could well write a paper on *cross-cultural psychology as history*, following Gergen's (1973) model! There are those who have shown a clear awareness of the issue, notably Patricia Greenfield (e.g., 1999). In offering an example, I have chosen an old study, one of my own, for the reason that is simple to present. In 1955 I used Piaget's 'bicycle-drawing' task, which tests the understanding of the mechanism. The sample consisted of children in several schools in Accra, in what was still the Gold Coast. Thirteen years later I returned to what had by then become Ghana, and repeated the study in the same schools. The results are shown in Figures 4 and 5, for boys and girls, respectively. In 1955, the performance of Accra boys was significantly inferior to that of Glasgow boys, but by 1968 they had caught up. By contrast, the Accra girls had not improved over the period; but if the study were repeated now, my guess would be that the girls would also have become significantly better at the task.

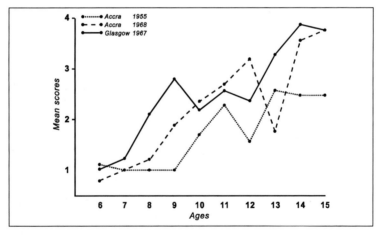

Figure 4: Comparative developmental trends (boys)

In my view, cross-cultural psychology should in the future become less parochial—in other words, establish closer relations with neighboring disciplines. An obvious one is of course anthropology; but while lip-service is paid to the importance of this neighbor, in practice it is too often ignored. This is probably a consequence of the methodological emphasis on tests and questionnaires already mentioned. A partner not usually considered at all is history, though a historical approach can throw a great deal of light on cultural variations (e.g., Diamond 1998); and archaeology provides some fascinating insights on ancient cognition (e.g., Renfrew and Zubrow 1994). One could of course list several other candidates, but one in particular deserves more detailed discussion, namely, evolutionary psychology, which has burgeoned over the last decade or so and could be a natural ally.

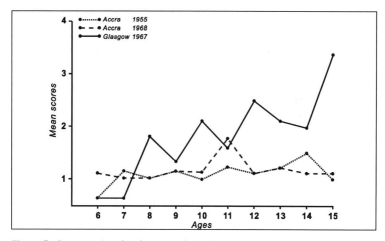

Figure 5: Comparative developmental trends (Girls)

Take for instance the goal of reaching towards psychological universals. It is highly unlikely that this could be achieved by the mere accumulation of more and more data, as tends to be assumed. Instead, a better prospect for arriving at approximations to psychological universals might be through hypotheses formulated on the basis of evolutionary theory. This is of course not to say that either the hypotheses themselves, or the findings, will be unaffected by culture. Any researcher inevitably lives and works within a given socio-cultural setting likely to influence their hypotheses to a greater or lesser extent. Moreover, research findings themselves are unlikely to be quite clear-cut—life is not so easy. Yet within these limitations it is likely that cross-cultural psychology could make a potentially valuable contribution. A start has already been made by, for instance, Buss et al. (1990), who, on the basis of evolutionary theory studied mate preferences in 37 societies. They found a consensus everywhere concerning certain key attributes sought in a long-term mate. This work was published in the *Journal of Cross-Cultural Psychology*, which I am glad to note has become sympathetic to the approach. However, this kind of cross-cultural work remains exceptional, and evolutionary psychologists themselves are sometimes guilty of assuming rather than demonstrating universality. Thus, Cosmides and Tooby (1992) argued on evolutionary grounds that there is a 'cheater-detection mechanism' operating in the course of social exchanges. They provided some supporting empirical evidence, based on American students. It was later replicated and refined by Shakelford (1997), but once again with undergraduate psychology students in the American Midwest! So we don't know if the cheater-detector is really a human universal or is just confined to American students. Another unanswered question remains (and I make no apology for stressing the same problem yet again) so long as studies, however widely spread across the globe, are confined to students and other educated people. This is because an apparent universal might in reality be a function of literacy and/or schooling rather than a product of evolution. So here, in sum, is where cross-cultural psychology could provide invaluable service, and might well in due course formulate and test its own evolutionary hypotheses.

Lastly, it seems clear to me that cross-cultural psychology, if it is to have a promising future, can no longer be content to proceed along wellworn grooves. There is, in my view, a need for a wide-ranging debate about fundamentals, and this constitutes my own contribution to such a debate. If I have been critical, it was with the intention of being constructive, and my hope is of a bright future, as expressed by Jauffret in his peroration two centuries ago:

"May this Society ... fulfil in due course the glorious destiny that seems to await it, and merit that one should say of it one day that its foundation proved useful at the same time for the advancement of science and the happiness of humankind!" (Jauffret 1801, cited in Copans and Jamin 1978: 85).

References

Amir, Y./Sharon, I. (1987). Are Social Psychological Laws Cross-culturally Valid? In: Journal of Cross-Cultural Psychology, 18, 383-470.

Berry, J.W. (1966): Temne and Eskimo Perceptual Skills. In: International Journal of Psychology, 1, 207-229.

Berry, J.W. (1990): Imposed Etics, Emics, and Derived Etics: Their Conceptual and Operational Status in Cross-Cultural Psychology. In: T.N. Headland/K.L. Pike/M. Harris (Eds.): Emics and Etics: The Insider/Outsider Debate (pp. 84-99). Newbury Park, CA: Sage.

Berry, J.W./Poortinga, Y.H./Segall, M.H./Dasen, P.R. (1992). Cross-Cultural Psychology. Research and Applications. Cambridge: Cambridge University Press.

Berry, J.W./Poortinga, Y.H./Segall, M.H./Dasen, P.R. (2002). Cross-Cultural Psychology. Research and Applications. Cambridge: Cambridge University Press.

Berry, J.W. (1997) Preface. In: J.W. Berry/Y.H. Poortinga/J. Pandey (Eds.): Handbook of Cross-Cultural Psychology, 2nd ed., Vol.1 (pp. X-XV). Boston: Allyn & Bacon.

Buss, D.M./Abbott, M./Angleitnot, A./Asherian, A./Biaggio, A./Blanco-Villasenor, A. (1990): International Preferences in Selecting Mates: A Study of 37 Societies. In: Journal of Cross-Cultural Psychology, 21, 4-57.

Campbell, D.T./Naroll, R. (1972): The Mutual Methodological Relevance of Anthropology and Psychology. In: F.L.K. Hsu (Ed.): Psychological Anthropology (pp. 435-463). Cambridge, Mass.: Schenkman.

Copans, J./Jamin, J. (1978): Aux origines de l'anthropologie francaise. Paris: Sycomore.

Cosmides, L./Tooby, J. (1992): Cognitive Adaptations for Social Exchange. In: J.H. Barkow/L. Cosmides/J. Tooby (Eds.): The Adapted Mind: Evolutionary Psychology and the Creation of Culture (pp. 163-228). New York: Oxford University Press.

Degérando, J.-M. (1969 [1800]): The Observation of Savage Peoples. Tr. F.T.C. Moore. London: Routledge & Kegan Paul.

Diamond, J. (1998): Guns, Germs and Steel: A short History of Everybody for the last 13,000 Years. London: Vintage.

Geertz, C. (1975): The Interpretation of Cultures. London: Hutchinson.

Gerard, H.B./Conolley, E.S. (1972): Conformity. In: C.G. McClintock (Ed.): Experimental Social Psychology (pp. 237-263). New York: Holt, Rinehart & Winston.

Gergen, K.J. (1973): Social Psychology as History. In: Journal of Personality and Social Psychology, 26, 309-320.

Greenfield, P. (1999): Historical Change and Cognitive Change: a Two-decade Follow-up Study in Zinacantan, a Maya Community in Chiapas, Mexico. In: Mind, Culture and Activity, 6, 92-108.

Jahoda, G. (1970): A Cross-Cultural Perspective in Psychology. In: The Advancement of Science, 27, 57-70.

Jahoda, G. (1979): On the Nature of Difficulties in a Spatial-Perceptual Task: Ethnic and Sex Differences. In: British Journal of Psychology, 70, 351-363.

Jahoda, G. (1979): On the Nature of Difficulties in a Spatial-Perceptual Task: Ethnic and Sex Differences. In: British Journal of Psychology, 70, 351-363.

Messick, D.M. (1988): On the Limitations of Cross-Cultural Research in Social Psychology. In: M.H. Bond (Ed.): The Cross-Cultural Challenge to Social Psychology (pp. 41-47). Newbury Park, CA.: Sage.

Poortinga, Y.H. /Malpass, R.S. (1986) Making Inferences from Cross-Cultural Data. In: W.J. Lonner/J.W, Berry (Eds.): Field Methods in Cross-Cultural Research (pp. 17-46). Beverly Hills: Sage.

Renfrew, C./Zubrow, E.B.W. (1994): The Ancient Mind: Elements of Cognitive Archaeology. Cambridge: Cambridge University Press.

Rivers, W.H.R. (1901): Part I. Introduction, and Vision. In: A.C. Haddon (Ed.): Reports of the Cambridge Anthropological Expedition to Torres Straits. Cambridge: Cambridge University Press.

Segall, M.H./Campbell, D.T./Herskovits, M.J. (1966): The Influence of Culture on Visual Perception. Indianapolis: Bobbs-Merrill.

Serpell, M.H. (1976). Culture's Influence on Behaviour. London: Methuen.

Shackelford, T.K. (1997): Perceptions of Betrayal and the Design of the Mind. In: J.A. Simpson/D.T. Kenrick (Eds.): Evolutionary Social Psychology (pp. 73-107). Mahwah, N.J.: Lawrence Erlbaum.

Spencer, Herbert (1876): Principles of Sociology. 3 vols. London: Williams & Norgate.

Titchener, E.B. (1916): On Ethnological Tests of Sensation and Perception. In: Proceedings of the American Philosophical Society, 55, 204-236.

Triandis, H.C. (1980): Preface. Handbook of Cross-Cultural Psychology, Vol.1. Boston: Allyn & Bacon.

Thurnwald, R. (1913): Ethno-psychologische Studien an Südseevölkern. In: Beihefte zur Zeitschrift für angewandte Psychologie und psychologische Sammelforschung; No. 6. Leipzig: Barth.

Wassmann, J./Dasen, P.R. (1994): "Hot" and "Cold": Classification and Sorting among Yupno of Papua New Guinea. In: International Journal of Psychology, 29, 19-38.

A Meditation on Message and Meaning

Ernest E. Boesch

I

Unexpectedly a twig breaks in a garden tree, a bird sings in front of the kitchen window, a nut tree sapling sprouts up from nowhere, or my computer strikes—as in so many other insignificant small events, Supanee, my wife, will say: "A message". A message of what? She won't tell. Of nothing specific, probably. It may be felt simply as an invitation to be open to life, to the wonders of nature, to the gift of being, to let nothing go by as insignificant. It may awaken her awareness of ever present, all pervading meanings.

This is indeed strange: message without a content one could spell out. Nothing else than a feeling of meaningfulness, somehow the opposite of what depressive patients complain about: that nothing makes sense, that all is meaningless. A real puzzle to a psychologist who wants to define meaning in terms of structure or information.

Such a feeling of meaningfulness may be experienced in other, yet equally puzzling ways. Joseph Campbell writes: "When you reach an advanced age and look back over your lifetime, it can seem to have had consistent order and plan, as though composed by some novelist. Events that when they occurred had seemed accidental and of little moment turn out to have been indispensable factors in the composition of a consistent plot. So who composed that plot? ..." And he goes on: "It is even as though there were a single intention behind it all, which always makes some kind of sense, though none of us knows what the sense might be, or has lived the life that he quite intended."[1] I confess having often felt exactly what Campbell describes. To recognize meaning in one's life or in some event, although unable to tell what this meaning is, seems to occur frequently. To experience such meaningfulness, even if scarcely articulate, is profoundly satisfying and reassuring. Should it be lacking, it seems, as mentioned, to qualify as depression. What then can it be?

---

1   In: Bond (1997), p. XVIII.

A first understanding might be that the feeling of meaningfulness marks the difference between familiarity and strangeness. I walk along a shopping street—windows full of all kinds of goods, clothes hanging on outside stalls, bargain-priced books on sidewalk tables, a noisy saxophonist at a corner, women with shopping bags, others with a pram or an unruly child, lovers, old people, bar tables in the pedestrian area and so on—all of it means something; although I may ignore its exact significance, it belongs to a society whose habits, customs, rules and language are familiar. However, should I walk in an Arabian Suk, even the smell would be strange, I would not know the goods displayed in narrow shops, would be baffled by cryptic sounds all around, and soon, without a guide, I would feel lost. All that, of course, means something to those living there, but to me it is meaningless—or rather, it signifies threat, loss of self confidence, helplessness.

The meaning of things and situations, thus, relates them to my cadres of orientation, and thereby qualifies my world view and my action potential. Yet, should we not distinguish degrees as well as kinds of meaning? Is the Arabian Suk really 'meaningless'? It may appear so at the moment, but it also promises meanings, otherwise I would not have gone there. Thus, meanings may be anticipated, hoped for or feared, although not yet specified. This prospective quality makes the meaninglessness in the Suk very different from the one in depression. For the depressive patient, the world is entirely void of meaning, he despairs even of his own meaningless self, while I still feel myself to exist in a meaningful world, the Suk being simply an island of provisional 'un-meaning', a 'not-yet-meaning' promising to become meaningful as far as I trust my action potential.

Yet, is this exact? The depressive patient knows of course that a knife serves to cut, a pen serves to write, and so on: the meaning of things, in the sense of their function and relationships, has not disappeared from his mind. Thus, although remaining conscious of the structural and functional significance of his world, it is bare of meaning.

Could it be that his meanings have lost their emotional quality? We might feel tempted here to establish a taxonomy of meanings, such as structural, functional, emotional, and search for examples to illustrate each of them. I fear that this would take the second step before the first. Therefore, instead of hastening to classify what we do not yet know enough about, I would rather look first at a real situation and try to disentangle its meanings. Since this can be done only with a situation intimately known, I may be allowed to reflect on the nearest situation at hand, namely the study in which I am working just now.

II

This study is a room in the house jointly owned by my wife Supanee and me. It was built some 25 years ago, after long looking around for a suitable location and assembling the finances needed. Today, the debts are paid, no limiting liabilities anymore. A garden with a large lotus pond, some bamboo and other bushes, surrounded by big trees—all planted by us—guaranties much privacy. Protected by a big pine tree, a slightly rising, decoratively paved walk leads up to the entrance—a bamboo bush near a big natural stone give it a rather Asian look. The flat roof carries a sun collector and a parabellum antenna. The neighborhood is quiet, modestly upper middle class, with agreeable relationships, helpful if needed, friendly, but not intrusive.

About a hundred meters from the house begins a big woods, a year-round recreational area, covering a hilly area that separates us from the town of Saarbruecken on the west, and the University on the north, the former about one hour's walking distance, the latter, half of that, so that, during my active years, I frequently walked through the woods to my institute. The small village in which we live is a relatively newly built, quiet part of an otherwise rather drab suburb. Let me add that Saarbruecken lies about 15 km from the French border—which to me greatly increased its attraction. And its 270-km distance from Switzerland still allowed relatively easy visits to my home country.

Our house lies in Germany, and I not only closely witnessed, after 1952, its turbulent social developments, but also remained painfully conscious of pre-war and war-time German history. Having grown up in war-torn Europe, although in the relatively protected Switzerland, made me indeed very sensitive to this side of our domicile.

The house, built according to my plans, conserved of course its basic structure, but in details it has changed progressively, adapted more intimately to our needs and tastes, so that today it offers all the amenities corresponding to our age and inclinations. Its large windows open on the garden, there are inside spaces for privacy as well as communality, a health area containing sauna and fitness room, comfort for relaxing, pictures and art objects for enjoyment.

All that, of course, is not yet my study, but the meaning of an object never derives from it alone, but also from its embeddedness in larger contexts. My office at the University, although in part serving similar activities, carried different connotations and meanings. And while that office lay at the end of a dark corridor lined by rooms of other members of the Institute, with all doors closed, my home study connects openly with areas of our private life, allowing an easy coming and going between the two.

So let me now present the study itself. It is a moderately-sized room, yet large enough for working as well as occasional resting. My working place, at an L-shaped desk, faces a view of the garden. On the side, a large glass door opens onto a small terrace, enclosed on three sides, paved in a yin-yang design, over which watches the iron sculpture of a mythical Thai-Burmese swan. A bookcase plus two cupboards filled mainly with books line two walls, while a third is taken up by a shelf holding amplifiers, recorders, and the rather voluminous collection of CDs, and flanked by two high-quality speakers. Two easy chairs complete the furniture, one of which can be extended for my siestas and was formerly used in psychoanalyses.

On the walls hang Thai paintings, two traditional, one modern in style, a gilded wooden Thai relief representing two intertwined Nagas, an African mask of a mythical animal, which my son Christophe brought back from his researches in the jungle of the Ivory Coast, a lithography by Picasso, signed and numbered, but not dated, an etching by the British painter Ben Nicholson, a Matakam hand harp from the North of Cameroun, and an engraved African calabash that our Africanist, Paul Hinderling, had given me in exchange for a native drum. Two Thai handdrums stand in a corner. On the music shelf a Sihing Buddha statue sits on the traditional lotus bed, while over my working desk presides a smaller sized sitting Buddha, delicately sculptured and dated B.A. 2517—the year (AD 1974) when it was cast and also 'entrusted' to me in response to a donation to the Sirirath-Hospital in Bangkok (Buddha images do not belong to anybody, so they cannot be bought, sold or given away). On top of the bookcases are, on one side, examples of artful Thai pottery, on the other a wooden statue of 'Mae Phra Thoranee', the Earth Goddess and protectoress of the Buddha in Thai mythology. It is flanked by silver bowls embossed with mythological or religious figures, which are a speciality of Northern Thailand and adjoining Burma. Also probably Northern Thai is a carved lintel over the door, which, traditionally, is believed to protect the house.[2] Be it added that all the furniture, except the chairs, was made according to my designs—a half exception is the music shelf which, originally, was a bookcase bought in Switzerland during my first marriage; later I had it transformed in order to contain the stereo equipment and the collection of CDs.

This is a dry, merely physical description of my study and its situation. Yet, it already hints at the complexity of enclosed meanings—the working desk with computer, telephone, and a lot of paper disorder,

2   See Nimmanahaeminda (1966).

books, a musical installation, Thai artistic, religious, and mythological objects, and, of course, much I have not mentioned, like the flute I played until a few years ago, the Thai opium weights arranged around the Buddha on my desk, the kinds of books kept here (while others are stored at different places in the house), the uncounted photographs kept in a cupboard, to mention only a few more examples. This constitutes a heterogeneous collection of things likely to have very different meanings. Let us therefore look more closely at some of them.

To begin with perhaps a very inconspicuous one, a glass wine carafe that incongruously stands in one of my bookcases. It is a plain vessel used all over Switzerland in the more popular restaurants and pubs. Its shape, although elegant, easily comparable with the artful Thai pottery in the study, is too common for attracting aesthetic appreciation. This particular carafe belonged to my cousin Dora who had spent a year in Japan and later married a Swiss painter of some renown. They settled in the Tessin, the southern part of Switzerland where, after the death of her husband, Dora kept a small pub in a rather remote village that clings to one of the steep slopes of a Tessin valley. We often went to see her in her big, yet simple, even uncomfortable country house, high over the canyon, with a small garden and a cool pergola, a pub room with large, old, shiningly polished wooden tables. She liked Supanee in a sometimes friendly teasing and protective way, and we sampled with her the country restaurants where she knew to get delicious roasted chicken. She liked white wine, was good friends with her village folk who regularly came to play cards in her pub, and she spread around her a healthy, cheerful outlook and wisdom. I was, of course, in a way jealous of her living in a part of Switzerland where all my life I had dreamed of settling one day, of her simple, undemanding, and still deeply satisfying life. When she was dying, I was able to arrange for her to enter a private hospital that provided her with kind care. My grandmother, too, died in her house of a stroke at the tea table, and was buried at a beautiful spot high above the village.

Thus, the carafe represents Dora, my only close cousin, the attraction of the Tessin, and my grandmother who, during my later childhood and adolescence, was even more important than my mother. But it is of course also a wine recipient. Slender, with the elegant curve of a young girl's narrow waist, it conveys more friendly hospitality than a wine bottle: the dark glass and rigid form makes a wine bottle look severe, it hides its contents, while in the carafe the wine shines a warm glowing red. Its large mouth and the unassuming simplicity of its form create an impression of spontaneous, informal generosity. I am, I confess, an amateur of good red wine (although in moderate quantities), and thus the carafe not only reminds me of Dora and her house on the mountain slope, but also of other festive moments. Let me add that Ben Nicholson, the artist I mentioned, seems to have understood the aesthetic attraction of these carafes—in an etching that hangs in my study he artfully combines three of them. So this unassuming glass vessel is in reality a symbol full of recollections, cheerful, but also sad ones; it associates images of a simple, good and hospitable life as well as the loss of much of it. I might say that it condensates part of my history, but also some of my vain hopes.

The Buddha Sihing on top of my music chest faces me each time when I sit listening to music. It is a sculpture of perfect beauty, sitting in a pose of relaxed and yet concentrated absorption[3], each time making me wish somehow to assimilate, to interiorize such perfect serenity. Imperceptibly, it seems even to influence my musical orientation—noisy, chaotic music just does not harmonize with it. The Buddha Sihing is the type of image that the Thais deeply venerate—it demonstrates, I would say, how intimately aesthetic beauty relates to religious sentiments. We met this statue accidentally in the display window of an antiquity dealer in Saarbruecken. Supanee attracted my attention to it, and I spontaneously went into the shop to "rent" it (since, as I mentioned above, Buddha images cannot be bought or sold). This is one of four Buddha images of which my Thai wife and friends tended to say: "It waited for you". One of them "met me" at the night market in Chiengmai, another in a back-street of Paris, a third one in a shop window of a noisy business street in down town Bangkok, and each one of them came or stayed in my possession in an improbable way. The Thais' saying that a Buddha statue "waited for me" might have been only half serious, but involuntarily it expressed the belief in an intimate relationship between things and man. Quite differently, the small Buddha on my desk was "entrusted" to me by a friend, Ouay Ketusinh, at that time professor of physiology at the Sirirath Faculty of Medicine. While this Buddha did not "wait for me", I would surmise that, knowing the Thais' attitude towards those objects of their faith, my friend must have considered me worthy of receiving it. And, of course, this Buddha reminds me also of a very impressive person I was lucky to know.

I knew very little of Buddhism before Unesco sent me, quite unprepared, to Thailand. And my wish to acquire a Buddha image did not stem from any religious interest. In the house of a Swiss friend, then already a Bangkok resident, I was struck by the beauty of a Khmer Buddha head. Now, although my father was an industrial artist and painter, we did not possess any sculpture—during the economic depression in which I grew

---

3   E.g. see The National Museum Volunteers (1987), p.44.

up, the idea of acquiring something like that would have been unthinkable. So the Buddha head in Kurt's house struck me not only by its
beauty, the serenity of its expression, but also as a token of luxury and
wealth. Such was the mundane origin of my wish for a Buddha statue—
soon fulfilled when a member of my Bangkok Institute led me to one of
his friends who agreed to 'lend' me one of his Buddhas.

In the meantime, of course, my interest had deepened. I had visited
the beautiful temples of Bangkok, observed the quiet devotion of the
faithful, had read about Thai mythology and Buddhism. I was impressed
by the airy, colorful luminosity of temples in contrast to our dark and
stale smelling churches, by the tolerance of the Thai Buddhists contrasting with the narrow sectarianism so often displayed by Christianity. And,
indeed, my sense for the aesthetic qualities of Thai Buddhist statues—
among the most beautiful of their kind—had been sharpened. Bob Textor, an American anthropologist who became a close friend during my
stay in Bangkok, was studying Buddhism intensively, and with his help I
also gained a deeper understanding for so-called superstitious practices.
In temple compounds I now looked on with sympathy at Thai women
shaking bowls with oracle sticks, reading eagerly the message on the one
ejected, and then, after having thanked the Buddha, quietly walking
away—some consoled, others worried. It was all so simple: lighting can-
dles and incense sticks at the right place, prostrating oneself in front of
the serenely watching Buddha image, was sufficient for creating hope.
There were, of course, other places with Brahmanic shrines one went to
in order to beg for success in business, examinations, or love, where all
kinds of offerings were deposited—food, elephants and other wooden
figures, flower garlands. But no Buddhist would consider that to be her-
esy; their faith included tolerance even for "paganism".

So in the course of time quite a number of Buddha statues "congre-
gated" in our home, and their meaning had not only progressively deepened, but had also accumulated various experiences—friendships like the
ones with Kurt, Bob Textor, Ouay Ketusinh, Kayoon Limtong, impressive encounters, like the one with the abbot of a temple in Baan Khaai,
memorable ceremonies, and touchingly beautiful religious places. Of
course, these images still move me by their aesthetic form, but the contexts of experience, learning, and imagination expanded their meaning to
become symbols of a relaxed, brighter faith. Or rather of something
which Buddhists tend to call "power of mindfulness". Against all rationality, they seem to emanate a message of peace, or at least to remind us
that peace has to begin in our mind, that it must be sought within ourselves; wisdom, they seem to insist, has to be the ultimate goal of life.
Wisdom, what does it mean? I am of course still far from knowing it, yet

65

the two Buddha statues in my study continuously present their message—a message that condenses much of my past and, beyond that, hints at a meaning which, although still hidden I somehow intuitively anticipate.

Let me turn to some other contents of the study, the books. I don't intend to mention any particular book, as an answer to the ubiquitous interview question: "Should you be allowed to take only one book with you on an island...." No, I could not name any particular book as being of special and permanent value to me, yet books, as a plural, are. There are books kept all over the house, many of them still not yet read. The ones in the study are partly needed for my work—a host of dictionaries and reference works; then there are publications by Piaget, Freud, Lévi-Strauss—my intellectual 'mentors'. The rest are a relatively heterogeneous collection, books which for various reasons are of particular interest to me—art volumes, publications on Thailand, on philosophy, mythology, ethnology, or religion, for instance. They are in German, English, or French, a few even in Thai (two of which I had hoped to translate, but I soon discovered that my knowledge of Thai did by far not allow me to understand all its intricate connotations. My intention to also include literary documents in studies of cultural psychology thus met a serious obstacle).

To be surrounded by books may give an agreeable feeling of intellectuality, but more precisely, what is their function? Books are potentials, they promise information, insight, broadening outlooks, all the more so when a library is multilingual. Each book I buy is a project, it stays on my shelves as a potential for action. Thus my daily activities are somehow lined by multiple taps that I can open according to need or wish, and in reading a book, the potential turns real, it strengthens my action or perhaps also changes it. Therefore, even the non-read books have their function—they contain the rescues needed in case of difficulties in my work. Our action always risks encountering unforeseen obstacles, and the reserve of books provides the potential to deal with them. For this reason I only rarely resort to our university libraries—books have to be available whenever needed, and moments of need may arise unexpectedly. But the availability of too many books may also worry—somehow, each unread book hints at a waiting project, at my limited action potential.

My associative links with books range wide and far. Very early on they provided me with vicarious experiences—first, as far as I remember, the Karl May stories of American Indians that I read as a boy, with hot cheeks, until late in the night. Then came, as a potent source of adolescent identification, the jungle adventures of Tarzan, later, more sophisticated, Hans Carossa, Rainer Maria Rilke, Hermann Hesse, plus of course writings by many other authors, important, though of lesser influence perhaps. Among them were, of course, the classics we read in high school—some of which, I confess, impressed me at that time, but did not stick in my memory as intimately as Rilke or Hesse. I wrote poetry, already at 18 or 19 wanted to become a writer, but after the war, when the extension and depth of Nazi German depravity became known, I began to suspect that evil could also have its roots in works of art, as for instance, I found, in the ruthless self-centredness of Goethe's Faust, and my admiration of German poets turned to deep distrust. For years to come I would stop reading German literature. It was probably at that time, too, that I began to realize that writers, even the ones of fiction, did bear a humane responsibility. Of course, writing, among other functions, helps to control and to construct one's self- and world-view; but as soon as it is published, this private function turns into a public one, the written text becomes model, appeal, warning, seduction, and thus no writer can evade responsibility towards his reader. Goethe's *Werther* is reported to have caused many suicides—should he not have been blamed for them? This was an example of the kind of questions, I found at that time, a writer should face. Justified as these thoughts were or not, they made me sensitive to the germs of evil hidden even in high culture.[4] Freud would of course agree—there is much repression behind art and philosophy. Which does not deny their value and function, but warns the creator of culture to remain wary. However, none of this stopped my wish to be a writer. Although I continued writing stories and poems, practical psychological and psychoanalytic experience strengthened those doubts and slowly pushed my literary ambitions into the background.

Not, however, by reducing the attraction of books. The volumes around me still sample the possible dimensions of writing—fiction, philosophy, science—including, too, the aesthetic quality of the written word. Beautiful page settings, beautiful letters always impress me, not least alien calligraphies, be they Chinese, Arabic, Sanskrit or Thai— which I struggled hard to learn. Thus, the aesthetic combined itself with the stylistic. Books, of course, contain language, and language, independent of its content, has an appeal of its own, by its sound, its rhythm, the elegance of its wording—which, in a sense, connects deeply with its honesty. I myself could never write without paying close attention to the rhythm and sound of the words and phrases, and I progressively discovered that these aesthetic aspects somehow connected with the honesty, or frankness, of content. The fluttering words, the puffed up phrasing one encounters in so many texts of social science or philosophy, frequently only hide carelessness—maybe even emptiness—of thought. It is surpris-

---

4   See also: Boesch (2005).

ing, by the way, that opaque language impresses many readers as deep thinking, and so untransparent texts written in a repulsive jargon of 'learned science' often receive the highest praise. Should one attempt to translate them into simple language, their message tends to lose its glamour. For this reason such authors, as famous as they may be, are almost totally lacking in my library. I am convinced, by the way, that a renewed discipline of honest and responsible writing would also greatly profit our public discussions.

So much for the books. A last look perhaps at the music shelf. Music, too, has a long past in my life. My first recollection was sitting under the piano while my father accompanied my mother's singing. That was, of course, before their divorce and the economic depression that made us poor—as was almost the whole town of St. Gallen. Later I learned by myself to play my grandfather's harmonium, and my father taught me to play the flute. In fact, music was important at home, although more as a kind of mastering of instruments than of higher musical culture. My father played the piano as long as he had one, plus the flute and the bassoon. I myself, in high school, first played the piccolo, then the trumpet in our cadet band and school orchestra. Later, I played the guitar to accompany my own singing, and finally, once we could afford one, I took great pleasure in playing the piano. The flute, however, remained the only instrument for which I took some systematic lessons, with the renowned flutist André Jaunet.

Most important for my musical experience was the friendship with Andreas Juon, an organist, pianist, conductor of a Bach choir, and composer himself. I certainly owe to him much of my musical culture, mainly a deepened understanding of Johann Sebastian Bach. I sang in Juon's choir, and played the flute with him on various occasions—I still vividly remember our serenades on chilly New Year's nights in front of the houses of some friends, my flute intonating a melody, his recorder embellishing it with lively variations. I also joined our local lay orchestra as a flutist, while my first wife sat among the violins. Towards the end of our marriage, to accompany her on the piano offered a welcome exception to an otherwise conflict-prone communication. During later years the piano became my preferred instrument.

All this, of course, somehow enters the connotations of the music shelf, which, though, also has a history of its own. I remember hearing a record player for the first time—it must have been around 1940—in the student room of Paul Osterrieth, a friend in Geneva, later a well-known professor in Brussels (who, by the way, once offered me a chair at his University—which I declined, feeling that Brussels was too distant from Switzerland). I think that it played one of Bach's Brandenburg Concertos, which impressed me very much—as did Paul's and his later wife Catherine's cultivated life style. Back in St. Gallen, we bought one of those early boxes to be wound up by hand, but the real 'revelation' came in Thailand. There, in my friend Kurt's seaside house, we sat on the terrace one night, over us a dark tropical sky dotted with brilliant stars, a mild breeze cooling the heat of the day, and from two loudspeakers sounded Smetana's "Moldau". That was the first and, of course, particularly attractive time that I heard stereophonic music.

At that time, the Saarland still being separated from Germany, it was impossible to buy such stereo equipment there. So I drove to Mannheim, bought two speakers, smuggled them back to Saarbruecken, where I had found a two-way amplifier, and connected the necessary elements for my first hi-fi installation. Which, of course, was progressively improved over the years, with the help of a friendly engineer-shop owner. And finally, I acquired the expensive speakers I own now (they work with electric arcs instead of membranes). They should compensate for my deteriorating eyesight, which more and more forbids me from attending concerts. I had, however, to locate this musical installation in my study—the musical tastes of Supanee, with her Thai background, being very different from mine. Yet, with time I acquired some understanding for Thai and other Asian music, too—still wondering what makes cultures elaborate such different musical forms, listening habits, and tastes; I still lack an answer.[5]

All these, plus many other objects, surround my working table. Each of them, of course, comprises multiple associations, memories, connotations, values which, should I try to pursue them exhaustively, would weave a multicolored net covering much of my life. They relate to situations, events, persons, actions, but somehow converge them all, although in complex ways, into the main function of my study, which is writing. In former times, this consisted mainly of writing the texts for my courses and lectures, but also articles, letters, and books; nowadays, letters, articles and books are my main occupation. Thus, I have at last become a writer, less of fiction, but still of more personal texts than is usual in 'science'. Let that remain undiscussed, and let me rather consider how these contents or the outlay of my study relate to the meaning of my writing.

---

5   See the chapter "Über Musik" in Boesch (2005).

III

In a book published some five years ago a chapter carries the title "The myth of the lurking chaos". It describes our frequent penchant to anticipate disasters or catastrophes, be they real, like thefts, accidents, earthquakes or other misfortunes, be they imaginary, like evil spirits, witches, the wrath of God, the end of times, or the Ultimate Judgement. A newer publication deals with the 'Janus-face' of culture, i.e., the ambivalent qualities of art, religion, and other cultural properties. The worried look on our cultures expressed in these chapters is of course amply justified by the events of our times. Yet, what I suggest there might be irritating all the same: namely, that evil, such as terror, undoubtedly has many roots, some in defects of the social system, others in human nature, but some also, unsuspectedly, in positive domains of culture. I tried to substantiate this concerning art and religion in particular, leaving aside philosophy and science, where similar demonstrations might have been possible. I added, too, that far from being as peaceful as we like to imagine ourselves, we all too often seem to need enemies or even to seek them actively for strengthening our self and our social identity.[6]

Now, the contents of my study seem not at all to tally with those rather pessimistic ideas. I am even surprised that, except perhaps for some books, there is nothing that relates to the anxieties or worries frequent in my life: real ones, due to the horrors of war and economic hardship, imaginary ones due to personal circumstances. Quite the contrary, the study surrounds me with symbols of a safe world and a happy or at least fortunate past. Why then do I, over and over again, conjure in my books the threats looming in our world? It looks like an exorcism—could it be that?

I like writing letters. Aside from mere administrative ones, letters tend to communicate personal views and opinions. In expounding my ideas, I somehow try to enlarge my private area into the external world. This requires, of course, finding a balance between what I know of the addressee and my own train of thought, a balance, so to speak, between the outside and the inside. Attempting such balance necessarily contributes to both: understanding the other as well as clarifying myself, it makes the private and the public attuned to each other. In other words, it diminishes the alienness of the non-I.

Might it be the same for books? In a sense, yes. Books are like letters, but with a large number of anonymous addressees. Their message, no doubt, also extends the private realm, but does so, too, by vying for a

---

6   See Boesch (2000 and 2005).

balance. In as far as my writings address psychological problems, they try to take into account the thinking and knowledge of informed readers; but I also look at facts and problems in my own way, wanting to make science 'in tune' not only with my private experience and existence, with the realities of daily life, but also with standards of humanity that should control scientific rules. This may, imperceptibly or voluntarily, shift my writing towards expressing personal ideas and images—from the scientific it might turn literary.

Or it may be, in a way, literary already from the start. Because writing means creating structures, transforming thoughts into language. Or, language is a recalcitrant medium: handled badly, it can be ugly, unpleasant to the eye and the ear as well as the mind. Writing, thus, means more than formulating a message—it requires giving the message a form that is no less pleasant than it is convincing. Beauty of form, sound, view, and thought is what the poet, of course, strives for more intimately than the prosaic writer—who, however, should feel similarly responsible. In this sense, writing sentences whose content is not only clear, but also sounds good, comes along in the right rhythm, both creates harmony for oneself, and makes one's message agreeable and understandable to the reader.

In a previous article I said that an artist, by surrounding himself with beautiful paintings symbolically erected a wall to protect his private area against the threats of the outside world. I compared it with the gardener who encloses his well-tended garden with a wall in order to keep out weeds and pests. He will not completely succeed: nettles, moles, and mice will always find a way in, yet the wall will make it easier to maintain the pleasantness of his private area. Endeavoring to maintain its beauty, he may, unconsciously, imagine a perfect harmony, somehow pursuing his private fantasm of paradise[7]. Could such not also be, unconsciously, the function of my writing? In some ways, I am 'writing against', against an outside which, though pleasant or seductive at times, always appears to be threatened by chaos. I might even be writing against a similar inside danger. Creating something like beauty, be it in form, color, sound, in attractive images, or simply in balanced sentences, is indeed a kind of exorcism. It defeats chaos by form.

That is a too simple, also perhaps a too ambitious formula. Yet, in a sense I do write less for communicating what I know, than for finding knowledge; more exactly, for organizing what is amorphous. Writing aims at giving form to what I feel to be unclear, even disturbing. Thus, writing is for me a process of exploration, of searching for the answer to a question. Not too rarely that answer may even differ from what I ex-

---

7   "Kunst, Glaube, Terror". In: Boesch (2005).

pected it to be—the search may lead me astray, but what looks astray could at times be the right direction. Thus, I often seem to need writing in order to think clearly. Hence it turns into a curious interaction. I may write down an idea, but the sentence or the paragraph somehow talks back at me, forces me to scrutinize it, urges my thoughts towards more clarity, perhaps, as I said, in an unforeseen direction. In a sense, writing incites a struggle between language and thought, uncovering now the inadequacy of language, then again the inadequacy of thought, and the result may finally be no more than provisionally satisfying—but satisfying all the same. Whatever that may be, the study considered here is a place for inner organisation. And in this organisation all its contents play their role. They symbolize key experiences in my life, they somehow circumscribe the area of questions important to me, and thus the values they represent implicitly permeate my thinking and direct my writing.

All this shows that to consider only the 'surface function' of my study, as a place for work and, intermittently, relaxation, in no way exhausts its meaning. We have uncovered, still incompletely, close interrelations between its location, its contents, and its function. We have seen that its contents, results as well as reminders of positive moments in my life, have been selected and arranged with no plan in mind, and yet with a pervasive purpose: to create a private, meaningful realm for my writing. This, of course, is again polyvalent and over-determined, it combines multiple origins and intentions into an action of complex significance. The complexitiy of the action corresponds with the heterogeneity of the collected objects. Thus, the study appears to be a focus concentrating a past and its many ramifications with purposes and fantasms of becoming.

IV

Would this long consideration of my study now give us a clearer idea of what is meant by the word 'meaning'? A twig breaks down in the garden, and Supanee says "message!"—does the event, although it "means something" to her, have a structure and a purpose? Or a child despairs about the broken arm of her doll—does its meaning 'bundle' a past with anticipations? While there are many little things that "mean something to us", do they really always relate a person to his or her world or action? The question, of course, could be answered only by analysing closely a number of such instances—I propose to look here only at one example, which I hope to be informative: a dream. Most of the time a dream is like a sealed 'message', it both announces and conceals a meaning. The message reveals its 'meaning' only when the seal is broken, when the dream is interpreted, either by oneself or by a more or less competent outsider. To interpret a dream, one has to relate its contents with the person's ongoing and past experiences. Once the dreamer feels this integration to 'fit consistently' her or his view of themselves and their situation, the dream becomes meaningful. Otherwise, the interpretation, be it 'true' or not, will be rejected (Let me note here, that no interpretation of a dream can be objectively true—individual situations are too complex for definite 'deciphering'; therefore, the 'feeling of consistent fit'—be it instant or delayed—remains a purely subjective evaluation, although perhaps useful to the dreamer.) Thus, a dream may be a message, but it turns meaningful only by relating it to a dreamer's experience and outlook.

Now, the breaking of the twig in front of my wife's garden window may be a message, but it is of course a 'sealed' one. To interpret it, she has to relate it in some way to herself. Which, basically, presupposes her being receptive to such 'messages', due to, I think, a belief in the close connectedness between outside and inside, between I and world. Such receptivity and watchfulness would somehow arise from her whole history. Even such tiny events can become meaningful only by being integrated into an individual's subjective world. 'Meaning', thus, relates an object, a situation, or an action to the continuity of one's existence. We might say that it concentrates the 'coming from' and the 'going to' into an actual metaphor, whereby 'going to' seems to be more important. Memories provide security, the confidence of being able to cope, but such coping potential derives its sense from anticipations; should the future be curtailed, in imagination or in fact, coping is not needed anymore and reality loses its meaning.

V

The things in my study have been designed, collected, selected by myself. Each of them has, of course, its own meaning, related in more or less close or distant ways to other objects, in or outside the study. All this has been constructed, but, as I said, not planned—it grew as my experience expanded. The network of its meanings is by far not exhausted by what I write here. This all the more, since meanings are often felt rather than analysed, difficult to verbalize, and may even change in my consciousness according to the situation. In spite of that, I sit here and write about them. What for? Might it perhaps be for countering these changes, for stabilizing the meanings in my world? Whatever those may be, speaking about the meanings in our world is important. It creates solid structures of valences, reliable orientations, stable contents for communication. We are, basically, 'narrators', as I wrote elsewhere[8]—might it not even be that the 'narrated' messages, rather than other experiences, create our values? Words create the world, said Saint John, although probably in a different vein.

The word creates the world. Indeed, all religions create their image of the world, political ideologists attempt the same, educators do it, philosophers, writers, even scientists compete for changing peoples' world view—by language. That is why manipulating words and images in information, politics, commerce, and entertainment has developed into an important and rewarding skill. People are easy to cheat because they want to live in a meaningful world. Reality often appears chaotic, therefore, words that seem to make it understandable, transparent and, above all, propitious to one's desires, will readily be believed. And we tend to think that what we believe is real, be it about our world or even ourselves.

And yet, to what extent do words really create meanings? After all, words are vague, unspecific markers of some kind of reality. A man tells a girl that he loves her. What does he mean? The girl, unless naïve and gullible, will want to know more. Which may embarrass even an honest lover—how to say what he really means by love? All too often the right words fail us in describing so many things—a feeling, a color, a sound, the taste of food, the impression we gain from a person. The poet attempts precision by metaphors, rhymes, sounds, and still may discover that language fails him. Of course, this blurredness of the language plays into the hands of various proselytizers: their message, interpretable in many ways, can please different listeners. Thus, words do not really specify meaning, they only mark limits within which meanings can be variably allotted. And so, a verbal message may be heard this by one, that way by another. A woman may say, "This poem moves me", and her friend says, "To me it's just empty words". So language, too, has to be made meaningful—but how?

The words we hear or use are of course understood in their common denominations. But they are loaded, too, with private experiences, expectations, emotional connotations, hopes, fears. Take again the word 'study'—the contents enumerated in these pages plus others not mentioned enter my understanding of the word, but someone else would give it a different meaning. Of course, a person whom I would invite to my study would understand the 'surface meaning' of it—yet, the reaction of a young girl or of a seasoned gentleman might be quite different.

Everything in my study is personal, and so is, in a sense, also what I write about it. Yet, is not everything in it also cultural? Objects, pictures,

---

8   "Homo narrator, der erzählende Mensch". In: Boesch (2005).

books, of course the computer, all are cultural products, and the same is true, after all, of the language that I use—and even of myself. I am a 'cultured individual', yet I transform culture, assimilate it, give it my personal form and meaning. About which I speak again in the cultural signs of language which, however, I use in a personal way. By evaluating and selecting, by assimilating and interpreting cultural contents, culture becomes meaningful for me, and by the same token, I define my role and function in it. But all this is regulated and steered by a purpose. Which one? Are my goals not cultural again?

So we move in a circle. Culture suggests meanings in numerous ways, which however, need to be understood, interpreted, qualified. So we seem to decide what they mean to us, seem to evaluate and select them according to our own intentions. Yet, how can we do that? Are we not ourselves mere cultural products, as some philosophers, sociologists, and psychologists maintain? Is there anything personal that empowers us to form meanings beyond cultural dictates? Perhaps a look at a very intimate experience may give us some clues.[9]

VI

I am walking. One step after the other, and each, potentially, carries a meaning. I may not notice it, yet I walk differently in a cheerful mood, in sorrow, or in deep thoughts. Might we say that my mood somehow 'commands' my style of walking? Of course, but the opposite is no less true: My walking commands my mood. Look at it more closely: each step, whether I am consciously aware of it or not, sends me a message— 'feedback' in the more sober terminology of science: it tells me that I walk easily or with effort, lightly or laboriously. This contains both, the basic information that I am able to move, and the more circumstantial one about the actual quality of my moving. This feedback immediately translates itself into a mood, a feeling of ease or strain, and it extends and generalizes: it makes me confident or doubting about reaching my aim, not only the present one I am going to, but also others, possible ones. In other words, the feedback from my walking, imperceptibly perhaps, but unavoidably influences my action potential. In our usual walking such feedbacks may pass unnoticed, but fatigued by a long march or with a strained ankle, they will provide obvious messages. The Buddhist meditation, walking slowly with attention, intends to strengthen awareness of messages emanating from the movement of muscles and senses, from the contact with the earth, and to widen thereby the meditator's conscious-

---

9   See Boesch (1992).

75

ness. What does that mean? What could be the messages he thus receives? Would they be cultural? Hardly. They are impressions before words, not yet conceptualized, the feeling of firmness of the ground he steps on, the caresses of wind and sun on his skin, somehow messages of belonging, of oneness with his world, a feeling of security or however one would awkwardly try to name them. They can be felt as being in tune, as an openness towards what surrounds the meditator, or simply as a rich inner firmness. Whatever it be, it is certainly genuinely personal.

This would be a special walking experience, but also our common walking commands mood, self-awareness, may even be a quality of I-world relationship. Of course, such immediate, intrinsically subjective messages accompany any of our actions, be they predominantly physical, like walking, be they mental, or even emotional. Emotions regulate actions, as we have known since Pierre Janet[10], but beyond that every emotion also signals an I-world relationship. Similarly, the ease or difficulties of my thinking reverberate on my self-feeling, they too are messages felt before words, spontaneously and intimately. All these, I would uphold, are pre-cultural messages, emanating from one's inner experience and—consciously or unconsciously—contributing to the way in which we interpret our world and act in it.

They will also color the cultural influences. Take a lover on the way to his sweetheart—his steps will be light, he may even be humming a tune, while the next day, going apprehensively to an examination, he would be likely to walk with a hesitant, even heavy gait. In both cases, his mood is not formed by the ongoing, but by the anticipated action: the expectation of a positive goal lightens, a feared one impedes the steps. But of course, both love and examination are strongly loaded with cultural values, promises, and constraints. Yet, self-confidence or self-doubts gained from previous intrinsic action messages will give these cultural values a personal tone. Furthermore, walking will retain its feedback function: the light-footedness of the lover would increase his cheerful mood, the heavy walking of the anxious candidate strengthen his self-doubts. Thus, the anticipated goal and the actual performance, cultural input and subjective experience amalgate to form their intrinsic message.

Naturally, not all messages are proprioceptive. The wind playing in the foliage of a tree, the birds singing, the sound of engines on the street and a thousand other impressions may be messages—most of them, however, already labelled by culture. Yet, those labels are flexible. Our surrounding culture is an immense pool of messages among which we search for those which promise adequate subjective-functional feedbacks. We select our food, choose where and how to relax, with whom to

---

10 See Boesch (1984).

socialize. The world of music is almost inexhaustible, and yet my CDs comprise only a small section of it; the books I read are a just a minimal sample of the millions available. Often we tentatively choose messages before knowing their meaning. I may search a book for a moving poem, discarding many before finding one which pleases me. The message turns to meaning when it fits an inner orientation, a vague anticipation or hope waiting to find its fulfilling content. In this hope we 'hunt for' promising messages, in leisure time, holidays, hobbies, friendships, and we feel at home in a culture which offers a sufficiently wide—or at least safe—range for our search. Messages are a promise, but they can also be a challenge, or even a threat. Therefore, interpreting them consists essentially in trying to balance the pre-cultural and the cultural, to equalize the relationship between me and the world. Meanings, thus, indicate the presence or absence of such balance.

VII

Let us then, to make these rather abstract reflections more tangible, look again at my study. The meaning of the objects considered so far was all connected with manifold past experiences. Let me then look at one in no way related to my past. On the wall above the Sihing Buddha hangs a red Japanese tray, a flat lacquered circle, with no decoration except two small slots for carrying it. I had bought it for no other reason than its perfect simple beauty, and it just lay around at home without being used in any way. Then, when I put the Sihing Buddha statue on the music shelf, I spontaneously filled the empty space above it with this tray. It resembles the emblem of the Japanese flag, the rising sun, and I somehow felt that it belonged there. Yet, in fact, to put it above the Buddha's head is irreverent. It might however also be thought to be behind rather than above, as in medieval paintings distant figures have to be put above the ones in the foreground. And indeed, looked at from Europe, Japan lies far 'behind' Thailand.

But what could it mean to put this Japanese emblem near the Buddha statue? I have never been in Japan, and do even not regret it. I have read enough about modern Tokyo, Kyoto, and other big towns, about the oppressive school system, the hectic quality of Japanese life, and even the behavior of its army during World War II. The few Japanese scholars I have met were meticulous, but uninspiring, and even Japanese women do not attract me particularly. All these, impressions from reading, films or occasional encounters are, of course, entirely subjective, yet, they suffice to limit my desire to know the reality of modern Japan.

But there is another Japan, corresponding in some ways to my personal fantasms. Its Noh theatre, with its masks and costumes, evokes my old and at times active interest in the marionette theatre. It is the country that attracts me with its Zen wisdom, its art and temples, the tea ceremony, the flower aesthetics, and the garden culture. In its Haikus I discovered a poetry able to express in three simple lines a profound wisdom uncovered in inconspicuous daily details; and, in spite of noisy TV pictures, I imagine it to be a country of soft and smooth movements and of smiling communication. All this, although I know it to be a merely subjective image, creates a land where beauty permeates life, where Buddhism finds its concrete realization. Thus, the Japanese emblem near the Buddha statue already makes much sense.

There is more to it. Japan is Asia, and my own life has been profoundly affected by the Asian experience, which, by the way, has stimulated and sustained my interest in two poet-writers who also appeared to have been influenced strongly by their contacts with Japan: the Dutch Cees Nooteboom and the Swiss Adolf Muschg. They appealed, of course, to my own writing ambitions, and the second, being of the same nationality and having married, too, an Asian wife, even fostered a tendency at identification.

I possess a lot of literature about Japan, a few novels, some poetry, art books, writings on Zen Buddhism, and quite a few on Japanese gardens. In its garden culture my imaginary Japan found a perfect balance between nature and art. This appeals, I think, to my wishes—although contradictory—to integrate harmony and spontaneity; spontaneity in nature implies chaotic growth, harmony on the contrary imposes restraint, compromise or even sacrifice. The Japanese garden seems to succeed in combining both—through much work, of course. Zen practice, I feel, pursues about the same goal.

All this justifies the proximity of the Japanese tray to the Sihing Buddha. This statue, although acquired (as described earlier) in Saarbruecken, represents both my real and imaginary Thai experience. Thai Buddhism, being of the Hinayana line, differs greatly from the Mahayana Japanese Zen, but in my imagination this difference melts away, and they both symbolize a kind of perfect wisdom. A message, relating to personal imaginations and emotions, found its expression in short stories I wrote about more or less mythical events in Thailand.[11]

The two items in my study, in front of a wall, somehow open an imaginary window into far reaching other dimensions—they negate the spatial seclusion. They reach towards the past, back even to the younger years when I constructed string puppets and wrote a play for them (which

---

11 Boesch (1993).

78

I sent to Hermann Hesse, receiving a kind answer from the then already old man—and Hesse, with his meditating sinologist Pater Jakobus, thus enters into the connotations of Asia, too). All this, of course, connects me with the emotions, the wishes and secret hopes I harbored at that time. And they also reach toward more recent years when I started reading about Japanese culture and got interested in the writers Nooteboom and Muschg. Another thread includes even the glass carafe of my cousin Dora, who had spent time in Japan. But the extensions reach out, too, towards a future, implying projects as well as memories (which, by coloring hopes or fears, concern the future, too).

VIII

All this is woven in my daily perception of the Japanese tray and the Thai Buddha image. Although unconscious most of the time, it permeates it, like the different tones and their harmonics melt indistinguishably into a musical chord. Thus, objects, things of the outside world, by being amalgated with my past and outlook, turn subjective-functional, are loaded with meanings. Perception, therefore, is more than recognition of external facts; it produces feedbacks of idiosyncratic content. They mean something to me, thereby structuring relationships between I and world.

These relationships are, first of all, actional. In a strange world I feel lost, deprived of my action potential. But once familiarized with the meaning of objects, of gestures and words, I can adequately act again. Meanings, thus, are sign-posts for action. Being surrounded in our culture by meaningful things, we feel familiar, "at home", confident of mastering usual as well as contingent action requirements.

This sounds obvious and easy, and is of course sufficiently true for daily communications and interactions. Yet, on closer analysis, the things around us are only individually meaningful; whether others attribute the same meanings to them, we will never know. Of course, usually it seems to be so. People act in similar ways, and therefore, commerce can count on a large communality of tastes and preferences. Yet, when a wife cannot agree with her husband on the kinds of curtains or china to buy, differences of meaning become obvious. The meaningfulness of my world depends on my personal action experience and outlook. There are large overlaps of meaning between people, but also persistent differences. Of course, close community, constraints of interaction foster a harmonization of meanings. Their overlap may be enlarged, the individual meanings modified in the course of life. Yet, experience shows that even after a long partnership in marriage divergences persist. They are often concealed by concessions, compromises, submissive yielding, but may reveal their presence in apparently trivial quarrels, secret dissatisfactions or even neurotic conflicts.

Still, such individual idiosyncrasies do not abolish the action significance of meanings. Yet concretely, would this apply to the objects filling my study? What might be the action significance of a Thai picture or of a Picasso lithograph on the wall, of a Buddha image on my desk or a glass carafe in a bookcase? Of course, in order to explain their meanings, I related their history and their associative links with events in my life—at some time they possessed an action value. Was that sufficient then, is it sufficient now for understanding their actual meaning?

All I wrote here about my study and its contents did not, by far, of course, exhaust its associative links. To do that, would fill an autobiography. I had to limit my observations to the most obvious connections. But, to finish these considerations, let me point out an additional aspect. The Japanese tray, the Buddha statues, the Thai paintings and silver bowls are all not of my culture, and they apparently don't anymore have an action significance for me. They may have had when I was in Thailand, maybe also later when I wrote the Thai Naga stories, although less directly. But they come from that immense part of the world which is unknown, alien to us, an area of darkness that perhaps may beckon the adventurous, but more often is imagined to be threatening. And so these alien cultural objects are messengers from that far-away world, they reduce its threat, may even promise familiarity. They enliven my curiosity, my wish to learn, which to me increases the transparency of their world, thereby enlarging the one in which I feel at home.

But there hangs, near the Sihing Buddha, a Picasso lithograph. It is, of course, not from a far-away world, but it is from a threatening one. Picasso was a chaotic man, destructive as much as creative, or destructive even in his creations. I studied much of his work, wrote about it, trying to unveil the sense behind his chaos[12]. I believe I was successful, and so to me the litho on the wall signifies something like a victory of order over the threat of destruction. It still hangs there en-igmatically: the shadow of a young bovine behind a bowl of fruits that could as well symbolize the face of a black woman—Picasso's life-long obsessions? Maybe, but they have lost their fascination for me. Psychological analysis as exorcism? Anyhow, the picture reminds me that working on Picasso increased my insight into modern art, another alien world losing its strangeness.

It is not sufficient, as one usually tends to do, to understand action as a pursuit of concrete goals. Similarly important is its function of extending the transparency of our world. This, of course, is imaginative rather

---

12 E.g., in Boesch (1991).

than practical action, but it is of prevailing importance. We continuously need to create a world in which we feel at home, mentally even more than practically. Strangeness limits our action potential, and therefore tends to be felt as a threat. This is the main reason for our striving at meanings. We want to be able to relate ourselves to our world. Which implies being aware of messages. Thus, to ask what this or that means is a basic question for human beings. We may refrain from it, may content ourselves with attaching conventional labels to events and thereby dull our perceptiveness for what might be surprising, even enriching—or dangerous. We need a live curiosity, ready to wonder at the apparently insignficant or common place, in order to open up a larger world. The action relevance of my study, thus, extends beyond writing, even in the polyvalent function we have considered. It is a place where messages converge, increasing the transparency of my world and expanding it beyond the confines of its physical walls and the daily restrictions of life.

A twig cracks, "a message", comments my wife. What does it say? Is it a warning? Do the tree and the wind know what will happen to me? What part of the universe, then, am I? And so the thoughts might run, unconsciously perhaps, and still probing, structuring, evaluating—the unending search for and the construction of meaning that accompany our days. Ours is a tiny section of the whole world, but by making it meaningful, we make it our world. A world of which we go on being a part, but which also becomes a part of us. And I wonder whether all this—we may know it or not—isn't a lasting expression of our longing for the basic meaning, the magic formula, which gives sense to our life and existence.

References

Boesch, E.E. (1984). The Development of Affective Schemata. In: Human Development, 27, 3-4.

Boesch, E.E. (1991). Symbolic Action Theory and Cultural Psychology. Heidelberg: Springer.

Boesch, E.E. (1992). Culture—Individual—Culture. In: M. v.Cranach/ W. Doise/G. Mugny (Eds.). Social Representations and the Social Bases of Knowledge (pp. 89-95). Lewiston: Hogrefe and Huber.

Boesch, E.E. (1993). Von Nagas, Drachen und Geistern. Bonn: Deutsch-Thailändische Gesellschaft.

Boesch, E.E. (2000). Das lauernde Chaos. Bern: Huber.

Boesch, E.E. (2005). Von Kunst bis Terror—über den Zwiespalt in der Kultur. Göttingen, Vandenhoeck und Ruprecht

Bond, M.H. (ed.) (1997). Working at the Interface of Cultures. London/New York: Routledge.

Campbell, J. (1949). The Hero with a Thousand Faces. New York: Meridian.

Hesse, H. (1943). Das Glasperlenspiel. Zürich: Fretz + Wasmuth.

Nimmanahaeminda, K. (1966). Ham Yong, the Magic Testicles. In: The Siam Society, The Kamthieng House. Bangkok: Siam Society.

The National Museum Volunteers (1987). Treasures from the National Museum Bangkok. Bangkok: National Museum.

Understanding as Relationship: Cultural Psychology in Global Context

Kenneth J. Gergen

Consciousness of difference—political, moral, ideological, ethnic—is ever present and ever expanding. This focus can be intense, as matters of life and death depend on how we confront such differences. In this context there is broad demand for a culturally sensitive and engaged psychology. The result has been a dramatic expansion in the number of scholars engaged in such pursuits, along with the range of theories and orientations contributing to the venture. Most important, there is increasing attention given to reflecting on the enterprise itself. Sharp contrasts now exist in prevailing conceptions concerning the subject matter of the field, the theories of greatest promise, and the optimal methods of study. Vastly complicating the question of 'whither cultural psychology', is the fact that any answer to the complex questions confronting the field will itself issue from a space of cultural life. One may set out to study psychological processes within comparative cultural settings, but the very forms of study will themselves bear the stamp of cultural tradition. In attempting to understand cultural inquiry, we cannot transcend our own cultural lodgment.

At the present time there are significant tensions among various orientations to inquiry—empiricist vs. interpretive, nomological vs. idiographic, etic vs. emic. However, in my view researchers in all these camps tend to embrace a range of assumptions that one may recognize as quintessentially Western. There are important exceptions to this general surmise; there are numerous qualifications applicable to specific cases; and one treads on dangerous ground in distinguishing between what is Western as opposed to non-Western (especially when speaking primarily as a Westerner). However, to press the dialogue forward on issues of future inquiry, I will first touch on three significant ways in which common inquiry in cultural psychology essentially recapitulates the Western tradition. In this sense, to presume that inquiry should be universally guided by these presumptions is deeply problematic. Not only would this mean that our forms of inquiry in cultural psychology would be severely limited, but that to extend the tradition globally would approximate a form of neocolonialism.

While it is important enough to bring these cultural orientations to the forefront, I will also examine significant limitations. To be sure, these critical assays will also reflect traditions of argument within a Western tradition. In effect, we are thus invited into a reflexive loop—Westernism turned back on itself, However, it is my hope that from this critical reflection we may locate ways of appreciating the multiplicities of cultural inquiry—as they exist now and as they will emerge in coming years. In effect, from this effort we may envision a cultural psychology that can confront its own limits, and more adequately encompass and embrace diverse forms of global life.

Beyond Western Modernism

In terms of the Western tradition, the most distinctive imprint on cultural inquiry in psychology is lodged in what is typically viewed as the Modernist period. As generally held, modernism commenced as Western culture moved from 'the dark ages' of medievalism into the Enlightenment. The Enlightenment was a historical watershed primarily owing to the dignity that its scholars and statesmen granted to the individual mind. For Enlightenment thinkers, it was no longer necessary to bend unquestioningly to the totalitarian force of royal or religious decree. For within each of us, it was proposed, lies a bounded and sacred sanctuary of the mind, a domain governed by our autonomous capacities for careful, conscious observation and rational deliberation. It is only *my thought* itself, proposed Descartes in 1637 that provides a certain foundation for all else.[1]

From this tradition I wish to focus on only three assumptions that currently center most inquiry in cultural psychology. By placing each of these assumptions under critical focus, we begin to locate avenues toward a more inclusive and globally beneficial psychology.

From Individual Knowledge to Social Construction

It is this 17th-century construction of the individual mind—and its further development in the 18th century, that served as the major rationalizing device for the 19th-century beginnings of a systematic psychology. The effects were twofold: first, the individual mind came to be a preeminent

---

1   The literature on Western modernism is vast. Engaging exemplars include Porter 2000.

object of study, and second, knowledge of the human mind could be understood as an achievement of the individual minds of scientific investigators. If individual mentality is the major source of human conduct, on the one hand, then to unlock the secrets of mental process is to gain a certain degree of control over human action. In Wilhelm Dilthey's (1914) terms, "The nexus of psychic life constitutes the originally primitive and fundamental datum (of scientific study) [...] the external organization of society in the ties of family, community, church and state, arise from the living nexus of the human mind" (76). At the same time, it is the individual investigator, endowed with capacities for observation and rationality, who is best equipped for such study. These twin assumptions continue to undergird most research in contemporary psychology, along with allied forms of cultural inquiry.

Within the modernist tradition a distinction is typically drawn between the 'inner world' of mind and the 'external world' of material. As traditionally held, knowledge is achieved when the internal world of the individual accurately assays the nature of the external world. An individual's knowledge of the world is revealed by the extent to which he or she can rationally predict its occurrences (and take appropriate action.) The dualistic presumption has virtually set the agenda for philosophers from Locke and Kant through Quine and Fodor. The chief question is that of epistemology: How is it that the individual mind can acquire accurate knowledge of the external world? Interestingly enough, a viable answer to the epistemological question has never been forthcoming. Variations on the empiricist approach (mind as blank slate) continue to vie with those of the rationalists (mind as constructing agent). After more than three centuries the epistemological riddle remains intractable. For many, it is Richard Rorty's *Philosophy and the Mirror of Nature* that signals its demise. As Rorty proposes, the epistemological problem is only a problem within a Western metaphysics of dualism. If we suspend the mind/world distinction (in effect, suspending the presumptions of Western modernism), the problem ceases to exist. We have been captivated by our linguistic tradition.

The effect of this argument is to press our concerns past the mind as the locus of knowledge to the communities in which distinctions such as mind/world come into prominence. We come to see that our ways of characterizing the person and the world are outgrowths of particular traditions—including both its linguistic genres and the institutions in which they are embedded. What we take to be 'the real', what we believe to be transparently true about human functioning, is a byproduct of communal construction. This is not to offer a form of linguistic solipsism or reductionism; it is not to say that 'nothing exists outside our linguistic con-

85

structions'. Whatever exists simply exists, irrespective of our linguistic practices. However, once we begin to describe or explain what exists, we inevitably proceed from a forestructure of shared intelligibility.[2]

To 'tell the truth', on this account, is not to furnish an accurate picture of 'what actually happened', but to participate in a set of social conventions, a way of putting things sanctioned within a given 'form of life'. To 'be objective' is to play by the rules within a given tradition of social practices. To illustrate, the terms 'serve', 'volley', and 'ace' gain their particular meaning from within the practices that constitute the game of tennis. One can be quite accurate in assessing whether an 'ace' has occurred within the practice of the game; but outside the tennis court the term loses its meaning. More broadly put, this is to say that language is world constituting; it assists in generating and/or sustaining certain forms of cultural practice.

From Reason to Rhetoric

Coupled with a belief in individual knowledge, cultural modernism places major importance on the power of individual reason. As traditionally held, it is through our capacities for abstract thought, conceptual manipulation, and systematic logic that we become effective agents in the world. In a Darwinian context, the superiority of the human species is often traced to precisely these capacities.

Yet, while seeming truisms, these assumptions prove deeply flawed. The problems are demonstrated most clearly in the case of literary and rhetorical critiques of individual reason (cf. Derrida 1976; Myerson 1994). Consider again the modernist assumption that one's language is an expression of one's reasoning about the world. As literary and semiotic theorists propose, language is a system unto itself, a system that both precedes and outlives the individual. Thus to speak as a rational agent is to participate in a system that is already constituted; it is to borrow from the existing genres, or to appropriate forms of talk (and related action) already in place. In this sense, private rationality is a form of cultural participation simply removed from the immediate exigencies of relationship. How could we deliberate privately on matters of justice, morality, or optimal strategies of action, for example, except through the terms of public culture? (See also Sandel 1982) When applied to the domain of scientific knowledge, we see that the individual scientist is only "rational" if he or she adopts the codes of discourse common to his/her particular community of science. In effect, scientific rationality is achieved

---

2   For more on social constructionism, see Gergen (1994, 1999).

through locally privileged uses of language (Nelson, Megill and McCloskey 1987; Simons 1990).

Traditionally we have assumed that if powers of reason are the key to effective action, then reason is not itself ideological or value invested. As commonly held, value commitments may indeed bias the reasoning process. However, when we understand that reasoning is an artifact of community life, the presumption of value neutrality drops away. To the extent that reason is lodged within communities, it will function in ways that sustain the community. Thus the logics employed within the sciences, for example, will reflect the values shared within this community and sustain its form of life. The logic of cause and effect, in this sense, is not a reflection of pure reason, but contributes to a particular way of life.

The oppressive potentials inhering in claims to pure reason have become increasingly apparent in the various feminist and multicultural critiques of psychology, along with writings on the colonizing effects of language more generally (Bohan and Russell 1999; Foucault 1980; M. Gergen 1988). As variously surmised, there are hierarchies of rationality within the culture. Some individuals are deemed more rational, and thus more worthy of leadership, social position, and wealth than others. Interestingly, those who occupy these positions are systematically drawn from a very small sector of the population (In the U.S., typically white male. Such categories as 'female' or 'black' are often associated with being irrational or emotional). In effect, while Enlightenment arguments have succeeded in unseating the totalitarian power of crown and cross, they now give rise to new structures of power and domination. And, if the exercise of rationality is, after all, an exercise in language, if convincing descriptions and explanations are, after all, rhetorically constituted, then there is no ultimate means of justifying one form of rationality, description, or explanation over another. If such justifications were offered, they would also prove to be exercises in linguistic convention. In effect, the very idea of 'superior reason' currently functions unjustifiably to exclude many people from the corridors of decision making.

Understanding: From Intersubjectivity to Relationship

The joint emphases on knowledge as a condition of the individual mind, and reason as the motor of (effective) action, we are in a position to appreciate the modernist view of how it is humans understand each other. This issue is of pivotal significance to the future of cultural inquiry, as the field is essentially dedicated to the understanding of others. On the traditional account, spoken and written language are the chief means by which we communicate. To understand another's language is to understand the private meanings he or she wishes to convey. John Locke (1689) captures the Enlightenment view of language when he writes that our words are "signs of internal conceptions". They stand as external "marks for the ideas within (the individual's) mind whereby they might be made known to others and the thoughts to man's [sic] mind might be conveyed from one to another" (212). Within the Western tradition, then, human understanding is a matter of intersubjective connection. When words enable one subjective agent to register correctly the subjective condition (intentions, reasons, motives, affect) of another, then we say that understanding has occurred.

Interestingly, neither philosophers nor hermeneutic theorists of the past three centuries have been able to establish a viable theory of how external signs (words, action) can be used to achieve accuracy about internal states. When there is never access to another's internal states themselves, all one can ever use to justify an interpretation of an external sign is to fall back on yet another interpretation (for further explication see Gergen 1994). How then are we to account for the sense that "we do understand each other?" The answer may be found in Wittgenstein's (1953) account of word meaning. As Wittgenstein proposed, words do not gain their meaning from their relationship to mental states, but from their use in action. Words are constituents of language games; as we participate within these games so do we come to use words effectively. Or, to put the case more broadly, as we coordinate our actions with others, so do we come into a state of understanding. To understand another is not, then, to have privileged access to a subjective condition, but to participate effectively in the process of mutual coordination. If a friend tells me she is sad about a recent loss, I do not understand her by making inferences from these words to an inner sanctum of her mind, but by the ways in which my words, posture, tone of voice (my full and active engagement) are coordinated with her revelation. If I were to launch into an excited account of my summer vacation, she would be fully justified in the conclusion that, by our traditional standards of coordination, I failed to understand. Understanding, then, does not reside in the heads of people in relationship, but rather in the process of relationship itself. To achieve understanding is a relational accomplishment. It is this view of understanding as relationship that will inform our subsequent discussions of cultural inquiry in psychology.

Cultural Inquiry in Relational Perspective

It is convenient at this point to summarize and integrate the various outcomes of the preceding exploration. This will prepare us to consider forms of inquiry in cultural psychology, as they now exist and in the emerging future. First we sketched a way of viewing all propositions about the real, the rational, and the good as constructed within particular traditions of relationship. Thus, there may be many 'objective truths', but each derived from the assumptions, discourses, and practices of particular communities. Further, we found that all candidates for rationality or objectivity within a particular community of meaning making are saturated with the value preferences or ideology of that community. Finally, these realities and values are not the byproduct of isolated individuals who come together to communicate about them. Rather, it is within the process of relationship that our forms of understanding come into being. Of particular significance, we found that interpersonal understanding can properly be viewed as a form of relational coordination. To understand others is not so much a matter of penetrating their mental states as it is carrying out mutually effective relations.

In light of these views, let us now consider modes of understanding of particular relevance to cultural inquiry in terms of their implications for effective coordinations among persons. When we undertake cultural inquiry, where does understanding as a relational process take place; who is included or excluded, what are the implications for life in the cultures of the world, what are the advantages of our contemporary forms of inquiry, and how might our efforts be expanded so as to enhance relational processes more globally?

Outside Understanding: The Other as Object

The vast share of cultural research in psychology is lodged most fully within the tradition of western dualism. We serve as scientists employing skills of reason and observation to generate theories and explanations regarding the behavior of human beings. In this case, we deduce hypotheses concerning the nature of cultural differences, prepare systematic methods (e.g., experiments, questionnaires, scale measures) for testing these hypotheses, gather data in such a way as to avoid biases, subject the data to statistical analyses, and report the findings in professional journals. We may view this form of research as *outside understanding*, which is to say, that the cultures under study function as exterior objects, the

89

behavior of which the investigator attempts both to describe with accuracy and integrate into a more general or comprehensive theory. We have come to speak of such research as *etic*, where the major conceptions and measures reflect the shared understanding of the culture undertaking the research.

How are we to consider such inquiry in terms of relational coordination? Where is the process of understanding as relationship to be located? Essentially, outside understanding represents a contribution to the forms of life within the culture in which the research originates. In a limited sense, this is to say that most cross-cultural research contributes to the relationships within the professional or academic culture. Concepts of cognitive dissonance, motivation, emotion, priming, and self-efficacy, along with ANOVAs and multiple regressions, are the discourses of 'our community', and reflect our values and ways of life. To negotiate agreements about 'what they are like' is to bring about solidarity, satisfaction, and the sense of achievement. (See, for example, the six-volume series, *Handbook of Cross-Cultural Psychology, Journal of Cross-Cultural Psychology*, Schaller and Crandall 2004) To be sure, 'our community' is also embedded within the broader array of relationships within what may roughly be called 'our culture'. Thus, academic studies of cross-cultural differences in depression, independence, and self-esteem are interesting to the more general population because such terms are also embedded within traditions of common value.

There is much to be said on behalf of outside understanding, particularly if one lives within Western culture. Western cross-cultural psychology is essentially an indigenous endeavor, and like most social institutions throughout the world, contributes to sustaining the home culture in important ways. In effect, empiricist research is essentially a way of supporting western ways of life, of reinforcing its values, and generating a local vocabulary of describing and explaining the world in ways that are congenial with its traditions. And too, such research may also carry with it useful practical implications. For example, the common finding that Western cultures differ from Asian cultures in their emphasis on individualism vs. collectivism (Triandis 1995), contains useful advice for any Western organizations that hope to establish business in Asian cultures.

At the same time, there are two prevailing dangers of outside understanding, one local and the other global. On the local level, a strong commitment to such an orientation means that the realities and values of the local culture become increasingly commanding. They cease to be constructions, and become essentialized and unquestioned. Within academic culture this lends itself toward a diminution of dialogue and constraints on the creative process. As we develop empirical tests and accu-

90

mulated data to verify the individualist-collectivist difference, for example, so does the reality of this difference and the methods of study become solidified. We cease to consider myriad alternatives in the way we might construct such differences along with alternative methods of inquiry.

This is not to say that such research lacks catalytic value. Indeed, cross-cultural inquiry does caution the field against unbridled generalization of its findings. However, such questioning is conservative; it does not ask the mainstream researcher to consider the cultural lodgment of both theory and method. For example, cross-cultural research may challenge the presumption of universal emotional expressions, but it will not raise questions concerning the universality of the 'underlying' emotions (a Western concept) or empirical methods as the tools of substantiation.

The greater danger of a univocal commitment to outside understanding lies in its implications for relationships within the world community more generally. When we approach the peoples of the world 'on our own terms', we place severe limits on our potential for coordinated activity. This is most obvious in the case of language. If all cultures remain only within their own linguistic traditions, the range of interdependency is radically truncated. For the Western psychologist to dismiss such terms as *atman*, *liget*, or *ki ga meiru* as 'folk terms', and unworthy as scientific explanations of behavior, is to build walls of isolation. More significantly, to presume that psychological inquiry should everywhere proceed on assumptions of Western empiricism is to participate in a form of subtle colonialism. Alienated and hostile reactions to the global expansion of Western psychology are already apparent. Thus, regardless of the accumulated data, when Western psychologists attempt to describe differences between cultures (e.g., Nisbett 2003), their characterizations are likely to draw attack from abroad. Or, as the Indian psychologist Gerishwar Misra writes: "When people from other cultures are exposed to western psychology they find their identities placed in question, and their conceptual repertoires rendered obsolete." (Gergen, Misra, Lock, and Gulerce 1996: 498)

More antagonistic are the words of the Maori scholar, Lawson-Te Aho (1993). He writes:

"Psychology, and clinical psychology in particular, has created the mass abnormalization of Maroi people by virtue of the fact that Maori people have been on the receiving end of psychological practice as the helpless recipients of (English) defined labels and treatments [...]. Clinical psychology is a form of social control derived from human intent and human action and offers no more truth about the realities of Maori people's lives than a regular reading of the horoscope page in the local newspaper" (26).

In effect, while outside research of the empiricist variety may be enormously useful within the home culture, there is danger in the tendency to universalize the local, and to export the concepts and methods of the field as if they contributed to transhistorical and transcultural knowledge.

Inside-Out Understanding:
The Other as Subject

Psychologists have long been sensitive to the problems of outside understanding, and increasingly turned their attention to the possibility of illumination from the inside. Rather than imposing concepts from the home culture, can research allow us to comprehend others 'in their own terms'. Such research is often termed *emic*; for those eschewing the kinds of standardized measures issuing from nomological empiricism, such inquiry may be called 'interpretive' or 'hermeneutic'. The emicially oriented researcher may employ standardized measures, but use them in such a way that 'differences in kind' as opposed to 'differences along a dimension' can be registered (see, for example, Marcus and Kitiyama 1991). For the more interpretively oriented, it is important to enter more fully the culture in question, grasp the indigenous concepts, values, and motives as they reveal themselves in cultural life. Ideally this might require 'living with the natives', entering rituals, mastering the language, and speaking at length with the denizens. To the extent that systematic methods are employed, they are more often qualitative than quantitative. Because psychological functioning is typically assumed to be particular to the culture, the researcher will often be sensitive to the historical and ecological context of the people in question. Psychological functioning must be understood, in this case, as embedded within a whole. From this immersion, the investigator returns to the home culture to fashion a report that enables the reader to 'get a feel' for the culture in question. It is in these kinds of endeavors that psychologists such as Michael Cole (1996) and Jaan Valsiner (1997) have much in common with cultural anthropologists such as Richard Shweder (1991) and Catherine Lutz (1988).

In contrast to outside understanding, we may in relational terms view such an orientation as *inside-out* understanding. That is, the attempt is to understand from within, but to report the results of such inquiry outward to the home culture. What, then, are the relational implications of this form of inquiry? At the outset, it should be realized that in spite of the attempt of such research to reflect other cultures in their own terms, such research as it is conducted by a participant in Western culture (either directly or via education), will invariably reflect Western conceptions and values. To join with symbolic anthropologists, for example, in the presumption that people's actions are guided by an underlying array of shared concepts, symbols or values, is already to sustain a form of Western (mind-body) dualism. Subjectivity remains regnant over public action. And this same set of presumptions places a stamp on the kinds of behavior to which the investigator attends and the questions that will be asked of informants. It is not action in itself that interests the interpretive scholar so much as the 'meaning behind the action'.

While many psychologists are acutely aware of the conceptual and methodological problems of outside understanding, the operation of Western biases has been far less apparent in the case of emic or interpretive inquiry. In part, this paucity of self-reflexivity can be traced to the belief that such research is maximally designed to liberate the West from itself and thereby foster greater understanding among peoples. For cultural anthropologists, however, the implicit biases of the interpretive orientation have become a matter of painful self-reflection. It was perhaps Edward Said's (1978) critique of Western area studies in its construction of *the oriental* that set the stage. As Markus and Fischer (1986) later argued, anthropological study was inherently ideological. Its portrait of others was inevitably an entry into the political economy. Further, as so deftly illustrated in Clifford and Markus' edited work, *Writing Culture*, the attempt to describe and explain other cultures was to enter into the textual genres of the home culture. By employing these genres the traditions of the home culture would be reasserted.

Informed by these critiques, many anthropologists now make a special effort to inform their audiences of what they see as the cultural biases inherent in their work. While a god's eye account of such biases is out of reach, such accounts are helpful in sensitizing readers to the objectifying tendencies otherwise inherent in our languages of representation. At the same time, others have pressed on to experiment with methods that may avoid some of the harsher critiques. Of particular interest is the development of auto-ethnography, a form of research in which an individual provides an autobiographical account of life within his or her particular culture or subculture (see, for example, Bochner and Ellis 2002). Slowly these issues are making their way into cultural psychology (see, for example, Jahoda 1999; Shi-xu 1997, and offerings of the journal, *Culture and Psychology*.) More searching dialogue is much to be desired.

Yet, in spite of the problematics of inside-out understanding, we should not lose sight of its significant contributions. The interpretive approach has two features of estimable significance. First, in contrast to 'outside understanding', understanding from the inside-out has a substantial catalytic or generative capacity within the home culture. In the case of outside understanding, whatever is 'found' by the investigator can only offer a minor challenge to the prevailing assumptions and values of the home culture. If one employs a scale of depression, for example, or a coding category of emotional expressions across cultures, one will never discover activity that fails to fit the linear model of depression, or that falls outside the vocabulary of Western emotions used for classification. The measures and experiments are specifically designed to produce data that instantiates the theoretical assumptions (and their attendant values and ways of life.) It is because of this that most research from the outside will tend to speak of universals of human behavior. If the researcher can find the means to translate actions in all cultures into his or her terms, then the terms of the research will suggest that the phenomena under study are of universal scope.

In contrast, inside-out understanding can provide dramatic challenges to the assumptions of the home culture. By attending to complex patterns of action; struggling to interpret words and phrases that can scarcely be slotted into convenient assumptions of the home culture; striving for a wholistic integration of cultural behavior, languages, and environment, the investigator will not typically emerge with the conclusion, 'just as we thought it would be'. Rather, the strong invitation is to articulate forms of life that are disjunctive with the home culture, that ask the home culture to recognize genuine and deep seated differences among people. It was once said of anthropological research that there are two master narratives underlying virtually all research: Either, "You thought people around the world were different, but they are the same," or "You thought people around the world were the same, but they are different." Inside-out research is effectively equipped to sustain the second of these narratives, and in doing so replace the common urge to arrogance with an abiding curiosity and openness to the other.

There is a second and less obvious advantage to inside-out understanding. To gather data in such an enterprise often requires that the researcher enter the culture in a significant way. The researcher cannot simply send his or her measures to a colleague in another culture, to be translated and administered impersonally, and recreated as entries to a statistical matrix. Rather, interpretive activity requires more substantial immersion in the culture of interest. Relations with 'informants' must be cemented, one must engage effectively with locals of many sorts, and ideally one should master the language. In effect, inside-out understanding requires the forging of a new set of relationships. The form of research contributes to new forms of collaborative activity. The network of relationship expands; understanding as relationship now transcends the boundaries of the home culture.

Understanding within:
Knowing as "Being There"

When we appreciate the process of understanding as relational coordination, our attention is directed beyond the existing traditions. Rather, we begin to realize that we have been overly concerned with relational outcomes in 'our culture' typically the academic culture in which research originates. To paraphrase, we implicitly ask, "How does my research contribute to (our) tradition of scholarship?" From a relational perspective, we are invited to extend our interest to the processes of understanding issuing from within alterior cultures themselves. The challenge here is not 'to report on them', but to participate in the process of coordination itself. In effect, our concern shifts from understanding the other to understanding *with* the other, i.e., not 'thinking like the native' but *entering* the native world.

In an important sense, one might term this understanding from within as *first order understanding*. That is, as people come together and generate coordinated patterns of action (including discourse) they are, in effect, moving toward the achievement of understanding. There is no distinction to be made at this level between effective functioning and understanding. The path to *second order understanding* begins when we attempt to reflect on first order understanding, to grasp its character in some form. The two previous forms of inquiry—understanding from without and inside-out understanding—are both forms of second order understanding.

With this distinction in place, there are two important points to be made regarding cultural inquiry in psychology. The first and most apparent is that first order understanding does not yet play a role in the configuration of cultural inquiry in psychology. We have exclusively confined understanding or knowledge to the second order. In effect, we might usefully consider ways in which our science might launch programs of first order understanding within alterior cultures. Programs of living abroad begin to work in this direction, but in these cases there is little systematic attention given to the potentials of deep immersion. At the same time, while 'going native' is not a viable option for most people, there are means of enabling outsiders to participate vicariously or indirectly within otherwise alien culture. Film is perhaps the most obvious vehicle for such participation. Here psychology can benefit substantially from the visual movements in both sociology and anthropology. (See Heider's *Ethnographic Film*.) Most interesting as well is the groundbreaking work of Victor Turner (1982) on performance as anthropological report. As Turner outlines, relying on written language to provide knowledge of other cultures is to be a victim of the linguistic conventions of the home culture. We cannot write about others' meaning systems, for example, without translating them into our local intelligibilities. Thus, rather than relying on linguistic representation, we may generate 'cultural experiences' enabling people to participate more directly in the rituals and activities of the culture in question. As Turner demonstrated, it is possible to fashion contexts in the home culture that roughly approximate activities of eating, drinking, dancing, and the like.

The second important implication of this focus on understanding within is the welcome it provides to truly indigenous psychologies. Concern with indigenous psychologies is scarcely new in the cultural wings of the field. From the groundbreaking work of Heelas and Lock (1981) to more recent reviews and explorations (Kim and Berry 1993; Paranjpe 1998), contrasting assumptions about the nature of mind, its content and processes, has demanded attention. However, such work has moved slowly to what might be viewed as authentic indigenous psychology. Much existing research on indigenous psychology has been based on either outside or inside-out modes of understanding. It represents an attempt to create the intelligibility of other cultures to a Western audience, often employing Western concepts and methods of inquiry to bolster the assembled insights. In effect, the relational impact is largely reserved for life within Western culture. In contrast, authentic indigenous psychologies make use of discourse and practices intrinsic to the cultural traditions themselves. For Westerners, the concepts and practices might indeed fall outside the realm of legitimate psychology. In the West, when we employ personality measures, experimental methods, and statistical analyses to understand samples of our own population, we are employing second order methods of understanding the West's indigenous psychology. However, such methods of research may have little relevance when the non-Western peoples of the earth turn an interested eye upon themselves. Here illumination might take many different forms, from meditation to chanting, dancing, or story telling. The development of authentic indigenous psychology is now in the chrysalis stage. Liberation psychology in the Philippines may stand as the primary exemplar (Enriquez 1988, 1990). However, with nurturing support, their development could add richly to the global dialogues and practices.

Fusion Understanding: Emergent Relations

In this final section we enter a largely uncharted landscape, and yet, a territory of increasing global and political significance. Although the concept of 'culture' remains contested, there is at least one broad conception that informs most psychological inquiry. This conception is a child of the 19th century, symbolized most concretely in Wilhelm Wundt's volume work, *Völkerpsychologie*. Within this tradition, the investigator presumes a bounded and stable entity, a 'people' who possess forms of life to which various investigators can return from time to time so as to build up an accurate and coherent structure of knowledge. All of the above orientations to cultural understanding are committed in varying degrees to this presumption. And yet, as the technologies of transportation and communication have burgeoned over the past century, not only is there rapid cultural change within various geographic regions, but there is enormous movement of people and media across traditional boundaries. There is dislocation, diaspora, and diffusion everywhere (Clifford 1997; Friedman 1994; Kahn 1995; Kirshenblatt-Gimblett 1998; Grunitzky 2004). Indeed, we now begin to approach the point where the very concept of 'a culture' in the traditional sense must be questioned. We might indeed abandon the more static term, *culture*, and replace it with the process term, *culturing*.

At this point the implications for inquiry are far from clear, and future dialogue is essential. At least two forms of relevant inquiry are already in motion. At the most basic level, the attempt to characterize cultures in general may be replaced with inquiry into highly specific subcultures. Avoiding concern with the porous boundaries of broad cultural groups, the focus is placed on more specifically identifiable enclaves. The contributions of anthropologists, sociologists, and cultural studies scholars to this literature are now substantial (see, for example, Espiritu 1995; Kwong 1996; Suro 1999). Within psychology this shift to subculture has yet to blossom. Although controversial, the work of Nisbett and Cohen (1996) on the culture of the Southern United States opens the door. However, even this focus may be too broad.

There is further reason to pursue such inquiry in psychology. Culturally oriented psychology has come to play an increasingly important catalytic role in the field of psychology more generally. Cross-cultural psychology has raised important questions regarding the claims to universality characteristic of the field more generally. Cultural psychologists, along with more interpretively oriented scholars, have raised important questions regarding the very presumption of universal mechanisms or processes of mind. Studies of subcultures press these concerns

97

even further. To the extent that substantial differences exist in subcultures (which studying would surely reveal), then the common practice of generalizing from experimental data to the population as a whole is placed in jeopardy. For example, if we come to recognize that New York City, like most cosmopolitan areas, is composed of myriad subcultures, then we would have to question whether the results of experiments on college sophomores at a local university illuminate anything beyond this particular subculture. We would finally have to face the long-avoided question in psychological research: What is the 'population' to which our statistical analyses allow us to generalize?

Of course, shifting the focus from cultures in general to more specific subcultural enclaves does not remove the problem of cultural dispersion so much as postpone it. Thus, a second form of inquiry is invited, in this case concerned with aspects of the dispersion process itself. Again, there is a growing body of relevant scholarship within the social sciences more generally. Scholars have variously been concerned, for example, with problems of maintaining cultural identity (Deloria 1998), conflicting claims to cultural traditions (Clifford 1988; Brown 2003), newly emerging cultures (Kibria 2002), intra-cultural confrontation and cohesion (Bernard 2004); and processes of transition within cultures and subcultures (Suro 1999; Hermans and Kempen 1998). Such work stands as an open invitation to future inquiry in cultural psychology.

Yet, we must also realize that inquiry into ongoing processes of cultural transformations is either from the outside or from the inside-out. As such it is limited in its relational potentials. Those who are served by such research are largely from the cultures in which the research originates. There are attempts to treat diffusion from within, but these are primarily the works of filmmakers concerned with the decay of their traditions, the conflicts attendant upon dispersion and diffusion (for example, *My Beautiful Launderette*, *Baghdad Café*, *Mississippi Marsala*, *Bombay Wedding*, *Ileana*, *Bend it Like Beckham*). How, then, might professional psychologists otherwise approach culture in motion? And more specifically, what kinds of practices might serve a broader array of relationships, including peoples in motion and our relationships with them?

In this context, I believe cultural psychology might usefully expand its repertoire of practices to include participatory action. The aim here would be to bring our voices into the mix of those in motion, and to work together to create viable cultural forms.

Research of the traditional varieties is largely backward looking; it reports on states and conditions existing at the time of inquiry. Whether such states or conditions will continue over time remains an open question (see Gergen 2001). Yet, in the case of cultural disintegration and transformation backward looking research is limited. More useful is to join in the process of coordination to create fusions for the future.

As Reason and Bradbury's *Handbook of Participatory Research* makes clear, there is ample precedent for participatory research within psychology. The journal *Action Research* also offers numerous cases in which researcher/participant fusion has been successfully achieved. Jim Scheurich offers a good example of how scholars may help to bring about positive fusion. Scheurich, teamed with Gerardo Lopez and Miguel Lopez to develop a performance piece concerned with the lives of Mexican American migrants. The performance includes music, video, and a carousel of slides, all operating simultaneously. In addition, there was a script that required the improvisational participation of a cast along with members of the audience. In effect, the performance provided the audience with possibilities for a rich engagement with the migration culture.

A Closing and an Opening

In my view, the increasing engagement of psychologists in cultural inquiry has enormous implications, not only for the field itself but in terms of potential contributions to the relations among the world's peoples. As we become increasingly aware of the ways in which our professional pursuits are expressions of cultural traditions, so must we confront the existence of multiple and potentially conflicting realities and values around the world. As the anthropologist, Renato Rosaldo (1989) once wrote about cultural research, "Cultural interpretations are both occasioned by and enter arenas of ideological conflict. Under such circumstances, neither the notion of a neutral language nor that of brute facts can prosper" (66). In effect, we are invited to look beyond the research findings we generate, to consider the relationships that they strengthen and destroy. Fully conscious cultural inquiry today stands precisely at the cutting edge of global history, where disparate peoples must creatively grapple with their differences, or perish. Cultural inquiry in psychology is bringing us into consciousness concerning the cultural limits of our research, and fostering the opening of psychology to important dialogues with anthropology, history, and philosophy. It is now time for us to broaden our vision of the field to include its impact and potentials within the global sphere more generally.

References

Bernard, E. (Ed.) (2004). Some of my Best Friends. Writing on Interracial Friendships. New York: Amistad.

Bochner, A.P./Ellis, C. (2002). Ethnographically Speaking. Walnut Creek, CA: AltaMira.

Bohan, J.S./Russel, G.M. (1999). Conversations about Psychology and Sexual Orientation. New York: New York University Press.

Brown, M.F. (2003). Who Owns Native Culture? Cambridge: Harvard University Press.

Clifford, J. (1988). The Predicament of Culture. Cambridge: Harvard University Press.

Clifford, J. (1997). Routes, Travel and Translation in the Late Twentieth Century. Cambridge: Harvard University Press.

Clifford, J./Markus, G. (Eds.) (1986). Writing Culture. Berkeley: University of California Press.

Cole, M. (1996): Cultural Psychology. Cambridge, MA: Belknap.

Deloria, P.J. (1998). Playing Indian. New Haven: Yale University Press.

Derrida, J. (1976). Of Grammatology. Baltimore: Johns Hopkins University Press.

Dilthey, W. (1984 [1914]). Selected Writings. In: H.B. Rickman (Ed.). Cambridge. Cambridge University Press.

Enriquez, V.G. (1988). From Colonial to Liberation Psychology: The Phillippine experience. Quezon City: University of Philippines Press.

Enriquez, V.G. (Ed.) (1990). Indigenous Psychology: A Book of Readings. Quezon City: New Horizons Press.

Espiritu, Y.L. (1995). Filipino American Lives. Philadelphia: Temple University Press.

Foucault, M. (1980). The History of Sexuality, V.1. New York: Random House.

Friedman, J. (1994). Cultural Identity and Global Process. London: Sage.

Gergen, K.J. (1994): Realities and Relationships. Cambridge: Harvard University Press.

Gergen, K.J. (1999). An Invitation to Social Construction. London: Sage.

Gergen, K.J. (2001). Social Construction in Context. London: Sage.

Gergen, K.J./Lock, A./Gulerce, A./Misra, G. (1996). Psychological Science in Cultural Context. In: American Psychologist, 51, 496-503.

Gergen, M.M. (1988). Toward a Feminist Metatheory and Methodology in the Social Sciences. In: M.M. Gergen (Ed.): Feminist Thought and the Structure of Knowledge (pp. 87-104). New York: New York University Press.

Grunitzky, C. (Ed.) (2004). Transculturalism. New York: True.

Heelas, P./Lock, A. (Eds.) (1981). Indigenous Psychologies: The Anthropology of the Self. London: Academic Press.

Heider, K.G. (1976). Ethnographic Film. Austin: University of Texas Press.

Hermans, H.J.M./Kempen, H.J.G. (1998): Moving Cultures: The Perilous Problems of Cultural Dichotomies in a Globalizing Society. In: American Psychologist, 53, 1111-1120.

Jahoda, G. (1999). The Images of Savages: Ancient Roots of Modern Prejudice in Western Culture. New York: Routledge.

Kahn, J.S. (1995). Culture, Multiculture, Postculture. London: Sage.

Kibria, N. (2002). Becoming Asian American. Baltimore: Johns Hopkinds Press.

Kim, U./Berry, J. (Eds.) (1993). Indigenous Psychologies. Thousand Oaks, CA: Sage.

Kirshenblatt-Gimblett, B. (1998). Destination Culture. Berkeley: University of California Press.

Kwong, P. (1996). The New Chinatown. N.Y.: Hill and Wang

Locke, J. (1989): Some Thoughts Concerning Education. Ed. J.& J. Yolton. Oxford: Clarendon Press.

Lawson-Te Aho, K. (1993). The Socially Constructed Nature of Psychology and the Abnormalisation of Maori. In: New Zealand Psychological Society Bulletin, 76, 25-30.

Lutz, C. (1988). Unnatural Emotions. Chicago: University of Chicago Press.

Markus, G.E./Fischer, M.M.J. (1986). Anthropology as Cultural Critique. Chicago: University of Chicago Press.

Markus, H./Kitayama, S. (1991). Culture and the Self: Implications for Cognition, Emotion, and Motivation. In: Psychological Review, 98, 224-253.

Myerson, G. (1994). Rhetoric, Reason and Society. London: Sage.

Nelson, J.S./Megill, A./McCloskey, D.N. (Eds.) (1987). The Rhetoric of the Human Sciences. Madison: University of Wisconsin Press.

Nisbett, R. (2003). The Geography of Thought: How Asians and Westerners Think Differently ... and Why? New York: Free Press.

Nisbett, R./Cohen, D. (1996). Culture of Honor: The Psychology of Violence in the South. Boulder, CO: Westview.

Paranjpe, A.C. (1998). Self and Identity in Modern Psychology and Indian Thought. New York: Plenum.

Porter, R. (2000). The Creation of the Modern World. New York: Norton.

Reason, P./Bradbury, H. (Eds.) (2000). Handbook of Action Research, Participative Inquiry and Practice. London: Sage.

Rorty, R (1979). Philosophy and the Mirror of Nature. Princeton, NJ: Princeton University Press.

Rosaldo, R. (1989). Culture and Truth. Boston: Beacon

Said, E. (1978). Orientalism. New York: Pantheon.

Sandel, M.J. (1982). Liberalism and the Limits of Justice. Cambridge: Cambridge University Press.

Schaller, M./Crandall, C.S. (Eds.) (2004). The Psychological Foundations of Culture. Mahwah, N.J.; London: Erlbaum.

Scheurich, J. (1997). Coloring Epistemology: Are our Epistemologies Racially Biased? In: Educational Researcher, 26, 4-16.

Shi-xu (1997). Cultural Representations: Analyzing the Discourse about the Other. New York: Peter Lang.

Shweder, R.A. (1991). Thinking Through Cultures. Cambridge: Harvard University Press.

Simons, H. (1990). Case Studies in the Rhetoric of the Human Sciences. Chicago: University of Chicago Press.

Suro, R. (1999). Strangers among Us, Latino Lives in Changing America. New York: Vintage.

Triandis, H. (1995). Individualism and Collectivism. Boulder: Westview.

Turner, V. (1982). From Ritual to Theatre. New York:Performing Arts Journal Publications.

Valsiner, J. (1997). Culture and the Development of Children's Action. 2nd ed. New York: Wiley.

Wittgenstein, L. (1953). Philosophical Investigations. Oxford: Blackwell.

Wundt, W. (1921). Elements of Folk Psychology. (English translation). London: Allen and Urwin.

ANALYZING SOCIAL INTERACTIONS IN A 'GLOCAL' SOCIETY: PROBLEMS AND POSSIBILITIES OF A CULTURAL PSYCHOLOGY

ULRIKE POPP-BAIER

Cultural Psychology as the Interpretative Paradigm in Psychology?

Cultural psychology or the culturalistic approach in psychology covers a broad range of meanings. According to one, cultural psychology is an alternative to the mainstream scientific approach in psychology. This approach deals with 'meaning' and 'sense' and aims to contribute to solving problems and overcoming conflicts that people experience in their everyday lives or to promote a kind of cultural critique. This cultural psychology is determined by practical tasks and methodological orientations that are justified with respect to the practical tasks. Sometimes it is identified as the so-called interpretative paradigm in psychology in which research relies on qualitative methods (cf. e.g., Popp-Baier 1997).

But this identification gives rise to problems in the absence of a clear set of qualitative methods and an agreed definition of qualitative research. Qualitative research involves multiple methods and does not privilege a single methodology: "Qualitative research means different things to many different people"—as Denzin and Lincoln (1994a: XI) stated in their first *Handbook of Qualitative Research*. In fact, the different modes of qualitative research are associated with quite different traditions and procedures. For example, some qualitative methodologies originate from linguistic analysis, while others arise from social theory, and still others draw on pragmatic, phenomenological, hermeneutic, poststructuralist, or postmodern philosophy. Moreover, each of these broad research traditions encompasses several radically different approaches. In the new *Handbook of Qualitative Research* (2000), some authors argue that we are already in the post 'post' period—post-

103

poststructuralist, post-postmodernist, and post-postexperimental (cf. Denzin and Lincoln 2000a). The exact significance of this diagnosis for qualitative research remains unclear. Methods clearly abound, including different forms of qualitative interviews, different forms of participant observations, research strategies such as the so-called grounded theory, methods of analysis such as objective hermeneutics, different forms of narrative analysis, content analysis, conversation analysis, discourse analysis, semiotic analysis, and, so on (cf. Denzin and Lincoln 1994, 2000; Flick et al. 1995).

These different meta-theoretical stances, methodologies, and methods have hardly anything in common anymore. The value of collectively labeling this diversity as cultural psychology or the cultural approach in psychology is therefore doubtful.

Furthermore, the article by Mary and Kenneth Gergen (2000) in the new *Handbook of Qualitative Research* reveals a distinction between two groups of qualitative researchers. One group criticizes the nomothetic methodologies for their inability to reflect the complexities of human experience and action. Such researchers turn to qualitative methods in the hope of generating richer and more subtle accounts of the social world and human experience. According to Gergen and Gergen (2000), these views remain widely accepted in today's qualitative community, with diverse proponents of grounded theory research and phenomenology, as well as feminist standpoint researchers. They also argue, however, that qualitative researchers have no justification for claiming that their methods are superior to quantitative ones in terms of accuracy or sensitivity to what exists. In the second group of qualitative researchers, attempts to replace the traditional effort to discover and record something like 'the truth' have led to some methodological innovations that challenge the traditional binary between research and representation, that is, between acts of observation or 'gathering data' and subsequent reports on this process. Gergen and Gergen (2000) refer to these innovations as multiple voicing, literary styling, and performance. In short, multiple voicing stands for including the different perspectives of the research subjects in the research report, literary styling means that the research report may take the form of fiction, poetry, or autobiographical invention, and performance denotes the use of communicative expressions such as graphic arts, video, drama, dance, magic and multimedia as forms of research and representation (cf. Gergen and Gergen 2000: 1028pp.).

Considering this second group of qualitative researchers raises the question as to whether the difference between the first group of 'traditional' qualitative research and the second 'innovative' group is bigger than the difference between some approaches in the context of the so-called quantitative research on the one hand and traditional qualitative research on the other.

The interesting question in this context remains whether the label cultural psychology or culturalistic approach in psychology still applies as a unifying label for all these very heterogeneous qualitative approaches. The common factors in all these approaches are that they are peripheral and are interpreted as alternatives to the so-called methods of positivism in the social sciences.

Some authors also stress a certain common model of man which underlies cultural psychological research: the so-called 'subject model' stresses man as a socially situated, intentional, and self-reflexive subject that gives meaning to his or her own actions and experiences (cf. e.g., Billmann-Mahecha 2001).[1] But the question remains: is this enough to identify a certain type of psychology that can be distinguished from other directions as 'cultural psychology'? In my opinion, this would only be the case if we could link certain methodological principles to a specific kind of analytical unit that constitutes the theoretical foundations of a 'cultural psychology'.[2]

At this moment, however, the different 'cultural psychologists' have not agreed on such a link. Nor is it even clear that all 'cultural psychologists' find this kind of unifying methodological-theoretical foundation desirable (cf. Billmann-Mahecha 2001).

Problems and Possibilities for Studying 'Culture' in Psychology, as Illustrated by Research Topics in the Psychology of Religion

Another way of defining cultural psychology is by relying on a certain notion of 'culture' or the 'cultural' that is often related to a kind of cross-cultural or intercultural research. Most people will agree that in our multicultural societies and in the context of globalization we need more studies about intercultural communication, intercultural actions, intercultural competence, and so on.

Here, the cultural psychological approach revolves around relating individual experience to something like 'culture'.

---

1   This approach corresponds with the so-called emic approach in studying 'cultures'. For recent contributions to the 'old' debate about the emic/etic distinction in cross-cultural psychology (and in cultural anthropology as well) see Helfrich (1999) and the comments from Chaudhary (1999), Berry (1999), and Lonner (1999).

2   For approaches in this direction, cf. e.g. Eckensberger (1990), Shweder (1990), and Straub (1999).

I will open my discussion with an example from my current research focus on the psychology of religion. The example is not truly based on a psychological approach. It is derived from psychological anthropology, but that does not matter in this context.[3] In the excellent article "The Afterlife of Stories: Genesis of a Man of God", anthropologist Susan Harding (1992: 60-75) analyzed the narrative of a Baptist preacher in Virginia, which I imagine she recorded in a research project. The Baptist Reverend Milton Cantrell told her a lot of stories to convert her to the Baptist faith. This meant convincing her to let Jesus Christ into her heart and to accept Christ as her personal saviour. The preacher was unsuccessful but eventually told her a story that she called unforgettable and analyzed in her article. The story was about how the reverend had accidentally killed his youngest son while operating a crane. After opening this story "with a wistful, philosophic lull, he rapidly lapsed into a humble, staccato rhythm and a string of homey details that terminated abruptly with his son's death" (1992: 61), the preacher having accidentally killed his son on a Saturday morning. "The details disappeared, the narrative stopped, and he reported three subsequent dialogues, one with God, another with his wife and [...] again with God" (1992: 61). In these dialogues he expressed that he accepted the death of his son, although neither he nor his wife understood it. Then he spoke to the anthropologist about God's son, who lives in his heart, and asked her to let God's son enter her heart.

According to Harding, there are some questions that everybody might ask him—or oneself—after listening to or reading this story:

"How did the boy die? How did Milton *really* feel about it? What about his pain? His sorrow? His guilt? How could he speak with such spareness, such calm, and such calculation to a stranger about what could be the most tragic moment in his life? The dialogues with God and with his wife sound like cloaks that conceal what he must have felt. At best, they ring of reinterpretation, of a retrospective story, one that, Milton suggests, renders him at peace with his loss" (1992: 61).

In the next part of her article Susan Harding outlines two possible perspectives on this story: a bad one and a good one. The bad one—the wrong outlook, according to Harding—is as follows: Milton's story can be examined

---

3   As Shweder (1990) puts it, 'modern' psychological anthropology is actually a kind of cultural psychology.

"as if it were a system of verbal clues about something outside itself—the tragic event, Milton's raw experience, the unmediated emotions of the moment, his subsequent effort to recover and reintegrate', and might appear 'distinctly odd, choppy, suspiciously elusive" (1992: 62).

The other perspective—which would also be the perspective of the born-again listener—the emic perspective, as Susan Harding suggests, would accept Milton's story as "true" in the sense of being an "integral and dynamic component" of what is being narrated. In this view

"the story is not a system of clues to extra-narrative realities (neither to prestoried emotions, experiences and events nor to posthoc psychological processes) but a generative moment in which the event, characters, narrator, feelings, motives, and moral and theological meanings are brought into existence through language. A faithful ear also would have heard a multidimensional, biblically storied universe of significance in Milton's words, cadence, phrases, story frames, and character references, as well as a juxtaposition of dialogue and description" (1992: 62).

Harding claims that "born-again stories 'speak' their narrators and their emotions, motives and experiences into existence and in this sense are invariably 'true' stories [...] Being born-again means entering into a specific narrative culture and speaking one's self, one's life, one's world, in its terms, and it is the task of gospel preachers to transmit the authority, ability and desire to speak born-again stories. They do so by 'opening up' the Christian biblical canon and thus become a kind of third testament in their speech and actions. They emerge out of the web of biblical allusions of which their stories are an intersection, out of the aesthetics of the biblical shape of their stories, and out of the trail of biblically framed stories which came before and prefigured them" (1992: 63). It is therefore pointless, according to Harding, to ask about the reverend's pain, sorrow, or guilt about the death of his son beyond the stories he has told, because his entire experience occurs within the born-again discourse.[4]

---

4   In the rest of her article Harding (1992: 67pp.) analyzes the reverend's story in detail. She highlights the biblical phrases he uses in his speech, the web of allusions, and the story's aesthetic form, which locates it (squarely) in the tradition of Hebrew Scripture (the Old Testament of the Christians). Harding also makes clear that the reverend's story "echoes" at least three major stories in the Bible: the story of Job, the story of Abraham and Isaac, and the story of Christ, of God sacrificing his son. By setting up a "dense and precisely nuanced system of intertextualities", Reverend Cantrell demonstrated the principles of "fundamentalist Baptist" interpretation. It is a kind of "figurative interpretation" that enables its adherents to read the New Testament as a "master type-story",

I have mentioned only the main principles of Harding's analysis of the reverend's narrative, but her analysis and interpretation are very convincing indeed. All the same, I disagree with Harding. In my view her article exemplifies a cultural approach in anthropology and psychology that relies on a certain notion of a coherent, uniform, and timeless culture. I disagree with Harding because her interpretation implicitly contains generalizations that she does not justify and which, in my opinion, are impossible to justify in the framework of her approach.

The first generalization concerns the pragmatic situation of the reverend's narrative. As she told us at the beginning of her analysis, the reverend's intention to convert her clearly influenced his narrative. In my opinion, Harding has no evidence to infer that he would speak to fellow born-again Christians the same way, or that the dialogue with his wife really took place as he related. Susan Harding knows a lot about Baptists' faith and principles for interpreting the Bible and their own life, and she considers these practices the religious or narrative culture of the Baptists. In her article, however, she does not base her statements on other interactions with born-again Christians, except for one interview with a Baptist preacher. She therefore has no means for detecting variations, diversities, problems, contradictions, or changes that might exist even in a Baptist community. Of course it makes no sense to oppose stories in the Baptist framework or to confront them with a kind of raw experience or human compassion that is natural in coping with the death of someone you have loved very much. Everyone, however, including the Baptist preacher Milton Cantrell, takes part in different discourses and has heard different stories in the course of his life about experiencing the death of a loved one. As a result, nobody can predict the exact framework that will be chosen and enacted. I would agree with Harding (1992: 62) that Milton's story is "true" in the sense of being "an integral and dynamic component of what is being narrated"—but perhaps there are more true stories in this sense because there are more integral and dynamic components of what is being narrated that have not been related in the interview setting. While the Baptist preacher and his wife may experience every occurrence in their lives according to the Baptist framework, one interview is not enough to reach this conclusion. Especially in an interview where the preacher tries to convert an 'outsider', he is most unlikely to speak about doubts, sorrows, and pain in his life that do not conform to the biblical

which establishes the perspective for reading the Old Testament as the prefiguration of the New Testament and events in the real world and their own life as a 'completion' of the story of Christ. The lives of the born-again Christians and the stories of their trials and victories and sufferings and blessings fulfil the biblical stories they tell in a manner that frames, prefigures, and foretells their own stories.

framework. While the imprint of the biblical framework on the structure and content of the story is amazing, this kind of analysis is insufficient to prove that it is the only one that Milton can tell about the tragic event. Harding's illustrations can only convince someone who is already—at least implicitly—used to an essentialized concept of culture. In my opinion, Harding's article is indisputably an excellent example of a kind of 'cultural analysis' in the framework of a certain perspective. It answers a certain question, although others are also possible in this context.

If we deny other possible perspectives and questions, we construct a homogeneous culture through a certain methodical approach. Our eye for the importance of 'the culture' for human experience and actions would lack a perspective for the possible heterogeneity of 'the culture' we are studying and using to interpret the narrative of one of its adherents.

Some anthropologists, such as Lila Abu-Lughod, have suggested omitting the word culture from the vocabulary of social scientists altogether because of its current misuse in public rhetoric and social science. Abu-Lughod (1991) objects to the tendency to overemphasize 'coherence', 'uniformity', and 'timelessness' in the meaning systems of a given group, and as a consequence, constructing fundamentally different, essentialized, and homogenized social units, which are connected to each other in a relationship of power. 'Making other' in this context is always connected with 'hierarchy', as difference tends to be a relationship of power.

Perhaps we can apply the concept of culture differently. I will present another example from religious studies, in which individual experience is related to a certain cultural or symbolic order. The psychological anthropologist Peter Stromberg (1993) devised this concept for the study of Christian conversions, especially for conversions to Evangelical Christianity. Social scientist have long been fascinated with Christian conversions, as a form of religious experience that believers say both strengthens their faith and changes their lives. Stromberg's study examines the performance of conversion narratives and argues that the performance itself is central to the efficacy of the conversion. In his analysis of conversion stories from Evangelical circles in the United States, he assumes that religious discourse is decisive in enabling believers to reconcile conflicting desires, and consequently to transform themselves. Stromberg (1993) distinguishes two forms of communicative behavior: the form of the referential and that of the constitutive. The referential use of linguistic symbols implicitly assumes a general consensus in a certain social reference group concerning the meaning of these symbols. Communicative behaviors that are visible as activities in which one communicates by doing something are designated as constitutive communicative behaviors. Their meanings depend upon the contexts in which they occur. According to Stromberg, these behaviors always entail a breakdown between communication and situation.

For example, the statement 'I have a headache' may be a referential communicative act if I only want to tell someone that I feel pain in my head, and I implicitly assume that everyone who understands English will understand this utterance. In different contexts, however, the same utterance may form different constitutive communicative acts, for example a polite hint for a visitor to leave because I am tired. In this case, the meaning of the communicative behavior depends on the surrounding social context. Another example of constitutive communicative behavior is communication that occurs through symbolic systems other than verbal language. For example, I might choose to convey that I am wealthy by purchasing an expensive car or by wearing expensive clothes.

Stromberg submits that converts who narrate their conversion story use a type of speech that always comprises both the referential and the constitutive forms of communication: canonic discourse, which refers to a certain religious context of meaning, becomes constitutive (i.e., meaningful) in a broader sense by establishing a direct link between canonic language and individual experience. In the conversion narrative individual experience is narrated in the framework of religious language and acquires meaning through the religious code. Stromberg argues that this connection enables verbal expression of previously inaccessible or unacceptable desires while deepening the commitment to faith. In this sense, the conversion narrative constitutes the self-transformation of the narrator. Usually this kind of self-transformation will be sustained dialogically by a variety of social interactions within the respective religious groups. According to this perspective, conversion does not seem like an isolated occurrence in the life of an individual. Rather, it concerns a gradual procedure in which subjects attribute meaning to their experiences. This attribution of meaning is not contained within a single story that is constantly repeated with each narration. Rather, Stromberg stresses—in part by regarding the conversion story as a ritual—that the story's actual performance is an essential constituent of the procedure that can be perceived as conversion in the sense of self-transformation.

This conception offers a framework for analyzing conversion stories in which converts relate how they have overcome serious personal problems (e.g., anxieties, shyness, or difficulties with their spouse) or illnesses (e.g., eating disorders, depressions, or lower back pain) by embracing, for example, the Charismatic-Evangelical version of Christianity. Stromberg's concept allows us to show how converts express and even transform their problems in the new religious language they are learning and alleviate or even solve their problems this way.[5]

Comparing the respective approaches of Stromberg and Harding reveals at least one major difference. Because Stromberg stresses a kind of acculturation process, he distinguishes individual orientations from elements of the new discourse or culture that people will embrace. He perceives no difference between the conversion narrative and a kind of 'raw experience' or 'extra-narrative realities' or 'pre-storied emotions', or the like. Stromberg's approach does, however, enable distinctions to be made between different narratives in which the individual participates and consequently between 'different realities' that occur in the framework of these narratives. In this manner, Stromberg stresses the process of constructing this kind of narrative and reveals that this process can lead to different results. Every religious community has its 'devotees', its 'fundamentalists' (and sometimes its 'terrorists'), its 'liberalists', its 'fellow travelers', its 'sceptics', its 'heretics', its 'apostates', etc. Over time, 'liberals' may also become 'fundamentalists' or 'sceptics', while 'sceptics' may turn into 'fundamentalists' etc. In my view, any psychological approach should offer analytical tools for analysing these kinds of processes and changes, as Stromberg (1993) does. Of course, Stromberg (1993) has more difficulties conceptualizing the linkage process between individual experience and religious discourse, although he nevertheless manages to conceptualize and analyze the heterogeneity within a religious 'culture' this way, which Harding (1992) cannot. He conceptualizes a process and the activities of the individual and the social interac-

---

5   Cf. for example Popp-Baier (2001, 2002) for the psychological analysis of women's conversion narratives from the Charismatic-Evangelical movement. In this context, for example, I analyzed the conversion story of a young woman who suffered from an eating disorder and overcame this disorder by embracing Charismatic-Evangelism (Popp-Baier 2001). In my analysis of this conversion narrative, I stressed that by telling her conversion story the young woman came to terms with her unbearable embodied aims. By using the canonic language of Charismatic-Evangelical Christianity, the woman formulated her life orientation before conversion (achievement orientation) and replaced it with another one after conversion (to enjoy life). The canonic language also became constitutive by reframing the experiential world of the convert. This transformation enabled her to abandon her achievement orientation and her desire for control at the level of referential meaning by structuring her new 'self-concept' at the level of constitutive meaning through an authoritarian relationship with God. This allowed her to follow her achievement orientation in her religious life and to live as controlled as usual in a universe of discourse in which the notion of control figures as an important 'motive'. Every new performance of her conversion narrative will improve this kind of self-transformation and will allow her to interpret this subjectively as a healing process.

tions that sustain, produce, and perhaps change the religious culture or— perhaps more accurately—the religious discourse and the individual experiences as well.[6]

Analytical Tools for Analyzing Diversity

Stromberg's distinction between two forms of communication (i.e., the referential and the constitutive forms) is decisive in his approach. This aspect may be crucial: we need at least a double concept of culture and an idea of how the 'two' are interrelated with psychological processes, otherwise, we risk overlooking the differences and heterogeneities within a so-called culture. This may be why researchers committed to a certain normative notion of multiculturality have the impression that the traditional concept of culture prevents us from conceptualizing the diversity and complexity of social interactions in a 'glocal' society influenced not only by processes of globalization but also by processes of localization (cf. Robertson 1992).[7]

Let us consider a classical concept of a cultural approach in anthropology: Clifford Geertz's concept of cultural analysis in his essay "Religion as a Cultural System" (Geertz 1993). According to Geertz, the culture concept denotes "an historically transmitted pattern of meanings embodied in symbols, a system of inherited conceptions expressed in symbolic forms by means of which men communicate, perpetuate, and develop

---

6 Cf. also Cooper and Denner (1998), who discuss seven theoretical perspectives linking culture and psychological processes (psychological development).

7 According to Robertson (1992, 1995), the terms 'glocal' and 'glocalization' were originally formulated in Japan and were devised in particular reference to marketing issues, as Japan became more successfully engaged in the global economy. "The idea of glocalization in its business sense is closely related to what in some contexts is called, in more straightforwardly economic terms, micro-marketing: the tailoring and advertising of goods and services on a global or near-global basis to increasingly differentiated local and particular markets" (Robertson 1995: 28). Robertson (1995) wants to use the general term 'glocalization' to discuss some points concerning the global-local-issue. In particular, he tries "to transcend the tendency to cast the idea of globalization as inevitably in tension with the idea of localization" (1995: 40). From his own analytical and interpretive, standpoint there is no polarity or opposition between globalization and 'the world of the local'. By contrast, Robertson maintains that "the concept of globalization has involved the simultaneity and the interpenetration of what are conventionally called the global and the local, or—in a more abstract vein—the universal and the particular" (1995: 30). The same is true for the processes of homogenization and heterogenization, which are complementary and interpenetrative.

their knowledge about and attitudes toward life" (1993: 89). Geertz warns against confusing cultural analysis with entering into a mentalistic world of introspective psychology, or failing to draw enough distinctions. "Cultural acts", he says,

"the construction, apprehension, and utilization of symbolic forms, are social events like any other; they are as public as marriages and as observable as agriculture. They are not, however, exactly the same thing; or more precisely, the symbolic dimension of social events is, like the psychological, itself theoretically abstractable from those events as empirical totalities. [...] No matter how deeply interfused the cultural, the social, and the psychological may be in the everyday life of houses, farms, poems and marriages, it is useful to distinguish them in analysis, and, so doing, to isolate the generic traits of each against the normalized background of the other two" (1993: 91p.).

According to Geertz, the cultural patterns are "extrinsic sources of information", which means that "they lie outside the boundaries of the individual organism in that intersubjective world of common understandings into which all human individuals are born, in which they pursue their separate careers, and which they leave persisting behind them after they die" (1993: 92). It also means that cultural patterns provide programs for social and psychological processes that shape public behavior.

In Geertz's view these cultural patterns have the status of 'models'— 'models' in a twofold sense. The most interesting aspect in Geertz's concept is his statement that cultural patterns have an 'intrinsic double aspect': they are not only 'models *of* reality', but they are also 'models *for* reality'. They attribute meaning, that is, objective conceptual form to social and psychological processes, both by molding themselves according to this reality and by molding this reality after themselves.

In this context Geertz discusses a Balinese theatrical cultural performance, in which a terrible witch called Rangda engages in a ritual combat with an amiable monster called Barong (1993: 114pp.). According to Geertz, this ritual performance makes clear how religious cultural patterns describe and shape reality at the same time. The Rangda -Barong combat depicts the interweaving of the malignant and the comic in Balinese everyday social life and individual behavior and at the same time shapes it during the performance. The figure of Rangda not only embodies and expresses fear (model-of-aspect) but also creates behavioral forms for everyday life and shapes behavior (model-for-aspect). In general, Geertz maintains that such patterns make religion sociologically interesting (and in my opinion, in psychological respects as well) by describing and above all shaping the social order (and human thought, action, and experience as well).[8]

This concept corresponds with Stromberg's approach in analyzing conversion narratives. Adding Geertz's distinction to Stromberg's distinction between the referential and the constitutive, the constitutive can be furthermore differentiated as a specific analytical appropriation of Geertz's general double concept of cultural patterns as models *for* and models *of* with regard to a certain form of cultural analysis: the analysis of the individual and social reproduction of a certain religious discourse, and the specific psychological aspects of this religious discourse which provides the believers with a certain language for shaping, expressing, and transforming their wishes, fears, experiences, convictions, world views, doubts, etc. Culture—or perhaps more appropriately the cultural—as a double concept might be a requirement for conceptualizing analytical tools suitable for analyzing diversity and the so-called multiculturalism in different societies without neglecting the unifying, constraining, or even programming aspects of cultural patterns in different kinds of social interactions.

Marshall Sahlins conducts a similar search for the relation between individual experience and cultural order. Drawing on concepts from Cassirer, Saussure, Mead, Heidegger, Sartre, and Ricoeur, he concludes:

"Never present as such to individual experience, the institutions of society thus become capable of ordering subjective interests and actions—that is, by virtue of a common membership with 'the generalized other'. Nor will my purposes be completely idiosyncratic: even when opposed to some other they are formulated on a common cultural logic. [...] The individual is a social being, but we must never forget that he is an individual social being, with a biography not the same as that of anyone else. [...] This means that life in society is not an automatic genuflection before the superorganic being but, rather a continuous rearrangement of its categories in the projects of personal being" (2000: 285).

Based on this quotation, we can argue in favour of the biographical approach in 'cultural psychology'. Examining individual biographies (or biographies of partners, families, or even communities) forces us to study diversity, variety, and heterogeneity. By studying biographies we explore the realization of opportunities, projects, and processes, changes, activities, decisions, etc., and thus variety as well. It is therefore no surprise,

---

8   The last statement is a kind of abstract of the 'real' processes taking place, because it is, of course, not 'religion' that describes or shapes anything.

for example, that Harding (1992), who wanted to demonstrate the determination or creation of individual orientations by a religious culture, analyzed only 'narratives', whereas Stromberg (1993) eventually analyzed 'life stories'.[9]

Moreover, Sahlins (1982) suggests that the classical distinction between language and speech (according to the tradition of Saussure) may be elaborated into an argument about culture in general. Likewise, culture has a "dual mode of existence", both in human projects and as a structure or system. "Intentionally arranged by the subject, it is also conventionally constituted in society." As a symbolic process, it is organized differently according to the two dimensions of "culture-as-lived" and "culture-as-constituted" (Sahlins 2000: 286).

Structure or culture-as-constituted is a state, whereas action or culture-as-lived unfolds as a temporal process:

"In structure, the meaning of a sign is fixed through differential relationships with other signs; in action, it is variously combined with other signs in implicational relationships [...] Moreover, in their several projects people effect contingent relationships between signs which are not necessarily those ordained in the culture-as-constituted" (Sahlins 2000: 286).

And that is the way cultural change takes place. But 'structure' in this sense has only a virtual existence, or perhaps we might say it has a kind of status that appears to combine the Kantian 'Ding an sich' and the Weberian 'ideal type' because it is thought to influence individual and social actions, while at the same time every identification of a 'structure' is already an individual or social act of identification and in this way belongs to 'culture-as-lived' and is influenced by temporal processes.

Sahlins identifies two forms of symbolic interaction between structure and action: "the functional displacement of sign relationships in personal action and practical revaluation of signs in the famous "context of the situation" (2000: 288). Compared to Geertz (1993), Sahlins (2000) proposes two modes of existence of culture and therefore different processes by which the two modes interact. Relying on Geertz's article "Religion as a Cultural System", we have thus far identified only an analyti-

---

9 Personality psychology also entails many efforts to search for concepts for analyzing diversity and heterogeneity. For example, in the discussion about the identity concept some authors stress that personal identity is to be conceptualized not as a homogenous unit but as a kind of 'synthesis of the heterogeneous' or as a 'multivoiced' or 'dialogical self'. Cf. for example Ricoeur (1990), Hermans and Kempen (1993), and Straub (2000). For a more radical concept of the self as the 'un-synthesized heterogeneous', cf. for example Gergen (1991); for a critical evaluation of these approaches, cf. Straub (2000).

cal difference between two aspects of one mode of existence: the model for and the model of aspects of cultural patterns. The same holds true for Stromberg (1993). Combining the distinction by Sahlins (2000) with the one by Geertz (1993) yields a threefold concept of cultural analysis: analysis of culture-as-constituted and analysis of the two aspects of culture-as-lived, respectively representing the model-of-aspect and the model-for-aspect. Relating this concept to Stromberg's concept allows us, for example, to elaborate the analytical or interpretative perspectives on conversion narrative by comparing the individual adjustment of the religious code to the religious code as it can be analyzed (as an 'ideal type') in 'texts'[10] in the specific religious community. In the next step, we analyze the constitutive aspects (the model for and the model of aspects) of this religious code by relating it to biographical processes as well.

Concepts like the ones by Geertz (1993) and Sahlins (1993) enable us to devise a perspective within the framework of a cultural psychology sensitive to varieties, differences, heterogeneity, contradictions, changes, and so on without the risk of esssentializing culture that determines or programs individual and social behavior completely. The distinctions are not elaborate theoretical models for cultural psychological research but sensitizing concepts that may inspire empirical research. The more elaborate, specific theoretical models (action approach, biographical approach, narrative approach, discourse approach, etc.) that we need for our empirical research depend on our specific research questions and practical interests.[11] Moreover, the twofold or threefold concept of culture (or

---

10 According to Robertson (1992, 1995), the terms 'glocal' and 'glocalization' were originally formulated in Japan and were devised in particular reference to marketing issues, as Japan became more successfully engaged in the global economy. "The idea of glocalization in its business sense is closely related to what in some contexts is called, in more straightforwardly economic terms, micro-marketing: the tailoring and advertising of goods and services on a global or near-global basis to increasingly differentiated local and particular markets" (Robertson 1995: 28). Robertson (1995) wants to use the general term 'glocalization' to discuss some points concerning the global-local-issue. In particular, he tries "to transcend the tendency to cast the idea of globalization as inevitably in tension with the idea of localization" (1995: 40). From his own analytical and interpretive, standpoint there is no polarity or opposition between globalization and 'the world of the local'. By contrast, Robertson maintains that "the concept of globalization has involved the simultaneity and the interpenetration of what are conventionally called the global and the local, or—in a more abstract vein—the universal and the particular" (1995: 30). The same is true for the processes of homogenization and heterogenization, which are complementary and interpenetrative.

11 For the discussion of some specific theoretical models and their applications to certain research questions, cf. for example Cooper and Denner (1998).

116

rather of the cultural) may be a test for formulating and using more specific theoretical models for empirical research: do the concepts enable this kind of twofold or threefold perspective and thus the sensitivity to agency, differences, contradictions, or changes?

Analyzing Social Interactions in 'Glocal' Societies

At present 'multiculturalism' may be one of the most demanding and exciting subjects for cultural psychology. In other words, we have to deal with social interactions and social conflicts in the so-called glocal societies structured by processes of globalization and localization (cf. Robertson 1992, 1995, see also footnote 6). In this context, individual or social actions should be interpreted in the context of the people's different cultural backgrounds. In formulating the issue this way, however, we may be on the wrong track from the very beginning of analyzing the phenomenon. A better description appears in Gerd Baumann's book *The Multicultural Riddle*, where the author writes: "Multiculturalism is not the old concept of culture multiplied by the number of groups that exist, but a new, and internally plural, praxis of culture applied to oneself and to others" (1999: VII).[12]

Baumann (1999) notes that adequate social-scientific analyses of multiculturalism demand a new understanding of culture. To obtain an adequate perspective on social interactions in a 'glocal' surrounding, we need to perceive culture first of all as something we make or remake and shape or reshape in everyday interaction, and thus not as something that we own or to which we belong.

"The essentialist understanding of culture (whether nationalist, ethnicist or religiously orthodox) has to be turned into a processual, and even discursive,

---

12 Turner (1994) distinguishes between "difference multiculturalism" and "critical multiculturalism". According to Turner, "difference multiculturalism" stresses ethnic identity and mystifies actual differences between groups by the "romancing of otherness": "As a form of reification or romantic essentialism, it presupposes the abstraction of cultural phenomena from their real social and political significance of the 'difference' as a vacuum filled in by the cultural theorist" (1994: 410). By contrast, "critical multiculturalism" seeks to use cultural diversity as a basis for challenging, revising, and relativizing basic notions and principles common to dominant and minority cultures alike, so as to construct a more vital, open, and democratic common culture' (Turner 1994: 408). With regard to these distinctions, a cultural psychological approach should avoid implicitly contributing to a "difference multiculturalism".

understanding of culture. Culture is not a giant photocopy machine that turns out clones, but the most sensitive capacity of humans who cannot but produce change even when they mean to produce stability" (Baumann 1999: 137).

The same statement in a new situation has a different meaning. Cultural identities as national, ethnic or religious identities are thus processes of identification that turn out to be dialogical: they emerge and crystallize or are "used creatively and turn subtle in the daily process of approaching so-called others" (Baumann 1999: 138).

Let us consider an example. About two years ago in a Dutch town a Turkish schoolboy shot another pupil at school. During the first round of interrogation, he said that he was instructed by his father to avenge the honor of his sister, who spent a few weeks with the boy he hurt without marrying him. He later denied receiving such an order, his father denied issuing one, and the whole family declared the revenge of honor issue to be complete nonsense. In the context of the court hearing, two experts were asked for their opinion, but they disagreed. One declared that it could be a case of revenge of honor, while the other expert declared that it obviously was not because important elements were missing. The whole issue remained unclear. The logic behind the opinion of the second expert is interesting to us. He argued that there is a cultural pattern called revenge of honor, and that determining whether an individual action matches this pattern is possible. The boy's actions in the case mentioned above, however, lend themselves to at least two possible interpretations. One is that the boy had certain reasons or motives for bringing a firearm to school (we know about other cases where children have brought firearms to school and used them) and tried—at first—to justify his course of action by invoking a cultural pattern that he knew would justify the use of a firearm. The other is that he received the order from his father, and the boy and his father or the boy and the whole family tried to reconcile an issue of family honor with the possibilities and realities in the Dutch society where they lived. In this case at least two people (and perhaps more than two) worked together to change important elements of the 'revenge of honor' cultural pattern to ensure the minimum penalty authorized under Dutch law.

If we find the second interpretation the most plausible and disregard the moral and legal aspects of this case for the moment, we can describe the act as the result of a certain 'bicultural' competence. In psychological respects it makes no sense to explain the boy's action solely in reference to the cultural pattern of revenge of honor. A psychological analysis of this case has at least to consider the role of this cultural pattern in the boy's everyday life and his understanding of its meaning, as well as the kind of social interactions that motivated him to bring a firearm to school and discharge it. Explaining the boy's action solely with reference to the pattern of revenge of honor would implicitly essentialize culture and would contribute to the construction of different cultures (i.e., a civilized European one and a less civilized one), where people still murder each other over questions of honor, and whereby the members of the civilized one are as much 'determined' by their culture as are those of the less civilized one (cf. also Baerveldt and Voestermans 2000). As Baumann has stated, multicultural writing should "not reify national, ethnic or religious identities". Rather, it should reflect the awareness "that all identities are identifications in context and that they are thus situational and flexible and imaginative and innovative"—even when they are not intended as such (1999: 138). It is therefore better, for example, not to construct a kind of Judaeo-Christian culture that forms 'our' background and to regard Islam as the alien other. On the one hand, Judaeo-Christian culture is very diverse,[13] while on the other hand people who call themselves Muslims belong to very different communities and practice very different forms of Islam. Islamic intellectuals in Germany, for example, often warn that we abet the intentions of the fundamentalist groups by constructing Islam as the alien entity in 'our' culture.[14]

---

13 That holds true for the Christian faith. In the context of comments on the tragic events in the United States on September 11, some Protestant church leaders as well as the president of the German Republic, Johannes Rau (who is a very devout Protestant), argued that the so-called inter-religious dialogue needed to be intensified, and that to this end Christians would have to become more aware of and reflect on the special characteristics of their own faith. Otherwise, they would not be able to have a dialogue with the adherents of other faiths (cf. for example the interview with Johannes Rau in Die Zeit, 27 December 2001: 8). To be honest, I am not sure what they really mean, but I am afraid that this will lead the diversity and plurality within Christianity to be neglected. Christianity is not one single religion but several, and I am not sure about their basic common principles or 'characteristics'. At this moment we cannot even mention the belief in Jesus Christ as the Son of God, because, increasingly, theologians (especially Protestant ones) view Jesus Christ as an exceptional human being but no longer as the Son of God and still call themselves Christians. There is more of a 'family resemblance' between the different 'Christian religions' than common basic principles of belief. Christians have to be aware of this before they can have a dialogue with adherents of 'other religions'.

14 Historically, Islam has figured prominently in the development of so-called Western culture. And as Abu-Lughod points out: "One of the most productive lines of thought made possible by Edward Said's Orientalism has been the reframing of world history as a global phenomenon, with the recognition that the division between West and East, and the representations of each, were produced in the historical encounter broadly labeled imperialism" (1998: 17). In general, Abu-Lughod wonders whether "the

By reifying cultural identity, we sustain the politics of elitists and fundamentalists (and perhaps even of terrorists). Considering the processual and dialogical nature of all identifications, however, provides an opportunity for examining multicultural realities at a level that reveals the internal plurality of all individual, social, or cultural 'units' or identities, respectively. At certain times and places, even at the level of social interactions in a glocal community, multiple identifications can be observed empirically.[15] According to Baumann, we can also empirically identify a discourse of culture, which is a vision of culture "that understands differences as relational, rather than absolute", and acknowledges that many different "cleavages cut across each other. Instead of viewing society as a patchwork of five or fifty cultural groups, it views social life as an elastic and crisscrossing web of multiple identifications." People choose whom to identify with and when and where and even when to engage the discourse (1999: 139). As social scientists, we have to adopt a perspective and adequate concepts, research methods, and strategies that sensitize us to the different processes of constructing 'multiple identities' and engaging in different forms of discourses.

In their article "The misconception of culture: Towards a psychology of biculturality",[16] Carl Baerveldt and Paul Voestermans (2000) maintain that in psychology we do not need the concept of culture to explain individual and social behavior. Rather, cultural psychology is the discipline for analyzing and explaining so-called cultural patterns (e.g., a cultural pattern like 'revenge of honor') in psychological terms by understanding them as cultural patterns of behavior that are regarded as the dynamic product of constant mutual adaptations. In this context the authors advocate the psychological study of biculturality in the multicultural society. "Instead of a one-sided emphasis on cultural differences, [...] (they) make a case for a psychology of biculturality concerned with the skills and competencies one has to draw upon to participate successfully in a multicultural society" (2000: 120). The question then arises why 'biculturality': why not immediately 'multiculturality'? This general use of the concept of biculturality eventually leads the authors to lapse into the mistake they commit throughout their article: they suggest examining how Turkish youngsters participate in two cultures when they arrive in the

---

notions of separate cultures have themselves been produced by the colonial encounter" (1998: 16). And according to Abu-Lughod it is especially "recent thinking in postcolonial studies" that "has the potential to get us beyond the impasse of this ossified notion of culture and the binaries that it underwrites" (1998: 17).

15 Cf. therefore for example Baumann's own empirical research in 'multi-ethnic' London (Baumann 1996).

16 The article is written in Dutch and entitled "Het misverstand cultuur: naar een psychologie van biculturaliteit".

Netherlands with their families. In this manner, they establish a general difference between 'the' culture of their parents and 'the' Dutch culture, which become homogenous units and are thus not understood as the internal plural realities that the authors would like to believe they are.

Hermans and Kempen (1998) also try to meet the challenges of the emergence of 'glocal' systems, the process of hybridisation, and the increasing cultural complexity. According to the authors, new forms of worldwide interconnectedness call into question basic assumptions of cross-cultural psychology: the geographical localization of culture and the conceptualization of cultural differences in terms of dichotomies (for example, collectivism versus individualism). Therefore, Hermans and Kempen also advocate "an alternative approach that is sensitive to the process of cultural interchange, the complexities of social positions, and the dynamics of global interconnectedness" (1998: 1112). Examining the alternative approach that Hermans and Kempen (1998) elaborate in their article, I wonder whether the approach is indeed 'alternative'. To give an example, they distinguish 'cores' of cultures from 'contact zones' between cultures and suggest that for research "the attention should shift from a comparison between countries or regions to the study of cultural processes on the contact zones as exemplified by the growing number of international contacts, networks, organizations, and institutions, which are populated by people from different cultural origin" (1998: 1117). By distinguishing 'cores' of cultures from 'contact zones' between cultures, however, they continue to reify culture as a spatial unit, and by mentioning 'cultural origins' in this context, they implicitly use 'culture' as a geographical unit.

Perhaps we should in fact refer to the 'cultural' instead of 'culture' and to 'cultural competence' instead of 'intercultural competence' to avoid such implicit essentialism in psychological research.[17] In their arti-

---

17 For recent discussions about the concept of culture and various attempts to avert an essentialist view of culture, cf. for example, Barth (1994), Borofsky (1994), Keesing (1994). Especially for suggestions on avoiding 'culture' and speaking about the 'cultural', see Sahlins (1994) and Vayda (1994). For a short overview about current debates concerning 'culture' in anthropology, see also Fuchs (2001).
Along the same lines, the sociologist Gilroy (1987) also detected a similar kind of essentialism in anti-racist campaigns and anti-racist politics in Great Britain concerning the definitions of 'race' and 'racism'. Gilroy advocates abandoning a general theory of anti-racist practice, which also requires discarding crude definitions of 'race' and 'racism': "'Race' is, after all, not the property of powerful, prejudiced individuals but an effect of complex relationships between dominant and subordinate social groups. If whites have shared the same job centers, schools, police cells, parties and streets with blacks in what sense can we speak of them as having additional power? The very complexity of these relations and the extent of difference that exists between the meanings and structures at-

cle, Baerveldt and Voestermans (2000) advance an interesting suggestion concerning adequate research strategies. They advocate action research, which means conducting research *with* people rather than *about* people. In a problem-centred approach, this method will eliminate the need to distinguish between 'cultures' before starting research.[18]

Nevertheless, we do not have to overlook the need to deal with an essentialist concept of culture as well because reified visions of culture belong to the social realities we study (sometimes as a so-called strategic essentialism). National, ethnic, and religious minorities, as well as other kinds of groups, use them (and probably need them in some cases) to achieve their goals, to impose their interests on other people, to resolve social conflicts, and to understand or explain their own feelings and behavior or that of other people. Again, the best strategy for social scientists may be to avoid defining cultures or so-called others before starting with empirical research and examining empirically how people construct communities and identities and how they use them in everyday life. This will help us appreciate the different reified and discursive visions of culture that people themselves use in our field of study, while at the same time we have to distinguish between the level of the 'visions', the 'ideas', the 'subjective theories', and the enactment of these 'visions', 'ideas', or 'subjective theories' in daily life in interactions between people from different nations, different ethnic backgrounds, different religious communities, etc. According to Baumann, an

"ethnographic study of multicultural realities as lived in one place can produce new clues that fill in the theoretical gap [...] between people claiming reified identities and their everyday necessity of crosscutting identifications. People who live in a multicultural milieu need to do both to achieve their personal, family or community goals. What develops in such an environment

tached to 'race' in different social formations are additional factors that undermine the possibility of a general theory of race relations and the sociologically inspired attempt to elevate that concept into an analytical rather than a merely descriptive one" (1987: 149). In his new book, Between Camps, Gilroy (2000) sketches visions of the future released from outmoded principles of differentiation and offering the possibility of a truly planetary humanism. In search of new analytical concepts that allow us to describe and understand the complex issue of sociality in which "displacement, flight, exile and forced migration are likely to be familiar and recurrent phenomena that transform the terms in which identity needs to be understood", the author perceives a valuable idea in the concept of 'diaspora': "As an alternative to the metaphysics of 'race', nation and bounded culture coded into the body, diaspora is a concept that problematizes the cultural and historical mechanics of belonging" (Gilroy 2000: 123).

18 For different approaches in action research, see for example Reason (1994).

is a double discursive competence: People know when to reify one of their identities, and they know when to question their own reifications. What also develops are processes of multicultural convergence: the simultaneous reorientation of otherwise separate traditions upon a new point of cross-cultural agreement" (Baumann 1999: 139, see also footnote 15).

In analyzing how and when people enact their reifications of culture, and how and when they abandon them, social scientists and especially psychologists have a crucial role. If we want to live in 'multicultural societies' and thereby sustain and contribute to a 'critical multiculturalism' (cf. Turner, 1994, see also footnote 12) through our scholarship, 'multicultural society' may figure as a 'regulative idea' for psychological research to explore the plural realities in practice within a theoretical perspective that retains the possibilities of a cultural perspective and discards the problems of this perspective in psychology.

Conclusions

The discussions mentioned above lead us to conclude that psychological analysis of variety and heterogeneity in 'glocal' societies requires a twofold or threefold concept of the 'cultural' and an idea about the interconnectedness between cultural patterns or cultural forms and psychological processes. Cultural psychology should be conceptualized as a discourse in which different specifications of theoretical models and methods for empirical research have to depend on concrete research questions. If we wish to emulate Gerd Baumann (1999) by speaking of the 'riddle' of cultural psychology, we must acknowledge that this article is not the solution to this riddle but merely contributes to defining the problem.

References

Abu-Lughod, L. (1991). Writing against Culture. In: R.G. Fox, (Ed.): Recapturing Anthropology. Working in the Present (pp. 137-162). Santa Fe: School of American Research Press.

Abu-Lughod, L. (1998). Remaking Women. Feminism and Modernity in the Middle East. Princeton: Princeton University Press.

Baerveldt, C./Voestermans, P. (2000). Het misverstand cultuur: naar een psychologie van biculturaliteit (The misconception of culture: Towards a psychology of biculturality). In: Nederlands Tijdschrift voor de Psychologie, 55, 109-120.

Barth, F. (1994). A Personal View of Present Tasks and Priorities in Cultural and Social Anthropology. In: R. Borofsky (Ed.). Assessing Cultural Anthropology (pp. 349-360). New York: McGraw-Hill.

Baumann, G. (1996). Contesting Culture: Discourses of Identity in Multi-Ethnic London. Cambridge: Cambridge University Press.

Baumann, G. (1999). The Multicultural Riddle. Rethinking National, Ethnic, and Religious Identities. New York and London: Routledge.

Berry, J.W. (1999). Emics and Etics: A Symbiotic Conception. In: Culture & Psychology, 2, 165-171.

Billmann-Mahecha, E. (2001). Kulturpsychologie (Cultural Psychology). In: Lexikon der Psychologie (pp. 1-4). Heidelberg: Spektrum Akademischer Verlag GmbH.

Borofsky, R. (1994). On the Knowledge and Knowing of Cultural Activities. In: R. Borofsky (Ed.). Assessing Cultural Anthropology (pp. 331-346). New York: McGraw-Hill.

Chaudhary, N. (1999). Diversity, Definitions and Dilemmas: A Commentary on Helfrich's Principle of Triarchic Resonance. In: Culture & Psychology, 2, 155-163.

Cooper, C.R./Denner, J. (1998). Theories Linking Culture and Psychology: Universal and Community-Specific Processes. In: Annual Review Psychology, 49, 559-584.

Csordas, Th.J. (1994). The Sacred Self: A Cultural Phenomenology of Charismatic Healing. Berkeley: University of California Press.

Denzin, N.K./Lincoln, Y.S. (1994a). Preface. In: N.K. Denzin/Y.S. Lincoln (Eds.). Handbook of Qualitative Research (pp. IX-XII). Thousand Oaks: Sage.

Denzin, N.K./Lincoln, Y.S. (Eds.) (1994). Handbook of Qualitative Research. Thousand Oaks: Sage.

Denzin, N.K./Lincoln, Y.S. (2000a). Introduction: The Discipline and Practice of Qualitative Research. In: N.K. Denzin/Y.S. Lincoln (Eds.). Handbook of Qualitative Research. 2nd ed. (pp. 1-28). Thousand Oaks: Sage.

Denzin, N.K./Lincoln, Y.S. (Eds.) (2000). Handbook of Qualitative Research. 2nd ed. Thousand Oaks: Sage.

Eckensberger, L.H. (1990). On the Necessity of the Culture Concept in Psychology: A View from Cross-Cultural Psychology. In: F.J.R. van de Vijver/G.J.M. Hutschemaekers (Eds.). The Investigation of Culture. Current Issues in Cultural Psychology (pp. 153-183). Tilburg: Tilburg University Press.

Flick, U./Kardorff, E. von/Keupp, H./Rosenstiel, L. von/Wolff, St. (Eds.) (1995). Handbuch Qualitative Sozialforschung. [Handbook Qualitative Social Research] 2nd ed. München: Psychologie Verlags Union.

Fuchs, M. (2001). Der Verlust der Totalität. Die Anthropologie der Kultur. [The Loss of Totality. The Anthropology of Culture]. In: H. Appelsmeyer/E. Billmann-Mahecha (Eds.). Kulturwissenschaft. Felder einer prozessorientierten wissenschaftlichen Praxis (pp. 18-53). Weilerswist: Velbrück.

Gergen, K.J. (1991). The Saturated Self. New York: Basic Books.

Gergen, M./Gergen, K. (2000). Qualitative Inquiry: Tensions and Transformations. In: N.K. Denzin/Y.S. Lincoln. (Eds.). Handbook of Qualitative Research. Second Edition (pp. 1025-1046). Thousand Oaks: Sage.

Geertz, C. (1993 [1973]). Religion as a Cultural System. In: C. Geertz. The Interpretation of Cultures. Selected Essays (pp. 87-125). London: Fontana Press.

Gilroy, P. (1987). There Ain't No Black in the Union Jack: The Cultural Politics of Race and Nation. London: Routledge.

Gilroy, P. (2000). Between Camps. Race, Identity and Nationalism at the End of the Colour Line. London: The Penguin Press.

Harding, S. (1992). The Afterlife of Stories: Genesis of a Man of God. In: G. Rosenwald/R.L. Ochberg (Eds.). Storied Lives. The Cultural Politic of Self-Understanding (pp. 60-75). New Haven and London: Yale University Press.

Hermans, H.J.M./Kempen, H.J.G. (1993). The Dialogical Self. Meaning as Movement. San Diego: Academic Press.

Hermans, H.J.M./Kempen, H.J.G. (1998). Moving Cultures. The Perilous Problems of Cultural Dichotomies in a Globalizing Society. In: American Psychologist, 10, 1111-1120.

Helfrich, H. (1999). Beyond the Dilemma of Cross-Cultural Psychology: Resolving the Tension between Etic and Emic Approaches. In: Culture & Psychology, 2, 131-153.

Keesing, R.M. (1994). Theories of Culture Revisited. In: R. Borofsky (Ed.). Assessing Cultural Anthropology (pp. 301-309). New York: McGraw-Hill.

Lonner, W.J. (1999). Helfrich's 'Principle of Triarchic Resonance': A Commentary on yet Another Perspective on the Ongoing and Tenacious Etic-Emic Debate, 2, 173-181.

Popp-Baier, U. (1997). Psychology of Religion as Hermeneutical Cultural Analysis. Some Reflections with Reference to Clifford Geertz. In: J.A. Belzen (Ed.). Hermeneutical Approaches in Psychology of Religion (pp. 195-212). Amsterdam: Rodopi.

Popp-Baier, U. (1998). Das Heilige im Profanen. Religiöse Orientierungen im Alltag. Eine qualitative Studie zu religiösen Orientierungen von Frauen aus der charismatisch-evangelikalen Bewegung. [The Sacred in the Profane. Religious Orientations among Women from the Charismatic-Evangelical Movement.] Amsterdam: Rodopi.

Popp-Baier, U. (2001). Narrating Embodied Aims. Qualitative Methods in Various Disciplines II: Cultural Sciences. http://www.qualitative-research.net/fqs/fqs-eng.htm.

Popp-Baier, U. (2002). Conversion as Social Construction. A Narrative Approach to Conversion Research. In: C.A.M. Hermans/G. Immink/A. de Jong/J. van der Lans (Eds.): Social Constructionism and Theology (pp. 41-61). Leiden: Brill.

Ricoeur, P. (1990). Soi-même comme un autre. [Self as an Other.] Paris: Editions du Seuil.

Reason, P. (1994). Three Approaches to Participative Inquiry. In: N.K. Denzin/Y.S. Lincoln (Eds.). Handbook of Qualitative Research (pp. 324-339). Thousand Oaks: Sage.

Robertson, R. (1992). Globalization. Social Theory and Global Culture. London: Sage.

Robertson, R. (1995). Glocalization: Time-Space and Homogeneity-Heterogeneity. In: M. Featherstone/S. Lash/R. Robertson (Eds.). Global Modernities (pp. 25-44). London: Sage.

Sahlins, M. (1982). Individual Experience and Cultural Order. In: M. Sahlins (2000). Culture in Practice. Selected Essays (pp. 277-291). New York: Zone Books.

Sahlins, M. (1994). Goodbye to Tristes Tropes: Ethnography in the Context of Modern World History. In: R. Borofsky (Ed.): Assessing Cultural Anthropology (pp. 377-393). New York: McGraw-Hill.

Straub, J. (1999). Handlung, Interpretation, Kritik. Grundzüge einer interpretativen Handlungs- und Kulturpsychologie. [Action, Interpretation, Critique. Foundations of an Interpretative Action and Culture psychology] Berlin: de Gruyter.

Straub, J. (2000). Identitätstheorie, empirische Identitätsforschung und die 'postmoderne' armchair psychology. [Identity Theory, Empirical Identity Research and the 'Post-Modern' Armchair Psychology] In: Zeitschrift für qualitative Bildungs-, Beratungs- und Sozialforschung, 1, 167-194.

Stromberg, P. (1993). Language and Self-Transformation. A Study of the Christian Conversion Narrative. New York: Cambridge University Press.

Shweder, R.A. (1990). Cultural Psychology—What is it? In: J.W. Stigler/R.A. Shweder/G. Herdt (Eds.): Cultural Psychology. Essays on Comparative Human Development (pp. 1-43). Cambridge: Cambridge University Press.

Turner, T. (1994). Anthropology and Multiculturalism: What Is Anthropology that Multiculturalists Should Be Mindful of It? In: D.Th. Goldberg (Ed.): Multiculturalism: A Critical Reader (pp. 406-425). Oxford: Blackwell.

Vayda, A.P. (1994). Actions, Variations, and Change: The Emerging Anti-Essentialist View in Anthropology. In: R. Borofsky (Ed.): Assessing Cultural Anthropology (pp. 320-328). New York: McGraw-Hill.

CULTURE AND THE 'DIALOGICAL SELF': TOWARD A SECULAR CULTURAL PSYCHOLOGY OF RELIGION

JACOB A. V. BELZEN

Varieties of Cultural Psychology

Conceptions of cultural psychology vary widely. Let me mention just three possible conceptions, each of which requires a quite different way of interdisciplinary research: Each calls for different approaches, methods, and techniques, as well as for different disciplinary partners with whom to collaborate in empirical research. Cultural psychology can be conceived of as the effort to interpret the works, or achievements, of a so-called high level of culture with the help of psychological theories. It is my impression that this is the conception of cultural psychology found most often within the so-called cultural studies one encounters within the Humaniora, located frequently and typically in a faculty of arts (or arts and letters). The conception of culture that goes along with it has a somewhat elitist ring; the pieces of culture analyzed in this branch of scholarship are mostly achievements in the various cultural domains: novels and poetry, film, opera and drama, sculpture, painting, etc. (cf., e.g., *Brief: Yearbook of the Amsterdam School for Cultural Analysis, Theory and Interpretation*, which has been published since 1996). The psychological theories employed here are mostly psychoanalytic in nature; it is a kind of 'application' of psychology: psychology is used to interpret and to theorize about pieces of 'high' culture. The analyses in this domain very often come from scholars without conventional training in psychology; here, the interdisciplinary collaboration is usually with other branches of the *Humaniora*.

A second conception of cultural psychology I want to mention only briefly is found where the focus of attention is drawn to the history of psychology. Throughout its history, psychology's theories and approaches have differed, sometimes enormously, and one of the most important factors determining the differences seems to be culture. Different cultures, and different eras within the same culture, have developed quite different kinds of psychologies. When one wants to investigate the roles that culture and history have played in the development of psychology, its various schools, theories, and approaches, collaboration with historians will typically be sought, not only because of their skills and experience in working with archives and other sources, but also because of their perspective and usually broader scope (Danziger 1990, 1997; Richards 1996).

A third conception of cultural psychology is found where human psychic functioning is understood as constituted, evoked, and facilitated by cultural forces and configurations. With this kind of reasoning, the aim is to contribute to the development of psychology as such, to contribute to a psychology that is sensitive to the cultural context and to the cultural momentum of human functioning. This enterprise is primarily carried out by psychologists, who are, however, heavily informed by experts on culture in general or on a specific culture, such as anthropologists, sociologists, folklorists, etc. Here, culture is not understood in an elitist way; on the contrary, it is understood as a necessary and powerful, though mostly unreflected, *conditio sine qua non* for psychic phenomena.

Within each of these conceptions of cultural psychology, one finds studies on religion, however this phenomenon is defined. In many works of art and other achievements of 'high' culture, the influence of religion is readily visible. One sometimes even finds studies that try to use psychological theories to explain, or partially explain, the existence of religion as such. It goes without saying that religion and religious philosophies have had a large impact on the different kinds of psychologies one finds in different cultures and eras. And the fact that religion is, or has been, a major part of common culture in most cultures, needs no argumentation. Even in the so-called secularized West, religion is still visible and traceable in the language, values, and habits of the cultural participants, and probably more people are engaged in some kind of religious activity than in all the arts, or even sports. Therefore, it should be understood readily that religion, however it is conceptualized, presents a major topic to the agenda of every form of cultural psychology. And the other way round, religion being a phenomenon that varies so widely across cultures and history, one would expect psychologists of religion to turn to a culturological approach in order to interpret 'the varieties of religious experience' (James 1902). However, for a number of historical reasons that we cannot go into now, this is not the case, or at least not to the extent one might have expected. Although the early pioneers of cultural psychology—for example, Wilhelm Wundt, but also including Traugott Konstantin Oesterreich and Willy Hellpach—published works on religion as a cultural phenomenon, in later years cultural psychologists have not paid prominent attention to religion. The personal disinterest in, or even hostility towards religion that has become so widespread among psychologists since World War II, is certainly one of the main reasons for this neglect of religion as a topic for psychological research (Ragan et al. 1980). And on the other hand, within the psychology of religion as it has developed in the past century, drawing on cultural psychological perspectives has been a rare approach; on the contrary, the psychology of religion is usually more interested in being part of the so-called mainstream within psychology.

Notwithstanding these historical developments and the current state of affairs, the prospects for cultural psychological approaches in the study of religion have seldom been as favorable as they are today. In the last few years, the antipathy towards religion within psychology seems to have faded, making it possible to deal with religion again, just as it was in the days of psychology's founding fathers (cf. for an instructive review Wulff 1997). The interest in the psychology of religion is clearly increasing, not only among students and the general public, but also among practitioners and researchers (cf., for example, publications by the American Psychological Association; e.g., Richards and Bergin 1997, 2000; Shafranske 1996; for a review of the larger field, cf. Belzen 1998, 2000). To a lesser extent this also applies to cultural psychology: there is certainly more interest in the field than there was, say, ten years ago. Some authors and journals associated with this renewed attention to cultural psychology are also devoting attention to religion; although usually not allied with the psychology of religion, they give examples from religious domains, and certainly no longer treat religion as taboo (cf. e.g., Gergen 1993, 1999; Gone et al. 1999; Much and Mahapatra 1995; Popp-Baier 1998; Sampson 1996). And perhaps even more important, a cultural psychological approach to the study of religion offers the opportunity to overcome some of the *a prioris* and moral biases that have dominated—and hindered—the psychology of religion for too long (especially the notion that religion is part of man's nature, and that it is therefore better, or more healthy or whatever, to be religious than non-religious; cf. Belzen 1999). When we understand religion as an element of culture, we need concepts and units of analysis that will enable us to investigate the nexus between a certain culture (or cultural context) and the person, such as activity, action, habitus, and also narrative or 'story'. The theorizing about the 'dialogical self' as initiated by Hermans and Kempen may count as such a case. Their work—which has been well received by the international cultural psychology 'movement' (Hermans 1999a, b; Valsiner 2001)—presents an example of the third type of cultural psychology just defined above, and is promising for a cultural psychological analysis of religion. It is particularly interesting to take a closer look at this body of theory since it simultaneously provides an opportunity for an analysis of the aforementioned second type: the development of the concept of the dialogical self is inextricably bound up with the history of psychology at the Catholic University of Nijmegen (the Netherlands). The dialogical self may be regarded as a belated result of a much older Dutch initiative to integrate cultural psychology and the psychology of religion, one that led to the establishment of a department for the psychology of culture and religion at Nijmegen in 1956 (although its roots reach back to the founding years of psychology in general in the Netherlands). In addition, it belatedly catches up with a stand that has been fundamental to all psychologies of religion for a long time: psychological research on religion must be performed from a secular perspective (cf. Belzen 2001). To corroborate these claims, it is necessary to draw substantially on historical information as well as on information about recent developments. I shall therefore present a mixture of historical and systematic argumentation.[1]

The Dialogical Self

One of the attractive aspects of the concept of the dialogical self as developed by Hermans and Kempen (1993) is that it is both firmly rooted in classical European traditions in psychology and it is compatible with contemporary discussions within international, nowadays USA-dominated, psychology. The concept of the dialogical self is a result of an ongoing reception of and conversation with authors as diverse as Heidegger and Merleau-Ponty as representatives of phenomenological thought, James and Mead as representatives of American pragmatism, and Sarbin and the Gergens as representatives of such contemporary movements as social constructionism and narrative psychology. The compatibility with developments presently taking place in philosophy, literary theory, and in various segments of interpretative psychologies is evident, as is made clear in *The Dialogical Self* and numerous other publications by Hermans and Kempen (Hermans and Kempen 1993, 1998; Hermans, Rijks and Kempen 1993), as well as in publications by other authors (McAdams 1999; Fogel 1993). In their effort to conceive of the

---

1   A personal note: Harry Kempen died suddenly on March 26, 2000. He was my—and every Dutch cultural psychologist's—teacher; more important, he was my colleague for many years. At the department for cultural psychology, our offices were next to one another, and we became good friends: for years, we had several conversations each day, during which we shared all sorts of issues, including matters of personal relevance. The present paper draws substantially on these conversations (our 'thousand hours', as I used to call them).

human person as a multiplex and changing, context-dependent, embodied self, Hermans and Kempen have clearly contributed to a cultural psychology as it is presently developing at various places and with different branches, but also because of its long tradition at Nijmegen, where both authors studied and worked for some forty years. The diversity of influences and sources manifest in their work has always been a feature—both a strength and a burden—of the Nijmegen department of cultural psychology. But first, let us consider the concept itself very briefly.

Hermans and Kempen proposed an idea of the self as a multiplicity of relatively autonomous *I* positions in an imaginal landscape. Drawing on Sarbin's (1986) proposal for a narrative psychology, assuming that in the self-narrative a single author tells a story about himself as actor, Hermans and Kempen conceived of the self as polyphonic: one and the same individual lives, or can live, in a multiplicity of worlds, with each world having its own author telling a story relatively independent of the authors of the other worlds. At times the various authors may even enter into a dialogue with one another. Moreover, the self, conceptualized as analogous with a polyphonic novel, also has the capacity to integrate the notions of imaginative narratives and dialogues. In their idea of the self, Hermans and Kempen no longer stipulated—in contrast to James and Mead—an overarching *I*, which would organize the several constituents of the *me*. Instead, the spatial character of the self leads to the supposition of a decentralized multiplicity of *I* positions that function as relatively independent authors, telling their stories about their respective *me's* as actors (Hermans and Kempen 1993). In their initial publication on the dialogical self, the authors pointed out three ways in which their conception differed from much of the received view in the West. In contrast to a conception of the self as individualistic, the *I* moves, in an imaginal space, from one position to another, from which different or even contrasting views of the world are possible. Second, the dialogical self is 'social', which does not mean that a self-contained individual enters into social interactions with other outside people, but that other people occupy positions in the multi-voiced self. The other person is a position the *I* can occupy and that creates an alternative perspective on the world (including the self). Finally, the conception of the dialogical self opposes the ideal of the self as a centralized equilibrium structure. Hermans and Kempen do not stipulate the self as the center of control: the different *I* positions in the self represent different anchor points, which—depending on the nature of the interaction—may organize the other *I* positions at a given point in time (Hermans, Kempen and van Loon 1992).

Having sketched the dialogical self, I will try to show the importance of the concept within contemporary cultural psychology, and especially its importance to a culturally sensitive psychology of religion. A brief historical exploration of the concept's intellectual context will lead me to the conclusion that the dialogical self is both a late realization of and a final breakthrough within a program for cultural psychology and the psychology of religion already called for well before World War II. I will start by first looking for an answer to the question of where the interest at Nijmegen in a culturally sensitive psychology, leading to the establishment of a rather unique chair in (and, later, department of) cultural psychology in 1956, found its inspiration. In a second return to the past, I will try to explain the equally uncommon Nijmegen desire to combine cultural psychology with the psychology of religion. In the next part of the paper, I will contextualize the developments a little more, and draw on the previous information in order to support my conclusion just stated.

The Origin of the Idea of Cultural Psychology

The idea of establishing a professorial chair in cultural psychology came from F.J.Th. Rutten (1899-1980), the man who built up the psychology department at Nijmegen. We need to take at least three factors into consideration if we want to understand his motivation, i.e., 1. his professional training; 2. his personal context, personality, and style; and 3. his vision of psychology.

Professional Training

Rutten had initially been appointed (in 1931) to teach psychology in the context of educational sciences, with the aim of training Roman Catholic teachers. It was a position in which he succeeded his teacher in psychology, F.J.M.A. Roels (1887-1962), whose assistant he had been for a number of years. In those days, empirical psychology was still a rare subject at Dutch universities. Theoretical, or philosophical, psychology had been taught for many decades by professors of philosophy, but the introduction and establishment of psychology as a separate, empirically working discipline was a late one, especially in comparison with neighboring countries. In fact, Roels seems to have been the first person to be appointed as a full-time professor of psychology at a Dutch university, i.e., at Utrecht University in 1918.[2]

---

2   To be historically correct and to use the proper terminology: Roels started out as an assistant to C. Winkler (1855-1941), Professor of Psychiatry and Neurology at Utrecht University. In 1916 he became a private teacher

At the Roman Catholic University in Nijmegen (est. 1923), the priest J. Hoogveld (1878-1942) was responsible for pedagogics. He wanted to follow the example of the Catholic University in Leuven (Belgium), where psychology had been given a place on the pedagogics curriculum. He had therefore recruited Roels—who had studied philosophy and psychology at Leuven with Michotte (1881-1965), a student of Wundt and Külpe—to become a part-time professor at Nijmegen University. Roels had a close colleague and friend in A.A. Grünbaum (1885-1932), who— born in Russia, but working in Germany—fled to the Netherlands at the onset of World War I and who was appointed honorary professor for developmental psychology at Utrecht University in 1928. He was one of the people who introduced the phenomenological movement to the Netherlands. In his work, one finds all kinds of anti-elementaristic themes as they were elaborated in Germany at the time: 'intentionality' (Brentano), 'totality' (Gestalt psychology), 'existence' (Husserl), and 'understanding' of life out of life itself (Dilthey). Grünbaum developed an 'organological' view of consciousness, i.e., the view that consciousness should be considered as a unity, and that unity is the result of the human being's commitment to a concrete situation requiring action. Within the, in those days, prevalent scientifically oriented psychology, the consciousness of, for example, a blacksmith working on a piece of hot iron would be described as an order of sensations, acts of attentions, and impulses of the will. But according to Grünbaum, such a description is artificial, as it contradicts the experience of the blacksmith. Precisely because he is involved in making something, "the whole complex of sensations, feelings and impulses is carried by the experience of the situation as a whole, in which there is no separation between an 'I' that is reacting, and an environment that is influencing the 'I'" since this appears to be the end of the quoted material (Grünbaum 1928: 13). The blacksmith does not see separate sensations, which are to be followed by impulses of the will, but a horseshoe that does not yet have the shape he wants it to have.

Roels was strongly influenced by the views propagated by Grünbaum. He too stressed that the person is a unity. The life-unlike character of experimental psychology was a result of its preoccupation—in line with Cartesian dualism—with consciousness. Roels agreed with William Stern (1917) that the basic principle of reality is not the fact that there are psychic and physical phenomena, but that there are concrete persons:

---

at the Faculty of Humanities and Philosophy. He was appointed 'lecturer' at Utrecht in 1918 and 'professor' in 1922. In 1980, the lectureships at Dutch universities were changed into professorates; neither function nor title exists anymore.

"The immediate experience teaches that the human being is a 'unitas multiplex': very divers elements unite in him" (Roels 1918: 25). Consciousness should not be regarded as isolated from activity, nor from the 'outside' world. Therefore, Roels considered Watson's (1913) definition of psychology as the study of behavior as equally one-sided, for Watson remained within Cartesian dualism, only this time focusing on the body. In Roels's view, the only adequate definition of psychology could be the study of the human being as a psychophysical unity.

Roels was far more than just a theoretician, however: he had a very practical orientation, and wanted to apply psychology in the search for solutions to all kinds of daily problems. In his opinion, applied psychology was as "necessary as bread" (1919: 13). But in a notable text from 1928, he had to conclude that the psychology of his days hardly had anything to offer when it came to answering practical questions. Applied psychology, or 'psychotechnics' in his terminology, was impossible without cultural psychology, he stated. Psychotechnics registers only the elements out of which psychical phenomena are constructed (Roels 1928: 82). Gestalt psychology had shown, according to Roels, that the whole cannot be constructed by simple addition of its elements. Consequently, he saw it as cultural psychology's task to regard phenomena as "constituting moments of a meaningful whole" (1928: 88). This much-needed, firm, cultural psychological basis was almost entirely lacking, not only with regard to pedagogical psychology, but also with regard to the psychology of worldviews, social psychology, and economic psychology.

Personal Background

Rutten acquired this interest in cultural psychology from his teacher and promoter, Roels. He seems to have been clearly fostered by Roels, who requested that Rutten be appointed to the Catholic University; they published together, and almost immediately after the defense of Rutten's dissertation, Roels took his leave from Nijmegen, thereby creating the opportunity to appoint Rutten as his successor. Rutten's study, 'The transition of the agrarian popular type into the industrial popular one' (1947), testifies to his continuing interest in cultural psychological questions. According to Harry Kempen, who—like Hubert Hermans—had been a student of Rutten, this study also must have had a personal-autobiographical background. Rutten came from the very rural, traditional Limburg (in the south of the Netherlands), which in those days was a rather undeveloped area. For his academic training, he moved to Utrecht (a major university city in the middle of the country), and then to the French-speaking university in Leuven (Belgium). The, in those days, substantial differences between these settings may have brought the importance of the relationship between culture and behavior to his attention. Like Roels, Rutten was interested in developing psychologies of the different subcultures to be found in the Netherlands. In order to practically apply psychology, exploration of the different worlds of subjects had to be undertaken. These were the worlds of the dock worker, peasant, and academic, and also of the different milieus within religiously divers segments of society. When, in later years, he traveled to the USA, he was struck by the very different style of approach taken by his colleagues there (Rutten 1954). He seems to have realized that the differences between European and American psychology were not simply the consequence of different scientific considerations, but that the different settings gave rise to different psychologies.

Vision of Psychology

Rutten's sensitivity to different contexts and cultures/subcultures also made him realize the—to use a Heideggerian phrase—*seinsgebunden* character of knowledge, as well as of scientific knowledge. Consequently, he strove for an open-minded psychology, one that would be all-round, and not restricted to one or only a few approaches. According to people who knew Rutten intimately, this striving must have been deeply characteristic. Fundamentally, he questioned several trends he perceived in modern Western culture: the rationalism that had invaded all segments of life, the increasing individualism, and the decline of mythical sensitivity. In his view, psychology should help to balance these trends. He wholeheartedly subscribed to the aims the American Psychological Association had formulated for the discipline, but realized that the application of psychology 'as a means of promoting human welfare' required at least a supplement to developments in contemporary psychology. The psychology he encountered in the USA struck him as being very 'narrow' (Rutten 1954). Rutten, contrarily, was interested in the development of a kind of *psychologia universalis*, in transcending locally valid knowledge. Cultural psychology should serve this interest, and from the beginning of the 1950s onward he started—despite resistance from various sides—to lobby for a professorial chair in the subject. On behalf of future generations of students, he intended to keep psychology in 'his' institute broad and diverse. When in the 1960s psychology in the Netherlands turned almost completely toward USA-inspired operationalization and the employment of statistics, Rutten must have been just as pleased with his assistants and successors who went to Tolmin and Coombs in the USA as he was with those who traveled to India and Thailand to explore

137

the Hindu and the Buddhist lifestyle and spirituality (cf. Fortmann 1968).[3]

The Combination of Cultural Psychology and the Psychology of Religion[4]

The professor holding the chair Rutten had created in cultural psychology had to pay, as it was initially formulated, 'special attention to the psychology of religion'. The question is whether Roels and Rutten had already conceived of the psychology of religion as necessarily conducted from the perspective of cultural psychology, or whether the combination had something to do with the first (and last) professor to hold this chair. Let us consider briefly the first possibility. In general, psychology of religion received virtually no attention from Dutch Roman Catholics before World War II, and when it did, the attention was deeply distrustful (cf. Belzen 2001). The first to speak positively about the subject, even in the sense of defending the subject, and calling for a Catholic institute for the subdiscipline, was—again—Roels. Psychology of religion had been led astray, in his opinion, by "wrong friends, Protestant theology and positivistic philosophy" (Roels 1919/20: 343), and Roman Catholics should not leave the subject to them. Yet, at the time (1919), he expected from a psychology of religion mainly 'contributions to apologetics': Catholics would be able, for example, to point out how gratifying the liturgy is to the soul, or how 'insane' it is to compare ritual with obsessive neurosis. But Roels did not get his way. It was years before the psychology of religion was again spoken of in Dutch Roman Catholic circles.[5]

---

3   In 1975, when operationalism and testing of hypotheses had also become dominant at his former institute, Rutten published a short article in which he recommended that psychologists read 'great literature' (philosophers, poets, novelists). He wrote that as psychologists, we "[...] are captured in a certain historical way of thinking. The professional language we have been taught, and the methods and techniques that we have learned to handle, orient the way in which we perceive behavior. There is real danger that the expertise we have gained will hinder new developments. We are constantly forced to struggle to get hold of and to overcome the doctrinary conformism required by any training" (Rutten 1975: 391).
4   For a broader account of the institutional development of the psychology of religion in the Netherlands: cf. Belzen (in press).
5   In his text on cultural psychology, some ten years later, Roels devotes only a small remark to religion: "A beginning has hardly been made with a psychology of worldviews, that is, a psychology that explores the psychic-spiritual structures or inner attitudes, from which different types of worldviews stem" (1928: 88). This sounds rather casual, unlike his earlier plea for the subdiscipline. But one cannot infer from this quotation that he had abandoned the apologetic aims he pursued with the psychology of

In 1937 Rutten gave a lecture at a meeting of the Roman Catholic Society for Thomistic Philosophy on 'the domain of psychology of religion'. In this methodological exposé, Rutten clearly distinguishes a religious, or theological, perspective from a psychological one. According to Rutten, both perspectives are legitimate, theology searching for the religious value and truth of the phenomena, and psychology investigating their psychical aspects and conditions. Scientific research into religious phenomena can never call upon supernatural factors to explain them; the work of 'grace' cannot be made visible in a psychological investigation, but cannot be denied either. As far as scientific psychology is concerned, it has to work with the conceptual and methodical instruments of psychology in general. (Although Rutten, like Roels (1919/20), denies that psychological experiments—as conducted by the German psychologist of religion, K. Girgensohn (1921), who applied *külpean* techniques in his research—could be employed.) Methodologically, psychology is neutral, according to Rutten, as it also is when it investigates religion. On the other hand (and he calls this a 'perplexing fact'), psychology of religion can, in his opinion, only be performed by a psychologist who is religious himself, as it will be necessary to participate intentionally in the phenomena under research in order to understand their significance. In this thoughtful text, Rutten makes only a few remarks that could be interpreted as being inspired by a cultural psychological perspective: "To the extent that certain forms of behavior as expressions of persons, each with their own disposition and development, coincide with certain circumstances of time and place, they are subject to empirical-psychological laws" (Rutten 1937: 10). By 'circumstances of time and place' Rutten meant not only factors that could be experimentally manipulated. He also mentioned 'forms of religion handed down' and the 'peculiarities of an epoch'. These phrases *could* be understood as a reference to a cultural and historical context, although the text as such is certainly not conceived from a cultural psychological perspective. Unlike Roels's text, Rutten's is not a plea for an apologetic use of a psychology of religion, although he does clearly point out that such a psychology can be of great value for pastoral care (Rutten 1937: 33-34).

As should be clear, neither Roels nor Rutten were very outspoken about the desirability of a cultural psychological approach to the psychology of religion. It is doubtful, therefore, whether they were acquainted with Wundt's thesis that "religion is not a topic for individual

religion: the 1919 text was addressed to a Roman Catholic audience, and the passage from 1928 comes from a publication by the Psychological Laboratory at the religiously neutral State University of Utrecht. To what 'psychology of worldviews' Roels is referring here, remains unclear. Perhaps to Jaspers (1922)?

psychology, but for cultural psychology" (Wundt 1915: 513).[6] Therefore, the reason for Rutten to combine his older interests in both cultural psychology and psychology of religion may—and this is the second possibility—have been of a more trivial nature. Several years after his lecture on psychology of religion, he supervised a doctoral dissertation on prayer, a project by Han Fortmann (1912-1970), a Roman Catholic priest who had studied classical languages and psychology. After he obtained his doctoral degree in 1945, Fortmann became involved in Roman Catholic youth work, also on a national-organizational level, and he was one of the editors of *Dux*, a periodical primarily oriented toward youth work, but which was read by a much broader audience. Fortmann published over a hundred articles in *Dux*, including such subjects as education in citizenship, the development of faith, the will, fantasy, conscience, and sexuality.

Over the years, he maintained contact with Rutten (as can be inferred from their correspondence, which is now in the archives of the psychology department at Nijmegen). At the beginning of the 1950s, Rutten became Minister of State for Education and the Sciences. In the mid-1950s, Fortmann joined a group of modern-minded Roman Catholics who wanted to change Catholic morals and customs with respect to sexuality. One of the group's members was the internationally renowned phenomenologist F.J.J. Buytendijk (1887-1974), who became president of the Catholic Central Society of Mental Health. In a recent historiography (Westhoff 1996), prominent members of this society are referred to as 'liberators'. They were deeply concerned with the mental health of Catholics, and perceived many spiritual problems as being caused by, or at least related to, mental health problems. At the time, the Roman Catholic leadership was suspicious of psychiatry, psychotherapy, and mental health care, and in later years the legendary 'pastoral commission' had to work in secret, as it was perceived as being almost subversive (Suèr 1969). When in the mid-1950s Rutten returned to his professorial work at Nijmegen, his former student Fortmann must have seemed the ideal person to perform tasks that Rutten meanwhile perceived as

---

6   It is possible, of course, that they had read this work, or that Roels had become aware of this part of Wundt's theorizing via his teacher, Michotte, in Leuven. Michotte was working at the Leipzig laboratory in 1906, precisely at the time when Wundt was working on his cultural psychology, which he considered a natural complement to his earlier, experimental work in psychology. According to Wundt, psychology would have to be plural. Psychology can only turn to experiment as an auxiliary method if it seeks to examine the 'elementary psychic processes'; but if it seeks to study the higher psychic processes it has to consult other sciences for orientation (Wundt 1900-1909). Wundt's own suggestion was that psychologists should consult history.

highly necessary: a. Fortmann had broad interests and would contribute to Rutten's ideal of keeping psychology open-minded, and interactive with such related knowledge fields as anthropology and history; b. He was able to contribute to the promotion of human welfare by taking a critical stance toward developments in society at large from a psychological perspective; and c. As a Roman Catholic priest who had written a dissertation on a religious topic, he would be able to develop a psychology of religion. The task Rutten assigned to Fortmann was a broad, and in some ways hybrid, one: 'cultural psychology with special attention to the psychology of religion', which very soon proved to be too large for the part-time chair Fortmann was offered in 1956: just three years later, the professorship was changed into a full-time position for 'general and comparative psychology of culture and religion'. It is irrelevant to follow the history of the professorship and its department here; for the purpose of our analysis, I only need to focus on the kind of cultural psychology Fortmann tried to develop.

Cultural Psychology: Program and Preliminary Achievements

To anticipate the end of the story: Fortmann was never able to fully meet the assigned task as he interpreted it, perhaps partly because he passed away at a relatively young age (he was only 57 when he died in 1970). The two domains—cultural psychology and the psychology of religion— only gradually merged in his work, and never became truly synthesized. This is most evident from his *Introduction to Cultural Psychology* (1971), in which he pays almost no attention to the psychology of religion. And the other way round, in his work on the psychology of religion, on which he published more than he did on cultural psychology, there is not much written from a cultural perspective. Although the subtitle of his main work, *Als ziende de onzienlijke* (1964-1968), is 'A cultural-psychological study on religious perception and so-called religious projection', it is more a programmatic phrase than the realization of a project. In this four-volume work, Fortmann takes a stand in the debate on religious projection as it was going on in the Netherlands at the turn of the 1960s. He provides summaries of the positions taken by important contributors to the debate (and also of the forerunners, such as Marx, Freud, and others), and from a phenomenologically informed viewpoint he argues that there exists no 'projection' in the sense of projecting something 'inner' onto something 'outer'. To give a brief characterization: *Als ziende de onzienlijke* is an in-depth treatment of its subject, yet

141

primarily on a theoretical level, taking into consideration notions from several disciplines (including theology); however, it seldom deals explicitly with culture and devotes only limited attention to such cultural anthropologists as Lévy-Bruhl and Lévi-Strauss; moreover, part IIIB (Volume 4) is entirely devoted to the relationship between mental health and religion, yet essentially from a non-cultural-psychological perspective. (Thus, in that sense, the volume is indeed in line with Rutten's wish for a psychological critique of contemporary culture, but not with Fortmann's own developing insight into the predominant importance of culture for the constitution and regulation of human experience and action).

In his major works on cultural psychology and the psychology of religion, one sees Fortmann still at work, preparing his project of integrating both fields, and collecting material for a future program. His broad orientation prevented him from adopting either a single perspective or only a few perspectives; he tried to become acquainted from several angles with many approaches and with literature that might prove useful for a future cultural psychology of religion. When he started out, there was not too much he could use to orient himself: the older psychology of religion as developed in the USA hardly fit into his cultural psychological interests; the German psychology of religion had become almost extinct after World War II, and the experimental methodology of its most important pre-War representative, Girgensohn, was not considered applicable; and about the psychoanalytic psychology of religion Fortmann was, and remained, somewhat suspicious. His discontent with the existing psychology of religion may have encouraged him to adopt a new approach, a cultural psychological one. But then again, on what types of cultural psychology could he have relied in those days? According to Harry Kempen, who became Fortmann's first assistant in the field of cultural psychology (and *not* that of the psychology of religion), it was mainly to nonpsychological theory Fortmann had to turn. From psychoanalysis there was only the society-oriented work of the older Freud, Jung, and the Frankfurt School. Then, from cultural anthropology there was the 'culture and personality' school, with work from such authors as Benedict, Hallowell, Kardiner, the Kluckhohns, Linton, Margaret Mead, and the Whitings. Finally, the older Durkheim was a sociological source of inspiration. Whereas the early Durkheim conceived of society as a 'thing' that exists exterior to the individual (and that therefore should not be studied from a psychological perspective), the later Durkheim abandoned this sociologism and realized that society exists only in and through individuals. The mediating concept between actor and society became 'collective representations', a forerunner of the contemporary concept of 'social representations' (Moscovici 1998). In his later years, as is clear from his posthumously published *Introduction to Cultural Psychology* (1971), Fortmann also proved himself to be an early Dutch recipient of the—in those days, primarily French—structuralist movement in psychoanalysis (Lacan) and literary theory (Barthes).

A mild critical remark on Fortmann's work is that much of his theory-oriented writing bears the character of summaries of important publications; it is as though he were collecting the stones to build a structure, for which he may have had some kind of architectural design. However, this design—his not-all-too-explicit view of a cultural psychology of religion—was not too well understood, and after his death, his department split up into three sections (cultural psychology, the psychology of religion, and pastoral psychology) that were not integrated, neither theoretically nor practically. Psychologists of religion in the department oriented themselves either on sociology and social psychology, or on clinical psychology. To a large extent, cultural psychologists continued to orient themselves on Fortmann's style: they read widely, were theoretically *pluriform*, but in order to get research going (and completed) they usually had to limit themselves to the perspective of some theoretical 'hero', or to the application of standard methods and techniques. The number of theoretical approaches drawn upon at the department of cultural psychology increased, however, by adding to Fortmann's reading the following:

- Social behaviorism and the sociology of behavior, notably 'social learning theory', an approach that perceives cultural processes from the perspective of behaviorist and neo-behaviorist learning and decision-making laws;
- Psychoanalysis as employed by leftist theorists, starting less from drive theory and the Id, and focusing instead on I and Superego processes (Althusser, Foucault);
- Symbolic interactionism, a branch of psychology inspired by George Herbert Mead and developed by sociologists;
- Cognitive psychology and cognitive anthropology, which reminds cognitive psychology—which is always in danger of conceiving of the subject as 'buried in thought'—of the existence of sociocultural systems, as reservoirs from which actors derive their information and 'input';
- Russian cultural-historical psychology, as developed by Vygotsky and Luria, and in later years by Bruner, Cole, Scribner, Wertsch, and others, and stating—in line with Wundt—that all higher processes of the mind are mediated by culture;
- Social constructionism, as seminally formulated by Berger and Luckmann and as nowadays eloquently defended and developed by Gergen, Sarbin, and others.

143

At the department, it was Harry Kempen especially who continued to explore contemporary psychology and other bodies of theory, in search of approaches that could contribute to a future synthesis of cultural psychology, a synthesis that was not likely to develop in the way theorizing took place at the department of cultural psychology. Instigated by Fortmann, and ideologically bound by the vacant chair in cultural psychology and the psychology of religion (a chair that was to be divided at the beginning of the 1980s, as no one could be found who was acceptable to both cultural psychologists and psychologists of religion), the several sections of the department remained loosely connected. The input from a related outsider was needed to achieve a theoretical breakthrough. This person was Hubert Hermans, an old friend and colleague of Harry Kempen, and also a student of both Rutten and Fortmann, but who had been granted a professorship in personality psychology in another department. Hermans's strategy was different from Kempen's: He published easily and widely; influenced by the same phenomenological orientation (among others, Merleau-Ponty), inherited from Buytendijk and Fortmann, he developed an original approach based on his successful work on motivational psychology (Hermans 1967, 1971; cf. also Hermans 1970). He conceived of the self as motivated by a number of coherent, but diverse, values, an idea he worked out empirically by constructing an elegant research technique: the Self-Confrontation Method (Hermans, 1974, 1981; Hermans and Hermans-Jansen 1995). The friendship and ongoing dialogue between Hermans and Kempen led to the development of the idea of the dialogical self, which is clearly compatible with and a contribution to cultural psychology: whatever the values around which a self may be organized, they are derived from some cultural context, and are developed in interaction with other persons from that context. Hermans and Kempen conceive of the self as evoked by culture, as structured by elements from culture, and as multiplex and changing because of a personal history within a culture at a certain sociohistorical stage. Elegantly adopting several theories from cultural psychology, and combining these with phenomenologically inspired self-psychology as initiated by William James (1890) and with Bakthinian ideas (Bakthin 1929/1973), they present the self as a multiplicity of voices, as a decentralized multiplicity of *I* positions, telling stories about their respective *me's*.

As my aim is not to present their theory at length here, but merely to provide some systematic reflections on it, let me proceed to point out ways in which Hermans' and Kempen's thinking is in line with, and is part of the line started by Rutten and Fortmann, and, even more importantly, in which way it is a further development of this line. I will deal with these two aspects under the headers 'Deconfessionalizing of the psychology of religion' and 'Toward a cultural psychology of religion'. In this account, we will be confronted with another clear example of the cultural embeddedness of science/psychological science, traditionally a topic high on the agenda of cultural psychology's research (cf. Hume 1997; Danziger 1990, 1997; Knorr Cetina 1999; Moscovici 1988; Valsiner and Van de Veer 2000).

Conclusions

Deconfessionalizing of the Psychology of Religion

The Roman Catholic University in Nijmegen was founded with the explicit aim of providing an academic training that would not be dominated by positivistic thinking and would not contradict Roman Catholic teaching. The reasoning was that as the natural sciences, and the philosophy of life many people (not only academics) derived from it, had—from Galileo to Darwin—seemed to be a series of attacks on the Catholic philosophy of life, students had to be protected. Psychology—which in those days was becoming experimental and scientific, orienting itself toward the natural sciences and emancipating itself from philosophy—was regarded with deep suspicion. When Rutten was appointed professor of empirical psychology, the bishop of Den Bosch (Mgr. Diepen), who was responsible for the University, summoned Rutten and demanded that he explain how he would proceed. Rutten could not really reassure the bishop, who told him to beware, as he was still young and inexperienced, and forbade him to discuss such topics as free will in his lectures. Mgr. Diepen promised Rutten to pray for the outcome of so risky an enterprise as lectures on empirical psychology (Abma 1983: 36). However, as we have seen, Rutten, while being a devout Catholic, did not develop his psychology on the basis of Roman Catholic philosophy, but empirically; he tried to create a kind of 'free space' for psychology, even if it turned to religious phenomena: psychology would not be able to make judgments regarding the value or truth of religious phenomena, but as far as they were human phenomena, they could be investigated by psychology. The theological factor of grace could not be denied by psychology, as that factor did not belong to its perspective; yet to safeguard religious phenomena from hostile psychological analysis, Rutten declared it necessary that a psychologist of religion be a religious person. Therefore, and although psychology in general would be 'methodically without confes-

145

sion', the psychology of religion had to remain reserved for religious, Roman Catholic psychologists only. In that way, the results of the psychology of religion would also be helpful for such religious activities as pastoral work and spiritual direction. Roels had earlier defended a similar position, but in comparison with Roels, Rutten took a more liberal stance: For him, the psychology of religion was no longer primarily an apologetic instrument in defense of Roman Catholicism, but only a potential source of general insight, useful to the ministry.

Fortmann made a further distinction: he separated the psychology of religion from pastoral psychology, recruiting different staff members for these divergent fields. With Fortmann, psychology of religion became a kind of neutral research into religiosity, the personal-human counterpart of religion. Fortmann kept in line with Rutten, however, in his use of psychology for criticizing defective manifestations of Catholic religiosity (and not of Catholic religion in general) and for elevating Catholic spirituality. Also, being a priest and working at a Roman Catholic university before the great secularization of the Netherlands, the topics he dealt with were Catholic ones and he was clearly recognizable as a religious Roman Catholic author. The psychology of religion was more or less a Catholic enterprise within secular psychology at Nijmegen.[7] In the post-Fortmann period, this remained the character of the psychology of religion at Nijmegen for a long time (the department was even known as the 'Catholic corner' of the building), not least because most staff members were, or had been, clergy. Increasingly, however, it was presented as an interest in religion in general. In many publications from the psychologists of religion at Nijmegen, a mildly apologetic undertone remained audible: during the days of disinterest in, or even contempt for, religion as a topic for psychological research, they strove to keep religion as a topic on psychology's agenda, using clinical-psychological argumentation. Reasoning was based on the *a priori* that religion is an inherent part of, and therefore benevolent to, human nature. Although staff members no longer tried to use psychology to elevate Catholic customs and spirituality (since the 1970s, these had no longer been dominant, and sometimes were no longer visible, in society at large), they did use the supposedly neutral terminology of psychology to show how religion can be positively related to mental health, and what impact religious and other

---

7   Of course, Roman Catholic influences on the psychology at Nijmegen can also be detected in the strong interest in phenomenological psychology, a psychology that tried not to be natural-scientific in nature, and therefore according to many Catholic psychologists, would be more apt for investigating the psyche. Relations between Catholicism and phenomenology can be clearly pointed out in the work of such well-known Nijmegen professors as Strasser and Buytendijk.

values may have in psychotherapy. They also tried to detect favorable conditions for faith development, and showed that new religious movements need not be a hazard to mental health. Funding for their research mainly came from Catholic sources. The general attitude was that, admittedly, religion can be a monster, but that—appropriately understood and practiced—it enhances human existence. In other words, in line with developments in society at large, there had been a steady deconfessionalization at the Nijmegen department of the psychology of religion since the days of Roels: Rutten had freed empirical psychology methodologically from Catholic patronizing and softened its apologetic aims; Fortmann strove for a psychology of religion that would be a neutral enterprise of research, although he remained focused on Roman Catholic topics; after Fortmann, non-Catholic topics were also investigated, and although the benevolent inclination toward religion was still dominant, efforts were made to participate in ordinary, non-religiously bound, psychological research, also to be financed by non-religious sources and to be published in non-religious media.

It is only with the concept of the dialogical self, however, that an original perspective has developed that is not religiously motivated or legitimated, that can be applied within the research on religious and nonreligious topics alike, and that, most importantly, no longer presupposes any superiority to being personally religious. The dialogical self acknowledges that human beings live in multiple social worlds, inhabited by both 'actual' and 'imaginary' others, persons known from both the past and from the multiple stories we live by. If a person is religious, or at least acquainted with some kind of religion, he or she may entertain relationships with gods, spirits, saints, and/or religious authorities, and may conduct a dialogue with them, and they may all be part of a narrative construction of the world (Hermans and Kempen 1993; Hermans and Hermans, in press). It is important, however, to realize that the concept of the dialogical self does not presuppose that relationships with religious 'others' should in any way be part of the self; such a presupposition would be a theological *a priori*, and theological reasoning or evaluation is alien to the dialogical self as a psychological concept.

Toward a Cultural Psychology of Religion

As will be understood by now, the dialogical self is the first original Nijmegen contribution to cultural psychological reasoning. Based on theories and concepts that were once in vogue in Nijmegen psychology, it formulates an original and elegant insight into the relationship between self and culture. Informed by a cultural psychological heritage, it opposes the idea of a unified, separate, and centralized self. It presents the self as being evoked and structured by a diversified cultural setting, and views the self as an ensemble of relationships with 'actual' as well as 'imagined' others from different realms: from history, from one's personal past, but also from a mythical past or some spiritual realm. A person may maintain relationships with persons actually met, but also with persons known from stories, television, or pictures or statues in a temple or other religious meeting place. Therefore, Hermans and Kempen represent the self as an embodied multiplicity of *I* positions in stories, made possible and available by cultural contexts. To the extent that a person is religious, or is familiar with religious discourse and practices, she or he will be acquainted with stories about gods, spirits, and saints; in other words, such a person will be familiar with religious signifiers, with whom she or he may or may not interact. Precisely to detect whether, why, and to what extent one or several relationships with religious signifiers constitute an essential part of one's narrative construction of the world, what their place is in the more general organization of the self, and why, when, and how such *I* positions will develop and where they will be moved to, are empirical questions that will be examined by a psychology of religion drawing on the theory of the dialogical self. Any psychology of religion employing the theory of the dialogical self will be a culturally sensitive psychology of religion, and therefore an example of the kind of psychology of religion for which Fortmann aimed.[8] Therefore, I conclude that this theory is a breakthrough in two related ways: 1. It is the first original Nijmegen contribution to cultural psychology, and 2. It is an integration of cultural psychology and the psychology of religion, which had been separated since Fortmann's death. The theory of the dialogical self is a worthy tribute to the heritage of Hermans and Kempen's old teachers Rutten and Fortmann—the initiators of cultural psychology in the Netherlands.

---

8   For a correct understanding, one should differentiate clearly between the employment of the theorizing about the dialogical self and the employment of the Self-Confrontation Method as developed by Hermans earlier. The use of the Self-Confrontation Method as such does not make an investigation a psychological one (it may be used in theological research too, cf. Putnam 1998), and is not necessarily associated with a cultural psychological perspective. Research from the perspective of the dialogical self, however, will always also be an exploration of a subject's personal culture.

References

Abma, R. (1983). 'Methodisch zonder confessie.' Uit de geschiedenis van de Nijmeegse psychologie. Nijmegen: Katholieke Universiteit Nijmegen, Psychologisch Laboratorium.

Bakthin, M. (1929/1973). Problems of Dostoevsky's poetics. 2nd ed. Ann Arbor, MI: Ardis. (Original Russian work published 1929).

Belzen, J.A. (1998). Verschuivende aandacht voor religie binnen de psychologie. Bespreking en signalement van recente ontwikkelingen in de godsdienstpsychologie. In: Psyche en Geloof, 9, 20-34.

Belzen, J.A. (1999). The Cultural-Psychological Approach to Religion: Contemporary Debates on the Object of the Discipline. In: Theory and Psychology, 9, 229-256.

Belzen, J.A. (2000). Ontwikkelingen in de godsdienstpsychologie. Noties aan de hand van enkele recente publicaties. In: Psyche en Geloof, 11, 21-46.

Belzen, J.A. (2001). The Introduction of Psychology of Religion to the Netherlands: Ambivalent Reception, Epistemological Concerns, and Persistent Patterns. In: Journal for the History of the Behavioral Sciences, 37, 45-62.

Belzen, J.A. (2002). Die Gleichzeitigkeit des Ungleichen—Anmerkungen zur Entwicklung der Religionspsychologie im niederländischen Sprachraum. In: Chr. Henning/E. Nestler (Eds.). Konversion —zur Aktualität eines Jahrhundertthemas (pp. 117-144). Frankfurt: Lang.

Danziger, K. (1990). Constructing the Subject: Historical Origins of Psychological Research. Cambridge: Cambridge University Press.

Danziger, K. (1997). Naming the Subject. How Psychology found its Language. London: Sage.

Fogel, A. (1993). Developing through Relationships. New York: Harvester Wheatsheaf.

Fortmann, H.M.M. (1946). Aandachtig bidden. Een psychologische studie over de eigenschappen, de mogelijkheden en de grenzen der gebedsconcentratie. Nijmegen-Utrecht: Dekker & Van de Vegt.

Fortmann, H.M.M. (1968). Hindoes en boeddhisten. Dagboekaantekeningen en reisbrieven. Baarn: Ambo.

Fortmann, H.M.M. (1964-68). Als ziende de Onzienlijke: een cultuurpsychologische studie over de religieuze waarneming en de zogenaamde religieuze projectie. Hilversum: Brand (4 delen).

Fortmann, H.M.M. (1971). Inleiding tot de cultuurpsychologie. Baarn: Ambo.

Gergen, K.J. (1993). Belief as Relational Resource. In: The International Journal for the Psychology of Religion, Vol.3, 4, 231-235.

Gergen, K.J. (1999). Invitation to Social Construction. London: Sage.

Girgensohn, K. (1921). Der seelische Aufbau des religiösen Erlebens. Eine religionspsychologische Untersuchung auf experimenteller Grundlage. Leipzig: Hirzel.

Gone, J.P./Miller, P.J./Rappaport, J. (1999). Conceptual Narrative as Normatively Oriented: The Suitability of Past Personal Narrative for the Study of Cultural Identity. In: Culture & Psychology, 5, 371-398.

Grünbaum, A.A. (1928). Het ik-bewustzijn en de psychische ontwikkeling. Utrecht: s.n.

Hermans, H.J.M. (1967). Motivatie en prestatie. Amsterdam: Swets & Zeitlinger.

Hermans, H.J.M. (1970). A Questionnaire Measure of Achievement Motivation. In: Journal of Applied Psychology, 54, 353-363.

Hermans, H.J.M. (1971). Prestatiemotief en faalangst in gezin en onderwijs; tevens handleiding bij de Prestatie Motivatie Test voor Kinderen (PMT-K). Amsterdam: Swets & Zeitlinger.

Hermans, H.J.M. (1974). Waardegebieden en hun ontwikkeling. Amsterdam: Swets & Zeitlinger.

Hermans, H.J.M. (1981). Persoonlijkheid en waardering; deel 1: organisatie en opbouw der waarderingen. Lisse: Swets en Zeitlinger.

Hermans, H.J.M. (1999a). Dialogical Thinking and Self-Innovation. In: Culture & Psychology, 5, 67-87.

Hermans, H.J.M. (1999b). The Innovative Potentials of Agreement and Disagreement in Dialogical History. In: Culture & Psychology, 5, 491-498.

Hermans, H.J.M./Hermans-Jansen E. (1995). Self-Narratives: The Construction of Meaning in Psychotherapy. New York: Guilford Press.

Hermans, H.J.M./Hermans-Jansen, E. (in press). Dialogical Processes and the Development of the Self.

Hermans, H.J.M./Kempen, H.J.G. (1993). The Dialogical Self: Meaning as Movement. San Diego, CA: Academic Press.

Hermans, H.J.M./Kempen, H.J.G. (1998). Moving Cultures: The Perilous Problem of Cultural Dichotomies in a Globalizing Society. In: American Psychologist, 53, 1111-1120.

Hermans, H.J.M./Kempen, H.J.G./van Loon, R.J.P. (1992). The Dialogical Self: Beyond Individualism and Rationalism. In: American Psychologist, 47, 23-33.

Hermans, H.J.M./Rijks, T.I./Kempen, H.J.G. (1993). Imaginal Dialogues of the Self: Theory and Method. In: Journal of Personality, Vol. 61, 2, 207-236.

Hume, H. (1997). Psychological Concepts, their Products and Consumers. In: Culture & Psychology, 3, 115-136.

James, W. (1890). The Principles of Psychology. London: MacMillan.

James, W. (1902). The Varieties of Religious Experience. A study in human nature. Hammondsworth: Penguin, 1982.

Jaspers, K. (1922). Psychologie der Weltanschauungen. Berlin: Springer.

Knorr-Cetina, K. (1999). Epistemic Cultures. How the Sciences make Knowledge. Cambridge, MA: Harvard University Press.

McAdams, D.P. (1999). Personal Narratives and the Life Story. In: L.A. Pervin/O. John (Eds.). Handbook of Personality: Theory and Research. 2nd ed. (pp. 478-500). New York: Guilford Press.

Moscovici, S. (1998). Social Consciousness and its History. In: Culture & Psychology, 4, 11-29.

Much, N.C./Mahapatra, M. (1995). Constructing Divinity. In: R. Harré/P. Stearns (Eds.). Discursive Psychology in Practice (pp. 55-86). London: Sage.

Popp-Baier, U. (1998). Das Heilige im Profanen: religiöse Orientierungen im Alltag; eine qualitative Studie zu religiösen Orientierungen von Frauen aus der charismatisch-evangelischen Bewegung. Amsterdam/Atlanta: Rodopi.

Putnam, W. (1998). Godsbeelden en levensverhaal. Een onderzoek met behulp van de Waarderingstheorie en de Zelfkonfrontatiemethode naar de betekenis van persoonlijke godsbeelden. Tilburg: Tilburg University Press.

Ragan, C.P., Malony, H.N./Beit-Hallahmi, B. (1980). Psychologists and Religion: Professional Factors and Personal Belief. In: Review of Religious Research, 21, 208-217.

Richards, G. (1996). Putting Psychology in its Place. An Introduction from a Critical Historical Perspective. New York/London: Routledge.

Richards, P.S./Bergin, A.E. (1997). A Spiritual Strategy for Counselling and Psychotherapy. Washington: American Psychological Association.

Richards, P.S./Bergin, A.E. (2000). Handbook of Psychotherapy and Religious Diversity. Washington: American Psychological Association.

Roels, F.J.M.A. (1918). De toekomst der psychologie. Den Bosch: Teulings.

Roels, F.J.M.A. (1919-20). Godsdienstpsychologie en apologetiek. In: De Beiaard, Vol.4, 2, 337-359.

Roels, F.J.M.A. (1928). Cultuurpsychologie en psychotechniek. In: Mededeelingen van het psychologisch laboratorium R.U. Utrecht, 77-95.

Rutten, F.J.Th. (1937). Het domein der godsdienstpsychologie. Nijmegen: Centrale Drukkerij.

Rutten, F.J.Th. (1947). De overgang van het agrarische volkstype in het industriële. Amsterdam: Koninklijke Nederlandse Academie van Wetenschappen.

Rutten, F.J. Th. (1954). Verschil tussen de Amerikaanse en Europese benadering der psychologische problemen. In: De Tijd, June 17, 3.

Rutten, F.J.Th. (1975). Een lijstje titels uit de wereldliteratuur. In: Gedrag, 6, 391-392.

Sampson, E.E. (1996). Establishing Embodiment in Psychology. In: Theory and Psychology, 6, 601-620.

Sarbin, T.R. (Ed.) (1986). Narrative Psychology: the Storied Nature of Human Conduct. New York: Praeger.

Shafranske, E.P. (Ed.) (1996). Religion and the Clinical Practice of Psychology. Washington: American Psychological Association.

Stern, W. (1917). Die menschliche Persönlichkeit. Leipzig: Barth.

Suèr, H. (1969). Niet te geloven. De geschiedenis van een pastorale commissie. Bussum: Paul Brand.

Valsiner, J. (2001). The First Six Years: Culture's Adventure in Psychology. In: Culture & Psychology, 7, 5-48.

Valsiner, J./van der Veer, R. (2000). The Social Mind. New York: Cambridge University Press.

Watson, J.B. (1913). Psychology as the Behaviorist Views it. In: Psychological Review, 20, 158-177.

Westhoff, H. (1996). Geestelijke bevrijders. Nederlandse katholieken en hun beweging voor geestelijke volksgezondheid in de twintigste eeuw. Nijmegen: Valkhof.

Wulff, D.M. (1997). Psychology of Religion: Classic and Contemporary. 2nd ed. New York: Wiley.

Wundt, W. (1915). Völkerpsychologie: eine Untersuchung der Entwicklungsgesetze von Sprache, Mythos und Sitte, Vol. 6. Leipzig: Kröner.

Universals and the Psychology of Music: An Exemplar for Cultural Studies

ROM HARRÉ

Introduction

The root question that needs to be resolved before any serious cross-cultural work can be undertaken is to decide how to distinguish what is universal from what is likely to be local. Setting aside the implausible idea that there is a universal human culture, the identification of the local aspects of a human practice is surely a first step to locating the cultural component in that practice. Cultural variability is to be set against universal stability, that is, against what is invariant through cultural transformations.

The most powerful case for this distinction has been based on the principle that certain biological features of the human organism are the best candidates for universality. And the best candidates from the range of such features are those that are strongly genetically determined. While some features of the human organism are genetically determined variables, such as height (bell shaped distribution) and sex (bipolar), others are not, for example, the anatomy of the brain, bipedalism, and so on.

From the point of view of psychology, both groups of features are of interest. Sex is culturally modified into gender, with all sorts of complex local patterns. Even height is subject to cultural interpretations. Radical cultural relativism moves from issues of interpretation of what is seemingly given, to the stronger claim that what is biologically given is itself a selection from a myriad of alternative foci by virtue of cultural imperatives. Why should the reproductive organs be of any interest? Why should height merit attention? To escape the clutches of radical relativism we need some biological feature that has never attracted any cultural interpretations, but is crucial to a human practice. Wittgenstein's assumptions of 'the human form of life' approximates a claim for a universal human ethology, based on Darwinian selection of such reactions as smiling to express pleasure and the ability to recognize a smile as such an

153

expression. Chomsky's theory of linguistic universals depends on the existence of the mysterious brain organ, the LAD. Despite the work of Lorenz and others more recently, and the prestige of the inventor of transformational grammar, it is surely arguable whether there is a common ethology and whether there is any such thing as the LAD. I confess to thinking that it is a fantasy to find a biological universal to sustain the cognitive universals of the Chomskian theory.

Happily for the psychology of music the cochlea is neither a myth like the LAD nor, unlike the limits of human ethology, is its anatomy, physiology, or function a matter of scientific controversy. It is not something that requires a cultural interest to pick it out from the rest of human anatomy, like sex or height. It is the organ of audition!

Before we can assess the role of the cochlea as the grounding for universals in music we must pause to run over some existing suggestions for universals in music. Chomsky's analyses of language forms to display putative linguistic universals parallel and power the search for the LAD. In a similar vein we must try to display some universals in the practices of music, i.e., the orderly production of sound. From this point on I shall take for granted that music is a phenomenon in which human beings produce sequences of sounds that differ in pitch (that is the frequency of the sonic wave), and are rhythmic (that is, cluster into repeated groups). I shall also take for granted that the products of this human practice generally give pleasure to those who hear them, those who produce them, and those who plan them, that is, to the audience, the performers and, where relevant, the composers.

Some Proposals for Music Universals

There is a distinction between putative universals in the structure of musical performances and the psychological effects that such performances have on people. Universals of both kinds have been suggested. Bearing in mind that the cochlea must serve as the ultimate test of such proposals, there have been a variety of suggestions.

Leonard Bernstein's proposals

In a very well known lecture series at Harvard (available on video), Bernstein linked the question of musical universals to the possibility of linguistic universals, or rather, to an analogy between language and music. His first proposal turned on the alleged universality of the melodic and rhythmic patter of children's chants. The rhythm 'da—da—d'da—

da' is widely heard. Absent further anthropological studies one does not know quite what to make of this. The fact that the melody follows the pattern of thirds and fifths may be the significant factor. This is a key point to which we will return.

Coupled with this suggestion, and perhaps linked to the melodic form exemplified in these chants, Bernstein suggested that there is a basic musical form. It is universal because it is derived from an underlying structural universal like the universal grammar proposed by Chomsky. What is this universal musical form and from whence is it derived? And why is it *music*?

Vibrating Things

Music does rest on universals because the two main scales, the melodic sequences of pitch differences, can be derived from the physical properties of vibrating things. This may need some explanation. The main musical cultures, Western European, Indian, Chinese, and Indonesian are each based on the sonic properties of different material things: strings, columns of air, and solids. Western European and Indian are grounded on the vibration of strings, going back to Pythgorean research. Chinese is based on vibrations of columns of air, going back to the researches of Hsung Ti, and Indonesian, or gamelan, is based on the sonic properties of solids.

When any objects of these categories are set vibrating, there is a universal pattern of frequencies of sound waves produced, caused by the pattern of vibrations of such objects. There is always a fundamental and a sequence of harmonics, precisely mathematically related to the frequency of the fundamental. Thinking in terms of the common diatonic scale, if the fundamental is C the first harmonic is the fifth, or G. This is easily demonstrated on a piano: by holding down the G key to raise the damper, and striking the C below, the G string will sound. Higher harmonics can also be caught by an acute listener.

Doubling the length of the string, air column, or bar gives the octave. The first harmonic to the fundamental or tonic, the fifth, is called the 'dominant'. The notes from which all scales in all cultures are derived come from the circle of fifths. Starting with middle C on the piano, the first harmonic is G, the fifth. Taking G as a new starting point, the next harmonic is the fifth above G, that is, D. Proceeding in this way, one will reach all the notes of the diatonic scale, and eventually the chromatic scale as well, as they were before the reforms of the eighteenth century and the equal tempered scale of Johann Sebastian Bach. This is the circle of fifths. The first five notes so produced are called the 'pentatonic' scale, 'C, D, E. G, A'.

If music is created by setting various material things vibrating, then physics is the determinate of the modes of vibration thereby created. Physics is the same everywhere. So, if we define music as that auditory phenomenon that is produced by the use of these classes of objects to produce vibrations, then we have a musical universal. Cultural variations in the choice of material stuff to set vibrating is irrelevant since the physics of sound waves is universal. (I have heard Pachelbel's Canon played on traditional Korean instruments by students of the Seoul Conservatoire.) Be it pipes, sitars, or sarons, the harmonics must be the same, and thereby, at least the pentatonic scale.

The move to the equal tempered scale in the eighteenth century is linked to the development of orchestral music, particularly in Germany and Austro-Hungary. How could one tune an orchestra when the clarinets (newly invented) use B-flat as the root note, the horns are in F, and so on. The circles of fifths from each starting point will differ. By dividing the octave into eight equal parts, the musicians of the time reached a compromise to which the human ear is insensitive. This is a cultural phenomenon!

Kinds of Psychological Effects of Music

Having reflected on the possibility of universals at the producing end of music, what about universals at the product end of the musical process? Performance must terminate in apprehension, and, ideally, appreciation. When a sequence of sounds is heard as music, does it display features that are recognizable in all cultures where the indigenous music has been studied? There have been considerable efforts to try to identify such universals and to substantiate them across wide cultural variations. Here are some of the more plausible proposals:

a) *Lullabies*: research has come up with some possible universal characteristics, such as slow tempo and descending intervals.

b) *Games*: Bernstein, and others, have pointed out the widespread melodic line of children's 'call/response' patterns.

c) *Work*: Musical accompaniments to everyday tasks were once very common in Western culture (for example, sea chanteys) and are still important in Africa and elsewhere. It has been claimed that the melodic line and rhythmic pattern of the call/response structure is such a universal. This seems to me implausible, given that the 'mechanics' of the task may be very different from place to place. Pounding corn and hauling up the sails are very different rhythms. It would be necessary to show that where corn is pounded and wherever sails are raised the music is sufficiently similar.

d) *Dance*: Rhythm, frequently enriched with melody, is necessary for maintaining the orderliness of a dance. The observation that dance and music are intimately related does not show the universality of rhythmic forms.

The same point could be made for observations concerning the role of music in recitation, though nowadays that is reduced to metre. Music has played a part in war, to coordinate marching, for example. Think of the derivation of the instruction 'andante'.

There is no difficulty in putting one's hands on plenty of examples of features of music as heard or performed that could not be the manifestation of universals. Here are some: ethnic identity as expressed in music, e.g., Irish dance music; the Australian Aboriginal song lines, melodic geography (Chatwin 1988); the Suomi or Lapps have personal songs, a musical practice I believe is unique—each individual 'possesses' a melodic line (Tacka 2000).

The final step in this line of argument is to return to human anatomy and physiology, in search of the musical MAD, 'Music Acquisition Device'. Unlike Chomsky's mythical LAD, the human MAD is well known and fully understood. It is the cochlea. All we need here is a brief sketch of how it works. The main frame of the organ is a threefold tube, fluid filled. Along the tube runs a basilar membrane, and two rows of hair cells, sensitive to pressure in fluid. Vibrations are passed from the ear drum via the minute bones of the inner ear to the oval window, a membrane separating the cochlea fluids from the inner ear. The incident vibrations are transmitted as pressure waves through the fluid. The hair cells react differentially to the frequency that has the maximum amplitude. This is the fundamental. The relevant harmonics are picked up by appropriately placed hair cells further along the cochlea. There are complex neural connections to the primary auditory cortex. In this brain region, cells are arranged in columns, each column tuned to a specific frequency.

Here we have the MAD, the bodily organ that makes possible the apprehension of sound in terms of fundamental and harmonics. Every culture is human, and every human has a pair of cochlea, and every cochlea functions alike. It is no surprise then to find the circle of fifths and pentatonic scale where human beings have been found plucking strings, banging lumps of wood, and blowing down reeds.

157

Analytical Universals:
Schenkerian Structures

Turning to the analysis of music itself, with only musicological concepts in hand, the key analytical technique is based on the work of Schenker (1954). He showed that the basic structure of most forms of music exemplifies two basic forms: the major triad, CEG, and the tonic dominate pair, CG. Add to this the principle that a musical phrase or melody or even a large musical item must end by resolution to the tonic, and we have a powerful analytical tool.

Here we have the match that we ere looking for. The analytical powers of the cochlea, an organ the structure of which is genetically determined, and no doubt of Darwinian provenance, yields the very same pitch patterns as are revealed by a musicological analysis of musical productions. The ubiquity of the pentatonic scale, CDEGA, underlines the generality of the Schenkerian structures, which in a scale the tonic of which is C, are CEG and CG.

Two Universalism Probing Questions
for Cognitive Psychology of Music

1) Is the material set-up of the human cochlea and its analytical powers, together with a material system for producing harmonica tuned vibrations, the same in all known musical cultures? The answer to this question must be 'Yes' since this organ is common to all human beings, at the same level of generality as five fingers and two eyes. The three major musical cultures are based on material entities that vibrate as fundamental and first and higher harmonics, from which scales can be recovered by instituting the circle of fifths.

2) Is the cognitive process of musical apprehension apparently the same? That is, is the presentation of music a matter of motivated departure and return from and to base structures, of pitch (Schenkerian) and of rhythm? Again the answer seems to be 'Yes'.

The next step will be look closely at three non-Western musical traditions to test the correctness of the affirmative answers to the above questions.

158

Chinese Classical Music

We know that Hsung Ti devised the diatonic scale by shortening and lengthening the columns of air in pipes. This depended on the *same formal* relations between fundamental and harmonics as Pythagorean based musical patterns using string lengths. For example, he produced the fifth or dominant by cutting one third off the pipe from which the fundamental or tonic would be produced. Similarly, though in a somewhat clumsy fashion, he produced the second from the fifth by adding a piece to the truncated pipe that was one third its length. By repeated cutting and adding the pentatonic and diatonic scales are relatively easily reached.

Chinese Psychology of Music: c. 500 B.C.

Chinese philosophers of the classical period were agreed on the psychological effects of music, but not on the moral aspects that derived from them. All agreed in the opinion that music could be calming and order inducing, but it could also be sensually exciting, particularly inducing a certain wild sexuality. Lao Tzu, taking notice particularly of the second class of effects, declared that music is corrupting.

Mo Tzu argued that music is useless because it has no economic value and distracts people from their proper work. This is interesting in that it suggests that there were no work songs in ancient China and that music was predominantly a leisure activity. Confucius made the distinction between relaxing and exciting music, but suggested that good music should be used to help regulate social life. Bad music induces strong emotions, predominantly sexual, and hence leads to social and family chaos.

The basic distinction between kinds of music was psychological: *Ya*: pure, elegant and in good taste; *Su*: common, vulgar and corrupting.

The universality thesis is confirmed so far, in that the neuropsychological and acoustical material set up for music production and appreciation are clearly displayed in Chinese classical musical culture. However, the Chinese do not seem to have made the distinction between the induction of emotional states, such as calm and excitation, and the expression of emotional states.

159

Indian Classical Music: Scales

This musical genre is based on the diatonic scale, the notes generated by the circle of fifths, but, so far as I know, has its origin in the Pythagorean divisions of a taut string. However, there is a very clear cultural overlay, in that, in principle, the octave is divided into 22 intervals. Nevertheless in the construction of ragas, the scales on which the improvisations of performance must be based, use a twelve-tone system. Each raga is a fixed set of notes, associated with time of day, season of year, and is expressive of just one emotion, according to Indian typology of emotions.

Ragas are constructed in accordance with the following Principles:

1) Tonic and Dominant are fixed, and do not admit of sharpening or flattening.
2) There are seven primary notes and five secondary notes.
3) Secondary notes relate to Western sharps and flats. Effectively, the repertoire of notes available for constructing a raga is the analog of the Western chromatic scale.
4) The octave is divided into two tetrachords: Sa, Ri, Ga, Ma, Pa, Dha, Ni, Sa.

The rules of construction can be summarized as follows:

1) Three-octave span
2) At least five notes
3) Tonic must be included.
4) At least two notes from each tetrachord
5) Harmonic constraints: There must be at least one note in the middle octave consonant with a note from the lower or upper octave. The Vedi/Samvedi principle requires that whatever note is the tonic the 4th and the 5th must also be in the raga, not necessarily in the same octave.

It should be obvious that the underlying principles are none other than the Schenkerian structures. In other words, the cochlea as universal organ of audition imposes a generic but universal order on music.

Can we go further? The next step might be to ask whether finer grain structural patterns of music as melody can also be discerned in the three great non-Western musical traditions. Elaborating on the famous analysis by Susanne K. Langer (1957), the strongest structural principle involves motivated departures and returns to the Schenkerian or base structures. This creates the key phenomenological aspects of music as heard, namely, tension and resolution. Testing this against what we know of ragas we get the following:

1) Is the method of creating music as motivated departures and returns from base structures used in Indian classical music? The answer is clearly, 'Yes'. The rules for raga construction show clearly how both 4th and 5th are required elements in the raga.

2) Is the way the meaning of music is understood the same? Answer clearly 'No'. Indian music is associated with emotions but in such a way that each raga expresses a particular emotion and is appropriate at a particular hour and season. Western musicologists base their analyses of meaning on melody, rhythm, and performance related rather than as scale or key related. However, composers sometimes have quite definite conceptions of the emotional color of a key. Mahler, for instance, took D minor to be the key of sadness and menace.

Indonesian Music

This musical style is becoming much better known in the West than heretofore. A Gamelan is an orchestra (also used for the musical tradition). The material basis for Gamelan music is the vibration of tunable objects. There are two categories of such objects: Sarons—metallophones with six or more brass bars over a sounding box, struck by mallet, and damped by hand. These provide the basic rhythmic and melodic forms. Then there are Gongs: large gongs mark divisions in the music while bonangs, racks of small kettle gongs, are used to elaborate basic forms.

The tonic, third, and dominant arise by tuning the metal bars and discs of the gongs by size. So the Schenkerian structures are available to the musicians. Tuning makes use of both pentatonic and diatonic scales. Every full size Gamelan has two sets of instruments, one tuned to the Slendro scale, with 5 tones in the octave, and the other to the Pelog scale with 7 tones in the octave.

Each scale has its particular emotional tone. In using Gamelan to accompany the recitation of an epic with accompanying puppetry, the switching from Slendro to Pelog, and back, marks important transitions in the meaning of the music and the emotion expressed.

It is worth emphasizing that both Indian and Javanese Gamelan classical music presume a distinction between expression of emotion, say the killing frenzy of great battle, and the induction of music, for example, a state of elegiac calm by a certain raga.

Conclusion

Since it can hardly be doubted that cultural systems are local in both space and time, the kind of cognitive transitions from culture to culture that are required by cross-cultural psychology, for example, must be grounded in well established trans-cultural aspects of human cognition. That requires that there be a common ground for any trans-cultural features of human practices that are to be candidates for universality. In its turn, such a ground is strongest when it can be shown to be independent of culture, for which common biological structures would be the best candidates. While most other cases are disputable, there can be no dispute whatever about the common structure and analytical function of the cochlea. It thus follows that wherever there is music there must be Schenkerian structures, however they are modified and decorated from tribe to tribe. The challenge for other claims for trans-cultural aspects of human life must meet at least as stringent criteria as music meets.

References[1]

Chatwin, B. (1988). The Song Lines. New York: Penguin Books.

Langer, S.K.K. (1957). Philosophy in a New Key. Cambridge, MA: Harvard University Press.

Schenker, H. (1954). Harmony. Trans. E.M. Borgese, Chicago: Chicago University Press.

Tacka, P. (2000). Personal communication.

---

1 There are many excellent treatments of Indian, Chinese, and Javanese musicology. I have not referenced any specific works for these sections.

UNDERSTANDING CULTURAL DIFFERENCES: RELATIONAL HERMENEUTICS AND COMPARATIVE ANALYSIS IN CULTURAL PSYCHOLOGY

JÜRGEN STRAUB

Progress and Relevance of "Verstehen": Glimpses of the Past

More than half a century ago, Theodore Abel (1948) turned an epistemological reflection and criticism toward "The Operation called Verstehen"—which failed miserably. With a lack of bias that can hardly be found these days, Abel considered 'Verstehen' an operation of thought that seemed to be entirely logical (Matthes 1992a), and which he tried to incorporate into the naturalistic research program of the nomological sciences. 'Verstehen', then, was given a rather marginal role within the explorative field of empirical research. It was considered a particular form of perception conceptualized solely to identify the object of the empirical investigation, as well as to find hypotheses; it was not meant to be given an independent status as a specified and indispensable form of knowledge-formation.

This claim, which according to Abel had constantly been raised in traditional debates on the process of understanding, could be set aside for good reasons. Abel stated that it was bereft of any objectivity or proven validity. The knowledge created through the process of 'Verstehen' merely consisted of speculations of what could be the case and, as Abel put it, referred to mere *possibilities* (which, however, were often equally plausible) instead of referring to proven *facts*. It did not add one new thought to scientific stores of knowledge, but confined itself to reproducing what we already knew, and believed in. Abel thus discredited what was understood as "misplaced familiarity". The falsities and limitations he had found "preclude[d] the operation of *Verstehen* as a scientific tool of analysis" (Abel 1948/1964: 186). "The probability of a connection"—and here Abel points to a causal-deterministic, or correlative-statistical relationship, allegedly required for any act of understand-ing—"can be ascertained only by means of objective, experimental, and statistical tests" (ibid.: 188).

Abel, as well as numerous critics before and after him, considered all variations of this obscure operation of 'Verstehen' metaphysical and theological. Quite often, they were considered psychological or 'psy-chologistic' misdirections of almost no use in neopositivist science. Abel accused Giambattista Vico and Auguste Comte, Wilhelm Dilthey and Max Weber, James Cooley and Florian Znaniecki, Pitirim Sorokin, and R. MacIver, along with some others (e.g., Dilthey scholars) of having caused much confusion by attempting to establish 'Verstehen' as an in-dispensable method of the humanities, social sciences, and 'Kulturwis-senschaften', while the systematic clarification of the actual processes had been neglected. This last point of criticism was quite justified: Many social scientists "have given it various names; they have insisted on its use [...]. Yet the advocates of *Verstehen* have continually neglected to specify how this operation of 'understanding' is performed—and what is singular about it. What, exactly, do we do when we say we practice *Ver-stehen*?" (ibid.: 179).

Abel's central question still seems inevitable and most welcome. In an attempt to resolve the problem, Abel found an answer which, how-ever, was too deficient to consider his conclusions adequate. 'Verstehen' was narrowed and shortened to the psychological aspect of empathetic understanding. (Quite notably, Abel attempted to provide evidence for the fact that empathy implies those deterministically or probabilistically formulated principles with which 'Verstehen' operates; however, provid-ing evidence for the validity of these principles as such requires experi-mental and statistical methods.) For Abel, it seemed obvious that one must 'verstehen' what cannot naturally be understood, since in the ab-sence of methodical control, the interpreter (researcher) would have to base any findings solely on his own, personal experiences, as well as those that he has shared with a certain number of other people. These shared experiences would then be unquestionably valid for all subjects involved. The interpreter thus investigates what seems inscrutable, or at least seems to require further interpretation; he does so in light of con-fided possibilities (which he shares with a number of contemporaries). He renders the behavior of other (possibly 'alien') persons plausible by *analogically transferring* his own everyday knowledge, which allows him to empathetically 'feel with' such persons. The 'others', or 'aliens', will have done just what oneself would have done in a similar situation. It is this kind of empathy that stabilizes 'Verstehen'; and which Abel calls "imagination" (ibid.: 183). 'Verstehen' is guaranteed by the imagination of the interpreter: in other words, it is kept up by a psychological disposition rooted in personal experiences, which feeds a certain capacity for and skill in empathetically constituting analogies.

Down to the present day, one still finds remnants of this opinion—particularly in the context of psychological research. Given that the act of empathy and imagination can scarcely be accurately allocated and defined, which means it is of little importance to the *logics* and *methodology* of empirical research, one might consider this a legitimate point of criticism. However, this criticism was not news even in 1948; neither did it indicate the ending of the debate (for details about the historical development of the debate, see Apel 1978; Grondin 1991; Riedel 1978; and Horstmann 2004; Scholz 2001; Schurz 1988, 2004). Indeed, no *retraceable path* leads us from empathetic 'Verstehen' (or similar operations, such as certain forms of 'geistiger Nachvollzug' [mental comprehension], see Schurz 2004: 156 and seq.) to conclusions that can be regarded as scientific. This judgment can hardly be disproved.[1]

As we know, there is no direct access to the 'Seelenleben' (soul life) of other, possibly alien persons. Here, "introspection and self-observation" (Abel 1948/1964: 184) reach their limits, leading us back to Abel's alleged emotional syllogism. Conclusion by analogy however, which is inseparably attached to such syllogisms, is at risk of becoming some sort of poorly reflected projection. Hardly anyone nowadays would postulate what Abel reconstructed and criticized in 1948; today, we are more than aware that Abel's operation called 'Verstehen' most often does not fulfil its self-set tacit requirements. It is the existence of substantial cultural differences that may cast such presumption into doubt. Even more so, the assumption of an existing general, mental, and soul-related affinity among all beings (e.g., postulated by Wilhelm Dilthey) that would indicate some "easy" way to empathetically understand others, has been proven wrong.[2] These doubts have subverted every act of

---

1   I believe that this judgment can be maintained even if one does not intend to deny the role of emotions and acts of empathy for processes of understanding (of texts, text-analogs such as actions, etc.), or even considers reflections of this relationship a desideratum of contemporary hermeneutics.

2   Dilthey's "geisteswissenschaftliche", humanities-oriented understanding, descriptive and analytical psychology ("beschreibende und zergliedernde Psychologie"), which he put in strong contrast to explanative psychology in his famous essay (Dilthey 1894), was far more dedicated to a model of *general* psychology assuming psychological universals, than has been acknowledged. This is of great interest for a modern cultural psychology which neither stands in the direct tradition of Dilthey's *geisteswissenschaftlicher* psychology, nor can be traced back to traditional or recent nomological approaches, even though some exponents of humanities-

'Verstehen', particularly where scientific, methodical hermeneutics is concerned. We cannot deny that psychology, too, has to acknowledge certain universal commonalities between individuals[3]; yet, this does not save us from having to take into consideration the severe challenges we face when we try to understand cultural differences. Thus, the use of 'Verstehen', of which Abel (ibid.: 185) writes, "at best it can only confirm what we already know", could turn out to be more than embarrassing when it is applied in an attempt to scientifically approach individuals or groups of other, alien cultures, with all their experiences and expectations, thinking, feeling, wishing, wanting, and acting.

When facing cultural difference, alterity, and alienation, we have to distance ourselves from our stores of knowledge, opinions, beliefs, etc. However, this is easier said than done: Even if we conceive of the diversity of life-forms as 'variations' of one general, human life-form, as Wittgenstein (1984) does when he uses both the singular and plural of 'life-form' (Lütterfelds and Roser 1999), understanding cultural differences remains a highly challenging task that is hard to perform. What exactly do we mean when we say 'Verstehen', given that introspection and self-observation, analogizing transference, emotional syllogisms, and empathy do not suffice to describe this process in its entirety? And what does it actually mean today to speak of 'verstehende Psychologie' (un-

---

oriented psychology (among others, Eduard Spranger, e.g., 1921, the most influential Dilthey scholar with respect to psychology and paedagogics), have emphasized the fact that their approach could be seen as "cultural psychology" (cf. Straub 2003a). In this context, we should also consider an important work that Dilthey himself never published, namely, "On Comparative Psychology" (Dilthey, 1895 and 1906/1975). In this treatise, Dilthey describes psychological comparisons as being entirely unproblematic since he considered human soul-life ('Seelenleben') universal, regardless of the diversity of its actual manifestations. "No diversity without unity!" This conclusion, plausible as it may seem, is based on an overhasty marginalization of the role differences play, and thereby unjustifiably minimizes the importance of comparisons. Dilthey relates psychologically relevant phenomena to an obscure yet largely 'known' universal soul-life (which, however, proves to be nothing else but his own, introspectively 'understood' psychic state!). Dilthey's psychology is a universalist *General Psychology, on the basis* of which one might discuss differences. Such thoughts regarding putative human universals exemplify those Eurocentric biases that (nomologic) cross-cultural and (understanding/interpretive) cultural psychology have *unisono* criticized in the second half of the 20th century (Boesch and Straub 2006; Straub 2001, 2003b; Straub and Thomas, 2003).

3 Such 'assumption' is a theoretical, logical, and methodological necessity if one seeks to give hermeneutic acts of translation and understanding a chance instead of 'taking refuge' in the biased dogma of radical incommensurability.

derstanding psychology) and regard cultural psychology as an interpretive, hermeneutic enterprise?

Once one has realized what broad range of opportunities and suggestions can be found beyond the already mentioned points of view, one finds ways of 'Verstehen' that seem of much greater use for cultural psychology. Martin Heidegger's (1927) "hermeneutics of facticity" and his fundamental-ontological determination of 'Verstehen' might serve as an example. In this concept 'Verstehen' is considered the "original form of execution of *Dasein*", which then becomes "being-in-the-world" (Gadamer 1960/1986: 264). This existential-ontological view of 'Verstehen', which particularly influenced the philosophical hermeneutics of Hans-Georg Gadamer, has undoubtedly paved the way for the now commonly accepted view of the human world, a view in which this world is in its essence symbolically constituted and hermeneutically imparted. In other words, human practices of life and action necessarily require continuous acts of interpretation; they are hermeneutically structured, long before 'Verstehen' can be considered and used as a specific method of scientific research. In this context, we must not overlook the prominent role of language. However, other 'presentative' or 'pre-predicative' systems of symbols can be considered (almost) equally important (on this differentiation see Langer 1942). What Heidegger and Gadamer presented as life-practical understanding ('lebenspraktisches Verstehen') was mainly considered as understanding-how-to ('sich-verstehen-auf'), such as the versed dealing with practical issues of daily life. Apparently, such a concept of life-practical understanding was of importance to specifically scientific tasks and research questions in the fields of humanities, social sciences, and 'Kulturwissenschaften'; even more so, it also proved necessary for the self-definitions of these disciplines and the definition of their epistemological particularities (Giddens 1976). However, the concept did not contribute much to the methodical regulation of the scientific formation of experience or the clarification and definition of certain procedures.

Friedrich Nietzsche's polemics against *all facts as such* ('Tatsachen an sich') had already freed language from its 'serving function' in terms of the *adaequatio intellectus ad rem*, and paved the way for the discovery of the 'interpretivity' of, among others, scientific endeavors[4]. However, these reflections did not contribute much to the definition of understanding as *regulated method*, which would have been useful for many scien-

---

4   Not only does philosophical hermeneutics share this view with its precursor and 'close relative', phenomenology, but with large parts of linguistic-analytical philosophy as well (cf. Richard Rorty's [1979] analysis of a epistemological metaphor, "Mirror of nature", or Nelson Goodman's (1979) reflections on "Ways of worldmaking").

tific disciplines. This is valid for Gadamer's standpoint, too, despite the fact that he never contradicted the necessity of methodical procedures in the field of humanities. Here we must concede much more relevance to the works of those who were considered the representatives of 'traditional' hermeneutics (in contrast to Gadamer's philosophical hermeneutics), such as Friedrich Schleiermacher, August Boeck, Gustav Droysen, Wilhelm Dilthey as well as his 'successors' Georg Misch, Otto Friedrich Bollnow, to mention just a few (Grondin 1991; Horstmann 1994). Anyway, there are more alternatives than the one between 'traditional' and 'philosophical' hermeneutics. In the 19th and early 20th century, one could already find a growing number of publications focusing on *explicitly* social-scientific, and 'kulturwissenschaftliche' concepts of 'Verstehen', and thereby separating themselves from traditional philologies *and* Gadamer's philosophy. They sought *expressis verbis* to establish an understanding, hermeneutic methodology of social science and 'Kulturwissenschaften', whereby they acknowledged the fact that scientific rationality inevitably implies the need for transparency.

Here, I would like to remind the reader of the following: the works of Max Weber; the phenomenological philosophy of Alfred Schütz, who built on Edmund Husserl's philosophy; and the so-called genetic, or documentary method of interpretation developed by Karl Mannheim, which I will refer to later (see also Bohnsack, 1989, 1991, 2003b). In addition, there are the groundbreaking approaches that integrated and added to pragmatic thought (e.g., John Dewey, Charles Sanders Peirce, and George Herbert Mead); symbolic interactionism (e. g., Herbert Blumer); and ethnomethodology (e.g., Harold Garfinkel). It was the ethnomethodological approaches in particular that were the most consequential in turning the well-known "what-questions" ("What is society?", "What is cultural/social/psychic reality?") into "how-questions" ("How is society or cultural/social/psychic reality constituted/stabilized/transformed?"; cf. Bohnsack, 2003b: 556 et seq.). Psychoanalysis also contributed important aspects to social and cultural hermeneutics, and several scholars have tried to integrate some of the different approaches mentioned above (e.g., Jürgen Habermas, 1982, in his literature report on the logics of social sciences). This, however, does not indicate the end of the story.

Cultural psychology benefits from another tradition, up until the present day. Progress has been made with the help of a philosophical school which has, as becomes more and more apparent, much in common with 'traditional', 'philosophical', and other discipline-specific hermeneutics, namely analytical philosophy, especially such concepts and theories of language and understanding that build on Ludwig Wittgenstein's works, and of those, especially the so-called 'Philosophical investigations' (Wittgenstein 1984). This philosophical school has led to numerous findings that often appear in connection with action theoretical investigations, and which are of direct relevance for the development of a theory, as well as a methodology, of hermeneutical interpretive sciences. We also owe to this school the specification of the concept of 'Verstehen' as well as the undiminished significance of the latter.

As I have demonstrated elsewhere (cf. Straub, 1999a; 1999b), a cultural psychology that perceives sense- and meaning-structured cultural action as its paradigmatic area of interest (Boesch 1991; Bruner 1990) can greatly benefit from action-theoretical and linguistic contributions to an analytical philosophy that aims at terminological and methodological precision. Despite the fact that some of these fundamental conclusions were drawn decades or even centuries ago, the significant advances regarding the understanding of 'Verstehen', namely, *differentiations and formalizations*, are owed to the more recent, groundbreaking work of authors like Peter Winch (1958), Arthur Danto (1965), and Georg H. von Wright (1971). These authors made it clear that from their point in time on, 'Verstehen' could not be equated with a rather vaguely described act of empathy; thus, 'Verstehen' was more and more seen as a methodical procedure. This regulated operation does not quite fit with the model of subsumption theory developed by Carl G. Hempel and Paul Oppenheim (1948; Hempel 1942), yet it is far from being 'unscientific'. (With the growing criticism concerning the monopoly claim of subsumption theory, the idea of a 'unified science' overarching all disciplines, and, more generally, certain 'neopositivist' concepts of science, became less important.). Winch, Danto, and von Wright have all contributed highly influential works that led to a new understanding of specific variants of 'Verstehen' as an accurately explicable procedure—just like deductive-nomologic and inductive-statistical models of explanation—which could even be *schematized* and *formalized*. (Similar opinions and conclusions can be found in numerous publications, e.g., William Dray's [1957] highly influential contributions). Thus, we owe to these authors the specification of those models which we refer to as *rule-related, narrative*, and *intentionalist modes of explanation* (*via specific schemas of understanding*; cf. Straub, 1999a: 103, 105, 110, 139, 148). However, for quite some time, action theoretical approaches in psychology have only acknowledged the model of intentionalist (i.e., teleological) explanation (e.g., the ones by Cranach and Harré 1982; Cranach and von Tschan 1997; Greve 1994, 2004; Groeben, 1986; Werbik, 1978, 1984). Since action theory stands in an Aristotelian tradition, it seemed obvious that actions could be explained by using a reversed practical syllogism. The fruitful specification of this point is owed to von Wright (1971; cf. Mischel 1968). It then became clear that the model of intentionalist or teleological explanation was restricted to only *one type* of human action. Differentiations built on, and integrating 'older' findings and conclusions—such as Max Weber's famous typology (on this matter see Straub, 1999a: 63 et seq.)—became inevitable. One possible result of these differentiations—which lead to a pluralist theory of explanation of actions—can be summarized as follows (Straub 1999a, 1999b): sense- and meaning-structured phenomena—e.g., a specific action—can be explained by understanding ('verstehendes Erklären') through the reconstruction of

a)   inherent intentions (i.e., purposes, goals, aims, etc.) and corresponding assumptions (knowledge, beliefs, opinions) regarding the adequacy of (instrumental, or strategic) action, or

b)   rules underlying specific action (particularly social norms and corresponding values), or

c)   narrations in which action is embedded, or that represent the latter in its own "temporal complexity" (Danto 1965).

In other words, the intentionalist (teleological) schema might be 'complemented' by adding the schema of rule-related, and narrative hermeneutical explanation. Such models of explanation immediately bring into play collective stores of knowledge that structure and facilitate the sense- and meaning-structured actions of the acting members of a specific cultural life-form. We can now determine the structure of such stores of knowledge: apart from collective systems of knowledge, belief, and opinion that relate to action goals and (factual or assumed) purpose-means-relations, we have to focus on rules or narrations that are known and shared by all members of a culture, and that are binding in a way that regulates, coordinates, and structures individual actions. To give an example, let us assume that a certain number of humans belong to a cultural life-form in which the cultural stores of knowledge comprise the belief that "rain" can be induced through ritualized, magic actions performed by 'qualified' persons—this belief will actually cause (motivate), coordinate, and structure action, i.e., the 'chosen' or 'qualified' persons, and only they, will act in due course. The same applies to any person who follows the rules of their culture, e.g., the rules defining the marriage of a man and a woman. It also applies to actions that only gain their meaning from their relation to collectively meaningful narrations, or which seem possible only in the light of such narrations (e.g., myths regarding the foundation of a culture, and other narratives regarding collective historical consciousness). Reconstruction of, and reference to, such stores of

knowledge, each having its specific structure and function for hermeneutical models of explanation, as well as their integration into logical-
argumentative schemas then results in what can now—more precisely
and specifically—be named as *the operations called 'Verstehen'*. The
concept of 'Verstehen' is a 'collective singular'. Its variations are specific modes of understanding and explaining different types of human
action.

Why should the mentioned concepts of understanding explanation be
well established in cultural psychology? As we know, the intentionalist
concept is suited to conceive (i.e., apprehend) the 'subjectively meant
sense' of an action (which is exactly what the 'early' Dilthey, Max Weber, and Alfred Schütz aimed at). However, this concept, followed by the
narrative concept of understanding explanation of action (and action-
analogs) might go beyond the scope of 'subjectivist', 'individuocentric'
thought, particularly in cases where a person's intention (including corresponding purposes, goals, etc., as well as essential concepts of relevant
purpose-means-relations) are regarded as *socially* constructed or imparted. The same can be said about narrations that an actor might present
in order to tell why he did or did not act in a certain way, and which assume a central position within the narrative concept of explanation. (Of
course, explaining stories can also be constructed and told by an observer
or interpreter.) Last, but not least, rule-related explanation always refers
to collective knowledge (since, as can be seen from Wittgenstein's famous objections against the possibility of a 'private language', rules and
compliance are related to social practice generally; cf., e.g., Baker and
Hacker 1980, 1984; Kripke 1987).

We can see now why the mentioned concepts of "understanding explanation" are useful for cultural psychology. Cultural psychologists refer to collective stores of knowledge, to language games, and life-forms
in order to understand and explain human actions (thoughts, feelings,
etc.). Cultural psychology as hermeneutic, interpretive empirical science
is concerned with all the above-mentioned "dimensions" and modes of
collective knowledge and social practice. Generally, we can say that by
relating certain behaviors to the previously mentioned collective stores of
knowledge, cultural psychology conceptualizes those behaviors in which
it takes interest as *acts of meaning*. Thus, when speaking of cultural actions I mean such actions for which the referring to such stores of knowledge enables clarification and identification of their structure of sense
and meaning (as opposed to merely referring to individual, personal motives, intentions, etc.). One will have to take into account here that cultural stores of knowledge always gain their action-regulating function in
the form of subjective representations, which means that the subject must

171

creatively acquire such representations (Boesch 1991; Boesch and Straub 2006). Through this process, culture is given a "personal touch". However, this does not rival the fact that behaviors perceived of as cultural actions are unthinkable without the existence, and methodical reference to transindividual or collective stores of knowledge. Quite obviously, this distinction between actions considered cultural, and those interpreted and identified in other ways and with reference to other factors, must be seen as an *accentuation*. It does not operate on an 'either/or' basis, but allows for the identification and interpretation of an action as cultural in one case, and (largely) independent of specific cultural stores of knowledge in others. Here, cultural psychology builds on Elizabeth Anscombe's (1957) widely accepted conclusion that *identifying action* always implies description; in other words, identified action finds itself *under a description*. Such—essentially interpretive—acts of identification and description might differ to a large extent since interpreters may 'choose' from various possibilities. Thus, description and identification depend on, among others, the vocabularies available to the interpreter, or the descriptive language ('Beschreibungssprache').

As one can now see, a differentiated concept of 'Verstehen' is still alive and useful. The operation called 'Verstehen' is no longer unclear and obscure. Hermeneutics is not an obsolete theory. It has been given unexpected attention even in the field of cognitive science (e.g., Kurthen 1994; Varela 1990; see Straub 1992) and remains crucial to any research that aims at understanding *cultural* differences. This task, which complements the traditionally dominant effort to 'translate' and 'bridge' *temporally* constituted differences between life-forms, is not exclusively assigned to cultural psychology; it has long found its way to the heart of numerous disciplines that perceive themselves as 'cultural studies' or—which is not the same—'Kulturwissenschaften' (Appelsmeyer and Billmann-Mahecha 2001; Jäger, Liebsch, Rüsen and Straub 2004; Nünning and Nünning 2003; Reckwitz 2000), and that have dedicated themselves to intercultural hermeneutics (on psychology as 'Kulturwissenschaft' cf. Kramer 2003; Straub 2001, 2003b, 2004a; on intercultural hermeneutics cf. Göller, 2000; Kögler, 1992).

In the following, I will sketch out in more detail a suitable mode of methodical understanding employable in the field of cultural psychology. This requires a first approach toward the concept of culture and the interest that cultural psychology takes in cultural differences, alterity, and alienness. However, I will restrict my scope to those aspects that seem to be of particular importance for the given context. Here, 'the given context' means that my aspects of choice are most relevant for the culture-psychological analysis of actions. It is important to note that reference to the context in which a term is used proves not at all superfluous, as change of context leads to change of purpose, which then results in a change of meaning. Context is of utmost importance, as we can also see from the so-called conception of *meaning as use* accredited to Wittgenstein, in which he states, among other things, that we do not define words by reference to things, but by the way they are used.

The explication of the meaning of the theoretical concept of 'culture' should—like any concept—be tied to the concrete analysis of the phenomena motivating such research. Furthermore, as Mieke Bal puts it, "Never just theorize, but allow the object 'to speak back'" (2002: 18). Bal describes the metaphoric transformation of any given objects of analysis of culture into (quasi) 'subjects' capable of teaching the receptive, theoretically and methodically adept researcher, and who can 'force' the latter to work on—and with—their terms and expressions. By doing so she refers to the aforementioned conclusion: semantics depends on pragmatics, thus the meaning of a theoretical term depends on the way it is used in a specific context in order to analyze concrete phenomena. In this one can identify the old phenomenological realization that phenomena never really submit to their terms, i.e., they are 'loaded' with a certain 'resistance' which, according to Bal, one has to articulate as objections, words of opposition ('Widerworte'). It is indeed true, when Bal (2002: 18), as a "professional theorist", claims "that theory in the field of research of culture can only make sense when used in close interaction with the objects to be analyzed". This conclusion has long been incorporated into the so-called 'grounded theory'-approach (Glaser and Strauss, 1967; Glaser, 1978; Strauss, 1987), a recommendable methodology not only for cultural psychology.

However, I cannot introduce such a 'closely interacting' definition of 'culture'. I have to restrict myself to the above remarks and a reference to adequate examples of analysis that validate and concretize the following definitions, some of which might also give reason to modifications and differentiations (e.g., Boesch 1998, 2000, 2005). Anyway, it should be clear that a short definition cannot suffice in the case of 'culture'. We must provide transparency and precision if we want to prevent the term from degenerating into a mere 'fashion label' of no scientific use. Clarity and precision in the case of the concept of 'culture', and some other theoretical terms of social science and 'Kulturwissenschaften', should not, however, be mistaken for the elegance in the shortness of definitions that determines "what is meant" in just one phrase. The term "culture" belongs to a *wide network of interwoven and interdefinable terms* (i.e., they all refer to each other) that can be related in all possible ways, relations that do not necessarily express *opposites* only (as Bal stated in her resume of the well-known poststructuralist criticism toward structuralism). Only a few parts of this pragma-semantic network of meaning—which contains a concept of culture useful for psychology—will be unravelled here. However, the following considerations should serve our purpose.

'Culture' and the Analysis of Cultural Actions: Theoretical and Epistemological Annotations

Culture can be regarded as being a social, *knowledge-based, symbolically imparted practice* comprising *objectivations* and *objectifications*. The term objectivations here means 'external' artifacts such as technical instruments, buildings, streets and squares, clothing, or a meal, whereas objectifications are traces of cultural practice *'within'* the members of a culture, i.e., 'within' the subjects themselves.[5] Certain psychosomatic diseases and their corresponding symptoms might illustrate this point: in certain cultures, these diseases occur quite regularly, while in others they are almost unknown. Thus, the term 'disease of civilization' was coined; it refers to the specific life-form in which these symptoms occur, and according to which they form a coherent, pragma-semantic meaning system. Culture-specific dispositions to think, feel, or act in a certain, habitualized way can serve as examples here as well; they are acquired in the course of socialization, enculturation, or acculturation processes. They might eventually change, yet they are relatively *stable* integral parts of the psychic structure, and hardly visible 'symptoms' of typical psychic structures of a number of people who have shared (and still share) certain 'conjunctive' fields of experience and horizons of expectation. These people have acquired communicative knowledge that enables understanding and coordination of actions, and allows them to verbalize their concepts of self and world. Recollections that are subject to negotiation processes of collective memory (be it the so called 'cultural' or the 'communicative' memory; Assmann 1992) can be 'consolidated' in the form of dispositions.

Culture and psyche refer to each other. Cultural psychologists regard the connection of 'psyche' and 'culture' as an intrinsic, pragma-semantic interrelation: just as culture is in all its aspects a product of social, collective practice, so is psyche culturally constituted (Boesch and Straub 2006; Miller 1997). Task completion as execution of action, e.g., 'eating a Host during the Lord's Supper', 'cutting a lamb's throat', 'playing ten-

---

5 See also the related distinction between 'externalization' and 'internalization' (Eckensberger 1991: 13 et seq.)

nis', 'driving a car', 'marrying', requires cultural knowledge. Referring to the latter is crucial for the identification and description of such actions since both are closely tied to hermeneutic efforts and acts of interpretation and meaning-construction. Quite obviously, then, culture cannot be regarded as an external condition (of the synthesis, development, modification, or manifestation) of 'the psyche'. Culture does not 'cause' or 'generate' anything in the sense of a causal factor. It does not cause an action, its sense, or its meaning). This causalist conceptualization of culture, which is prevalent in nomothetic, cross-cultural psychology, regards culture and psyche as two logically unconnected, independent factors, or discrete variables. It is this assumption that allows studies to be conducted by means of experimental or quasi-experimental research designs in order to 'detect' contingent empirical relationships. And it is this assumption with which cultural psychology does not agree.[6]

Every cultural practice is, in a 'constitutive', intrinsic sense, interwoven with 'orientation-founding', 'action-regulative' knowledge (Straub 1999a; Zielke 2004). This is true for any psychological phenomena that are culturally 'impregnated' in their synthesis, development, and actual occurrence. It might be helpful here to refer to the common division of *explicit* and *implicit* knowledge. Implicit, i.e., practical knowledge in the stricter sense (Bourdieu 1976, 1987; Gadamer, 1930; Giddens, 1984; Polanyi, 1962, 1969) means certain proficiencies, capabilities, or know-how that are necessary in order to participate in corresponding language games, practices, and life-forms. Practical knowledge enables members of a culture to 'do the right thing at the right time', perform expedient, meaningful actions, answer questions (even by asking back), and to demonstrate their proficiency in handling things and situations. Such tacit knowledge is, as the term already suggests, 'silently' acquired through experiences, events that 'simply happen' ('Widerfahrnisse'), and the way in which we respond to these phenomena. Thus, following Aristotle's explication of the concept ἐμπειρία (empeiría, experiential, experience), and resulting knowledge, φρόνεζισ (phrónesis, pru-

---

6 Please see the mentioned references in Boesch and Straub (2006) on the potential dichotomy of culture and operationalization in the context of experimental and quasi-experimental research designs (see also Valsiner 1988). Furthermore, the given arguments point to the problematic that necessarily renders the common dichotomic classification of 'culture' and 'nature' difficult (yet not obsolete). The fact that cultural knowledge forms the basis of perception (i.e., enables us to 'see' something—any given phenomena—as something specific, one will hardly find any nature left 'untouched' by such process. Not only do we "create" nature as part of our cultural practices, e.g., man-made forests and other recreation areas, as soon as perception assumes an intermediating position, nature is no longer mere 'biological environment', but part of or the basis for cultural actions, symbols, and reaction patterns.

dential, prudence), practical, atheoretical knowledge can be regarded as implicit 'knowledge of handling' ('Umgangswissen') or know how (Mittelstraß 1974; Schwemmer 1987; Straub 1989: 199-212). Knowledge increases a person's *action potential* (on action potential, see Boesch 1991; practical applications of the term can be found in Boesch 1998, 2000, 2005). It is important to note that one is unaware of one's implicit knowledge. It is part of a practice, i.e., it does not constitute or belong to an individual's concept or awareness of this practice. Bohnsack (e.g., 2003b) speaks of *conjunctive* knowledge, following Karl Mannheim (1980) and his documentary method of interpretation. Conjunctive knowledge is based on shared spaces of experience and horizons of expectation; it is action-implicit. Actors know something that enables them to appropriately perform actions; however, actors are not aware that they know something, and thus cannot verbalize what exactly it is they know. Two examples: it is the trained hands that 'know' how to play Beethoven's Sonata op. 111 on a pianoforte, or how to shake hands, be it to greet someone or to close a contract. It is not conscious knowledge that 'tells' us how to do something; it is the face as part of the body ('Leib') that 'knows' how to express respect or contempt for someone, how to make others feel one's own longing or antipathy, trust or distrust. (The fact that the aspect of 'feeling' is brought up here also indicates the *implicity* of knowledge as part of the prereflexive, prelinguistic reason of individuals capable of acting). Investigating implicit, action-regulating knowledge is one of the most central tasks of reconstructive research in social science and 'Kulturwissenschaften', as well as in cultural psychology; yet, besides being crucial, it might also prove most difficult. Cultural psychology reconstructs *conjunctive* knowledge, as it forms the basis of relations of self and world of groups or individuals, as well as *how* these persons construct 'normality' within the scope of their life-worlds.

Excursus: Normative Acceptance of Normality as a Problem of Understanding

Bohnsack (2003b: 552) points out that some approaches in qualitative research and/or the underlying concepts of hermeneutics do not easily accept the great diversity of cultural, social, and psychological normalities. Both Gadamer's philosophical hermeneutics and Jürgen Habermas' approach might illustrate this point: Gadamer defines "true" interaction as a dialogue based on a *matter (of fact)*, as 'rotating around' claims of truth; thus, he excludes (merely psychological) understanding of the position and perspective, as well as the world(-views) of other people. Based on his theory of communicative action, Habermas ties the understanding of sense ('Sinnverstehen') to the (at least virtual) judgment of, as he puts it, validity claims (for factual truth, normative correctness, aesthetic shapeliness, or subjective authenticity) inherent in human actions and utterances. He thereby concludes that theoretical, universalist, and rationalist presuppostitions 'tie' understanding to the (reasonable) judgment 'of something'. Thus, understanding does not exhaust itself with reconstructive analyses of concepts of self and world and corresponding *modus operandi* that are conceived of as 'normal'.

We can summarize once again that the mentioned *reconstructive* task is indispensable, regardless of the question of whether normative attitudes must be entirely suspended in every stage of research, or whether validity claims can simply be "parenthesized" (as Bohnsack, 2003b: 552, demands). No matter whether or not such an approach is feasible and necessary on the way to longed-for 'socio-genetic' interpretation of life-forms, language-games, and actions, and whether or not the normative question of 'rationally justified' acceptance inevitably influences the task of 'understanding sense' in the social sciences or 'Kulturwissenschaften', does not alter the fact that reconstructive analysis of practical and discursive relations of self and the world of cultural actors still proves the most important goal of cultural psychology.

The aforementioned rational-theoretical controversy is a highly delicate issue; thus, every possible solution inevitably entails a number of 'severe' consequences. It is indeed difficult to pave a path between a universalist, rationalist concept of understanding, which seems nothing more but ethnocentrism and Eurocentrism in disguise, and the rationalized indifference regarding other cultures and their ways of thinking and living, which we call radical (normative or moral) relativism. In this context, one might easily see the reference to *Scylla and Charybdis* in Greek mythology. This explains why Bohnsack postulates that reconstructive research should be tied to mere description and explication of action-regulative knowledge of relevant groups, while normative questions and possible validity claims should be left untouched. Accordingly, he describes *different normalities*, as well as corresponding *rationalities*. That means, among other things, that scientific rationality is not a 'higher degree' of human reason; (one might agree with this 'modest' point of view as long as scientific reasoning keeps its claim for superiority toward everyday knowledge). Moreover, it means that one has to assume—and this is quite questionable—that scientific practice, in comparison to any non-scientific kinds of rationality, is not superior in itself, but *merely differs from other rationalities* (i.e., it is one possible rationality). Furthermore, such knowledge is, as Bohnsack points out, solely based on the attitude of the reseacher (who, if he is *up to date*, perceives of himself as second-degree observer merely exploring how any given person 'negotiates', 'creates', 'reproduces', or 'transforms' their sociocultural or psychosocial reality; he refrains from entering into the controversy regarding 'what-questions', and does not normatively discuss validity claims).

If normality is tied to corresponding rationalities, there must be as many normalities as we find rationalities, each of which must be accepted, not only because science cannot assume a 'superior' position or perspective, but also because we cannot 'make clear' *how* a given standpoint or perspective, utterance, or action could possibly be criticized, justified, or defended. If rationality is omnipresent, merely assuming different shapes, paradoxically it is 'everywhere and nowhere' to be found. (As a consequence, the above mentioned must also be valid in cases involving actions that one might regard as bizarre symptoms of some pathological disorder). Under these circumstances, the term loses its differentiating function.

Congenial as this 'egalitarian' criticism of the biased 'hierarchy of knowing-it-all' ('Hierarchisierung des Besserwissens'; Luhmann 1990: 510; Bohnsack 2003b: 558) might be, giving up on the possibility of rationally discussing and deciding on validity claims remains a questionable option, especially in light of the fact that such 'loss' would not only affect constructions of cultural and social realities, but individual *self-concepts* as well. In psychotherapeutic contexts, such self-concepts might in some cases be diagnosed as cases of self-delusion (e.g., of a patient). (On this matter, see Ian Hacking's convincing statement in which he gives numerous reasons why analyses of self-concepts should include differentiations between 'true' and 'false' self-concepts rather than merely stating different underlying rationalities; Hacking 1995). This task of analyzing self-delusions could also be taken on by non-normative scientists who do not confine themselves to the mentioned 'hierarchy of knowing-it-all'. Such 'second-degree-construction' (Schütz 1971, 1972), however, seems to encompass more than a mere reconstruction of 'first-degree-constructs'.[7]

---

7 Suspending such claims is obviously both challenging and complicated, as can easily be seen from numerous 'empirical' findings and resulting theoretical-terminological distinctions. For a truly palpable example, see the normatively imbued, allegedly 'objective' typifying differentiations in a study conducted to determine how different Turkish youth in Berlin distinguish practical rules and relations of 'inside' and 'outside' spheres of everyday life (Bohnsack 2003; Nohl 2001a). Therein, a schematic, 4-quadrant depiction of possible strategies makes it obvious which strategies are judged as being 'more complex', 'sympathetic', 'more elegant', or simply 'better than others'¤implicit judgments that do not necessarily imply a (temporary) suspension of validity claims, which the authors had initially demanded.

Let me recapitulate some relatively common aspects of (among others) cultural psychological research: sociocultural life-forms, as well as practical relations of self and world linked to corresponding psychological dispositions, represent different kinds of 'normality'. In closing the excursus, I recapitulate: for analytical purposes, empirical research *has to* consider the actors' practices and knowledges—most often in the form of documents or 'protocols' (e.g., audio recordings, transcriptions of group discussion or interviews, drawings, pictures, observation protocols based on photos or videos, etc.). However, cultural psychology does not exhaust its possibilities by mere adoption and reproduction of the participants' views of their selves and worlds. Reconstruction of a subjectively or socially constructed sense, as the actors are aware of it (see Groeben 1986; Straub and Weidemann, 2006), is one of the goals of action-theoretical (as well as cultural) psychology, yet that is not its only possible purpose. Cultural psychology is also particularly interested in, as mentioned above, implicit, practical, habitualized knowledge. This knowledge is neither subjective nor conscious, thus it cannot easily be accessed through processes of reflection. Habitus is active "socialized subjectivity" (Bourdieu & Warrant 1996: 7; cf. Raphael 2004), i.e., it is an empractically acquired, constantly modified and adjusted system of dispositions that regulates both routinized and creative actions. These habitualized implicit stores of knowledge are objects of, e.g., genetic and documentary methods of interpretive research.[8]

However, it is obvious that culture as knowledge-based social practice also encompasses explicit, discursive, reflexive, propositional knowledge. This knowledge proves equally important for the symbolic practice and orientated action of humans. Science itself takes part in the creation and transformation of such knowledge by adding highly specialized and specified contributions. As is known, scientific findings are usually directed toward everyday practice, which they also might 'colonialize' in return (cf. Habermas 1981b). Methodically controlled reconstruction of implicit and explicit knowledge, language games, practices, and life-forms can be considered part of this process as well. To summarize, it is crucial to distinguish practical, i.e., implicit, knowledge from its discursive, explicit 'counterpart', especially with regard to scientific approaches to cultural differences, intercultural communication, and similar phenomena. Contrary to explicit knowledge, which can easily be laid open due to its discursive nature, implicit knowledge can only be derived

---

8   Reconstruction of implicit knowledge is always tied to transformation of the latter (Renn 2006); it is more than mere articulation of formerly tacit knowledge. In other words, reconstruction does not solely represent something of which the knowing person is not aware, but necessarily induces a kind of metamorphosis of implicit knowledge.

179

by interpretive means, i.e., analyzing its practical, performative manifestations, objectivations, and objectifications. This requires systematic *verbalization* of culture as knowledge-based practice. Cultural realities (e. g., again, actions) must reach the level of distinct verbalization; they must be articulated in a sufficiently explicit way. The adoption of 'emic', 'indigenous' perspectives is imperative, yet it is equally important to also add 'etic' perspectives.[9]

We can now concretize the idea that 'culture' is more than an umbrella term used to describe knowledge-based, symbolically imparted social practice. On the level of explicit scientific knowledge, 'culture' is an interpreting construct ('Interpretationskonstrukt') that refers to this practice. We employ 'culture' as a key concept in cultural psychology, serving as a theoretical construct for interpretive and meaning-constructive purposes; this construction is then used to specify other (psychological) constructs, e.g., 'action'.[10] This highly abstract definition is primarily owed to a well-known, yet rather trivial realization: 'culture' can neither be reified nor identified in an objectivist manner[11], even when used to merely describe selected aspects of cultural realities, for which one does not necessarily perceive of culture as "a whole" (Fuchs 2001; Müller 2003; Reckwitz 2000; Welsch 1999).

Events or incidents ('Widerfahrnisse'), thoughts, imaginations, feelings, motives, intentions, volitions, actions, are not 'things' (i.e., objects), thus they cannot simply be 'located', 'observed', and 'grasped'. This is why essentialist as well as substancialist concepts of culture have in recent years been replaced by alternative terms that all refer to the constructive or interpretive character of cultural phenomena (Reckwitz 2000). Being concrete, determined cultural 'matters of fact', the mentioned concepts are represented in the form of explicit, discursive knowledge, and possibly qualified by propositional, 'predicative' utterances and statements. Scientific formation of knowledge and experiences thus requires *linguistically* qualified manifestations of, for instance, cultural

---

9   This oft-quoted differentiation was initially introduced by Pike (1954, 1967), who, subsequent to the linguistic division of phonemics and phonetics, rendered it suitable for empirical-methodological purposes in connection with the social sciences and 'Kulturwissenschaften'.

10 (Boesch 1991; Bruner 1990; especially Straub 1999a, which includes a more detailed explanation of the already mentioned 'constructs of meaning-formation and interpretation', which I have taken over from the 'interpretationalist' philosophies of Lenk (1978, 1987, 1993) and Abel (1989, 1993)). It is important to note that I distinguish everyday processes of meaning-formation (first-degree constructions) from scientific, self-reflectively structured, systematic, methodic interpretation (second-degree constructions).

11 On the precise meaning of 'objectivist' as predicate, see Zitterbarth (1987, chapter 1).

language games, actions, and life-forms. In this context, however, unambiguousness and terminating specification are far out of reach. The interesting phenomena are polyvalent. Like intentional actions, other *qualitatively defined cultural facts*, can only be analyzed in their *descriptions*. There is no *factum brutum*. A 'fact' is always a reality under a certain description. Every phenomenon can be described (i.e., identified and represented) in *different ways*. Often descriptions change in the course of time, i.e., under the pressure of new experiences. From this it follows that descriptions, identifications, and representations are *in some way undetermined* (Hacking 1995), which is not to say they are arbitrary; if used in scientific contexts, they need to be related to the cultural practice that is to be described, identified, and represented. This relationship can be established by claiming validity or empirical cogency. Such claims may appear in different shapes, some of which will be introduced below.

Thus, we can now conclude that 'cultures' are constructs used for interpretation and meaning-formation. In cultural psychology, cultures appear as explicit, action-regulating stores of knowledge. It seems precarious, yet, to some extent, unavoidable to objectify 'culture' in scientific discourse. This poses several normative problems, most of which have been thoroughly discussed in cultural anthropology and ethnography (particularly in connection with the so-called 'crisis of representation', and the debate on 'writing culture'; Clifford and Marcus 1986; Berg and Fuchs 1993). These problems have arisen in connection with some severe criticism regarding the distribution of power between 'the self' and 'the others' (as members of other, alien cultures). The latter were to be assigned the 'right to be heard' and the claim to be recognized. In other words, the debate was based on the claim to having a say in the representation of one's self. These rights have long become a challenge for scientific efforts to describe 'the others' and 'the alien'.

Apart from the 'political' issues involved, one should also consider epistemological arguments: these prove all objectivist conceptualizations which consider representations as mere reproductions of reality wrong and challenge us to cast linguistic references to cultural realities in a new light, (one might think of, among others, Paul Ricoeur's [1988, 1991] proposed 'indirect reference', or Hilary Putnam's [1988, 1990, 1997] "realism with a human face"; from a relativistic point of view: Rorty 1979, 1982, 1989). However, I will not discuss such complex (political, moral, and epistemological) topics at this point. It might be helpful, though, to bear the mentioned challenges in mind in order to avert the widely-spread yet untenable idea of constructivist epistemologies generally undermining the empirical claim for referring to realities and, after the completion of research, formulating fallible 'matters of facts' which can be distinguished from mere fiction, and fictional utterances. The mentioned demand might be much more complex and complicated than can be dealt with by means of objectivist, 'empiricist' concepts; this, however, does not render it obsolete. Empirical constructions of cultural realities are more than mere inventions, i.e., they are not 'fiction'. Certainly, one cannot state any direct reference between such constructs and the reality that they represent. However, empirical constructs are not arbitrary in their nature. The concept of (indirect) 'reference' ('Stellvertretung') implies a complex relation between signifier and signified. The fact that scientific languages and practices have much in common with their literary 'counterparts'—such as the use of metaphors and other tropics, and similarities regarding narrative structures—has long been used as an (inappropriate) argument against the accentuated distinction between experience-scientific prose and fictional literature, including all aspects of their geneses, which from both the genetic and systematic points of view in fact lead to a remarkable difference between these 'genres' and their corresponding functions and validity claims (cf. Eggert, Profitlich and Schierpe 1990).

As I have mentioned before, analyzing cultural realities motivates and specifies our interest in sense- and meaning-structured *actions*. Such actions can be analyzed within their processual sequence and interactivity in social communicative situations, e.g., in order to trace back interaction-related difficulties that might (might have) become manifest in the form of misunderstandings and confusions, conflicts and crises. Once actors and the social, mutually linked actions (thoughts, emotions, motives, etc.) they perform are analyzed in terms of their implicit cultural *differences*, 'culture' serves as both an explicative and explanatory theoretical construct. In other words, cultural actions become evident within their structures of sense and meaning only if the interpreter consciously relates them to cultural stores of knowledge, and identifies, represents, interprets, describes, understands, and explains them in the light of these findings.

Actors might broach the issue of cultural differences *themselves*, particularly in cases where they have faced severe challenges in their communicative practice. However, cultural differences of particular communicative relevance are often vague in their actual appearance. If that is the case, researchers might pick up relevant utterances and hints, and start their empirical-interpretive analysis of intercultural communication, cooperation, or coexistence (i.e., an analysis focused on methodic operations regarding cultural difference, alterity, and alienness) from there. In other cases, researchers might take the initiative and relate identified communicative particularities (misunderstandings, conflicts, crises) to cultural differences. In any case, researchers must acknowledge the fact that mere reconstruction and reproduction of knowledge articulated in the interpretanda (i.e., texts at hand, e.g., transcripts of audio-visually recorded, everyday face-to-face interactions) will not suffice to identify all communicatively relevant differences. This, however, requires some 'close reading' of the protocols (records) of the social practice one seeks to analyze.

One can say that, regardless of the actual theoretical approach of choice—e.g., contrastive pragmatics or 'theory of contextualization cues' in linguistic contexts, cultural dimensions or cultural standards, relational hermeneutics in connection with psychological and sociological research —they all operate within and *beyond the limits* of the knowledge they have gained from their empirical materials and data. Any research in which interpreters consciously connect human practice (thoughts, feelings, desires, and actions) to differing , 'incompatible', or even 'incommensurable' world views, language games, or life-forms, will thereby introduce and operate within the scope of stores of knowledge, differentiations, and determinations accessible to the researcher. Thus, analyses and comparisons of cultures, cultural actions, and intercultural communication, cooperation, and coexistence are also *cultural (i.e., culture-bound) analyses.* Interpreters operate on the basis of multifaceted knowledge that they apply to texts (which are regarded as objectivations of knowledge-based [inter]cultural practice). However, as I have mentioned above, one will not accumulate sufficient knowledge about cultures, cultural language games, forms of action, or life-forms by interpreting only those texts that constitute the interpretanda of qualitative-empirical social research. The accumulation and 'mobilization' of such knowledge (i.e., knowledge that renders analysis possible and facilitates it) requires intertextual references. (The texts and reference systems used, once again, refer 'back' to the practical contexts in which they are rooted.)

As we have seen, cultural psychology—following the differential typology of concepts of action and modes of explanation—reconstructs knowledge that encompasses (a) collectively meaningful goals as well as knowledge about appropriate means, and (b) action-constituting and action-regulating rules, particularly social norms and the underlying values, as well as (c) narrations belonging to specific life-forms and corresponding language games: they, too, shape the concepts of the self and world, and define collective identities (regarding this problematic term see Straub 2004b, 2004c); furthermore, narrations influence, to a great extent, the formation of sense- and meaning-structures of numerous actions. This knowledge, as well as those psychological phenomena in which cultural psychology is interested, are subject to cultural variability. Per-

sons might act in different ways, and they do so because of certain incongruities regarding their implicit and explicit knowledge; as actors
embedded in a sense- and meaning-structured practice, they reveal to us
their competence to participate in different cultural life-forms and language games. So, how do we proceed from here in order to methodically
analyze such differences?

Comparative Analysis: Identification of Cultural Actions as Methodical Operation of 'Comparative Thinking'

'Culture' is a relational concept. That is a polyvalent definition; it first of
all refers to the constitution, traditions, and transformations rooted in
cultural contact and exchange, which can be found in any culture (Burke
2000; Shimada 1994; 2000; a much discussed, normative perspective can
be found in Said 1979); moreover, it inevitably implies that analysis of
culture always depends on the *differentiation possibilities* that are accessible to the person who is trying to understand. Practical concepts of self
and world—whatever the actual aspect of interest might be—can only be
'grasped' and 'represented' through application, and explication of differentiations available to the interpreter. Thus, the interpreter's points of
view ('Sehepunkte' in the sense of Chladenius) and his or her world
views ('Weltansichten' in the sense of W. von Humboldt) again come
into play. What seems to be 'different' and 'alien' can only be seen from
one's 'own' perspective—this applies to scientific research as well:
otherness and alienness are relationally structured. Analyzing these concepts is a kind of translation from one set of cultural life-forms and language games into another (on linguistic-pragmatic theories regarding the
'translation of cultures' see Bachmann-Medick 1993; Renn, 2006; Renn,
Straub and Shimada 2002). This means that all efforts toward the understanding of differences require such acts of comparison, at least if one
seeks to arrive at significant conclusions regarding cultural and intercultural phenomena. What we call 'prayer' or 'oblation', 'music', or 'art'
has already been distinguished from other cultural actions and objectivations. It seems obvious that the lines between these concepts can be
blurry; the mentioned differentiations are neither historically nor culturally invariant. The idea of what we call 'art' might change as much as
what we consider 'religious' or the actions that we condemn as 'violent'.
Such historical changes result from comparative thinking; one might
consider this a truly trivial conclusion—however, it is anything but trivial
in its consequences.

A general theory, methodology, and methodics of culture and cultural modes of acting will inevitably draw its focus on the concept of horizons of comparison. After having differentiated types of *horizons of comparison* and their functions for interpretive analysis dedicated to determinative and reflective reasoning (Kant 1790; see below), we can identify what we actually do when we analyze, for instance, cultural actions, and how we methodically proceed in order to describe, understand, and explain them. (This, however, does not include those details that 'merely' result from specific theoretical approaches, or methods and techniques). What is interpretive analysis, and how can we identify such analysis as methodically controlled action? The following sections will be restricted to analysis of textually imparted phenomena, e.g., transcripts of group discussions or narrative interviews that deal with a variety of action(s). These kinds of representations will be looked at and analyzed more closely in order to identify cultural differences.[12]

Interpretive analysis of 'recorded' practice—even single actions that are embedded in a specific time frame as well as a 'material' and 'social' everyday context—is a complex operation that requires "reason, emotion, imagination, experience, and experience-based activities on a sustainable basis" (Schulte 1990: 6). This, however, applies to any act of reading and understanding; *scientific interpretation* in the stricter sense requires intentional and conscious realization; it is an explicit, methodically controlled, transparency-oriented effort based on potential intersubjective consent that aims at understanding texts and text-analogs such as actions and other practical or pathic aspects of human existence. Interpretations are conducted *ex post facto*, i.e., when the action to be analyzed has already been performed, and texts thereof have been completed (Soeffner 1989a, 1989b; Straub 1989: 213 et seq.). Scientific interpretation can be seen as a self-reflectively structured process of meaning-construction. *Scientific* also means that such interpretations include detailed descriptions of basic assumptions and theoretical backgrounds, arguments that serve to justify and explain such interpretation, as well as details regarding specific methods. In any case, transparency will reach certain limits since the knowledge applied by the interpreter can never entirely be made explicit. However, we can still say that scientific inter-

---

12 I will restrict myself to a summary of what has been thoroughly described elsewhere (Straub 1999a: 201 et seq.). Once again, examples of recent empirical research practice can be found in Boesch (1998, 2000, 2005), and in the following studies, which are based on different methods: Kölbl (2004), Kölbl and Straub (2001, 2003), (Straub [1993] or Weidemann (2004). See also the descriptions of the dissertation projects which belong to the research program of our 'Graduate School on Intercultural Communication and Intercultural Competence [www.tu-chemnitz.de/phil/ikk].

pretations do attempt to methodically control the arbitrariness of every-day efforts toward understanding and meaning-construction.

In order to more thoroughly explain the process of interpretation, I will refer to Bohnsack's 'investigations' (1989: 343 et seq.; 1991: 127 et seq.; 2003b, 2005) which I, however, differentiate and extend considerably (leading to terminological, among other changes). Bohnsack's work builds on the achievements of Mannheim (1952; 1964; 1980), especially in terms of his so-called documentary method of interpretation. Least of all, the following explications cannot be seen as specifications of the methodology of comparative analysis. The mentioned methodology (see also Glaser and Strauss 1967) aims at scientific 'second-degree constructions' in the form of 'typifications', which can then be included in typics and typologies (for a short summary, see Bohnsack 2003b: 567; in more detail: Bohnsack 1989; 2001; Nentwig-Gesemann 2001; Nohl 2001a, 2001b; Straub 1993). Interpretive research is—in cultural psychology as well as in any other discipline—closely tied to the systematic program of the *typological* formation of knowledge and experience.[13]

In terms of structures and processes, interpretive sequential analysis can be dissected into several components. It is crucial here to differentiate between two stages of interpretation, which I call *formulating* interpretation, and *comparative* interpretation. The latter can again be differentiated, which leads us to *determinating* and *reflecting* interpretations (see below). Performing such acts of interpretation necessarily requires certain preparatory actions, (which need not be described in detail at this point), e.g., segmenting the text (transcript) according to content-related or formal criteria, compiling an overview of relevant subjects, or 'creating' a collection of text segments in terms of a specific theme, etc.[14]

---

13 This, however, has nothing in common with the methods and goals of outlived psychological typologies (as have been used in rightfully criticized characterology). On a more suitable program of typological formation of experience and knowledge, turned against the monopoly claim of the nomological model, as well as the misleading distinction between nomothetic and ideographic research, see also Gerhardt (1985, 1986), Kelle (1994), Kelle and Kluge (1999). In psychology, the comparison of ideographic and nomological (or nomothetic) approaches is still popular, whereby the former is commonly seen as research into the individual, whereas the latter is conceptualized as aiming for more general conclusions ('psychological laws'). Direct association of this misleading comparison with the distinction of qualitative and quantitative methods then draws the anachronistic caricature of qualitative research being merely interested in the individuality of individuals and other 'unique, isolated cases', and unable to arrive at general conclusions.

14 One will find numerous methodological text books dealing with these rather 'technical' issues (e.g., Deppermann 1999; Deppermann and Lucius-Hoehne 2002; Flick, von Kardorff and Steinke 2005; Lamnek, 1995; Mayring, 1990; Strauss 1987).

Formulating interpretation remains as close as possible to the given text (interpretandum). It creates an initial understanding of the text (or single segments and utterances thereof) in its own context. In order to achieve this, the interpreter explicates—either in a shorter summary or in greater detail—what each segment 'deals with'. By estimating the relevance of a specific segment within the over-all context of the text the interpreter defines the degree of detail in which the segment is to be noted down. Quite obviously, it is the segments that have been written down in the greatest detail that will later be used for comparative purposes; that is, these segments will influence the construction of types, typics, and typologies.

It is important to note that at this stage, the interpreter works in closest possible, i.e., direct relation to the text, and operates within both the experience space and experiential horizon (in other words, the sign system as well as the system of knowledge and orientation) of his or her 'informant'. Utterances are reproduced, might be slightly summarized, and compiled regarding certain subjects or themes; thus, formulating interpretation can be seen as *reproductive* understanding of the concepts of world and self of an actor; it is "interpretation that operates within the framework [...] of those whose actions and texts are to be analyzed, and whose systems of expectation [...] are neither transcended nor expatiated upon" (Bohnsack 1989: 343). Thus, formulating interpretation adds nothing to what the actor has already 'said'; however, it is an important stage of interpretation since it directly links scientific knowledge with textually imparted concepts of action, self, and world. Formulating interpretation therefore illustrates how we can arrive at scientific second-degree constructions by reconstructing and utilizing everyday first-degree constructions. Of course, the next step is crucial in order to reach this aim.

Comparative interpretation is a more creative and extensive analytical procedure, with which the now re-phrased segments are analyzed in more detail. In most cases, one will not analyze single segments alone, but a certain sequence of segments, or such segments that can in some way be related to each other. In other words, interpreters focus on segments from which certain *patterns* of experience, expectation, meaning-formation, orientation, action, and/or development can be 'extracted'. As I have already mentioned, comparative interpretation builds on the findings of formulating interpretation, i.e., in the comparative stage of interpretation, one extends and more thoroughly determines what has been re-phrased, and (re-)structured beforehand. As the name suggests, comparative analysis means that certain utterances or passages are now related to, i.e., compared with, each other. It is in this process of comparative thinking that utterances or passages are identified as symbolic constructs that 'comprehend' and impart sense and meaning (which can now be explicated more precisely). Comparative interpretations are constructive semantic operations that derive sense-and meaning-constructs through reference to other texts or text passages. Predications, identifications, re-identifications, differentiations, 'relationalizations', and constructions of sense- and meaning-relations can only be achieved through comparative interpretation, as Glaser and Strauss (1967; Glaser 1978; Strauss, 1991) pointed out by coining the apt term 'comparative analysis' to describe their approach toward, and practices of, empirical research.

Cultural stores of knowledge are understood through reference to other stores of knowledge and experience;[15] the latter can be regarded as pragma-semantically relevant counter-horizons. In the light of such comparative *counter-horizons*, one successively arrives at a higher degree of elaboration regarding one's initial determinations and descriptions of the *interpretanda, and comparanda.* Such determinations are the core of relational hermeneutics. Successive use of the above-mentioned horizons of comparison lead to differentiations that are often initially identified as being binary oppositions until, in the course of interpretation, they become more subtle, complex linguistic differentiations, or widely-spread pragma-semantic systems of reference.

Counter-horizons used for comparative interpretation should always be explicitly introduced and described, i.e., they should be used in a methodically controlled, intersubjectively retraceable way that also allows for criticism. Much—if not everything—depends on the specific horizons of comparison of which the interpreter (or group of interpreters) makes use; creative interpretations are never entirely free from certain amounts of contingency, resulting from the fact that the horizons of comparison used are rooted in the interpreter's knowledge. This inevitable embeddedness must be reflected upon and made clear. It is at this very point that 'reasonable' demands for transparency come into play, demands that can now either be accepted or rejected. However, contingency should not be mistaken for arbitrariness. In contrast to the latter, contingency cannot be avoided (at least not entirely). The interpreter depends on her or his stores of knowledge in many ways; his or her creativity, fantasy, imagination and judgment, logical competence regarding the use of deductive, inductive, and abductive procedures are essential parts of his or her per-

---

15 Again, knowledge is understood in a very wide sense of the term: it encompasses (a) scientific knowledge and experience as well as everyday knowledge in the narrower sense, i.e., all rationally explicable statements and systems of statements interrelated with "redeemable" validity claims; (b) beliefs that provide certainty to the believer only; and (c) mere opinions, for which one can neither claim nor prove any validity.

sonality and subjectivity; furthermore, they also form, just as the interpreter's knowledge does, her or his action potential.

As researchers, our operations are always based on our experiences and knowledges, which are commonly reproduced in socio-cultural practice, and which we have consciously and intentionally acquired or in other ways 'adopted' in the course of our lives. This base can neither be articulated and reflected upon in its entirety, nor can we 'suspend' it since certain parts of it are 'located' beyond the limits of our reason, explanatory competence, and methodical control. Methodical rationality is a regulative idea as well as a useful rule with which we, however, can never fully comply, mainly because we are 'forced' to act according to our own stores of partially *implicit* knowledge.

Horizons of comparison provide either 'minimum' or 'maximum' contrasts, i.e., they serve to identify phenomena that are either very similar, or are such that they form strong contrasts. We then structure phenomena that appear similar (or almost identical) as *types*, in such a way that these types serve as 'umbrella terms' for the given phenomena. By doing so, we also distinguish a type from other possible types and phenomena. Thematically relevant types—e.g., those related to certain cultural, generational, gender-related, or milieu-specific particularities—form so-called typics. Several related typics can be considered a typology.

As I have indicated before, interpretive research might gain its comparative counter-horizons from different sources (of knowledge). Thus, we can schematically dissect the given horizons of comparison according to their sources, as figure 1 illustrates.

Knowledges, particularly those that allow for the identification or specifying and enhancing analysis of psychologically relevant cultural differences, play a multiple role in this schematic differentiation. As we already know, the scope of empirical findings, as well as the empirical validity of identification processes regarding cultural differences, depends on a number of knowledge-related preconditions. First of all, let us consider *empirically grounded* horizons of comparison that have been derived from the interpreter's own research, and that belong to one's own text body. Not only do these horizons stem from one's own, methodically controlled research; one also finds in them manifestations of the cultural knowledge of one's research partners. They are direct evidence of the latter's life-forms and language-games, i.e., they symbolize the thoughts, feelings, wishes, and actions of 'the others' and potential 'aliens'. Thus, comparative analysis of these materials or data is the *via regia* that enables us to understand such 'alien' phenomena. It is the basis of empirical research, at least of such research that aims at providing the "experi-

189

ence of the experience" of others (Matthes 1992b), in other words, of being 'different' or 'alien'.

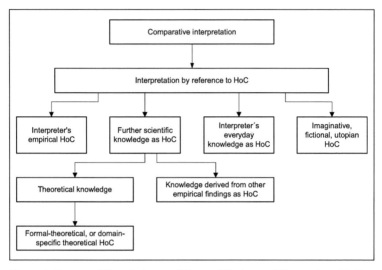

Figure 1: Sources of Knowledge, and Types of Horizons of Comparison (HoC)

However, empirical research cannot solely draw upon these grounds. In empirical research, one will always bring into play different variants of other stores of knowledge and experience. In order to analyze and discriminate an interpretandum, researchers might also refer to *empirical findings that were not derived from their own research*, but belong to the generally accessible store of empirical research results that have already been published. Exploring these publicly accessible stores can be of great benefit; however, they might prove to be of no avail for innovative research projects focussing on topics that have not yet been well investigated.

Furthermore, *theories* considered helpful in investigating the phenomena of interest also come into play. In interpretive research, theories (or isolated theoretical hypotheses) are not just 'tested'; they fulfill a heuristic, often even constitutive function. (As a side note, this function undermines the common idea of 'empirical testings' of theories, as the relation of theory and practice is based on a non-vicious hermeneutic circle; thus, one cannot follow the general idea of theory-free empirical facts ('facta bruta') on one side, and theoretical hypotheses regarding these facts, including their contingent relation, on the other.) Such theories are often linked to specific methods, e.g., depth hermeneutical procedures that would simply be unthinkable without at least some aspects of psychoanalytical theory. These methods, too, are not only relevant when directly applied to empirical data; they already play an important role in the constitutive processes regarding the interpretanda. The way in which the latter is constituted and 'understood' depends on the theories and methods that the interpreters apply, and which have most often been applied long before the actual research is conducted, namely to develop an initial idea of their objects of research and the research project itself. In this respect, we can distinguish *general, formal-theoretical* concepts and approaches (such as concepts of action and action theories) from *domain-specific, material theories* (e.g., psychological theories of developmental tasks during adolescence, or theories of gender-specific socialization).

However, scientific interpretation does not merely draw upon such stores of empirical knowledge, theoretical patterns of thinking, and methodological approaches that are constantly discussed by the scientific community, and which then influence the actual research practice. It is the *everyday-knowledge* of the interpreter, his experience of life, and his reflections on the latter, which again come into play, and which can hardly be overestimated. No researcher can abandon or suppress his experience of life—in fact, no one can—while interpreting texts or text analogs for scientific purposes. He is a human being, shaped by what he has experienced and what he has not, a person who has gained experience through proactivity and partially autonomous actions, fortunate events and appreciated incidents as well as undesirable circumstances and dreadful occurrences. The way in which interpreters 'read' their empirical material, the things that they can—or cannot—'find' and consider, depends to a large extent on prior experiences and corresponding emotional, affective, and cognitive coping strategies, including dispositions resulting therefrom. However, 'physical' experience is not the only possible source; one might also gain experiences from books and movies or other media, and, not least of all, narrations—to give only a few examples to illustrate how one can temporarily 'share' someone else's life and knowledge.

A certain familiarity concerning certain phenomena, rooted in one's own experiences and imparted in the above-mentioned way—irrespective of the actual event from which it stems—is an indispensable premise of understanding. This is one of the reasons why understanding can never be a process that anyone can learn, or teach in the same way: one always understands 'something'. 'Understanding' (to understand, 'verstehen') is at least a 'two-folded', double predicator (including a subject and an object). It refers to incidents and experiences in which different persons will recognize different degrees of familiarity; some might also consider them 'completely alien'. Interpreters might have enhanced their knowledge with respect to certain experiences, which they can then articulate to some extent and creatively make use of. As scholars and researchers, we make use of such knowledge, too: Our knowledge becomes part of implicit or explicit horizons of comparison. Whoever attempts to 'exclude' this knowledge from empirical research undoubtedly adheres to an unrealistic, contra-productive view of scientific formation of knowledge. Empirical findings do not solely result from methodical meticulousness in prior data collection, analysis, and evaluation; nor do theoretical expertise and fantasy automatically lead to significant, noteworthy conclusions. Significant results that add to the recipients' knowledges can only be reached in cases where researchers are able to integrate their own, everyday practical knowledge into empirical horizons of comparisons—knowledge that is all but arbitrary.

Creative interpreters must be able to "access" and activate knowledge that provides *productive* comparative horizons in terms of the subject matter they seek to analyze. (One cannot determine in advance whether this knowledge actually serves—however, cultural psychology knows that some crucial knowledges and abilities prove relevant to almost any research one can think of, such as language proficiency.) Everyday knowledge is crucial, too, since it structures the interpreter's perspective and perception, and enhances his heuristic fantasy, imagination, and judgment. This allows us to distinguish the expert from the novice not only by referring to theoretical knowledge, and methodical skills. Experiences and practical knowledge are other criteria for this accentuated distinction (which is useful even though we might not attempt to accurately measure these differences). Due to the lack of essential cultural and, not least of all, practical knowledge, junior scientists would have hardly been able to carry out such research projects as those implemented, for instance, by Clifford Geertz, Ernst Boesch, or Jerome Bruner.

An interpreter's everyday knowledge is an important but not sufficient condition of experience- and empirical knowledge-formation with regard to the interpretive sciences. There is no need to disdain or ignore this rich source of comparative horizons. However, we must not overlook some risks of such everyday knowledge: Together with the mentioned scientific—in particular, theoretical—horizons of comparison, the horizons related to the interpreter's everyday knowledge might lead to 'comparisons' that merely assimilate relevant differences (i.e., adapt them to his or her own concepts and knowledges). It is obvious that this process of 'understanding' might then establish a basis for misunderstandings and misconceptions. Egocentric or *nostrocentric* appropriation of 'other' and 'alien' phenomena are a risk with many sources, yet interpretive science cannot fully disengage itself from it. Here, everyday knowledge proves particularly challenging, as it can never be articulated in its entirety. As hermeneutical findings have shown, its structures of prejudice are difficult to assess (Gadamer 1960/1986; on the same matter, including a discussion of Gadamer's controversial rehabilitation of prejudice, see also Straub, 1999: 250 et seq.). Such prejudices can only be partially reflected and transcended (whereby the former are changed again, in a way that cannot be entirely retraced). Quite obviously, these prejudices not only enable us to form scientific knowledge; at the same time, they prove to be potential obstacles on our way toward a methodically controlled understanding of 'alien' phenomena.

Everyday knowledge provides opportunities to compare what seems 'alien' with what we 'already know' and offers perspectives that might facilitate our thinking; however, it may also disable us in our efforts to approach other, 'alien' life-forms and the people who participate in such cultural life-forms. This risk cannot be eliminated; however, interpretive researchers can reduce it by at least avoiding more evident potential 'mistakes'. This means that one has to distance oneself from one's own knowledge, to 'suspend' it (temporarily, in some stages of interpretation), as far as this is possible and necessary. This is particularly possible in cases where comparative analyses include explicitly, empirically grounded horizons of comparison, i.e., such stores of knowledge which—as implicit and explicit knowledge—symbolize other, 'alien' life-forms. Another way to 'distance' oneself from one's own cultural matters of course is the formation of research *groups* in which members of the culture of interest also take part. In spite of the often demanded internationalization of research, and the intercultural orientation and organization of such enterprises, such cooperations are still rare. If they actually happen, they are often (mis)used in order to pretend interculturality. In reality, true cultural exchange and intercultural communication with regard to necessary discussions and debates are more often suppressed (e.g., due to time constraints), particularly among group members who have internalized the same 'international style' of scientific reasoning and researching in the course of their scientific socializations. Still, such (multicultural) groups might well serve as a corrective here since they might guard against 'one's own knowledge', which I have, in the above as well as elsewhere, identified as assimilating and *nostrifying appropriation* (Straub 1999b).

Similarly, *communicative validation* of interpretation may serve the same purpose, provided that one's research partners are able to participate. However, this strategy is limited; apart from practical limitations—most often of an economic nature—we should not overlook, e.g.,

193

language-related challenges, including severe translation problems regarding science-specific language games and their 'everyday counterparts', or, to give another example, questions of ethics and morals involved in the process of communicative validation. As we know, some research results simply cannot be communicated without further comment, as is most often the case with results that seem to undermine and question the self- and world-concepts of certain people.

To summarize, scientific comparative interpretation requires the interpreter's everyday knowledge. This knowledge may constrict or facilitate the interpreter's attempt to understand "alien" phenomena. This knowledge also indicates the interpreter's subjectivity and individuality, and what is most important is the fact that the interpreter is himself a cultural being who represents collective stores of knowledge and experience that he or she has acquired by participating in one—or more—life-form(s). In this context, it is important to note that experiencing one's self (as part of the development of one's self-concept) can *already be* strongly influenced by experiences of cultural differences, alterity, and alienness. Since this is a very individual process, one will always find interindividual differences regarding the mentioned experiences, and it is these differences that turn out to be of great relevance in the given context. Whoever seeks to understand 'alien' life-forms, and the ways of thinking, feeling, wishing, and acting that are connected with them, is far more than a so-called 'tabula rasa'. One might assume that work and private life, science and the everyday world, methodical empiricism and informal experience-formation cannot be kept entirely separate—those aspects that researchers intentionally articulate, distinguish, and accentuate in their research, e.g., in the form of empirical horizons of comparison, is unseparated and undistinguished within their very selves. However, we can still say that an interpreter's everyday knowledge might be imbued, shaped, and sharpened by experiences of cultural differences, alterity, and alienness, it might be rooted in—to a greater or lesser extent—intercultural communication, cooperation, and coexistence, and it might or might not include intercultural competence (Bolten 2001; Taylor 1994; Thomas 2001; Weidemann 2004). Some empirical results are only possible on the basis of personal, long-term, and complex experiences of life, which become part of one's everyday knowledge, which is then used to form productive horizons of comparison within empirical research. The usefulness of an interpreter's everyday knowledge regarding cultural-psychological research is incapable of ('accurate') measuring, particularly prior to the actual research process. However, recipients of cultural-psychological findings can still estimate and judge whether an interpreter's everyday knowledge has proven advantageous, or whether it has prevented the interpreter from drawing significant conclusions.

We can now resume and specify: comparative interpretation means analyzing an interpretandum by referring to constructions of relations of similarity or difference that are based on certain horizons of comparison. Here one has to distinguish two forms of judgment (or reason) of which interpreters can make use, namely, *determinating* and *reflective* judgment. These expressions were coined by Immanuel Kant (1790), to whose "Critique of the Power of Judgment" I (partly) refer. *Determinating* judgment means that phenomena (e.g., actions) are identified and described in a familiar way, i.e., words that are recognized as belonging to a commonly used term, category, schema, or script. (Methodical operations of content-related analysis, for instance, draw upon determinating reason as they "place" empirical data in known and familiar structures, and thereby subordinate the former; cf. Mayring 1990). *Reflective* judgment has its place not only in philosophical aethetics and Kant's teleology of nature; it proves important for a general theory and methodology of empirical formation of knowledge in interpretive science. Kant's concept can be applied to a broad range of experiences that cannot easily be subsumed within common terms, categories, schemata, and scripts. Reflective reason is needed whenever we seek to gain or articulate experiences, but cannot easily do so since we have not yet sufficiently identified what should be articulated and how we can articulate it in an appropriate way.

Such underdetermined, at most vaguely described phenomena are well known in action- and cultural-psychological research, especially when other, alien cultures are involved. Thus, cultural-psychological research requires reflective judgment whenever it reaches research-strategically relevant issues, namely whenever the interpreter attempts to analyze and describe phenomena with which he has not been in touch before, i.e., 'new' phenomena.[16] While determinating reason uses common terms, categories, schemata, and scripts in order to identify the given phenomena, reflective reason operates without such acts of *subsumption* and *assimilation*, whereby the interpreter's vocabulary is altered and extended, i.e., it is adjusted to the formerly 'new' phenomena, not the other way round. Reflective interpretation is associated with, as Jean Piaget would have phrased it, *accommodation*. In other words, reflective reason makes deals with what is not identical (Adorno, 1973,

---

16 The parallel to Peirce's concept of abduction is obvious (see Reichertz 1993); contrary to Peirce, Kant did not introduce his concept as a formal-logical method like deduction and induction.

speaks of "the nonidentical"), and it does so in order to identify and define it (and thereby transform it into an object of determinative reason).[17]

Reflective and determinating reason complement each other. Thus, they are equally relevant. Reflective judgment broadens and differentiates the interpreter's horizon, enriches his symbolic world and the language in which he describes, understands, and explains the empirical phenomena that have caught his interest. Both reflective and determinative reason lead to operations that are necessary and productive with regard to comparative-analytical understanding of other, eventually alien cultural life-forms and language games, as well as corresponding ways of thinking, feeling, wishing, and acting.

On the Validity of Comparative Interpretation of Cultural Action

Comparative analyses of cultural actions can either reach the heart of its 'object', or fail miserably. Both options are equally possible. Provided that we do not expect to find one 'true', or maybe 'the best' interpretation—as we acknowledge the polyvalence of all aspects of human life, and, in particular, the fact that any given way to 'read' a text or record of human practice inevitably depends on the interpreter's standpoint and perspective—we still separate rather 'misleading' interpretations from 'valid' ones. This can be exemplified by 'negative' extremes. Let us assume that a person interprets this essay in the following way: the central message is that the firework planned for tonight in order to celebrate a commonly known, happy occasion was relocated from the castle courtyard to the ballroom. Based on the given essay, the interpreter would have failed, of course, and such a person would hardly be considered an 'interpreter'. One can think of numerous—perhaps slightly less extreme—other examples. Our interpretations might fail to meet the investigated practices, life-forms, and language games, albeit in less bizarre ways than was described in the above 'absurd' example. Some cultures do not include the idea of, for instance, anthropomorphic and anthropopathic gods; 'religion' as well might mean different things in different cultures, and might provide inadequate concepts of comparison for phenomena which, at first glance, appear to be somehow related (Popp-Baier 2006; Straub and Shimada 1999).

---

17 Countless examples might illustrate how difficult and time-consuming this can be. See for example some of the creative works by François Jullien (e.g., 2002).

Separating 'better' interpretations from 'rather bad' ones is undoubtedly a challenging task, for which one might not find adequate, general criteria or regulations (since one would have to consider the entire range of purposes and intentions that a given interpretive analysis is to serve). However, following the above explications it might have become clear that one aspect assumes a central position in this context: it proves to be of great importance if one seeks to reasonably judge whether a given interpretandum—i.e., certain concepts and language games, forms of action, life-forms, etc.—has been adequately translated, and identified. The term 'translation' refers to pragma-linguistic theories, which conceive of translation as 'transmission' or 'transfer' of terms and utterances from one culture to another, i.e., as translation of cultural language games and life-forms in which individuals can participate *practically* (Bachmann-Medick 1993; Renn, Straub and Shimada 2002). This emphasizes the *multidimensionality* of approaching cultures. The differentiation between practical approaches to culture (including its language games, forms of action, and language games) on one side, and the symbolic, particularly linguistic reference on the other, which Joachim Renn (2005, 2006), among others, has pointed out, leads to the conclusion that practical experience may serve as a potential corrective regarding references and representations. Methodical empiricism, which usually excludes such experience, or restricts it to a greater or less extent—must acknowledge this fact, too. Paradoxically, such experience cannot initially be identified; it is perceived as mere 'feeling', 'anticipation', or 'presentiment' of potential cultural difference, alterity, and alienness, which must be verbalized in order to turn initial, vague 'perceptions' into articulated representations—experiences—which might then force one to revise previous representations.

Experiences such as 'witnessing' is what happens on the way 'toward' a culture. As mentioned before, experience is not tied to 'physical' or 'material' processes. Empirical knowledge about other, potentially alien cultures, cultural differences and intercultural communication, cooperation and coexistence stems from different sources: in most cases, only a few parts can be traced back to 'physical' experiences of the researcher, and the reflexive 'compensation' thereof; far more often, experience-formation is based on methodical reconstruction of experiences made by others, preferably those individuals who are familiar with the cultural language games, actions, and life-forms to be analyzed, and who can therefore 'mobilize' their *practical* knowledge to 'correct' inadequate representations. Overlooking practical approaches regarding specific terms and language games, actions, and life-forms, as well as methodical ignorance might all too easily result in misleading, nostrifying

197

interpretations, which might then be unreflectedly reproduced. Such interpretations leave no space for alterity or alienness, but simply assimilate and subordinate them.

Quite evidently, subsumption-logical appropriations and assimilation cannot be entirely avoided. At no stage of knowledge- and research-formation—which is a potentially infinite process which one only 'terminates' for pragmatic reasons—can we understand other, alien phenomena without nostrifying the other and alien. Here, the initial stages of understanding are the most challenging: they might easily lead to assimilative processes (or, on the contrary, might cause the interpreter to believe in the total incommensurability and incomprehensibility of the other, and alien.) Trivial as it may seem, the only thing that can possibly help is open-mindedness. In connection with this, theories, methodologies, and methods of empirical research that attach the necessary comparisons to determinating and reflective judgment prove helpful, which prevents us from *merely applying* putative *tertia comparationis*. This requires accommodation of one's own horizons, concepts, categories, schemata, and scripts.

Understanding differences, alterity, and alienness is always achieved 'by someone' and 'for someone'; it is situation-related and 'addressed to someone'. Successful research modifies, at the very least, one's own *action potential*, which is tied to one's linguistic differentiation possibilities. (Or, in the same way, the action potential of a group to which one belongs). Theoretical and empirical advances in interpretive cultural-psychological contexts become evident in an extended symbolic horizon, particularly in the linguistic universes of the researchers, the scientific community, and other recipients of scientific findings who integrate such results into their concepts of self and world, and their action potentials.

Ontic and Radical Differences: Epistemic Limits and Moral Challenges of Scientific Understanding of the 'Alien'

Understanding cultural differences, alterity, and alienness holds another challenge: this challenge, however, cannot be identified unless one differentiates the differences that we use to define what is 'different' or 'alien'. With regard to empirical social science and 'Kulturwissenschaften', such terms as 'cultural differences' 'alterity', and 'alienness' imply the assumption that 'alien' phenomena *can* in fact *be understood*—however laborious and incomplete this process and its results might be. Following this assumption, one is—*in principle*—capable of understanding *everything*, so that nothing needs to remain 'alien' for good. Difference, alterity, and alienness are thus seen as terms describing *bridgeable* distances, or *'surmountable'* experiences. Cultural language games, actions, and life-forms can be translated, which means that as long as one acknowledges the fact that total equivalence of (theoretical) terms and descriptions does not exist, we can assume potential 'understandability' of culturally different and alien phenomena (and, following from this essay, we actually *have to*). Of course, comparative analysis and interpretation, as they are perceived in this essay, share this view.

Such a conclusion initially 'reassured' a scientific community that had been not only confused, but utterly shaken by the sudden occurrence of differences and alienness; this reassurance, however, met strong opposition from exponents of philosophical concepts of *radical* difference, alterity, and alienness. However, I will not focus on the descriptive-logically inconsistent assertion of factual incommensurability of cultures, which would indeed require comparison of such 'incommensurable' phenomena (on the concept of incommensurability also see Rosa, 1999). Bernhard Waldenfels (1998, 1999; Waldenfels and Därmann 1998), among others, has emphasized the radicality of experience, as well as the *radical aspect* inherent in every experience related to alterity and alienness (as well as, one might add, intercultural communication, cooperation, and coexistence). These authors attempt to conceive of the other and the alien 'as such', and thereby 'perpetuate' them; it can be seen as an attempt to 'save' the other and the alien from scientific research, which would, according to the authors, inevitably lead to their elimination by means of understanding. Whether or not this approach belongs instead to the field of philosophical metaphysics, remains to be seen. What is verbalized here from a phenomenological perspective is a well-known *experience*. Basically, what the referred to authors describe is an experience of 'withdrawal' or 'denial': what is to be understood is withdrawn from the process of understanding. This includes the so-called 'self-withdrawal' that affects all attempts to gain 'self-understanding' and 'self-consciousness'. In order to achieve this, one can differentiate between (at least) two concepts of difference, alterity, and alienness: 'Merely' *ontic* (relative, comparative) difference, and *radical* difference, alterity, and alienness.

Emanuel Levinas—as well as those authors who have dedicated themselves to those aspects of his work that are concerned with otherness—has emphasized this point even more. Burkhard Liebsch (2001: 155 et seq.)—among others—has established the above-mentioned (theoretical) distinction. Relative difference is, as Liebsch states, characterized by conscious acts of 'superficial' categorizations, classifications, and group-formations through which human beings achieve positive distinction (which is precisely what has been discussed above). Thinking radical difference, however, does not allow for such processes (of comparison and distinction); it deals with 'the actual otherness' of others, hence it does not comply with the relative 'otherness' that one can find in commensurable phenomena. Radical difference of human beings can be, however, (physically, pre-reflectively, pre-linguistically) experienced prior to any conscious comparison. This kind of radical otherness is of a fundamental and irreducible nature. As fundamental otherness (*Anderheit*), it distinguishes every human being. In contrast to this, relative otherness (*Andersheit*) implies that individuals are distinguished in relation to what they *share*.

The philosophical concept of *Anderheit* perpetuates the relevance of lasting difference and alienness, e.g, of cultures, cultural language games, actions, and life-forms. Radical difference, *Anderheit*, or radical alienness does not result "from comparisons, but from something which has happened to us [Widerfahrnis] [...], something in which we are involved before we can actually adopt a point of view which allows for comparison" (ibid.: 158). This radical difference is not constituted by certain identifiable characteristics or dispositions. One cannot physically perceive, remember, describe, verbalize, or symbolize radical difference. *Who* a person is (in his own or in another person's view) in terms of his qualitative identity is exactly *who he is not* in terms of his radical, fundamental otherness or *Anderheit*. 'The other', or 'alien', is not a concrete, definable 'being'. This applies to close friends and relatives and anonymous, unknown people alike, even though we might feel familiar with the former, while the latter spontaneously might seem 'alien'. Otherness and alienness withdraw from conscious realization, be it in connection with loved ones or situations in which people come face to face with each other for the first time. Thus, 'the other' or 'alien' can only be experienced as a paradoxical 'absent presence' or 'present absence'; there is no such thing as a mere 'presence' or 'absence'.

This withdrawal, which phenomenology conceives of as experience, is of utmost *ethical* importance, as Levinas has pointed out again and again. It is this withdrawal (of the other) that concerns and challenges us. It is the process of witnessing, of 'experiencing the other' that confronts us with radical otherness, alterity, and alienation, and not those epistemological-cognitive comparisons that require a tertium comparationis, i.e., a *common* point of reference with which the 'comparanda' can be judged, according to their similarity or difference. Every such tertium comparationis comprises some similarity and 'sameness' that 'destroy' (Levinas) radical difference, alterity, and alienness. This points to an ethical issue;

200

however, the mentioned withdrawal, as well as the corresponding with-drawal of self might *not only be ethically* relevant since it also has some implications for psychology that deserve further consideration. Contacts between members of different cultures and (inter)cultural interaction re-quire translation of cultural language games, actions, and life-forms, and might enhance the action potential, as well as broaden the horizons of all the individuals involved; at the same time, they comprise an experience that one can 'stay aware of', even when productive acts of comparison have already been performed and practically relevant differences have been identified (possibly in a new language of perspicuous contrast; see Taylor 1981). This experience is exactly what phenomenologists call radical difference, *Anderheit*, and alienness.

Phenomenologists can designate a topic as being a legitimate subject of an action-theoretical and cultural psychology in such a way that it does not restrict the empirical research on that topic to the analysis of ontic, relative, or comparative differences and their psychosocial impli-cations. Of course, analyses of ontic differences are highly relevant and, as has been pointed out before, methodically challenging. However, as soon as cultural differences come into play, psychology cannot confine itself to 'listing' such ontic differences, as is the case with other disci-plines. It is in psychological contexts in particular that the unsettling ex-perience of the 'withdrawing' other and self in relation to intercultural communication, cooperation, and coexistence, which might also decrease one's action potential, becomes a central point of scientific interest. Those who neglect this point withhold and ignore the crucial, yet subtle experiences of radical alienness and alterity. However, these kinds of (cultural) differences are also, regardless of such neglect, inseparably interwoven with our lives.

References

Abel, G. (1989). Interpretations-Welten. Philosophisches Jahrbuch, 96, 1-19.

Abel, G. (1993). Interpretationswelten. Gegenwartsphilosophie jenseits von Essentialismus und Relativismus. Frankfurt a.M.: Suhrkamp.

Abel, T. (1948/1964). The Operation Called Verstehen. In: American Journal of Sociology, 54, 211-218 (reprinted in: Hans Albert (Ed.) (1964): Theorie und Realität (pp. 177-188). Tübingen: Mohr).

Adorno, T.W. (1973). Negative Dialektik. Gesammelte Schriften, Bd. 6. Frankfurt a.M.: Suhrkamp.

Anscombe, G.E.M. (1957). Intention. Oxford: Blackwell.

Apel, K.-O./Manninen, J./Tuomela, R. (Eds.) (1978). Neue Versuche über Erklären und Verstehen. Frankfurt a.M.: Suhrkamp.

Appelsmeyer, H./Billmann-Mahecha, E. (Eds.) (2001). Kulturwissenschaft. Kulturwissenschaftliche Analysen als prozeßorientierte wissenschaftliche Praxis. Weilerswiest: Velbrück.

Assmann, J. (1992). Das kulturelle Gedächtnis. Schrift, Erinnerung und politische Identität in frühen Hochkulturen. München: C.H. Beck.

Bachmann-Medick, D. (Ed.) (1993). Übersetzung als Repräsentation fremder Kulturen. Göttingen: Erich Schmidt.

Baker, G.P./Hacker, P.M.S. (1980). Wittgenstein: Understanding and Meaning? An Analytical Commentary on the Philosophical Investigations. Oxford: Blackwell.

Baker, G.P./Hacker, P.M.S. (1984). Scepticism, Rules and Language. Oxford: Blackwell.

Bal, M. (2002). Kulturanalyse. Frankfurt a.M.: Suhrkamp.

Berg, E./Fuchs, M. (Eds.) (1993). Kultur, soziale Praxis, Text. Die Krise der ethnographischen Repräsentation. Frankfurt a.M.: Suhrkamp.

Boesch, E.E. (1991). Symbolic Action Theory and Cultural Psychology. Berlin, Heidelberg, New York: Springer.

Boesch, E.E. (1998). Sehnsucht. Von der Suche nach Glück und Sinn. Bern, Göttingen, Toronto, Seattle: Huber

Boesch, E.E. (2000). Das lauernde Chaos. Mythen und Fiktionen im Alltag. Bern, Göttingen, Toronto, Seattle: Huber

Boesch, E.E. (2005). Von Kunst bis Terror. Über den Zwiespalt in der Kultur. Göttingen: Vandenhoeck & Ruprecht.

Boesch, E.E./Straub, J. (2006). Kulturpsychologie. Prinzipien, Orientierungen, Konzeptionen. In: G. Trommsdorff/H.-J. Kornadt (Eds.). Kulturvergleichende Psychologie. Enzyklopädie der Psychologie. Serie VII. Themenbereich C "Theorie und Forschung". Göttingen: Hogrefe. (In Press).

Bohnsack, R. (1989). Generation, Milieu, Geschlecht. Ergebnisse aus Gruppendiskussionen mit Jugendlichen. Opladen: Leske + Budrich.

Bohnsack, R. (1991). Rekonstruktive Sozialforschung. Einführung in Methodologie und Praxis qualitativer Forschung. Opladen: Leske + Budrich.

Bohnsack, R. (2003a). Differenzerfahrungen der Identität und des Habitus. Eine empirische Untersuchung auf der Basis der dokumentarischen Methode. In: B. Liebsch/J. Straub (Eds.). Lebensformen im Widerstreit. Integrations- und Identitätskonflikte in pluralen Gesellschaften (pp. 136-160). Frankfurt a.M.: Campus.

Bohnsack, R. (2003b). Dokumentarische Methode und sozialwissenschaftliche Hermeneutik. In: Zeitschrift für Erziehungswissenschaft, 6 (4), 550-570.

Bohnsack, R. (2005). Standards nicht-standardisierter Forschung in den Erziehungs- und Sozialwissenschaften. Zeitschrift für Erziehungswissenschaft, 8, Beiheft 4, 63-81.

Bolten, J. (2001). Interkulturelle Kompetenz. Erfurt: Landeszentrale für Politische Bildung.

Bourdieu, P. (1976). Entwurf einer Theorie der Praxis auf der ethnologischen Grundlage der kabylischen Gesellschaft. Frankfurt a.M.: Suhrkamp.

Bourdieu, P. (1987). Sozialer Sinn. Kritik der theoretischen Vernunft. Frankfurt a.M.: Suhrkamp.

Bourdieu, P./Wacquant Loïc J. D. (1996). Reflexive Anthropologie. Frankfurt a. M.: Suhrkamp.

Bruner, J.S. (1990). Acts of meaning. Cambridge/MA: Harvard University Press.

Burke, P. (2000). Kultureller Austausch. Frankfurt a.M.: Suhrkamp

Clifford, J./Marcus, G. (Eds.) (1986). Writing Culture. The Poetics and Politics of Ethnography. Berkeley: University of California Press.

Cranach, M. von/Harré, R. (Eds.) (1982). The Analysis of Action. Recent Theoretical and Empirical Advances. Cambridge: Cambridge University Press.

Cranach, M. von/Tschan, F. (1997). Handlungspsychologie. In: Straub, J./Kempf, W./Werbik, H. (Eds.). Psychologie. Eine Einführung. Grundlagen, Methoden, Perspektiven (pp. 124-158). München: Deutscher Taschenbuch Verlag.

Danto, A.C. (1980 [1965]). Analytische Philosophie der Geschichte. Frankfurt a.M.: Suhrkamp.

Deppermann, A. (1999). Gespräche analysieren. Opladen: Leske + Budrich.

Deppermann, A./Lucius-Hoehne, G. (2002). Rekonstruktion narrativer Identität. Ein Arbeitsbuch zur Analyse narrativer Interviews. Opladen: Leske + Budrich.

Dilthey, W. (1957 [1895, 1906]). [Über vergleichende Psychologie.] Beiträge zum Studium der Individualität. In: W. Dilthey. Gesammelte Schriften V: Die geistige Welt. Einleitung in die Philosophie des Lebens. Abhandlungen zur Grundlegung der Geisteswissenschaften. Herausgegeben von Georg Misch. (pp. 241-316). Stuttgart: Teubner & Göttingen: Vandenhoeck & Ruprecht, (Original, nur teilweise publiziert 1895 und 1906).

Dilthey, W. (1957/1894). Ideen über eine beschreibende und zergliedernde Psychologie. In W. Dilthey. Gesammelte Schriften V: Die geistige Welt. Einleitung in die Philosophie des Lebens. Erste Hälfte. Abhandlungen zur Grundlegung der Geisteswissenschaften (pp. 139-240). Herausgegeben von Georg Misch. Stuttgart: Teubner & Göttingen: Vandenhoeck & Ruprecht.

Dray, W. (1957). Laws and Explanation in History. Oxford: Clarendon Press.

Eckensberger, L.H. (1991). Die Perspektive einer transkulturellen Psychologie und die Notwendigkeit, Psychologie als Kulturwissenschaft zu betreiben. Vortrag, gehalten auf dem Kongreß "Erneuerung der Psychologie" am 17.-20.2.1991 in Berlin. Saarbrücken: unpublished manuscript.

Eggert, H./Profitlich, U./Schierpe, K.R. (Eds.). Geschichte als Literatur. Formen und Grenzen der Repräsentation von Vergangenheit. Stuttgart: Metzler.

Flick, U./Kardorff; E. von/Steinke, I. (Eds.) (2005). Qualitative Forschung. Ein Handbuch. Reinbek: Rowohlt.

Fuchs, M. (2001). Der Verlust der Totalität. Die Anthropologie der Kultur. In: H. Appelsmeyer/E. Billmann-Mahecha (Eds.). Kulturwissenschaft. Felder einer prozessorientierten wissenschaftlichen Praxis (pp. 18-53). Weilerswist: Velbrück.

Gadamer, H.-G. (1930/1967). Praktisches Wissen. In: H.-G. Gadamer. Kleine Schriften I. Philosophie. Hermeneutik. Tübingen: Mohr.

Gadamer, H. (1986 [1960]). Truth and Method. New York: Continuum.

Gerhardt, U. (1985). Patientenkarrieren. Eine medizinsoziologische Studie. Frankfurt a.M.: Suhrkamp.

Gerhardt, U. (1986). Verstehende Strukturanalyse: Die Konstruktion von Idealtypen als Analyseschritt bei der Auswertung qualitativer Forschungsmaterialien. In H.-G. Soeffner (Ed.). Sozialstruktur und soziale Typik (pp. 31-83). Frankfurt a.M., New York: Campus.

Giddens, A. (1984 [1976]). Interpretative Soziologie. Frankfurt a.m.: Campus.

Giddens, A. (1988 [1984]). Die Konstitution der Gesellschaft. Grundzüge einer Theorie der Strukturierung. Mit einer Einführung von Hans Joas. Frankfurt a.m.: Campus.

Göller, T. (2000): Kulturverstehen. Grundprobleme einer epistemologischen Theorie der Kulturalität und kulturellen Erlenntnis. Würzburg: Königshausen & Neumann.

Goodman, N. (1979). Ways of Worldmaking. Indianapolis: Hackett.

Glaser, B.G. (1978). Theoretical Sensitivity. Advances in the Methodology of Grounded Theory. Mill Valley: The Sociology Press.

Glaser, B.G./Strauss, A.L. (1967). The Discovery of Grounded Theory. Strategies for Qualitative Research. Chicago: Aldine.

Greve, W. (1994). Handlungsklärung. Die psychologische Erklärung menschlicher Handlungen. Bern: Huber.

Greve, W. (2004). Handeln in Widerfahrniskontexten. Handlungsabsichten, Handlungsbedingungen und Bedingungen von Handlungsabsichten. In: F. Jäger/J. Straub (Eds.). Handbuch der Kulturwissenschaften. Band 2: Paradigmen und Disziplinen (pp. 220-248). Stuttgart: Metzler.

Groeben, N. (1986). Handeln, Tun, Verhalten als Einheiten einer verstehend-erklärenden Psychologie. Wissenschaftstheoretischer Überblick und Programmentwurf zur Integration von Hermeneutik und Empirismus. Tübingen: Francke.

Grondin, J. (1991). Einführung in die philosophische Hermeneutik. Darmstadt: Wissenschaftliche Buchgesellschaft.

Habermas, J. (1981a). Theorie des kommunikativen Handelns. Frankfurt a.M.: Suhrkamp. Band 1: Handlungsrationalität und gesellschaftliche Rationalisierung. Frankfurt a.M.: Suhrkamp.

Habermas, J. (1981b). Theorie des kommunikativen Handelns. Band 2: Zur Kritik der funktionalistischen Vernunft. Frankfurt a.M.: Suhrkamp.

Habermas, J. (1967/1982). Ein Literaturbericht: Zur Logik der Sozialwissenschaften. In: J. Habermas. Zur Logik der Sozialwissenschaften (pp. 89-330). Fünfte, erweiterte Auflage. Frankfurt a.M.: Suhrkamp.

Hacking, I. (1995). Rewriting the Soul. Multiple Personality and the the Sciences of Memory. Princeton: Princeton University Press.

Heidegger, M. (1927). Sein und Zeit. Tübingen: Max Niemeyer.

Hempel, C.G.(1942). The Function of General Laws in History. The Journal of Philosophy, 39, 35-48.

Hempel, C.G./Oppenheim, P. (1948). Studies in the Logic of Explanation. Philosophy of Science, 15, 135-175.

Horstmann, A. (2004). Positionen des Verstehens—Hermeneutik zwischen Wissenschaft und Lebenspraxis. In: F. Jäger/J. Straub (Eds.). Handbuch der Kulturwissenschaften. Band 2: Paradigmen und Disziplinen (pp. 341-363). Stuttgart: Metzler.

Jäger, F./Liebsch, B./Rüsen, J./Straub, J. (2004). Handbuch der Kulturwissenschaften. 3 Bände. Stuttgart: Metzler.

Jullien, François (2002). Der Umweg über China. Ein Ortswechsel des Denkens. Berlin: Merve.

Kant, I. (1790/2000). Critique of the Power of Judgment. Cambridge: University of Cambridge Press.

Kelle, U. (1994). Empirisch begründete Theoriebildung. Zur Logik und Methodologie interpretativer Sozialforschung. Weinheim: Deutscher Studien Verlag.

Kelle, U./Kluge, S. (1999). Vom Einzelfall zum Typus: Fallvergleich und Fallkontrastierung in der qualitativen Sozialforschung. Opladen: Leske + Budrich.

Kögler, H.-H. (1992). Die Macht des Dialogs. Kritische Hermeneutik nach Gadamer, Foucault und Rorty. Stuttgart: Metzler.

Kölbl, C. (2004). Geschichtsbewußtsein im Jugendalter. Grundzüge einer Entwicklungspsychologie historischer Sinnbildung. Bielefeld: Transcript.

Kölbl, C./Straub, J. (2001). Historical Consciousness in Youth Age. Theoretical and Exemplary Empirical Analyses [118 paragraphs] (auch dt: Geschichtsbewußtsein im Jugendalter. Theoretische und empirische Analysen. In: Forum Qualitative Sozialforschung/Forum: Qualitative Social Research, [On-line Journal] 2, 3 [http://www.qualitative-research.net/fqs/fqs-eng.htm]

Kölbl, C./Straub, J. (2003). Geschichtsbewusstsein als psychologischer Begriff. In: Journal für Psychologie, 11 (1), 75-102.

Kripke, S. (1987 [1982]). Wittgenstein über Regeln und Privatsprache. Eine elementare Darstellung. Frankfurt a.M.: Suhrkamp.

Kurthen, M. (1994). Hermeneutische Kognitionswissenschaft. Die Krise der Orthodoxie. Bonn: Djre.

Lamnek, U. (1995). Qualitative Sozialforschung. Band 1: Methodologie. Band 2: Methoden und Techniken. Weinheim: Psychologie Verlags Union.

Langer, S. K. (1942). Philosophy in a New Key: A Study in the Symbolism of Reason, Rite, and Art. Cambridge/Mass.: Harvard University Press.

Lenk, H. (1978). Handlung als Interpretationskonstrukt. Entwurf einer konstituenten- und beschreibungstheoretischen Handlungsphilosophie. In H. Lenk (Ed.). Handlungstheorien interdisziplinär II. Handlungserklärungen und philosophische Handlungsinterpretation. Erster Halbband (pp. 279-350). München: Fink.

Lenk, H. (1987). Zwischen Sozialpsychologie und Sozialphilosophie (pp. 183-206). Frankfurt a.M.: Suhrkamp.

Lenk, H. (1993). Philosophie und Interpretation. Vorlesungen zur Entwicklung konstruktionistischer Interpretationsansätze. Frankfurt a.M.: Suhrkamp.

Liebsch, B. (2001). Zerbrechliche Lebensformen. Widerstreit, Differenz, Gewalt. Berlin: Akademie Verlag.

Luhmann, N. (1990). Die Wissenschaft der Gesellschaft. Frankfurt a.M.: Suhrkamp.

Lütterfelds, W./Roser, A. (1999). Der Konflikt der Lebensformen in Wittgensteins Philosophie der Sprache. Frankfurt a.M.: Suhrkamp.

Mannheim, K. (1952 [1931]). Wissenssoziologie. In: K. Mannheim. Ideologie und Utopie (pp. 227-267). Frankfurt a. M.: Klostermann.

Mannheim, K. (1964 [1921/22]). Beiträge zur Theorie der Weltanschauungsinterpretation. In: K. Mannheim. Wissenssoziologie (pp. 91-154). Neuwied: Luchterhand.

Mannheim, K. (1980). Strukturen des Denkens. (Unveröffentlichte Manuskripte 1922-1925). Frankfurt a. M.: Suhrkamp.

Matthes, J. (1992a). The Operation Called "Vergleichen". In: J. Matthes (Ed.). Zwischen den Kulturen? Die Sozialwissenschaften vor dem Problem des Kulturvergleichs. Soziale Welt, Sonderband 8, (pp. 75-102). Göttingen: Schwartz.

Matthes, J. (1992b). Über das Erfahren von Erfahrung (oder: Von den Schwierigkeiten des erfahrungswissenschaftlich orientierten Soziologen, mit gesellschaftlicher Erfahrung umzugehen). In: H.J. Schneider/R. Inhetveen (Eds.). Enteignen uns die Wissenschaften? Zum Verhältnis zwischen Erfahrung und Empirie (pp. 101-123). München: Fink.

Mayring, P. (1990). Qualitative Inhaltsanalyse: Grundlagen und Techniken. Deutscher Studienverlag: Weinheim.

Miller, J.G. (1997). Theoretical Issues in Cultural Psychology. In: J.W. Berry/Y.H. Poortinga/J. Pandey (Eds.). Handbook of Cross-Cultural Psychology. Vol. 1: Theory and Method (pp. 85-128). Second Edition. Boston, London, Toronto, Sydney, Tokyo, Singapore: Allyn and Bacon.

Mischel, T. (1968). Psychology and Explanation of Human Behaviour. In: N.S. Care/Landesman, C. (Eds.). Readings in the Theory of Action (pp. 214-237). Blomington: Indiana University Press.

Mittelstraß, J. (1974). Erfahrung und Begründung. In: J. Mittelstraß. Die Möglichkeit von Wissenschaft (pp. 56-83). Frankfurt a.M.: Suhrkamp.

Müller, K.E. (2003). Das Unbehagen mit der Kultur. In: K.E. Müller. Phänomen Kultur. Perspektiven und Aufgaben der Kulturwissenschaften (pp. 13-48). Bielefeld: transcript.

Müller-Jacquier, B. (1986): Interkulturelle Verstehensstrategien— Vergleich und Empathie. In: G. Neuner (Ed.). Kulturkontraste im DaF-Unterricht (pp. 33-84). München: Iudicium.

Nentwig-Gesemann, I. (2001): Die Typenbildung der dokumentarischen Methode. In: R. Bohnsack/I. Nentwig-Gesemann/A.-M. Nohl (Eds.). Die dokumentarische Methode und ihre Forschungspraxis (pp. 275-300). Opladen: Leske + Budrich.

Nohl, A.-M. (2001a): Migration und Differenzerfahrung. Junge Einheimische und Migranten im rekonstruktiven Milieuvergleich. Opladen: Leske + Budrich.

Nohl, A.-M. (2001b): Komparative Analyse: Forschungspraxis und Methodologie dokumentarischer Interpretation. In: R. Bohnsack/I. Nentwig-Gesemann/A.-M. Nohl (Eds.). Die dokumentarische Methode und ihre Forschungspraxis (pp. 253-273). Opladen: Leske + Budrich.

Nünning, A./Nünning, V. (Eds.) (2003). Konzepte der Kulturwissenshaften. Theoretische Grundlagen, Ansätze, Perspektiven. Stuttgart, Weimar: Metzler.

Pike, K.L. (1954). Emic and Etic Standpoints for the Description of Behavior. In: K.L. Pike (Ed.). Language in Relation to a Unified Theory of the Structure of Human Behavior. Glendale/IL: Summer Institute of Linguistics.

Pike, K.L. (1967). Language in Relation to a Unified Theory of the Structure of Human Behavior. 2nd (enlarged) edition. The Hague: Mouton.

Polanyi, M. (1962). Personal Knowledge. Towards a Post-Critical Philosophy. Chicago, London: University of Chicago Press.

Polanyi, M. (1969). Knowing and Being. Essays edited by Marjorie Grene. Chicago/London: University of Chicago Press.

Popp-Baier, U. (2006). Zwischen Himmel und Erde: Kulturwissenschaftliche Überlegungen zur gegenwärtigen Religionspsychologie. Handlung, Kultur, Interpretation. Zeitschrift für Sozial- und Kulturwissenschaften, 15 (1), 132-148.

Putnam, H. (1988). Repräsentation and Reality. Cambridge/Mass.: MIT Press.

Putnam, H. (1990). Realism With a Human Face. Cambridge/Mass.: Harvard University Press.

Putnam, H. (1997). Für eine Erneuerung der Philosophie. Stuttgart: Reclam.

Raphael, L. (2004). Habitus und sozialer Sinn: Der Ansatz der Praxistheorie Pierre Bourdieus. In: F. Jäger/J. Straub (Eds.). Handbuch der Kulturwissenschaften. Band 2: Paradigmen und Disziplinen (pp. 266-276). Stuttgart: Metzler.

Reckwitz, A. (2000). Die Transformation der Kulturtheorien. Zur Entwicklung eines Theorieprogramms. Weilerswist: Velbrück.

Reichertz, J. (1993). Abduktives Schlußfolgern und Typen(re)konstruktion. In T. Jung/S. Müller-Doohm (Eds.). "Wirklichkeit" im Deutungsprozeß. Verstehen und Methoden in den Sozialwissenschaften (pp. 258-282). Frankfurt a.M.: Suhrkamp.

Renn, J. (2005). Die gemeinsame menschliche Handlungsweise. Das doppelte Übersetzungsproblem des sozialwissenschaftlichen Kulturvergleichs. In: Srubar, I./Renn, J./Wenzel, U. (Eds.). Kulturen vergleichen. Wiesbaden. Verlag für Sozialwissenschaften. (In Press).

Renn, J. (2006). Übersetzungsverhältnisse. Perspektiven einer pragmatischen Gesellschaftstheorie. Weilerswist: Velbrück.

Renn, J./Straub, J./Shimada, S. (Eds.) (2002). Übersetzung als Medium des Kulturverstehens und sozialer Integration. Frankfurt a. M./New York: Campus.

Ricœur, P. (1988). Zeit und Erzählung. Band I: Zeit und historische Erzählung. München: Fink.

Ricœur, P. (1991). Zeit und Erzählung. Band III: Die erzählte Zeit. München: Fink.

Riedel, M. (1978). Verstehen oder Erklären. Zur Theorie und Geschichte der hermeneutischen Wissenschaften. Stuttgart: Klett-Cotta.

Rorty, R. (1979). Philosophy and the Mirror of Nature. Princeton: Princeton University Press.

Rorty, R. (1982). Consequences of Pragmatism. Minneapolis: University of Minnesota Press.

Rorty, R. (1989). Contingency, Irony and Solidarity. Cambridge: Cambridge University Press.

Rosa, H. (1999). Lebensformen vergleichen und verstehen. Eine Theorie der dimensionalen Kommensurabilität von Kontexten und Kulturen. Handlung Kultur Interpretation. Zeitschrift für Sozial- und Kulturwissenschaften, 8 (1), 10-42.

Said, E.W. (1979). Orientalism. New York: Vintage.

Scholtz, O.R. (2001). Verstehen und Rationalität. Untersuchungen zu den Grundlagen von Hermeneutik und Sprachphilosophie. Frankfurt a.M.: Klostermann.

Schulte, J. (1990). Chor und Gesetz. Wittgenstein im Kontext. Frankfurt a.M.: Suhrkamp.

Schütz, A. (1971). Gesammelte Aufsätze. Band 1. Das Problem der sozialen Wirklichkeit. Teil I. Mit einer Einführung von Aron Gurwitsch und einem Vorwort von H. L. van Breda. Den Haag: Nijhoff.

Schütz, A. (1972). Gesammelte Aufsätze. Band 2. Studien zur soziologischen Theorie. Den Haag: Nijhoff.

Schurz, G. (1988). Erklären und Verstehen in der Wissenschaft, München: Oldenbourg.

Schurz, G. (2004). Erklären und Verstehen: Tradition, Transformation und Aktualität einer klassischen Kontroverse. In: F. Jäger/J. Straub (Eds.) (2004). Handbuch der Kulturwissenschaften. Band 2: Paradigmen und Disziplinen (pp. 156-174). Stuttgart: Metzler.

Schwemmer, O. (1987). Handlung und Struktur. Zur Wissenschaftstheorie der Kulturwissenschaften. Frankfurt a.M.: Suhrkamp.

Shimada, S. (1994). Grenzgänge—Fremdgänge. Japan und Europa im Kulturvergleich. Frankfurt a.M.: Campus.

Shimada, S. (2000). Die Erfindung Japans. Kulturelle Wechselwirkungen und nationale Identitätskonstruktion. Frankfurt a.M., New York: Campus.

Soeffner, H.-G. (1989a). Alltagsverstand und Wissenschaft. Anmerkungen zu einem alltäglichen Mißverständnis von Wissenschaft. In ders. Auslegung des Alltags—Der Alltag der Auslegung. Zur wissenssoziologischen Konzeption einer sozialwissenschaftlichen Hermeneutik. Frankfurt a.M.: Suhrkamp, 10-50.

Soeffner, H.-G. (1989b). Prämissen einer sozialwissenschaftlichen Hermeneutik. In ders. Auslegung des Alltags—Der Alltag der Auslegung. Zur wissenssoziologischen Konzeption einer sozialwissenschaftlichen Hermeneutik. Frankfurt a.M.: Suhrkamp, 66-97.

Spranger, E. (1921): Lebensformen. Geisteswissenschaftliche Psychologie und Ethik der Persönlichkeit. Zweite, völlig neu bearbeitete und erweiterte Auflage. Halle: Niemeyer.

Straub, J. (1989). Historisch-psychologische Biographieforschung. Theoretische, methodologische und methodische Argumentationen in systematischer Absicht. Mit einem Vorwort von Heiner Legewie. Heidelberg: Asanger.

Straub, J. (1992). Von der Information zu Sprache und Praxis. In: Handlung Kultur Interpretation. Bulletin für Psychologie und Nachbardisziplinen, 1 (1), 79-82.

Straub, J. (1993). Geschichte, Biographie und friedenspolitisches Handeln. Biographieanalytische und sozialpsychologische Studien auf der Basis von narrativen Interviews mit Naturwissenschaftlern und Naturwissenschaftlerinnen. Opladen: Leske + Budrich.

Straub, J. (1999a). Handlung, Interpretation, Kritik. Grundzüge einer textwissenschaftlichen Handlungs- und Kulturpsychologie. Berlin, New York: de Gruyter.

Straub, J. (1999b). Verstehen, Kritik, Anerkennung. Das Eigene und das Fremde in den interpretativen Wissenschaften. Göttingen: Wallstein.

Straub, J. (2001). Psychologie und Kultur, Psychologie als Kulturwissenschaft. In: H. Appelsmeyer/E. Billmann-Mahecha (Eds.). Kulturwissenschaft. Kulturwissenschaftliche Analysen als prozeßorientierte wissenschaftliche Praxis (pp. 125-168). Weilerswiest: Velbrück.

Straub, J. (2003a). Sprangers Lebensformen. In: Burkhard Liebsch u. Jürgen Straub (Hg.): Lebensformen im Widerstreit (pp. 217-296). Frankfurt a. M., New York: Campus.

Straub, J. (2003b). Was hat die Psychologie unter den Kulturwissenschaften verloren? In: K.E. Müller (Ed.): Phänomen Kultur. Perspektiven und Aufgaben der Kulturwissenschaften (pp. 131-156). Bielefeld: transcript.

Straub, J. (2003c). Psychologie und die Kulturen in einer globalisierten Welt. In: A. Thomas (Ed.): Kulturvergleichende Psychologie (pp. 543-566). Göttingen u.a.: Hogrefe.

Straub, J. (2004a). Kulturwissenschaftliche Psychologie. In: F. Jäger/ J. Straub (Eds.): Handbuch der Kulturwissenschaften. Band 2: Paradigmen und Disziplinen (pp. 568-591). Stuttgart: Metzler.

Straub, J. (2004b). Identität. In: F. Jäger/B. Liebsch (Eds.): Kulturwissenschaften. Ein Handbuch. Band 1: Kontexte und Grundbegriffe (pp. 277-303). Stuttgart: Metzler.

Straub, J. (2004c): Personal and Collective Identity. In: H. Friese (Ed.). Identities (pp. 57-76). New York, Oxford: Berghan.

Straub, J. (Ed.) (2005). Narration, Identity and Historical Consciousness. The psychological construction of time and history. New York, Oxford: Berghan.

Straub, J. (2006). Historische Positionen und Entwicklungslinien einer Kultur integrierenden Psychologie. In: G. Trommsdorff/H.-J. Kornadt (Eds.): Kulturvergleichende Psychologie. Enzyklopädie der Psychologie. Serie VII. Themenbereich C "Theorie und Forschung". Göttingen: Hogrefe. (In Press).

Straub, J./Shimada, S. (1999). Relationale Hermeneutik im Kontext interkulturellen Verstehens. In: Deutsche Zeitschrift für Philosophie, 47 (3), 449-477.

211

Straub, J./Thomas, A. (2003): Positionen, Ziele und Entwicklungslinien der kulturvergleichenden Psychologie. In: A. Thomas (Ed.): Kulturvergleichende Psychologie (pp. 29-80). Göttingen u.a.: Hogrefe.

Straub, J./Weidemann, A./Weidemann, D. (2007). Handbuch Interkulturelle Kommunikation und Interkulturelle Kompetenz. Stuttgart: Metzler.

Straub, J./Weidemann, D. (2006). Die verstehend-erklärende Psychologie und das Forschungsprogramm Subjektive Theorien. Göttingen: Vandenhoeck & Ruprecht.

Strauss, A. (1991 [1987]). Grundlagen qualitativer Sozialforschung. Datenanalyse und Theoriebildung in der empirischen soziologischen Forschung. Mit einem Vorwort von Bruno Hildenbrand. München: Fink.

Taylor, C. (1981). Understanding and the Explanation in the Geisteswissenschaften. In: S.H. Holtzmann/C. Leich (Eds.). Wittgenstein: To Follow a Rule (pp. 191-210). London: Routledge & Kegan Paul.

Taylor, E.W. (1994). A Learning Model for Becoming Interculturally Competent. In: International Journal of International Relations, 18 (3), 389-408.

Thomas, A. (2001). Interkulturelle Kompetenz—Grundlagen, Probleme und Konzepte. Erwägen Wissen Ethik—Streitformen für Erwägungskultur, 14, 137-228.

Valsiner, J. (1988). Culture is not an Independent Variable: A Lesson from Cross-Cultural Psychology. Paper Presented at the 24th International Congress of Psychology, Sydney.

Varela, F. (1990). Kognitionswissenschaft—Kognitionstechnik. Eine Skizze aktueller Perspektiven. Frankfurt a.M.: Suhrkamp.

Waldenfels, B. (1998). Grenzen der Normalisierung. Studien zur Phänomenologie des Fremden, Band 2. Frankfurt a. M.: Suhrkamp.

Waldenfels, B. (1999). Topographie des Fremden. Studien zur Phänomenologie des Fremden, Band 1. Frankfurt a. M.: Suhrkamp.

Waldenfels, B./Därmann, I. (Eds.) (1998). Der Anspruch des Anderen. Perspektiven phänomenologischer Ethik. München: Fink.

Weidemann, D. (2004). Interkulturelles Lernen. Erfahrungen mit dem chinesischen "Gesicht": Deutsche in Taiwan. Bielefeld: transcript.

Welsch, W. (1999). Transkulturalität. In: Interkulturalität—Grundprobleme der Kulturbegegnung. Mainzer Universitätsgespräche Sommersemester 1998 (pp. 45-72). Trier: Paulinus-Druckerei.

Werbik, H. (1978). Handlungstheorien. Stuttgart: Kohlhammer.

Werbik, H. (1984). Über die nomologische Auslegung von Handlungstheorien. In: H. Lenk (Ed.). Handlungstheorien interdisziplinär III.

Verhaltenswissenschaftliche und psychologische Handlungstheorien. Zweiter Halbband (pp. 633-651). München: Fink.

Winch, P. (1958). The Idea of a Social Science and its Relation to Philosophy. London: Routledge and Kegan Paul.

Wittgenstein, L. (1984). Philosophische Untersuchungen. Werkausgabe Band 1. Frankfurt a. M.: Suhrkamp.

Wright, G.H. von (1974 [1971]). Erklären und Verstehen. Frankfurt a.M.: Athenäum.

Zielke, B. (2004). Kognition und soziale Praxis. Der Soziale Konstruktionismus und die Perspektiven einer postkognitivistischen Psychologie. Bielefeld: transcript

Zitterbarth, W. (1987). Postmaterialismus und Lebensorientierung. Systematische Argumentation und exemplarische Erfahrungsbildung für eine Psychologie in kulturwissenschaftlicher Absicht. Frankfurt a.M.: Lang.

HISTORICALLY STRUCTURED SAMPLING (HSS): HOW CAN PSYCHOLOGY'S METHODOLOGY BECOME TUNED IN TO THE REALITY OF THE HISTORICAL NATURE OF CULTURAL PSYCHOLOGY?

JAAN VALSINER & TATSUYA SATO

Whom do we Study? The Question of Sampling

A major problem that blocks research in cultural psychology from developing new methodology is the issue of sampling. This block is due to the social norm widely accepted by psychologists that sampling should be 'random' and 'representative'—both of these labels cover up reality that is necessarily very different from these set ideal in everyday practice (see Table 1) we here prove that such ideals of sampling are theoretically flawed and cannot be implemented even if their applicability were to be logistically achievable.

Sampling is an inevitable operation in any research project. Any research effort—unless it analyzes the whole realm of the given phenomena—requires some way of sampling. Some specimens of the existing (known) pool of all specimens are selected—which means others are left out. The researcher generalizes from the studied specimens (sample) to all specimens (population)—and is likely to assume that what is generalized as it is posited to be applicable to the unstudied cases. Yet, as we show, this assumption is unwarranted, since it is not the cases that are in our focus of investigation, but the processes that are represented in each case.

As is obvious from Table 1, different traditions in the social sciences have tried to modify the canonical version of sampling—that of random sampling—in ways that fit their epistemological goals (theoretical or representative sampling) or by giving particular practical means of finding research participants a fancy label (e.g., convenience, practice-based, etc.). That makes sense since the belief in random sampling is nothing more than a belief—since in practice the randomness of any single choice (e.g., of a specimen from a population to make a sample) is in principle impossible to ascertain[1]. Yet there is a bigger issue beyond the practical impossibility of randomness of the "random sampling"—the role of the open-systemic phenomena in the selection schemes of sampling. The crucial issue for cultural psychology is whether any of the sampling schemes open researchers' access to the phenomena of culture in psychological processes, or keep these phenomena out of the scientists' reach. Psychology at large has been active in keeping researchers away from the crucial aspects of their phenomena (see demonstration in the case of personality inventories—Valsiner, Diriwächter, and Sauck 2004). But what is the situation in cultural psychology—the "up and coming" area in psychology (Cole 1996)?

Culture as a Problem for the Social Sciences

Culture is a historically emergent phenomenon. It emerged from the historical interchange of the species that was to become Homo sapiens, and the environment. In Max Weber's words, "[...] culture is a finite segment of the meaningless infinity of the world process, a segment *on which human beings confer meaning and significance*" (Weber 1949: 81, added emphasis).

Weber's comment recognizes the unique, personal nature of experience that becomes organized by cultural tools—instruments and signs (semiotic mediators). It is the functional focus on cultural tools used within the psychological functioning of human beings that distinguishes cultural psychology from its cross-cultural cousin (see Valsiner 2003 for elaboration of this distinction).

Our contemporary cultural psychology looks upon human psyche as social in its ontogeny and constructive in its microgenesis (Valsiner 2000). Thus, cultural psychology *is necessarily* a *historical psychology*—where the question of higher-level phenomena as those relate to the lower-level psychological functions is the central question. Relating of these levels when seen in time entails the synthesis of new (higher) levels, and de-differentiation (demolition) of previous higher structures.

---

1   Randomness of a series of numbers can be mathematically determined—but statements about randomness (or nonrandomness) of each single number in the series cannot (see Chaitin 1975). Social scientists' sampling efforts are necessarily single decisions—take X rather than Y or Z at time t, and thus cannot be random, even if "randomization machines" like tossing coins, using random number generators, etc. are practically used in the sampling process.

Emergence and dissipation go hand in hand in the cultural organization of human psychological life.

Random:	A sample of objects is selected for study from a larger group (called population). Each object is chosen by procedures that are designated to be random— it is "by chance" that the objects are selected. Each object in the population has an equal chance of being selected into the sample. Within that sampling mode sub-types exist: cluster sampling (population is divided into clusters, followed by random selection of the clusters), or independent sampling (samples selected from population are mutually free of affecting one another).
Representative:	The act of selection is based on the proportional representativeness of the objects in the population. The sample includes a comparable cross-section of varied backgrounds that are present in the population. Sub-types are stratified sampling (first divide the population into sub-groups, then select from these groups) and matched sampling (each object in one group is matched with a counterpart in another).
Theoretical:	the underlying theory if the researcher determines whom to select for the study. Our new introduction—HSS—belongs here.
Practice based:	A practitioner—a clinical psychologist, teacher, nurse— who wants to do research on their field and experience treats his or her clients as research subjects. Ethical protections of subjects' rights are in place, but the agreement by persons to participate is set up within the field of their indebtedness to the researcher as the provider of some other practically needed services.
One-point breakthrough:	Even if researchers hope to access the ideal kinds of subjects, exceptional circumstances and/or special conditions may prohibit that. In such cases, the researchers struggle to access anyone who accepts the research proposal—literally fighting against tight access barriers. Undoubtedly such sampling is far from being 'nonbiased' or 'random'—yet there is no need to criticize such a sampling as "biased". Depending on the research theme, it's

	preferable to do something rather than nothing. And it may develop into a version of relational network based sampling as below.
Relational network based (i.e. the 'Snowball Method'):	The researcher engages the members of the first selected (and agreeing) participants to bring to the sample the members of their relationships networks. A crude sub-type is quote sampling (researcher may be given a "quota" of how many and what kinds of objects s/he needs to bring into the study.
Convenient:	Researchers in universities ask students to participate in their research. Cognitive Psychologists like to regard students as adults, developmental psychologists like to regard them as adolescent, and comparative psychologists like to regard them as human beings. So university students are convenient samples for psychology studies.
Capricious:	The researcher takes whoever happens to agree to participate.

Table 1: Different notions of sampling in the social sciences

The issue of how to make sense of part◇whole relationships that has haunted psychology all through its history re-surfaces in contemporary cultural psychology. In cultural psychology, it is that latter link—"vertical consistency" between general assumptions, theories, methods, and phenomena (Branco and Valsiner 1997) that determines the adequacy of one or another look at sampling. The issue of sampling cannot be taken out of a wider epistemological context where the question—how do we arrive at generalized knowledge—is central for our inquiry.

Design Failures: 'Blind Spots' of 'Random' Sampling

Despite use of the notion of population in our methodological discourse, there is a paradox—we talk about population as if it were fixed and finite (even if not possible to study, in full—for practical reasons), but in reality it is fluid, ever-changing, and infinite[2]. The population does not exist

---

2   The traditional statistical inference philosophy recognizes the unknowability of the "hypothetically infinite population" but *considers it to be stable in its infinity*. That legitimizes the notion of getting to know it through random sampling techniques (Gigerenzer and Murray 1987: 15) and the reliance on the "law of large numbers". In contrast, *if the infinite nature of population is assumed to entail any form of change of the*

as a given—it develops as the specimens in it act, produce, reproduce, and change their own ways of being. Thus, in reality the conglomerate we call "population" is some collectivity of functioning systems that not just "merely is" but exists in its own processes of movement—of the whole, and of its parts. The basic assumptions of the systemic (in contrast with the elementaristic) view on the phenomenon of "population" make the difference in the ways the notion of sampling becomes crafted. Population is a collection of specimens assumed to be independent and coexistent with one another. Population is not a system—a unit where different parts are in functional relationships with one another.

Psychology has borrowed from the business accounting ethos—rather than physics—the notion of selecting a sample of independent objects from a bigger pile of a similarly designated object universe. The examples usually used in introductory psychology classes entail the omni-powerful researcher involved in the task of drawing marbles out of an urn, supposedly randomly—as given in Figure 1.

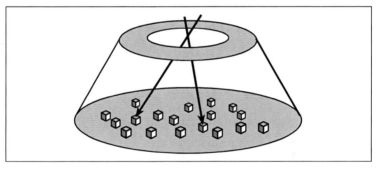

Figure 1: A common example of how sampling works in case of nonsystemic phenomena.

This action—drawing marbles out of an urn—exemplifies the tradition of an atomistic world view where no systemic organization needs to be presumed. The objects to be sampled are assumed to be independent of one another, and of the context, and not possess any "counter-intentionality"[3] to the sampling efforts.

Given the surface of the box and the homogeneous nature of each of the marbles, each of them can be said to "have" equal probability of be-

---

whole population, random sampling would lead to creation of systematic artifacts.

3   The ideas of sampling do not consider the prerogative of sampled subjects to refuse to participate, or to undermine the investigation by way of self-presentational or any other intentional goal. The marbles do not "escape" the sampling efforts.

ing drawn to the sample[4]—and hence any sub-group of the marbles drawn would provide evidence about the homogeneous category of these objects. This situation is still the same in case the marbles become unevenly distributed in the box (Figure 2)—as long as they are homogeneous and the boundaries of the box ("search ground") are known, the sampling of the objects is sufficient for generalization from a homogeneous sample to a homogeneous population.

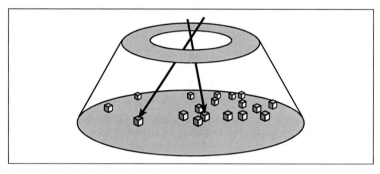

Figure 2: A physical example of how sampling still works in case of nonsystemic phenomena—unevenly distributed in the box

The picture becomes complicated if the different specimens of the population vary quantitatively—while maintaining their homogeneous class nature in qualitative terms (Figure 3). Some marbles are bigger; others smaller—the sample drawn from the box will be heterogeneous in quantity while still being homogeneous in quality.

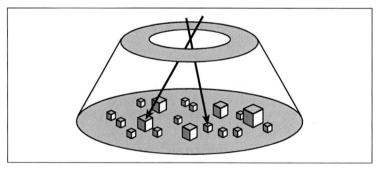

Figure 3: An example of how sampling marginally works in case of nonsystemic phenomena that form a quantitatively heterogeneous class

---

4   Note the attribution error in this way of phrasing the issue—the language use implies some property that is inherent in each of the marbles, while the actual outcome of being selected (or not) depends fully on the interaction of the selected marble and the field.

Such separation of the qualitative and quantitative features of objects of investigation has been axiomatically accepted in psychology, and has made certain uses of statistical techniques (e.g., correlations—Valsiner, 1986) possible. Yet this assumption is untenable—in any systemic phenomena, quality and quantity are directly mutually co-constructive—quantitative alterations lead to qualitative irreversible shifts (Prigogine 1978, 1987).

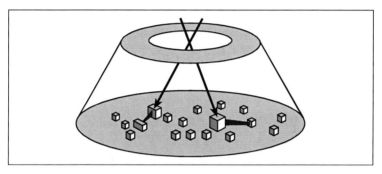

Figure 4: An example of how sampling fails to work in case of nonsystemic—yet linked—phenomena

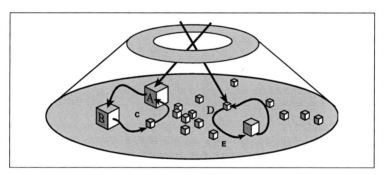

Figure 5: An example of how sampling creates an error in case of treating systemic phenomena as if these were nonsystemic objects

Thus, traditional sampling as described in Figure 3 misses the most crucial issue—that of systemic organization. Figure 4 illustrates the case where different systemic linkages exist between the members of the population. Yet, these links are not (yet) examples of systemic interdependencies; rather, they are physical links. In the case depicted in Figure 5, the traditional sampling (that would create a "sample" {A, D}) is not representative of the systemic relations among the "members of the population" (systems A-B-C-A and D-E-D), but breaks down that functional systemic relation. Yet, without any doubt, all the "items" in the

221

"box" can be viewed as detectable forms—like in Figure 3. *The tradi-*
tional sampling philosophy has a "blind spot" in axiomatically granted
overlook of the interdependence of the elements in the field. In other
words, sampling from an unknown "population" and hoping to generalize the results of the study to "the population" cannot answer any questions in cases where the phenomena need to be considered systemically
organized.

Why Has the Sample-to-Population Line of Generalization Survived?

Science is a social enterprise—and hence vulnerable to nonlinear historical development. Technological progress does not automatically mean
new breakthroughs in ideas, even if it may make such breakthroughs
possible. The thinking in science is intellectually interdependent with the
sociohistorical context that scientists inhabit (Valsiner 2004; Valsiner
and van der Veer 2000). Even within the same historical period and
within the same society, large differences exist between various disciplines in their way of generating knowledge.

The development of quantification of data in psychology is a good
example of a search for precision that has ended in its opposite. In the
name of consensually validated methods and data analysis techniques,
the nature of phenomena has been lost from consideration (Cairns 1986).
Statistical methodology has redirected the discipline in ways that have
elevated methods to the status of theories (Gigerenzer 1993) and led to
the proliferation of pseudoempirical research (Smedslund 1995). The
"inference revolution" (approximately 1940-1955—Gigerenzer and
Murray 1987. chapter 1) created a monovocal orthodoxy of the inferen-
tial techniques and introduced it as standard scientific practice in psychology.

One of the results of these social tendencies in mid-20th-century psychology has been the loss of precision. This statement may seem paradoxical—given the multitude of numerical data presented in abundance
in contemporary psychology journals. Yet precision is not in numbers but
in what the numbers represent, and psychology's data have become
largely unrepresentative of the phenomena from which they are derived
(Cairns, 1986). The result for knowledge construction is a conceptual
dead-end of contemporary psychology. It continues to be in a crisis—
hence new areas of research—such as cultural psychology—may have a
chance of restoring the phenomena <> data relationship for improved
precision in our science.

The Self-Constructed Limitation of the Social Sciences

Above we have proven that sampling of specimens from populations is based on premises that render the study of any structured systemic phenomena—of the cultural and developmental kind—in principle impossible. Social sciences have moved into a dead-end street as they have, historically, tried to deal with the issue of multiple causality in phenomena. The roots of the notion of random sampling—uncontrollability of multiple assumed causes that operate within a population—creates the need for randomization of a sample selected from the population. It is based on the assumption of the independence of the objects of sampling. In the case of human populations, the notion of randomness is misplaced, as it is applied to structurally interdependent human worlds (Shvyrkov and Persidsky 1991).

Sampling in Case of Non-Independent Phenomena

The above analysis is still incomplete: we have not demonstrated how the philosophy of sampling of elements (of systemic units) also overlooks the autopoietic nature of the systems themselves. The systems are not "just there" to be found, and "collected" (Kindermann and Valsiner 1989), but are self-organizing systems that develop in relation with the environment. Their survival depends upon that environment, and by their actions they change the environmental niche they inhabit (Odling-Smee et al 2003). Hence an additional oversight is to treat the "sampling box" as if it is merely a "container" that keeps together the specimens to be sampled from (Figures 1-5). Instead, the "box" is the environmental basis for survival and development (Figure 6). It is the processes of development based on organism-environment relating that need to be sampled— not selected (and disconnected) surface outcome features of the specimens that have developed.

In the case depicted in Figure 6, the traditional sampling, which would create a "sample" and later would make generalizing statements about "populations", shows its fundamental misfit. The causal system that operates for the functioning and development of the discernible phenomena (A,B,C,D, E, and others in Figures 1-6) are not located at the plane of their ontological (manifest) level at all, but in between the systemic organization (that can be detected at the manifest level) and the related plane of ecological basis for survival. Any analysis of the phenomena that transcends the immediate ontology of their being of some (or another) kind (category) needs to study (a) their systemic nature, together with (b) their functional relations with their ecological niches.

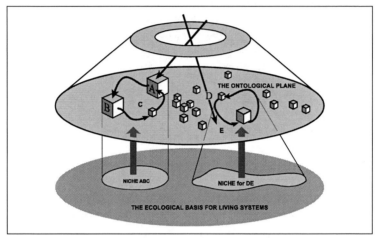

Figure 6: An example of how traditional sampling bypasses the crucial feature of the living systems—interdependency with environments

Living systems develop, and development entails creation of trails, of life trajectories. So even Figure 6 is limited: it shows the interdependency of the system and the ecological niche, *but not its history*. Yet it is the history that distinguishes the open-systemic phenomena from their closed-systemic or nonsystemic counterparts. Thus, any study of human psychology (or sociology) is necessarily historical in its scope if it is to maintain its focus on the issues the researchers declare they are studying.

We propose that the adequate sampling of the specimens of systems proceeds through the sampling of system-historical trajectories that include the past (retrospective base), the present, and an analysis of the construction of the future trajectories. Any cultural system, whether personal or collective, can be understood only through its history[5].

Systemic View: Axiomatic Acceptance of Interdependence

The interdependence of human psychological worlds is the axiom in cultural psychology—here sampling need not represent a population, but reflects the cultural histories of the cases studied. There is no value in

---

5   Here we paraphrase the point emphasized by Lev Vygotski—after his fellow paedologist Pavel Blonski: behavior can be understood only as history of behavior (van der Veer and Valsiner 1991).

taking any "random" set of individuals from a population since the individual cases are supposed to reflect the range of variation not in the population, but in the ways in which specific adaptations to concrete conditions exist. Thus, a new concept is proposed—Historically Structured Sampling (HSS). HSS utilizes the property of open-systemic phenomena—convergence at temporary equifinality points in their individual development.

Historically Structured Sampling (HSS): Selection by Histories

The notion of HSS relies heavily upon the notion of equifinality that originated in the general systems theory (GST) of von Bertalanffy (von Bertalanffy 1968) and is rooted in the early work of Hans Driesch. Von Bertalanffy pioneered the organismic conception of biology from which the GST developed. He regarded living organisms, including human beings, not as closed but as open systems.

Closed systems are considered not to depend upon their environments for their functioning. If phenomena in a particular science can be assumed to be of the kind of closed systems, the traditional sampling techniques (Figures 1-2. above) would be sufficient and there would be no need for developing an alternative like HSS. Yet no biological, psychological, or social system can be reasonably conceived as closed—hence the need for HSS[6].

On the other hand, open systems receive information and interact dynamically or in an exchange with their environment. Incorporating the concept of the open system into his theory, von Bertalanffy (1968) outlined the principle of the equifinality as crucial for the open systems:

"In any closed system, the final state is unequivocally determined by the initial condition: e.g., the motion in a planetary system where the positions of the planets at a time t are unequivocally determined by their positions at a time t_0 [...] If either the initial conditions and or the process are altered, the final state will also be changed. This is not so in open systems. Here same final state may be reached from initial conditions and in different ways. This is what is called equifinality, and it has a significant meaning for the phenomena of biological regulation" (von Bertalanffy 1968: 40).

---

6   It is important to note that the decision about whether a given system is "open" or "closed" is an axiomatic one—where the centrality of the basic assumptions and phenomena connection in the methodology cycle (see Branco and Valsiner 1997) is crucial.

The open-systemic nature of social and psychological phenomena has led to the need to consider complex events in their history. Sociologists' efforts at "event history analysis" (Blossfeld, Hamerle, and Mayer 1989; Yamaguchi 1991) and developmental psychology's look at person-context analysis (Cairns, Elder, and Costello 1996) are some of the existing recent efforts to move beyond the myopia for open-systemic nature in the traditional research habits.

Equifinality

Equifinality means that the same state may be reached from different initial conditions and in different ways in the course of time. We propose to call a trajectory model such as in Figure 7 a Trajectory Equifinality Model. Equifinality is a general property of open systems. In the minimal case, the open systems dynamics entail the notion of individual trajectories (A and B) that may converge (at equifinality points), as in Figure 7. They may diverge after passing through the equifinality point—leading to further multifinality (see multifinality points in Figure 7).

It is important to emphasize that equifinality does not imply sameness, which is an impossible condition in any historical system. Rather, it entails a region of similarity in the temporal courses of different trajectories. It is only by our conventional use of language that we easily consider similarity to be sameness (Sovran 1992), a move in language use that is unproblematic in the sciences where history is not relevant. In biology, psychology, sociology, and beyond, we only operate on the basis of functional similarities. "Sameness" of open-systemic objects is in principle impossible, given the self-maintenance that necessarily involves creation of novelty, even in a miniscule version. Thus, what we consider colloquially "same" is at most "similar", and the issue at stake is the extent of dissimilarity in the case of "similar"-labeled groups of objects. In the development of our HSS model we locate that *extent of dissimilarity*[7] in the qualitative differences of the trajectories of the past (A and B in Figure 7) as the different developing systems arrive at the equifinality point.

---

7   This issue has been constructively approached in fuzzy set theory that emphasizes the open-endedness of human thinking thanks to the fuzziness of the concepts with which we operate (Zadeh 1978).

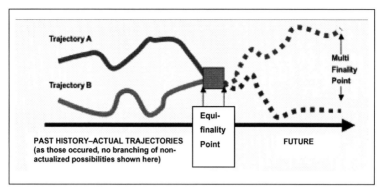

Figure 7: Equifinality point within irreversible time (past-to-future movement)

There are only two fundamentally general equifinality points in each human life that are universally shared by all—birth and death. But in most psychological studies, these two points are not often investigated. There is, of course, the possibility of looking at the prenatal developmental trajectories as the antecedents toward the varied trajectories of postnatal development as an example of utilization of the equifinality point of birth for developmental research (see Hepper 2003). Similar uses of the second universal equifinality points in psychological research are limited only to the trajectories of arrival at the equifinality point: the biological realities set severe limits on any further speculations.

The equifinality point is a "point in-between"—it is *both* a place for temporary similarity in the life courses of the systems and a bifurcation point for further development. It plays the *central role in the selection of cases* of developing systems in case of HSS. Any psychological states and/or life events in which researchers are interested are structured historically. Of course the equifinality point is defined by the specific parameters on which the investigator focuses. The researcher decides which aspects of the historically organized system are the objects of investigation: the EFP becomes a part of the conceptual scheme in the researchers' thinking.

An example of an equifinality point in human development is the case of infants' beginning to walk independently. The usual, textbook-depiction of such development is that of a linear sequence: infants begin to creep and crawl, then stand up and begin to walk. However, this picture simplifies the complex reality of open systems, that develop by nonlinear trajectories. The usual trajectory of the development of locomotion is not the only one (Valsiner 2001b). As the work of Trettien (1900) showed, there exists another (less frequent) trajectory. Some infants never creep or crawl, but move from the sitting position to standing position, and from there, to independent walking. And after beginning to walk, infants learn and acquire the many other ways of locomotion. So independent walking for the infant becomes the equifinality point en route to becoming an adult: both "crawling babies" and "sitting position babies" will get their licenses to drive a car, where the sitting position suffices. Like many other developmentally relevant equifinality points in ontogeny, the arrival at independent walking is relevant for moving further along in the life trajectories of the developing person. Some of these equifinality points are biologically and culturally predefined, i.e., they are obligatory.

Obligatory Passage Points in the Trajectories Equifinality Model (TEM)

There exist some additional basic concepts to outline this model. TEM is based on the assumption that all historical phenomena move in time on their unique trajectories that at times converge at equifinality points. History occurs in irreversible time and the varied trajectories may entail obligatory passage points (OPP), depicted in Figure 8. Irreversible time is the characteristic of real time to never repeat any happening of the previous time period. Time flows from an infinite past towards an infinite future (Valsiner, 2001b). Yet human beings exist as finite organisms—living from birth to death and creating their own personal lives through cultural means.

To understand the diversity of the trajectory of development, it is important to examine the passage points that lead to EFP. Then another concept is needed to understand the trajectory—passage points. Before reaching the EFP, people experience many events and things. We call them passage points. Passage points are important events for subjects (or informants). And they are always—not anytime—bifurcation points.

In this figure "the rectangle J" is the supposed EFP on which researchers focus in their research. For this EFP, there are many pathways to pass. "Ellipses B through H" are BFPs in this *TEM*. We can call them passage points. Of course, many passage points are both EFP and BFP, but the main EFP should be focused along the researchers' interests.

It is necessary to emphasize that TEM is our theoretical representation of complex reality of development. Different researchers may find many different passage points that they consider theoretically relevant. After all, all ongoing decision making about action—to act or not to act in context C at time T—can be viewed as a bifurcation point. However, no matter how many points we can find, the nature of all points is not equal. Some points are trivial, and the others are crucial. Some are inevitable, others suggested as if they were inevitable. What is—and is not—meaningful for a researcher is determined by the theoretical framework of the researcher and its mapping onto the phenomena (Branco and Valsiner 1997), not on social conventions or ease of finding the equifinality or bifurcation points.

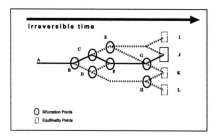

Figure 8: Depicting the Equifinality Trajectories Model (modified after Valsiner 2001b: 62)

Obligatory Passage Points (OPP)

This concept originally emerged in the context of the sociology of science (Latour 1988). In our course of development there are two types of OPP, the indigenous and the exogenous. The former includes species-specific biological transition points, such as cutting of teeth in infancy, menarche, or menopause. The exogenous is set up by the environment and/or custom. The cessation of menstruation in women during times of hardship ("war-time amenorrhea") is a result of an environmentally produced transition phase. Adolescent initiation rituals that exist in many societies are culturally set exogenous OPPs. So is obligatory formal schooling—children are sent to school as a socially set OPP that lasts for years.

By focusing the research theme, some points other than birth and/or death are found to be essential. For example, in research on the life course of infertile woman, heteromarriage (whether legal or de-facto) is an OPP. For someone who wants to make his/her own new family, infertility is a negative, blocking biological factor that disallows the move through species-specific (reproductive) OPP.

How Historically Structured Sampling Works

Up to now we have outlined the theoretical landscape for making sense of cultural-psychological phenomena as open-systemic, multitrajectory historical processes. This only sets the stage for defining a fitting way to solve the problem of sampling. Starting from the analysis of past trajectories of the personal life trajectories and their contextual structures at every EFP and BFP—seeing what OPP kinds of demands existed at the bifurcation points—the researcher moves to select the participants on the basis of theoretically meaningful past histories. Note that all the persons singled out for study *are at the given moment in a similar state* (EFP). What makes the difference is their past histories and their concrete organization (see contrast of Trajectory A and Trajectory B in Figure 7, above).

The OPP is the basic structure and/or canalization system of life trajectories upon which our sampling technique—HSS—is set up. The act of HSS entails

a) locating the relevant equifinality point (EFP), as well as all relevant OPPs, in the generic map of trajectories necessarily present for the generic system of the processes under investigation (theoretically-based activity),

b) empirical mapping out of all particular cases, i.e., systems open to study that move through these points, and

c) comparison of different actual trajectories as these approach to the equifinality point by superimposing onto each trajectory a pattern of a theoretically meaningful "range measure"—derived from (a)—that specifies whether the given trajectory fits into the realm of selectable cases.

HSS thus maps the individual histories of particular systems onto the wider general system of possible trajectories of arrival at the equifinality point. HSS sets up contrasts between different trajectories, and between the same trajectory and its possible future under new OPPs beyond the EFP. It calls for an analysis of the sets of possibilities for the given system to proceed through, and sampling of that particular set out of all that are known, for further sampling of individual cases that have reached the selected point.

Such sampling of cases, based on the past historic trajectory differences *that are currently absent* (all systems are in the same equifinality area at the time of sampling), is the opposite of traditional sampling of contrasting groups based on outcome data. In HSS the traditional notion of "experimental" versus "control" *groups* is not applicable. Instead, all the cases selected through HSS—who are currently in a specified similar EFP—can be contrasted with one (or more) *virtual comparison* condition (VCC)—conditions which *clearly are absent now*, but which *could have been realistic had the persons involved at relevant BFPs in the past moved in different directions* than they actually did (see the example of coping with infertility, below). It is the personal history of not reaching the VCC state—contrastive state to the current actual EFP—that is relevant for the researcher who uses HSS. HSS operates by focusing on the contrast of what historically did happen, and what potentially could have happened, but did not.

HSS allows for the use of various methods to analyze past trajectories for all potential participants in the investigation. Triangulation of methods is necessary. Preliminary open-ended questionnaires, intensive interview data, historical knowledge, theoretical knowledge, and even common sense are all useful for empirical elaboration of the TEM as the basis for HSS. HSS thus capitalizes on the "life courses" of the objects of our investigation by selecting various cases on the basis of their movement through relations with environments. Yet it is not another label for life history, rather, it is a technique of sampling for the study of some other—prospective—processes of cultural development that have not yet emerged. HSS may set the stage for prospective longitudinal observation of what would emerge in "natural contexts", or for a microgenetic intervention experiment.

Likewise, HSS can be the basis for social intervention in a community (based on the HSS verified past movements in the community) and in clinical settings. HSS is a tool for researchers that replaces the reliance on the axiomatically accepted notion of "random sampling" in particular (as there is no "randomness" in history, but moves from uncertainty to certainty) as well as the notion of "sample" as a set out of a bigger set ("population"). HSS is based on different axioms than the ideology of "random sampling": systemic and autopoietic nature of cultural phenomena, unique construction of life experiences in irreversible time, and relative structure of the landscape of the life course (by structure of OPPs, and EFPs/BFPs).

Possible Applications of HSS in Research Practices

Given the needs of cultural psychology, it is useful to understand the three levels of the process on irreversible time; i.e., history, life-course development, and decision making. Three levels of organization of phenomena at which HSS is applicable are:

1. macro-genetic level: history of a society, social group, or institution,
2. meso-genetic level: human individual life-course development (ontogeny),
3. micro-genetic level: decision making in semiotically over-determined everyday life situations.

The application of HSS unites different levels: sampling by HSS takes place at one level, while the study to be conducted occurs at another. Thus, by selecting persons within a society that is undergoing dramatic change (*macro*-genetic level HSS), it becomes possible to study ongoing *meso*-genetic (ontogenetic) level changes. Likewise, if HSS is made at the *meso*-genetic level (e.g., selecting people with different life-course trajectories, but who have all reached a given equifinality point, e.g,. have all reached a certain point in school, or an adolescent transition ritual place) the door is opened to the micro-genetic study of the relevant processes. The HSS *always occurs at one level more general than the actual study* for which the sampling is done, is to be conducted.

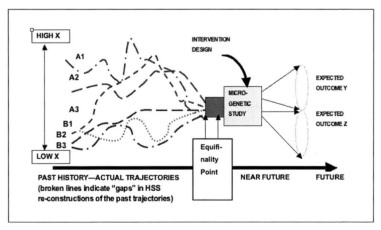

Figure 9: HSS as basis for a study of emergence (broken lines indicate "gaps" in HSS reconstructions of the past trajectories)

If one is to compare HSS with the traditional sampling procedures, the difference is in the acceptance of directionality of development in case of HSS. Different systems may be selected as examples of basically opposite movement at the more general (macro- or meso-genetic level) in order to test the properties of their further development at one level lower. Figure 9 provides a generic example.

HSS leads to the selection of two sets of individual systems by their similar trajectories (A1, A2, A3 and B1, B2, B3) that all at the present time are located in the equifinality zone. All of these cases have been analyzed as to their past trajectories, and any reconstruction of this kind is uneven in its access to the life course as it actually happened. Yet it is documented how their ontogentic life courses fluctuated over time, on the dimension HIGH X <> LOW X. Even if the specific reconstructions of the past are vulnerable to selective recall and constructive confabulation, its directions between different BFPs can be ascertained.

Based on HSS, each of the selected systemic cases is subjected to a microgenetic intervention procedure, the result of which is expected to be further life-course trajectories in directions Y and Z. Such study entails the setting of new kinds of hypotheses of the kind—"GIVEN HISTORY {range A} and INTERVENTION Z the individual cases are expected to precede in direction Z (or Y) with specifiable ranges of X." Note that what is absent in such hypotheses building is any notion of "control group": since all hypotheses are to be tested within a single case, the trajectories discovered in the course of HSS operate as "control conditions". This orientation is analogous to behavioral single-case designs.

How Trajectories are Made:
The Landscape Model

Trajectories are possible only in models where time is retained. A point has no direction, a sequence of two points forms a line—which can be interpreted as having a direction—and becomes a trajectory. Not surprisingly, it is in the realm of developmental sciences—biology or psychology—that the notion of trajectories is theoretically important.

Trajectories can be posited either with (see Figure 6 above) or without (see Figure 9, above) depicting their generative context. The former entails a field model where directional vectors (trajectories) are depicted within the context of a field parts of which they are. Perhaps the most widely known example of the former is Waddington's (1956) classic epigenetic landscape model of the linking of genetic and environmental factors in development. In Waddington's own words,

"One can make a mental picture [...] of development of a particular part of an egg as a ball running down a valley. It will, of course, tend to run down to the bottom of the valley, and if something temporarily pushes it up to one side, it will again have a tendency to run down to the bottom and finally finish up in its normal place. If one thinks of all the different parts of the egg, developing into wings, eyes, legs, and so on, one would have to represent the whole system by a series of different valleys, all starting out from the fertilized egg but gradually diverging and finishing up at a number of different adult organs." (Waddington 1966: 49)

Waddington's interest was in the explanation of how biological organisms' morphogenesis takes place. After considerable search for a visual representation of that process (see Gilbert 1991, for a detailed history of his schemes), he ended up with a model as depicted in Figure 10.

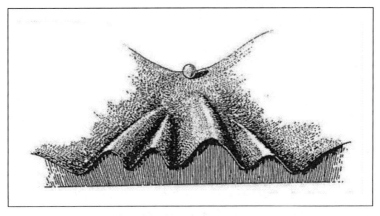

Figure 10: Waddington's "Epigenetic landscape" (Waddington 1966: 49)

This model describes the nature of trajectories as diverging—the whole landscape broadens toward the end. This fits the biological differentiation of morphological structures (e.g., where the finally formed body parts do not "grow into" one another). From the viewpoint of HSS this landscape model is limited as it fails to include equifinality points (while being rich in bifurcation points).

If psychology or other social sciences were to consider an analog of his "landscape," both bifurcation and equifinality points would need to be included. Furthermore, if the "ball" is the equivalent of the developing system in an open-systemic way, its relations with the landscape are not those of mere direction, but include the mutually active role of both—the "ball" is "digging its way" thus making the valleys, while the system of existing valleys resists and acts upon the "ball", attempting to direct it actively toward one or another location of "digging".

Given the absence of EFPs in Waddington's model, it represents only one example of trajectory-based theoretical thought in the history of biology. Waddington's model serves merely as a reminder of a class of models that include the idea of trajectory but has no unification point for the sake of selection of developing systems for their baseline contemporary similarity.

Examples of Empirical Projects
Where HSS is Productive

Comparison of people from different societies acquires a new meaning with the adoption of HSS. In terms of cultural histories, we look at the transition from the oral to the written literature traditions in the histories of two societies—Japan and Persia. Both—by the present time—have reached, albeit by different historical trajectories, the equifinality point of the focus on written literature in formal schooling, if we take a historical view of a time frame of something like 2000 years.

Yet the different histories of the two societies lead individual people of the current generation—while similar in their selected equifinality point (focus on written texts in formal education)—to different personal histories of arriving at that point, and different potentials for moving further ahead. In Figure 11, below, the right arrow points to the alleged position of the Japanese condition. In Japan, written literature prevails. But for example, present conditions in Iran are different from those in Japan. Young adults (e.g., 30-year-olds) in Iran can be expected to be much more familiar with oral literature (the left arrow) than their counterparts in Japan. This intersociety difference can be found from looking at the cultural histories of each country prior to any study of any person in each. The continuity of the generic focus on oral<>written communication interchange in the histories of the societies sets up the expectations for what kinds of foci one can find within people of the current generation. However, the point of HSS is not to demonstrate that the history of a society determines the mentality of its people. That would amount to the kind of linguistic/cultural determinism that has governed the thinking of social minds in the Occident (Valsiner and van der Veer 2000).

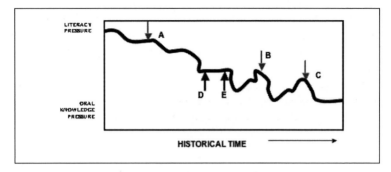

Figure 11: Sociohistorical pressures (arrows) upon the proportional prevalence of written (versus oral) transfer of cultural knowledge

The scheme (Figure 11) shows how a society at different periods of time may prioritize the reliance of its members on written or oral communication of knowledge. This macro-sociological history can be plotted as to the proportions of oral/written transfer at different periods, with pressures toward an increase in either the share of literacy (arrows A, B, C) or that of oral transfer (arrows D, E) at different times. For example, in the historical periods where the main communication means were those of writing (and exchanging) paper-based documents, the pressures toward increased reliance on writing and reading can be observed. Thus, in pre-Gutenberg Europe, the majority of communication was based on oral communication channels. Together with the invention of the printing press that changed—and the additional social change of the Lutheran Reformation delegating to the individual the most important communication task (i.e., that of communion with God through one's own reading of the Bible) increased the pressure of literacy to take over the dominant role from oral knowledge transfer. Similarly, one may wonder if a reverse process is going on now in the 21st century—the age of cellular telephones, MTV, shredding machines, and saving knowledge in virtual rather than physically tangible forms. Reading and writing are being replaced by mouse-clicking, and relevant information on computer screens is no longer organized for reading, just for detection and reaction to pregiven choices.

Figure 11 gives us a macro-historical background for HSS. Different individuals within a society at the given time occupy different social role positions in relation to the oral/written literature relation—some (scholars) operate primarily within the written tradition, others (bards)—within the oral tradition. This would be similar for example both in Japan and in Iran in our time. Where the differences in the histories begin to play a major role is at the transition from the dominance of one to that of the other. Children entering formal education systems move from the dominance of one to the other. Their personal trajectories of past encounters with written and oral literatures can be determined from interviewing their caregivers when the children enter school. The results of such interviews allow the researcher to chart out the systemic trajectories up to the selected equifinality point. So here, the HSS procedure makes use of two levels—macrogenetic (histories of the two societies) and ontogenetic (individual children's developmental trajectories). The study of the making of the future can now proceed at the microgenetic level—as a kind of teaching/learning experiment in the classrooms. It is expected that the children—in the context of new literacy tasks—will bring their past personal-cultural histories to function as tools to adapt to the educational setting. For many Iranian children it may mean that they need to confabulate—create an oral "story" around a writing task. For many Japanese children, the way to handle the microgenetic task may reflect their past focus on writing, rather than oral construction. Thus, the basic features of the past trajectories of individual children in their macro-social backgrounds guide the process of handling a new microgenetic task.

Yet children do not just follow the guidance of the past—they reconstruct it, and do it largely by acting in some form of contrast to their pasts. Resistance to learning can lead to learning (Poddiakov 2001), or—work on one's deficiencies can lead to overcompensating excellence in precisely those areas. Hence, HSS leads to the possibility of studying individual cases where personal histories differ cardinally from others in the same category. For instance, some children in Japan may have "Iranian-like" personal-cultural histories when it comes to the uses of literacy texts, and some Iranian children may have histories similar to those of Japanese children. These single cases—let us call them "cross-over cases"-- are identified by HSS and can be studied in the microgenetic procedure. It is precisely such "cross-over cases" that can provide the most important comparisons between societies.

From the individual's perspective, we can consider two historical trajectories in different societies. We—human beings—cannot choose our birthplaces. It's very first point, any baby enters the realm of oral communication—people around him or her making speech sounds that only slowly begin to make any sense. But, suppose that one baby is in the "oral transfer of knowledge" dominant society and another is in the "written transfer of knowledge" dominant society. So, babies in the former society tend to be in the oral communication culture and babies in the latter society tend to be in the written communication culture. It's important for us to recognize that both oral and literary societies are equally equivalent for babies.

237

We can set up the EFPs on the communication style such as oral and literary in our theoretical schemes, but these are both usable by people in their everyday lives. We may also call them *polarized equifinality points* (PEFP). PEFPs operate in "doubles"—they unite the opposites between which the developmental or historical processes proceed—guided by the promotional field one level more general than the phenomena under investigation.

Obviously, babies are not ready for written communication right after their birth. At the first Bifurcation Point "A", some go up to "B" where "written transfer of knowledge" dominates in the society, and the others go down to "C" where "oral transfer of knowledge" is dominant. In the former, children may start to learn reading and writing as early as kindergarten. In the latter, they might start it late—if at all. After all, human cultural transfer occurred in pre-literate societies as well as literate ones—albeit with a different role played by memory functions (Vygotsky and Luria 1993, chapter 2)

In Figure 12, "D" is the supposed Obligatory Passage Point (OPP) of entering elementary school. Many societies today force children to go to elementary school. "E" is another BFP. In a "written transfer of knowledge" dominant society, a child may quit studying at school because of health problems. In an "oral transfer of knowledge" dominant society a child may quit studying because of gender. For instance, girls have been underrepresented in formal schooling contexts in many societies—while women's role in the informal education context in any society has been central.

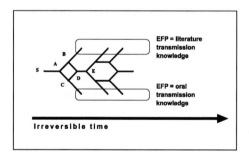

Figure 12: The system of Polarized EFP for the case of people in between the Oral and Written texts-dependence context—and the system of trajectories

Re-Considering Ontogeny of Tactile Contact

We can consider a classic "intervention design" known in child psychology—the role of extra tactile contact between mothers and newborns in further development of the infants. In the usual habit of psychology,

238

studies in child psychology have focused on something considered as "independent variable" at time t0 as "having an effect" on some "dependent variable" at t1. For example, Klaus and Kennell (1976) were pioneers in claiming the importance of early mother-baby tactile contact for later development. Yet such selection of "independent" and "dependent" variables denies the systemic organization of development both before the earlier antecedent condition (increased tactile contact) and from the experiences within the interval until the "dependent variables" were investigated. Of course, the act of giving mothers and newborns more time (than U.S. pediatric wards allowed in the early 1970s) to sleep with one another cannot in itself operate as any "independent variable". It is merely a contextual arrangement to which causal properties cannot be attributed. It is a newly introduced life-course event—a short period of stability of contact—that is part of the history of the life course—an equifinality point (or period)—for all the mothers and babies included in the Klaus & Kennell research program. Correlational analysis of finding relations between the "earlier" and the "later" indicators at the level of the sample do not represent the life-course processes that are taking place. The "effects" of neonatal tactile contact are of a systemic kind—instead of one form of such possible "effects" there are at least five possible ones (see Blossfeld and Rohwer 1997: 368). Any correlational (or regression)-analytic finding of "an effect" is completely blind to which of these five (or other possible) forms of these "effects" might be in place. The early mother-child bonding hypothesis is one of many mythical hypotheses that proliferate in psychology—supported by the common sense ideology that guides psychologists' thinking.

How would the Kennel and Klaus research tradition fare from the perspective of HSS? Their intervention—provision of extra tactile mother/baby contact opportunity—introduced an EFP to all of the participants in the "experimental groups". In contrast, the "control groups" —mother-baby pairs without such events—did not share any pointedly similar experience. Yet mothers and babies from both groups were confined to similar hospital settings.

The personal life histories of each mother and her baby—if analyzed in terms of the trajectory through the pregnancy and birth process—would be the basis for our HSS effort. The "experimental manipulation" (more tactile contact—or not) would be part of the microgenetic intervention. The follow-up of each mother/baby pair after the extra tactile contact would entail an analysis of other relevant life-course episodes in the relations of the mothers and babies, such as processes of breastfeeding, of exploration of the environment in toddlerhood, etc. Comparisons between individual cases would be made based on the distinctions

239

of their HSS trajectory histories (see Figure 9, above). The "control group"—where mothers and babies were *not* subjected to the extra tactile contact—would be irrelevant for the analysis of the construction of further trajectories given the EFP experience. It will be treated as a second experimental group—one where the EFP of giving birth is followed by a slight modification of tactile access patterns. Through HSS, the differences in the life histories that led to EFP are expected to make a further difference—*not* the presence *versus* absence of a minor contextual variation at the given time.

Cultural Psychology Abandons the Discourse of "Variables"

Our example here illuminates a more important general point. Conventional psychology tends to regard *attributes* of subjects (or informants) as important for the generalization of results. "Controlling" the variables such as nationality, sex, age, and many others, is expected to guarantee the objectivity and/or validity of the research. Yet no researcher can actually "control" psychological "variables" since those have auto-regulatory properties—the person acts in ways that neutralize or resist the efforts of the researcher to systematically vary the "variables". Some of the features referred to as "variables" in psychology are merely indices of fixed *status quo*—so, gender (male/female) is not controllable by way of the experimenter's intervention, but only in a manner of speaking (recognizing existing gender differences). Interestingly, the notion of "controllable variables" is easily generalized in the minds of researchers—these "variables" become freed from their contextual dependencies, and of the time.

Same Event—Different Personal Experiences

Using the HSS, wartime can be a point of sampling and we can see the diversity of trajectories that subjects experienced at this equifinality point with unraveling the interaction between human and environment. Here we can see the covariation pattern or configuration of cultural variables (Kojima 1997: 318). Such covariation does not reveal causes of development (which are systemic) but allows for an overview of the high variety of forms in organism-environment relations.

Contemporary life-course sociology provides examples of equifinality points in the social domain (economic depression, war) that are inevitable for people (especially young people) to move through in their development. Because human beings as an open system interact with their environments, sometimes almost all people in the same environment are affected by one big event, such as war and disaster. The experiences of such an equifinality point are similar (not the same) in almost all people, but the influences tend to be different (not similar). Shanahan, Valsiner, and Gottlieb (1997) pointed out that, in biology and psychology, interest in time had been limited to a concern for development as "temporal accretion" or "critical periods". If we use the concept of equifinality to describe the interaction of people in any age with social events, it is possible to understand diversities in people in any age. Essentially, an equifinality point is also a bifurcation point—for anything that is to come in the move from the present to the future (e.g., through interventions—Figure 9, above).

It is also an example of meso-genetic HSS that the different levels of ontogenetic development can operate as "trajectories" of entrance to the same life experience—but from different perspectives on the life-world. Lev Vygotsky's example—from his clinical experience—of the same episodic event (mother's drunken state) being experienced by her three sons is an example of how HSS can be used in the system of interrelated systems (within a family):

"The essential circumstances were very straightforward. The mother drinks and, as a result, apparently suffers from several nervous and psychological disorders. The children find themselves in a very difficult situation. When drunk, and during these breakdowns, the mother had once attempted to throw one of the children out of the window and she regularly beat them or threw them onto the floor. In a word, the children are living in conditions of dread and fear due to these circumstances.

The three children are brought to our clinic, but each of them presents a completely different picture of disrupted development, caused by the same situation. The same circumstances result in an entirely different picture for the three children.

As far as the youngest of these children is concerned, what we find is the commonly encountered picture in such cases among the younger age group. He reacts to the situation by developing a number of neurotic symptoms, i.e. symptoms of defensive nature. He is simply overwhelmed by the horror of what is happening to him. As a result, he develops attacks of terror, enuresis and he develops a stammer, sometimes being unable to speak at all as he loses his voice. In other words, the child's reaction amounts to a state of complete depression and helplessness in the face of this situation.

The second child is developing an extremely agonizing condition, what is called a state of inner conflict, which is a condition frequently found in certain cases when contrasting emotional attitudes towards the mother make their appearance... ambivalent attitude. On the one hand, from the child's point of view, the mother is an object of painful attachment, and on the other, she represents a source of all kinds of terrors and terrible emotional

241

experiences... The second child is brought to us with this kind of deeply pronounced conflict and sharply colliding internal contradiction expressed in a
simultaneously positive and negative attitude towards the mother, a terrible
attachment to her and an equally terrible hate for her, combined with terri-
bly contradictory behaviour. He asked to be sent home immediately, but expressed terror when the subject of his going home was brought up.

[...] the third and the eldest child presented us with a completely unexpected picture. This child had a limited mental ability but, at the same time,
showed signs of precocious maturity, seriousness, and solicitude. He already
understood the situation. He understood that their mother was ill and pitied
her. He could see that the younger children found themselves in danger when
the mother was in one of her states of frenzy. And he had a special role. He
must calm his mother down, make certain that she is prevented from harm-
ing the little ones and comfort them. Quite simply, he has become the senior
member of the family, the only one whose duty it was to look after everyone
else." (Vygotsky 1994: 340-341)

While Vygotsky himself found the situation of all three children traumatic (which it obviously was), here we can look at the example as an
extension of the usefulness of meso-genetic HSS. By sampling of families of multiple members—children, or other adults (in extended families)—the researcher can investigate the contrasts between mutually connected parts of the social organism (system), where the personal histories
of each member are known. Life-course sociology does not maintain this
kind of systemic unit, but separates people of different backgrounds into
traditional "samples" that go through similar experiences. However, in
terms of cultural psychology, these experiences are personally constructed—on the basis of the shared social history.

An Example at the Micro-Genetic Level

HSS is useful for using the decision-making process of the subject in the
life course in the past to study the re-construction of the future. Yet the
HSS perspective transcends the decision-theoretic legacy of psychology
in two ways. First, most of psychological works treat the "one shot" decision only. Even if process is being emphasized—such as in Cognitive
Dissonance Theory (Festinger 1957)—the decision-making process remains a "one shot" deal, not a trajectory of decisions in a sequence.

The reason why dissonance *after* a decision has been made should be
focused upon is needed as we look at the life processes at large that cannot be reduced to the episodes that Cognitive Dissonance Theory covers.
So, after making a decision, people must cope with cognitive dissonance;
however, in daily life situations, few people actually try to re-make the

earlier decision. Everyday life situation is under a redundant control mechanism (Valsiner 2001b), so decision making tends to be semiotically overdetermined. In addition, we have many things to decide to do or not do—everyday decisions are a kind of sequence of ill-defined problems, one feeding into the next. They are not independent, discrete problems that have simple solutions—each solution feeds forward to the emergence of a new problem.

Ironically, the stronger the exogenous settings (institution, custom, and so on) are, the less people feel the pressure to make decisions. Entering to primary school is one of the examples. Contemporary citizens never bother about whether to make their children enter primary school or not. But in everyday life situations, we have some kind of "degree of freedom" for decision making—"do I or don't I? If I do, when and how?" For example, mothers may spend time thinking about when to start giving pocket money to their children.

Culture and Personal Life Trajectories

Our introduction of HSS as a tool for investigation leads to selecting people who face sequential, interdependent decisions—such as a young woman's decision of how to wear make-up. The act of changing the appearance of the face has a long history in culturally symbolic body painting and the making of ritual masks. These cultural-historical forms set the stage for our contemporary cosmetics use, practices that function for beautification purposes.

Here it would be fitting to mention recent studies using the HSS and the equifinality trajectories idea (Sato, Yasuda and Kido 2004). Yasuda (2004) approached the infertile experiences of married women in Japan by looking at their reconstructed histories of moving between the PFEP containing FERTILITY and INFERTILITY as the two opposites within the same whole. Historically, women who cannot bear children had been maltreated. Barren women were called "umazume", which literally means "stone woman". Scorn was poured only on the women in childless couples. One old, often-quoted Japanese saying was that "If a wife cannot bear children for three years after one's marriage, she ought to be divorced". This saying may be the product of the feudal era, and though today Japan is not at feudal but modern, the baseless accusation against barren women still remains.

But psychological study should be free of value judgment: either having or not having children should be a valid option for all couples.

Because it's very difficult for graduate students to recruit such partici-pants, with one exception, all were recruited at the internet BBS of an association of adoption. The restriction of participants recruit method is not considered a "sampling error", but a part of the HSS is determined by the participants themselves (their motivation to participate in the study on the topic of their life-course desire—becoming parents).

First, Yasuda (2004) ambiguously treated the infertile experiences as EFP. But the restriction of participants made her focus on the two polar-ized results of infertile experiences, i.e., couples with children and cou-ples without children. In this study, equifinality point is not necessary defined as one single point. If a researcher tries to investigate the married women's TEM by HSS, both having children and having no children should be considered as equivalent equifinality points. And there are dif-ferent trajectories for equivalent equifinality points. We again call such equifinality points as equivalent and/or polarized equifinality points (PEFP). EFP depends on the researcher's focus and/or research ques-tions. If one wants to investigate the stability of a married couple's life, the presence or absence of children is only one of the passage points and another EFP should be set.

After theoretically charting out the Polarized EFP for her study, Ya-suda (2004) highlighted different OPPs in the field. The first OPP is the point when infertility treatments couples become aware of the adoption system as a solution that they could use. Yet this is an exclusive option: in Japan, people who expect to adopt must stop any infertility treatments. So this is the second OPP—both of them being of social-psychological nature. The Japanese Association of Adoption requires that the couples give up infertility treatments before entering into the adoption procedure. So stopping the infertility treatments is a social-institutional OPP for couples interested in adoption.

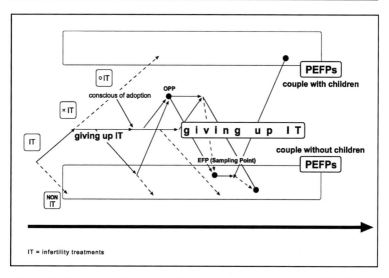

Figure 13. Observed trajectories in 9 women moving towards the EFP of having children in contrast to not having children

So far, the EFPs and OPPs were set up on the basis of the social and psychological decision structures in the social environment of the Japanese society at the present time. Yasuda conducted semistructured interviews with nine cases (6 women and 3 couples, all motivated to undergo intertility treatments). She could reveal the richness of the nine life stories about the women with infertility treatments. She struggled to map the life events and psychological phenomena of the participants to a summary of actual trajectories (Figure 13). The starting point is medical labeling—"infertility". Even though the medical definition of infertility is rather difficult to prove—it is a diagnosis based on the documented *non*-happening of something expected (pregnancy)—, once people are conscious of that label, they usually reflect upon it through two options—"Let it be" or "try infertility treatments". So they see it as a bifurcation point for their life course.

This look at the multitude of possible and actualized trajectories makes it possible to understand the trajectory of infertile experiences from the viewpoint of individuals who chose the infertility treatments and took adoption into consideration. Both "being conscious of infertility" and "taking the adoption into consideration" are not only personal experiences but also historically structured ones. Actually, this figure looks different from deductively derivable formal models of trajectories unfolding within the field of PEFP {FERTILITY<>INFERTILITY}. Yet it reflects the real trajectories of movement of the women who were involved in the study. In this figure, solid lines express the possible and real courses. Dashed lines express possible (supposed), but not captured trajectories in this research.

If the picture in Figure 12—depicting different ontogenetic trajectories of the equifinality trajectories model—is used as a basis for HSS, one could study women of different trajectories—those of direct and repeated efforts to arrive at fertility (repeated infertility treatments), and others with "up-and-down" trajectories (still ending up in efforts to bear children). It would be reasonable to expect that any microgenetic next event in their life course, e.g., their personal ways of relating to the next episode of infertility treatment, would be organized differently by way of their personal cultures. (Valsiner 2000)

General Conclusion

In any psychological research effort, sampling is inevitable. Actually, many kinds of sampling methods are used in psychology. We have expanded the notion of sampling to include its historical-developmental version—HSS. It is an alternative to the usual way of random sampling.

The difficulty of random sampling has been elaborated in this chapter. Its reliance on the assumed "randomness" of the singular acts of selection of individuals from populations into "samples", and its built-in overlooking of the person-environment interaction (Figure 6, above) are sufficient reasons to refrain from using such sampling techniques in cultural psychology. However, after demonstrating the misfit of the traditional technique we needed to develop a more promising alternative—and our notion of Historically Structured Sampling (HSS) is meant as such. Aside from being open to history and uniqueness of the life course, it is also an example of theoretically-based sampling. Psychology at large has moved away from theory-based empirical efforts, much to its epistemological detriment. Our hope is that HSS in cultural psychology will restore the centrality of theory.

There are also practical matters. In any real-life situation where the investigator operates, access to the phenomena is institutionally constrained. The researcher may be in a position of not just being unable to choose the participants, but not even being able to choose the institution where the potential participants are socially embedded. If a researcher wants to enter one high school, it is not the researcher but the high school administrator, or perhaps teacher or director, who makes the decision. The strategy of HSS may render this obstacle less dangerous to research: even if one high school rejects the researcher's request, another school may grant it. Sampling like this is not random, but not capricious. From the perspective of HSS, any school of similar background constitutes an EFP. So it's worth studying whenever access is possible. Contrasting such study with a study involving a large number of college student questionnaire responses is not worthwhile. Sampling such large study is convenient and capricious—and far from the unreachable traditional ideal of "randomness".

Furthermore, a person is not a pile of traits or an automaton that provides answers to vaguely formed items on personality questionnaires and surveys. A human being—or a social group, or community—as an open system lives with cultural historical events. In its history different potential events might occur (at bifurcation points), but are either made not to happen, or they just do not happen. The focus on HSS brings into our empirical research practices a contrast much discussed by philosophers, but not implemented in empirical research, i.e., that between *potential* events and *actual* events. HSS is based on the contrast of the real (what did happen in the past) and the functional non-real (what could have happened at the particular bifurcation points, but did not—White 1972).

How will cultural psychology's knowledge base be improved by use of HSS? We think HSS will have a couple of implications, just as Freud's theory has at least three implications for psychiatry, psychology and our life: etiology of mental disease, the therapeutic method, and the theory of human development. HSS should be the theory for sampling in psychology by integrating the three levels of historicity, i.e., macro-, meso-, and micro-geneses. It lives up to the general claim that psychological systems can be studied only through the history of their emergence and trajectories to the present state. Depicting the TEM makes it possible for us to grasp the trajectory with irreversible time.

Lastly HSS—based on TEM trajectories—helps the researcher to identify the individuals who are involved in important life decisions. Consider the sorrow and/or trouble of a mother of mildly mentally handicapped children. She could select the "normal" class or "special" classrooms as her EFP for the children's education. She may have selected the latter, but has been worrying about it ever since. The HSS-based research helps psychologists to advise such a mother in order to mitigate her sorrow and/or trouble: either the "normal" or the "special" classroom ought to lead anyone to the same equifinality points later on. HSS allows different historical opportunities for further development to be seen beyond each EFP. Similarly, HSS-based knowledge would support special education teachers in arranging the environment differently for children of unusual pasts at the equifinality points.

The HSS trajectory need not assume linearity and/or unidimensional nature of the life course. Although the HSS started from criticism of the sampling methods in developmental psychology, the developmental theory derived from the HSS has the power to change the epistemology of developmental psychology. HSS restores the central role of time—duration of life forms—to the study of social and psychological systems. *Behavior of such systems—in the widest sense—is only understandable as the history of such systems*—a point made in the 1920s by the Russian pedologist Pavel Blonskii, and which fascinated Lev Vygotsky but failed to gain ground in psychology in subsequent decades. Perhaps we are now in an OPP for the social sciences to consider the historicity of the phenomena we study in an internally coherent way, rather than following the preaching of missionaries for the "right methods" in science. The latter are normative claims—basically power assertions—which may lead psychology astray in its complicated efforts to make sense of human beings.

Acknowledgments

The authors are grateful to the Ritsumeikan University for bringing the first author to Kyoto in February 2004 for a series of seminars in cultural psychology, and where the idea of HSS was collectively conceived. Discussions in the "kitchen seminar" at Clark on October, 20, 2004, and feedback from Wolfram Fischer, Alexander Poddiakov, Emily Abbey, Roger Bibace, Tania Zittoun, and Nandita Chaudhary is gratefully acknowledged.

References

Blossfield, H.-P./Hamerle, A./Mayer, K.U. (Eds.) (1989). Event History Analysis. Hillsdale, N.J.: Erlbaum.

Blossfeld, H.-P./Rohwer, G. (1997). Causal Inference, Time and Observation Plans in the Social Sciences. In: Quality & Quantity, 31, 361-384.

Branco, A.U./Valsiner, J. (1997). Changing Methodologies: A Co-Constructivist Study of Goal Orientations in Social Interactions. In: Psychology and Developing Societies, 9, 1, 35-64.

Cairns, R.B. (1986). Phenomena lost. In: Valsiner, J. (Ed.). The Individual Subject and Scientific Psychology (pp. 97-111). New York: Plenum.

Cairns, R.B./Elder, G./Costello, E.J. (Eds.) (1996). Developmental Science. New York: Cambridge University Press.

Chaitin, G.J. (1975). Randomness and Mathematical Proof. In: Scientific American, 232, 5, 47-52.

Cole, M. (1996). Cultural Psychology. Cambridge, Ma,: Harvard University Press.

Diriwächter, R. (2004). Völkerpsychologie: The Synthesis that Never was. In: Culture & Psychology, 10, 1, 85-109.

Festinger, L. (1957). A Theory of Cognitive Dissonance. Stanford, CA : Stanford University Press.

Gigerenzer, G. (1993). The Superego, the Ego, and the Id in Statistical Reasoning. In: Keren, G./Lewis, C. (Eds.). A Handbook for Data Analysis in the Behavioral Sciences: Methodological Issues (pp. 311-339). Hillsdale, N.J.: Erlbaum.

Gigerenzer, G./Murray, D.J. (1987). Cognition as Intuitive Statistics. Hillsdale, N.J.: Erlbaum.

Gilbert, S.F. (1991). Epigenetic landscaping: Waddington's Use of Cell Fate Bifurcation Diagrams. In: Biology & Philosophy, 6, 135-154.

Hepper, P. (2003). Prenatal Psychological and Behavioural Development. In: Valsiner, J./Connolly, K.J. (Eds.). Handbook of Developmental Psychology (pp. 91-113). London: Sage.

Kindermann, T./Valsiner, J. (1989). Strategies for Empirical Research in Context-Inclusive Developmental Psychology. In: Valsiner, J. (Ed.). Cultural Context and Child Development (pp. 13-50). Toronto-Göttingen-Bern: C.J. Hofgrefe and H. Huber.

Klaus, M.H./Kennell, J.H. (1976). Maternal-Infant Bonding. St.Louis: Mosby.

Kojima, H. (1997) Problems of Comparison. In: Tudge, J./Shanahan, M.J./Valsiner, J. (Eds.). Comparisons in Human Development— Understanding Time and Context (pp. 318-333). Cambridge University Press.

Latour, B. (1988). The Pasteurization of France. Cambridge, MA: Harvard University Press.

Odling-Smee F.J./Lakland, K.N./Feldman, M.W. (2003). Niche Construction: The Neglected Process in Evolution. Princeton, N.J.: Princeton University Press.

Poddiakov, A.N. (2001). Counteraction as a Crucial Factor of Learning, Education and Development: Opposition to Help. FQS:Forum Qualitative Sozialforschung / Forum: Qualitative Social Research, 2 (3). [http://www.qualitative-research.net/fqs/fqs-eng.htm]

Prigogine, I. (1978). Time, Structure, and Fluctuations. In: Science, 201, No. 4358, 777-785.

Prigogine, I. (1987). Exploring Complexity. In: European Journal of Operational Research, 30, 97-103.

Sato, T./Yasuda, Y./Kido, A. (2004). Historically Structured Sampling (HSS) Model: A Contribution from Cultural Psychology. Paper presented at the 28th International Congress of Psychology, Beijing, China, August 12.

Shanahan, M.J./Valsiner, J./Gottlieb, G. (1997). Developmental Concepts across Disciplines. In: Tudge, J./Shanahan, M.J./Valsiner, J. (Eds.). Comparisons in Human Development—Understanding Time and Context (pp. 34-71), New York: Cambridge University Press.

Shvyrkov, V./Persidsky, A. (1991). The Importance of Being Earnest in Statistics. In: Quality & Quantity, 25, 19-28.

Smedslund, J. (1995). Psychologic: Common Sense and the Pseudoempirical. In: Smith, J.A./Harré, R./van Langenhove, L. (Eds.). Rethinking Psychology (pp. 196-206). London: Sage.

Sovran, T. (1992). Between Similarity and Sameness. In: Journal of Pragmatics, 18, 4, 329-344.

Trettien, A. (1900). Creeping and Walking. In: American Journal of Psychology, 12, 1-57.

Valsiner, J. (1986). Between Groups and Individuals: Psychologists' and Laypersons' Interpretations of Correlational Findings. In: Valsiner, J. (Ed.). The Individual Subject and Scientific Psychology (pp. 113-152). New York: Plenum.

Valsiner, J. (2000). Culture and Human Development. London: Sage.

Valsiner, J. (2001a). The First Six Years: Culture's Adventures in Psychology. Culture & Psychology, 7, 1, 5-48.

Valsiner, J. (2001b). Comparative Study of Human Cultural Development. Madrid: Fundacion Infancia y Aprendizaje.

Valsiner, J. (2003). Culture and its Transfer: Ways of Creating General Knowledge through the Study of Cultural Particulars. In: Lonner, W. J./Dinnel, D.L./Hayes, S.A../Sattler, D.N. (Eds.). Online Readings in Psychology and Culture (Unit 2, Chapter 12), (http://www. wwu.edu/~culture), Center for Cross-Cultural Research, Western Washington University, Bellingham, Washington, USA.

Valsiner, J. (2004). Three Years Later: Culture in Psychology—between Social Positioning and Producing new Knowledge. Culture & Psychology, 10, 1, 5-27.

Valsiner, J./van der Veer, R. (2000). The Social Mind: Construction of the Idea. New York: Cambridge University Press.

Valsiner, J./Diriwächter, R./Sauck, C. (2004). Diversity in Unity: Standard Questions and Non-Standard Interpretations. In: Bibace, R./Laird, J./Noller, K./Valsiner. J. (Eds.). Science and Medicine in Dialogue. Stamford, Ct.: Greenwood Press.

Van der Veer, R./Valsiner, J. (1991). Understanding Vygotsky: A Quest for Synthesis. Oxford: Basil Blackwell.

Von Bertalanffy, L. (1968). General Systems Theory. New York: Braziller.

Vygotsky, L.S. (1994). The Problem of the Environment. In: van der Veer, R./Valsiner, J. (Eds.). The Vygotsky Reader (pp. 338-354). Oxford: Blackwell.

Vygotsky, L.S./Luria, A.R. (1993). Etiudy po istorii povedenia: obezjana, primitiv, rebenok [Studies in the history of behavior: Ape, Primitive, and Child]. Moscow: Pedagogika-Press.

Waddington, C.H. (1956). Principles of Embryology. London, Macmillan .

Waddington, C.H. (1966). Principles of Development and Differentiation. New York: MacMillan.

White, M. (1972). On What Could Have Happened. In: Rudner, R./Scheffler, I. (Eds.). Logic & Art: Essays in Honor of Nelson Goodman (pp. 310-325). Indianapolis: Bobbs-Merrill.

Yamaguchi, K. (1991). Event History Analysis. Newbury Park, Ca.: Sage.

Yasuda, Y. (2004). The Processes of Reminiscing Themselves through Experiences of Being Infertility. Unpublished Master's thesis, Ritsumeikan University (In Japanese).

Zadeh, L.A. (1978). Fuzzy Sets as a Basis for a Theory of Possibility. In: Fuzzy Sets & Systems, 1, 3-28.

Beyond the Dilemma of Cultural and Cross-Cultural Psychology: Resolving the Tension between Nomothetic and Idiographic Approaches

Hede Helfrich-Hölter

There are two major approaches to the psychological study of human beings of different cultures, the *nomothetic* and the *idiographic* approach. The nomothetically oriented researcher approaches the study from a trans- or metacultural perspective, while the *idiographically* oriented researcher attempts to view phenomena through the eyes of his/her subjects.

The nomothetic/idiographic distinction partly parallels the distinction between *etic* and *emic* orientation as extrapolated from a distinction in linguistics between *phonetics* and *phonemics* (Pike 1954, 1967). While *phonetics* is the study of *universal* sounds used in human language, irrespective of their meanings in a particular language, *phonemics* studies sounds whose meaning-bearing roles are *unique* to a particular language (cf. Berry et al. 1992: 232).

The Nomothetic Approach

The nomothetic approach demands a descriptive system that is equally valid for all cultures and which allows for the representation of *similarities* as well as *differences* between individual cultures. Consequently, both the *objects* and the *standards* of comparison must be equivalent across cultures (cf. Helfrich 1993).

Comparisons serve to examine susceptibility or resistance in individual actions and thinking to cultural influences. *Culture* is viewed as a factor of *influence* with which we should be able to explain differences in cognition, learning, and behavior. The term 'influence' has to be understood here in a twofold sense: as a

1) systematic treatment factor
2) random factor.

In the first case, cultural variables are investigated as antecedents of individual behavior (cf. Lonner and Adamopoulos 1996). An example is the differential susceptibility to visual illusions as a function of the ecological context (Segall et al. 1966). In the second case, the cross-cultural comparison serves to test our current psychological knowledge and perspectives by using them in other cultures in order to learn if they are valid (cf. Berry 1999). An example is the testing of the validity of models of cognitive development proposed by Western psychologists in non-Western cultures.

The Idiographic Approach

According to the idiographic or emic approach, 'culture' is not an external factor whose effects on the individual must be examined, but rather an *integral part* of human behavior (e.g., see Gergen 1985). Human acts cannot be separated from their cultural contexts. They are determined not by *causes,* which can be studied using the methods of the natural sciences, but rather by *reasons,* which are under the control of the acting individual, and must be understood through the eyes of the individuals under investigation. What is emphasized in this approach is human self-determination and self-reflection.

In addition, the idiographic approach shows us that it is not only the subjects of the research who are culture-dependent, but also the whole system of psychological thought and its underlying assumptions. And these, of course, are informed by Western technological and scientific views of the world. So-called 'indigenous' psychology (cf. Berry et al. 1992: 380; Kagitcibasi and Berry 1989; Lonner and Adamopoulos 1996: 60) therefore attempts to explore cognition and behavior from the point of view of researchers from the culture under study, thus highlighting the relativity of insights gained from Western perspectives (see also Straub and Shimada 1999).

Critique of the Nomothetic Approach

The nomothetic approach is based upon a model of static influence. 'Culture' is considered a set of independent variables whose influence on individual competencies and states can be investigated in terms of dependent variables. However, there are two reasons, why 'culture' does not represent an independent variable in the usual sense.

'Cultural Membership' as an Organismic Factor

The first reason is that cultural factors, such as ecological elements, child-rearing styles, or educational systems do not represent experimental *treatment* factors, but rather *organismic* variables. While in an experiment, subjects are arbitrarily or randomly assigned to a treatment factor, the assignment of subjects to the different organismic factor levels is, at best, a selection which is based on their natural membership in a particular factor level which already exists independent of the investigation. The difficulty with this 'natural' membership is that, in most cases, it covaries with other features or traits, preventing the influence of the independent variable of interest from being examined in isolation. Instead, it is 'bundled' together with other variables (cf. Matsumoto 1996: 68), such as formal education (Pettigrew and van de Vijver 1990), industrialization (Inkeles and Smith 1974), or even biological factors (Bornstein 1975). Due to this lack of separation, differences in the dependent variable cannot be causally explained by differences in the cultural factor under study (see also van de Vijver and Leung 2000). A causal interpretation can be justified only within a theoretical framework in which the plausibility of context variables is specified a priori.

Individual Control of Cultural Influence

There is an even more fundamental criticism of the use of cultural factors as independent variables. At the heart of this criticism lies the fact that 'culture' does not represent an unavoidable unidirectional influence, but rather a systemic framework circumscribing possible courses of action (see Boesch 1991; Valsiner 1997). That is, the quality and extent of cultural penetration varies significantly between individuals because each individual constructs his/her 'personal culture' (cf. Valsiner 1994: 16). This is especially so as societies become less homogeneous, and the contemporary world increasingly dominated by cultural change rather than by cultural tradition (cf. Chaudhary 1999).

Definition and Measurement of Dependent Variables

The dependent variables to be studied should be constructs, i.e., certain cognitive competencies or psychological states. These are, however, only measurable in the form of indicators such as an observable behavior or performance on a test task. The relationship between the indicators of underlying constructs and the constructs themselves needs theoretical explanation. In most cases, this relationship varies in culture-specific ways. Thus, for instance, the behaviors indicating aggression are different across cultures. Raising one's voice may indicate hostility in some cultures but not in others. If cognitive competencies are studied, the structure of the demands of a given task may not be equivalent because the solutions needed for the task may not be the same within all cultures. For example, children from cultures with regular school education are more often familiar with prepared solutions, or at least solution schemes. Therefore, they may sometimes be able to solve a problem without having to go through all the steps considered necessary. This means that for some children, certain problem solving strategies may be more habituated than they are for others.

Critique of the Idiographic Approach

Proceeding from the assumption of human self-determination and self-reflection, the idiographic approach attempts to reconstruct the experiential world of the individual through his/her own reports and explanations. Inherent in this view is Lloyd Morgan's notion of the '*doubly induction*' necessary to reach psychological conclusions (Lloyd Morgan 1903). That is, inductions reached through the objective study of certain observable phenomena must be interpreted in terms of inductions reached through the hermeneutic study of mental processes. From the idiographic perspective, the latter induction needs reports and explanations given by the individuals themselves, who must verbally communicate the nature of their individual experience to the researcher.

There are two dangers associated with this approach: systematic bias and relativism. *Systematic bias* occurs when individuals misrepresent or misinterpret their own behavior. *Relativism* refers to the subjective status of scientific knowledge.

Norm and Behavior

The problem with using self-reports as a data source is that individuals may systematically misrepresent or misinterpret their own behavior (cf. Paulhus 1986: 144). Explanations given by individuals often tend to be guided by behavior norms and stereotypes rather than by behavior itself. In other words, self-reports tend to be biased by the social and personal desirability of actions. Empirical studies show that actual behavior may deviate considerably from the standards inferred from self-reports (see, e.g., Helfrich 1996). While there may be conscious dissimulation designed to create a favorable impression ('impression management'), there may mostly be 'self-deception', i.e., positively biased reports that the respondent actually believes to be true (cf. Paulhus 1986: 144).

Outcome and Process

A further reason for the misinterpretation of one's own behavior may be described as 'hindsight bias' (cf. Hawkins and Hastie 1990). Reports and explanations of one's own actions proceed retrospectively with the awareness of the outcome of those actions, both the intended and unintended consequences and the expected and the unexpected ones. It is precisely this awareness of unexpected and/or unintended consequences that biases the retrospective view of the source and progress of actions. The retrospective observation favors the 'product' or outcome of actions and does not reflect the process that led to this product.

It follows from this criticism that one must differentiate between the completion of a series of actions and the reflection about these actions. Reflection on past actions takes place under the influence of a normative valuation of the outcomes of actions. In contrast, behavior research emphasizes processes and unintended influences.

The Danger of Relativism

The idiographic approach is just as culture-bound and culturally dependent as the premises and methods of the nomothetic approach. After all, even the image of the self-determined, active individual is culture-dependent. Similarly, the assumption that knowledge can be made explicit, is a typical Western assumption. In some cultures, knowledge is only implicitly represented and cannot be verbalized.

The retreat to 'indigenous' or native psychology (see Berry et al. 1992: 380; Dasen and Mishra 2000; Kim 2000) does not represent a solution; the logical consequence of its radical form is an extreme cultural relativism that not only prevents comparison but also appears to reject the possibility of scientific knowledge. The insights gained in this way remain at a historicizing level, and earn the status of arbitrariness.

Conclusion

Both nomothetic and idiographic approaches have their specific short-comings. Underlying the nomothetic approach is a model of static influence. 'Culture' is considered as a set of independent variables whose influence on individual competencies and states can be investigated in terms of dependent variables. Here, it is easy to overlook the differential effects of cultural impact as well as the fact that the definition of dependent variables is itself culture-bound. The idiographic approach tries to compensate for this culture-boundness by giving the individuals under study their own say. The emphasis placed on so-called narrative techniques reflects the fact that the idiographic approach is based on a model of self-determination. The individual is seen as a self-determined being, acting within a cultural framework, whose actions are susceptible to self-reflection. The difficulty with this approach is that forces and biases that limit self-determination and self-reflection are ignored. As such, the dynamics of action are not automatically accessible to retrospective self-observation, which tends to be guided by outcomes and norms rather than by processes and actions.

These weaknesses in both the nomothetic and the idiographic approaches indicate the need for an alternative approach. I will now present a conceptual framework that synthesizes the two approaches. The new framework, called the 'principle of triarchic resonance', takes advantage of the strengths of both approaches while minimizing their weaknesses.

The Principle of Triarchic Resonance

General Outline

Each observable performance is taken to be the result of an interaction of three distinct components: the *individual*, the *task,* and the *culture*— hence the name 'triarchic'.

The 'resonance' metaphor is used to describe the specific form of interaction between the three components. The term, which implies a dynamic relationship, is borrowed from acoustics, where it means that a physical body/organism with a natural tendency to vibrate at certain frequencies builds up large amplitude vibrations when set in motion by another body/organism vibrating at similar frequencies. The amplitude of the forced vibrations increases the closer the frequencies of the driving system are to the natural frequencies of the resonator (the original system). Thus, if a body/organism has a range of natural frequencies, some of them can be amplified through external forces while others cannot. Depending on the existing frequencies of the resonator as well as on the strength of impact through the external force, the resulting resonance varies with respect to the range of amplified frequencies as well as to their respective amplitude. Generally speaking, the term 'resonance' means that existing tendencies are selectively amplified or muted through external stimulation.

Applied as a metaphor to human beings, *resonance* here suggests that every individual has a basic biological 'endowment' whose characteristics can be amplified or suppressed by external forces (see also Eccles 1989). The external forces can be described as the totality of experiences to which the individual has been exposed. Categorized in a simplified manner, the exponents of these experiences are the situational demands (*task*) and the traditional (or historically derived and selected) patterns, i.e., *culture*. Although it is mainly the individual who acts as a resonator, resonance is not restricted to the unidirectional effects of the task or culture on the individual. Instead, each of the three components— individual, task, culture—influence the others, although to different degrees. This difference results from the fact that culture can exist independent of particular individuals and remains relatively stable in comparison to them (Kroeber 1917; see Berry et al. 1992: 167). This does not rule out that an individual can at times enter into a power-dominance role over culture, and over the task. The triarchic resonance principle thus describes the dynamic interaction of all three components.

Amplification and suppression are *dynamic* processes unfolding over *time* as follows:

1) A condition, once achieved, affects subsequent states, but its effects become weaker in the course of time.

2) The results of a single event without any repetition also weaken with time, either fading or being overlaid by new events.

3) The impact of an external force depends on the state of the resonating system and the position on its developmental path. That is, the impact of situational demands and cultural influences on an individual varies with his/her developmental phases.

Therefore, the time dimension must be regarded from three perspectives: first, from the *microgenetic* perspective of the *task*; second, from the *ontogenetic* perspective of the individual; and third, from the perspective of *culture genesis*.

Microgenetic Perspective

The *microgenetic* perspective of the task refers to the developmental time course from the task as an external demand to its completion as a principally observable performance. The term 'task' here is not to be understood in the narrower sense of a test item but rather in the broader sense of situational demands or needs of a cognitive, social, or emotional nature. The task, as an external force, challenges the competence and stimulates the motivation of the individual as the resonating system, and the evoked intellectual or psychological processes lead to an observable performance. The task evokes different types of processes, depending on the extent and time of the subject's prior experience with that particular task. Completion of a relatively novel task may require full attention. In contrast, when a task has been carried out repeatedly, its completion becomes automatic.

Three levels of familiarity can be differentiated (after Rasmussen 1986; Reason 1990; see Helfrich 1999): the *skill-based* level, the rule-based level, and the *knowledge-based* level. Automatic actions are carried out at the skill-based or habitual level, novel actions at the knowledge-based level, whereas the rule-based level occupies an intermediate position. The same task may be carried out at different levels, depending on the individual and his/her cultural experience. Top-down shifts tend to occur along with increasing expertise; actions originally carried out at the rule- or knowledge-based level tend to shift to the next lower level as the number of successful repetitions increases. Concomitant with the top-down shift, there is a decrease of attention and awareness in carrying out the action. This shows that the level of processes evoked by the task not only depends on the amount of experience but also on the developmental stage at which the task is encountered. Bottom-up transitions can be seen, too; some tasks may be mastered in childhood at a skill-based level without explicit instruction, but require conscious mastering at a knowledge-based level when initially faced in adulthood.

Ontogenetic Perspective

The *ontogenetic* perspective refers to prior individual experience during the course of biological development. The quality and the quantity of the prior experiences, as well as the developmental point at which these experiences take place, affect subsequent behavior and shape subsequent states of competence. The strength (i.e., amplitude) and quality (i.e., range) of resonance depends on the individual's developmental phase, with the impact of situational demands and cultural influences probably being of greatest influence during childhood. The quality of impact may also be different in childhood; much of what is learned in childhood is acquired implicitly, i.e., without explicit teaching. Learning a language provides a good example of how cultural tradition takes place at different behavioral levels. Language learning during childhood occurs at the skill-based level, both because the language is acquired in a period of considerable sensitivity without explicit teaching and because of extensive practice. In contrast, language acquisition as an adult occurs at the knowledge-based level, which has intellectual consequences in terms of the accessibility of the competence. While, in the latter case, language may be accessible only as conscious application, in the former it is accessible as unconscious or automatic mastery.

Culture-Genetic Perspective

'Culture' has been defined as a system of patterns that is transmitted from generation to generation. In this definition tradition is seen as an outcome, i.e., as an already established entity. This tradition itself is, however, subject to development. The perspective of *cultural genesis* focuses on the dynamics of a society's pattern system being product and process at the same time. As a process, the value system is modified both by external situational demands and the actions of the individuals. Retrospectively viewed, cultural genesis may have transformed the epistemic structure of a task by changing the affected competence level. Modern industrial cultures have transferred arithmetical tasks, for example, calculating the cube root of a given number, to the pocket calculator, which enables us to obtain the solution without knowing the solution process. Applied to cross-cultural research, the process of solution required by a given task may not be the same in all cultures because of culture-specific variations in the availability of prepared solutions, or in solution schemes (see also Diamond 1997). What represents an action at the skill-based or rule-based level for members of one culture may be an action at the knowledge-based level for members of a different culture. It is clear that specifying the level valid for the culture under study requires incorporating the indigenous view.

Acting as a product, a society's value system modifies individual traits and competencies, insofar as these are strengthened or weakened depending on cultural evaluation. Thus, for example, the development of individual motives, interests, and competencies is culture-specifically influenced since certain achievements are highly valued within a culture while others receive little attention (see Durham 1990; Poortinga et al. 1990). Parents, teachers, and peers play an important role in transmitting this evaluation by reinforcing certain behaviors and ignoring or suppressing others (cf. Grossmann 1993: 59). Berry (1976) has pointed out that spatial skills are of higher value, and hence more developed, in hunting societies than they are in rural ones; in the latter, spatial abilities are needed for survival (cf. van de Vijver and Leung 2000). The relationship between evaluation and ecological demands is less evident elsewhere, but it is still present. Consider musical abilities, which are evaluated differently across cultures. Western schooling favors these abilities to a much lesser extent than the ability to reason logically. Consequently, when confronted with a musical task, the motivation to master it tends to be less pronounced than, for instance, in some traditional African cultures. Culture genesis thus interacts with both: the individual ontogenesis and the microgenesis of the task.

Interaction between Culture, Individual, and Task

Figure 1 summarizes the mutual relationships between culture, individual, and task in terms of the principle of triarchic resonance. The arrows symbolize the mutual impacts, the shadowed areas the temporal displays. Given a task as a situational demand, a specific behavior performance is displayed by the individual. The microgenetic process leading to the specific type and level of this observable performance (as indicated by the solid arrows) is affected by the activated motivation and competence levels which, in turn, are modified by ontogenetic as well as by culture-genetic processes (as indicated by the broken arrows). Although the process of responding to situational demands is universal, the same situation can generate multiple behaviors, depending on the particular culture and the particular individual. Even the definition of a given situation as a *task* to be mastered differs across cultures and individuals and is subjected to cultural and individual development. The way a situation is mastered affects subsequent individual and cultural development (as indicated by the broken arrows leading from the observable performance to the individual and from there to culture).

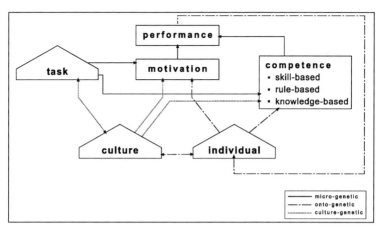

Figure 1: The principle of triarchic resonance

Relationship between Nomothetic and Idiographic Approaches

The principle of triarchic resonance provides a universal framework for the study of cultural variability. In this sense, it is a nomothetic approach. Yet, in order to explain an observed behavior as a product of the interaction between culture, individual, and task, both the nomothetic and the idiographic approach are needed. Comparisons require a nomothetic view, but the comparability can only be assured through incorporation of the idiographic view. An exclusively nomothetic approach runs the risk of incorrectly inferring from differences in observed performance to the impact of culture because the relationship between task, competence, and performance is erroneously assumed to be constant across cultures. The idiographic approach must be incorporated to explicate the particular form of this relationship. The idiographic view can shed light on the culture-specific meaning of a task, the way it is conceived, and the relevance attributed to it. But the idiographic approach also has its limitations; cultural and individual self-interpretation tend to accentuate the normative desirable behavior and to attenuate the undesirable. For example, a purely idiographic view may not reveal that a particular ecological situation could be alternatively interpreted as a task to be mastered. Moreover, cultural and individual self-interpretation bear systematic biases regarding time-bound processes; retrospective observation favors the product or outcome of actions and tends to 'smooth' the process leading to that outcome. Therefore, the study of the relationship between task, competence, and performance must be extended through the metacultural view.

Similarity to Other Models

The principle of triarchic resonance shows some similarities to two other theoretical proposals: Berry's 'derived etic' (Berry 1989; see also Berry 1999), and Vygotsky's theory of the 'sociohistorical formation of higher mental processes' (Vygotsky 1978).

Berry (1989), mediating between nomothetic and idiographic approaches, has suggested a 'derived etic' approach as an advanced stage in a research process. As in the present proposal, Berry's framework incorporates aspects of task (called 'context'), cultural adaptation to task, and individual behaviors (both competence and performance aspects) in adaptation to task, culture and task (cf. Berry 1999). Thus, Berry's model provides a guideline for empirical research in cross-cultural psychology at the operational level, and the consequences for research strategies partly overlap with those derived from the principle of triarchic resonance. Both models attempt to restrain the researcher from generalizing cultural idiosyncrasies, but the principle of triarchic resonance provides additional theoretical considerations to account for the cultural idiosyncrasies.

Essential parts of the principle of triarchic resonance resemble Vygotsky's theory of the "sociohistorical formation of higher mental processes" (Vygotsky 1978; 1981).

Similar to Vygotsky, different levels of development are specified; the 'microgenetic' level is specified as the development of a cognitive skill, while the ontogenetic level is seen as the 'subject's individual history' (Vygotsky 1978), and the culture-genetic level is specified as the 'cultural development' (Vygotsky 1978). However, unlike Vygotsky's notion of 'historical laws', which are the key to discovering the development of higher forms of behavior (Vygotsky 1978: 20), the metaphor of resonance indicates that there is not necessarily an opposition between the 'laws of nature' and the 'laws of spirit'. Instead, it emphasizes that new qualities may emerge from the encounter of external demands with internal tendencies.

Summary

A unifying theoretical framework called the 'principle of triarchic resonance' has been proposed here in order to overcome the weaknesses of both nomothetic and idiographic approaches. This model attempts to account for the mutual relationship between individual, cultural, and situational demands as a dynamic interaction unfolding over time. The metaphor of 'resonance' is used to describe this process, and to emphasize that existing characteristics of a system can be substantially modified by selective amplification or suppression through external stimulation. It also emphasizes that this process is neither completely passive nor completely active. Based on its three components, the principle of resonance is to be applied from three perspectives: the microgenetic perspective of the completion of the task, the ontogenetic perspective of individual development, and the culture-genetic perspective of task transformation through cultural tradition. In this way, the model attempts to compensate for the weaknesses of both the idiographic and the nomothetic approach. Unlike the idiographic approach, it incorporates time-bound processes neglected by self-interpretation of behavior, while, unlike the nomothetic approach, it explicitly incorporates the dynamics of the task whose culture-specific genesis can be accounted for only through the incorporation of 'indigenous' perspectives.

The principle of triarchic resonance provides a framework for the evaluation and planning of cross-cultural comparisons. As with all metaphors and analogies, the scope of its applicability should not be overgeneralized. Designed for comparability of psychological states or processes and their cultural antecedents, the principle of triarchic resonance currently does not encompass the scope of phylogenetic development where changes such as mutations may require additional theoretical models. However, the principle does provide a methodological framework for future cross-cultural psychological investigations and can aid researchers in overcoming the problems now inherent in cross-cultural investigations.

References

Berry, J.W. (1976). Human Ecology and Cognitive Style. Comparative Studies in Cultural and Psychological Adaptation. Beverly Hills, Cal.: Sage.

Berry, J.W.(1989). Imposed Etics, Emics, Derived Etics. In: International Journal of Psychology, 24, 721-735.

Berry, J.W. (1999). Emics and Etics: A Symbiotic Conception. In: Culture & Psychology, 5, 165-172.

Berry, J.W./Poortinga, Y.H./Segall, M.H./Dasen, P.R. (1992). Cross-Cultural Psychology. Cambridge: Cambridge University Press.

Boesch, E.E. (1991). Symbolic Action Theory and Cultural Psychology. Berlin: Springer.

Bornstein, M.H. (1975). The Influence of Visual Perception on Culture. In: American Anthropologist, 77, 774-798.

Chaudhary, N. (1999). Diversity, Definitions and Dilemmas: A Commentary on Helfrich's Principle of Triarchic Resonance. In: Culture & Psychology, 5, 155-163.

Dasen, P.R./Mishra, R.C.(2000). Cross-Cultural Views on Human Development in the Third Millennium. In: International Journal of Behavioral Development, 24, 428-434.

Diamond, J. (1997). Guns, Germs, and Steel. The Fates of Human Societies. New York: Norton.

Durham, W.H. (1990). Advances in Evolutionary Culture Theory. In: Annual Review of Anthropology, 19, 187-210.

Eccles, J.C. (1989). Evolution of the Brain: Creation of the Self. London: Routledge.

Gergen, K.J. (1985). Social Constructionist Inquiry: Context and Implications. In: K.J. Gergen/K.E. Davis (Eds.). The Social Construction of the Person (pp. 3-18). New York, Berlin: Springer.

Grossmann, K.E. (1993). Universalismus und kultureller Relativismus. In: A. Thomas (Ed.). Kulturvergleichende Psychologie (pp. 53-80). Göttingen: Hogrefe.

Hawkins, S.A./Hastie, R. (1990). Hindsight: Biased Judgments of Past Events After the Outcomes are Known. In: Psychological Bulletin, 107, 311-327.

Helfrich, H. (1993). Methodologie kulturvergleichender Forschung. In: A. Thomas (Ed.). Kulturvergleichende Psychologie (pp. 81-102). Göttingen: Hogrefe.

Helfrich, H. (1996). Soziale Handlungsmuster im Vergleich zwischen Japan und Deutschland. In: G. Trommsdorf/H.-J. Kornadt (Eds.). Gesellschaftliche und individuelle Entwicklung in Japan und Deutschland (pp. 319-330). Konstanz: Universitätsverlag Konstanz.

Helfrich, H. (1999). Human Reliability from a Social-Psychological Perspective. In: International Journal of Human-Computer Studies, 50, 193-212.

Inkeles, A./Smith, D.H. (1974). Becoming Modern. Cambridge, MA.: Harvard University Press.

Kagitcibasi, C./Berry, J.W. (1989). Cross-Cultural Psychology: Current Research and Trends. In: Annual Review of Psychology, 493-531.

Kim, U. (2000). Indigenous, Cultural, and Cross-Cultural Psychology: A Theoretical, Conceptual, and Epistemological Analysis. In: Asian Journal of Social Psychology, 3, 265-287.

Kroeber, A.L. (1917). The Superorganic. In: American Anthroplogist, 19, 163-213.

Lonner, W.J./Adamopoulos, J. (1996). Culture as Antecedent to Behavior. In W. Berry/Y.H. Poortinga/J. Pandey (Eds.). Handbook of Cross-Cultural Psychology, Vol. 1 (pp. 43-83). Theory and Method. 2nd ed. Boston: Allyn & Bacon.

Lloyd Morgan, C. (1903). An Introduction to Comparative Psychology. 2nd edition. London: Walter Scott.

Matsumoto, D. (1996). Culture and Psychology. Pacific Grove: Brooks/Cole.

Paulhus, D.L. (1986). Self-Deception and Impression Management in Test Responses. In: A. Angleitner/J.S. Wiggins (Eds.). Personality Assessment via Questionnaires (pp. 143-165). Berlin: Springer.

Pettigrew, T.F./van de Vijver, F.J.R. (1990). Thinking Both Bigger and Smaller: Finding the Basic Level for Cross-Cultural Psychology. In P.J.D. Drenth/J. A. Sergeant/R. J. Takens (Eds.). European Perspectives in Psychology, Vol.3 (pp. 339-353). Chichester: John Wiley..

Pike, K. L. (1954). Emic and Etic Standpoints for the Description of Behavior. In: K.L. Pike (Ed.). Language in Relation to a Unified Theory of the Structure of Human Behavior (pp. 8-28). Glendale: Summer Institute of Linguistics.

Pike, K.L. (1967). Language in Relation to a Unified Theory of the Structure of Human Behavior. Den Haag: Mouton.

Poortinga, Y.H./Kop, P.F.M./van de Vijver, F.J.R. (1990). Differences Between Psychological Domains in the Range of Cross-Cultural Variation. In: P.J.D. Drenth/J.A. Sergeant/R.J. Takens (Eds.). European Perspectives in Psychology, Vol. 3 (pp. 355-376). Chichester: John Wiley.

Rasmussen, J. (1986). Information Processing and Human-Machine Interaction. Amsterdam: North Holland.

Reason, J. (1990). Human Error. Cambridge: Cambridge University Press.

Segall, M.H./Campbell, D.T./Herskovits, M.J. (1966). The Influence of Culture on Visual Perception. Indianapolis: Bobbs-Merrill.

Straub, J./Shimada, S. (1999). Relationale Hermeneutik im Kontext interkulturellen Verstehens. In: Deutsche Zeitschrift für Philosophie, 47, 449-477.

Valsiner, J. (1994). What is "natural" about "natural contexts"?: Cultural Construction of Human Development (and its Study). In: Infancia-y-Aprendizaje, 66, 11-19.

Valsiner, J. (1997). The Saarbrücken Tradition in Cultural Psychology, and Its Legacy. In: Culture & Psychology, 3, 243-245.

van de Vijver, F.J.R./Leung, K. (2000). Methodological Issues in Psychological Research on Culture. In: Journal of Cross-Cultural Psychology, 31, 33-51.

Vygotsky, L.S. (1978). Mind in Society: The Development of Higher
Mental Processes. Cambridge, MA: Harvard University Press.

Vygotsky, L.S. (1981). The Genesis of Higher Mental Functions. In J.V.
Wertsch (Ed.). The Concept of Activity in Soviet Psychology.
Armonk, N.Y.: Sharpe.

THE SOLUTION OF FUNDAMENTAL METHODOLOGICAL PROBLEMS IN CROSS-CULTURAL PSYCHOLOGY BY GUARANTEEING THE EQUIVALENCE OF MEASUREMENTS

PATRICIA SIMON

The Impossibility of Accomplishing Experiments in Cross-Cultural Psychology

Cross-cultural psychology has for a long time been treated in literature—even by its own representatives—not as a discipline of its own or an individual branch of psychology, but solely as a method or research strategy in its own right (Berry 1980; Boesch and Eckensberger 1969; Eckensberger 1990; Helfrich 1993; Jahoda 1980; Triandis 1980). This line of thinking obscures the fact that cross-cultural psychology is actually dealing with the experience and behavior of humans in different cultures. The fact that cross-cultural psychology was originally reduced to a mere method can paradoxically be traced back to the fact that this research topic suffers from strong methodological problems. This becomes particularly apparent when it is considered from the perspective of the methodological standards borrowed from the natural sciences. For experiments cannot be conducted in cross-cultural psychology since this topic deals with so-called 'organism variables' or 'assigned variables' (Boesch and Eckensberger 1969; Edwards 1971; Helfrich 1993). Therefore, the subjects under study cannot be randomly assigned to experimental treatments and, hence, no strict logical causal assertions can be made.

However, this is not the only branch of psychology that is confronted with this problem; rather, due to their high level of complexity and the interdependence of the independent variables in their impact on the dependent variable, there are many psychological questions that cannot be solved by carrying out experiments. A powerful illustration of this is a question that has engaged small-group research since the 1930s, and that focuses on the factors determining the effectiveness of work groups. Although this question has been researched for decades, only a few single factors could be identified, which has led in part to rather contradictory results (Guzzo and Shea 1992; Hackman 1990; Hackman and Walton 1986; McGrath 1991). The contradictory findings of this small-group research can, in part, be traced back to the unquestioned acceptance of the assumption that an experiment is the research method of choice. Due to the methodological constraints of experiments, the impact of a factor determining effectiveness was often investigated in these studies—without taking into consideration the interdependence of the determinants in their impact on group effectiveness. This did not do justice to the complexity of group processes (Simon 2002). Only after the determinants of effectiveness were simultaneously subjected to a multivariate analysis in an observation study, was it possible to develop a powerful model of group effectiveness (Simon 2002).

This example clearly illustrates the fact that not only does cross-cultural psychology have to accept a reduction in the choice of methods in order to solve its problems, but other fields of psychology must do the same when their research focuses on the complexity of human nature.

Since experiments cannot be conducted in cross-cultural psychology, many researchers were afraid that this could lead to the belief that the discipline would be deemed unscientific (cf. for example Boesch and Eckensberger 1969: 557). However, this fear proved to be unjustified, as can be recognized by the growing tendency of mainstream psychology to also unfetter itself from the constraints of the experiment in recent years. This development is accompanied by the realization that a given research method should serve a particular research question and not vice versa, that is, that the research method determines the research question. This latter example is just as unscientific as not carrying out an experiment allegedly is. For, "if priority is given to the method, as clean as it may be, over and above the question, this can undoubtedly result in the emergence of a theoretical model of psychology that does not fit the object, or that methodological weaknesses (or rather an incompatibility between method and question) never really come to light" (Boesch and Eckensberger 1969: 515; translated by the author).

Undoubtedly, the experiment enjoys a high status in the empirical sciences since it is still the only method with which it is possible to make causal statements. Nevertheless, this does not mean that the experiment is the only scientific method available with which to gather data. Further methods exist, such as systematic observations, tests, questionnaires, and interviews, which are not less scientific. However, it is impossible to make causal statements employing these methods, when in the data collection situation disturbance variables are not controlled. If, however, one deals with complex relationships, one or more such methods can prove to be superior to the experimental method, which can be seen from the work groups example mentioned above. Only after a systematic observation and a multivariate statistical analysis procedure were used, was it possible to develop a model of group effectiveness that adequately describes the complex relationships of the determinants of effectiveness (Simon 2002).

Furthermore, in times when everyone can make use of computers, the problem of causality can also be tackled with multivariate statistical procedures such as path analysis or structure equation models. Of course, with such procedures no causal statements can be made in a stricter sense since it is not the statistical procedure that determines the causal status of an investigation, but rather the situation of data gathering itself. Nevertheless, such procedures make it possible to clarify how strong the impact of a predictor variable on a criterion variable might be.

On the other hand, in a discussion concerning causality one should not forget that the capacity to explore the cause of an effect only enjoys such a high status in the empirical sciences because with knowledge of the cause of an effect one is able to make exact predictions, which is the essential aim of science. However, such predictions can also be made based on a regression model that has been developed on the basis of observational data. If one knows—referring back to the example above regarding group effectiveness research—*in which way* effective work groups interact, one can then reliably predict the performance potential of a particular group, based on an analysis of its interaction process (Simon 2002). In order to embrace the essential goal of empirical sciences, the cause need not necessarily be known, but the knowledge of the way in which the complex relationships between the variables function can be sufficient to make predictions. The question, as to why it precisely functions in this way, perhaps, can never be solved when we focus on such complex relationships. This recognition may not be easy to accept; such a recognition drove poor Faust, in Goethe's popular tragic drama, into the arms of Mephisto:

"Ye instruments, ye surely jeer at me,
With handle, wheel and cogs and cylinder.
I stood beside the gate, ye were to be the key.
True, intricate your ward, but no bolts do ye stir.
Inscrutable upon a sunlit day,
Her veil will Nature never let you steal,
And what she will not to your mind reveal,
You will not wrest from her with levers and with screws" (Goethe, 1899: 22).

Without becoming lofty at this point, a great deal of truth lies in these words of Faust, which will become clear in the following section. This section deals with one of the greatest problems of cross-cultural psychology, which is that no 'neutral point of view' exists from which it is possible to analyze data from different cultures.

The Problem of the Missing 'Neutral Point of View'

Indeed, although it is not as directly evident as in the case of cross-cultural psychology, the problem of the 'missing neutral point of view' also exists in mainstream psychology. Popper (1984) had already drawn attention to the fact that no theory-free observation exists, and to quote yet another philosopher, this problem also becomes clear by the uncovering of Habermas' (1968) *'erkenntnisleitenden Interessen'*, or one could say 'cognition-led interests', of a researcher. That means, every study is determined by the antecedents of a researcher. Since the researcher is always a part of the research process, it is impossible to assume a neutral point of view. Therefore, we can conclude that we are not able to detect the truth. Indeed, scientific theory offers different theories of cognition that are all coherent, and each of which deliver to us an alleged fundament for recognition. In spite of their internal coherence, however, no external criterion exists that would make it possible to decide which theory of cognition is true. So the question arises, which theory of cognition should one choose as a basis for one's studies? Should one choose Pascal's (1937) theory of cognition? He states that it is not possible to understand the whole without knowing anything about the parts and that the different parts cannot be understood without knowing the whole. According to Pascal, this boils down to the fact that we are unable to detect the truth due to the original sin. Only when we turn ourselves to God will he perhaps, in an act of grace, bestow on us the truth (cf. Heess 1977). Or is it better, to avoid religious aspects, to follow Hume's (1882) theory, which was the first to direct full attention to the problem of induction in the empirical sciences. According to Hume, we are unable to detect the cause of an effect since every conclusion drawn on the basis of an experience presupposes the thesis of the uniformity of natural processes (*Gleichförmigkeitsthese des Naturverlaufs*), which cannot be proven. This obviously also applies to any experiment, and the causal inferences that are based on it. Seen epistemologically, it is devoid of any foundation. The belief that a causal relationship exists between two events arises, according to Hume (1882), only from habituation to the coincidental appearance of the two events. This belief is a kind of natural instinct that no rationality can produce or prevent.

For those who are not satisfied with this explanation, as Hume assumes that a subjective necessity based only on habit can be objective, we might bring into play Kant's (1783) solution to the induction problem. He postulates that an inherent idea of cognitive understanding of cause exists with which we come to know our world. According to this theory, we find in nature the laws of our own mind. Since cognitive ideas do not, however, correspond to empirically verifiable phenomena, Kant's solution of the induction problem has come into the cross fire of criticism, especially from the Logical Empiricists (Stegmüller 1978). Later, Popper (1979) tried to circumvent the problem of induction through his deductive methodology, and believed that he had reformulated the problem: "In this way the problem of induction becomes solvable. The solution is, that induction does not exist, since general theories cannot be derived from singular statements" (Popper 1979: 118). According to Popper, one has to give up the purist striving of scientific theories toward an absolute, doubtless, presupposition free fundament of knowledge. Such an idea is not realistic, and the source of this idea simply lies in the psycho-structure of human beings, their need for certainty, and their emotional striving for security.

A Solution for the Problem of Cognition in Cross-Cultural Psychology

The treatise of different theories of cognition has shown that no fundamental basis of knowledge exists. If a researcher follows a specific theory of cognition, which are all true in their own way, he runs the risk of becoming ideological. Therefore, from my point of view, there is only one pragmatic solution, namely, to secure the findings of a study with the help of criteria, just as mainstream psychology does when it tries to determine the objectivity, reliability, and validity of its findings. Knowledge can be understood as objective—to use Kant's words—when several researchers express the same opinion about an object. Indeed, in this case, one cannot be sure that this judgement corresponds to the circumstances in the world and thus that *it* is absolutely true, either, but this judgement comes closest to the truth of the human perception and cognition system.

However, it is just at this point that the problems of cross-cultural psychology begin. Due to the fact that the interpretation of data greatly depends on the researcher's culture, various measures must be imple-

273

mented to ensure that two researchers from different cultures will arrive at the same judgement about an object, or until it is certain that a researcher will interpret the data from a foreign country in a culturally adequate way. According to classical test theory, a researcher must subject his method of data collection to different tests in order to achieve objective, reliable, and valid results. For example, in order to be able to work with a questionnaire measuring a psychological construct, it must be ensured that the data does not undergo subjective biases in the data collection situation. Furthermore, it must be ensured that the questionnaire can reliably measure the construct, and that the questionnaire measures what should be measured.

Transferring this problem to cross-cultural research, it will become clear that in this case too, it is a question of objectivity, reliability, and validity, namely the problem of ensuring the reliable collection and interpretation of the data in a culturally adequate way. Since a researcher in cross-cultural research is, however, confronted with at least two different populations, the techniques for producing and proving the criteria developed in classical test theory alone are not sufficient. However, these techniques can be combined with concepts already developed in cross-cultural psychology to guarantee the measurement and interpretation of data in a culturally adequate way, so that objective, reliable, and valid instruments for cross-cultural research can be obtained.

For precisely such aspects, Helfrich (1993) compiled a list of four postulates that must be fulfilled in order to measure and interpret data in a culturally adequate way. According to Helfrich (1993), the measuring process can be divided into four levels, each of which must be equivalent in order to be able to compare data from different cultures.

The first measurement level on which equivalence is required is the hypothetical construct that should be measured. The hypothetical construct must possess a conceptual equivalence in the cultures under examination. The second level—deviating from the order of the four levels suggested by Helfrich (1993)—forms the scale on which the comparison is made, which must possess equivalence in scale. The third level presents the indicators with which the construct is measured. In order to guarantee a comparison of data from different cultures, they must be operationally equivalent. The fourth and last level refers to the comparison of the data collection situation for which a collecting equivalence is required. These four types of equivalence in measurement are summarized in Figure 1.

Conceptual equivalence of the hypothetical construct means that the construct has the same meaning in all cultures under examination. Transferring this to classical test theory, the question of content validity must be addressed. The question as to the content validity of a test is often only answered for reasons of plausibility (Lienert and Raatz 1994). So, for example, the content validity of tasks in a school test can be derived from logical reasons. Thus, this type of validity can correspondingly be described as logical validity (Lienert and Raatz 1994). Also, in cross-cultural psychology one need not necessarily implement extravagant investigations to determine the content validity, particularly when the construct under consideration is a human universal such as thinking, learning, problem solving, or language usage (Berry 1980; Helfrich 1993). If it is not possible to accept a test based on plausibility, it might be that experts can/will judge the test items in terms of how representative they are for the construct. However, for reasons of expense, the calculation of a numerical validity value is waived most of the time (Lienert and Raatz 1994). In an analogous way, in cross-cultural psychology there is the option of asking experts from the different cultures under consideration about the content validity of the construct. Under such circumstances it might be necessary to use different terms for measuring the same construct in different cultures (Helfrich 1993).

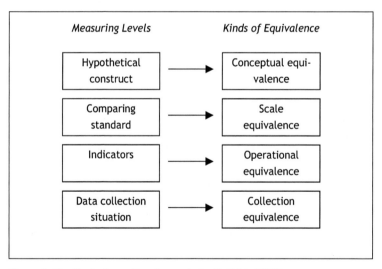

Figure 1: The Equivalence Requirements by Helfrich (1993)

Equivalence of scales means that the construct is measured on the same scale in every culture under consideration (Helfrich 1993). The term scale denotes the level on which a construct is measured. With Stevens (1951), four levels (or scales) can be differentiated: the nominal, the ordinal, the interval, and the ratio scale. Thus, this is also an area in which the methodological problems that cross-cultural psychology is confronted

275

with do not significantly differ from those methodological problems discussed in mainstream psychology. Here, the same theoretical problems of measurement must first be solved before one can start with an investigation. Suggestions regarding the creation of scale equivalence in cross-cultural psychology have been made by Poortinga (1975), Poortinga and van de Vijver (1988) as well as Vijver und Poortinga (1982), and are summarized by Helfrich (1993).

The operational equivalence of indicators requires that the operationalization of the indicators measuring a construct possess adequate construct validity in terms of classical test theory in all cultures under examination. The construct validity is often not numerically substantiated due to the enormous technical effort and economic resources required (Lienert and Raatz 1994); rather, it is substantiated with arguments and reasons of plausibility. In cross-cultural research, the test of construct validity can lead to the need for two different indicators for measuring the same construct in two different cultures: indicators that measure different behaviors from a phenomenal point of view, but measure the same construct from a functional point of view (Berry 1980; Boesch and Eckensberger 1969; Frijda and Jahoda 1966; Helfrich 1993).

The requirement for data collection equivalence is comparable to test theoretical criterion objectivity, which can be divided into three types: objectivity in the execution, scoring, and interpretation of a test. The test execution objectivity criterion requires that a test be performed under the same conditions across all subjects. Carrying this demand over to cross-cultural psychology, this means that the test situation is the same across all cultures, or, to say it in the words of Helfrich (1993), that the subjects from different cultures have an equal chance of scoring well on the test, which means that the test must be constructed in a culturally adequate way.

The scoring objectivity refers to the numerical or categorial calculation of the registered test behavior (Lienert and Raatz 1994). When dealing with standardized tests with fixed instructions for mathematical operations, a complete agreement between two investigators normally occurs (with the exception of mistakes in the calculation). In cross-cultural psychology, the scoring objectivity of standardized tests is fulfilled when the scale equivalence and operational equivalence of the indicators are satisfied. Under these conditions, the test results of subjects from different cultures can be calculated in the same manner.

Interpretation objectivity refers to the degree to which the interpretation of the test results is independent of the person who interprets the results (Lienert and Raatz 1994). The interpretation objectivity is trivial in cases of tests with fixed norms (Lienert and Raatz 1994). In cross-cultural psychology, the interpretation objectivity of a normed test is fulfilled when the requirements of conceptual equivalence of the to-be-measured construct is satisfied, as well as the equivalence of the indicators and the scale level.

From this illustration it becomes clear that the four postulates of measurement equivalence in cross-cultural psychology are nothing more than the requirement of objectivity, reliability, and validity in classical test theory. At this point the reader might have noticed, however, that none of the four equivalence postulates are related to the reliability of a test. This is due to the fact that the reliability of a test can only be determined *after* the test has been constructed. The four equivalence postulates, however, are the prerequisites that must be considered when constructing an instrument for cross-cultural research. Only when these prerequisites have been fulfilled is it at all possible to achieve reliable values with a test. Naturally, in cross-cultural psychology as well, the reliability of a measurement instrument must be determined once it has been developed.

An Exemplary Depiction of the Application of the Suggested Solution by Means of the Interaction-Observation System SYNPRO

The following example of the interaction-observation system SYNPRO demonstrates the usefulness of combining the equivalence requirements suggested by Helfrich (1993) with the test theoretical criterion to achieve culturally adequate instruments for cross-cultural research.

The Interaction-Observation System SYNPRO

The interaction-observation system SYNPRO was specifically developed to measure interaction behavior in work groups that are confronted with complex problems (Simon 2002). In SYNPRO, the problem-solving process occurring in a work group is structured by means of five main categories: goal clarification, process clarification, problem analysis, problem-solving phase, and process reflection. The main category, *goal clarification,* serves to measure group discussion about work objectives, whereas *process clarification entails the registration of* all planning components, that means the coordination of the particular work steps, and the strategies and methods of problem solving. *Problem analysis as a category* serves to provide insight into the problem by gathering information, exchanging information, and generating hypotheses as to how the system works. In the *problem-solving phase*, concrete suggestions for solutions are made on the basis of the foregoing problem analysis. The last category, *process reflection*, comprises the reflection of the discussion and work processes (Simon 2002).

The cooperation of group members within the particular problem-solving phases is depicted in the form of sub-categories. According to what the particular phases mean, the *suggestions made for solutions* in the three main categories—goal clarification, process clarification, and problem-solving phase—have different functions. For the main category goal clarification, it is a question of target suggestions, for the main category process clarification, it is a question of procedural, strategy, and method suggestions, and for the main category problem solving it is a question of suggestions for concrete solutions. Expressed statements in response to particular suggestions by group members were categorized as positive, negative, or neutral. In order to reflect the interrelatedness of the discussion process between group members, a further distinction was made between *detailed suggestions* and *contrary suggestions*.

Furthermore, particular attention was paid to the decision-making process by distinguishing between making *concrete decisions about suggestions* and *trying to make such decisions*. In the main category *process clarification*, decisions not preceded by discussion about suggestions are treated separately as so-called *coordination decisions*.

In addition to the discussion about suggestions in the three main categories, *analyzing questions* and *situation analysis* also occur while working on the problem. In the main category *goal clarification* analyzing questions relate to questions about targets *per definitionem*, in the main category *process clarification* they relate to questions about the process, and in the problem-solving phase they relate to questions about the way of handling a problem. For these three main categories the sub-category situation analysis refers to the summary of the decisions made, and for the main category process clarification, to the summary of the accomplished work steps.

Within the main category *problem analysis*, the exchange of information between group members as well as the analysis of the problem is depicted. The gathering of information and the exchange of information is measured through the sub-categories *information questions* and *information transport*. Questions requesting information from the experimenter are registered in the sub-category *questions to the experimenter*. The sub-categories *situation analysis* and *analyzing questions* serve in this main category to analyze the essential problem. The sub-category situation analysis comprises the gathered knowledge of a group about the problem, and the analyzing questions serve to assess the questions a group asks about various aspects of the problem.

The main category *process reflection* comprises the coordination of the discussion process, the estimation and reflection of the discussion process as well as the problem-solving process, and the organization of the work utilities. Furthermore, the category *mood-barometer* measures the various moods of a group during the problem-solving process, recognizable by laughing, jokes, or sighing.

Table 1 gives an overview of the categories. Complete definitions of the particular categories with coding examples and rules for distinguishing between the categories, as well as the coding manual, can be found in Simon (1997).

With the help of this system, for example, the complexity of the decision-making process regarding a concrete suggestion for a solution can be reproduced starting from the evaluations, to the controversies that might arise and the further differentiations of the suggestions down to the concrete decision making. In this manner the decision-making process within a group can be analyzed according to its crucial units (Simon 2002).

The observation unit of SYNPRO, in terms of the smallest meaningful unit within the interaction process that can be assigned to a category, is made up of the function of an utterance in the problem-solving process and on the cooperative level (Simon 2002). Therefore, the function of the interactions in the problem-solving process, and on the cooperative level, represents the dimension in which the interaction behavior of a group is portrayed. The hypothetical construct underlying this dimension is 'problem-solving' in groups.

1. goal clarification (Zk)	(St)	- statement
	(Sa)	- situation analysis
	(Fa)	- analyzing question
	(V)	- suggestion
	(DV)	- detailed suggestion
	(GV)	- contrary suggestion
	(Ef)	- decision-making
2. process clarification (Pk)	(St)	- statement
	(Sa)	- situation analysis
	(Fa)	- analyzing question
	(V)	- suggestion
	(DV)	- detailed suggestion
	(GV)	- contrary suggestion
	(Ef)	- decision-making
	(KE)	- coordination decision
3. problem analysis (Pa)	(St)	- statement
	(Sa)	- situation analysis
	(Fa)	- analyzing question
	(If)	- information question
	(Iw)	- information transport
	(Fv)	- questions to the experimenter
	(Rv)	- reactions to the experimenter
4. problem-solving phase (Pr)	(St)	- statement
	(Sa)	- situation analysis
	(Fa)	- analyzing question
	(V)	- suggestion
	(DV)	- detailed suggestion
	(GV)	- contrary suggestion
	(Ef)	- decision-making
5. process reflection (Pl)	(KD)	- coordination of the discussion process
	(BD)	- estimation and reflection of the discussion process
	(OA)	- organization of the work utilities
	(BP)	- estimation and reflection of the problem-solving process
6. mood-barometer	(EV)	- transport of the decisions to the experimenter

Table 1: The Categories of the SYNPRO Interaction Observation System

The Further Development of the Interaction Observation System SYNPRO into a Culturally Adequate System

When carrying over this system to another culture for cross-cultural research, the conceptual equivalence of the hypothetical construct must first be guaranteed. The construct 'problem solving' underlying this system can certainly be understood as a human universality, so that the conceptual equivalence can be assumed. The ascertainment that problem solving is a human universality, however, is not sufficient to carry this system over to another culture. This system consists of several categories according to which problem-solving behavior in groups is structured. Thus, not only must the content validity of the hypothetical construct be inspected, but the content validity of the individual categories as well.

The content validity of the SYNPRO categories was determined by the agreement of experts as to the extent to which the categories were representative of the interaction behavior that they are supposed to measure (Simon 2002). Analogous to this, the transfer of this system to another culture would require the help of an indigenous expert, one who examines whether the categorization of the interaction contributions of group members belonging to this culture can be achieved utilizing the same categorizing principles upon which the SYNPRO system is based. For it is possible that a contribution from a group member, such as "It seems like it would be a good idea to [...]", which in German cultural circles, because of the indirect subjunctive wording, is an opinion coded as a statement, could, in the North American culture, function as a suggestion, expressed within what that culture considers to be the appropriate courtesy.

This basically means that the function of these individual statements in different cultures must be reviewed. The function of an utterance is considerably dependent on the sentence intonation and the situational context. Depending on how something is expressed, the same content can take on different functions. So, for example, the proposition "Let's produce five thousand shirts, okay?", depending on how it is expressed, in one instance can take on one unit (interact) in the observation system, or in a different instance, can take on two different functions. If the proposition is quickly announced in one sentence, the word "okay" serves as a mode of expressing the suggestion in an especially polite form. In this case, the entire proposition is coded as a suggestion. If, however, the proposition is not announced quickly enough, and the "okay" is emphasized after a short pause, the addition of this word asks group members to express their opinions regarding this suggestion. In this case, we are deal-

281

ing with two different functions for the problem-solving process and co-operation, and the word "okay", which is added to the suggestion, is coded as an individual unit in the sense of an analyzing question.

Depending on the sentence intonation, the same content can have different functions for the problem-solving process, and cooperation. Thus, when coding interaction behavior in a foreign culture, merely translating the words of these foreign group members is insufficient. Rather, to adequately categorize their statements, the observer must know their culture, and based on this cultural context, must decide when a statement takes on which function.

For the analysis of interaction behavior in German work groups, it is clearly defined in the manual for coding with SYNPRO under which conditions the different utterances take on certain functions. To achieve content validity of the SYNPRO categories in another culture, a new coding manual must be written (in cooperation with an expert) in which the culturally specific linguistic connotations of that culture are clearly defined.

For the development of an observation system, a general rule is that an observer who is independent of the developer of the instrument has to learn, with the help of the manual, how to code interaction behavior using SYNPRO in order to guarantee the reproducibility of the coding data. Analogous to this, when a new manual is developed, for example, for the American culture, a German observer can learn, with the help of the manual, to code the interaction behavior of an American work-group, naturally only with the presupposition that the observer has mastered the American language. When carrying over the categories of this system to another cultural circle, we are essentially dealing with a learning process comparable to the learning of vocabulary, except that we are not dealing with the learning of German or American vocabulary, but the learning of the functionality of the interaction behavior of American group members.

The degree to which one has been successful in carrying over SYNPRO to another culture, with the help of the development of a new coding manual, can be investigated through the determination of the reliability of the new system. This can be examined with the help of two German and two American observers who have mastered both the German and the American coding manual. Using a German and an American work group whether or not the coding of the observers is in agreement, can be examined. If the inter-rater reliability between observers of the same culture is significantly higher than the inter-rater reliability between observers of different cultures, this is an indicator that the carrying over of the system into the American culture was not satisfactory. If the coding of the Germans observing the American group is worse than the coding of the German group, and vice versa, this is also an indicator that the transformation of the system to the American culture was unsuccessful. If the coding of the American work group by a German as well as an American observer is in agreement at approximately the same level as the inter-rater reliability between the two American observers, this is an indication that a successful transformation of the system to the American culture has been achieved.

This would also substantiate that the interaction behavior in American work groups can be structured along the same principles as those in German work groups. Thus, this would be evidence for the universality of the SYNPRO categories, which would then represent a universal dimension for the structuring of interaction behavior in work groups. In this case, one could speak of a 'dimensional identity' of the system in the sense of Frijda and Jahoda (1966), so that an essential goal of cross-cultural research would be fulfilled, namely the detection of commonalities between cultures. (Of course this statement can only be made with restrictions. Naturally, to prove the universality of the categories additional cultures must be examined.)

Since the interaction behavior in German and American work groups can be portrayed along the same dimension—namely, the dimension defined by the main categories, and their sub-categories—the problem of scale equivalence would also be solved. SYNPRO operates on the level of a nominal scale that would form a culturally equivalent standard of comparison if the transformation of the system to fit the American culture was successful.

However, the goal of a cross-cultural study is not only to detect cultural commonalities, but also differences. Indeed, it is entirely possible that the interaction behavior of culturally different work groups can be portrayed along the same dimension—represented through the categories of SYNPRO—but that the progress of the problem-solving process can vary among different cultures. To identify culturally dependent problem-solving styles, different indicators need to be constructed that possess operational equivalence across both cultures. In a German work group, for example, the extent of controversies in the problem-solving process can be operationalized based on the ratio of the number of contrary suggestions to the total number of suggestions made in the group, as shown in the work of Simon (2002). When measuring the construct controversies in a Japanese work group, however, it could be possible that the operationalization of controversies on the basis of contrary suggestions form an inadequate indicator. For in Japanese work groups the direct exchange of controversies is avoided due to the prevalence of the work philosophy of 'ningensei'. According to this work philosophy, as a general rule, relationships free of conflict must be established by investing sensitivity, consideration, and genuineness into the group (Kashima and Callan 1994). Therefore, contrary suggestions are not expressed in a direct manner; instead, the contrary opinion of a group member is rather expressed in a more subtle way, so that a more adequate indicator for measuring the construct 'controversies' in Japanese work groups is required.

The equivalence of construct validity of those indicators measuring culturally dependent problem-solving styles can again be examined with the help of an expert from the respective culture. In the German culture as well, the construct validity of indicators cannot be numerically substantiated, rather, most often it is corroborated by argumentation and accepted for reasons of plausibility (Simon 1997, 2002).

Under certain circumstances, it could turn out—as the previous example shows—that a construct must be operationalized on the basis of different behaviors (such as the operationalization of the construct controversies based on contrary suggestions in German groups and based on other statements in Japanese groups), which, when viewed functionally, express the same thing on the level of the problem-solving process and cooperation, namely, an opinion contrary to the suggestion of a group member.

The comparability of the situation in which the data is collected, in terms of Helfrich's (1993) fourth postulate—equivalence of data collection—can be assured in that the interaction behavior of a German work group is measured in a typically German setting and that the interaction behavior of a culturally different group is measured in a setting that is typical for that culture. Through this procedure the execution objectivity is ensured so that every culture has the same chance of solving the problem.

Due to the scale equivalence then given by SYNPRO, and the operational equivalence of the indicators measuring different aspects of the problem-solving process and which are ensured by the representatives of the respective cultures, the scoring objectivity—in terms of the numerical computation of the values of the different indicators—would likewise be guaranteed. Additionally, with the given comparability of the data collection situation, the interpretation objectivity would also be guaranteed. Therefore, it would be possible to make cross-cultural assertions about whether, for example, controversies are expressed more often in German and American work groups than in Japanese groups.

The Problem of Population Dependence in Measurements

Exploring the above example of a culturally adequate instrument—SYNPRO—which fulfills Helfrich's (1993) equivalence requirements, and inspecting these requirements using the test theoretical criteria, make it clear that cross-cultural psychology is based on the same principles as other branches of psychology. The crucial difference consists merely in the fact that here an instrument is not developed with respect to one target population, but with respect to two or more populations, depending on how many different cultures are included in the study. This inevitably results in multiple steps of analysis in the development of an instrument, and can mean that, under certain circumstances, phenomenally different instruments must be used, which from a functional point of view, measure the same phenomena. Herein lies a component of cross-cultural psychology that alienates researchers focussed primarily on methods because data sets from two populations can only be compared if they were collected under the same conditions. In cross-cultural psychology, however, we might deal with phenomenally different but functionally equal conditions, as different populations are examined.

From these comments it becomes clear how dependent the construction of an instrument is on the population. With this realization we have arrived at a further important methodological problem in psychology with which not only cross-cultural psychology struggles. The dependence of measurements on the population has been heavily criticized in cross-cultural psychology, as well as in classical test theory. Population dependence means that the test parameters are dependent on the parameters of the subjects. Therefore, these are socially normed tests that can only be reasonably interpreted with relation to a reference group. This led to the demand for so-called 'specifically objective' tests in which the test parameters are independent of the subject parameters. According to this kind of test, the degree of difficulty of an individual test item should be independent of any type of reference group, as Rasch (1960) tried to implement in a probabilistic approach. However, with this approach, the problem arises in that the test and subject parameters can only be estimated through an effortful iterative procedure. Independent of the mathematical difficulty of this approach—which can perhaps be interpreted as an indicator of the artificiality of such a construction, as the saying goes 'in simplicity lies the recipe'—this poses the question of how much sense the postulate of population independence makes.

This becomes very clear with reference to the above mentioned question of cross-cultural psychology, which is the question of culturally dependent, different problem-solving styles. Here the question immediately arises as to what a specific objective problem-solving style should look like. In my opinion, the same fallacy is hidden behind the demand for specific objectivity, as behind the search for a fundamental basis of cognition. In both cases, it is a matter of the missing neutral point of view, which, in the case of Rasch's (1960) model, is only dressed in a new coat, so that it is not immediately apparent.

An alternative to reference-group oriented tests that can be taken seriously is the criterion-oriented test (Fricke 1974; Klauer et al. 1972). In this case, one could still say there is something like an optimal problem-solving style as a criterion. Here, however, the test would be restricted to tasks for which a formally correct solution exists. For a great deal of the problems we are confronted with in everyday life, or that work groups in organizational practice are entrusted with, a correct solution does not exist; in most cases 'many roads lead to Rome'.

If one tries to develop criterion-oriented tests for such problems, the same difficulties arise as have been previously noted. This becomes especially clear in complex problem-solving research, in which one tries to construct complex computer-simulated scenarios in terms of a test according to the guidelines of criterion-oriented measurement. Representatives of this field of research view standards of discrepancy as an optimal criterion for the quality of the output in such scenarios. Standards of discrepancy indicate how far the output values achieved by the subjects in specific system variables diverge from the optimal goal values for these respective system variables, or the divergence of the subject's interventions from optimal interventions (Funke 1992; Funke 1993, 1995; Hübner, 1989; Kolb et al. 1992). However, a prerequisite for this is the formalization of the system to be able to calculate the optimal values at the expense of the close to reality configuration of the scenario (Funke 1993). Here again, the artificiality that inevitably occurs when one tries to take a neutral point of view becomes clear. In close to reality scenarios no optimal reference points can be specified, not only because more than one way leads to the solution of the problem—so an optimal way does not exist—, but because there is simply no point of reference from which one could say that it is definitely the most effective solution. What the most effective solution is, in terms of a criterion, can only be stated based on a comparison with the output hitherto achieved in the handling of a computer-simulated scenario. The same problem is also present in intelligence tests since what constitutes a high intelligence quotient can only be determined in contrast to a reference group. We are not in a position to be able to take a neutral point of view outside of our system, as we are all part of the system. The demand for an optimal point of reference represents, in my opinion, a chimera that arises from the unreflected adoption of standards taken from the natural sciences. But even the reference points available in physics are relative (cf. Einstein's Theory of Relativity).

Criterion-oriented measurements only make sense in those areas in which an optimal criterion really does exist; *criteria* such as *correct* or *incorrect,* used, for example, in criterion-oriented school performance tests (cf. Lukesch 1998). If, however, one wants to identify culturally dependent problem-solving styles—to stay with the example cited above —then no objective criterion exists. In this case, it makes sense to measure, dependent on the population, the different problem-solving procedures of different cultures. The different procedures for problem-solving can only be identified from the vantage point of a reference group. The difference between cross-cultural psychology and other branches of psychology is merely that in cross-cultural psychology, a single individual or group is not evaluated with respect to the population to which they belong, but rather, an entire population is placed in reference to another population.

A Few Closing Words

With all of the criticism aimed at classical test theory it should not be forgotten that this theory was originally developed in order to implement it in personality psychology, with the goal of measuring inter-individual differences at a sufficient level of exactness, meaning it is objective, reliable, and valid (Lukesch 1998). Indeed, in cross-cultural psychology the primary objective is not to measure differences between people but to measure differences between cultures. In this light, the criteria of classical test theory in combination with the equivalence requirements of Helfrich (1993) represent a thoroughly adequate way of helping cross-cultural psychology out of its methodological problems and to measure differences in experience and behavior of persons from different cultures at a sufficient level of exactness.

References

Berry, J.W. (1980). Introduction to Methodology. In H.C. Triandis/J.W. Berry (Eds.). In: Handbook of Cross-Cultural Psychology. Vol. 2, (pp. 1-28). Boston: Allyn & Bacon.

Boesch, E.E./Eckensberger, L.H. (1969). Methodische Probleme des interkulturellen Vergleichs [Methodological Problems of Cross-cultural Comparisons]. In: K. Gottschaldt/P. Lersch/F. Sander /H. Thomae (Hrsg.). Handbuch der Psychologie in 12 Bänden [Handbook of Psychology in 12 Volumes] (Bd. 7,1) herausgegeben von C. F. Graumann: Sozialpsychologie (pp. 515-566). Göttingen: Hogrefe.

Eckensberger, L.H. (1990). On the Necessity of the Culture Concept in Psychology: A View from Cross-Cultural Psychology. In: F.J.R. van de Vijver/G.J.M. Hutschemaekers (Eds.). The Investigation of Culture. Current Issues in Cultural Psychology. Tilburg: University Press.

Edwards, A.L. (1971). Versuchsplanung in der psychologischen Forschung [Planning Designs in Psychological Research]. Weinheim: Beltz.

Fricke, R. (1974). Kriteriumsorientierte Leistungsmessung [Criterion-oriented Measurement of Performance]. Stuttgart: Kohlhammer.

Frijda, N.H./Jahoda, G. (1966). On the Scope and Methods of Cross-Cultural Research. In: International Journal of Psychology, 1, 110-127.

Funke, J. (1992). Wissen über dynamische Systeme: Erwerb, Repräsentation und Anwendung [Knowledge about Dynamical Systems: Acquisition, Representation, and Application]. Berlin: Springer.

Funke, U. (1993). Computergestützte Eignungsdiagnostik mit komplexen dynamischen Szenarios [Computer Supported Aptitude Tests and Complex Dynamic Scenarios]. In: Zeitschrift für Arbeits- und Organisationspsychologie [Journal of Occupational and Organizational Psychology], 37, 109-118.

Funke, U. (1995). Szenarien in der Eignungsdiagnostik und im Personaltraining [Scenarios in Aptitude Tests and Personnel Training]. In: B. Strauß/M. Kleinmann (Hrsg.). Computersimulierte Szenarien in der Personalarbeit [Computer-Simulated Scenarios in Human Resource Management]. Göttingen: Verlag für Angewandte Psychologie.

Goethe, Johann W. (1971 [1899]). Faust. Der Tragödie erster Teil [Faust: The Tragedy's First Part]. Stuttgart: Reclam.

Guzzo, R./Shea, G.P. (1992). Group Performance and Intergroup Relations in Organizations. In: M.D. Dunnettte/L.M. Hough (Eds.).

Handbook of Industrial and Organizational Psychology, Vol. 3, p. 269-314. Palo Alto: Consulting Psychology Press.

Habermas, J. (1968). Erkenntnis und Interesse [Cognition and Interests]. Frankfurt: Suhrkamp.

Hackman, J.R./Walton, R.E. (1986). Leading Groups in Organizations. In: P.S. Goodman and Associates (Eds.). Designing Effective Work Groups. San Francisco: Jossey-Bass.

Hackman, J.R. (1990). Creating More Effective Work Groups in Organizations. In: J.R. Hackman (Ed.). Groups That Work (and Those That Don't). Creating Conditions for Effective Team Work. San Francisco: Jossey-Bass.

Heess, M. (1977). Blaise Pascal. Wissenschaftliches Denken und christlicher Glaube [Scientific Thinking and Christian Belief]. München: Wilhelm Fink Verlag.

Helfrich, H. (1993). Methodologie kulturvergleichender psychologischer Forschung [Methodology of Cross-Cultural Psychological Research]. In: A. Thomas (Hrsg.). Kulturvergleichende Psychologie. Eine Einführung [Cross-Cultural Psychology: An Introduction]. Göttingen: Hofgrefe.

Hübner, R. (1989). Methoden zur Analyse und Konstruktion von Aufgaben zur kognitiven Steuerung dynamischer Systeme [Methods for Analyzing and Constructing Tasks for the Cognitive Steering of Dynamical Systems]. In: Zeitschrift für Experimentelle und Angewandte Psychologie [Journal of Experimental and Applied Psychology], 36, 221-238.

Hume, D. (1967 [1882]). Eine Untersuchung über den menschlichen Verstand [An Enquiry Concerning Human Understanding]. Stuttgart: Reclam

Jahoda, G. (1980). Theoretical and Systematic Approaches in Cross-Cultural Psychology. In: H.C. Triandis/W.W. Lambert (Eds.). Handbook of Cross-Cultural Psychology. Vol. 1, (pp. 69-142) Boston: Allyn & Bacon.

Kant, I. (1989 [1783]). Prolegomena zu einer jeden künftigen Metaphysik, die als Wissenschaft wird auftreten können [Prolegomena for Every Future Metaphysics which Could Appear as Science]. Stuttgart: Reclam.

Kashima, Y./Callan, V.J. (1994). The Japanese Work Groups. In: H.C. Triandis/H. Dunnette/L.M. Hough (Eds.). Handbook of Industrial and Organizational Psychology. Palo Alto: Consulting Psychologist.

Klauer, K. J./Fricke, R./Herbig, M./Ruprecht, H./Schott, F. (1972). Lehrzielorientierte Tests [Learning Outcomes-oriented Tests]. Düsseldorf: Schwann.

Kolb, S./Petzing, F./Stumpf, S. (1992). Komplexes Problemlösen: Bestimmung der Problemlösegüte von Probanden mittels Verfahren des Operation Research—ein interdisziplinärer Ansatz [Complex Problem Solving: Determining the Quality of the Subject's Solution with Procedures of Operation Research—an Interdisciplinary Appproach]. In: Sprache & Kognition [Language and Cognition], 11 (3), 115-128.

Lienert, G.A./Raatz, U. (1994). Testaufbau und Testanalyse [Test Construction and Test Analysis]. 5th ed. Weinheim: Beltz.

Lukesch, H. (1998). Einführung in die pädagogisch-psychologische Diagnostik [Introduction to Pedagogical-psychological Diagnostics]. 2nd ed. Regensburg: Roderer.

McGrath, J.E. (1991). Time, Interaction, and Performance: A Theory of Groups. In: Small Group Research, 22, 147-174.

Pascal, B. (1937). Pensées. Über die Religion und über einige andere Gegenstände [On Religion and Some Other Objectives]. (herausgegeben von E. Wasmuth). Berlin: Lambert Schneider.

Poortinga, Y. (1975). Limitations on International Comparison of Psychological Data. In: Nederlands Tijdschrift voor de Psychologie, 30, 23-39.

Poortinga, Y./van de Vijver, F. (1988). Culturally Invariant Parameters of Cognitive Functioning. In: J.W. Berry/S.H. Irvine/E.B. Hunt (Eds.). Indigenous Cognition: Functioning in Cultural Context (p. 19-36). Dordrecht: Hijhoff.

Popper, Karl R. (1979). Ausgangspunkte. Meine intellektuelle Entwicklung [Starting Points: My Intellectual Development]. Hamburg: Hoffmann & Campe.

Popper, Karl R. (1984 [1935]). Logik der Forschung [Logic of Research]. 8th ed. Tübingen: Mohr.

Rasch, G. (1960). Probabilistic Models for Some Intelligence and Attainment Tests. Studies in Mathematical Psychology. Kopenhagen.

Simon, P. (1997). Die Entwicklung eines Beobachtungssystems zur Erfassung von Interaktionsmustern und Leistungsdeterminanten in plurinationalen Arbeitsgruppen [The Development of an Observation System for Measuring Interaction Patterns and Determinants of Effectiveness in Multi-National Work Groups]. Unveröffentl. Diplomarbeit [Unpublished Diploma]. Universität Regensburg.

Simon, P. (2002). Die Entwicklung eines Modells der Gruppeneffektivität und eines Analyse-Instruments zur Erfassung des Leistungspotentials von Arbeitsgruppen [The Development of a Group Effectiveness Model and an Analysis Instrument for Measuring the Output Potential of Work Groups]. Landau: Verlag für empirische Pädagogik.

Stegmüller, W. (1978). Hauptströmungen der Gegenwartsphilosophie [Main Streams in Contemporary Philosophy]. Stuttgart: Alfred Kröner Verlag.

Stevens, S.S. (1951). Handbook of Experimental Psychology. New York: Wiley.

Triandis, H.C. (1980). Introduction. In: H.C. Triandis/W.W. Lambert (Eds.). Handbook of Cross-Cultural Psychology. Vol. 1, (pp. 1-14). Boston: Allyn & Bacon.

Van de Vijver, F.J.R./Poortinga, Y.H. (1982). Cross-Cultural Generalization and Universality. In: Journal of Cross-Cultural Psychology, 13, 287-408.

QUANTITATIVE AND QUALITATIVE CROSS-CULTURAL COMPARISON: THE ROLE OF CULTURAL METRICS

WOLFGANG WAGNER, NICOLE KRONBERGER, JOSÉ VALENCIA &
MARIA LUCIA DUARTE PEREIRA

Paradoxically, the issue of psychological comparisons across cultures becomes all the more pressing the more the modern world undergoes processes of economic, political, and social unification. Globalization, as it is called nowadays, highlights cultural differences and draws attention to even minor variations in understanding and behavior between people from different countries. As long as the representatives of each culture *grosso modo* acted only within their geographically limited areas, it was of little importance that Austrians exhibited a different mentality than Japanese, and that the work values of Egyptian Arabs differed from US-American-Caucasian values. It is under the conditions of a global market and the earth-spanning Internet that Austrian, Japanese, Egyptian, and US-American mentalities, to name just a few, meet on a regular basis and challenge psychology's understanding of cultural differences.

In the following it will be argued that straightforward comparison of measurements, in the quantitative domain, and of semantic interpretations, in the qualitative domain, across cultures easily leads to inadequate results. This is due to the fact that scales, questionnaire items, and texts produced through interview techniques or open-ended questions have culturally specific meanings, that is, they cannot be mapped onto the same semantic metric unless otherwise proven. These culture-specific structures are called, metaphorically, cultural metrics. The claim will be illustrated by examples taken from quantitative and qualitative research.

Conceptual Ethnocentrism in Cross-Cultural Comparison

Researching culture has never been an easy exercise for psychology. There are now three distinct approaches that deal with this issue: cultural psychology, indigenous psychology, and cross-cultural psychology. Cultural psychology is informed by anthropology and maintains that

- psychological pluralism exists despite many universals, where researching the latter is not its aim;
- it is interested in studying ethnic and cultural sources of psychological and social diversity;
- thick description is needed to understand local stimulus conditions;
- local sense-making and action patterns of intentional actors can be seen as a consequence of socially inherited values and representations;
- mentalities rather than the mind is the subject matter of cultural psychology (Shweder 2000: 209p.).

A mentality in the present understanding is 'the actual cognitive functioning of a particular person or people. To describe a "mentality" ... is to get specific about the particular conceptual contents (the "ideas") that have actually been cognised and activated by the person or people. To describe a "mentality" is also to get specific about the particular mental processes (the particular senses, feelings, memories, desires, inferences, imaginings, etc.) that have been recruited by this or that person or people to make their cognising and activation of "ideas" (conceptual contents) visible.' (Shweder 2000: 210) Cultural psychology, hence, attempts to do justice to the particularities of cultures and their capacity to shape the workings of the psychological faculties. Being a descriptive approach to local worlds, cultural psychology assumes neither that psychological theories ('classical' ethnocentrism) nor any dimension or construct ('conceptual' ethnocentrism) developed in the West apply to non-Western cultures, unless otherwise proven. It emphasizes local description and not comparison between cultures, which presupposes at least one dimension onto which the cultures can be mapped.

The potential danger of conceptual ethnocentrism lingers with cross-cultural psychological comparison. Cross-cultural psychologists 'find differences in the meaning of constructs annoying, since such differences make the equivalent measurement of constructs more difficult', as Triandis acknowledges in a recent paper (Triandis 2000: 188). Their research depends on cross-culturally valid dimensions of measurement, but this validity cannot be established by local standardization of scales, as has often been suggested. A scale can only be standardized by statistical means after the scale has been conceptually defined, that is, after it has been established that the meaning of the underlying psychological construct is the same and that the same metric applies across cultures.

This problem has always preoccupied cross-cultural psychologists, and several statistical and other methods have been developed to check for bias and for correcting its effects. Building upon an extended literature, van de Vijver and Leung (1997) identified three biases involving items, methods, and constructs. Item bias, in their understanding, is a measurement artefact at the level of scales and items. It involves inadequate translation or formulation of items as well as the fact that the real-world referent of an item might not exist in one or the other of the cultures being compared. Method bias refers to differential tendencies of acquiescence and extremity in scale use and differential familiarity with a stimulus as well as differences in the situations where a test is being applied. Item and method bias are both technical problems, and can be avoided by adequate assessment and measurement procedures.

The third, construct bias, results if the construct investigated in a study is not the same in each of the cultures involved. This comes closest to what here will be called 'conceptual ethnocentrism'. Van de Vijver and Leung (1997) suggested several approaches for how to avoid this problem. One would be the 'decentered approach' where the researchers employ culturally divergent perspectives in the theoretical development and design of a study and try to give equal weight to all cultures under examination. This approach would yield a set of constructs and items that cannot automatically be assumed to be valid in all culture specific samples. The other, the 'convergence approach', starts with local researchers from each culture developing an indigenous conceptual structure and instrument for tackling the problem under scrutiny in their culture. If, in the course of the investigation and comparison, it is found that the local results converge across cultures, there is good reason to assume cross-cultural validity of the phenomenon. As ideal as the convergence approach might be in correcting for ethnocentric bias, it is difficult in practice.

The problem of construct bias is at the heart of *conceptual ethnocentrism*. This is understood as the assumption that a theoretical variable or parameter found to be a relevant characteristic of one culture can be used to map the variability of other cultures. One must keep in mind, however, that this is neither a statistical problem nor one related to measurement, and therefore the term 'bias', with its strong methodological connotation, seems not to be well chosen. The classic example is the individualism-collectivism variable often used as an independent variable to distinguish cultures from each other. The idea of this variable and the associated scale resulted from the Western individualism trait as one pole of an assumed variable, where all non-individualist cultural groups can be mapped onto a position between the poles of strong individualism and strong collectivism. It is, however, ethnocentric to suppose that such a variable can capture the complexities of non-Western cultures that happen not to fall squarely into the Western individualistic mold. While the individualism pole might adequately capture a Western trait, the collectivism pole is likely not to capture the varieties of non-individualist cultures (e.g., Minoura 1996). Indigenous psychological research enriched the conceptual inventory of cross-cultural psychology with variables such as 'tightness', 'complexity', 'activity', 'honour', and 'verticality' (Triandis 1996: 408f.). Their usefulness and translatability into different cultural understandings has still to be proven. Until then, indigenous psychologies should not be seen as modifications of contemporary (Western) psychology, but as contemporary local psychologies in their own right and with their own variables (Wagner 1997; Yang 2000). Otherwise, while pretending to investigate culture, cross-cultural psychology might in fact only investigate nature as it was 'discovered' in Western laboratories (Jahoda 1986).

Cross-cultural comparison of mentalities such as values and beliefs are prime candidates for conceptual ethnocentrism. If, for example, 'persistence' appears to be a cultural value in Hong Kong but not with Illinois undergraduates, and 'to be well adjusted' is claimed to be a value in both samples, the question arises whether 'persistence' and 'being well adjusted' designate the same things in both cultures. This cannot be established by comparing scores on a common scale, even with proper translation. The results derived from a study by Triandis, Bontempo, Leung and Hui (1990) show that what is thought in Illinois of the expression in English, 'being well adjusted', is widely shared among Illinois undergraduates, and that in Hong Kong, what is thought of the Chinese language equivalent of 'being well adjusted' is widely shared among Hong Kong undergraduates. It is not shown, however, that the cultural 'things' designated by the respective English and Hong Kong Chinese words 'being well adjusted' are socially and culturally equivalent.

The local values contained in the respective Illinois and Hong Kong understandings of 'being well adjusted' would in fact only be equivalent if it meant in both cases
a) either 'to talk, think and behave like others in my group',
b) or 'to appear like talking, thinking and behaving like others in my group',

c) or 'to talk, think and behave as I wish as long as it does not annoy anybody else in my group'.

The expression 'being well adjusted' would not be equivalent if in one sample it meant one thing and in the other sample it meant another thing. For example, being well adjusted in the sense of (c) could very well be a US-American understanding; being well adjusted in the sense of (a) or (b) have more the flavour of an Asian culture (although we admit that this is a guess). Even if all three have the same literal translation of 'being well adjusted', the specific content is crucially different.

Conceptual ethnocentrism is not a matter of incorrect translation even if translating such sensitive concepts is quite problematic. We can translate virtually every word existing in Chinese or English into any other language. But translations, though literally correct, rarely capture what an indigenous concept means in the local world. Understanding words and concepts means defining the very phenomena they designate by virtue of the specific local context of cultural practices and language use. Conceptual ethnocentrism assumes that the very psychological concepts like mind, perception, emotion, motivation, personality, etc. are valid concepts for constructing non-Western variants of general theories. Evidence suggests that local theories can only be built with local psychological concepts, as the indigenous psychology and the cultural psychology program attempt to do (Jodelet 1993; Kim 2000; Yang 2000).

A theory-guided cross-cultural study, which investigated interpersonal processes, serves as a final example for potential ethnocentrism (Wagner, Kirchler, Clack, Tekarslan and Verma 1990). The study compared spouses' interdependences in conflicts in traditional cultures where strong gender-role segregation and associated male dominance exist (India, Turkey) with cultures characterized by gender-role integration and egalitarian values (Austria, USA). It was found that spousal emotional interdependence is much less in more traditional countries than in Western ones. The degree of emotional interdependence in conflict was operationalized as a variable computed from three scores. The scores were the subjects' ratings of well-being in a purchasing conflict where they were asked to imagine situations (a) where they buy a personally desired commodity despite their spouse's disagreement, (b) where they do not buy the commodity because of their spouse's disagreement, and (c) where they buy the commodity with their spouse's agreement.

In this study, purchasing was considered a sufficiently comparable activity in all four countries. People buy and sell commodities all over the world. On superficial appearance, purchasing is the act of exchanging a token (money) for a product of a certain utility. What the authors did not consider is that purchasing under the auspices of the spouse agreeing or disagreeing may mean something completely different in cultures with profound role-segregation than purchasing in cultures with role-integration. First, marriages in traditional cultures are often arranged, and not autonomous decisions of spouses, as is the case in the West; second, love in the Western sense of sexual attraction and shared personal interests does not necessarily characterize marriages in other regions of the world; third, culturally gender-segregated activities, responsibilities, competencies, and spaces in the house already imply that the other spouse is not supposed to share in the same activities, responsibilities, competencies, and spaces. By this very cultural implication alone it is clear that spouses must be much more independent in traditional cultures than in Western ones. What the authors conceptualized as conflict by virtue of our Western experience (also the Indian and Turkish collaborators can be said to be Westernized to a certain degree) very probably is no conflict at all in traditional cultures.

This study was not on mentalities but on interaction patterns, and it obeyed the rules that the Laboratory of Comparative Cognition (1979) set for cross-cultural comparison, that is, to statistically compare only within-country-interactions across countries instead of main effects. Nevertheless, the study described above was based on the unwarranted assumption that the cultural meaning of the construct 'marital conflict' is the same in all four countries. Mind, mentality, and social interaction are more closely interdependent than usually acknowledged.

Cultural Metrics

Culture as a Functionally Organized System

In most contexts, culture must be seen as a semantic structure of meanings, "a pattern of shared attitudes, beliefs, categorisations, self-definitions, norms, role definitions, and values [...]" (Triandis 1996: 408), and as

"an organized body of rules concerning the ways in which individuals in a population should communicate with one another, think about themselves and toward objects in their environments. The rules are not universally or constantly obeyed, but they are recognized by all and they ordinarily operate to limit the range of variation in patterns of communication, belief, value, and social behaviour in that population." (LeVine 1982)

This system cannot be divided into rules, attitudes, beliefs, categorizations, self-definitions, norms, role definitions, or values without losing the essential meaning inherent in their delicate cross-reference with other meanings, cognitions, and feelings. Each of these is functionally related to many others.

Consider the following metaphorical illustration:[1] If you ask chemists what a hormone is, they will tell you its chemical composition and molecular structure as a polypeptide, a steroid, or an amino-acid derivative. Note that this is a chemical characterization of a hormone, and that the chemical character is not a sufficient definition for a hormone (e.g., there are polypeptides that are not hormones and hormones belong to different chemical classes). Instead, a hormone is a substance that is released from gland cells under certain physiological conditions and acts on receptors that trigger a reaction functionally related to the trigger of the hormone release. A hormone is thus defined by the way the cells 'use' it in their physiological activities.

In the same way, the simple clause 'He did x because of y' can either be an attribution statement or something else, depending on the context. In any case, a linguistic analysis of such a clause is insufficient. For it to be an attribution, it is necessary to prove that the sentence was uttered in a context that called for an explanation and not just for a free association or a recital of a text; that '…did x' is a salient activity in the culture, otherwise it would not call for an attribution; that '…because of y' gives a sensible reason in that culture; and that the reason given can be classified as internal or external, stable or unstable. A reason like '…because he needed to win' can be internal if conceived as a 'need' or intention, or external, if conceived as the pressures of his trainer in a sports competition. One needs to connect a complex clause such as this one to a whole range of contexts that make up the respective culture before one can call it an interpersonal attribution. In other words, just as a hormone is defined by the functional role it plays in certain biological contexts, an interpersonal attribution is defined by the functional role it plays in certain cultural contexts, and both—the definitions of hormones and of attributions—are thus structurally similar to the meaning of words being defined by the way of its situated use (Wittgenstein 1958).

Cultural Metrics in Quantitative Methods

Given the importance of functional and other relationships between variables in characterising cultures, Triandis (1996: 407), suggests considering 'cultural syndromes'. 'Cultural syndromes are conceived as dimen-

---

1   Personal communication by Günter P. Wagner, New Haven.

sions of cultural variation that can be used as parameters of psychological theories ... In that way, the current psychological theories will become special cases of the universal theories.' Although the author's latter claim may be overly optimistic, the concept of cultural syndromes is an important one. If culture comprises systems of beliefs and practices that belong together and are meaningfully interrelated, dependent measures can only be sets of overt and verbal behaviors. It is the '...use of theoretically motivated, *within-group* (emphasis in the original) observation as a means of specifying culturally patterned activities that can be used as "measures" by procedures which maximize representativeness' (Laboratory of Comparative Human Cognition 1979: 168).

Using bundles of overt and/or verbal behavior variables as dependent measure addresses two issues simultaneously: First it allows to compare statistical interactions between variables instead of the main effect of single variables across cultures. ... Using bundles of variables obliges the researcher to look at interactions within cultures and comparing these interactions between cultures. In the statistical sense, only an interaction found in one culture which is replicated in another culture allows to conclude that the effect is shared by those cultures (Campbell 1961). But, as Amir and Sharon (1987) have impressively demonstrated, statistical interactions in experimental data can rarely be replicated across cultures. Second, bundles of variables allow the pinning down of local interrelated meanings within a semantic field of cognitive and/or evaluative behaviors. Bundles of dependent measures also address the issue of semantics. It is very difficult, if not impossible, to assess the local meaning of the response to an attitude, value, or belief item without any reference to other attitudes, values, beliefs, or practices. A set of responses on continuous or categorical scales, be they answers to closed questions or word associations to stimuli, can be analyzed by nonlinear multivariate statistics. The resulting pattern of the responses then gives an impression of the semantic relationships—or *semantic metric*—in each culture.

A 'semantic metric' will be defined here as *the pattern of implicit meanings respondents attribute to a questionnaire item or to a word or proposition in talk and writing.* These meanings determine the relationship of one measure to another measure, of one scale difference to a difference on another scale, and of one proposition to another proposition in text. Thereby, respondents of the same culture define a metric—in a loose sense of the term—within which all their measures and text are defined. That is to say that measurement patterns are semantically mediated by the culture of the respondents. As Berry (2000: 197) put it: "in studying behaviour one has to be 'cultural' before being 'cross'."

Cultural Metrics in Qualitative Methods

What applies to quantitative research and statistical comparison applies to some types of qualitative comparisons as well. Discourse and text are as much embedded in local contexts as responses to questionnaires. But while quantitative data easily evoke the illusion of being decontextualized and therefore objective and equivalent across cultural samples, qualitative researchers are acutely aware of the potential fallacies of context and interpretation (cf. Straub 1999). This does not mean, however, that the problem of semantic metrics does not apply to the comparison of qualitative data.

Interview transcripts and other qualitative material can be compared across languages and cultures using two approaches. One approach is to translate the transcripts from the cultural groups, to pool them, and to analyze them jointly. The second is to analyze and interpret the qualitative material locally through researchers native to the respective culture or language and to compare the results in a second step. Both are being used in the not too numerous cross-cultural qualitative research literature.

An example of the first approach, pooling and joint analysis, is the work of Dahlin and Watkins (2000) on Chinese and German students' views of the role of repetition and memorizing in understanding and learning. The interviewees from both samples were living, or, in the case of the Germans, had been living in Hong Kong for some years. The Chinese were interviewed in Cantonese and the interview recordings were translated and transcribed verbatim into English by the respective interviewer. The German students were interviewed in English. Finally, the pooled English transcripts were analyzed and interpreted by two trained researchers who maintained close communication during this work.

Gibbons et al. (1993) provide a good example of the second approach, that is local interpretation and subsequent comparison. They used pictures of women doing housework and office work drawn by adolescents from three cultures, Guatemalan, Filipino and US-American, and had other adolescents from the three cultures content analyze the drawings. Naturally, using pictorial material complicates the comparative problem further, but by having indigenous coders doing the content analysis of the drawings they first established a local frame of category interpretation that was later used for comparison.

The two approaches are quite different in their implications because straightforward translation of the original text is a completely different business than translating interpretations. Translating a natural text from one language to another, even if done with all precautions, cannot guarantee that the translation leaves the implicit and contextual meanings of propositions, phrases, and paragraphs unaltered. Furthermore, the process is uneconomical and laborious. This is the problem professional translators of novels and poems face in their daily work. Local qualitative analysis of text is less affected by this problem. Linguistically and culturally competent researchers doing text analysis on the spot are more likely to make implicit and contextual meanings explicit in their interpretations. These interpretations are supposed to capture structural semantic features of text as well as its content on a more general level. That means, in a metaphorical sense, that the interpretation is done within the local semantic metric.

Translating interpretations, particularly if the researchers cooperate closely in a face-to-face situation, is a much better warrant of comparability or, in the alternative case, of incomparability, than translation of the original material. Even the failure to prove equivalence of semantic metrics and spaces is an interesting result in its own right and can enrich psychology's insight into the variability of mentalities and the functioning of culturally diverse minds. These issues will be illustrated in the next sections.

Examples of Research

In this section we will present four examples of research that span the spectrum from using quantitative to qualitative methods in cross-cultural comparison, and which first investigated the local metrics before proceeding to comparison. The first example, a straightforward quantitative study on the cross-cultural understanding of work values, was published by an international research team (Meaning of Work Research Team 1987); the present authors were involved in the remaining three. One is a study on the understanding of war and peace in Spain and Nicaragua (Wagner, Valencia and Elejabarrieta 1996), and the other examines the meaning of biotechnology in six European countries (Wagner et al. 2002); both can be labeled 'semi-quantitative' since they use qualitative data, i.e. word associations and free responses, that are statistically analyzed. The fourth study is of people's concerns about biotechnology; it is a qualitative analysis of focus-group discussions in ten European countries (Wagner et al. 2001).

Quantitative Comparison of Questionnaire Data

The 'Meaning of Work' research team conducted an international comparative study on the meaning of work. The key variable in the research was the 'work centrality score', which was obtained by having respondents indicate the following: 'Assign a total of 100 points to indicate how important areas are in your life at the present time—Leisure, Community, Work, Religion, and Family.' The points assigned to Work constituted the work centrality score. It was thought to reflect the relative significance of work in a respondent's life space.

The authors state that 'when making international comparison, it is important to consider response frequency distributions and averages. This, however, is not sufficient, and in some instances, may lead to erroneous or incomplete interpretations' (Meaning of Work Research Team 1987: 221). Consequently, they did not only compare the scores of work centrality across several countries, but also conducted a nonlinear multivariate analysis called 'quantification on response pattern' within each sample (Hayashi 1950). This technique is basically the same as correspondence analysis and allows the interrelationship among multivariate categorical data to be analyzed. In the present research it was used to elucidate interrelationships between work centrality and more than 30 items about the respondents' definition of work, their reasons for working, how they feel at work, etc. The result of this procedure is the position of each variable category in a multidimensional space. The closer two categories are mapped in the space, the more highly the two categories are related. By looking at the trace of the respondents' work centrality scores within each country's space, the meaning of a high or low score can be determined for each culture (Figure 1).

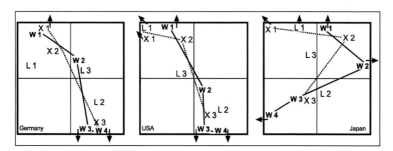

Figure 1: Trace of 4-point work centrality scale (bold line, W1-W4) among trace of 7-point work centrality (trichomised, X1-X3) and lottery item (L1-L3) for Germany, Japan and USA.[2]

---

2 Note: Graphs adapted from Meaning of Work Research Team (1987), pp 230, 232, 234. Note that the axes were rotated to match the work centrality scale as closely as possible among the three countries. Points with little arrows at the frame border indicate the point being positioned outside of the drawing.

Note that, to allow easy visual inspection, Figure 1 depicts only three variables of the study. Further, the graphs were rotated to match the general orientation of the work centrality scores in all three countries. It contains an alternative scale of work centrality (L1 to L3) and a 'lottery item' (X1 to X3) asking subjects what they would do if they won a lot of money: to stop working (L1), to continue working in the same job (L2), or to continue work but with changed conditions (L3). Visual inspection of the simplified graphs makes it immediately clear that the meaning of work as expressed by the trace of the centrality index is not the same in either Japan, Germany, or the USA.

Using more variables from the original data, the authors further determined that the Japan scored the highest and the US the lowest on the work centrality scale. This might result in drawing the misleading conclusion that US workers are less motivated to work than are Japanese. In reality, the response pattern analysis reveals that the meaning of a US-score between 20 and 39 points (i.e., moderately high; people who define work positively as something that produces social value) is to place importance on expressive aspects of work. Japanese workers scoring between 20 and 39 are characterized by trust in others and seeking good interpersonal relations; they put interpersonal matters in their workplace first and work itself second. Further on, the meaning of a 20 to 39 points score in the US is equivalent to the meaning of a score between 40 and 59 in Japan. Only the meaning of scores less than 20 (i.e., a negative view of work that one is forced to do, and an emphasis on economic and material conditions of work) is the same in the two countries.

In sum, the analyses reveal that the work centrality scale spans the same semantic metric in the German and US-American sample, but a different one in the Japanese sample. One and the same work centrality score may indicate a completely different attitude in different cultures, while two different scores or means may be an expression of the same attitude. Purely quantitative scores are hard to compare and interpret if the researcher cannot ascertain that they have the same meaning in the compared cultures.

Comparing the Structure of Word Associations

A study by Wagner, Valencia, and Elejabarrieta (1996) illustrates a similar problem. The authors investigated the structure of word associations dependent on the context in which they are assessed. Respondents from Spain and Nicaragua produced free associations about international conflict/war and peace.

While the goal of the original research does not concern us here, the data can still serve to illustrate a method that allows bundles of variables to be dealt with, even if they are free associations and therefore different in the two cultures. The variables were the words that the subjects associated with the stimulus words 'international conflict'. Figure 2, which is not included in the original article, shows how the associations about international conflict in Spain and Nicaragua are related to each other (a) within and (b) between the two countries.

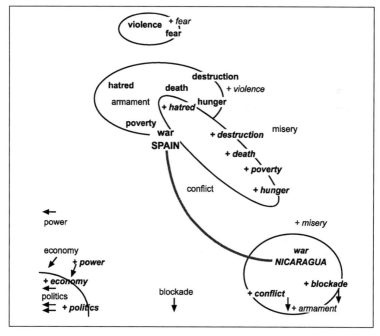

Figure 2: Semantic space of correspondences between associated words about war and peace for Nicaragua and Spain.[3]

A correspondence analysis of the stacked co-occurrence matrices of the 15 most frequent words in each country yields a multidimensional space of which the first two dimensions are depicted. They explain about 50% of the variance. This space can be interpreted as the semantic space of the word associations. A cluster-analysis yields two well connected clus-

---

3 Note: Data from Wagner, Valencia and Elejabarrieta (1996). Words from Nicaraguan subjects have a '+' in front and are in italics. Light grey clusters: Nicaraguan. Dark grey clusters: Spanish. Bold type: Words pertaining to the enveloping cluster. The arc points to the relevant word 'war'. Points with little arrows at the frame border indicate the point being positioned outside of the drawing

ters for each country (in the center of the figure). Nicaragua contains 5 words (destruction, death, hatred, poverty, hunger), Spain 6 (the same plus 'war'). They indicate that the majority of subjects from both countries have a similar lexicon of proximal and affectively laden word associations about international conflict. Spanish subjects also exhibit a loose cluster connecting 'violence' and 'fear' (upper center of Figure 3). Other Nicaraguan subjects produce a loosely connected cluster connecting 'economy' and 'politics' (lower left corner of Figure 3) and still others a well connected cluster encompassing 'conflict', 'blockade' and 'war' (lower right corner of Figure 3).

The case in point is the position of the word 'war'. While there is no doubt that most Nicaraguans and Spaniards share some basic understanding of international conflict as indicated by the two central clusters, Nicaraguan subjects do not place the word 'war' in this central cluster. It is a sub-sample of Nicaraguans who associate it together with 'blockade' and 'conflict' (see the two-pointed arrow in Figure 3). This is a semantic complex of more 'intellectual' words produced by a sub-sample that can easily be interpreted as resulting from their—then recent—experience of unrest, civil war, and US intervention. The example shows that Nicaraguans have a differently patterned perception of 'international conflict' than Spaniards. Hence, their scores on a 'conflict scale' and the resulting 'conflict score' would be situated within a different semantic metric than the score of Spanish respondents.

Comparing Text through Automatic Analysis

The comparison of text across cultures or groups speaking different languages constitutes a particularly difficult task and is relatively rarely done. The present example is taken from an international research group investigating the perception of biotechnology in various European countries (Wagner et al., forthcoming). An open-ended question in a Eurobarometer survey covering all member countries of the European Union asked respondents to write down what comes to mind when thinking of modern biotechnology. The respondents produced everything from no response to several fully formulated sentences.

This kind of data is influenced by several conditions: First, data collection was run in each country by different sub-contractors and within each country many different interviewers conducted the interviews. Some may have let the respondents write their comments themselves, others may have summarized only the gist of the response themselves. Second, the complete sample comprises responses in 13 separate languages and, if language and nationhood has anything to do with culture, the national samples constituted 15 different cultural sub-groups of what might be called the common European cultural heritage. The shortcomings in data quality that one might expect in the present data were at least in part alleviated by the sample size, which was statistically representative within each country.

According to the available groups of collaborators in various countries, the open-ended responses from six countries, Austria, France, Germany, Norway, Sweden, and the United Kingdom, were analyzed using ALCESTE (Reinert 1983, 1990). This program allows text data to be analyzed automatically and uses descendent hierarchical classification, segmentation, correspondence analysis, and the theory of dynamic clouds in its procedure. The algorithm produces matrices of co-occurrences of all words, which are then decomposed and the words descendingly clustered according to their occurrence in proximity in the text or not. If the size of the text-corpus is sufficiently large, the program allows 'discursive spaces' that describe the principal topics mentioned in the text-corpus to be identified (for an overview on the procedure see Kronberger and Wagner 2000).

To preserve local meanings and linguistic idiosyncrasies in the data, the texts entering the analysis could, of course, not be translated and merged to a single data file. The principle of maintaining the local semantic metrics demands that each national sample be analyzed independently. Hence, in the first step, each of the six national corpuses of text data were analyzed separately and, in the second step, the resulting cluster solutions were collected and interpreted in comparison. All this was done in close collaboration with the national and language-native researchers. The overall result is presented in Table 1.

Table 1 cross tabulates the countries in the rows and the discursive clusters in the columns. The cells contain a short description of each cluster in each country. They are left blank if the cluster was not found.

It can be seen that the discursive clusters found independently in each country's text data consistently match across countries. Besides this surprising match of the cluster solutions, the cluster comprising ideas of meddling and interfering with nature reappears in each country and can be said to be a shared concern in all six countries. This finding is independent of any bias that might have been introduced by translating the original responses into one language, and it is also independent of any biased interpretations that might ensue when researchers interpret responses from cultures to which they are not native. Both of these problems are frequently introduced in cross-cultural research.

307

| | What is Biotechnology: Focus on Content | | | | | Is Biotechnology Good or Bad? Focus on Evaluation | | | | | Country specific | Lacking knowledge | | |
| | General (rather neutral) | | Specific: Domains of Application (evaluation involved) | | | Positive | Ambivalent | Negative Evaluation | | | | | | |
	Research /pro-gress	Manipulation/ Alteration	Food	Reprod-uction	Medicine	Good	Good but risky (1)	Risky/Dang erous (2)	Expression of fear	Interfering with nature		Echo (3)	Guessing (4)	Don't know
Austria	Biotechnology is a scientific activity applicated to plants, animals and humans (food, reproduction, medicine) (27%)						Good but risky/ dan-gerous (fear) (22%)	Unknown efects/ dangerous (16%)		Interfering with nature STOP! (36%)		See inter-fering with nature		See unknown effects
France	Research (11%)	Manipulation/ Alteration (16%)	Food/ Agricul-ture (15%)	Reprod-uction (2%)	Medicine (14%)	Improve-ment (10%)	Dangerous/risky although there can be good effects (also morally dangerous) (8%)	Fear	Against nature (18%)			Echo (3%)	Guessed (16%)	Don't know (3%)
Ger-many		Manipulation of plants, an-imals, humans agriculture (16%)	Food (also medicine and reproduction) (15%)		Medicine (12%)		Good but risky Risky/dange rous (fear) (37%)			Interfering with nature STOP! (11%)		See Medicine Good but risky		Don't know (10 %)
Norway	Research (8%)	Alteration of plants, anim-als, humans (21%)	Food (8%)	Food and reproduc-tion (16%)	Medicine (14%)	Good but frightening Unspecific worry (22%)				Interfering with nature (10%)		See Medicine Good but frightening		

	Research (19%)	Manipulation of plants and animals (11%)	Food and reproduction (7%)			Good if used the right way/dangerous (15%)	Fear too fast (19%)	Interfering with nature (21%)	Belgian Blue (9%)	See Research	Don't know (17%)
Sweden	Research (19%)	Manipulation of plants and animals (11%)	Food and reproduction (7%)			Good if used the right way/dangerous (15%)	Fear too fast (19%)	Interfering with nature (21%)	Belgian Blue (9%)	See Research	Don't know (17%)
UK			Food (21%)	Reproduction (7%)	Medicine (21%)	Unspecific worry/ dangerous (fear) (16%)		Interfering with nature (18%)		see Medicine	

Table 1: Lexical classes of ALCESTE crosstabulated by countries

(1) Good but risky: may have good effects but is risky and dangerous, therefore must be applied properly, demand for control

(2) Risky and Dangerous: biotechnology is unpredictable and therefore dangerous, fear of loss of control

(3) Respondents repeat technologies mentioned in the preceeding question ('telecommunication', 'solar energy', etc.)

(4) Associations evoked by the terms 'bio', 'gene' and 'technology' (mostly positive: e.g. ecologically beneficial or optimistic view of science)

Numbers in parenthesis indicate for each country the percentage of responses being classified to a specific discourse

'Qualitative purists', it must be admitted, must view automatic analysis of text with suspicion since the method uses structural features of text, that is, proximity of words, as a means to reconstruct classes of meaning. To check whether or not the assumption that structure allows the extraction of meaning is valid, Allum (1998) compared two independent analyses of the UK-data set: one was the ALCESTE solution used in the present example and the other was a manual content analysis and categorization of the same response set. Figure 3 depicts the automatically derived classes and the manually derived categories projected into the same correspondence analytic space.

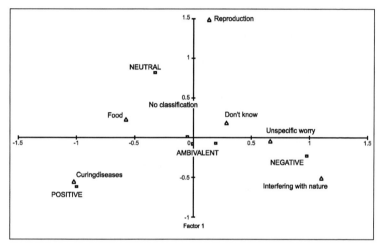

Figure 3: ALCESTE classes (triangles) and evaluative categories from manual analysis (squares, capital letters) of open responses in a questionnaire about biotechnology in the UK projected into same correspondence space[4].

Figure 3 depicts the categories found in a classical content analysis of the evaluative tone of the open-ended responses (little squares, capital letters) and some of the discursive classes found in the automatic analysis (little triangles). The surprisingly good coincidence of the two independently derived results corroborates the validity of ALCESTE's automatic analysis.

---

4   Reproduced with friendly permission by Nick Allum (Allum 1998).

Comparison of Focus-Group Discourse

This last example is from research derived from the above investigation. The European research group on public concerns about biotechnology attempted to corroborate and to understand more profoundly the afore-mentioned results from an automatic text analysis by conducting focus-group discussions on people's concerns about biotechnology in various European countries (Kronberger et al. 2001; Wagner et al. 2001). Here, as with other methods, it was necessary to observe local meaning systems in the analysis. Therefore, translation of the focus-group transcripts and simultaneous qualitative analysis was impossible.

The study involved ten countries: Austria, Denmark, Finland, France, Germany, Great Britain, Italy, Portugal, Sweden, and Switzerland. In each country a local team of researchers was responsible for this task. The research was conducted in seven steps (originally suggested by G. Gaskell, LSE):

a) The research teams of all ten countries convened and agreed on shared interview guidelines, the sampling rules of the focus-group participants, and the general procedure. It was agreed, for example, that the groups should be homogeneous with regard to education levels because less educated subjects are likely to be mute in the presence of better educated participants.

b) The researchers ran the focus-groups in their own countries according to the agreed upon guidelines and at approximately the same time of the year. In most countries the focus-groups were recorded, using both audio and video, and their talk and discussion subsequently transcribed. The video footage was useful in determining who said what in the focus-groups, particularly in the case of simultaneous speech.

c) The transcript was analyzed locally, i.e., in each original language and culture by experienced qualitative researchers using ATLAS/ti or NUD•IST. This analysis was intended to reveal the most prominent features appearing in the material. Besides topical content, particular attention was paid to metaphors used and the way focus-group participants referred to different applications of biotechnology.

d) The results of the first analysis were brought to a joint meeting of all research groups, presented, and discussed. This workshop allowed universal topics, images, and metaphors to be identified as well as features of the transcripts that had only local significance. Subsequently, the workshop participants developed a grid of those categories and features that were deemed relevant to the research, whether universal or local. The grid allowed content categories and discursive features to be cross-tabulated. It was to be used in a second local analysis of the texts and allowed any local content that was considered relevant by an analyst to be entered.

e) In a second analysis of the texts the researchers were supposed to search for the categories and features constituting the grid in their own material. For the task of comparison, the principle content of the grid was two or three examples for each feature and content category. Table 2 presents the general format of this grid.

f) Once each research group had completed the grids, a final joint meeting of the researchers established the bases for comparison, such that researchers checked their own grid against the background of other grids. This procedure helped to correct interpretational biases and resulted in minor corrections.

Table 2 crudely shows the scheme of analysis and comparison. For each country a separate cross tabulation of interpretive category and associated discursive features was constructed. The cells contained examples of focus-group text that local researchers considered a typical illustration of the way a certain topic was talked about in the focus-group sample. No need to say that this procedure resulted in rather extensive cross-tabulations that were subsequently used for comparison.

A qualitative research such as the present one is, of course, prone to attract many problems. First, the selection of the samples is hard if not impossible to make parallel in different countries. Second, qualitative analysts are likely to have their own styles of analysing text even if a shared method is agreed on, such as the grounded theory approach (Strauss 1987) in the present case. Since qualitative researchers can hardly be 'parallelized', this approach appeared to be the best common denominator, although it allows a very high degree of freedom. This freedom, however, was kept under control through the regular meetings. Finally, the biggest problem for professional qualitative researchers is perhaps the fact that a comparative analysis such as this one prohibits analysing the 'deep structure' of the texts. Because of the comparative goal, the grids used to present the results were a methodological compromise and automatically led to simplifications and polishing idiosyncratic edges of focus-group discourse. This contrasts with much of qualitative analysis, which usually strives for an in-depth understanding of texts beyond mere content analysis. Such an in-depth analysis is favored by cultural psychologists but it would probably not allow cross-country comparison.

	Situational or discursive feature A	Situational or discursive feature B	Situational or discursive feature C	Etc.
Country 1				
Interpretative Category 1		Specific examples of text for country 1, category 1, and feature B		
Interpretative Category 2				
Etc.				
Country 2				
Interpretative Category 1				
Interpretative Category 2			Specific examples of text for country 2, category 2, and feature C	
Etc.				
Country X				
Interpretative Category 1				
Interpretative Category 2				
Etc.				Specific examples of text for country X, category Y, and feature Z

Table 2: Scheme for comparing focus-group results across countries.

Conclusions

The examples presented in the foregoing sections provide an illustration of how the local semantic metric of cultures and language groups can be respected in comparative research. In the quantitative domain a social psychological scale needs to be based on an equivalent semantic metric if it is used across cultures. Without this, warrant scale scores and what they mean for the respondents cannot be compared. Statistical methods to check for comparable metrics in such data do exist. Van de Vijver and Leung (1997), for example, suggest parametric methods such as exploratory factor analysis and subsequent target rotation, among others. While such methods may yield reliable results if the data can legitimately be considered to be of a parametric quality; but this is a big 'if', given the potential biases such as item and method bias introduced by different research teams collecting the data under varying circumstances. An alternative approach are nonparametric methods such as the one illustrated by the 'Meaning of Work' research team (Meaning of Work Research Team 1987) as well as in the example of word associations using data from the Wagner, Valencia, and Elejabarrieta (1996) 'war-peace' study. The validity of these methods does not depend upon precarious parametric assumptions and they allow the internal relationships among a set of variables to be visualized. They are, therefore, more intuitive to the researcher (cf. van de Geer 1993).

Automatic classification of text through ALCESTE (Reinert 1990) is also a nonparametric structural method. The resulting clusters describe discursive classes, i.e., words and phrases that occur in context in a large corpus of text. Using this method on culturally homogeneous text and comparing the obtained cluster solutions in a second step allows similarities and discrepancies of discourse between culture and language groups to be established.

It might appear inappropriate to talk of semantic metrics in the example of cross-country qualitative analysis of focus-groups, but there is some justification for it. In principle, the basic problem in qualitative comparison is the same as in the quantitative domain. Comparing two data sets presupposes identical meaning of items and scores, i.e., a comparable semantic metric. With qualitative material this can only be established by doing content-analyses and interpretations locally without prior translation. Only in second step interpretations and category systems can be translated and brought to bear on a comparative perspective.

Pike's (1967) idea of distinguishing the emic from the etic approach in cross-cultural psychology was a fruitful one and instigated decades of methodological discussions. Nowadays none of the two is exclusively favored and the most promising methodological developments have been combinations or integrations of both (e.g., Berry 1989; Helfrich 1999; Van de Vijver and Leung, 1997, to name but a few), as well as Valsiner's attempt to keep the journal 'Culture and Psychology' free of simple numerical cross-cultural comparison research (Valsiner 2001).

By the same token, the concept of a cultural metric allows quantitative and qualitative comparative methodology to be viewed within a framework integrating emics and etics. This perspective needs further analysis as to what degree it may allow the simultaneous consideration of quantitative and qualitative material bearing on the same phenomenon. Attempts to use both data sources have been made but found to be notoriously difficult. This issue is being discussed under the heading of validity and 'triangulation' of qualitative methods (c.f. Fielding & Fielding, 1986; Flick, 1992). In any case, the debate is far from over and promises more exciting "culture's adventures in psychology" (Valsiner 2001: 5).

References

Allum, N.C. (1998). A Social Representations Approach to the Comparison of Three Textual Corpora Using ALCESTE. Unpublished Thesis, London School of Economics and Political Science, UK.

Amir, Y./Sharon, I (1987). Are Social Psychological Laws Cross-Culturally valid? In: Journal of Cross-Cultural Psychology, 18, 383-470.

Berry, J.W. (1989). Imposed Etics, Emics, Derived Etics. In: International Journal of Psychology, 24, 721-735.

Berry, J.W. (2000). Cross-Cultural Psychology: a Symbiosis of Cultural and Comparative Approaches. In: Asian Journal of Social Psychology, 3, 197-205.

Campbell, D.R. (1961). The Mutual Methodological Relevance of Anthropology and Psychology. In: F.L.K. Hsu (Ed.). Psychological Anthropology. Homewood, Ill: Dorsey.

Dahlin, B./Watkins, D. (2000). The Role of Repetition in the Processes of Memorising and Understanding: A Comparison of the Views of German and Chinese Secondary School Students in Hong Kong. In: British Journal of Educational Psychology, 70, 65-84.

Fielding, N.G./Fielding, J.L. (1986). Linking Data. London: Sage.

Flick, U. (1992). Triangulation Revisited: Strategy of Validation or Alternative? In: Journal for the Theory of Social Behaviour, 22, 175-198.

Gibbons, J.L./Lynn, M./Stiles, D.A./Jerez de Berducido, E./Richter, R./Walker, K./Wiley, D. (1993). Guatemalan, Filipino, and U.S.A. Adolescents' Images of Women as Office Workers and Homemakers. In: Psychology of Women Quarterly, 17, 373-388.

Hayashi, C. (1950). On the Quantification of Qualitative Data from the Mathematics-Statistical Point of View. In: Annals of Statistical Mathematics, 2.

Helfrich, H. (1999). Beyond the Dilemma of Cross-Cultural Psychology: Resolving the Tension between Etic and Emic Approaches. In: Culture and Psychology, 5, 131-153.

Jahoda, G. (1986). Nature, Culture and Social Psychology. In: European Journal of Social Psychology, 16, 17-30.

Jodelet, D. (1993). Indigenous Psychologies and Social Representations of the Body and Self. In U. Kim/J.W. Berry (Eds.). Indigenous Psychologies. London: Sage

Kim, U. (2000). Indigenous, Cultural, and Cross-Cultural Psychology: A Theoretical, Conceptual, and Epistemological Analysis. In: Asian Journal of Social Psychology, 3, 265-288.

Kronberger, N./Wagner, W. (2000). Keywords in Context: Statistical Analysis of Text Features. In: M. Bauer/G. Gaskell (Eds.). Qualitative Researching with Text, Image and Sound. A Practical Handbook. London: Sage.

Kronberger, N./Dahinden, U./Allansdottir, A./Seger, N./Pfenning, U./Gaskell, G./Allum, N./Rusanen, T./Montali, L./Wagner, W./ Cheveigné, S./Diego, C./Mortensen, A. (2001). 'The Train Departed without us'—Public Perceptions of Biotechnology in ten European Countries. In: Politeia, 63, 26-36.

Laboratory of Comparative Human Cognition (1979). What's Cultural about Cross-Cultural Cognitive Psychology? In: Annual Review of Psychology, 30, 145-172.

LeVine, R.A. (1982). Culture, Behaviour and Personality. New York: Aldine.

Meaning of Work Research Team (1987). International Comparison of the Relationships between MOW Variables. In: Meaning of Work Research Team (Eds.). The Meaning of Working. New York: Academic Press.

Minoura, Y. (1996). A Plea for a Hypothesis-Generating approach to Link the Individual's World of Meaning and Society's Cultural Orientation. In: Culture and Psychology, 2, 53-62.

Pike, K.L. (1967). Language in Relation to a Unified Theory of the Structure of Human Behavior. The Hague: Mouton.

Reinert, M. (1983). 'Une méthode de classification descendante hiérarchique: application a l'analyse lexicale par contexte'. In: Les Cahiers de l'Analyse des Données, Vol. 8, 2, 187-198.

Reinert, M. (1990). 'ALCESTE. Une méthodologie d'analyse des données textuelles et une application: Aurélia de Gérard de Nerval'. In: Bulletin de méthodologie sociologique, 26, 24-54.

Shweder, R.A. (2000). The Psychology of Practice and the Practice of the three Psychologies. In: Asian Journal of Social Psychology, 3, 207-222.

Straub, J. (1999). Handlung, Interpretation, Kritik. Grundzüge einer textwissenschaftlichen Handlungs- und Kulturpsychologie [Action, interpretation, critique. An outline of a text-scientific psychology of action and culture]. Berlin: de Gruyter.

Strauss, A.L. (1987). Qualitative Analysis for Social Scientists. Cambridge: Cambridge University Press.

Triandis, H.C. (1996). The Psychological Measurement of Cultural Syndromes. In: American Psychologist, 51, 407-415.

Triandis, H.C. (2000). Dialectics between Cultural and Cross-Cultural Psychology. In: Asian Journal of Social Psychology, 3, 185-196.

Triandis, H.C./Bontempo, R./Leung, K./Hui, C.K. (1990). A Method for Determining Cultural, Demographic, and Personal Constructs. In: Journal of Cross-Cultural Psychology, 21, 302-318.

Valsiner, J. (2001). Editorial: the First Six Years: Culture's Adventures in Psychology. In: Culture and Psychology, 7, 5-48.

Van de Geer, J.P. (1993). Multivariate Analysis of Categorical Data: Applications. London: Sage.

Van de Vijver, F./Leung, K. (1997). Methods and Data Analysis for Cross-Cultural Research. London: Sage.

Wagner, W. (1997). Local Knowledge, Social Representations and Psychological Theory. In: K. Leung/U. Kim/S. Yamaguchi/Y. Kashima (Eds.). Progress in Asian Social Psychology. Vol. 1. Singapore: Wiley.

Wagner, W./Kirchler, E./Clack, F./Tekarslan, E./Verma, J. (1990). Male Dominance, Role Segregation and Spouses' Interdependence in Conflict. In: Journal of Cross-Cultural Psychology, 21, 48-70.

Wagner, W./Kronberger, N./Allum, N./Correia Jesuino, J./De Cheveigné, S./Diego, C./Gaskell, G./Heinßen, M./Midden, C./Odegaard, M./Olsson, S./Rizzo, B./Rusanen, T./Stathopoulou, A. (2002). Pandora's Genes—Images of Biotechnology and Nature in Europe. In: G. Gaskell et al. (Eds.). Biotechnology in the Public Eye. Cambridge: Cambridge University Press.

ault:

Wagner, W./Kronberger, N./Gaskell, G./Allum, N./Allansdottir, A./ Cheveigné, S./Dahinden, U./Diego, C./Montali, L./Mortensen, A./ Pfenning, U./Rusanen, T./Seger, N. (2001). Nature in Disorder: The Troubled Public of Biotechnology. In: G. Gaskell/M. Bauer (Eds.). Biotechnology 1996-2000: The Years of Controversy. London: Museum of Science and Industry.

Wagner, W./Valencia, J./Elejabarrieta, F. (1996). Relevance, Discourse and the 'Hot' Stable Core of Social Representations—A Structural Analysis of Word Associations. In: British Journal of Social Psychology, 35, 331-351.

Wittgenstein, L. (1958). Philosophical Investigations. Oxford: Blackwell.

Yang, K.-S. (2000). Monocultural and Cross-Cultural Indigenous Approaches: The Royal Road to the Development of a Balanced Global Psychology. In: Asian Journal of Social Psychology, 3, 241-264.

EXPLORING INTERCULTURAL LEARNING: POTENTIAL AND LIMITS OF THE STRUCTURE FORMATION TECHNIQUE

DORIS WEIDEMANN

Introduction

Intercultural experiences of social researchers have been one of the pro-
pelling forces behind the development of cross-cultural and cultural psychology. In many cases, the insight that exported concepts, methods, and
interpretations could not be applied to a foreign setting was the starting
point for a lifelong search for alternative psychological theories or commitment to cross-cultural research (the life stories of social scientists collected by Bond (1997) are a case in point). Quite obviously, overseas
sojourns have the potential to forcefully demonstrate the cultural foundations of human psychological functioning. Extended intercultural contact
makes alternative cultural systems visible and thereby reveals the cultural
preconditions of one's own world view. Frontiers between 'the familiar'
and 'the foreign' become tangible, are negotiated and continuously re-
drawn, resulting in changes of emotional states, attitudes, values, knowledge, judgment, or behavior. Evidently, this experience is not restricted
to social scientists but is equally true for large numbers of international
students, managers, and other culture-travelers. A heightened cultural
awareness and the adoption of new behavioral patterns and culturally
adequate social skills are reported by (and expected of!) representatives
of all these groups. It is precisely because international sojourns possess
a potential for the acquisition of these as well as other cross-cultural
communication skills that international work and study experience is
widely regarded as an important prerequisite for international job positions and has therefore become an integral part of many university study
programs.

The aim of this chapter is to explore theoretical and methodical approaches to the studying of intercultural learning processes during inter-

national sojourns. After a short review of the adjustment research framework, central elements of a qualitative, cultural psychological approach to intercultural learning are spelled out. An empirical, longitudinal study on German sojourners in Taiwan is presented as an example of such an approach and serves to describe the structure formation technique as an innovative and fruitful method for documenting learning processes. Finally, potentials and limitations of this method for studying intercultural interactions and intercultural learning are critically discussed.

Intercultural Learning and the Adjustment Research Framework

Despite the universally acknowledged effectiveness of international sojourns in developing cultural awareness and cross-cultural communication skills, empirical research on related learning processes has been sparse. Corresponding studies have mainly been carried out within the narrow methodical and theoretical confines of the *adjustment research* framework. While this line of research has proven extremely fruitful and provided valuable insights into the general nature and importance of cultural adaptation, it has not systematically addressed individual learning processes. Instead, causes of and remedies for adjustment problems and acculturative strategies have been at the center of attention.

The choice of research focus cannot solely be explained by scientific reasons but obviously reflects the needs of the American international organizations that were among the first sponsors of sojourners research. Then (as now) concerns about organizational performance in an international context were the key stimulants of research funding. In line with early findings that suggested a 'culture shock' phenomenon (Lysgaard 1955, Oberg 1960), researchers, as well as their sponsors, were alarmed by the fact that overseas stays were accompanied by considerable stress and maladjustment that impaired the effectiveness of experts and managers sent to international postings. Consequently, cross-cultural adjustment came to be regarded as the key to effectiveness and overseas success and, eventually, even as its reliable *indicator*. Measuring degrees of overseas adjustment thus gained crucial practical importance. As a result, research mainly concentrated on developing and testing adjustment models that helped to assess and to predict acculturative outcomes. As Church had already noted in 1982, by stressing adjustment *outcomes*, researchers largely neglected the study of adjustment *dynamics and processes*. Despite a few notable exceptions, this trend continues today.

Within the framework of adjustment research, learning is largely treated as an implicit psychological process that is assumed to take place between 'cultural contact' and 'adjustment outcomes', yet it has rarely been precisely defined nor directly addressed by empirical research. Learning is broadly conceptualized as *response* to the skills and knowledge *deficits* that become apparent in intercultural contact and that can be regarded as the central reason for initial adjustment problems. Learning activities beyond 'deficit-repair' that may take place irrespective of reaching the normative goal of 'adjustment' are thus denied or ignored. As a result, little is known about what stimulates culture-related learning in an overseas setting, which phases, preconditions, and moderating factors can be observed, or how the process is affected by inter-individual differences.

The almost exclusive reliance on questionnaires (that sometimes employ ill-defined constructs) in sojourner studies has further contributed to this situation. As Church comments, "[s]uch studies tend to be superficial and generally fail to relate sojourn behaviour and adjustment difficulties to specific sojourn experiences or cultural differences" (Church 1982: 561). In order to gain a deeper understanding of learning and adjustment processes, a multi-methodical approach as well as a longitudinal research design are indispensable.

Despite considerable advances during the last two decades (especially with regard to employed theories, see, e.g., Ward 2004), much of Church's criticism still applies today. Even though current adjustment models build on a broad theoretical and empirical basis, the above identified shortcomings have not entirely been overcome. A recently proposed acculturation model (Ward 1996, Ward, Furnham and Bochner 2001) may serve to illustrate this point and also to identify *additional factors* that have contributed to the neglect of individual learning processes. Among these, unsatisfactory theories of 'culture' and 'culture contact' are the most notable. Since Ward's model builds on profound knowledge of adjustment research and explicitly integrates approaches by different authors, its central assumptions and general outline may well be regarded as representative. It is therefore well suited for pointing out characteristic topics and general suppositions, and may thus also serve to spot shortcomings that need to be overcome if an understanding of individual intercultural learning is to be achieved.

According to this model, the acculturation process is set off by "cultural contact". The culture contact situation makes skills deficits obvious and is experienced as stressful by the individual. It stimulates psychological responses on affective, behavioral, and cognitive levels, which then result in certain (nonstatic) adjustment outcomes. Adjustment outcomes are conceptualized as encompassing a psychological dimension (which mainly relates to physical and psychological well-being, Ward 1996: 127) and a sociocultural dimension (which mainly relates to behavioral competence, ibid.). Moderating factors of the culture contact situation and of the acculturation process are spelled out.

A central, instigating element of the acculturation process is the "cultural contact" situation. As Ward explains:

"The model considers culture contact as a major life event that is characterized by stress, disorientation, and learning deficits and demands cognitive appraisal of the situation and behavioural, cognitive, and affective responses for stress management and the acquisition of culture-specific skills. These factors, as well as their psychological and sociocultural outcomes, are likely to be influenced by both societal-level and individual-level variables" (Ward 1996: 128).

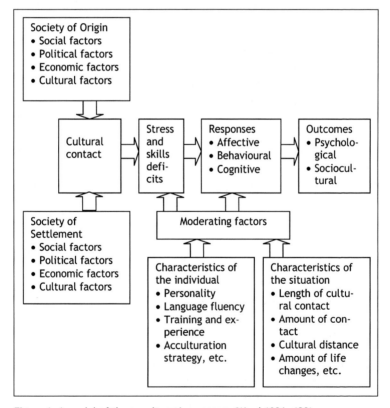

Figure 1: A model of the acculturation process (Ward 1996: 129)

Despite its central position in the theoretical foundation of the acculturation (and adjustment) concept, which is also apparent in the above statement, 'culture contact' is not a very well defined construct, nor is this lack of definition usually deplored. Yet, a precise conceptualization is not only necessary for a deeper understanding of the acculturation process itself but also in order to identify the specific *cultural* components of an otherwise general psychological stress and coping (or social skills acquisition) model. Apparently, Ward's model—as with other popular adjustment theories—is based on the implicit understanding that cultural contact automatically takes place once a person crosses national borders. Though the crossing of borders is not regarded as a *necessary* condition for cultural contact (most authors conceptually allow for in-country cultural contact as well, see, for example, Grove and Torbiörn 1985, Ward, Furnham and Bochner 2001), it is certainly treated as a *sufficient* one. Obviously, this view implies a concept of cultures as fixed, nation-bound entities as well as an understanding of individuals as representatives of 'their' national cultures, which they then transport to the foreign environment (this view also underlies the idea of "cultural distance" that is included as a moderating factor in Ward's model). The objective existence of cultural difference is taken for granted and expected to produce negative effects in cultural contact situations.

This simplified view is bound to raise a number of questions, such as why *positive* aspects of cultural contact are ignored. Certainly, cultural contact is also accompanied by feelings of excitement, joy, or self-effectiveness that can be expected to shape the adjustment process just as powerfully and that must be taken into account when explaining why people actively seek international travel, study, or employment at all.

Another unanswered question is whether *all* interactions of a sojourner with his or her host country environment count as culture contact, even if these interactions take place on the basis of *shared* cultural values, norms, and behavioral rules. The definition of cultural contact quoted earlier as a "major life event that is characterized by stress, disorientation, and learning deficits" (ibid.) presupposes that cultural difference is a *sine qua non* of cultural contact. Additional unanswered questions include whether or not the experienced sojourner who has become familiar with local ways remains involved in 'cultural contact' and, if not, what degree of adjustment would be sufficient for this effect.

Most likely, in Ward's model cultural contact is meant to describe the *general* context of international sojourners in their *new* environment and not intended to be used as a diagnostic label for isolated interaction episodes. If 'cultural contact' is to be used as an explanatory construct in micro-level analyses, further clarification is warranted. Even in a meta-level model, the implicit assumption that moving across national borders inevitably leads to the experiencing of cultural difference (and thus to cultural contact) is unsatisfactory. As Hermans and Kempen (1998) have convincingly argued, present-day glocalized and multicultural societies have made the assumption of homogenous national cultures that 'clash' in international interactions obsolete. However, the implications of this insight for adjustment and sojourners research have yet to be spelled out.

Clearly, conceptions of 'cultural contact', of adjustment and intercultural learning, will have to account for multicultural ownership and for positive experiences of cultural difference. Acculturation models, such as the one presented above, do not yet provide the theoretical foundation to sufficiently explain these phenomena. The development of more sophisticated adjustment models has without doubt been impaired by inconsistent definitions of central concepts and the associated difficulty of integrating research results that are based on differing constructs, operationalizations, and methods (Church 1982, Ward 1996). A major obstacle to theory development, however, is the unchanged focus on acculturation outcomes that can also be observed in the Ward's model. Even if process moderators are addressed, the relevance of understanding the acculturation process derives from the interest in more effectively predicting and explaining acculturation outcomes. Taking into account that the evaluation of adjustment outcomes and the conceptualization of adjustment dimensions are closely linked to organizational goals of effectiveness or to other normative horizons, this appears as an unacceptably narrow perspective on psychological change during international sojourns.

Towards a Cultural Psychological Approach to Intercultural Learning

In order to grasp and to explain the learning processes of sojourners, such as the ones mentioned at the start of this chapter, the adjustment research framework seems inadequate. Instead, I propose a cultural psychological approach that allows for a nonnormative outlook on individual experiences and (intercultural) learning during overseas sojourns.

This approach is based on an understanding of culture as the entirety of discourses, practices, and objectivations, which are based on a collective meaning system (comprising, e.g., goals, norms, stories, and symbols) that is characterized by a certain coherence and continuity (Straub, 1999; Weidemann and Straub 2000). This definition implies that culture may refer to collectives of different sizes and also to relatively transient life forms. It is regarded as a discursive construct because it rests on so-

324

cial constructions of reality and is discursively negotiated and defined; it is relational because the demarcation of different 'cultures' implies acts of comparison and judgment (Matthes 1992). Individuals are thus understood to 'belong' to many different cultures, though belongingness may be accorded (or denied) on the basis of different criteria or interests.

For an understanding of learning processes during international sojourns, this conceptualization has significant implications. If cultures are denied ontological status, there is *no objective means* to identify cultural difference. Instead, as 'culture' itself, cultural difference is a relational construct that may gain relevance and explanatory power in certain situations and with respect to the discursive traditions, perspectives, and goals of the involved individuals or collectives (whether they be the involved actors, accidental onlookers, or detached scientists).

Different conclusions may be drawn as to whether 'culture' is a relevant construct in explaining actual situations and whether an interaction should be classified as 'intercultural', depending on who interprets the situation (and to which end). Yet, in order to understand how sojourners develop an understanding of cultural difference and of different cultural systems, their perspective and experiences must be taken into account. In doing so, any investigation must be both open for *subjective perspectives* as well as able to transcend the assumption that cultural difference will (only) be experienced with respect to different national cultures and that cultural difference is intrinsically stressful and aversive. This can only be achieved by a *qualitative research approach* that allows participants to express and comment if and in which situations they experience cultural difference, how they react to and what they conclude from this experience. By changing the focus from adjustment outcomes to an *open* interest in individual meaning making, new aspects of adjustment and learning may come into view that have hitherto been ignored.

German Sojourners in Taiwan: an Example of a Cultural Psychological Approach to Intercultural Learning

The choice of a cultural psychological approach and a qualitative methodological framework offer a theoretical foundation for a broad variety of research questions, methods, and constructs. The following study on German sojourners in Taiwan will be introduced and discussed as *one example* of such an approach. Based on a cultural psychological outlook on human beings as inhabitants of "intentional worlds" (Shweder 1991), this particular study focused on implicit lay theories that German sojourners held and developed in order to explain the functioning of their Taiwanese environment. The concept of lay theories (alternatively known as "implicit theories", or "subjective theories", also see below[1]) refers to the assumptions, interpretations, and explanations by 'ordinary people' (i.e., of actors who do not possess specific scientific knowledge about the explained phenomenon) of the social and material world around them. In comparison to scientific theories, 'lay theories' are less coherent and consistent, and often implicit rather than explicit, yet they effectively serve the important function of orientation in everyday life (Heider 1958, Furnham 1988, Wegner and Vallacher 1977). Following the interest in *learning processes* during international sojourns, the study further aimed at documenting and interpreting *changes* of implicit theories. Insofar as these theories concern *cultural* practice, changes of implicit theories were understood as expression of *intercultural learning*.

In light of the breadth and number of lay theories that any one person holds, restriction to a selected topic was mandatory. This topic had to be a) complex enough to stimulate elaborate lay theories; b) distinct enough to be the object of clearly focused theories; c) expected to become relevant to Germans in Taiwan; and d) likely to be perceived as a cultural phenomenon by my research partners. Based on reviewing both German and Taiwanese social psychological and comparative research, I decided on the topic of 'face' (see below). The study thus centered on German sojourners' implicit theories of the Taiwanese concept of 'face' and the changes in these theories over time. In the following paragraphs, design, methods, and results of this study will be presented and critically discussed.

Intercultural Learning of Germans in Taiwan

According to the concept of culture employed here (cf. Straub 1999, Weidemann and Straub 2000), German-Taiwanese interactions cannot uniformly and uncritically be regarded as 'intercultural'. However, scientific as well as anecdotal reports suggest that these interactions possess a significant potential for feelings of cultural difference (Günthner 1993, Nagels 1996, Thomas and Schenk 2001). Indeed, the notion that 'Chinese culture' (uncritically subsuming everything Taiwanese) and 'Ger-

---

1   In this contribution, the terms 'implicit theory' and 'lay theory' are used interchangeably. The term 'subjective theory' will be reserved for the specific approach of the Research Programme Subjective Theories that is introduced below.

man culture' differ in *almost all* important respects seems to be wide-spread. As a result, German-Chinese interactions are perceived as highly demanding and especially failure-prone. German introductory texts to intercultural communication thus almost never fail to include a critical incident with 'Chinese clients' that vividly demonstrates the negative consequences of communication failure (see, e.g., various chapters of the recent German language *Handbook of Intercultural Communication and Cooperation* by Thomas, Kinast and Schroll-Machl 2003). The abundance of intercultural guidebooks that coach Germans on 'Chinese' interaction rules can be regarded as another impressive indicator of a pronounced feeling of significant difference between 'German' and 'Chinese' cultures as well as of a self-attested knowledge and skills deficit. In light of these findings, it appears highly likely that German sojourners in Taiwan will be confronted with cultural difference that will require and stimulate intercultural learning.

One of the issues that figures most prominently in guidebooks and scientific texts alike is the Chinese concern for 'face'. Invariably, skillful handling of 'face' is mentioned as an important challenge and prerequisite for managerial success in China and Taiwan. The high incidence and surprisingly stereotypical format of 'face'-related stories (of German language guidebooks as well as of scientific texts), suggests that the Chinese concept of 'face' is not only regarded as a 'technical problem' in intercultural contacts, but possesses special symbolic meaning. A cursory analysis of such stories reveals that they typically conform to the following uniform rhetoric format: German actor "A" meets Chinese actor "B". "A" acts with best intentions and according to 'normal' German social rules and inadvertently hurts "B's" 'face'. "B" breaks off the contact altogether and "A" is left without the means for repairing the break. Interestingly, this story line (which can be considered to express a well-intended person's ultimate horror of intercultural contact) is specifically linked to the Chinese concept of 'face'[2]. 'Face' here takes on the role of a looming, uncontrollable threat that may bring intercultural contact to an immediate end, yet is almost never treated as a positive concept that opens up opportunities in social intercourse. These findings suggest the existence of (German) collective representations of 'the Chinese' that link the notion of general cultural difference, the Chinese concept of 'face', and a generalized fear of communication failure. Germans who plan to move to Taiwan are thus very likely aware of the existence and importance of the Chinese concept of 'face' and can be expected to hold implicit theories on Chinese 'face' even prior to their arrival in Taiwan.

---

2 Corresponding examples may be found in Sader (1999) and Thomas (1996); for an elaboration of this point see Weidemann (2004).

The Chinese Concept of 'Face'

It has been argued that if social judgment is a universal phenomenon, then so is the personal need for 'face'. The concept of 'face' has gained entry in international sociological and sociolinguistic discourse (Goffman 1955, Brown and Levinson 1978) and is usually regarded as a universal principle, although local variations are assumed to exist. Even though universality is broadly acknowledged, most publications treat 'face' as a distinctly (East) Asian phenomenon. This reflects the great importance of this concept for the social reality of East Asian societies as well as the important role the concept of 'face' has played in the development of Chinese/Taiwanese indigenous psychologies (cf. Jia 1997, Hsu 1996, Ho 1976, 1994, 1998, Bond and Hwang 1986, Hwang 1987).

The conventional distinction of two components of 'face'—*lian* and *mianzi*—, first suggested by Hu (1944), emphasizes that 'face' must be regarded as a multidimensional construct that encompasses concepts such as status, moral integrity, reputation, and dignity. Based on results of his own empirical research, Hsu suggests four components of 'face':

- *Morality*: Situations that evoke moral judgment and evaluation of one's personal character are highly 'face'-sensitive. For example, "bullying children or the elderly, being caught stealing things, being exposed about one's extra-marital affair(s), being exposed about one's corruption, and pretending that one is knowledgeable about a subject but is exposed on the spot" (Hsu 1996: 109) are situations that will call into question one's moral integrity, and thus entail a severe loss of 'face'. On the other hand, affirming one's good moral standing will contribute positively to one's social image.
- *Ability*: Proving to be a capable person, "to succeed in various significant endeavours in life" (ibid. 114), immediately adds to one's 'face'. On the contrary, failing to produce expected results, to be exposed as incompetent are considered to result in a loss of 'face'.
- *Social standing*: Social standing refers to the 'status' a person holds in social intercourse. "To be recognized as possessing a higher social standing than one's interactant(s) and to be treated accordingly (e.g., with appropriate honorifics, address terms, and suitable gifts and such other niceties) is an important achievement in life and endows an individual with a substantial gain of 'face'; to be positioned lower than others, by contrast, is a major cause for a poor public image and constitutes a serious 'face'-loss" (Hsu 1996: 117).
- *Culturedness*: This aspect concerns one's own education and 'breeding', which may show in aspects such as proper dress, appropriate speech, polite behavior, or table manners. On the other hand,

"[d]ressing improperly in public (such as having one's fly open), acting impolite to other people (such as showing disrespect for one's
teacher and telling improper jokes in mixed company, overpraising
oneself, and getting drunk at a formal party) [...] are felt to be seriously 'face'-losing" (Hsu 1996: 120).

'Face' can be regarded as an attribute as well as an unstable result of social interaction and judgment (Ho 1994). As can also be seen in these
examples, 'face' is continuously at stake, is being negotiated, claimed,
hurt, or accorded. According to Bond and Hwang (1986), 'face'-related
behavior can be classified into the following six categories:

- Enhancing one's own 'face';
- Enhancing other's 'face';
- Losing one's own 'face';
- Hurting other's 'face';
- Saving one's own 'face';
- Saving other's 'face'.

The validity of this classification is further supported by everyday Chinese terminology, which includes specific terms for all of these (and associated) aspects of 'face'-behavior (see, for example, Hsu 1996).

Aim and Design of the Study

Research results of Chinese, Taiwanese, and German scientists confirm
the high relevance of 'face' for social interactions in Taiwan as well as
typical knowledge and skills deficits of Germans who are unfamiliar with
the Chinese concept of 'face'. These results suggest that German sojourners in Taiwan will most likely be confronted with 'face'-related behavior, are likely to perceive 'face'-related behavior as a cultural phenomenon, and may be expected to extend their implicit understanding of
'face' during the course of their stay. The study thus aimed at documenting the changes of German sojourners' lay theories about the Taiwanese
concept of 'face'. For the purpose of this study, changes in the lay theories of my interviewees were understood to represent 'intercultural learning'.

The study followed a longitudinal design and a multi-methodical approach. Methods included structured interviews on 'face', open interviews on general living experiences in Taiwan, and an adapted form of
structure formation technique (see below). Fifteen German students and

managers were interviewed four times during their first year in Taiwan[3]. Three of the interviews were accompanied by the structure formation technique that was used to represent subjective knowledge structures of the Taiwanese concept of 'face'. Since the use of structure formation technique to document intercultural learning in an overseas setting can be regarded as innovative, this method will be presented in more detail.

Structure Formation Technique

Structure formation techniques were developed in the context of educational research by the German psychologists Scheele, Groeben, and colleagues in the 1970s and 1980s, and have since been widely used in German health and educational research. Because their development and application are closely linked to the Research Programme Subjective Theories (RPST) (Dann 1983, Groeben, Wahl, Schlee and Scheele 1988) this approach will be briefly presented.[4] Originally conceived in critical response to the then popular behaviorist paradigm, the RPST stresses a humanistic approach that is linked to a specific action theory. It regards human beings as self-reflective and (potentially) rational actors who hold their own (subjective) theories about the 'why' and 'how' of their environment, regulating their actions accordingly. Subjective theories resemble concepts such as 'lay theories' (e.g., Furnham 1988), 'implicit theories' (e.g., Wegner and Vallacher 1977), and 'everyday understanding' (Semin and Gergen 1990), yet, the explicit assumptions about structure and function of *subjective theories* are unique to this approach. Subjective theories are defined as

"cognitions relating to the self and the world constituting a complex aggregate with an (at least implicit) argumentational structure; these cognitions fulfil functions parallel to those of objective 'scientific' theories, namely those of explanation, prediction and technology" (Groeben 1990: 21).

---

3   Data collection was carried out during a research stay in Taiwan from 1998 to 2000. Initial interviews took place shortly after my interview partners' arrival. The second meeting took place about two weeks after the first and was devoted to theory construction by use of the structure formation technique. Third and fourth meetings took place after six months and one year of stay in Taiwan, respectively. For a more detailed description of the research design see Weidemann (2001, 2004).

4   For English language introductions see Dann (1990, 1992a), Groeben (1990), Groeben and Scheele (2001), Grotjahn (1991), Christmann and Groeben (1996).

Being complex cognitive aggregates, subjective theories are understood to encompass less complex social psychological constructs, for example, 'attribution', 'personal constructs', 'schema', or 'script' (Groeben et al. 1988).

An important assumption of the RPST is that subjective theories can be verbally explicated and reconstructed by way of dialogue between researcher and research participant. Expressing the underlying humanistic view, the role of the participant in this dialogue is that of an equal partner who actively participates in the research process. Subjective theories are reconstructed in a two-step research design that encompasses a semi-standardized interview and a graphic representation of the theory structure on paper. To avoid strains on the interview partner, both activities usually take place on different days. The visualization of the theory structure follows pre-set representational rules and is undertaken jointly by interviewer and research participant. The visualization is considered final when agreement (dialogue-consensus) on the structure is achieved between researcher and interview partner, thus ensuring subjective validity of the graphic representation as well as an optimal understanding of the participant's view by the researcher ("communicative validation", Groeben et al. 1988).

Because the RPST is grounded in the view of human beings as self-reflective actors and acknowledges the importance of intentionality, Boesch and Straub (2006) view this approach in close vicinity to cultural psychology. However, its underlying intentionalistic action theory and rationalistic ideals have met with considerable criticism. The claim that subjective theories exist as complex cognitive aggregates even prior to the interview situation, and only have to be 'brought to light' in the research setting, as well as the assumption that subjective theories are *causally* related to actual behavior (and thus allow prediction as well as modification of behavior) have in particular been contested (Straub 1996; Straub and Weidemann 2006; Weidemann 2001, 2004; Steinke 1998, Flick 1989).

Among the various methods that were developed to explicate subjective theories, structure formation techniques have been the most popular. In the context of the above-mentioned two-step research procedure, they are used to produce a visualization of implicit theories. This is achieved by writing theory contents on small pieces of cardboard that are then assembled into a larger picture by linking them with specific relational indicators (e.g., "is equal to", "is an example of" "leads to", etc.). The statement: "If someone loses control in public, this will be regarded as a loss of face" may thus be represented in the following way:

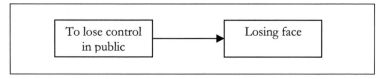

Figure 2: Example of graphic representation by structure formation technique

Based on the prototype of the Heidelberg structure formation technique (Groeben et al. 1988, Scheele and Groeben 1992) different variants have been developed and applied to a broad range of research questions (Dann 1992b, Scheele, Groeben and Christmann 1992). Irrespective of these variations, structure formation techniques generally fulfil the following functions (Dann 1992b: 3-4):

- By introducing a graphic (instead of purely verbal) representational mode they enforce precision and support concentration on the most relevant theory elements.
- They allow for repeated corrections and modifications during the construction process until the interview partner considers the result an adequate representation of his/her individual theory structure.
- Because the construction process is accompanied by questions, explanations, and 'loud thinking', structure formation techniques enhance understanding of the interviewer (thus fulfilling the ideal of 'dialogical hermeneutics').
- Finally, the use of SFT results in a direct representation of knowledge that does not depend on computational or interpretive analysis.[5]

While all structure formation techniques supply a pre-defined set of rules for the graphic representation of the individual theory structure, these rules may differ in number, content, and level of abstraction. The selection and definition of rules follows theoretical standpoints of the researcher (that are not necessarily in full accordance with the RPST) and is based on the research question as well as on the characteristics of the interview partners.

In the present context, a specific variant of SFT was developed that a) reflects partial disagreement with the theoretical assumptions of the RPST, and b) fits the specific research setting. In particular (and in con-

---

5 Besides these functions, Dann adds that structure formation techniques help to identify inadequate beliefs that can then be modified in training sessions in order to cause more adequate or efficient behavior (the issue of subjective theories and behavior modification is treated in greater detail by Mutzeck, Schlee and Wahl (2002)). As mentioned above, the hypothesis that subjective theories are causally related to behavior is not universally accepted. I have not, therefore, listed 'behavior modification' as a general function of SFT.

trast to the RPST), the graphic representation of the theory structure is *not* considered a *reconstruction* of an already existing implicit theory. Instead, it is regarded as the outcome of an *active construction* process and thus as an artefact that results from a particular interview situation. A causal relationship between explicated theory and actual behavior is not assumed. Though implicit theories include knowledge about action rules, explanations, and goals of actions, they do not allow predictions of actual behavior (though parallels might be observed). However, the resulting graphic *is* considered an adequate visualization of the interview partner's knowledge about 'face' at a certain point in time.

Adaptation to the present research interest required three changes: First, the method was adapted to meet the needs of a longitudinal design. Instead of repeating the same procedure (and thus creating entirely new theory structures) during each interview session, changes of implicit theories were documented on the basis of the previous visualization, which was then discussed and modified during subsequent sessions. Interview partners were thus liberated from the boring task of having to repeat *unchanged* theory contents during each subsequent meeting and invited to reflect on *new* insights. Second, the set of representational rules was reduced to a small number of rules that were intuitively understandable to my interview partners. The fact that some SFTs require research participants to spend considerable time on studying (alien) representational rules has been criticized on the ground that this is hardly reconcilable with the ideal of research participants as equal partners who freely express their subjective views. Also, in the case of verbally constituted representations of subjective psychological theories, the use of complicated representational rules hardly achieves more than pseudoprecision, and leads to abstract visualizations that unnecessarily reduce 'rich' statements and narratives to 'poor' theory structures[6]. I have therefore opted for a minimum number of representational rules while allowing for maximum verbal content in theory structures. Finally, I adjusted interview questions to my interview partners' level of knowledge. Be-

---

6   Verbal statements can always be transformed into various graphic representations. The already quoted statement "If someone loses control in public, this will be regarded as a loss of face" may thus be visualized in the following (increasingly formal) ways (relations are printed in italics): ["losing control in public"—*leads to*—"losing face"], as ["losing control in public"—*has a negative impact on/diminishes*—"face"], or as [*absence of*—"personal control"—*under the condition that*—"public"—*has a negative impact on/diminishes*—"face"]. While the last version suggests higher formal precision, it does in fact offer less information than the first version ("negative impact on face" is less precise than "losing face", which can be related to the interview partner's explanations of what 'losing face' means to her).

cause they typically had very little experience with the Taiwanese concept of 'face' at the time of the first interview, I chose mainly open interview questions, which were followed by more focused questions only when interview partners provided more detailed observations or comments (also see Weidemann 2001).

Interview questions followed a pre-set structure that aimed at a systematic approach to the multifaceted phenomenon of 'face'. Interview questions were thus grouped into four sections that addressed the topics of a) losing 'face'; b) gaining 'face'; c) hurting other's 'face'; d) giving 'face' (see above). Because 'saving face' is mainly achieved by *avoiding* everything that might result in a loss of 'face' (on either side) and was therefore unlikely to generate additional information, I did not specifically ask about this alternative. Only when interview partners mentioned 'face' being 'saved' were comments included in the subjective theory structure.

Interview questions asked for general knowledge, personal experiences, or observations concerning 'face'-related situations, actions, and reactions. Apart from reports of 'face'-related situations that were addressed in open questions, questions on actions/antecedents and reactions/outcomes implied a temporal or even causal order that later served to structure the visualization of the subjective theory. All questions were explicitly directed at experiences in Taiwan or at perceived Taiwanese social norms.

Interviews were then transcribed and served as reference for a first draft of the subjective theory that was presented to the interview partner during the following meeting. During the subsequent discussion, new aspects that had not been mentioned during the first interview were introduced and integrated into the subjective theory structure. Since theory contents and symbols representing logical relations were written on small pieces of cardboard, they could easily be moved, added, or exchanged.

Because the aim was to get as full a picture of each participant's understanding of 'face' as possible, many examples were included and original wording was used wherever possible. The general aim was to arrive at a point where reduction made the structure as simple as necessary while leaving it as 'rich' (in terms of meaning) as possible.

After dialogue-consensus was reached, the resulting visualization served as a basis for renegotiation during subsequent interviews. During following interviews the discussion on 'face' was introduced by questions concerning any situation that might have struck the interview partner as 'face'-related since the last interview. Starting from these comments the subjective theory structure was partly altered and corrected (according to the new standpoint or insights), again, until dialogue-consensus was reached.

Results

The use of three different methods (open interview on general living situation in Taiwan, structured interview on 'face', structure formation technique) resulted in three different data formats: interview transcripts of open interviews, interview transcripts of structured interviews, and structure graphics. As will become apparent, a full picture emerges only when data from all three sources are related to one another.

Theory graphics

The use of a structure formation technique to document learning processes of sojourners was an innovative undertaking that implied a certain risk of failure. What if my research partners lacked the motivation or knowledge about 'face' to work on theory graphics, and what if subsequent sessions failed to arrive at theory modifications? The fact that all interview partners constructed theory graphics during all interview sessions and that theory structures grew more complex over time, was, therefore, a first, immediate result and served as an indicator of the method's applicability to the specific research interest. Figure 2 presents the example of theory graphics that were constructed during three consecutive interview sessions by Mister Weber, a German engineer, for whom Taiwan was the first international posting in his career.[7]

---

7 This figure combines three consecutive theory graphics. New elements that were added during the second structure formation session are indicated by broken lines ("----"). New elements that were added during the last meeting are highlighted by "·····".

335

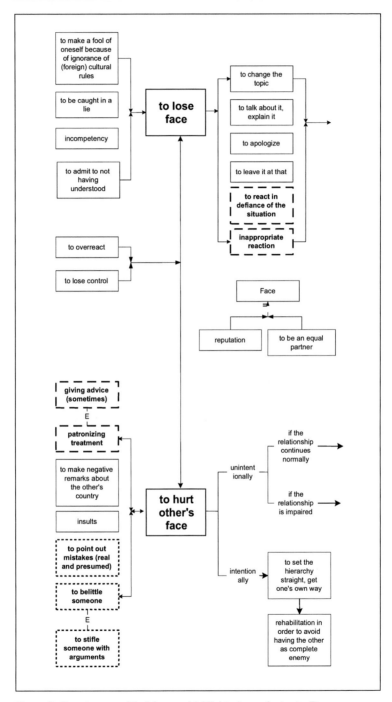

Figure 3: Structure graphic (changes highlighted, see footnote 7)

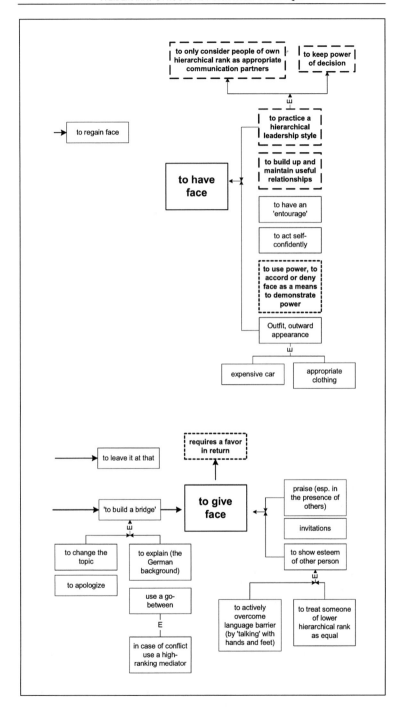

A systematic, cross-cutting analysis of theory graphics shows certain regularities of theory contents and changes over time. Almost invariably, different aspects of 'face' are represented unequally: knowledge about *losing 'face'* is typically much more elaborate than knowledge about having and giving 'face'. These latter aspects of 'face' are, however, central learning fields, i.e., while knowledge increases in relation to all four aspects; there is a special increase in knowledge about having and giving 'face'. The unequal distribution of knowledge is in accordance with German linguistic usage that includes an expression for losing 'face', yet lacks direct translations of having and giving 'face'. Surprisingly, in some cases blanks or near-blanks in the theory graphic indicate that *giving 'face'* remains a foreign concept even after a one-year stay in Taiwan.

A closer look at *new contents* of theory structures reveals three tendencies: first, new contents are usually generated from personally experienced episodes that are either integrated as 'face'-related 'examples' or serve as indicators for a deducted abstract principle that is then added to the theory structure. The following example may serve as an illustration: During the second interview, Paul, a German student, recounts how he felt forced to drink liquor with the father of his Taiwanese girlfriend in order not to hurt the father's 'face', even though he did not like to drink alcohol and would have normally refused the drink. This episode may either be integrated into the theory graphic as: "refusing to drink with the father of one's girl friend"—*leads to*—"hurting other's face". It may, however, also serve to deduct a general principle that manifests itself in this specific episode, but that concerns other (not yet personally experienced) situations as well. In this particular case, Paul concluded that the situation was most adequately interpreted as an example of the more general rule that in order not to hurt the other's 'face', invitations in general should not be refused.[8] Second, a high proportion of new contents are negatively tinged. This is especially striking when considering that first theory structures are mostly nonjudgmental and emotionally neutral. Thus, the need to save 'face' is considered as detrimental to efficient problem solving, or behavior that aims to increase one's own 'face', such as owning an overly expensive car, is regarded as irrational and boastful. Third, as time passes, 'face' is increasingly perceived to possess power-related aspects. These are perceived in behavior, such as intentionally hurting other's 'face' in order to push personal interests or in giving 'face' in order to be granted a favour in reciprocity. Some interview part-

---

8   The representation in the theory graphic was thus as follows: "Refusing to drink with the father of one's girlfriend"—is an example of—"refusing an invitation"—leads to—"hurting other's face".

ners also observe that, as a rule, investment in one's own 'face' increases the general power potential. Since demonstration of power often implies hurting others' interests, many power-related aspects are evaluated negatively by my interview partners, which partially explains the increase of negatively tinged contents mentioned above.

Despite these general tendencies, there exist striking differences between individual theory structures that concern differences in contents, in complexity, or in abstraction level. None of these differences can be explained by demographic data (age, gender, occupational status), nor by analysis of theory structures only. *Why* some interview partners learn what they learn and remain ignorant of aspects that other participants consider important, can only be explained by drawing on additional information of the interview transcripts.

Structured Interviews on 'Face'

If, as the theory graphics suggest, new theory contents are closely linked to personal experiences, the frequency and nature of 'face'-related incidents in which my interview partners are involved certainly play a role in explaining their learning processes. People who have to deal with 'face' on an everyday basis can be expected to gain new insights much faster than individuals who are rarely confronted with 'face'. While theory graphics do not inform us about the frequency and importance of 'face'-related incidents in my interview partners' lives, interview statements are more instructive. Even before being explicitly asked, most interview partners offered their personal views on the relevance of 'face' in daily Taiwanese life. Typically, during the first interviews 'face' is perceived as an interesting phenomenon that the interview partner has heard a lot about but that she or he does not consider very important in her or his personal living context. Text analysis reveals that statements on the relevance of 'face' fall into three distinct categories:

a) *'Face' is regarded as an irrelevant aspect of Taiwanese social life.* Since this view is in obvious contrast to guidebook wisdom, collective representation of 'the Chinese' (see above), and to the interviewer's research interest, this standpoint requires a justification. Invariably, statements about the irrelevance of 'face' are backed up by the argument that 'face' is a phenomenon of the past that does not apply to modern Taiwanese society.

b) *'Face' is considered vaguely relevant.* A typical comment is that 'face' is felt to be "subliminally present", yet cannot be named and identified. This feeling is accompanied by expression of a vague fear of unintentionally hurting someone else's 'face' and then being left with a situation beyond control and repair.

c) *'Face' is considered an important and all-pervasive element of Taiwanese social interactions* that can be clearly described and identified in many examples. Sometimes, this standpoint is in contrast to earlier views that were expressed during preceding interviews and is therefore complemented by an explanation of this fact. Thus, Stefan, a German manager, observes that he had obviously failed to see 'face'-related aspects during the beginning of his stay but has now become very aware of them. Interview partners who consider 'face' an obvious and all-pervasive principle of Taiwanese social life typically use the term 'face' much more frequently in the interview and also apply it to interpretations of non-Taiwanese episodes.

Comparisons of statements over time show a distinct pattern: if evaluations of the relevance of 'face' change at all, the change occurs only in the above listed order (from category "a" statements to category "c" statements). Again, there are distinct inter-individual differences: while some interview partners consider 'face' an obvious and relevant phenomenon during their first interview (and stay with that opinion), some participants perceive 'face' to be vaguely relevant during all interviews or later on change their first impression of irrelevance to that position (category "b"). One interview partner regarded 'face' as irrelevant during all three interviews.

Without commenting on the adequacy of the different types of evaluations (based on the available data, there is no way to ascertain whether an interview partner is actually confronted with 'face'-related situations or not), they may be considered an expression of different grades of *awareness* of 'face'.

If learning about 'face' rests on personal experiences, awareness of 'face' is crucial. Only if actual situations are perceived to contain 'face'-related elements do they serve as learning opportunities. This relationship is also partly supported by the theory graphics: when interview partners report higher awareness of 'face', they are able to point out many more examples (which are sometimes structured by second order principles); however, self-expressed awareness of 'face' does not automatically address all four different aspects of 'face' that are represented in theory graphics. High self-expressed awareness of 'face' does not, therefore, automatically coincide with a more encompassing theory structure.

Yet, different levels of awareness of 'face' are a remarkable finding in themselves since this lends support to the argument that cultural difference is not objective fact but an interpretive construct and that the understanding of learning processes requires the reconstruction of subjective view points. However, neither theory graphics nor structured interviews offer explanations as to *why* participants arrive at different evaluations and insights on 'face'. For a more complete understanding, analysis of the open interview transcripts is indispensable.

Interviews on General Living Experiences

The case of Denise will serve as an illustration. Because of its complexity, Denise's theory structure makes a strong impression, even during the first interview session. Three aspects of 'face' are linked to a great number of contents that in parts even feature a meta-level structuring. Surprisingly, the aspect of 'giving face' remains an exception; it remains basically blank even during the last meeting, which took place after Denise had been in Taiwan for ten months. Interview statements confirm that Denise does not perceive any of her social relations to ever 'give face'. While the theory structure allows the analysis of its contents, it does not offer an explanation for this unbalanced representation. Why does Denise learn so much about having and losing 'face', and so little about 'giving face'? The interpretation of the biographical interviews suggests an explanation:

Denise came to the south of Taiwan to study at the language institute of a local university. Soon after her arrival, she noticed that curious stares followed her wherever she went. After the initial surprise that many people would start a conversation with her to find out about where she came from and why she was in Taiwan, she soon felt harassed by the number of young men who tried to engage her in conversation and by the women who wanted to touch her blonde hair. She started to resent the lack of privacy and the feeling that she stood out as a 'foreigner' in any group or crowd. As her Chinese progressed, she realized that many of her ideas, such as convictions about the importance of environmental protection, about homosexuality, or the right of young adults to choose their own way of life, met with little understanding in her new environment. At the same time she was appalled by the attitudes and life plans of her Taiwanese acquaintances, which to her appeared outdated and unacceptable. She interpreted these attitudes as expression of a different cultural system and responded by an effort to enhance endurance and to develop a "thick skin". Because this effort for "tolerance" did not increase her understanding, nor her acceptance of the 'strange culture', she was caught in a state where she was continuously and painfully confronted with cultural difference, yet lacked creative and positive ways of handling it. Her interpretation of the Taiwanese concept of 'face' is in accordance with this negative and passive outlook on local culture. Almost everything that Denise learned about 'face' consisted in—to her—aversive practice and nothing appeared to increase her personal action potential. Since giving 'face' is by nature an active strategy that creates options in social space, this part of the theory structure remains empty. In her general outlook on Taiwanese cultural practice as something to "endure", active and positive ways of investing and giving 'face' were ignored.

Conclusion

For the purpose of studying individual learning processes during international sojourns, the adjustment research framework was rejected because of the lack of precision of its central constructs (such as 'culture' and 'cultural contact') and the normative implication of adjustment models. Instead, a cultural psychological approach was proposed that conceptualizes intercultural learning as an open-ended process of personal change in reaction to perceived cultural difference, without postulating 'adjustment' as a normative goal of this process. Based on the theoretical foundations of a qualitative cultural psychological approach (as has been, e.g., proposed by Straub 1999, Ratner 1997), and in order to arrive at a closer understanding of individual learning processes, a longitudinal study on German sojourners in Taiwan was carried out. Based on the operationalization of intercultural learning as 'change of lay theories of the Taiwanese concept of 'face' over time', a structure formation technique was successfully used to document individual learning processes of Germans in Taiwan over the period of approximately one year. In the following, the potential as well as the limitations of this method for studying intercultural interactions and intercultural learning will be critically appraised.

Corresponding to cultural psychological principles, structure formation techniques—like qualitative research methods in general—assign participants the role of an equal research partner who is invited to relate his or her subjective views on a certain (research) topic. In contrast to other qualitative methods, however, structure formation techniques also involve research participants in the act of (communicative) validation of theory graphics. As a result, central terms and constructs can be clarified in dialogue between researcher and participant and the subjective validity attested to by the interview partner.

The use of structure formation techniques is preceded by a structured interview on the research topic, yet their use does not merely replicate interview contents in a different data format but stimulates further discussion on the topic at hand. Structure formation sessions provide an opportunity to explain, correct, and extend interview statements. Consequently, structure graphics may include additional or corrected information and thus serve the important purpose of a triangulation of methods.

As the presented results demonstrate, structure formation techniques result in easy-to-grasp graphic representations of lay theories and allow—by repeated use in longitudinal studies—the documentation of changes over time. Theory graphics not only provide an immediate overview of individual theory structures but may also help to spot missing elements (as in the case of Denise), inconsistencies, and other special characteristics that may stimulate further exploration and explanation (on the side of both the research participant and the researcher).

Yet, results from the study presented here also reveal methodical limitations. As the example of Denise also shows, interpretations of theory graphics require context information that is contained neither in the visualization nor in the structured interview on which it is based. In order to arrive at meaningful and 'rich' reconstructions of individual viewpoints, structure formation techniques must be supplemented by additional instruments, such as open or narrative interviews that serve to contextualize the focused data, both situationally as well as biographically. Even in multi-methodical designs, it should be noted that:

- Structure formation techniques focus almost exclusively on cognitive content. The failure to pay adequate attention to emotion (attitudes) and behavior results in a less than full understanding of intercultural learning processes. Supplementary methods may be used in compensation.

- Structure formation techniques impose a structured form on possibly unstructured or differently structured knowledge. The method thus sets limits on the research participant's free articulation and on his or her equal role, both of which are basic postulates of qualitative methodology.

- Structure formation techniques reduce complexity. While this fact is one of the method's strong points, the inevitable loss of information may be a problem in some contexts. However, the degree of complexity reduction partly depends on the choice of representational rules, which may be defined with respect to particular research aims and participants.

- If employed repeatedly in longitudinal designs, structure formation techniques may be used to document change processes. However, even if processes can be reconstructed from comparisons of consecutive (static) theory structures, the actual dynamic is lost in the representation. An understanding of change (learning or adaptation) processes may be supported by narratives of participants that reconstruct and explain processes in their temporal order, and/or by more frequent structure formation sessions. In the presented study, six-month intervals proved long enough for significant changes to occur, yet too long to exactly reconstruct minor learning effects. Shorter intervals may produce a more thorough understanding of micro-level learning processes.

• As mentioned in the discussion of the Research Programme Subjective Theories, the action theoretical foundation of SFT is underdeveloped and should be further explored.

Taking these limitations into account, structure formation techniques appear as a promising method in the context of *multi-methodical* research designs. They may support an understanding of how elements of a foreign environment are perceived, if and in which regard cultural difference becomes relevant, and of how originally foreign elements are integrated into subjective psychological theories. In the context of the cultural psychological endeavour to understand how "psyche and culture […] make each other up" (Shweder 1991: 73), they provide a means for investigating subjective meaning construction in intercultural contexts.

In view of the specific functions and potential of structure formation techniques, their use for further research questions may be further explored. Some possible research and application contexts include, e.g., their use as a stimulant for learning in intercultural training programs.

Because structure graphics bring theory deficits to light, they may be used as a means for focused reflection and learning. They may also be applied to the evaluation of such training programs: By comparing pre-training theory graphics and post-training theory structure, learning effects may be documented. Finally, structure formation techniques may be used to cover (subjective) semantic fields of central concepts, such as, 'intercultural competence' or 'acculturation'.[9] As the study on 'irony' (Scheele and Groeben 1988) demonstrates, structure formation techniques can serve as a *heuristic instrument* and systematically contribute to the aim of employing lay theories for *scientific theory generation* (cf. Heider 1958).

As has been demonstrated, the use of a cultural psychological approach to intercultural learning during overseas sojourns offers new in-

---

9   Lummer (1994), for example, uses a structure formation technique to document subjective theories on 'integration' of Vietnamese refugees in Germany and relates these to experienced difficulties and integration processes of his research participants.

344

sights beyond the 'adjustment' perspective. A cultural psychological approach provides a theoretical framework that enforces the focus on individual actors in cultural perspective and conceptually accommodates present-day phenomena such as multicultural ownership, mixed cultural identity, and intercultural learning. It does not take cultural difference for granted, yet will explore how such difference is perceived, created, and negotiated in real-life interactions, and which role it is accorded in individual lives.

On the other hand, cultural psychology has a lot to gain from investigating intercultural contact situations, as these may bring to light processes of culturally embedded meaning making and (by way of conflict or aversion) stress cultural components of psychological functioning that otherwise would go unnoticed. Different from enculturation processes that occur during early childhood, international transfers of adults offer an opportunity to engage people in dialogue in order to study identity formation and the role that culture(s) play(s) in this process. As has been argued, structure formation techniques may be put to good use in this endeavor.

References

Boesch, E.E./Straub, J. (2006). Kulturpsychologie: Prinzipien, Orientierungen, Konzeptionen. In: G. Trommsdorff/H.-J. Kornadt (Eds.). Kulturvergleichende Psychologie. Band 1—Theorien und Methoden in der kulturvergleichenden und kulturpsychologischen Forschung. Göttingen: Hogrefe. (In Press).

Bond, M. (Ed.) (1997). Working at the Interface of Cultures: Eighteen Lives in Social Science. London: Routledge.

Bond, M. Harris/Hwang, K.-K. (1986). The Social Psychology of the Chinese People. In: M.H. Bond (Ed.). The Psychology of the Chinese People (pp. 213-266). Hongkong: Oxford University Press.

Brown, P./Levinson, S.C. (1978). Politeness. Some Universals in Language Usage. London, New York: Cambridge University Press.

Christmann, U./Groeben, N. (1996). Reflexivity and Learning: Problems, Perspectives, and Solutions. In: J. Valsiner/H.-G. Voss (Eds.), The Structure of Learning Processes (pp. 45-85). Norwood: Ables.

Church, A.T. (1982). Sojourner Adjustment. In: Psychological Bulletin, 91 (3), 540-572.

Dann, H.-D. (1983). Subjektive Theorien: Irrweg oder Forschungsprogramm? Zwischenbilanz eines kognitiven Konstrukts. In: L. Montada/K. Reusser/G. Steiner (Eds.). Kognition und Handeln (pp. 77-92). Stuttgart: Klett-Cotta.

Dann, H.-D. (1990). Subjective Theories: A New Approach to Psychological Research and Educational Practice. In: G.R. Semin/K.J. Gergen (Eds.), Everyday Understanding. Social and Scientific Implications (pp. 227-243). Newbury Park, London, New Delhi: Sage.

Dann, H.-D. (1992a). Subjective Theories and Their Social Foundation in Education. In: M. von Cranach/W. Doise/G. Mugny (Eds.). Social Representations and the Social Bases of Knowledge (pp. 161-168). Lewiston: Hogrefe/Huber.

Dann, H.-D. (1992b). Variation von Lege-Strukturen zur Wissensrepräsentation. In: B. Scheele (Ed.). Struktur-Lege-Verfahren als Dialog-Konsens-Methodik (pp. 2-41). Münster: Aschendorff.

Flick, U. (1989). Vertrauen, Verwalten, Einweisen. Subjektive Vertrauenstheorien in sozialpsychiatrischer Beratung. Wiesbaden: Deutscher Universitäts-Verlag.

Furnham, A. (1988). Lay Theories: Everyday Understanding of Problems in the Social Sciences. Oxford: Pergamon.

Goffman, E. (1955). On Face Work. An Analysis of Ritual Elements in Social Interaction. In: Psychiatry, 18, 213-231.

Groeben, N. (1990). Subjective Theories and the Explanation of Human Action. In: G.R. Semin/K.J. Gergen (Eds.). Everyday Understanding. Social and Scientific Implications (pp. 19-44). Newbury Park, London, New Delhi: Sage.

Groeben, N./Scheele, B. (2001, February). Dialogue-Hermeneutic Method and the "Research Program Subjective Theories". *Forum Qualitative Sozialforschung / Forum: Qualitative Social Research* [On-line Journal], *2*(1). Available at: http://www.qualitative-research.net/fqs-texte/2-00/2-00groebenscheele-e.htm.

Groeben, N./Wahl, D./Schlee, J./Scheele, B. (Eds.) (1988). Das Forschungsprogramm Subjektive Theorien. Eine Einführung in die Theorie des reflexiven Subjekts. Tübingen: Francke.

Grotjahn, R. (1991). The Research Programme Subjective Theories. A New Approach in Second Language Research. In: Studies in Second Language Acquisition, 13, 187-214.

Grove, C.L./Torbiörn, I. (1985). A New Conceptualization of Intercultural Adjustment and the Goals of Training. In: International Journal of Intercultural Relations, 9, 205-233.

Günthner, S. (1993). Diskursstrategien in der interkulturellen Kommunikation. Tübingen: Niemeyer.

Heider, F. (1958). The Psychology of Interpersonal Relations. New York: Wiley.

Hermans, H.J.M./Kempen, H.J.G. (1998). Moving Cultures. The Perilous Problems of Cultural Dichotomies in a Globalizing Society. In: American Psychologist, 53 (10), 1111 - 1120.

Ho, D.Y.-F. (1976). On the Concept of Face. In: American Journal of Sociology, 81, 867-884.

Ho, D.Y.-F. (1994). Face Dynamics: From Conceptualization to Measurement. In: S. Ting-Toomey (Ed.). The Challenge of Facework (pp. 269-286). New York, Albany: State University of New York Press.

Ho, D.Y.-F. (1998). Indigenous Psychologies: Asian Perspectives. In: Journal of Cross-Cultural Psychology, 29 (1), 88-103.

Hsu, C.S. (1996). Face: An Ethnographic Study of Chinese Social Behavior. Ann Arbor: UMI.

Hu, H.-C. (1944). The Chinese Concept of Face. In: American Anthropology, 46, 45-64.

Hwang, K.-K. (1987). Face and Favor: The Chinese Power Game. In: American Journal of Sociology, 92 (4), 944-974.

Jia, W. (1997). Facework as a Chinese Conflict-Preventive Mechanism - a Cultural/Discourse Analysis. In: Intercultural Communication Studies, 7 (1), 43-62.

Lummer, C. (1994). Subjektive Theorien und Integration. Die Einwanderungsproblematik aus Zuwanderersicht, dargestellt am Beispiel von Vietnamflüchtlingen in Deutschland. Weinheim: Deutscher Studien Verlag.

Lysgaard, S. (1955). Adjustment in a Foreign Society: Norwegian Fulbright Grantees Visiting the United States. In: International Social Science Bulletin, 7, 45-51.

Matthes, J. (1992). The Operation Called "Vergleichen". In: J. Matthes (Ed.). Zwischen den Kulturen? Soziale Welt: Sonderband 8, 57- 9. Göttingen: Schwartz.

Mutzeck, W./Schlee, J./Wahl, D. (Eds.) (2002). Psychologie der Veränderung: Subjektive Theorien als Zentrum nachhaltiger Modifikationsprozesse. Weinheim u. Basel: Beltz.

Nagels, K. (1996). Interkulturelle Kommunikation in der Deutsch-Chinesischen Zusammenarbeit. Bremen: Schriftenreihe des Fachbereichs Wirtschaft der Hochschule Bremen.

Oberg, K. (1960). Culture Shock: Adjustment to New Cultural Environments. In: Practical Anthropology, 7, 177-182.

Ratner, C. (1997). Cultural Psychology and Qualitative Methodology.Theoretical and Empirical Considerations. New York and London: Plenum Press.

Sader, K. (1999). Deutsche Mitarbeiter in China. Eine Analyse und Bewertung verschiedener Akkulturationsmuster. Berlin: Mensch & Buch Verlag.

Scheele, B./Groeben, N./Christmann, U. (1992). Ein alltagssprachliches Struktur-Lege-Spiel als Flexibilisierungsversion der Dialog-Konsens-Methodik. In: B. Scheele (Ed.). Struktur-Lege-Verfahren als Dialog-Konsens-Methodik (pp. 152-195). Münster: Aschendorff.

Scheele, B./Groeben, N. (1988). Dialog-Konsens-Methoden zur Rekonstruktion Subjektiver Theorien. Tübingen: Narr.

Semin, G.R./ Gergen, K.J. (Eds.) (1990). Everyday Understanding. Social and Scientific Implications. London, Newbury Park, New Delhi: Sage.

Shweder, R.A. (1991). Thinking Through Cultures: Expeditions in Cultural Psychology. Cambridge, MA. and London: Harvard University Press.

Steinke, I. (1998). Validierung: Ansprüche und dessen Einlösung im Forschungsprogramm Subjektive Theorien. In: E.H. Witte (Ed.), Sozialpsychologie der Kognition: Soziale Repräsentationen, subjektive Theorien, soziale Einstellungen (pp. 120-148). Lengerich: Pabst.

Straub, J. (1999). Handlung, Interpretation, Kritik - Grundzüge einer textwissenschaftlichen Handlungs- und Kulturpsychologie. Berlin, New York: de Gruyter.

Straub, J./Weidemann, D. (2006). Die verstehend-erklärende Psychologie und das Forschungsprogramm Subjektive Theorien. Göttingen: Vandenhoeck & Ruprecht. (Forthcoming)

Thomas, A. (1996). Analyse der Handlungswirksamkeit von Kulturstandards. In: A. Thomas (Ed.). Psychologie interkulturellen Handelns (pp. 107-135). Göttingen: Hogrefe.

Thomas, A./Kinast, E.-U./Schroll-Machl, S. (Eds.) (2003). Handbuch Interkulturelle Kommunikation und Kooperation. Band 1: Grundlagen und Praxisfelder. Göttingen: Vandenhoeck & Ruprecht.

Thomas, A./Schenk, E. (2001). Beruflich in China: Trainingsprogramm für Manager, Fach- und Führungskräfte. Göttingen: Vandenhoeck & Ruprecht.

Ward, C. (1996). Acculturation. In: D. Landis /R.S. Bhagat (Eds.). Handbook of Intercultural Training (pp. 124-147). Thousand Oaks: Sage.

Ward, C. (2004). Psychological Theories of Culture Contact and Their Implications for Intercultural Training and Interventions. In: D. Landis/J. M. Bennett/M. J. Bennett (Eds.). Handbook of Intercultural Training (pp. 185-216). Thousand Oaks: Sage.

Ward, C./Bochner, S./Furnham, A. (2001). The Psychology of Culture Shock. Hove: Routledge.

Wegner, D.M./Vallacher, R.R. (1977). Implicit Psychology: An Introduction to Social Cognition. New York: Oxford University Press.

Weidemann, D. (2001, Sept). Learning About "Face"—"Subjective Theories" as a Construct in Analysing Intercultural Learning Processes of Germans in Taiwan. In: Forum Qualitative Sozialforschung / Forum: Qualitative Social Research [On-line Journal], 2(3). Available at: http://www.qualitative-research.net/fqs-texte/3-01/3-01weide mann-e.htm.

Weidemann, D. (2004). Interkulturelles Lernen. Erfahrungen mit dem chinesischen 'Gesicht': Deutsche in Taiwan. Bielefeld: transcript.

Weidemann, D./Straub, J. (2000). Psychologie interkulturellen Handelns. In: J. Straub/A. Kochinka/H. Werbik (Eds.), Psychologie in der Praxis. Anwendungs- und Berufsfelder einer modernen Wissenschaft (pp. 830-855). München: Deutscher Taschenbuch Verlag.

How to Orient Yourself in Balinese Space: Combining Ethnographic and Psychological Methods for the Study of Cognitive Processes

Jürg Wassmann & Pierre R. Dasen

Introduction

We have worked for a few years, even if sporadically, towards establishing a true collaboration that combines our two disciplines, social anthropology (in particular, cognitive anthropology) and cross-cultural psychology (in the area of cognitive development). We have had the opportunity of working together in the field in Papua New Guinea (Wassmann and Dasen 1994a; 1994b) and Bali (Wassmann and Dasen 1998) as well as to discuss our ideas with colleagues during a workshop that we organised jointly (Wassmann and Dasen 1993). Hence, we have worked towards defining a shared methodology, as described below, and intend to apply it in the context of field research in Bali and elsewhere (Mishra, Dasen and Niraula 2003).

Anthropology and Psychology: Combining Methods

We have already put forth, in German (Wassmann 1993a) as well as in English (Wassmann and Dasen 1994a), the choice of methods that seems most adequate to us. Consequently, in the present context we will focus only on discussing our research strategy (composed of three main stages) without further reference to the analyses and critiques that justify our choices.

We propose a strategy of three stages that requires the integration of (1) a description of the cultural and linguistic system, obtained mainly through interviews, (2) a study of behaviour in daily situations, derived from observation, and (3) induced situations. It goes without saying that these three stages will not remain the same throughout the process of study. Nor will they be equally important for each research. That is, the sequence of stages is not rigid, but rather will provide a wider range of options. There is only one restriction: the third stage must begin after the first two.

Description of the Cultural and Linguistic System

Upon arrival in the field, the ethnographer (anthropologist) normally starts questioning some key informants who, due to their position or status possess overall knowledge, and should be capable of presenting a coherent image of the normative cultural system. With these key informants, who come to work closely with the anthropologist, one obtains the qualitative base of the entire ethnography. In some cases (such as in the case described below), this information is already widely available in the form of previously published materials.

With key informants it is also possible to acquire an array of linguistic material, such as for example, the breakdown of concepts in semantic structures. Knowledge of one informant is then verified by cross checking with other informants. This is done in various ways, as for example, through participant observation.

There was a time when the ethnographic research would go no further. Within the field of anthropology, for instance, there was a tendency for the anthropologist to be satisfied in obtaining a taxonomy that was considered to reflect the knowledge of a given culture. Presently, this no longer suffices. In fact, knowledge, including linguistic knowledge, is not necessarily shared by a collectivity of people. It is necessary to scrutinise the distribution of knowledge by age, gender, social status, education, experience and so on (Wallace 1961; Boster 1985; Romney, Waller and Batchelder 1986; Borofsky 1994). Therefore, following the tenants of sociology or psychology, the anthropologist will conduct interviews with as many people as possible. For the most part, he or she will engage in semi-structured interchanges, to be followed later by a qualitative analysis. The administration of questionnaires is not feasible in most contexts where anthropologists work.

Often taxonomies do not correspond to the ways that people talk in daily life, that is, what people state as rules does not necessarily correspond to what they actually do. Knowledge is not the same as knowing (how to do). One might ask then, how do people apply normative systems to specific situations? How do the 'jpfs' (just plain folks, cf. Wassmann 1994b; see also Dasen and Bossel-Lagos 1989; Fournier, Schurmans and Dasen. 1999) adjust to the realm of daily life carrying with them knowledge that is partial or even deviant? To address questions such as these, observation is crucial.

Daily Life

The study of ordinary situations, happening every day, allows for the verification of whether verbal descriptions of a cultural system are merely a theoretical construction or whether they are embedded in action. On the one hand, one is to determine whether the cultural system is identified across various segments of the population or whether there is segmentation across a socially differentiated population.

Participant observation has been, since the inception of anthropology, an integral component of fieldwork. Moreover, as circumstances have changed, the anthropologist is required to observe in a more systematic manner a bigger range of the population studied.

However, observation is not always possible. If one wishes to study, for example, problem solving, there is no certainty that a situation amenable to inquiry will emerge spontaneously. In the event that a problem does actually take place, there is the risk that it may be solved in a hidden manner, sometimes even without the agent being aware of it. This poses great difficulties to the understanding of the processes.

Induced Situations

To study phenomena that do not occur spontaneously with sufficient frequency, or in which the processes are difficult to observe, the fieldworker resorts to placing the informants in situations that will prompt the phenomena he or she intends to study. Although these are not experimental situations in the strict sense of laboratory psychology, these situations are, nonetheless, always new, unusual, and artificial. For instance, they can take the form of a psychological test.

It is a necessary condition that these induced situations always be situated in the ethnographic context established through the first two phases of the investigation. The issue for study is chosen precisely on the basis of this knowledge of culture and so are the criteria for organising the experiment. Sometimes this may consist of organising a 'game' whereby the subjects interact almost without intervention from the researchers, or, of situations that are minimally intrusive such as asking for drawings (Toren 1990; Wassmann 1993a). On other occasions tasks can be invented as a replacement (e.g. the classification of objects picked out from the local culture, cf. Wassmann and Dasen 1994a). In certain cases, as we will illustrate below, the use of more standardised tasks can also be justified provided that they are adapted to the situation.

Although the methodologies of experimentation and observation have become common in the social sciences, anthropology generally does not accept such an intrusion as easily. If the situation must be new in order to fit the goals of research, does this not risk being so artificial, so unusual and bizarre that it cannot lead to reliable and valid observations?

These problems, quite real in nature, have been discussed various times (e.g. Ciborowski 1980; Berry and Lonner 1986; Poon, Rubin and Wilson 1992); we have also revealed previously (Wassmann 1993a) the extent to which the interventions can be intrusive and destabilise relationships of trust established during the first two stages of research. One must then proceed with great caution, not only to secure the validity of results, but also to guarantee good relations with informants as well as amongst researchers. To be sure, these problems can be solved, as the work of M. Cole & collaborators has demonstrated in the setting of 'experimental anthropology', or more recently in the context of work exploring practical knowledge (for a review, see Berry, Poortinga, Segall and Dasen 2002).

We will now illustrate the methodology we propose, through a study conducted in Bali that focused on systems of spatial orientation that are particularly important in Balinese language and culture. We will present this system at the cultural and linguistic level, describe how it is applied differently depending on context as well as how it is used in daily life and, discuss the use of induced situations that allows for examining the influence that this system has upon processes of memorisation and spatial representation. In short, this study analyses the relationship between language and cognition and, therefore, contributes to re-launch the debate about linguistic relativity.

The Cultural and Linguistic System

Kaja-Kelod

Numerous authors have described the Balinese orientation system and its centrality in Balinese culture (Belo 1935; Covarrubias 1937; James 1973; Hooykaas 1974; Hobart 1978; Howe 1980; Eiseman 1990, Reuter 1996, Hauser-Schäublin 1997, Ramseyer 2002). Hence, we will refer to existing literature on this topic as a replacement for interviews with key informants.

All these authors agree that orientation is extremely important for the Balinese. A direction describes not only a vector in physical space, but also cultural, religious, and social points of reference. Orientation begins with the volcano in the centre of the island, Gunung Agung (3142m) where the Balinese Hindu Gods live; 'towards the mountain' or 'upwards', the sacred, pure direction is called *kaja* and, the opposite, 'towards the ocean', 'downwards', *kelod*. It should be noted that the ocean, however, is not evil or impure. On the contrary, it can purify and supply sacred water. *Kaja* can be translated into English or Indonesian as 'north'. However, this translation is only correct in the south of Bali; the *kaja-kelod* axis, as will be described below, rotates as one moves around the island. On the northern side of the island *kaja* is actually to the south. This system of orientation can also be found in other South-East Asian and Oceanian languages (Barnes 1993).

Another direction considered to be sacred is *kangin*, the direction of the sunrise, that is seen as another important manifestation of God; opposite to it is *kauh*. In principle the axis *kangin-kauh* is orthogonal to the axis *kaja-kelod*, with kangin to the east. East and west, *kangin-kauh*, are identified by all in the island, states Eiseman (1990: 230), wrongly as we shall see below.

According to the literature, intermediary dimensions of *kaja-kangin*, *kelod-kauh*, are also frequently used. To each of the eight possible directions, as well as for the centre, corresponds a God and a colour. All of the Balinese cosmology is structured along three points—high, middle, and low—oriented along the axis *kaja-kelod*, from the human body to the organisation of the universe, including the structures of temples and villages, the social structure, and even stages of life. The goal is to preserve at all times the equilibrium of this structure.

Numerous aspects of Balinese life are thus organised according to this schemata. The villages are aligned *kaja-kelod*, with its main temple, dedicated to Wisnu, on the side of the mountain, and the cemetery on the side of the ocean. Each temple is aligned in the same way and, in their interior, so are the several altars. The houses of a lineage of families are oriented in a similar fashion, with the family's temple at the most sacred juncture, *kaja-kangin*. The family's chief lives on the *kaja* side and everyone must sleep in the direction of *kaja* or *kangin*; so too the disposition of other house-elements must follow similar rules. The kitchen is on the *kelod* side, and the animals are placed at the least sacred extreme, *kelod-kauh*. The symbolism of the eight directions (and the centre), and its related colours, is important in the preparation and disposition of gifts.

The level of disorientation that the Balinese feel when they 'loose their north' has been frequently mentioned. Geertz (1983 [1972]: 207), for example, wrote that for the Balinese, life is not organised if they cannot keep precise orientation in space ('not to know where north is to be crazy'). Eiseman (1990: 3) wrote: "Each Balinese seems to have a keen sense of orientation and if, for any reason this sense is gone, the individual feels visibly uncomfortable and disoriented". Similarly, McPhee (1944) described the total inhibition (verging on depression) of a young boy he had recruited in another village for a dance lesson. It was not until he was shown Gunung Agung beyond the nearest landscape, that he was able to start to dance[1]. Talking of fear and anxiety related to disorientation, Bateson and Mead (1942) mention that these could lead people to become sick. Jensen and Suryani (1992), two psychiatrists—one of whom is Balinese—find these terms exaggerated, and think that the example reported by McPhee is atypical. According to these two psychiatrists, when a Balinese arrives to an unknown place where he cannot orient himself, he conforms rather than becoming sick. However, these authors do agree that disorientation induces tensions and a "state of confusion (*bingung*) in which it is difficult to pursue one's thoughts and speech clearly" (Jensen and Suryani 1992: 76).

The use of this system of orientation seems to be learned quite early by children. According to Bateson and Mead (1942: 6), "the words for the cardinal points are among the first that a child learns and are used even for the geography of the body". A Balinese will tell you that 'there is a fly on the 'West' side of your face'. Moreover, Balinese babies learn very early that they should not confuse their left hand with their right hand. The latter is used for touching food, while the left hand is used for bathing. The left hand should never be used to touch food, point at something, or receive a gift.

The Spoken Language: Space Games[2]

In order to complete these descriptions, one of us (Wassmann) administered a linguistic survey by using a standard procedure called 'space games', developed by the research group of cognitive anthropology at the Max-Planck Institute of Psycholinguistics in Nijmegen (de Leon 1991; Levinson 1992b). In order to ascertain how language is used in the de-

---

1   This anecdote is interesting because it shows how directions are utilised during the process of learning how to dance: the teacher gives instructions of the type 'three steps to the east, then turn yourself south-west' (McPhee 1994: 124)
2   We thank Nengah Danta, who worked as interpreter, translator, and assistant and Prof. Gede I Pitana for fruitful discussions.

scription of spatial points of reference, an imaginary situation that stimulates two people to talk is organised, such that they do so almost without the participation of the researcher. It is therefore, an induced situation that allows a further step forward compared to a simple ethnographic description consisting of the variations in use of language from one individual to another.

Each 'player' is given a series of similar pictures that represent two persons in different positions and orientations, sometimes with a common element of reference such as a tree or an animal. The two players are separated by a screen. The conversations take place in Balinese language, are taped, and later transcribed and translated. This part of the study took place in two villages in the south of Bali, as well as in several villages in the north and west of the island. A total of 174 description were obtained from 29 pairs of players, both children and adults. The analysis reported here counted with the presence, for each picture, of at least one—absolute, egocentric, or intrinsic, —descriptor (a, e, i).

In order to explain these terms, let us consider as an illustration one of the pictures that were used. In our own habitual language, we describe it in the following way:

"Two men are side by side, at a certain distance. They have a stick in their right hand. The man on the right looks at me, the one on the left looks to the other side."

The descriptors such as 'on the right' and 'on the left', 'towards me' are said to be egocentric (or egomorphic, projective or deictic) because they are relative to the observer. 'Two men side by side' at 'a certain distance' are intrinsic descriptors, because they refer to the relative position of an object in relation to another, independent of the person who does the description.

These two types of descriptions are familiar to us because these are the same that are used in Indo-European languages. However, there exists a large number of languages that use (in addition to intrinsic descriptions that seem to occur in all languages), preferably, and at times exclusively, absolute descriptions, as for example, Guugu Yimithirr aboriginal language in Queensland (Haviland 1993), and Tzeltal, a language of the Maya from the Chiapas region in Mexico (Brown and Levinson 1993b). This entails descriptors that are independent from the observer, as well as of other objects, fixed on the exterior, such as the landscape: upwards/downwards, towards the mountain/the ocean, facing sunrise/sunset, etc.

On occasion, some languages use both absolute and relative descriptors, but with a preference for the first. This applies to the Yupno from

Papua New Guinea (Wassmann 1994b) who use the concepts of right and left only to refer to the localisation of objects that are in direct contact with the body, and absolute referents otherwise.

The Balinese language allows for the use of the three types of descriptors—absolute, egocentric, and intrinsic, but with a preference to absolute referents (*kaja, kelod, kangin* and *kauh*). Therefore, a typical description of the same photo mentioned above is the following (the observer is oriented towards kaja):

"A man is at *kauh* and the other at *kangin*. The one at *kauh* faces *kaja,* and the one at *kangin* faces *kelod*. They are a bit separated. The one at *kangin* has a stick in his *kauh* hand; the right hand of the one at *kauh* also has a stick."

Such a description entails at least an example of each type of descriptor—absolute, intrinsic, and egocentric. The great majority (98%) out of a group of 29 pairs of observers used at least one absolute descriptor for each picture. Egocentric descriptors are very rare, with the exception of the adults of the South side of the island, where they are used for 36% of the pictures though almost always in combination with absolute describers. This difference between the north-east and the south is due to a greater familiarity in the south with the Indonesian, as well as the factors of acculturation emerging from travelling by motor bike or car. Young children (7-9 years old) use only absolute describers, while the older children (11-15) and adults also use intrinsic descriptors for half of the pictures.

The almost exclusive use of the absolute system of reference in the Balinese language corresponds greatly to its symbolic importance in this culture. In other words, there is coherence between the cultural system and the language system.

The System of Orientation in Everyday Life

It is easy to observe the importance of the system of orientation in ordinary Balinese life. At all times, the terms in question appeared in conversations. People use the absolute terms to indicate a path or where they are going ('I am going kauh in the afternoon.'), or to explain a route 'turn left, then go kangin', or during a meal, one can say 'pass me the dish that is at kaja'. On reporting about a meeting, one refers to a person as 'the one sitting kelod'; one memorises, it seems, the positions in absolute terms.

Children must learn to follow instructions by using this system of orientation, at home or outside. It seems that some elementary schools use this knowledge as a criteria of aptitude for beginning school. During the process of teaching in Indonesian they insist on relative descriptors. For example, in order to draw the attention of students to the difference between a 'b' and a 'd', instead of using front/back or right/left, they rely on *kaja*/*kelod* in order to make students understand the difference.

The system of orientation appears in a great number of social situations. During cock fights, for example, at the moment of deciding which is the favourite for placing bets, supporters shout as loudly as possible a word that refers to the chosen cock; this can be the colour of its feathers, but also its location.

Another example of a situation where directions are an intervening factor, is the game of chance called kelos or kece. The players are divided into four groups and sit down according to the four directions. They decide for one direction in the following way: the director takes by chance one hand-full of coins and throws them into the groups until he has only four or less left. This number indicates the winner direction which corresponds to a sitting direction of one particular group (1=*kaja*, 2=*kauh*, 3=*kelod*, 4=*kangin*).

On one occasion we observed in detail in the village of Lean, North-East Bali, where players of a neighbouring village were visiting, the beginning of a game that gave place to the following exchange:

"Which system will we use, Bunutan or Lean?
The Lean system.
In Bunutan and here, *kaja* and *kelod* are in the same direction
kangin and *kauh* are different.
Here, *kauh* is on this side (towards Seraya).
For *kangin*, is four coins; *kangin* is there, on the side of Bunutan."

In this case, the players had to be able to arrive at an agreement about the chosen system of orientation, since, as we will see below, it is not identical in the two villages.

In effect, contrary to the descriptions that exist in the literature, we realised that the system is not uniform, but rather that it adapts to the topographic conditions of localities, that it may depend on specific historical circumstances, or that the systems may even be used differently by individuals within a place. Therefore, if *kaja* does indeed refer to the direction of the mountain, it does not necessarily refer to Mount Agung, especially when it is not visible, but to another closer elevation. In certain cases, as we will demonstrate below, *kaja* refers to a direction even where there is no mountain, such as the ocean.

We have examined in detail how the inhabitants of different localities in the north-east peninsula of Bali use the system. Going around the peninsula opposite to clock direction, kaja remains oriented towards the closest elevation, usually the mountains in the centre of the peninsula, while the *kangin-kauh* axis changes following the curvature of the coast. For the inhabitants of the east end of the island then, the sun rises at *kelod*, and *kangin* refers to the north.

One might think that *kangin* and *kauh* are always situated, respectively, to the right and to the left of the *kaja-kelod* axis, somewhat like the directions east and west which stay the same as one travels around the world along the equator. However, this is not the case: at a given moment, the system is inverted. The inhabitants of the two villages where this reversal occurs are well aware of this situation, and, as the example above indicates, they adjust their way of talking accordingly when they visit their neighbours. There is even a place between the two, where the two systems coexist. Apparently, this situation emerges form the history of populating the region. Further away, beyond the coastal area, the system changes even more. Within the peninsula, one finds three additional systems, with, at each border, an intermediary system that is relevant for only a small distance.

In this way one sees that there isn't a single translation of kaja that can be applied to all possible situations; not only is 'north' (or *utara* in Indonesian) inadequate and 'uphill' is more correct than 'towards the mountain'. *Kangin* is usually located to the right of the axis, but is sometimes left, referring more or less to the direction of sunrise in most cases, though not always.

In certain cases, the adaptation to local topography, combined with historical elements, results in the complete change of the system in comparison to the normative description. Therefore, the Balinese use this system in a localised manner. One could even say that their absolute system is relative! Or, using the terminology of Frake (1990), 'contingent'. The system is absolute (geocentric) in the sense that it refers to distant referents, not linked to the body nor to the immediate environment, but contingent, because it is linked to topography.

If the system of orientation established from the cultural knowledge of south Bali constitutes a complex system that entails spiritual dimensions, this aspect remains the affair of experts, detached from the lives of most other people, at least in the East of the island. We conducted 25 interviews about this topic, many of them with small groups of people.

No one knew the colours or the Gods in terms of the eight directions. They knew these existed for the four main directions but did not know details, responded by chance or made errors, referring to the need to rely on a specialist for this matter.

And how are the terms right and left used in ordinary life? These are mostly used to refer to the body or people and objects close to the observer (at a maximum distance of about one meter). However, absolute descriptors are also often used for these situations. Children, trying to distinguish their right hand from their left hand, always used absolute directions, even for objects that they are holding. Describing which way to follow, adults often use 'turn right or left' but systematically add 'towards' and one of the absolute directions (for example, 'I turn right towards kaja'). There is hence, in Balinese language, the possibility to combine the two systems of spatial reference, with considerable tendency to use the absolute system.

We can now ask how this influences representations of space. When the issue is, for example, to memorise a certain disposition of objects in space, there are two ways of encoding information: using only relative referents, or only absolute referents, or a combination of both.

It is virtually impossible to determine which spatial representation the Balinese use by means of interviews or even observation. To be sure, this encoding is automatic and unconscious, which inhibits us from provoking introspection in daily contexts. Consequently, we found ourselves forced to use induced situations.

Induced Situations: Encoding for Spatial Representation

For this component of our research we have used two tests invented by the Cognitive Anthropology Group (Levinson 1992a; Brown and Levinson 1993a; Danziger 1993; Wilkins 1995; Levinson and Nagy 1998; for a recent complete review, see Levinson 2003). These tests are called 'Animals in a Row' and 'Steve's Mazes'. The standardised nature of these tests allows different groups of researchers of this team to obtain observations that can be compared across linguistic groups[3]. Hence in the

---

3 Details about the procedure can be found in the manual (Danziger 1993 and Levinson 2003). For the first part of the experiment we followed closely the established procedures except that we maintained a constant order during the presentation of the trials (instead of randomly changing the order). In addition, after the fifth trial we asked our subjects how they had memorised the display. Finally, if on the maze test they had chosen a wrong solution, we demonstrated why this was not a correct an-

present case, the induced situations were not developed directly from our ethnographic observations, but we used them only because we felt they were easily adaptable.

All the tests are based on a single, simple, paradigm: one presents the subject with a stimulus entailing spatial information; he/she is then asked to turn 180 degrees, and is then asked to perform an action related to a similar stimulus.

For example, let us suppose that we place on the table in front of you an arrow pointing left; you turn around 180 degrees, and we present two arrows, one pointing to the left and one pointing to the right, and you are then asked which of the two arrows is identical to the one on the first table. If you choose the one pointing to the left, you have relied on ego-centric encoding, relative to your own body. However, if you encode space in absolute terms, you choose the arrow pointing to the right, since it displays the same absolute direction (i.e. to the west if you were oriented to the north at the beginning of the experiment).

Note that the relative coding leads to choose a stimulus that is identical to the visual image of the arrow on the first table, while absolute coding leads you to choose a stimulus that is the mirror image of the former, and thus entails a transformation of sensory information. Therefore, it is possible to conclude from a non verbal behaviour what type of coding is being used.

All of those who speak mainly an European language have the habit of choosing the relative system. An absolute coding will appear to them to be bizarre if not incomprehensible, to the point where developmental psychology, the cognitive sciences, and even our philosophical traditions, have considered that the conception of space belongs necessarily to the body proper, establishing this view as a 'canonical position' (Clark 1973: 34), adding that the relative conceptualisation of space was universal, since it was 'more natural and primordial' (Miller and Johnson-Laird 1976: 34). (For a more detailed discussion of the ethnocentric character of this assertion see Wassmann 1994b.)

Method

During the initial phase of our research we have relied on two tests in their standardised form. The experiment took place on the veranda of the house of one of the researchers, in the village of Bunutan on the northeast coast of Bali. Moving from one table to the other, the subject had to perform a 180 degree rotation, after a pause of 30 seconds (without any

---

swer (by returning to the first table), and allowed them to make another attempt.

other distraction but to look at a clock)[4]. During this first part of the experiment, no verbal clues were given in the instructions that might incite the subject to use a particular spatial system of orientation (in other words, we would not mention neither right or left, nor kaja, and so on).

For the animals test, a series of three animals (chosen from four available figures, a duck, a goat, a frog and a turtle) was presented on the table, for five successive trial after an initial training session. The subject was asked to remember the display in order to reproduce it on the second table. We took notes of the order of the animals as well as of the direction of the alignment.

For the second test (maze), the drawing of a landscape, with a house, a river, and trees was presented on the first table. A path was indicated in the form of an irregular line stopping at some distance from the house. The test included five of these drawings plus a demonstration (see figure 1). The researcher explained to the subject that the goal was to find the way back to the house, without crossing the river or the forest tracing this pathway with a finger, and informed the subject that he or she should memorise the pathway. On the second table there were three cards to choose from, with drawings of alternative pathways, one representing a relative solution, another an absolute solution, and a third one with a false solution (D for distractor).

---

4   This break is meant to avoid iconic-visual memorisation which could lead the subjects to opt for relative solutions (Danziger, 1993: 7). We followed this precaution systematically for all experiments even through trials indicated that similar results could be obtained with a 5 second break.

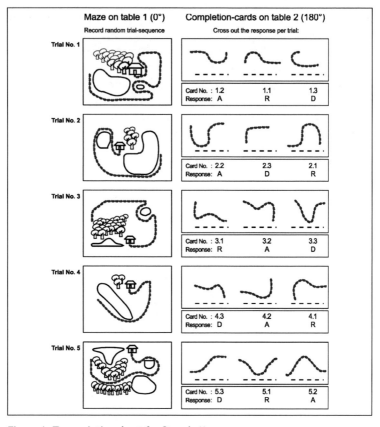

Figure 1: Transcription sheet for Steve's Maze

This experiment was conducted with 28 subjects, of which 8 were children aged 7 to 9 years old (0 to 2 years of schooling), 8 children aged form 10 to 15 years old (2 to 5 years of schooling), and 12 adults (between 20 and 60 years old, 0 to 6 years of schooling), with equal representation of gender. In addition, a simplified version of the animal test (two figures instead of three, intervals from 5 to 10 seconds) was administered to 10 children aged between 4 and 5 years old[5].

After 6 or 7 weeks, we repeated the experiment with the same subjects[6], but with some modifications meant to induce the opposite type of encoding from the one they used spontaneously. For example to influ-

---

5 We tried the test with 17 children of this age. However, 7 of these did not manage to understand the instructions. It proved to be impossible to use Steve's maze with children of his age-group.
6 Only one subject could not participate in the second part of the experiment.

ence relative encoding we used relative referents ('all animals look to the right'; 'the pathway moves away from you, and then turns right'). Also, the two tables were moved by 30 degrees in relation to the *kaja/kelod* axis, and the animals on the table was put on an angle of 30 degrees in relation to the borders of the table. For the maze test, the drawings were presented on a base with a 45 degree inclination, instead of disposed flatly on the table.

Results

Note that memorisation is not what interests us in the performance on these tasks, but rather we aim to obtain information on which type of spatial orientation is used. Memorisation is indicative of the difficulty of the task, that should be sufficiently easy for children to execute, and still remain interesting for the adults. We believe that this was achieved. In the first test, 17 errors (inversion of the order of the animals) were made during the first session (out of a total of 140 tests administered to 28 subjects), and 9 (out of 135) during the second session[7]. Perfectly adequate for the children, the situation was somewhat ludicrous for the adults, which might be the main reason why the later made as many mistakes as the children. The maze test is somewhat more difficult, with 25 errors (choice of the distractor, which was always corrected on the second attempt) out of 149 items during the first session (9/135 during the second), especially by younger children (13 errors, in comparison to 5 and 7 for the other groups). The behaviour and comments of adults indicates that this was a bit of a challenge for them, a real problem to solve.

First Session

The results from the first part of the experiment are presented in table 1.

	Animals	Steve's Maze	N
4-5	.96	-	9
6-8	.80	.58	8
9-11	.73	.58	7
12-14 + Adults	.86	.49	14

Table 1: R-A gradients on spatial encoding tasks by age-group

---

7   The first animal in the sequence was always correct and even when there was an inversion of the two other animals we could still classify the answer.

On the animals' test, the majority of subjects displayed systematically absolute reactions, and none showed systematically relative reactions. Comparing these results with those of Brown and Levinson (1993a), we observe that they are similar to the ones obtained amongst the speakers of Tzeltal of Tenejapa in Mexico, and opposed to results obtained amongst the Dutch who reacted mainly in a relative manner.

In the case of the maze test, only one quarter of the subjects reacted systematically towards the absolute, while the majority mixed absolute and relative choices. Another quarter of the subjects made systematically relative choices. This result resembles that of Brown and Levinson in Tenejapa, not for the same test which they apparently did not use, but for other tests of the same kind.

One may add to these results, for the first test, the reactions of 10 children aged between 4 and 5 years old. These only give systematically absolute answers. This corresponds closely to the language they use, which is completely absolute: even for an object held in the hand they never use left and right, but always absolute directions. Children aged 7 to 9 years old, use an absolute coding for the first test, though for the second test half of their answers are relative. The increase of relative answers is also noticeable in the 11 to 15 years old group for the first test, and for the adults in the second. It would appear therefore, that there is slight tendency for a developmental change with age (or with the number of years of schooling) whereby the amount of relative answers increases with time. Nonetheless, this trend is not statistically significant (Fisher-Yates).

The fact that a test is non-verbal does not necessarily mean that it does not lead to linguistic coding. Our first task certainly has a higher tendency to promote this form of coding, in the form of sentences of the type 'the duck is in front, and the turtle in the middle, and all look towards *kaja*'. Obviously, linguistic coding would be equally easy in the relative form ('they all look right') but we have noticed that in the use of language the absolute system clearly predominates. This linguistic strategy is much less applicable to the maze test, where the configurations seem more likely to be encoded iconically.

This difference in strategy is reflected in the introspection obtained on the fifth trial: first, the subjects express themselves more easily in reference to strategies used in the first test than in reference to the second. For the first test, the majority of subjects stated 'down there (on the first table) the animals faced *kaja*, so here they face *kaja*'. On the second test, the subjects who gave mainly absolute answers claimed to have memorised the image of a route, sometimes describing its shape ('like the letter U', like a belly whose curve faces *kauh*'). Those who gave relative answers talked of following the route, e.g. from right to left. An adult who made five relative choices stated 'I remember the shape the route goes from left to right; one cannot describe it with *kaja-kelod*'. On the first test, however, he had provided five absolute answers.

In conclusion, our subjects have the possibility of using two systems of coding, just as the Balinese language allows for a choice between relative and absolute descriptors. However, the preference for the absolute system was evident, especially in the first test, for which a single word in the absolute system is sufficient for coding the orientation of the display. A relative system of coding is chosen more often for the second test, that is more difficult to code verbally.

If one takes into account the two tests at the same time, only five subjects provided systematically absolute answers. Consequently, it appears that the choice between absolute and relative systems of coding is not inherently a personal characteristics, related to some internal cognitive orientation, but that all subjects, except possibly the younger ones, can indeed 'choose', or be lead by the task's demands or the experimentator's instructions, to use one or the other.

The layout of the tables might have favoured absolute answers, since everything (the subject and the objects) was ordered according to the main directions of the absolute system. On the other hand, for the second test, some features, for example the projective nature of the drawings of the trees and house, could favour more relative choices.

These observations have lead us to repeat the same experiments while introducing some changes to the display and the instructions, somewhat like Brown and Levinson (1993a) did in order to clarify the mixture of absolute and relative answers that they found among the Tenejapan. These authors presented the hypothesis of the coexistence of the two systems: 'Tenejapans would thus have two competing conceptual coding systems that can both be utilised in tasks of the sort presented' (p.48). We extend these authors' hypothesis for the Balinese case, particularly since the two systems are available in the Balinese language.

Second Session

Recall that in the second session the instructions and object were prepared in such a way as to lead the subjects to change their type of predominant answer (from absolute A to relative R, or vice versa). Table 2 presents the number of subjects who changed, as well as those who did not change; for the first category a change in encoding had to occur on at least two items (e.g. from 4 or 5 A to 1 or 2 A, or 3A to 0 or 1 A, but not 3A to 2A).

	Animals		Steve's Maze	
	No changes	Changes	No changes	changes
Age				
6-8	8	0	6	2
9-11	4	4	4	4
12-14 + a-dults	6	5	2	9
Total	18	9	12	15

Table 2a): Changes of answers between first and second session (N=27): Changes by age -group

	Animals		Steve's Maze	
Session	Second		Second	
	3-5 A	0-2 A	3-5 A	0-2 A
First				
3-5 A	18	7	6	8
0-2 A	2	0	10	3

Table 2b): Changes of answers between first and second session (N=27): Changes according the answers in the first session

We observed that, for the first test, a third of the subjects changed the type of response, which is statistically significant (Chi square = 8.02, p < .01). The young children (7 to 9 years old), stayed with absolute answers in spite of changes in the instructions and display and half of the older children (ages 11 to 15) and adults changed their type of answer; this difference between age groups is statistically significant (Fisher-Yates, p < .05). The same age trend is visible in the second test, for which half of the subjects changed their type of response: the very young children displayed lack of flexibility, while half of the older children changed, as well as most adults; the difference is statistically significant between the younger group and the adults (Fisher-Yates, p < .025).

In the first test, with one exception, none of the subjects took over the relative language of the instructions when we asked what they did in order to remember the display. One subject even stated 'well, when you say 'to the right' you must mean *kelod*'.

For the second test, that is more difficult to verbalise, the changes were more pronounced than for the first: 8 subjects out of 14 changed from absolute answers to relative answers, and 10 out of 13 in the opposite direction (these changes are statistical significant at p < .01, Fisher-Yates). Almost all subjects adapt systematically the type of language used for the instructions, in general in a manner consistent with the type of choice used for the second table. Eight subjects adopted the language of instruction without changing the type of response. They stated, for example, 'over there the curve of the path faces *kauh*, and here *kangin*' in order to justify a relative choice after receiving instructions in absolute language.

Numerous subjects experienced a dilemma, a conflict between two possible solutions. One adult stated 'over there the curve was at *kauh*, but here at *kangin*' [relative choice with absolute vocabulary]; 'the belly of the path moved away from me down there, but here, it should come towards me or away from me? I do not know'.

Even if this conflict between the two systems becomes almost conscious, it is never completely explicit. Therefore, there is not a conscious 'choice', but the fact that the majority of subjects above a certain age can change their predominant type of answer indicates the flexibility of possible encoding. At the same time, one can argue that the other subjects resist the suggestion, and maintain their type of answer regardless of the changes in the instructions. A few subjects, instead of allowing themselves to be influenced, even re-enforce the systematic character of their original answers.

Discussion and Conclusion

Our research addresses the old problem of linguistic relativism: to what extent is cognitive functioning dependent on language? The debate has swung through several pendular movements, and is without doubt not closed (Gumperz and Levinson 1992; Lucy 1992). In a recent paper, Li and Gleitman (2002) seek to undermine the large cross-cultural comparison of spatial language and cognition which claims to have demonstrated that language and conceptual coding in the spatial domain covary (Peterson, Danziger, Wilkins, Levinson, Kita and Senft 1998). According to Levinson (2003) the most plausible interpretation is that different languages induce distinct conceptual codings. Arguing against this, the cognitive scientists Li and Gleitman in the tradition of nativism, attempt to show that in an American student population they can obtain any of the relevant conceptual codings just by varying spatial cues, ignoring linguistic variation and the highly variable communication systems in different cultures (for a convincing refutation, see Levinson, Kita, Haun and Rasch 2002).

Berry, Poortinga, Segall and Dasen (1992: 105) summarise the empirical evidence as follows:

"In general, we can conclude that there is at best limited support for the linguistic relativity hypothesis at the lexical level, but the last word has probably not been spoken about this issue. [...] At the grammatical level, [...] the hypothesis that the structure of a language has a broad effect on thinking can be shelved."

It is this type of compromise, of moderate linguistic relativism, that our results demonstrate. In Bali, the system of absolute spatial references is so pervasive that it determines not only forms of linguistic expression, but also ways of representing space, and of encoding for memory. This absolute encoding represents a dissociation from sensory information, that is necessarily relative, which proves its strength. In other words, language and spatial representation are consistent which a strong cultural feature, but this does not mean that language determines thinking.

The majority of subjects, for the first task, and a bit more than half for the second, use absolute encoding. However, they also have at their disposal the possibility of a relative encoding even if it is not normally expressed in current language. In the second test, which does not easily allow a verbal formulation, half of the subjects used this relative mode spontaneously, and for those who reacted in absolute manner during the first session, more than half changed their type of response when the disposition of the display and the instructions motivated them to do so. The reverse change, however, was even easier: 10 out of 13 subjects changed from the relative type to the absolute between the first and the second sessions.

While the 'choice' of a system of coding is to a great extent determined by the context of the task and is not fixed as a personality trait would be, the characteristics of the subjects intervene; certain subjects have a clear preference for one of the systems, and oppose the attempts to 'manipulate' them by changing the context: for example, they followed the researcher in the language used but not in action. For them, the encoding of spatial representation is independent from language.

Amongst these personal characteristics, there is age. The very young children (4 to 5 years old) use only the absolute system in their language, and, as far as we can ascertain from the single test that was used with them, so do they encode spatial objects for memory. This predominance of the absolute system lasts throughout childhood in language, though for tasks of memorisation there seems to be a trend towards relative solutions, perhaps related to schooling in Indonesian (a relative language), or through increasing contact with western life. Without having been able to include a group of unschooled children, we could not distinguish factors resulting from schooling from factors related to age (the latter can itself contain a plethora of possible influences). While this developmental trend should be verified with a larger number of subjects, the second session showed clearly the progression towards greater flexibility in the use of either one or the other system.

In more recent research in India and Nepal, using the same paradigm, Mishra, Dasen and Niraula (2003) were able to work with larger samples, and to compare schooled with unschooled children (Dasen, Mishra and Niraula 2003), as well as comparing urban and rural locations (Mishra and Dasen, in press). This research confirmed the links between spatial orientation systems, ecology, culture and religion and the development and use of spatial language, links between these and spatial encoding at the group level more than at the individual level, and a link between spatial language (but not frames of encoding) and spatial concept development. Ongoing research is exploring the correlates of egocentric and geocentric encoding, and the possibility of these two frames marking two developmental paths. A follow-up study in Bali explores the influence of acculturation (in terms of urban/rural contexts and use of Balinese vs. Indonesian language).

This perspective leads us to discuss the compromises of this study. For the anthropologist, the number of subjects used in the research is impressive. In comparison with other places where access to a great number of subjects is more difficult, verging on the impossible (e.g. among the Yupno of Papua New Guinea, see Wassmann 1993a), the limitation was mostly a matter of time and means, and a voluntary decision to invest more time in ethnography. For the psychologist, this remains a pilot study, some aspects such as the developmental trends needing a confirmation with larger samples. In relation to the joint management of time during fieldwork, the achieved compromise, from both parts, seems to be ideal: that is, the combination of qualitative 'thick' description, that assures cultural validity, with quantitative data, both linguistic and cognitive, without which this study would have remained at the anecdotal level.

During our previous joint research, the extension of interviews to a relatively large group of subjects allowed us to discover an astonishing inter-individual variety (for the Yupno numeric system, see Wassmann and Dasen 1994b). The observation of daily situations as well as induced situations revealed a social distribution of knowledge and a divergence between the taxonomic system and its use in daily life (Wassmann 1993b; Wassmann and Dasen 1994a). In this study, the application of our methodology in three complementary phases provided very interesting results. The multiplication of subjects in the linguistic questionnaire allowed us to detect a small differences between the adults from the south of Bali and those of the north with more frequent use of egocentric referents amongst the first, as well as an increase of intrinsic descriptors with age. Extending our inquiry into the daily use of the system especially in the Eastern peninsula of Bali has provided us with some surprises: contrary to the system described in the literature, where only a reversal in the *kaja-kelod* axis between the northern and the southern side of the island is mentioned, we encountered a plethora of different systems, and numerous local adaptations of the system. Similarly, the use of induced situations allowed us to demonstrate that the absolute system obtained by means of ethnographic and linguistic research is not the only one at the cognitive level, where a relative system is also available even if it tends to remain relatively secondary. A controversy that has not been settled is whether the relative, egocentric system is necessarily more 'natural' than the absolute, geocentric one, as many authors seem to believe. In Bali, the geocentric system seems to be learned first; why should it not also be, in this cultural context, more natural?

References

Barnes, R.H. (1993). Everyday Space: Some Considerations on the Representation and Use of Space in Indonesia. In: J. Wassmann/P.R. Dasen (Eds.). Savoirs quotidiens. Les sciences cognitives dans le dialogue interdisciplinaire (pp. 159-180). Fribourg: Presses de l'Université de Fribourg.

Bateson, G./Mead, M. (1942). Balinese Character. A Photographic Analysis. New York: New York Academy of Sciences.

Belo, J. (Ed.). (1935). Traditional Balinese Culture. New York: Columbia University Press.

Berry, J.W./Lonner, W. (1986). Cross-Cultural Research Methods. Beverly Hills: Sage.

Berry, J.W./Poortinga, Y.H./Segall, M.H./Dasen, P.R. (2002). Cross-Cultural Psychology. Cambridge: Cambridge University Press.

Berry, J.W./Dasen, P.R./Saraswathi, T.S. (Eds.) (1997). Handbook of Cross-cultural Psychology. Boston: Allyn & Bacon.

Borofsky, R. (1994).On the Knowledge and Knowing of Cultural Activities. In: R. Borofsky (Ed.). Assessing Cultural Anthropology. New York: McGraw-Hill. 311-346.

Boster, J. (1985). Requiem for the Omniscient Informant: There's Life in the Old Girl yet. In: J.W.D. Dougherty (Ed.). Directions in Cognitive Anthropology. Urbana, IL: University of Illinois Press. 177-197.

Brown, P./Levinson, S.C. (1993a). Linguistic and Nonlinguistic Coding of Spatial Arrays: Explorations in Mayan Cognition (Working paper No. 24). Cognitive Anthropology Research Group, Max Planck Institute for Psycholinguistics.

Brown, P./Levinson, S.C. (1993b). 'Uphill' and 'Downhill' in Tzeltal. In: Journal of Linguistic Anthropology, Vol.3, 1, 46-74.

Ciborowski, T. (1980). The Role of Context, Skill and Transfer in Cross-cultural Experimentation. In H.C. Triandis/J.W. Berry (Eds.). Handbook of Cross-Cultural Psychology. Vol. 2: Methodology. Boston: Allyn & Bacon. 279-296.

Clark, H. (1973). Space, Time, Semantics, and the Child. In: T.E. Moore (Ed.). Cognitive Development and the Acquisition of Language. New York: Academic Press.

Covarrubias, M. (1937). Island of Bali. New York: Alfred A. Knopf.

Danziger, E. (Ed.) (1993). Cognition and Space Kit, Version 1.0. Nijmegen: Cognitive Anthropology Research Groupe, Max Planck Institute for Psycholinguistics.

Dasen, P.R./Bossel-Lagos, M. (1989). L'étude interculturelle des savoirs quotidiens: revue de la littérature. In: J. Retschitzki, M. Bossel-Lagos/P.R. Dasen (Eds.). La recherche interculturelle. Vol. 2. Paris: L'Harmattan. 98-114.

Dasen, P.R./Mishra, R.C. (2003). The Influence of Schooling on Cognitive Development: a Review of Research in India. In: B.N. Setiadi/A. Supratiknya/W.J. Lonner/Y.H. Poortinga (Eds.). Ongoing Themes in Psychology and Culture. Selected Papers from the Sixteenth International Congress of the International Association for Cross-Cultural Psychology (pp. 258-275). Yogyakarta: Kanisius.

Eiseman, F.B.J. (1990). Bali. Sekala & Niskala. 2 Vol. Hong Kong: Periplus.

Fournier, M./Schurmans, M.-N./Dasen, P.R. (1999). Représentations sociales de l'intelligence: effets de l'utilisation de langues différentes. In: B. Bril/P.R. Dasen/C. Sabatier/B. Krewer (Eds.). Propos sur l'enfant et l'adolescent : quels enfants pour quelles cultures? (pp. 279-296). Paris: L'Harmattan.

Frake, C.O. (1990). The Ethnographic Study of Cognitive Systems, II: Conceptual Frameworks of Directional Orientation and their Representations in the Physical World. In: CogSci News (UCSD), Vol. 3, 2, 4-6.

Geertz, C.C. (1983 [1972]). Jeu d'enfer. Notes sur le combat de coq balinais. In C.C. Geertz (Eds.). Bali. Interprétation d'une culture. Paris: Gallimard.

Gumperz, J.J./Levinson, S.C. (Eds.) (1992). Rethinking Linguistic Relativity. Cambridge: Cambridge University Press.

Hauser-Schäublin, B. (1997). Traces of Gods and Men. Temples and Rituals as Landmarks of Social Events and Processes in a South Bali Village. Berlin: Dietrich Reimer.

Haviland, J. (1993). Anchoring, Iconicity and Orientation in Guugu Yimithirr Pointing Gestures. In: Journal of Linguistic Anthropology, Vol. 3, 1, 3-45.

Hobart, M. (1978). The Path of the Soul: The Legitimacy of Nature in Balinese Conceptions of Space. In: G.B. Milner (Ed.). Natural Symbols in South East Asia. London: School of Oriental and African Studies, University of London. 5-28.

Hoykaas, C. (1947). Cosmogony and Creating in Balinese Tradition. The Hague: Nijhoff.

Howe, L.E.A. (1980). Pujung. An Investigation into the Foundations of Balinese Culture. Ph.D. thesis, University of Edinburgh.

Jahoda, G. (1992). Crossroads between Culture and Mind. New York: Harvester/Wheatsheaf.

James, J. (1973). Sacred Geometry on the Island of Bali. In: Journal of the Royal Asiatic Society of Great Britain and Ireland, 1, 141-154.

Jensen, G.D./Suryani, L.K. (1992). The Balinese People. A Reinvestigation of Character. London: Oxford University Press.

León, L. de (1991). Space Games in Tzotzil: Creating a Context for Spatial Reference (Working Paper No. 4). Cognitive Anthropology Research Group, Max Planck Institute for Psycholinguistics.

Levinson, S.C. (1992a). Language and Cognition: The Cognitive Consequences of Spatial Description in Guggu Yimithirr (Working Paper No. 13). Cognitive Anthropology Research Group, Max Planck Institute for Psycholinguistics.

Levinson, S.C. (1992b). Primer for the Field Investigation of Spatial Description and Conception. In: Pragmatics, Vol. 2, 1, 5-47.

Levinson, S.C. (2003). Space in Language and Cognition. Cambridge: Cambridge University Press.

Levinson, S.C./Nagy, L.K. (1998). Look at your Southern Leg. A Statistical Approach to Cross-Cultural Studies of Language and Spatial Orientation. Unpublished manuscript.

Levinson, S.C./Kita, S./Haun, D./Rasch, B. (2002). Language in Mind. Linguistic Effects on Cognition are Real. A Response to Li & Gleitman. Unpublished manuscript.

Li, P./Gleitman, L. (2002). Turning the Tables. Language and Spatial Reasoning. In: Cognition 83, 265-294.

Lucy, J.A. (1992). Grammatical Categories and Cognition: a Case Study of the Linguistic Relativity Hypothesis. Cambridge: Cambridge University Press.

McPhee, C. (1944). A House in Bali. Singapore: Oxford University Press.

Miller, G./Johnson-Laird, P. (1976). Language and Perception. Cambridge: Cambridge University Press.

Mishra, R./Dasen, P.R./Niraula, S. (2003). Ecology, Language, and Performance on Spatial Cognitive Tasks. International Journal of Psychology, in press.

Mishra, R.C./Dasen, P.R. (in press). Spatial Language and Cognitive Development in India: an urban/rural Comparison. In W. Friedlmeier, P. Chakkarath/B. Schwarz (Eds.). Culture and Human Development: The Importance of Cross-Cultural Research to the Social Sciences (in honor of Gisela Trommsdorff's 60th birthday). Lisse, NL: Swets & Zeitlinger.

Peterson, E./Danziger, E./Wilkins, D./Levinson, S./Kita, S./Senft, G. (1998). Semantic Typology and Spatial Conceptualization. In: Language 74, 557-589.

Poon, L. W./Rubin, D.C./Wilson, B.C. (Eds.). (1992). Everyday Cognition in Adulthood and Late Life. Cambridge: Cambridge University Press.

Ramseyer, U. (2002). Kunst und Kultur in Bali. Basel: Schwabe.

Reuter, T. (1996). Custodians of the Sacred Mountains. The Ritual Domains of Highland Bali. Canberra: ANU thesis.

Romney, A.K./Waller, S.C./Batchelder, W.H. (1986). Culture as Consensus: A Theory of Culture and Informant Accuracy. In: American Anthropologist, 88, 313-338.

Toren, C. (1990). Making Sense of Hierarchy. Cognition as Social Process in Fiji. London: The Athlone Press.

Wallace, A.F.C. (1961). Culture and Personality. New York: Random House.

Wassmann, J. (1993a). Das Ideal des leicht gebeugten Menschen. Eine ethno-kognitive Analyse der Yupno in Papua New Guinea. Berlin: Reimer Verlag.

Wassmann, J. (1993b). When Actions Speak Louder than Words. The Classification of Food among the Yupno of Papua New Guinea. In:

Quarterly Newsletter of the Laboratory of Comparative Human Cognition, Vol. 15, 1, 30-40.

Wassmann, J. (1994a). Worlds in Mind. The Experience of an Outside World in a Community of the Finisterre Range of Papua New Guinea. In: Oceania, 64, 117-145.

Wassmann, J. (1994b). The Yupno as Post-Newtonian Scientists. The Question of What is "Natural" in Spatial Description. Man, 29, 1-24.

Wassmann, J./Dasen, P.R. (Eds.) (1993). Alltagswissen. Les savoirs quotidiens. Everyday Cognition. Fribourg: Presses universitaires.

Wassmann, J./Dasen, P.R. (1994a). "Hot" and "Cold": Classification and Sorting Among the Yupno of Papua New Guinea. In: International Journal of Psychology, 29, 19-38.

Wassmann, J./Dasen, P.R. (1994b). Yupno Number System and Counting. In: Journal of Cross-Cultural Psychology, 25, 78-94.

Wassmann, J./Dasen, P.R. (1998). Balinese Spatial Orientation. Some Empirical Evidence of Moderate Linguistic Relativity. In: The Journal of the Royal Anthropological Institute Vol. 4, 4, 689-711.

Wilkins, D. (Ed) (1995). Extensions of Space and Beyond: Manual for Field Elicitation for the 1995 Field Season. Working Paper Cognitive Anthropology Research Group, Max Planck Institute, Nijmegen.

Rituals of Manliness in Western Films of the 90's: Psychoanalysis as a Method of Cultural Comparison

Hans-Dieter König

To start with, I would like to take up two lines of thinking[1]. First, I wish to present a psychoanalytical method of cultural psychology developed by Lorenzer (1986) within the framework of cultural studies in the Frankfort School and which he called depth hermeneutics[2]. Then, through the reconstruction of certain exemplary case studies, I would like to show how we may investigate and then compare socio-psychological processes in various cultures with the help of this method.

The Depth Hermeneutical Method of Cultural Research

Let us address the first question: Adorno again and again made use of psychoanalysis as a method of research. For example, he (Adorno et al. 1950) utilized psychoanalysis for investigating 'the authoritarian personality'—individuals who are prone to antidemocratic agitation—as well as for investigating the techniques employed by the fascists in their anti-Semitic propaganda. Further, together with Horkheimer (1947), he took psychoanalysis as a basis for analysing the culture industry; as he described it, the culture industry manipulates individuals by appealing to their unconscious. However, Adorno (1970) refused to interpret works of art psychoanalytically: as he pointed out in the initial pages of his *Theory of Aesthetics*, psychoanalysis commits the mistake of analysing art as if it were nothing other than the interpretation of a patient's associations[3]. He had three main objections to the way psychoanalysis was traditionally applied to art.

---

1 I would like to thank my friend Douglas Urton for the translation.
2 The method is explicated in König (1997b, 2001b, 2004).
3 For a critical treatment of Adorno's criticism of the psychoanalytical interpretation of art, cf. also König (1996: 319-334).

377

First, psychoanalysis psychologizes the work of art by putting it on a level with the artist's 'daydreams' and thus considering it as belonging to his inner world.

Second, psychoanalysis pathologizes the work of art by equating it with the case history of a neurotic: works of art—just as a patient's statements—are seen as symptomatic phenomena resulting from repressed desires and thus manifesting particular psychopathological forms.

Third, psychoanalysis overlooks the social meaning of a work of art; it ignores what 'the product itself' means and that it has a collectively fascinating effect on the basis of its uniqueness.

In retrospect, we can say that Adorno's criticism laid the foundation for Lorenzer's (1986) psychoanalytical project of cultural research based on the latter's (1970, 1974, 1981) understanding of Freudian practize and theory illuminated by social science[4]. According to Lorenzer, the traditional application of psychoanalysis is naïve because it ignores the methodological problem bound up with its (now) being applied to a field of research beyond the couch. The psychoanalytical concepts developed in and tailored to practical therapeutic experience cannot simply be transposed to cultural life, for this is a completely different area of research.

If we wish to develop the Freudian theory systematically as a science of culture—and thus avoid subsuming straightaway the dramatic course of interaction arranged in a text or in a series of pictures under fragments of psychoanalytical theory—then we are obliged to take up the quite advanced method of therapeutic psychoanalysis and develop it still further through our experience in the new area of research; subsequently, an independent theory of culture may be outlined. Accordingly, depth hermeneutics proceeds from the consideration that methodological steps are necessary for modifying the method of psychoanalytical hermeneutics—as developed in therapeutic practice and given the name 'scenic understanding' (Lorenzer 1970)—in such a way that in accordance with practical research in the field of cultural sciences it becomes suited to make new discoveries there.

Depth hermeneutics may be described as a psychoanalytic method of cultural psychology that opens up the narrative content of pictures and texts by examining their effect on the individuals who have experienced them. Here we are concerned not only with spontaneous protocol reports of, for example, interviews or group discussions. but also with artistic documents such as literature, films, or other works of art. Analysis is

---

4   I have tried to answer the question how depth hermeneutics corresponds to the methodology and method developed by Adorno (1957, 1969a, 1969b) in the field of cultural studies of the Frankfort School, in König 1996, 2000.

directed towards conscious and unconscious impulses working into the life plans portrayed in such a text or series of pictures, as staged in the social interaction between actors. It assumes an ambiguity in the way social acts take place; correspondingly, the meaning of interactions unfolds in the tension between a manifest and a latent significance. On the level of manifest significance, the actors interpret intentions and expectations, rules and norms, in the medium of a system of collective symbols. On the level of latent significance, interaction comes to expression through unconscious motives which an individual has repressed in the course of his biography due to social pressure or which he has suppressed in a momentary crisis; however, the socially offensive impulses in a subject's life-plan do assert themselves effectively in behavior, but 'behind one's back'. I want to illustrate this by referring to a Freudian slip described by Freud (1901) in his "Psychopathology of Everyday Life". He describes a man who invites his colleagues to drink a glass of champagne to their superior (he wants to cheer the boss)—quite evidently with the intention of congratulating him. That would be the manifest meaning of this verbal action. To be sure, the Freudian slip committed by the employee contradicts his verbally articulated intention, for he says "Let's jeer the boss!". His words reveal what is going on between him and his boss on a latent level of meaning. It is possible that at the same time not only the employee's individual unconscious but also the social unconscious of the entire group of colleagues comes to expression in this Freudian slip. If the other employees proved to be embarrassed by this slip of the tongue, then it would be the personal unconscious of the one employee that manifests itself in the mistake, and if an interview were carried out, one might possibly determine that the employee is bound up in a conflict of authority with his boss that has grown so acute due to an unresolved infantile conflict with the father. If, on the other hand, the colleagues were to show sympathy for the employee and find malicious delight in the mistake, then we could infer that this involves the social unconscious within an organization: through his Freudian slip, the employee verbalizes something that his colleagues sense as well but themselves do not dare to express, since the irritable boss tolerates neither questions nor criticism. These hypothetical thoughts illustrate how depth hermeneutics systematically reconstructs the inconsistencies, contradictions, and ruptures obtaining in scenes of interaction and aspires, thereby, to uncover the latent meaning camouflaged by the manifest meaning.

Let us ask this: How can depth hermeneutics contribute to the development of a methodically controlled approach to the life plans that are held back on the level of latent significance and inaccessible to the subject's verbal reflections? To this we may answer as follows: Depth hermeneutics relies on group interpretations. Participants expose themselves to a text, for example, to be analyzed, and the depth hermeneutical assumption is that in the group, too, interaction unfolds within the tension between a manifest and a latent meaning. Whereas the cognitive communication about the text's meaning is connected with the manifest level, the emotional understanding of the text is concerned with the latent level of meaning. What do we mean by this? The latent meaning of a quoted passage evades rational understanding; for this reason, it is accessible only when the seminar participants let themselves in on the text emotionally. They take on—not only cognitively but also emotionally—the roles that the text offers.

The affective understanding can lead to the discovery of something completely new if one follows Freud's (1912) recommendations for the practize of psychoanalytical interpretation: the technique consists 'in not directing one's notice to anything in particular and in maintaining the same, evenly-suspended attention' towards the text (111). At the same time, the seminar participants have to practize Freud's rule of 'free association'. The question, which scenes of interactions are to be analyzed, should be answered according to the associations spontaneously arising after the reading of the text. This means that by engaging their imagination, the participants open up a quite practical approach to the vivid experience contained in the text. When they picture this interactive experience arranged in the text as a 'scene' unfolding before their inner eye, they then sense 'what the text is doing with them'.

Undoubtedly, the most important associations are those which can be recorded in relation to confusing scenes of interaction. Confusions are cognitive and affective reactions to contradictory and inconsistent scenes of interaction. In the attempt to interpret the systematic meaning of these confusing scenes, one finds that they open up a new version that contradicts the versions arising from a simply routine process of text comprehension. Now these confusions direct the interpreter's evenly-suspended attention to key scenes that open up access to a level of latent meaning.

Thus, to begin with, associations and confusions—based on the text and verbalized within the group—open the way for understanding how the interaction of the actors unfolds in its concrete pictorial-scenic form. The process of interpretation begins with the understanding of individual scenes: those that show a structural similarity, even if they are to be found in a completely different nexus of action in the text. The scenes of interaction drawn into relation with one another are then grouped into various scenic complexes of action. These different scenic sequences are then compared and combined with one another until they are then welded into a single scenic configuration that illuminates the whole. The process of scenic interpretation may be considered as concluded when the manifest and also latent meaning of the scenically developed acts in the drama can be defined in a convincing and comprehensible way.

In the attempt to gain a comprehension of the text, the participants may make use of theoretical suppositions instead of their own practical life experience, or vice versa; what matters most is that the process of scenic interpretation takes place in everyday language, for this alone is suited to grasp the pictorial-scenic meaning of the interaction. When the process of scenic interpretation has been concluded, a second step is taken. This concerns the theoretical understanding of the case structure. Here, the theoretical foundations of psychoanalysis and cultural science provide insights that help us to standardize the case structure and to answer the question as to which general conclusions may be drawn from the reconstructed case study.

Concluding now the description of the method, I wish to proceed to the application of depth hermeneutics to the field of cultural research.

The Psychoanalytical Interpretation of the Films

I will now take up the second question: how can we research and compare psychic and social processes in different cultures with the help of depth hermeneutics? For this I wish to utilize three films of the 1990s from different western cultures, which I reconstructed psychoanalytically a few years ago. Here, in order to compare these films with one another, I would like to take up a question that can be developed from a theoretical supposition based on psychoanalytical as well as sociological viewpoints. In agreement with Erikson (1968) I wish to maintain that in modern societies, adolescence portrays a psychosocial moratorium which leads individuals growing up in a youth-subculture to experiment with cultural offers, which has the effect that they break their family ties and become established in a position in one or the other area of social life. I also agree with Parsons (1947), who authored a programmatic work on male aggressiveness in the social structure of modern industrial nations—a work which was also of great significance for Chodorow (1978) in her study of the division of labor in western industrial societies in relation to the sexes—and I thus wish to formulate the following hypothesis. In spite of considerable cultural change—which is manifest, among other aspects, in the integration of women in the occupational world as well as in the demands for emancipation arising in the women's liberation movement—there exists within the family-unit of modern industrial societies a still wide-spread division of labor according to sex, and this means that chiefly the men go about earning money whereas for the most part, women take up managing the household and raising the children. For this reason, boys as well as girls identify with the mother during the first two or three years of life; she serves as their primary object of affection and as the most significant person in their upbringing. In this way, because boys first develop a female identity, which they later on have to repress when their own sexual identity begins to evolve, they often develop a compulsive masculinity. In line with Parsons, I presume that boys are frequently aggressive during the period of latency because of the pressure they feel about not daring to reveal any trace of femininity; and therefore they prefer to get into fights and take up reckless adventures to give proof of their masculinity. During adolescence, infantile conflicts are lived out once more. At the same time, the identifications with the parents are abandoned, rejected, or partially reintegrated into a new form of identity-formation. Thus, male youths who show close ties to their mother and an unsatisfactory identification with their father attempt to prove their sexual identity and masculine strength in a compulsory way by rebelling against authority, by provoking others, or through hazardous undertakings. We are concerned here with a theory of socialization which describes a crisis in the male search for identity: a crisis grown even more acute due to the emancipation of women, and I wish to demonstrate this by means of a media-analysis in which three films—an American, a British, and a German—are examined as to the way in which the problem of the male search for identity is taken up and variably treated according to socio-cultural milieu.

The American Film *Basic Instinct*

Basic Instinct—a Hollywood film produced in 1992—fascinated many adolescents[5]. It concerns an adventurous detective, Nick, who works for the homicide commission in San Francisco. He investigates a case in which a former rock singer, while having sexual intercourse, was butchered with an ice pick in a way described in a certain novel. Nick casts suspicion on the attractive author of this novel, Catherine, as having committed the crime. Despite this he succumbs to her seductive approaches in a discotheque. At this point in time Nick is going through an identity crisis; he had been involved in several gun battles and is thus receiving counseling from a woman police psychologist. Nick reestablishes his masculinity by freeing himself from the motherly care provided

---

5   For a depth hermeneutic interpretation of Basic Instinct cf. König (1995).

by his counselor and then getting involved in a dangerous game of desires and the threat of death. Although Catherine binds Nick—just like
the murder victim—to the bed on the first love night, he shows no fear
and proves himself as a potent lover. The manifest meaning is that the
film portrays the archaic fear of sexual intercourse with a woman; particularly subject to this are adolescents who recoil from interpersonal
intimacy due to a weak sense of masculine identity (cf. Erikson 1968:
130pp.).

Confusing seems to be the fact that Catherine simultaneously loves a
good-looking woman who in her youth had killed her two brothers with a
razor blade, and the fact that she is acquainted with an older lady who
had killed her husband and children with a carving knife during the first
years of marriage, but this provides an approach to understanding the
latent meaning. The author, having written a book about how an ex-rock
star was stabbed to death by his girl-friend, proves to be a self-conscious
feminist because she wanted to demonstrate in a literary manner that
women carry out murders in order to take revenge on men for their acts
of violence.

Thus we may indicate the relationship between manifest and latent
meaning in the following way: On the one hand it is manifest that young
men with mother fixations are obliged to overcome their sexual fears and
take up the battle with women in order to prove their potency. On the
other hand, Nick's aggressiveness (he also rapes the woman police psychologist) is relegated to the level of latent meaning. Similarly, the manifest meaning, connected with the fact that an attractive writer has been
suspected of murder, camouflages the latent meaning, namely, that she is
dangerous because she is emancipated. Moreover, she is dangerous because, through her wealth and academic background, an economic and
cultural capital stands at her disposal, which gives her independence.

Basic Instinct takes up the topic of women's liberation—so much
dealt with in public discussions—in order to work against it by reverting
to the ruling ideology. The streets of San Francisco are transformed into
the stage upon which a sheriff appears who is like a hot-headed western
cowboy whose reputation has been marred by a series of shoot-outs. But
like his archetypal model, Nick proves himself, too, by remaining cold-
blooded during the decisive showdown, a matter of life or death, when he
shoots and kills the police psychologist—who turns out to be the mur-
derer. Just as the cowboy's killings are justified as a reaction against enemy aggression, so, too, is the use of violence justifiable as a means of
helping the detective to reestablish law and order—to preserve the status
quo threatened by dangerous adherents of the women's lib movement.
Basic Instinct takes sides with the dominant culture in so far as the ques-

tion of emancipation raised by the women's subculture is dealt with and rejected. For someone who is a real man like Detective Nick, it is not possible to let oneself in at all on a discussion with women on the questions they raise. Rather, it is a question of action: of going into battle against women and taming them. Thus, *Basic Instinct* utilizes the American dream in order to condemn the interests brought to public expression by the women's movement and to denounce these as dangerous demands which a man must defend himself against.

The British Film *Trainspotting*

Trainspotting became a cult film in Great Britain in 1996[6]. Every second teenager there saw it. The movie involves a group of adolescent drug addicts living in a run-down section of Edinburgh. As one of the junkies explained, heroin makes it possible for them to enjoy a kick that is a thousand times better than an orgasm. The extent to which these adolescents experience uncertainty in their masculine identity may be read from their sexual inhibitions. This is most evident in the unhappy figure of Spud: on the very day his girl friend takes him to her home, he is so drunk that he not only fails sexually in bed but also defecates later while sleeping. The grotesqueness of this catastrophic situation is underscored in that his wish to abandon drugs by initiating a sexual relationship with a girl turns out a complete flop (the wish 'makes a mess in its own pants'). Mark Renton, who is the intellectual head of this group of youths but who also shows a mother fixation, illustrates the way in which the junkies' sexual problems and their addiction to drugs may be explained. A pub scene demonstrates this. Here, Mark's mother disgraces him in front of his friends by kissing him on the cheek and saying "I love you", then adding that she still remembers when he was 'a little baby'. Mark is not capable of defending himself against these motherly excesses; he clams up, ashamed, and flees at once from the pub. Without thinking, he then breaks his attempt at withdrawal by taking a dose of methadone. The surrealistic scenes showing how he climbs up a high wall and flies off through the air to his dealer to get himself an overdose (which he only survives, by the way, through medical assistance), dramatize the fact that Mark needs the drugs in order to overcome the feeling of helplessness with which he reacts toward his mother, who treats him like a small child. The manifest meaning of this scene is that he frees himself from the mother by proving his masculinity: he takes up a dangerous

---

6   A depth hermeneutic reconstruction of this film is to be found in König (1998).

game with the drug, confident that he will emerge as victor over the danger.

The confusing term by which the junkies call their dealer ('Mother Superior'—because drugs are 'his Bible') provides an access to the latent meaning. This confusing idea—that the junkies thus fall into the role of pupils in a nunnery under a mother superior—reveals how the desire for drugs unfolds within the tension between a manifest and a latent meaning. Manifest is Mark's attempt to free himself from the mother with the help of drugs; latent is, on the other hand, that he—along with his friends—has found a new mother in the figure of the dealer. This new mother provides him the milk—in the form of drugs—which he still requires because of the unresolved mother fixation.

To be sure, the young people turn to drugs not only because of instinctive forces of destiny but also because they suffer under social grievances. They have grown up in a run-down working-class neighborhood, and in view of the prevailing mass unemployment in Thatcher's Great Britain, as well as the lack of prospects for the future, their use of drugs is also a protest against a social order whose laws, standards of achievement, and consumer promises they hate. Patriotic feelings are also revolting to them, precisely because they refuse to be integrated. Mark shouts into the landscape, 'I don't give a damn about being a Scotsman! We're nothing but a piece of rubbish, the scum of humanity, the most pitiful, miserable, subservient, and deplorable vermin that ever got shitted into life.' No matter how dangerous the submersion into heroin addiction may be, for Mark Renton the life within this subculture is a chance for individuation. In the end, as Mark succeeds in his withdrawal from heroin and then departs Scotland to seek a position in the business world of London, it becomes clear that his life as a junkie signifies a psychosocial moratorium which assists in his liberation from the sociocultural milieu of his origins and also helps to break the spell cast by the traditional religious certainties upheld by both his parents.

Confusing to us—when we see how Mark Renton has changed completely (he has turned into a smart yuppie working in a broker's office and having fun earning money)—is that despite all the discrepancies, there is a certain continuity to be found. Specifically, just as he lied, swindled, and stole as a junkie in order to get enough money for the next shot, he likewise is now concerned not only with 'loaning' and 'renting' in his brokerage work, but also with 'cheating'. No matter whether we observe the lives of drug addicts in a dilapidated working-man's section of Edinburgh or focus on a real estate office in modern London's business world, in the film we find questionable features in both worlds of experience; in neither is there room for morality. These inconsistencies indicate that the borderlines have grown blurry. Thus, the life of a junkie is a 'full-time job' in which no room for feelings of shame or guilt exists, since it is only possible through 'hard work' to get money for the next shot. And the stressful office work, too, has the effect of a drug that transforms Mark Renton into a workaholic who shows no moral scruples.

The German Film *Occupation Neo-nazi*

The documentary film *Occupation Neo-nazi* ran in the year 1993 in Germany's movie-theatres[7]. It led to a fierce controversy after the magazine *Der Spiegel* spoke of a "Brown shirts' publicity stunt" and the Jewish central advisory board brought charges against the filmmakers. The rapid cuts create an atmosphere filled with tension; Bonengel, the producer, dispensed with directives and left it to a Neo-nazi from Munich, Althans, to stage actions in front of the camera however he liked. These elements have given rise to a unique mix between documentary and feature film.

The particular form of masculinity propagated by Althans, the Neo-nazi leader, may be read from the film sequence in which he addresses a group of young people in a beer cellar in the town of Cottbus[8]. By explaining that it all depends on being a "good model", a "comrade" who is "faithful and willing to sacrifice" and "to take a place not only alongside one's comrades but also, if necessary when things get serious, in front of them", he thus revives the antidemocratic spirit of the old Weimar Republic. This spirit gave rise to the formation of a great myth among those of the 1914 generation who voluntarily joined the colors in a desire to escape the chains of middle-class society (ibid.). As Ernst Jünger (1926) later described, these Storm Troopers of the First World War thus proved their manliness in the trenches: "steel-nerved men who, half wasted away and day after day awaiting certain death, sat on their haunches behind red-hot machine guns, their nests surrounded by enemy forces and piled up with corpses" (76). We know that the Nazis viewed the comradeship among the German soldiers of the First World War as a "cell from which a new nation, pure in body and soul, may develop" (Mosse 1985: 162); likewise, Althans challenges the young people to unite under his leadership in a 'comradeship' of loyalty and willingness to sacrifice and thereby to create something which would not only radiate into this present-day world but also beyond (cf. Aust et al. 1995: 55-58). Rather he

---

7   A depth hermeneutic reconstruction of the scandalous key scenes in this film, in which the Neo-nazi makes a visit to Auschwitz, can be found in König (2001a).

8   A depth hermeneutic reconstruction of this speech to young people in Cottbus is to be found in König (1997a).

challenges the young people either to conquer or to die in the battle against the vicious, venom-spitting enemy whose encroachments demand the liberation of the "German lands". In this way, Althans entrusts his listeners with the task of taking up the legacy of the heroic fighters through the centuries who battled against the enemies of the fatherland: those who in the Middle Ages fought for the 'Holy Roman Empire of German Nations', those who participated in the Napoleonic wars, and those who fought in the two World Wars. Althans, revealing his world-view, answers to the social and political questions which arise from the structural problems immanent in progressive industrial societies by saying that all social grievance in Germany is rooted in the people's suffer-ance under foreign rule; this is what must be shaken off in a war of lib-eration.

Confusion arises through Althans's advice to the young people not to be swayed by the "external world" which entices them with "drugs" and "discotheques". The manifest meaning: that Althans is filled with enthu-siasm when he talks about the strength and masculinity of his listeners hides the latent meaning that he at the same time fears their weakness—that they could succumb to a dangerous encounter with the female sex. This would threaten their manliness in a double way: first, 'drugs' point to an addictive dependence which threatens to trap a man into oral de-pendence on a mother-like surrogate; secondly, 'discotheques' symbolize the sexual danger connected with the possibility that women could se-duce his listeners. This means, however, that Althans completely snubs the masculinity plans realized by Detective Nick in *Basic Instinct* and Mark Renton in *Trainspotting*. Precisely in the way Adorno et al. (1950) describe the authoritarian manner of dealing with inner conflicts, the un-compromising subjugation under Althans' leadership is to go hand in hand with an ascetic life-style which profits from the refusal to allow oneself sexual or oral pleasure. For indeed, the Neo-nazi leader demands of the young people "sacrifice" and "deprivation". The aggression rising on the heels of this self-denial is to be displaced, in an authoritarian manner, onto the political enemy—the scapegoat who is to pay for all suffering.

By means of his ideological agitation Althans promises a solution to social and political problems, and likewise he also gives an answer to the question of one's personal masculine identity. Agreeing with Lorenzer (1981) we may say that Althans, via "stereotypes as the core of a false ego", pursues an ideological agitation that welds "the wrong answer for the social problem [...]" together "with the wrong name for the conflict of instincts" (122). For, as we see, the Neo-nazi from Munich recom-mends that the young people take the Storm Troopers of World War I as models for their own search for identity—an image-world of mythical excess, by means of which the extreme right-wing answer to social and political questions (i.e., wars against enemies of the nation, instead of fighting for social change) is connected with the authoritarian answer for the conflict of instincts (the unconditional suppression of sexual impulses and letting aggressive instincts run free).

A confusing contradiction to this extreme right-wing agitation arises for us in the casual appearances of a well-groomed yuppie. Althans certainly gives the impression of being 'smart', with his expensive, brand name outfits, his fashionably styled short haircut, his youthful grin, and of being 'cool' just as well: his self-confident, easy-going behavior and the ability to provoke the older generation shows this. This confusion provides us an approach to the understanding of the peculiar nature of Althans' political agitation, which develops a ramified meaning through the combination of incongruent behavioral figures. Althans calls the middle-class "bourgeois rabble" that "lives at the cost of our people" and "wallows in our ancestors' castles", and the young people buy this anti-modern message from him because he appears as a yuppie who knows his way in the modern world. And, whereas he demands "sacrifice" and "deprivation" from the young people, he also signals through his appearance as a yuppie, that everything won't turn out so badly in the end. Thus, Althans takes the shock out of his Neo-nazi agitation by appearing as a cool yuppie who sells right-wing extremism as a 'life-style': he sells this to his listeners, with the wink of an eye as his very last exclamation.

Theoretical Understanding of the Scenic Interpretation

This analysis shows that all three films are able to assume a role in socialization because they appeal to young people's search for identity and because they offer various strategies for managing this search by staging specific rituals of growth into manhood. *Basic Instinct* illustrates a theme having to do with the type of manliness that one can develop by standing the test of sexual adventures with a dangerous woman; *Trainspotting* illustrates the theme involving the way in which one becomes a man by proving oneself stronger than the mortal danger inherent in the use of hard drugs; *Occupation Neo-nazi* deals with the type of manliness attained through the acquisition of a 'steel nature', on the basis of which one is then armed for the life and death battle against the enemy.

Here we see that the solutions proposed in these films for coping with a personal identity crisis are coupled with quite divergent social questions. In *Basic Instinct* the central point is the battle between the sexes, in accordance with which the women's demands for emancipation are rejected; *Occupation Neo-nazi* concerns the battle fought by right-wing extremists against democracy and foreigners; and in *Trainspotting* we are involved with the drug scene, which offers young people a chance for individualization—when they free themselves from the social milieu of their origins and when the spell cast by the traditional moral code of the working class is broken.

In this way each film codifies the social question in a specific, culture-bound manner. *Basic Instinct* utilizes the western myth to stylize the American male's battle against women as an archetypal, unavoidable drama unfolding on the borders of the wild west. In the film *Occupation Neo-nazi*, Althans promulgates the myth growing out of the legendary actions of the Storm Troopers in the First World War, thereby stylising the struggle against democracy and foreigners, likewise as an unavoidable war against the enemies of the entire fatherland. In *Basic Instinct* as well as in *Occupation Neo-nazi*, certain myths are dealt with in the intention of transforming history into nature, exactly as Barthes (1957: 113) says, since the battle of the sexes as well as war itself are regarded as irrevocable relationships of nature. The film *Trainspotting*, on the other hand, presents the view that the existing power structures result from conditions in the social realm. Thus, it turns to the destruction of national myths: just as the junkies refuse to take up the national identity developed by the Scotch in accord with the beauty of their landscapes, so, too, does Mark Renton undermine a possible idealization of Great Britain by turning his back on London (after a fascinating film sequence on this British metropolis) and planning a new start on the European continent.

The psychoanalytical reconstruction of these three films shows how its meanings are built up in scenes set within the tension between manifest and latent significance. Likewise we are also enabled to investigate the question of how these films codify wishes and drives. The manifest meaning of *Basic Instinct* is that young people on the way to manhood are able to prove their masculinity by taking up the battle with women; the confusions reveal the latent meaning that women are characterized as dangerous because they fight for their emancipation. So the film combines a solution for an inner conflict—to become an adult by leaving behind one's mother and to become a man by fighting alone against all his enemies—with a sexist solution to a social problem: how to deal with the emancipation of women. The discriminating answer—to become a man by defeating such women—is given in reference to the myth of the westerner who proves his masculinity by leaving his mother behind and living in the wilderness on his own. The manifest meaning of *Occupation Neo-*

nazi is that young people may develop their freedom and manliness when they transform themselves into 'steel natures' acting out their aggressive impulses; confusions illuminate the latent meaning that the unconditional subjugation to their leader means frustration of oral and genital drives. Thus, the film combines the authoritarian answer to a personal conflict—to become an adult by joining a group of strong fighting men—with an extreme right-wing answer to the question of how to solve social problems—by fighting the Jews instead of fighting for social change. And this message is given by referring to the national myth of Storm Troopers of World War I. In contrast, the manifest meaning of *Trainspotting* is to be found in the portrayal of both drug use and the real estate business as involving a great sense of freedom and adventure; the latent meaning contradicts this, however, by indicating that not only junkies but also the yuppies who have turned into workaholics are both succumbing to an addiction. The confusing insight into inner conflicts—adolescents trying to leave their mothers behind by becoming junkies who become addicted to their mothers in another way—is combined with a critical view of the suffering of adolescents under the social grievances in Thatcher's Great Britain. The elucidating effect of the film becomes palpable through the confusions that point out that the drug culture's lovely sheen is just as superficial as the glamour of London's business world. The contradictions and inconsistencies of both worlds confront movie goers with the problem of how the ruthless, dog-eat-dog style of modern economic life—also characteristic of the drug scene, by the way—leads to an eradication of moral principles. So the depth hermeneutical analysis proves how the three films may socialize adolescents: *Basic Instinct* and *Occupation Neo-nazi* have an *affirmative effect* by transforming social processes into conditions of nature young people have to endure. In contrast, *Trainspotting* has an *illuminating effect* by showing how adolescents rebel against a society—which makes the rich richer and the poor poorer—and become addicted to it, too.

I would like to finish this article by briefly indicating my way of proceeding methodically. After having reconstructed the depth structure of each film, I tried to generalize the results of the scenic interpretations to the extent that typical patterns in the rituals of manliness, as they appear in films of the 1990s, grew visible to us. To be able to grasp the specific cultural differences in the films, it was necessary to interpret them from a psychoanalytic as well as a cultural scientific point of view. For *Basic Instinct* and *Occupation Neo-nazi*, depth hermeneutics was combined with ideological criticism; for *Trainspotting* a combination of psychoanalytic theory and the theory of socialization was utilized and then coupled with the knowledge of social structures, ever drawing on the power of explanation inherent in the theory of individualization.

References

Adorno, T.W./Frenkel-Brunswik, E./Levinson, D.J./Sanford, R.N (1950). The Authoritarian Personality. New York.

Adorno, T.W. (1957). Soziologie und empirische Forschung. In: Gesammelte Werke. Vol. 8 (pp. 196-216).

Adorno, T.W. (1969a). Einleitung zum 'Positivismusstreit in der deutschen Soziologie'. In: Gesammelte Werke. Vol. 8 (pp. 280-353).

Adorno, T.W. (1969b). Gesellschaftstheorie und empirische Forschung. In: Gesammelte Werke. Vol. 8 (pp. 538-546).

Adorno, T.W. (1970). Ästhetische Theorie. Frankfurt a. M. 1973.

Aust, O. (1995). Protokoll der wichtigsten Sequenzen des Bonengel-Films 'Beruf Neonazi'. Typoskript.

Barthes, R. (1957). Mythen des Alltags. Frankfurt a. M. 1970.

Chodorow, N. (1978). Das Erbe der Mütter. Psychoanalyse und Soziologie der Geschlechter. München 1990.

Erikson, E.H. (1968). Jugend und Krise. Die Psychodynamik im sozialen Wandel. München 1988.

Jünger, E. (1926). Der Kampf als inneres Erlebnis. 2nd ed. Berlin.

Freud, S. (1901). Zur Psychopathologie des Alltagslebens. In: Gesammelte Werke. Vol. IV. Frankfurt a. M. 1999.

Freud, S. (1912). Recommendations to Physicians Practising Psycho-Analysis. Standard Edition Volume XII (pp.109-120). London 1958.

Horkheimer, M./Adorno, T.W. (1947). Dialektik der Aufklärung. Philosophische Fragmente. In: Gesammelte Werke. Vol. 5 (pp.11-290). Frankfurt a. M.

König, H.-D. (1995). Sexualität zwischen Lust und Tod. Der in dem Film Basic Instinct inszenierte Geschlechterkampf. In: S. Müller-Doohm/ K Neumann-Braun (Eds.). Kulturinszenierungen (pp.141-164). Frankfurt a. M.: Suhrkamp.

König, H.-D. (1996). Methodologie und Methode der tiefen-hermeneutischen Kultursoziologie in der Perspektive von Adornos Verständnis kritischer Sozialforschung. In: H.-D. König (Ed.). Neue Versuche, Becketts Endspiel zu verstehen. Sozialwissenschaftliches Interpretieren nach Adorno (pp 314-387). Frankfurt a. M.: Suhrkamp.

König, H.-D. (1997a). 'Ihr seid Ihr selbst und müsst Euch selber befreien!' Ideologiekritische und sozialpsychologische Rekonstruktion der

Rede eines Neonazis vor Jugendlichen in Cottbus. In: R. Heim/H.-D. König (Eds.) (pp. 69-90).

König, H.-D. (1997b). Tiefenhermeneutik als Methode kultur-soziologischer Forschung. In: R. Hitzler/A. Honer (Eds.). Sozialwissenschaftliche Hermeneutik (pp. 213-241). Leverkusen: Leske + Budrich.

König, H.-D. (1998). Junkiespiele zwischen Lust und Tod. Eine tiefenhermeneutische Filmanalyse zu Boyles Trainspotting. In: Texte. Sonderheft der Zeitschrift medien praktisch, 1, 9-23.

König, H.-D. (2000). Adornos psychoanalytische Kulturkritik und die Tiefenhermeneutik. Zugleich eine Sekundäranalyse des 24. Aphorismus der Minima Moralia. In: Zeitschrift für kritische Theorie VI, 10, 7-26.

König, H.-D. (2001a). A Neo-Nazi in Auschwitz. A Psychoanalytic Reconstruction of a Documentary Film on Right-Wing Extremism. [58 paragraphs]. Forum Qualitative Sozialforschung / Forum: Qualitative Social Research [On-line Journal], 2(3). Available at: http://www. qualitative-research.net/fqs/fqs-eng.htm.

König, H.-D. (2001b). Tiefenhermeneutik als Methode psychoanalytischer Kulturforschung. In: H. Appelsmeyer/E. Billmann-Mahecha (Eds.). Kulturwissenschaft (pp. 168-194). Weilerswist.

König, H.-D. (2004). Deep-structure Hermeneutics. In: U. Flick/E. von Kardoff/I. Steinke (Eds.). A Companion to Qualitative Research (pp. 313-320). London, Thousand Oaks, New Dehli: Sage.

Lorenzer, A. (1970). Sprachzerstörung und Rekonstruktion. Frankfurt a. M.

Lorenzer, A. (1974). Die Wahrheit der psychoanalytischen Erkenntnis. Ein historisch-materialistischer Entwurf. Frankfurt a. M.

Lorenzer, A. (1981). Das Konzil der Buchhalter. Die Zerstörung der Sinnlichkeit. Eine Religionskritik. Frankfurt a. M.

Lorenzer, A. (1986). Tiefenhermeneutische Kulturanalyse. In: H.-D. König/A. Lorenzer et al. (Eds.). Kultur-Analysen (pp. 11-98).Frankfurt a. M.

Mosse, G. L. (1985). Nationalismus und Sexualität. Bürgerliche Moral und sexuelle Normen. Reinbek bei Hamburg 1987.

Parsons, T. (1947). Über wesentliche Ursachen und Formen der Aggressivität in der Sozialstruktur westlicher Industriegesellschaften. In: T. Parsons. Beiträge zur soziologischen Theorie (pp. 223-255). Darmstadt: Neuwied 1973.

NEGOTIATING THE MIDDLE GROUND BETWEEN THE OSTENSIBLE AND SHARED HORIZONS: A DYNAMIC APPROACH TO CROSS-CULTURAL COMMUNICATION ABOUT HUMAN DEVELOPMENT[1]

ROBERT SERPELL

Making Sense of Behavior and Experiences within their Cultural Context

The central paradox of human cultural diversity arises from the possibility of intercultural communication despite the irreducibility of cultural differences. The challenge this poses for cultural psychology is how to facilitate a dynamic process of communication among participants with different perspectives, rather than a search for equivalence among static representations[2] (Serpell 1990). In this paper, I will discuss an approach to generating such a process. It emerged from a program of research in the Katete district of Zambia designed to explore indigenous conceptions of intelligence, in relation to parental caregiving practices, formal schooling, and developmental outcomes for children born into a subsistence, agricultural community (Serpell 1974, 1982, 1993). In the present paper, I will draw illustrative examples from two more recent, culturally focused lines of research. The first is a longitudinal study of early literacy development in the American city of Baltimore (Serpell, Baker, and Sonnenschein 2005). One strand of the study sought to document caregiver ethnotheories of child development and socialization in a sample of

---

1 An earlier version of this paper was presented at the conference on 'Cultural and Cross-Cultural Psychology in the Field of Cultural Studies: theoretical and methodological alternatives and controversies', Essen, Germany: Kulturwissenschaftliches Institut: May 17-19, 2001.
2 The seminal formulation by Pike (1954, 1967) of 'etic and emic standpoints for the description of behavior' has been widely invoked in discussions of research methodology for the field of cross-cultural psychology (Berry 1969; Triandis 1972; Headland, Pike and Harris 1990). However, its application to categories has also been roundly criticized for raising serious conceptual problems (Jahoda 1977, 1983).

parents stratified by race and class, and to investigate their influence on educational outcomes for the children in question. We also explored related beliefs of teachers regarding their and their students' parents' complementary responsibilities for the socialization of children during the preschool and early primary school years (Akkari et al. 1998). And we examined the potential of parent-teacher relationships for cooperative communication concerning the children's development (Danseco 1997; Serpell et al. 1996).

The second line of research is a collaborative, participatory study of educational innovation based on the principles of Child-to-Child (Hawes 1988) at a government primary school in the rural district of Mpika, Zambia (Adamson-Holley 1999; Mumba 1996; Mwape and Serpell 1996; Serpell and Mwape 1998/99; Udell 2001). The project has sought to document the wide range of activities through which the curricular principles of the Child-to-Child approach were instantiated at the school, to clarify the ideological and theoretical grounding of the curriculum, and to interpret the social history of their dissemination and appropriation. We have also attempted to assess the developmental benefits in various domains for boys and for girls, for youth who are promoted to more advanced stages of the formal educational system, and for those who discontinue their schooling at an earlier age. Concurrently, we have supported contact and exchange of ideas between the teachers responsible for the program and teachers at other schools, with a view to appropriation of this educational model by other schools and communities. The aspect of this project that I will describe was designed to investigate the conceptions of selected dimensions of child development held by teachers in primary, basic, and secondary schools, as a function of their curricular orientation and related parental attitudes.

In each of these studies, the process of cross-cultural communication about human development begins by identifying two complementary bridgeheads (Horton 1982) for cross-cultural communication: ostensible referents, and shared horizons. The investigator then proceeds to invite each research participant to articulate an account in his or her own words of how the ostensible referents are related to the shared horizons. This is followed by a process of negotiation to arrive at a set of intermediary constructs that both make sense to the owner-members of a particular culture for communication in terms of its existing system of meanings, and are also intelligible within another meaning-system that is shared by the investigator with an audience to whom the interpretation is addressed. The overarching methodological goal in this process is not to arrive at some definitive construct or set of constructs that eliminate differences (what Berry [1969] and others [Berry et al. 1992] have termed 'derived etics'), but rather to protect the process of communication against the hazards of oversimplification, trivialization, or systematic distortion (in the sense articulated by Habermas, cf. McCarthy 1978).

Interpretation in the context of cross-cultural communication involves a process akin to translation, where the goal, according to Gadamer (1965), is "a hermeneutic mediation between different life-worlds", each of which is a product of particular sociocultural conditions and is "caught up in the movement of history". An interpreter, like a translator, must "conceptualize his material in such a way that while its foreignness is preserved, it is nevertheless brought into intelligible relation with his own life-world" (McCarthy 1978: 173-4). A kindred formulation was proposed by the poet T. S. Eliot (1950) as the hallmark of good poetry, "the making the familiar strange, and the strange familiar". Spiro (1990) made a compelling case for adopting this precept as a goal for anthropological research. However, the ethnographic tradition in anthropology tends to presume the primacy of a 'home base' as audience for the investigator's discoveries, thus affording a rather one-sided perspective on who is to be enlightened by the research.

A well-known example of research in cultural psychology that has begun to 'make the strange familiar' to Western audiences is Doi's (1971) articulation of the Japanese concept of *amae* (cf. Azuma 1994; Lebra 1994; Tobin, Wu, and Davidson 1989). But, as Azuma (1984) points out, the original purpose of this explication of an indigenous construct was not to enlighten a Western audience, but to promote reflection within Japanese culture on the nature of human relationships, child development, and socialization. Enriquez and his colleagues in the Philippines were very clear on this point when they embarked on the program of systematically developing and promoting an indigenous *Pilipino* psychology, focusing on distinctive indigenous concepts that are hard to translate into English, such as *kapwa* (Enriquez 1994; Enriquez and Marcellino 1984; Pe-Pua 1998). Likewise, Boykin's (1983) purpose in articulating a set of distinctive themes of Afro-cultural tradition including 'verve', and 'expressive individualism,' was not so much to explain African-American behavior to the owner-bearers of mainstream American culture, as it was to stimulate enhanced awareness among African Americans of the 'integrity' of a set of cultural resources accessible to them for the interpretation of their own behavior and experience.

On the other hand, historical and comparative cultural studies that have 'made the familiar strange' include the problematization of American mainstream parental practices, such as separate sleeping arrangements for infants (Harkness and Super 1992; Morelli et al. 1992; Shweder et al. 1995); and teaching practices, such as the liberal use of praise (Stigler and Perry 1990). Perhaps more profoundly challenging for the mainstream of Western psychology, however, are studies that problematize constructs, such as authoritarianism (Chao 1994; Kagitcibasi 1992), or plagiarism (Wertsch 1991), which have become axiomatic elements of the frame of reference for Western intellectual discourse about psychology and other topics. Recognizing that these constructs are not part of the shared horizons for psychological interpretation in other cultures gives rise to a re-examination of their epistemological and axiological status. Such soul-searching in the West (Kagitcibasi 1992) may enhance both the subtlety of discourse within Western societies and their capacity to incorporate insights originating from contact with other cultures. However, focusing on reflexive benefits of cross-cultural inquiry to the investigator's culture of origin tends to obscure the fact that they are secondary consequences of what I conceive to be the primary goal of cultural psychology, namely, to make sense of behavior and experience within the cultural context in which it is set.

The relative success with which cultural research proceeds in this direction depends, I suspect, much less on adherence to a formally definable sequence of strategic steps or particular types of instrument, than on sensitive deployment of the imagination. Gombrich (1960), for instance, has shown how in the history of Western art, the Impressionist School were able to generate 'comparisons that worked', through a subtle synthesis of principles enshrined in existing tradition, careful observation of the external world, and inductive extrapolation of new modes of representation. Likewise, both in poetry (Barfield 1947) and in science (Boyd 1979), the use of metaphor serves both to build a bridge between alternative worldviews (Pylyshyn 1979), and to activate pre-existing structures of thought (Lakoff and Johnson, 1980). Thus, I have argued that cultural validation of explanations in developmental psychology cannot be separated from the perspectives of the particular audiences to which they are addressed. The acid test of a theoretical construct includes not only criteria favored by the scientific community, such as comprehensiveness, parsimony, and predictive accuracy, but also its capacity to resonate with broader cultural preoccupations of the audience (Serpell 1990, 1994).

Nevertheless, a systematic presentation of strategy and method may serve a number of valuable functions: first, as an informative resource for novices embarking on cultural psychological research. Second, the very existence of a systematic approach may provide armament for those engaged in a rearguard action against pressures from mainstream science and technology to adopt standardized instruments. The benefits of the latter, in my view, are generally outweighed by the hazards they incur, since they tend to by-pass or short-cut important preliminaries to the design of methods for research in cultural contexts for which the instruments were not designed, thus placing the entire enterprise of research at risk for systematic distortion. Yet, as Straub (2001) noted, "the voices warning against any universalist doctrine often throw out the baby with the bath water when they take refuge in a relativism that can make it incomprehensible that we do reach understandings across cultural borders, or how we do so, or how we might begin to do so without the imposition of power". I hope to illustrate for the research described below how psychological investigation may proceed cautiously, and yet methodically to reach out and recruit the participation of individuals whose enculturation is very different from that of the primary investigators. A third justification for articulating in detail the research methods described below is as a response to Lincoln and Guba's (1985) call for qualitative researchers, as one way of fulfilling their responsibility to remain accountable for their inquiries, to leave an 'audit trail' that would enable others to systematically check the validity of the original findings.

In earlier publications on this topic (Serpell 1990, 1993, 1994), I have applied the concepts of *horizon* and *negotiation* metaphorically to the domain of communication. I will take this opportunity to further develop these analogies, with reference to the schema shown in Figure 1.

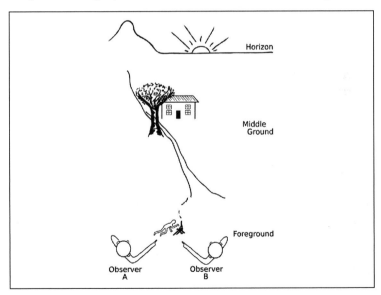

Figure 1: The middle ground

In the bottom left and right corners of the schema are the head and shoulders of two observers of the world. In the foreground, close to both of them a young child is approaching a fire. This is an ostensible element of the world they can both reach out and touch. They are both pointing at it, and are in a position to include it within their secondary intersubjectivity (Trevarthen 1980). There is little doubt they can agree on what is happening, but their interpretation of its significance may differ in view of how such events feature in the larger cultural worlds of which they are a part. If the child is part of the rural East African community of Nyansongo[3], the indigenous observer may wait and see if the child touches the fire, and if the infant does get burned and cry, this observer may laugh out loud in acknowledgment that this is an inevitable experience, part of growing up, and one the child will likely not repeat. But, if the observer is from another culture, she may feel she should intervene to prevent the child from getting burned, and view with strong disapproval the behavior of her counterpart. They both agree on what they see, and understand why the child is taking this risk, but they differ on how to interpret the event and on how to act appropriately in relation to it. At the top of the schema is the horizon, which looks much the same to both observers: a mountain sloping down to the shore of the lake and the sun setting over the water. In the middle ground is a cluster of items. Both observers can see the tree, and the house next to it. But from where observer A stands, the view of the path as it reaches the tree is obscured, so that she cannot tell exactly whether the path leads up to the front door of the house, or merely passes by the house. Observer B, on the other hand, can see, from where she stands, that the path goes right between the house and the tree, and continues on towards the mountain. What observer B cannot see is the sack leaning up against the tree, although it is clearly visible to observer A. In short, certain features of the world they both observe are clearly visible to one observer and invisible to the other. Communication about these features of the middle ground, between the ostensible scene close to them and the distant horizon that they share, will require reciprocal efforts of the imagination from both of them to incorporate them in an intersubjectively shared view of the world.

Table 1 summarizes the analogy between this schema and certain aspects of the three research projects in cultural psychology that I will discuss below. The middle ground for which a shared interpretation was negotiated in these studies concerned psychological and social relations rather than the spatial ones depicted in Figure 1. Interlocutors approached the topics of child development, socialization, and education with alternative perspectives that emphasized different dimensions and constructs,

---

3   The community of Nyansongo was described by Barbara LeVine in the Whiting and Whiting 'six cultures' project (See Whiting 1963; Whiting and Whiting 1975).

and negotiated an integrative interpretation of the phenomena on which those perspectives intersected.

Ostensible referents	Invitation, negotiation, intermediary constructs	Shared horizons
Katete study (adult interviews)		
Actual children + naturalistic vignettes of situations arising in village life	Selection of individuals for task responsibilities + explanation of criteria for selection	Authority of adults to assign children task responsibilities
Baltimore study (parental ethnotheory interviews)		
Actual children and netword of kin + inventory of recurrent activities in child's home	Interpretation of meaning of selected recurrent joint activities for the focal child + interpretation /evaluation of the same activities from the primary caregiver's perspective	Existence of a developmental niche constituted by a stable activity structure
Mpika study (teacher questionnaires)		
Events and behaviors recalled by informant as having been observed in students	Assigning behaviors as concrete exemplars of abstract dimensions	Relevance of formal education to some, but not all, dimensions of child development

Table 1: Components of the process of cross-cultural communication: examples from the different studies.

The Rural Chewa Perspective
on Child Development and Intelligence
in Katete, Zambia

My fourteen-year, trace study of 'the significance of schooling: life journeys in an African society' (Serpell 1993) began with an attempt to understand the context of primary socialization of children born into a rural community in eastern Zambia before they entered the local primary school. A major methodological concern at the outset was how to avoid biasing the elicitation procedure toward the perspective on which public schooling is based. We therefore introduced our interviews as an opportunity for us (teachers from the national university and a local primary school) to learn from the respondents (responsible adults in the context of village life) about the development and socialization of children in that context. We focused the entry-point for cross-cultural communication on actual children as ostensible referents by assembling a group of children of approximately the same age (based on information that we had collected through a preliminary demographic survey), and first establishing that our informant knew each of them by name. We also made allusion to some shared horizons such as the authority of adults to assign children practical task responsibilities in the course of everyday life, while setting the scene for our naturalistic vignettes of hypothetical situations that might arise in village life. (These vignettes had been generated in advance through a process of brain-storming among researchers, teachers, and parents familiar with the pattern of life in a Chewa village.)

We then invited our informants to indicate which of the designated individual children they would select for a given task responsibility in that hypothetical situation. For instance, one of the vignettes was as follows.

"Suppose that one day you are down by the stream, washing your clothes, and you see that the place where you usually spread them out to dry is muddy today, and this group of girls is with you. Which of them would you send to search for another good place to spread your clothes?"

Once the informant had nominated a specific child for the assignment, we went on to ask her to explain her criteria for that selection. Sometimes the respondent's initial reply would focus on such variables as age or kinship status. But in such cases we always pressed for a more substantive reason, pointing out that all the children in the designated group were of similar age, and all were members of the village, kinship-based community. Out of this semistructured interview process, we negotiated with our informants a set of constructs that were meaningful to them for the evaluation of children's behavior in relation to the demands of everyday life in the sociocultural context of the village. These constructs were intermediary in conceptual level between concrete, ostensible individuals of a particular gender, name, and place of residence, as well as a particular age and kinship status, on the one hand, and certain highly abstract, general principles that served, on the other hand, as a shared horizon that warranted the possibility of a meaningful conversation.

Articulating the system of meanings embedded in Chewa culture that informs those intermediary constructs, including *nzelu*, *ku-chenjela*, and *ku-tumikila* has been the subject of extensive subsequent research, and on which I have drawn to interpret various aspects of the life journeys of the young people whose behavior we first viewed through the lens of conversations with adults who knew them in the context of their home community. The constructs have been systematically compared with English constructs such as *intelligence*, *cleverness*, and *responsibility*, as well as constructs in French, Baoule, Bemba, and several other African languages (Serpell 1989), highlighting commonalities and contrasts. And I have drawn on that contrastive analysis as a frame of reference for interpreting the interweaving of European and African cultural systems of representation in the bicultural repertoire of Zambian school teachers and their students (Serpell 1993, Chapter 4; Serpell 1996, 1999). The middle ground between ostensible referents (actual children and concrete tasks) and shared horizons has thus been gradually articulated as a focus of contestation between different cultural systems of meaning and practice, each of which lays claim to defining important pathways of opportunity for children growing up in contemporary Zambian society. Such cross-cultural contestation of child socialization is not confined to societies that inherited their educational systems from a recent period of colonization. Similar issues arise at the interface between home and school for many children growing up in the U.S. (Serpell 1997).

Parental Ethnotheories of Development and Socialization in Baltimore, Maryland

The Early Childhood Project in Baltimore is an attempt to understand, in several contrastive sociocultural groups, the interactive processes through which children explore and gradually appropriate cultural resources in the environment, including the practices and technology of literacy. Since society takes an active interest in promoting this aspect of child development, our study also focuses on the context and processes of cognitive socialization. The city in which the study was situated, like many other American cities in the 1990s, included an impoverished center characterized by high rates of adult illiteracy and high school 'drop out', along with other features of what some authors have termed a growing urban 'underclass' (e.g., Wilson 1990). The city also contained a few wealthy neighborhoods and a substantial, middle-income residential zone where school attendance and adult literacy rates were much higher. In order to permit valid comparisons across such diverse groups, we considered it methodologically essential to define the focus of our inquiry broadly enough for parents with limited, weak, or aversive personal histories of contact with the school system and its agenda not to perceive us simply as agents of the school. This approach has afforded us opportunities to learn about parents' views concerning emergent literacy within a wider array of issues confronting all parents than has commonly been the case in literacy research.

The cultural context of child development constitutes both a set of constraints to which a child must adapt, and a conceptual framework for interpreting developmental change. Early theoretical treatments of context as external stimulation have given way to the more complex perspective of an incorporating system of social activity, informed by a system of cultural meanings (Serpell 1999a). This theoretical shift has methodological implications. Rather than describing the behavior of a caregiver as an external causal influence on the development of a child, researchers can learn more from engaging her in interpretive discussion of the hopes and fears, goals and beliefs that inform her interactions with the child. Such hermeneutical discussion acknowledges the common humanity of researchers, parents, and teachers, and their responsibility to co-construct or negotiate a shared understanding of possibilities for the enhancement of children's developmental opportunities (Serpell 1994).

Connecting with Everyday Understanding[4]

The approach we adopted to this complex area was to ground our discussion of ideas with parental caregivers in their own, relatively spontaneous formulations of what are salient activities in their child's everyday life.

This called for a gradual process of invitation to dialogue, which I have broken down (somewhat arbitrarily) into a series of strategic steps (see Table 2).

Step 1: building rapport in the recruitment process
Step 2: inviting participants to define their world in the Diary
Step 3: broadening the scope of discussion with the Ecological Inventory
Step 4: eliciting the insider's "meanings" attributed to recurrent activities
Step 5: inference and tentative formulation of socialization goals
Step 6: negotiated specification of socialization goals

Table 2: Connecting with caregivers' everyday understanding of child development and socialization: steps in the process adopted by the Baltimore Early Childhood project.

Setting the Scene

Step 1: Building Rapport during Recruitment

A stratified sample of schools was chosen to represent four contrasting 'social addresses' (Bronfenbrenner and Crouter 1983) within Baltimore City's complex ecosystem: low-income, African-American, low-income, European-American, middle-income, African-American, and middle-

4   This section of the paper is based on a joint presentation by Robert Ser-
    pell, Victoria Goddard-Truitt, Evangeline Danseco, and Susan Hill, to the
    Advanced Research Training Seminar on Qualitative Approaches in Cul-
    tural Psychology, at the University of Maryland Baltimore County (UMBC):
    July 29-August 1, 1998, co-sponsored by the IUPsyS, IAAP, IACCP, and
    UMBC (cf. Serpell and Akkari, in press).
    The Early Childhood Project is a longitudinal, collaborative study by the
    co-principal investigators, Robert Serpell, Linda Baker, and Susan Sonnen-
    schein, supported by the National Reading Research Center, under the
    Educational Research and Development Centers Program (PR/AWARD NO.
    117A20007) as administered by OERI, U. S. Department of Education, and
    by the National Institute of Child Health and Human Development (PRO-
    JECT NO. R01 HD29737-01A1). We appreciate the contributions of other
    members of our research team during the time these data were col-
    lected: Dorothy Adamson, Adrianna Amari, Yvonne Bush, Marie Dorsey,
    Sylvia Fernandez-Fein, Linda Gorham, Susan Hill, Tunde Morakinyo, Bev-
    erly Pringle, Nicole Talley, Sharon Teuben-Rowe, and Yolanda Vauss.

income, European-American. School Principals were approached by a multicultural team of researchers with the request that their school host the five-year, longitudinal project. Each of the schools that we approached catered to a neighborhood with a demographic profile that represented one or more of these social addresses. Letters were sent home inviting parents to meet with one or more members of the research team at the school, where an individualized, face-to-face discussion was held of the objectives and methods of the study, and parents were invited to give their informed consent to the participation of their child and family in the project. These discussions afforded an opportunity to build rapport with parents, setting the tone for subsequent interviews, and highlighting the theme that our purpose was to learn about the family's approach to child-rearing rather than to impose or advocate an 'expert' point of view.

Step 2: Inviting Participants to Define their World

By inviting her first to maintain a record for a week of what happens in each day of her child's life, we left each respondent free to define her own focus. Low literacy levels were accommodated by offering participating parents the choice of recording their diary on a cassette recorder or in a booklet. Some illustrative excerpts from two of the diaries, one recounted orally and recorded on tape, the other written, feature in the case studies presented below.

Home visits were arranged to follow up the diary with a series of semistructured interviews, and observations, which took place one or two times a year over the next five years. The first home visit included steps 3 and 4:

Step 3: Broadening the Scope of Discussion

Our Ecological Inventory has been described by Sonnenschein, Baker, and Serpell (1995). Based on the work of Baine (1988) and Gallimore et al. (1989), it served as a checklist for systematically reviewing with the informant each of several distinct types of literacy-related activity in which the focal child participated.

Step 4: Eliciting the Insider's 'Meanings' for Ostensible Activities

From the diary's initial description of the child's daily life, (in some cases further elaborated in response to the Ecological Inventory) we selected a set of recurrent activities in which the child engaged with a familiar co-participant, and probed the caregiver to articulate the personal meanings that she imputed to each activity and what she thought it meant to her child.

"What do you think this activity means to (the focal child)?"
"What does it mean to you as her parent?" (or other caregiving role, as appropriate)

When responding to these requests, caregivers often illustrated their views with prototypical episodes (cf. Quinn and Holland 1987). Our informants varied considerably in the degree to which they volunteered explicit integrative schemes to situate or reinforce their explanations of what a given activity meant to their child and/or to themselves as caregivers. Sometimes they invoked explicit cultural themes in their formulation of explanatory schemas. Three cultural themes that were frequently invoked were the rejection of violence, the promotion of fun, and the cultivation of motivation for educational success.

Such themes are expressed not only by individuals in their everyday, private discourse, but also in various public media, such as television, radio and print news items, comment, entertainment, and commercial advertising (cf. Lightfoot and Valsiner 1992). Rodrigo and Triana (1996) have suggested that parents' knowledge about child development is generally represented in schematic, prototypical form, stored in their memory as multiple episodic traces of a network of personal experiences, rather than as the well structured entity that we generally think of as a theory. These episodic traces are only occasionally abstracted at the time of retrieval in order to meet a particular situational demand. For instance, a selective sample of representational knowledge may be deployed within a hierarchy of plans of action addressed to the demands of a proximal social context. Or a different selective sample of knowledge may be activated when trying to understand another person's point of view.

Explanatory schemas may thus be considered an intermediary level of representation between the details of prototypical episodes and general cultural themes. Each of these elements of ethnotheory is illustrated in the following examples.

Case Study 1: Mrs A. (European-American, low-income mother of a preschool girl, Anna)

In this first case, the caregiver expresses a very explicit commitment to supporting the pedagogical process that she sees her child going through at school in the Pre K class. First, she contrasts her own attitude with that of her parents when she was a schoolchild. Later, she articulates the function of homework as an opportunity for students to display to their teacher what they have mastered in class, without the instructional support or what we might call the scaffolding (Wood, Bruner, and Ross 1976) in the child's zone of proximal development (Vygotsky 1978).

405

This European American mother who dropped out of high school, first talks about the activity she described in her handwritten diary as 'Mom read them there [sic] Bedtime Story,' and later about her four-year-old daughter's recurrent activity, which she referred to on several pages of the diary as 'we did her homework,' or 'did homework.'

Interviewer:	What does it mean to her when you read her a bedtime story?
Mother:	I dunno, I think she just likes it that I read to her. Cause J <her sister> reads to her but not like I do. I, like, try to express some parts and I just read it on through. I try to make it exciting or whatever, you know. Why make reading boring? Just stops the person from reading. < laughs > That's the way I see it. Cause I know when I went to school, my parents didn't likely give a hoot. If I did my homework, I did it. If I didn't, I didn't. If I went to school, oh well. You know? My kids, no! I know how my parents was and I'm not about...
I:	What does it mean to her when you do her homework with her?
M:	I don't know. I don't know, it's like her way of learning something. 'Cause I try to express to them that if you don't do your homework you don't actually learn anything out of class. I mean... when they are in class, the teacher has them to do something, they're learning with the teacher. But homework gives them the opportunity to show their teacher what they do know without their teacher being around, like without supervision. I mean, that's just like, like, ah, when Anna started writing her name, she started writing some letters backwards, you know. I didn't.... I corrected her on it when it was on our time, but when homework time I don't. Because that gives their teacher a chance to know what they really do know and what really needs to be worked on. I don't correct it on their homework. I think that's ... it would be bad on my half. Cause if her name's right, Ms. T. <the class teacher> will think: 'Wow, she can know what she's doing,' but, no, she can't, cause she needs help on it and Ms. T ain't going to know it. You know? What am I supposed to do, write a letter everyday to Ms. T. 'I fixed her....?' You know, no, that's o.k., I'll let Ms. T do it for her. That way Ms. T. can tell her: 'that's wrong, this is the way it's supposed to go.'

In this articulation of a personal philosophy, the mother invokes a public cultural theme, that parents should take an interest in their children's progress in school and show their support by attending to homework assignments, contrasting her own attitude with her parents' delinquency. However, she puts her own twist on it by focusing on the process of attending and insisting that it is different from instruction: 'I corrected her on it when it was on our time, but when homework time I don't.' The explanatory schema that she advances to justify this distinction is very succinct: 'Because that gives the teacher a chance to know what they really do know and what needs to be worked on.' Earlier in the same passage, she advances another explanatory schema to justify her practice of 'trying to make' her reading of bed time stories 'exciting': 'Why make reading boring? Just stops the person from reading.' Note also that a key part of her representation of the socialization function of 'doing homework' with her child is in the form of a prototypical episode: 'like when Anna started writing her name, she started writing some letters backwards, you know.'

Case study 2: Mrs B (African-American, low-income mother of a preschool boy, Bud):

The second case expresses the mutual socioemotional gratification that a caregiver and child experience when engaged in a recurrent helping focused activity. This African American mother who dropped out of school at the end of sixth grade, is talking about her four-year-old son's recurrent activity, which she described as follows in her audio taped diary:

He knew he didn't have to go to school but he got up early today anyway because I had to get up early to get ready for work. And he likes to help me a lot, so he got my little knick knacks together, like my little jewelry, things like that he likes to see me wear, put these all onto the bed.

Interviewer:	How do you think that makes him feel? What do you think it means to him to help you get ready like that?
Mother:	Well, probably I think it makes him feel more like he's the father and I'm the child...
I:	Mhmm...
M:	I never really thought about it, to tell you the truth. It never even came to me about how he felt about doing it. He just had this thing of I don't know, I can't really describe the way I feel about it. It's this thing about he want to be a part of it... He got this father side thing. It's kind of hard for me to explain.
I:	And how does it make you feel when he helps you out, and...?

407

M: It makes me feel good, because a lot of times he surprises me with it because... he just makes me feel like... like not my son, but my friend: he looks out for me, you know? Special it makes me feel special!

The prototypical episode in this case is described in the diary entry that the mother dictated into the tape recorder: 'he likes to help me a lot, so he got my little knick knacks together ... things that he likes to see me wear, put these all onto the bed.' In response to the (avowedly unfamiliar) task demand of a request to explain what it means to the child, she advances a striking simile by way of explanatory schema: 'probably I think it makes him feel more like he's the father and I'm the child,' which she later summarizes as 'He got this father side thing.' In an early report about this phase of the study (Serpell et al 1993) we noted: 'it seems to us significant that, in an earlier interview, this mother had described feelings of jealousy and bafflement about her son's intimate relationship with his father, who was living with them as part of the family. She attributed her unease to the fact that she herself had been raised without a father-figure and that she had raised her elder children without the support of their father, but nevertheless stated that she thought it was a good thing to have both parents around. Thus her choice of simile as an explanatory schema for a highly valued aspect of her relationship with her son is perhaps more than a generically apt symbol. It also resonates with a theme in her own personal life: the nature of paternal nurturance.'

Gallimore et al. (1989) describe several such recurrent, organizing themes in the lives of families raising a developmentally delayed child. How might one seek to validate such an interpretation? One approach is to search for independent evidence pointing in the same direction. Sameroff and Fiese (1992) have proposed that between the level of societal, collective representations and that of individual cognition a 'family code' can often be identified that is shared by members of a family, comprising a set of rituals, routines, and stories. Thus, stories that represent key aspects of a family's shared experience may serve as important points of reference for the understanding of human relationships (Fiese et al. 1999). In the final round of parent interviews of the Baltimore Early Childhood Project, as follows, we advised our informants ahead of time that we would be presenting them with an invitation to share with us some narratives of 'famous family events':

"In many families there are certain events that get talked about over and over again—sometimes the talk is about something that happened to one of the children ... Other times it's about something two or more of you in the family experienced together—something that made you all laugh, or made you scared or sad, or made you all happy. Do you and your children have any family events like that that you often recall?"

Such stories may be regarded as cognitive resources for integrating the diachronic dimension of family culture, interpreting the interactions of personalities, and incorporating anomalous events into a coherent, shared representation.

The following response to our request for family stories by Mrs B seems to provide striking confirmation of our above interpretation of the excerpt from an interview with her that took place three years earlier:

Interviewer:	Do you and your children have any family events like that that you often recall?
Mother:	I was constantly telling Bud about how he used to call his father Mommy.
I:	(to the Focal Child, Bud) Do you remember that story your mom tells you?
M:	He called his father Mommy and didn't call me nothing, He just didn't call me anything. He called his father Mommy though. And he was real, real close to his father. ... He loved to go to work with his father, every morning, six o'clock every single morning.
FC:	I still do that. I still get up at six o'clock.
M:	Every single ... even though his father don't work. But he used to do that.[5]

---

5   The Early Childhood Project research team is conscious of having somewhat neglected the roles and perspectives of fathers in the socialization of the children in our sample. Although we were careful to designate as our preferred informant 'the primary caregiver of the focal child,' in practice the people whom we ended up getting to know and interview over an extended period of time were in all but two cases the child's biological mother. The exceptions, one father and two grandmothers in a sample of 70 families we visited at least six times over a three- to five-year period, illustrate that it is a social rather than a biological relationship that defines this role, but in practice the two were confounded for the majority of cases, reflecting the social reality that the primary caregivers of most children are their biological mothers.

Step 5: Inference and Tentative Formulation of Parental Goals: Negotiating the Middle Ground

From these samples of the caregiver's ideas, as well as a lengthy conversation focused around an ecological inventory of the child's home environment, we inductively extrapolated a tentative formulation of several developmental goals informing the caregiver's approach to child-rearing.

This step of our elicitation procedure may be regarded as the most constructively hermeneutical part of our investigation of caregiver ethnotheories. Each interviewer met with one of the principal investigators of the project to review in detail the caregiver's responses to the first ethnotheory interview. Together they searched the responses for expressions of value by the respondent, and inductively derived a set of implicit socialization goals that appeared to inform the meanings she had imputed to the various recurrent activities in her child's everyday life. For Mrs A (the first case cited above), for instance, the inferred goals were as follows:

	(Rank)	Reliability index	domain (category)
a. learn to take care of things	(4)	perfect consensus	personal (17)
b. use her imagination	(3)	perfect consensus	personal (16)
c. prepare for the future	(7)	3/4 consensus	personal (14)
d. learn to get along with other people	(2)	perfect consensus	social/moral (5)
e. learn to make her own judgements, choices	(5)	semantic match	personal (15)
f. learn about the world and other people*	(1)	perfect consensus	intellectual (20)
g. become independent*	(6)	perfect consensus	personal (18)

Table 3: Inferred parental goals of Mrs. A

Step 6: Negotiated Specification of Socialization Goals

These focused interpretations were presented to the caregiver in a further round of discussion, conducted on the second home visit, and she was invited to reject, reformulate, and/or endorse each of them as one of her goals for her child, and then to add to the list.

The process of negotiating consensus about the definition of her goals for her child often involved the mother citing illustrative examples. Thus, with respect to the goal of 'using imagination', Mrs A. recounted how Anna, faced with a prohibition by their landlord on keeping a cat in the house, had created a fantasy:

"So she imagine it, you know, all her cats, that she has ... She says they're down the basement. You can't see them because they got invisible cages, when you go down there. So, no wonder I haven't seen them ! < laughs > And I hope they don't come out while I'm down there. I might trip on them or something. She said, 'Oh no, you won't never trip on them; they'll never come out when you're down there.' I said, 'Oh, OK' Then, when I'm down there hanging clothes, or something, I'll think 'I thought I heard a cat'. She goes, 'shh ... be quiet, Blackie. Mother can hear you.' ... I say 'OK' ."

Parents also sometimes took this as an opportunity to enunciate an explicit philosophical principle. When she was reminded that she had mentioned it was important that Anna (d) 'learn to get on with other people,' Mrs A. replied:

"Yeah. You see the way I am is ... I think more of other people's feelings than I think of my own. Because I say, well, put myself in their place and see how they would feel ... And I tell Anna, 'if someone's mad or angry at you, just stay away from them—say excuse me, and just get away from them. Or, if they're happy and want to play with you and all, then you, and maybe even if you don't like them, I says you know, 'cause everybody's on this earth to get along together ... no matter who they are or how they look or what they got ...' So I try to teach her that way."

Each caregiver was also encouraged to add goals that they felt were important but had not been identified by the investigator. The parent from Case Study 2, Mrs B, responded to this invitation to expand her representation of goals by sharing her insights about a specific developmental concern. She remarked:

"I think he needs a sense of security all the time and that basically has to come from somebody that he's close to—not somebody that's close to him, somebody that he's close to. (I: right) 'Cause he, he's scared, he's got this: he panics when he thinks he alone, or when he think that person that he's with is gone, you know, he'll cry uncontrollably and you would think somebody like threw him down the steps or something, that really uncontrollable kind of cry that children have when you know somebody that did something wrong. He gets that kind of panicky when he think that the persons that he's with, which is only three people in his entire life, that is me, his father, and his aunt. ... His brother, and he and his brother they real tight, but as far as like grown ups, strangers, family, he don't deal like that. I don't know why. That's the only child I ever had that only dealt with a small amount, other kids deal with my family, he don't, he won't go nowhere..."

Note how this mother highlighted a subtle distinction by careful deployment of very simple vocabulary ("somebody that he's close to"—not "somebody that's close to him"), expressing an insight derived from her reflection on personal experience and pointing towards an elusive dimension of interpersonal relationships that she perceives as having important implications for her family's socialization strategy. Further discussion led to the formulation for this mother of the goal that her son develop a sense of security—an item that had not emerged from the research team's preliminary analysis of the caregiver's diary or her responses during the first ethnotheory interview. When she was asked to place her goals in rank order of importance, this mother ranked the eight goals that she had endorsed as follows:

	(Rank)	Reliability index	Domain (category)
a. Have his own, healthy imagination	(5)	semantic match	personal (16)
b. Learn as much as possible, learn widely	(4)	+ (see note [6])	intellectual (? 29)
c. Feel free to tell when he thinks something is wrong*	(6)	medium consensus	social/moral (4/9)
d. Show that he is looking out for you	(7)	+ (see note 5)	social (? 6)
e. be safe	(3)	semantic match	social (1)
f. Feel his efforts are appreciated*	(8)	perfect consensus	personal (12)
g. be happy, have fun	(1)	semantic match	personal (13)
h. sense of security	(2)	unresolved disssent	pers./social (12/4)

Table 4: Inferred parental goals of Mrs. B

---

6   Our records do not indicate what degree of consensus was achieved for the assignment of this parent's goals b and d to specific categories on the menu, but it is clear that they belong respectively in the intellectual and social domains.

The goals expressed by Mrs A for Anna ranged widely over the domains of social, moral, personal, and intellectual development. When she was asked to place them in rank order of importance, she hesitated at first, then decided to place the intellectual goal 'learn about the world and other people' first, the social/moral goal 'learn to get along with other people' second, and the personal goal 'use her imagination' third. The ranks she assigned to each goal are shown in parentheses to the right of the list. This mother's account of her investment in her daughter's intellectual development at the age of four was phrased in broad terms without explicit reference to mastery of literacy or other, specific academic skills. Some of the other parents in our sample, however, cited as their top socialization goals such outcomes as doing well in school, enjoyment of reading, or motivation to learn.

Socialization goals are part of the middle ground that was negotiated in our ethnotheory interviews. Caregivers described their child's life in terms that made sense to them, and the research team inferred from those descriptions what appeared to us to be socialization goals. We presented our tentative hypotheses to the caregiver and asked whether they were a good match for the world as seen from her perspective. She, in turn, elaborated, corrected, or confirmed our draft list of her goals, prompting us to revise and or extend it. Eventually the two parties reached consensus on a list of goals that the caregiver endorsed as her own.

Condensation and Classification for Purposes of Aggregated Analysis: Establishing Validity and Reliability

The resulting list of endorsed developmental goals (numbering from 4 to 9 for each respondent) became our frame of reference for a subsequent series of questions designed to clarify the caregiver's understanding of child development and socialization. The goals were clustered by the principal investigators into a set of 30 categories, which were classified in turn into a taxonomy of five domains: social, moral, personal, intellectual, and academic (see Table 5). This condensation of the data afforded us several opportunities for further analysis:

- analysis of the distribution of endorsed goals across families with different social addresses;
- examination of the endurance of a caregiver's socialization goals over time; and
- ranking of the full range of goals by each respondent in order of perceived importance, or priority.

413

The outcome of our quantitative research on those issues is reported elsewhere (Serpell, Baker, and Sonnenschein, in preparation). Grouping the goals into domains, however, also raised questions of validity.

In our third round of Ethnotheory Interviews, a menu of goals was presented to the caregiver for ranking. The items on this menu were selected by the principal investigators from the goals endorsed during Ethnotheory Interview #2 in order to represent the full range of caregiver concerns. However, inspection of the full set of 210 'inferred goals' revealed that only about half of them corresponded unambiguously to one of the set of 30 menu items presented in Ethno #3, while 104 of them were not phrased in terms that permitted an *exact semantic match* to one of the items on the menu. A validation analysis was therefore conducted as follows. For this subset of 104 of the total 210 'endorsed goals', the transcript of the Diary, the Ecological inventory, and Ethno #1 were searched for all information relevant to the 'inferred goals' that were proposed to the respondent as: "...things you see as important for your child as s/he is growing up;... goals or hopes that you have for your child." This information was tabulated in summary form next to each of the Ethno #2 'endorsed goals'. Four raters then independently compared each of the Ethno #2 'inferred goals' with the menu of goals presented in Ethno #3 to determine which of the latter set corresponds most closely to the caregiver's intended meaning. These independent determinations were then pooled for comparison, and cases of disagreement were discussed. Various levels of reliability were distinguished among the results of this matching procedure:

- *Perfect*: complete consensus was achieved among the four raters on the best Ethno #3 goal match for 71 out of a total of 104 of the Ethno #2 'endorsed goals'.

  The 33 cases where this highest level of consensus was not achieved by independent rating were reviewed by the four raters as a group. Disagreements were discussed and the grounds for the initial disagreement were categorized in the following manner:
- *High*: three out of the four raters selected the same Ethno #3 goal as the best match in 16 cases.
- *Medium*: In 2 cases, two different Ethno #3 goals were selected, each by two of the independent raters. Review of these initial disagreements revealed that either three or four of the raters had independently acknowledged the other Ethno #3 goal as a plausible match, or this conclusion was reached following discussion, and a consensus was achieved on which of the two Ethno #3 goals was the better match. In the case of Mrs B, for instance, her endorsed goal (c) 'feel free to tell when he thinks something is wrong' was clarified in the

course of the interview as including both the notion of 'being open about his feelings' and that of 'being concerned about acting right'. All of the researchers reviewing this case interpreted this as indicating that the goal in question fell within the Social/Moral domain, but two of them assigned it to category (4) 'form close, trusting relationships,' whereas one assigned it to the category (9) 'learn right from wrong', and one to category (1) 'grow up safely'. The last of these interpretations was withdrawn in the light of discussion, and a consensual decision was reached by the group to treat this goal as case of both categories 4 and 9.

In four cases of this initial type, the review did not generate consensus on which of the two alternative matches was the best, and these cases were classified as 'low in reliability' and grouped with the others of that level described below.

- *Low*: In 11 cases, three or four different Ethno #3 goals were selected as the best match across the four independent raters, and in two cases the review of independent ratings failed to convince the 'odd one out' of the four raters to shift her/his preferred match to that chosen by the other three raters. For instance, Mrs B's endorsed goal (h) sense of security was assigned by two of the raters to the Social domain category (4) 'form close, trusting relationships,' whereas two others assigned it to the Personal domain category (12) 'be sure of himself, know that he has something to contribute'. Two rounds of discussion failed to resolve this disagreement. We decided, therefore, to treat this goal as a case straddling both categories, illustrating, in my view, not so much a lack of clarity or stability in our conceptual distinction between the social/moral and personal domains, but rather that these domains represent complementary facets of the psychological construct of socialization goals.

Matches between the Ethno #2 endorsed goals and the Ethno #3 selected goals were considered to be reliable if they met the criteria for perfect or high reliability as described above. In this way it was determined that 87 or 84% of the matches were reliable.

Our overall assessment of the validity of the goals attributed to our informants was thus based on a mix of independent ratings with discussion and consensus-building. In this respect, we concur with Moss (1994: 5), who argued that 'reliability, as it is typically defined and operationalized in the measurement literature ... privileges standardized forms of assessment,' whereas 'hermeneutic alternatives' may sometimes serve even better the important epistemological and ethical purposes that reliability serves. The hermeneutical traditions of Gadamer and Habermas highlight the power of egalitarian dialogue among knowledgeable interpreters for generating an insightful and illuminating, consensual account of a phenomenon under investigation. In the context of cross-cultural inquiry, such characteristics become extremely relevant to the specification of 'validity' (Serpell 1994).

The results of the investigation described above gave us confidence in the usefulness of caregiver goals established in this way for further analysis of the ways in which the implicit theories or models held by caregivers contribute to the eco-cultural niche of child development. For the subset of 'endorsed goals' investigated (as described above), we were able to document, in the transcripts of earlier interviews, one or more relatively spontaneous allusions by the parent to what was eventually designated as one of her goals. Thus our presentation of 'inferred goals' appears to have either reflected caregiver concerns or stimulated discussion by which her goals were clarified. Our elicitation procedure was designed to a ground caregiver's expression of their implicit theoretical ideas about child development in a discussion of concrete, ostensible activities in their children's everyday lives at home and in the community. Caregiver comments were extracted from these conversations and reflected back to them for further elaboration and explanation, so that our more theoretical conversation with them about their understanding of child development was generated from an analysis of child activities they had directly observed. By the time a menu of goals was presented to the caregivers, they could also see their 'endorsed goals' reflected in the list and they were informed that the menu represented the goals generated by caregivers throughout the six neighborhoods sampled in the study. This served to build a link between the expression of personal beliefs and shared cultural themes. We have described elsewhere the degree to which the socialization goals that we identified in our initial series of interviews (described above) proved to be enduring preoccupations of the parents over the ensuing three or four years of their child's development (Serpell et al. 2005). Meanwhile, for completeness, I have indicated with a star (*) those goals identified for the two cases of Mrs A and Mrs B that remained highly salient for them three years later.

We classified the developmental goals endorsed by the 42 parents in the first wave of participants when the child was in pre-Kindergarten into 30 categories, spread across the following broad domains, for the purpose of exploring each parent's goal hierarchy in the context of a wide range of explicit alternatives.

Social and moral development
1. Grow up safely
2. Stay away from violence
3. Share things with friends
4. Form close trusting relationships
5. Learn to get along with others
6. Be considerate of others
7. Learn how to act in public
8. Learn faith in God
9. Learn right from wrong
10. Learn to be respectful to adults and parents
11. Learn to use good judgement

Personal development
1. Be sure of him- or herself
2. Grow up happy, and enjoy life
3. Get to be what s/he wants
4. Set his or her own goals, and make her own choices
5. Be imaginative, develop his or her imagination
6. Learn to be responsible
7. Become independent

Intellectual and academic development
1. Express him- or herself
2. Learn about the world
3. Develop attention span
4. Learn to plan
5. Learn to do things for him or herself
6. Learn the value of money
7. Learn to read
8. Stay in school, and get an education
9. Learn skills for doing well in school
10. Be persistent, motivated to learn
11. Learn to take responsibility
12. Find pleasure in reading

Table 5: Taxonomy of parental socialization goals identified in the Baltimore Early Childhood Project.

Methodological Reflections

Because of our interest in ensuring that our participants had the opportunity to produce their own formulations, the research team has devoted detailed attention to an examination of the validity and reliability of our elicitation methods. What did we gain by taking so much trouble to ground our data in the everyday lives and discourse of the participating families and communities? Perhaps a greater degree of confidence in the authenticity of the value judgements and interpretations that we attribute to our informants than we could have had if they had responded to pre-structured categories designed by us without such intense engagement with them. One finding that stands out as less likely to have emerged if we had taken less trouble to allow the parents to express their own priorities with minimal constraints is that parental goals more often empha-sized the moral/social and personal domains of development than intel-lectual and academic skills. Many other researchers have proceeded di-rectly to the academic domain in their interviews with parents and have reported that across all socioeconomic and ethnocultural groups in Amer-ica there is a strong consensus among parents on the importance of their child's academic success (e.g., Stevenson and Newman 1986; Okagaki and Sternberg 1993). Our data do not contradict this generalization, but they set the enthusiasm for academic development in a broader context, showing that it is only one of a number of socialization goals held by American parents for their children, and not necessarily the preeminent one, at least in the early phases of the child's development.

In terms of the conceptualization advanced in Table 1, our communi-cation with indigenous informants in the Baltimore study was anchored at one end by our focus on the ostensible referent of the caregiver's own child. Longitudinal study of this focal child's life was the explicit reason for the relationship between the two parties to the interview, the child was known to both of them, and was generally present in the home at the time of the interview. Other members of the family and many of the loca-tions and objects mentioned in the Ecological Inventory were also often ostensible referents in this context, as caregivers would bring out toys, books, or photographs to show the interviewer during the home visits. At the other end, the Diary served to highlight the existence of a recurrent activity structure in the focal child's developmental niche. By inviting the caregiver early in her relationship with the project to fill in the con-crete details of this activity structure, we established as another element of common ground that such a structure exists, and that the caregiver is a definitive authority on what it includes. With these two bridgeheads es-tablished, the interviewer and caregiver were able to explore the more complex intermediary domain of the caregiver's socialization goals for the child and how they are expressed in the child's home life. What emerged from those exploratory conversations was a set of goals grounded in descriptions of concrete everyday activities.

Mapping those socialization goals and other features of the implicit theories of child-rearing that the caregivers articulated for us, onto their social addresses is a topic that goes beyond the scope of the present paper. Suffice it to say that, although we have found some significant differences among the four sociocultural groups, they do not yield an overall picture of a strong correlation between either race or class and the constructs that appear to be influential on the child's rate of early literacy development. Rather than concluding from this that culture is an unimportant factor in literacy development, we argue that race and class are only indirect indicators of the effective culture of literacy socialization. A more appropriate level at which to characterize cultural influences on this domain of psychological development is that of the family. Families have what we term an 'intimate culture', representing a nexus of multiple factors, shared among a particular group of persons, with some endurance over time (Serpell 2001). It is the structure of recurrent activities that constitutes a family's intimate culture and the system of meanings informing them that is shared among the members of a family, and that influences to a significant degree the literacy development of the family's children (Serpell et al. 2005).

Despite our efforts to restrain the dominance of our cultural preconceptions by grounding the investigation in the lived experience of the families, some critics might argue that our research agenda inexorably controlled the process and thus tended to exploit the participants. Compensating participant families for their time with a modest honorarium is clearly an insufficient response to this challenge. In my view, the 'therapeutic' metaphor of Wittgenstein cited by Winch (1958) offers a more responsible avenue of redress. The interview guide for our final interview with parents ended with an invitation for them to tell us about their own expectations of the research. Mrs B replied as follows:

> "The attitude I had about all this in the beginning ... I was curious. I wanted to help ... and if it was gonna help other children, other families; I was more than willing to participate. Well, I learned ... actually I learned a lot out of it.

Interviewer: By thinking about ...

Mother: By me ... and I learned a lot from myself ... 'cause a lot of this are things that I feel, but I don't get to discuss 'cause it's not a lot of people that's interested. You understand? Certain questions that you ask me, and I have to tend to think or I could just come right off the bat, those are questions, those are things that I always knew about me and how I felt about my children. But I never really, actually, heard it until I said it, and the more I say, the more I think, the more I learn on my own about who I am, and how I see things, and myself as a parent or a person, and what I really want for my children."

Later in the same conversation, this articulate mother reflected on what made it possible for the ECP interviews to trigger this type of self-discovery:

"I think y'all really got it put together. The questions that y'all ask are very interesting ... because you really know there's someone out there that really, really cares about the children, and not just the children, the families. You know, it's not just a quiz thing or a survey thing. It's more personal. You know, me and you, me and Jamina (*the first interviewer to establish contact with this family*). It's personal to me. It's a lot of personal stuff in it. But I could never sit down and do this with one of his teachers. I could never do that. I'd never feel comfortable enough to give my opinions or my feelings on a lot of the things that me and you discuss, whether it was on tape or not."

Communication between Parents and Teachers

Over and above any such 'therapeutic' benefits to participating parents, documentation of a family's intimate culture with respect to early childhood socialization may be a valuable resource for those wishing to promote enhanced communication between school teachers and parents. Working with some of the low-income, African-American families participating in the Baltimore Early Childhood Project, as well as a comparison sample of families of children with special educational needs enrolled in separate classes at the same schools, Danseco (1997) developed a method of comparing the independent assessments by teachers and parents of the same individual child's strengths and needs. In addition to conducting an analysis of the degree of congruence between the perceptions of these children's complementary socialization agents, she also asked them directly about the frequency and quality of their communication with one another about the child, and found that they often underestimated the degree of discrepancy between their respective assessments of the child.

We also conducted a small-scale, exploratory intervention project with a sample of pre-K and Kindergarten teachers through whose classes the Early Childhood Project cohort had passed (Serpell et al. 1996). The greatest challenge of this work was to foster a productive integration between the teachers's prior lived experience of communication with their students' families, which had often been quite frustrating, and the research literature on more successful, cooperative forms of teacher-parent communication. A unique contribution to this process was made by Linda Gorham, an experienced preschool teacher who, as a Graduate Research Assistant, had conducted interviews with families of the Early Childhood Project, gaining a strong appreciation for its empathetic perspective on parental ethnotheories, and mastery of the theoretical literature informing this and other cultural studies of early literacy socialization in low-income, urban American families. In the 'instructional conversations' (Tharp and Gallimore 1988) that we held with in-service teachers, the ostensive referents were their actual students, who subsequently became the focus of these teacher-researchers' cooperative communication with the students' families as part of the action-research projects they designed and carried out. While the principal investigators, all university faculty without preschool teaching experience, shared as a horizon with the teachers a general desire to enhance the effectiveness of teacher-parent communication, the negotiation of middle ground in defining and implementing the teacher-research projects was facilitated by the bicultural mediation of Linda Gorham who shared with the teachers one body of knowledge and expertise, grounded in her experience as a practitioner, and shared with the university researchers another, complementary body of concepts grounded in research. Note that the credibility of a bicultural mediator in such discussions arises from the fact that both parties know that she has seen the world from their perspective.

Bicultural mediation is also one of the task demands of basic school teaching in many contemporary African societies, where the culture of institutionalized, public, basic schooling contrasts in conspicuous ways with that of most students' homes (Serpell and Hatano 1997). Reflecting a history of hegemonic imposition by Christian missionaries and colonial governments, the practices of these schools are steeped in Western culture at many levels, including the content of the curriculum, the linguistic medium of instruction, and the organizational pattern of activities in terms of schedules, classrooms, exercises, and texts, etc. The indigenous personnel who now administer this system as teachers face the challenging task, especially in the more elementary grades, of bicultural mediation between the indigenous life-world of their students' home community and the pedagogical agenda of the school (Serpell 1993). One inno-

vative approach to addressing this challenge has been the curricular ideology of Child-to-Child (CtC)—a programmatic orientation with a linked
set of explicit methods addressed to specific goals (Hawes 1988; Pridmore and Stephens 1999). The Participatory Appropriation Project (Serpell and Mwape 1998/9)[7] documented the activities of primary school
teachers in the Mpika district of Zambia applying CtC concepts to integrate science and mathematics with primary health care and growth
monitoring of younger children in the community. The educational goals
of these activities include not only imparting knowledge and intellectual
skills, but also cultivating social and moral dispositions such as a healthy
life-style, social responsibility, cooperation, and nurturance.

Among these, the concept of nurturance is of particular interest because it is highly valued in many indigenous African traditions of child-
rearing (Harkness and Super 1992; Nsamenang 1992; Rabain 1979; Serpell 1992; Weisner 1997; Whittemore and Beverly 1989), but seldom
acknowledged in the educational curriculum of public schooling. One
strand of our research was designed to investigate how parents and
teachers conceptualized the significance of this dimension of human development, and the social distribution of responsibilities for promoting it.

The focus of our questionnaire was to invite teachers already familiar
with CtC to illustrate the construct of nurturance with examples of student behavior they had observed in the context of their professional
work. We also requested them to gauge on numerical scales (a) how important each of several dimensions, including nurturance, is for the development of the whole child, and (b) how essential it is to a teacher's
job to foster each dimension (Serpell and Mwape 1998/99). The behaviors cited by teachers in response to the questionnaire were subsequently
incorporated, essentially in the teachers' own words, in the instructions
for use of a rating scale. In this way, teachers were oriented to the task of
assessing students on this dimension through a framework of ostensible
referents drawn from their own experience and that of their colleagues in
the context of public schooling in Mpika District.

In the case of the parents and other caregivers in children's homes,
we approached the task of grounding the discussion in their own experience somewhat differently (Serpell, in press). Recognizing that many of
them would be insufficiently literate to read a questionnaire, we designed
an oral interview schedule in the local language, Ichi-Bemba. The interviews were conducted by students of the University of Zambia fluent in

---

7   The project 'Participatory appropriation of health science and technol-
    ogy: a case study of innovation in basic education in a rural district of
    Zambia', was supported by a grant to the University of Zambia from the
    Rockefeller Foundation (1995-97), under the auspices of the African Fo-
    rum for Children's Literacy in Science and Technology.

the language, and began by inquiring whether the parent/caregiver was aware of the practice in CtC of assigning responsibility to an older child for the nurturant care of a younger child either in the school or in the child's home neighborhood. Next the caregiver was asked if s/he regarded this as a new concept or an old one; whether it was something s/he remembered from her own upbringing as a child, at home and/or at school; and whether it was something that s/he currently practices as a parent. The 30 primary caregivers of pupils enrolled in two CtC classes who were interviewed in their homes were virtually unanimous in declaring that the concept was an old one, which they had experienced themselves as part of their own upbringing at home, and which they currently practiced as a parent. However, only about half of them recalled such practices being part of their own childhood experience at school, and many expressed some surprise on being informed that it was part of the CtC curriculum at their child's school. Almost all of them, however, expressed approval of this practice.

The interview went on to inquire about what benefits, if any, these parents believed would accrue to the older child from participation in such nurturant relationships. Responses to this question included both cognitive and behavioral outcomes, such as growth of a kindly, caring attitude (known in the Bemba language as *icikuku*), growth of a sense of responsibility, increasing competence with child care, preparation for parenthood, acquisition of practical knowledge, and more subjective experiences, such as gratification and pride from observing the younger child's cooperative response to nurturance, sense of virtue for doing good, respect from the younger child, and gratitude for the care s/he received from others when young, intrinsic gratification, or simply that this is a duty, part of growing up, something the older child needs to learn.

In deciding to interview the teachers in English and the parents in Bemba, we were guided by more than the simple criterion of English competence. Public school teachers in Zambia are required to work in the medium of English, it was therefore highly appropriate to invite them to cite examples in that language of what they had observed in the context of their professional interactions with students. For the parents, on the other hand, even though many of them were fluent in English, there was a cultural reason to pose our questions in the medium of Ichi-Bemba. We were asking them to think back to their own childhood experience as well as reflect on their current practices within their own homes. As Fishman (1967) has observed, in many postcolonial states, language use is stratified in a fashion resembling Ferguson's (1959) account of 'diglossia': the language of the former colonial administration is superposed as a 'high' code, functionally specialized for the public domains of law and government, over the indigenous language or languages, which remain the preferred medium of expression for socioemotionally important functions, thus not just a 'low' prestige code, but also the treasured 'language of hearth and home'. This sociolinguistic analysis may be complemented by a cultural, developmental account of the contexts in which individuals acquire their competence in one or more cultures. Insights about intimate subjects such as the subjective benefits to be derived from engaging in nurturant behavior may remain more accessible in the language of hearth and home, even after a second (or third, etc.) language has been acquired to the point where it has become one's dominant language. Thus, even a more highly educated sample of Zambian parents, although fluent in English, would probably have found it easier to express their opinions on such matters in an indigenous language.

Understanding, on the one hand, how teachers operationalize the ideological construct of nurturance in their observation and evaluation of their students, and, on the other hand, the various benefits perceived by parents of their children's taking on nurturant responsibilities provides a basis for 'building bridges' between these two groups of adults responsible for the upbringing of children (Danseco 1997). This kind of applied research deploys cultural psychology to facilitate a process of cooperative communication between children's families and their schools, exploring areas of consensus and disagreement, as a basis on which to promote local accountability of public educational institutions (Serpell 1999b). Rather than focusing only on incongruities between the cultures of home and school, it seeks to enhance the quality of mutual understanding among parents and teachers, and to generate a socioculturally productive relationship between public education and the community it is mandated to serve (Serpell 1997).

The Complementarity of Perspectives

I have described multiple types and levels of dialogue across the different studies reviewed in this paper. One of the defining properties they have in common is uncertainty about what elements of a complex topic can be taken for granted as shared, which are construed by the vying parties as incommensurably different, and which are open to the possibility of negotiated mutual understanding, if not necessarily complete consensus. I have suggested that a way forward may be to identify ostensible referents on the one hand and shared horizons on the other, as a way of anchoring the process of negotiation that must take place in the middle ground. The outcome of such negotiation is likely to be acceptance of a pattern of complementary perspectives based on mutual respect, rather than homogenization. This is consistent with a pluralistic approach to public policy in culturally diverse societies.

My analysis also favors a gradualist approach to international cross-cultural communication among sociocultural researchers. The accessibility of quantitative data analytic methods in the form of packaged computer software tends to promote a homogenizing pattern of research design, which as Cherns (1984) noted, may easily pass the filter of political monitors, because the software is increasingly buried in the hardware under the rubric of 'user-friendliness'. Yet, such 'uncovenanted cultural transmission' may eventually backfire by generating local resistance to culturally insensitive innovations. Given the complexity of the issues involved in negotiating mutual understanding across cultural boundaries, qualitative methods are probably better suited as an entry-point for egalitarian, cross-cultural discourse among researchers (Serpell and Akkari 2001).

Many of the growing number of active researchers in cultural psychology from Third World countries received their primary socialization in the medium of a language other than the one in which they now write and publish their findings, placing them in a privileged strategic position to act as bicultural mediators. As they draw on their dual cultural heritage to interpret the psychological phenomena they investigate, it may be that what they saw through the lens of their childhood language is more difficult to overlook than what they did not see. Referring to the schema in Figure 1, even if observer B goes on to learn the language of observer A, she will never forget that she saw from standpoint B how the path goes between the house and the tree, but she may have more difficulty remembering that the sack she now knows all about from standpoint A was quite simply invisible from standpoint B. The degree to which bicultural/bilingual interpreters conceive of their conceptual repertoire as integrated or compartmentalized is probably determined less by any objective characteristics of the two representational systems they compare than by the interpreter's experience of trying to build bridges between them. For, although we do inhabit one physical world, the counterparts to sacks and paths in our social world, constructs such as *nzelu*, intelligence, *icikuku* and nurturance are, as Taylor (1971) observed, 'grounded in the shape of social practice,' and thus constitutive of the very world we live in, which would not make sense without them.

References

Adamson-Holley, D. (1999). Personal Dimensions and their Relation to Education: a Follow-Up Study of Students Graduating from the Child-to-Child Program in Mpika, Zambia. Baltimore, MD: Unpublished PhD dissertation, University of Maryland Baltimore County.

Akkari, A./Serpell, R./Baker, L./Sonnenschein, S. (1998). An Analysis of Teacher Ethnotheories. In: The Professional Educator, 21, 45-61.

Azuma, H. (1984). Psychology in a Non-Western Country. In: International Journal of Psychology, 19, 45-55.

Azuma, H. (1994). Two Modes of Cognitive Socialization in Japan and in the United States. In: P.M. Greenfield/R.R. Cocking (Eds.). Cross-Cultural Roots of Minority Child Development (pp. 275-284). Hillsdale, NJ: Erlbaum.

Baine, D. (1988). Handicapped Children in Developing Countries: Assessment, Curriculum, and Instruction. Edmonton, Alberta: University of Alberta Press.

Barfield, O. (1947). Poetic Diction and Legal Fiction. In: M. Black (Ed.). The Importance of Language. Englewood Cliffs, NJ: Prentice-Hall.

Berry, J.W. (1969). On Cross-Cultural Comparability. In: International Journal of Psychology, 4, 119-128.

Berry, J.W./Poortinga, Y.H./Segall, M.H./Dasen, P.R. (1992). Cross-Cultural Psychology: Research and Applications. Cambridge University Press.

Boyd, R. (1979). Metaphor and Theory Change: What is 'Metaphor', a Metaphor for? In: A. Ortony (Ed.). Metaphor and Thought (pp. 356-408). Cambridge University Press.

Boykin, A.W. (1983). The Academic Performance of Afro-American Children. In: J. Spence (Ed.). Achievement and Achievement Motives. San Francisco: W. Freeman.

Bronfenbrenner, U./Crouter, A.C. (1983). The Evolution of Environmental Models in Developmental Research. In: W. Kessen (Ed.). History, Theory and Methods, Vol. I, Handbook of Child Psychology. New York: Wiley.

Chao, R.K. (1994). Beyond Parental Control and Authoritarian Parenting Style: Understanding Chinese Parenting through the Cultural Notion of Training. In: Child Development, 65, 1111-1119.

Cherns, A. (1984). Contribution to Social Psychology to the Nature and Function of Work an its Relevance to Societies of the Third World, In: International Journal of Psychology, 19, 97-111.

Danseco, E.R. (1997). Building Bridges: African-American Mothers' and Teachers' Ethnotheories on Child Development, Child Problems, and

Home School Relations for Children with and without Disabilities. Ph.D., University of Maryland Baltimore County.

Doi, T. (1971). The Anatomy of Dependence. New York: Kodansha International.

Eliot, T.S. (1950). Selected Essays. New York: Harcourt Brace.

Enriquez, V.G. (1994). Pagbabangong Dangal: Indigenous Psychology & Cultural Empowerment. Quezon City, Philippines: Akademya ng Sikolohiya at Kulturang Pilipino.

Enriquez, V.G./Protacio-Marcellino, E. (1984). Neo-colonial Politics and Language Struggle in the Philippines: National Consciousness and Language in Philippine Psychology. Quezon City, Philippines: Akademya Ng Sikolohiyang Pilipino.

Ferguson, G.A. (1959). Diglossia. Word, 15, 325-340.

Fishman, J.A. (1967). Bilingualism with and without Diglossia; Diglossia with and without Bilingualism. Journal of Social Issues, 23 (2), 29-38.

Gadamer, H. G. (1965). Truth and Method. London: Sheed & Ward.

Gallimore, R./Weisner, T.S./Kaufman, S.Z./Berneheimer, L.P.(1989). The Social Construction of Ecocultural Niches: Family Accomodation of Developmentally Delayed Children. In: American Journal on Mental Retardation, Vol. 94, 3, 216-230.

Gombrich, E. H. (1960). Art and Illusion. London: Phaidon.

Harkness, S./Super, C.M. (1992a). Parental Ethnotheories in Action. In: E.E. Sigel/A.V. McGillicuddy-DeLisi/J.J. Goodnow (Eds.). Parental Belief Systems: The Psychological Consequences for Children (pp. 373-391). 2nd Ed. Hillsdale, NJ: Erlbaum.

Harkness, S./Super, C.M. (1992b). Shared Child Care in East Africa: Sociocultural Origins and Developmental Consequences. In: M.E. Lamb, K.J. Sternberg/C.P. Hwang/A. Broberg (Eds.). Child Care in Context. Hillsdale, NJ: Erlbaum.

Hawes, H. (1988). Child-to-Child: Another Path to Learning. Hamburg, Germany: UNESCO Institute for Education.

Headland, T.N./Pike, K.L./ Harris, M. (1990) (Eds.). Emics and Etics: the Insider/Outsider Debate. Newbury Park: Sage.

Horton, R. (1982). Tradition and Modernity Revisited. In: M. Hollis/ S. Lukes (Eds): Rationality and Relativism. Oxford: Blackwell

Jahoda, G. (1977). In Pursuit of the Emic-Etic Distinction: Can we ever Capture it? In: Y.H. Poortinga (Ed.). Basic Problems in Cross-Cultural Psychology. Lisse, Netherlands: Swets & Zeitlinger.

Jahoda, G. (1983). The Cross-Cultural Emperor's Conceptual Clothes: the Emic-Etic Issue Revisited. In: J.B. Deregowski/S. Dzurawiecz/R.C. Annis (Eds.).Expiscations in Cross-Cultural Psychology. Lisse, Netherlands: Swets & Zeitlinger.

Kagitcibasi, C. (1992). Linking the Indigenous and Universtalist Orientations. In: S. Iwawaki et al. (Eds.). Innovations in Cross-Cultural Psychology. Selected papers from the 10th International Confrence of the International Association for Cross-Cultural Psychology held at Nara, Japan (pp. 29-37). Amsterdamm: Swest/Zeitlinger.

Lakoff, G./Johnson, M. (1980). Metaphors we Live by. Chicago University Press.

Lebra, T.S. (1994). Mother and Child in Japanese Socialization: a Japan-US Comparison. In: P.M. Greenfield/R.R. Cocking (Eds.).Cross-Cultural Roots of Minority Child Development (pp. 259-274). Hillsdale, NJ: Erlbaum.

Lightfoot, C./Valsiner, J. (1992). Parental Belief Systems under the Influence: Social Guidance of the Construction of Personal Cultures. In: I.E. Sigel/A.V. McGillicuddy-DeLisi/J.J. Goodnow (Eds.). Parental Belief Systems: The Psychological Consequences for Children (pp. 393-414). 2nd Ed. Hillsdale, NJ: Erlbaum.

Lincoln, Y.S./Guba, E.G. (1985). Naturalistic Inquiry. Beverly Hills CA: Serge.

McCarthy, T. (1978). The Critical Theory of Jürgen Habermas. London: Hutchinson.

Morelli, G.A./Rogoff, B./Oppenheim, D./Goldsmith, D. (1992). Cultural Variation in Infants' Sleeping Arrangements: Questions of Independence. In: Developmental Psychology, 28, 604-613.

Moss, P.A. (1994). Can There be Validity without Reliability? In: Educational Researcher, March 1994, 5-12.

Mumba, P. (1996). Democratisation of Primary Classrooms in Zambia: A Case Study of its Implementation in a Rural Primary School of Mpika. Mimeographed MS (Kabale Primary School, P.O.Box T144, Mpika, N.Prov. Zambia).

Mwape, G./Serpell, R. (1996). Participatory Appropriation of Health Science by Primary School Students in Rural Zambia. Poster Presentation at the International Conference of the International Society for the Study of Behavioural Development (ISSBD): Quebec, Canada: August 1996.

Nsamenang, A.B. (1992). Early Childhood Care and Education in Cameroon. In: M.E. Lamb/K.J. Sternberg/C.P. Hwang/A. Broberg (Eds.). Child Care in Context. Hillsdale, NJ: Erlbaum.

Okagaki, L./Sternberg, R. J. (1993). Parental beliefs and children's school performance. Child Development, 64, 36-56.

Palacios, J. (1990). Parents' Ideas about the Development and Education of Their Children. Answers to Some Questions. In: International Journal of Behavioural Development, 13, 137-155.

Pe-Pua, R. (1998). Paper Presented at the IACCP Congress, Bellingham, WA: July 1998.

Pike, K.L. (1954). Emic and Etic Standpoints for the Description of Behavior. In: K.L. Pike (Ed.). Language in Relation to a Unified Theory of the Structure of Human Behavior. Glendale: Summer Institute of Linguistics. 8-28.

Pike, K.L. (1967). Language in Relation to a Unified Theory of the Structure of Human Behavior. The Hague: Mouton.

Pridmore, P./Stephens, D. (1999). Children as Partners for Health: a Critical Review of the Child-to-Child Approach. London: Zed Press.

Pylyshyn, Z.W. (1979) Metaphorical Imprecision and the 'top-down' Research Strategy. In: A. Ortony (Ed.). Metaphor and Thought (pp. 420-436). Cambridge University Press.

Quinn, N./Holland, D. (1987). Culture and Cognition. In: D. Holland/N. Quinn (Eds.). Cultural Models in Language and Thought (pp. 3-40). Cambridge: Cambridge University Press.

Rabain, J. (1979). L'enfant du lignage. Paris: Payot.

Rodrigo, M.J./Triana, B. (1996). Parental Beliefs about Child Development and Parental Inferences about Actions during Child-Rearing Episodes. In: European Journal of Educational Psychology, 11, 1, 55-78.

Sameroff, A..J./Feil, L.A. (1985). Parental Concepts of Development. In: I. Sigel (Ed.). Parental Belief Systems: The Psychological Consequences for Children. Hillsdale, NJ: Erlbaum.

Sameroff, A.J./Fiese, (1992). Family Representations of Development. In: I.E. Sigel/A.V. Mcgillicuddy-DeLisi/J.J. Goodnow (Eds.). Parental Belief Systems: The Psychological Consequences for Children (pp. 347-369). 2nd Ed. Hillsdale, NJ: Erlbaum.

Serpell, R. (1974). Estimates of Intelligence in a Rural Community of Eastern Zambia. Human Development Research Unit Reports, 25. Lusaka, Zambia: University of Zambia (mimeo). Reprinted in F.M.Okatcha (Ed.) (1977): Modern Psychology and Cultural Adaptation (pp.179-216). Nairobi: Swahili Language Consultants and Publishers.

Serpell, R. (1982). Measures of Perception, Skills, and Intelligence: The Growth of a new Perspective on Children in a Third World Country. In: W.W. Hartup (Ed.). Review of Child Development Research, Vol. 6 (pp. 392-440). Chicago: University of Chicago Press.

Serpell, R. (1989). Dimensions endogenes de l'intelligence chez les A Chewa et autres peuples Africains. In: J. Retschitzki/M. Bossel Lagos/P. Dasen (Eds): La recherche interculturelle, Tome II (pp. 164-179). Paris, France: Editions l'Harmattan.

Serpell, R. (1990). Audience, Culture and Psychological Explanation: a Reformulation of the Emic-Etic Problem in Cross-Cultural Psychology. In: Quarterly Newsletter of the Laboratory Comparative Human Cognition, 12 (3), 99-132.

Serpell, R. (1992). African dimensions of child care and nurturance. In: M.E. Lamb/K.J. Sternberg/C.P. Hwang/A. Broberg (Eds.).Child care in context. Hillsdale, NJ: Erlbaum.

Serpell, R. (1993). The Significance of Schooling: Life Journeys in an African Society. Cambridge: Cambridge University Press.

Serpell, R. (1994). Negotiating a Fusion of Horizons: a Process View of Cultural Validation in Developmental Psychology. In: Mind, Culture and Activity, 1, 43-68.

Serpell, R. (1996). Cultural Models in Indigenous Socialization, and Formal Schooling in Zambia. In: C.-P. Hwang/M.E. Lamb/I. Sigel (Eds.). Images of Childhood (pp. 129-142). Hillsdale, NJ: Erlbaum.

Serpell, R. (1997). Literacy Connections Between School and Home: How Should we Evaluate Them? In: Journal of Literacy Research, 29 (4), 587-616.

Serpell, R. (1998). Participatory Appropriation in Sociocultural Context: a Multi Level Strategy for Applied Developmental Science. Keynote Address to the 4th Regional African Workshop of the International Society for the Study of Behavioural Development (ISSBD). Windhoek, Namibia: July 1998.

Serpell, R. (1999a). Theoretical Conceptions of Human Development. In: L. Eldering/P. Leseman (Eds.).Effective early intervention: cross-cultural perspectives (pp. 41-66). New York: Falmer.

Serpell, R. (1999b). Local Accountability to Rural Communities: a Challenge for Educational Planning in Africa. In: F. Leach/A. Little (Eds.). Education, Cultures and Economics: Dilemmas for Development (pp. 107 135). New York: Garland.

Serpell, R. (2001). Cultural Dimensions of Literacy Promotion and Schooling. In: L. Verhoeven/C. Snow (Eds.). Literacy and Motivation (pp. 243-273). Mahwah, NJ: Erlbaum.

Serpell, R./Akkari, A. (2001). Qualitative Approaches to Cultural Psychology: A Point of Entry for Egalitarian Cross-Cultural Communication among Researchers. In: M. Lahlou/G. Vinsonneau (Eds.). La psychologie au regard des contacts de cultures (pp. 65-85). Limonest, France: l'Interdisciplinaire.

Serpell, R./Baker, L./Sonnenschein, S. (2005). Becoming Literate in the City: the Baltimore Early Childhood Project. New York, NY and Cambridge, UK: Cambridge University Press.

Serpell, R./Baker, L./Sonnenschein, S./Hill, S. (1993). Contexts for the Early Appropriation of Literacy: Caregiver Meanings of Recurrent Activities. Paper presented in the Symposium on learning and development in cultural context, at the Conference of the American Psychological Society. Chicago, IL: June 1993.

Serpell, R./Baker, L./Sonnenschein, S./Gorham, L./Hill, S./Britt, G./Butler, B./Guelta, J./Holmes, D. (1996). Cooperative Communication among Teachers and Parents about the Emergence of Literacy in Sociocultural Context. Final Project Report to the National Reading Research Center (University of Georgia, University of Maryland College Park). (ERIC document)

Serpell, R./Hatano, G. (1997). Education, Literacy and Schooling in Cross-Cultural Perspective. In: J.W. Berry/P.R. Dasen/T.M. Saraswathi (Eds.).Handbook of Cross-Cultural Psychology (pp. 345-382). 2nd Ed. Volume 2. Boston, MA: Allyn & Bacon.

Serpell, R./Mwape, G. (1998/99). Participatory Appropriation of Health Science and Technology: A Case Study of Innovation in Basic Education in a Rural District of Zambia. In: African Social Research, 41/42, 60 89.

Shweder et al. (1995). Who Sleeps with Whom? In: J.J. Goodnow/P. Miller,/F. Kessel (Eds.).Cultural Practices as Contexts for Development. San Francisco: Jossey-Bass.

Sonnenschein, S./Baker, L./Serpell, R. (1995). Documenting the Child's Everyday Home Experiences: The Ecological Inventory as a Resource for Teachers. (NRRC Instructional resource No.11). National Reading Research Center, Universities of Georgia and Maryland.

Spiro, M. (1990). On the Strange and the Familiar in Recent Anthropological thought. In: In J.W. Stigler/R.A. Shweder/G. Herdt (Eds.). Cultural Psychology (pp. 47-61). Cambridge: Cambridge University Press.

Stevenson, H./Newman, R. (1986). Long-Term Prediction of Achievement and Attitudes in Mathematics and Reading. In: Child Development, 57, 646-659.

Stigler, J.W./Perry, M. (1990) Mathematics Learning in Japanee, Chinese, and American Classrooms. In: J.W. Stigler/R.A. Shweder/G. Herdt (Eds.). Cultural Psychology (pp. 328-353). Cambridge: Cambridge University Press.

Straub, J. (2001). Psychology, Culture and the Methodology of Cultural and Cross-Cultural Studies: A Topography of the Problem Field. Paper presented at the International Conference on Cultural and Cross-Cultural psychology: methodological controversies and alternatives. Essen, Germany: Kulturwissenschaftliches Institut, May 2001.

Taylor, C. (1971). Interpretation and the Sciences of Man. In: Review of Metaphysics, 25, 3-51.

Tharp, R./Gallimore, R. (1988). Rousing Minds to Life: Teaching, Learning, and Schooling in Social Context. Cambridge: Cambridge University Press.

Tobin, J.J./Wu, D./Davidson, D.H. (1989). Preschool in Three Cultures: Japan, China, and the United States. New Haven, CT: Yale University Press.

Trevarthen, C. (1980). The Foundations of Intersubjectivity: Development of Interpersonal and Cooperative Understanding in Infants. In: D.R. Olson (Ed.). The Social Foundations of Language and Thought: Essays in Honor of Jerome S. Bruner (pp. 316-342). New York: Norton.

Triandis, H.C. (1972). The Analysis of Subjective Culture. New York: Wiley.

Udell, C. (2001). Educational Innovation: A Case Study of Child-to-Child in Zambia. Baltimore, MD: Unpublished Masters thesis, University of Maryland Baltimore County.

Vygotsky, L.S. (1978). Mind in Society: The Development of Higher Psychological Processes. (Edited by M. Cole/V. John Steiner/S. Scribner/E. Souberman.) Cambridge: Harvard University Press.

Weisner, T.S. (1997). Support for Children and the African Family Crisis. In: T.S. Weisner/C. Bradley/P.L. Kilbride (Eds.). African Families and the Crisis of Social Change (pp. 20-44). Westport, CT: Bergin & Garvey.

Wertsch, J.V. (1991). Voices of the Mind. Cambridge, MA: Harvard University Press.

Whiting, B.B. (1963). Six Cultures. Studies of Child Rearing. New York, London: John Wiley & Sons.

Whiting, B.B./Whiting, J.W.M. (1975). Children of Six Cultures. A Psycho-Cultural Analysis. Cambridge, MA: Harvard University Press.

Whittemore, R.D./Beverly, E. (1989). Trust in the Mandinka Way: The Cultural Context of Sibling Care. In: P. Zukow (Ed.). Sibling Interaction Across Cultures: Theoretical and Methodological Issues (pp. 26-53). New York: Springer.

Wilson, W.J. (1990). The Truly Disadvantaged: The Inner City, the Underclass, and Public Policy. Chicago: Chicago University Press.

Winch, P. (1958). The Idea of a Social Science and its Relation to Philosophy. London: Routledge & Kegan Paul.

Wittgenstein, L. (1958). Philosophical Investigations. Oxford: Blackwell.

Wood, D./Bruner, J.S./Ross, G. (1976). The Role of Tutoring in Problem-Solving. In: Journal of Child Psychology and Psychiatry, 17, 89-100

ETHNIC SELF-UNDERSTANDING: ETHNIC CULTURAL PSYCHOLOGY AS AN ACTION TOWARD CULTURE AND ETHNICITY

WEI-LUN LEE

Introductory Background Discussion

The carrying out of studies concerning culture and ethnicity as a kind of action has become an issue in cultural and cross-cultural psychology, especially when considered in a multicultural and multiethnic environment, either within a society itself or in the context of globalization. As culture and ethnicity are no longer viewed as stable constructions that remain unchanged over time, and as researchers try to go beyond the methods of simply identifying and measuring the components of cultural and ethnic phenomena in order to see their interrelationship or compare them across different ethnic groups, reflections on defining the primary phenomena of investigation and searches for alternatives in methodology are undertaken in order to obtain a proper research action (or process) to the psychological phenomena concerning culture and ethnicity. This issue of research as action is particularly significant for a researcher like me, someone committed to the psychology of culture and ethnicity while situated in the multiethnic society of Taiwan, which is simultaneously a marginal country in the network of globalization. In light of this position, I am interested in the following questions: What is the nature of 'ethnicity', and accordingly, 'ethnic culture', in the context of globalization? How do researchers, with their particular cultural and ethnic involvements, relate themselves to the ethnic cultural phenomena under investigation? And, what is the proper approach for such inquiries?

From what I have observed in the field of psychology concerning issues of culture and ethnicity, several trends (or patterns) of reflection exist—though each with their own emphases—that attempt to answer the above questions regarding the issue of the research action dimension. These trends can be characterized as pointing in at least three different directions. The first trend is directed toward reconceptualizing the concepts of culture and ethnicity, and understands that a proper grasp of them can lead to a proper grasp of the research approach taken toward them. The second one is directed toward the researcher's own relationship to culture and ethnicity and recognizes the impact of individual cultural and ethnic background on the research process. This type of reflection suggests several methodological guidelines for minimizing cultural bias toward the research phenomena. The third trend is directed toward the action of studying culture and ethnicity in the context of power structures, and understands that this kind of study is itself a social action that will inevitably contribute to ethnic interaction in the larger society. Each of these approaches has made advances in this field of study, and each of them has, in turn, pointed to an additional challenge presented by the research action dimension of studies concerning culture and ethnicity. Before proposing my own alternative to this issue, I will provide a brief discussion of the three patterns of reflection, which will also serve as the backdrop for the significance of the approach I intend to introduce.

Reflections on the Conceptualization of Culture and Ethnicity

The first type of reflection delves into a metatheoretical examination of the conceptualizations of culture and ethnicity. The result of this examination suggests that some of the difficulties found in the current study of ethnicity may be due to a conceptual misusage. Howard (1991) pointed out that race, culture, and ethnicity are 'social categories' employed by people to understand themselves and others, and to generate action in everyday life. They are parts of the 'story' people tell about themselves and others and therefore, are discursive in nature. Torres and Ngin (1995) further pointed out that these discursive categories have been turned into 'analytical categories' in the process of 'racialization'. Therefore, the transformation of discursive categories into analytical categories contains logical and empirical pitfalls for research; for example, falsely assuming that people named under a single ethnicity are the same, without recognizing the heterogeneity within ethnic groups.

Weinreich focused particularly on the misconceptualization aspect in the study of ethnic identity, and proposed an alternative framework for such studies. In Weinreich's framework, "people's ethnic identity is not a *thing*. Rather it is itself a complex of processes by means of which people construct and reconstruct their ethnicity" (1988: 150). This complex of processes is thus reconceptualized with inspirations from the social anthropological perspective, social symbolic interactionists, Erikson's psychodynamics, personal construct theory, and cognitive-affective consistency theory, and presents itself as a contextualized, interactive, constructive, and affective phenomenon. Weinreich accordingly provided several theoretical postulates concerning conflicted identification, resolution of conflicted identification, formation of new identification, and the use of personal constructs in order to help "the investigator to generate theoretical propositions about the sociopsychological processes of identity development in the sociohistorical and biographical context under investigation" (1988: 162).

The same effort toward the conceptualization of culture and ethnicity can also be found in the works of Ratner (1996, 1999, and 2000). Ratner proposed a theory for conducting psychological studies concerning culture and ethnicity that looks at people's activities. In his view, "the central principle of a revised cultural psychology is that psychological functions are formed as individuals engage in practical social activities" (1996: 411). This emphasis on activity, therefore, turns the primary phenomena of investigation from mental processes to social activities. Through an integrative articulation of the relationship between psychological phenomena and social activity, this activity-based approach provides proper guidance for choosing the primary phenomena of investigation, characterizing their interrelated aspects, and uncovering the interaction among these aspects.

By reflecting on the conceptualizations of culture and ethnicity, the works described above do provide modifications for carrying out studies of cultural and ethnic psychology. The recognition of culture and ethnicity as being embedded in social activities or processes in which people live their lives, however, may imply a deeper impact on cultural and ethnic psychology than researchers would expect. If culture and ethnicity are not stable constructions, but rather pervade human activities and processes, are studies concerning culture and ethnicity themselves cultural and ethnic activities/processes? If the answer is yes, how should they be carried out and what is the meaning of such practice? These questions point to a further challenge, which will be the main issue of the following discussion.

Reflections on the Cultural and Ethnic Impact on the Research Process

The second pattern of reflection discussed here may be called a metamethodological one because the researchers are not only aware that culture impacts psychological phenomena, but also that "culture intersects the research process" (Hughes et al. 1993). The researchers in this trend of thought have proposed several changes in the formation of a research project in order to incorporate cultural factors, minimize cultural biases, and enhance research credibility. For example, Sue (1991) proposed a 'parallel research design' in which researchers are asked to articulate two 'conceptual frameworks' for understanding the target phenomenon, one based on the dominant group's viewpoint and the other reflecting the perspective of the ethnic minority. Some researchers (Hughes et al. 1993; Sasao and Sue 1993) have reflected on the process of research and suggested a systematic examination of the decisions made at each of the major research steps. Putting their suggestions together for developing a "culturally anchored methodology", they propose that researchers should—in their research design—deal with issues such as question formation, ethnic-cultural group identification, the choice of methodology, and data analyses and interpretation.

One particular topic that is closely related to the issue of the cultural impact on the researchers' carrying out their researches is the topic of etic and emic dimensions. Although Sue warned that "in ethnic minority issues, we need to recognize that some standards or criteria assumed to be universal (etics) are actually specific (emics) to mainstream American society" (1991: 74), he nevertheless suggested that both emic and etic perspectives have their own validity and should both be preserved in a manner of 'coexistence'. Hughes et al. (1993) related emic assertions to a qualitative method and etic to a quantitative, and thus brought the dispute down to a choice of methodology. However, the opposition between emics and etics is not just a matter of choice, and it may not be dismissed by this 'adding together' approach alone.

This paradoxical pair of emics and etics, nevertheless, illustrates the contradiction among the guidelines suggested in the foregoing metamethodological reflections. The consequence of the statement "culture intersects the research process" may be way beyond, or even against, some of these guidelines. The understanding that culture provides the 'blueprints' of our every behavior (emic perspective) in fact undermines the possibility of handling cultural influence in the research process (etic intention). That is, are the research questions not identified by certain conceptualizations that only represent a cultural view of how problems should be solved? Are not the data and results, through quantitative measurement and statistical analyses, to be filtered through a certain cultural perspective on how knowledge should be obtained? After all, how can we be certain that the whole idea of research and the research process is not simply a cultural construct that is unsuitable for application to people from other ethnic cultures? These questions all point to an inescapable cultural context, and the final conclusion seems to be an extreme cultural relativism wherein no understanding of other cultures is possible. However, in everyday life, no matter how frustrating it is, we do experi-

ence valid communication with people from different cultures. Therefore, a metamethodological approach to the study of culture and ethnicity
would only be a partial approach if it just tries to add on the control of
cultural influence to traditional research principles. A complete reflection
on cultural influence on research must deal with the issue of *action for
communication.*

Reflections on the Power Issues
Related to Culture and Ethnicity

Finally, the third type of reflection points to an understanding that insists
that the structure of power is the most important single factor behind the
various issues of the research action concerning culture and ethnicity.
This statement differs from the foregoing reflections in several ways.
First, the authors possessing this perspective usually explicitly express
their stance of being sympathetic to ethnic minorities or non-dominant
cultures. Their critiques are, thus, mostly aimed at the majority/dominant
group's control over the value- and knowledge-making process, including that of psychological research. Second, they emphasize the stressful,
even traumatic, experiences of ethnic minorities and non-dominant cultures, both in past and present, as the result of external colonialism and
internal colonialism. The efforts by ethnic minorities or non-dominant
cultures to resolve such problems are thus characterized as 'decolonization' (Blauner 1987; Darder 1995). This emphasis is, then, not just another research topic on ethnicity, but a powerful social and political discourse in itself that legitimates the authors' standpoint.

And third, this perspective radically challenges the political dimension; that is, the dimension concerning the production of psychological
knowledge within sociopolitical processes and its effect on psychological
research on culture and ethnicity. As Van Dijk has pointed out, academic
scholars, as social elites, are not only influenced by, but also contribute
to, the prevalence of power structures in ethnic relations. They do this
not only by an open support or defense of certain perspectives, but also
by the implication of ethnocentric ideology "under the surface of sometimes sophisticated scholarly analysis and description of other races,
peoples, or groups" (1993: 160). Accordingly, "if knowledge is power,
then knowledge of other people may be an instrument of power over
other people" (1993: 158). This challenge is one that psychologists cannot avoid because it not only questions the methodological or theoretical
issues of psychological research, but the credibility of psychology as a
social enterprise. In the search for a better approach to carrying out stud-

ies concerning culture and ethnicity, this perspective on power structures should receive appropriate consideration.

A radical reflection on power issues in psychological research has been provided by Sampson (1993). Sampson criticized the common strategy of 'adding on' in psychological research as a response to the challenges and demands of minority or non-dominant groups. As minority groups try to raise their own voices in the psychological domain, the dominant approach responds only by granting them a seat at its table, as if this move will result in a full representation of minority perspectives. With this arrangement, the voices of minority groups can be heard only by speaking as the dominant perspective expects them to, rather than speaking as themselves. The result of this 'adding on' strategy is, therefore, that the dominant point of view is saved from change and the special interest which it is accorded is preserved. Furthermore, potential damage may be done to minority groups since their efforts to raise their voices become distorted: that is, from initially seeking transformation of the dominant framework in psychology to asking permission for representation.

A discursive framework is thus suggested by Sampson (1993) so as to replace the 'adding on' approach as a response to this problem of power structures in psychological research. The discursive framework sees human realities as constituted through human discourse. People all live in a meaningful surrounding that is shaped, and continues to be re-shaped, by various forms of conversation and communication with others. To claim a particular understanding of reality as the objective (or primary) one is simply a discourse that intends to privilege a certain perspective over others in the construction of reality. Therefore, a discursive framework looks for the power issues in the way a discourse is generated and how it serves to construct reality. By taking reality as a human construction in discourse, the discursive perspective also intends to engage dominant and non-dominant voices in a transformative dialogic process. Thus, the goal of the discursive approach aims at the growth of 'discourse partnership' that can facilitate collective action so as to resolve the suffering and oppression of minority groups and non-dominant cultures.

Decolonization and discourse partnership, the two solutions suggested for resolving the power structure in dominant/majority—non-dominant/minority relationships, are also two discourses that indicate two different standpoints and two different directions for action. Decolonization provides oppressed people with a vision of how to achieve self-determination. Discourse partnership, as understood by people who radically reflect on their own power advantage, is an action toward co-

440

constituted realities in terms of genuine dialogue with minority groups. As power issues always involve two groups of people, any resolution of them should engage people from both groups. However, because of the difficulties accompanying both of these approaches, finding a way to work together is not an easy task. The oppositional mentality found in decolonization may make it difficult for minority groups to trust any contact and establishment with people of the majority group in the process of decolonization. And the accommodative 'adding on' strategy is always a possible pitfall for people with unequal power status in achieving discourse partnership.

Summary and Directions of the Following Presentation

The above discussion indicates an important emerging characteristic in the field of psychological study concerning culture and ethnicity. That is, as the issues of culture and ethnicity are introduced to the field of psychology, they not only pervade psychological phenomena, but they also affect the research by transforming it into a kind of social cultural activity. Ethnic cultural psychology, as it may be named, can no longer adopt a universal standpoint to which psychological phenomena appear to be the products of a stable and objective reality, a standpoint adopted by traditional positivist psychology. Ethnic cultural psychology has to recognize that it is inevitably situated in a context constituted by cultural and ethnic dimensions, including the related power structure. It is precisely within this ethnic cultural context that ethnic cultural psychology raises its concerns and tries to answer them. In other words, a psychological study as such always has, in its essence, an impact on the cultural and ethnic context within which it is situated. The practice of ethnic cultural psychology is, thus, itself an action toward culture and ethnicity.

Besides the recognition of ethnic cultural psychology as an action toward culture and ethnicity, the above discussion also provides several concrete conditions or challenges that should be acknowledged and responded to in an intended approach to ethnic cultural psychology. These conditions/challenges include, first, that instead of being a thing-like entity with definite properties, culture or ethnic culture may be better understood as a contextualized, interactive, creative, affective, and temporal phenomenon embedded in social processes and activities. Second, the impact of ethnic culture on the researchers themselves also indicates that a new understanding of the relationship between the researchers and their own cultures is necessary in order to resolve the difficulty arising from cultural relativism. And third, research on culture and ethnicity is itself a social action that can contribute either to the power structure in ethnic relations or to the growth of genuine dialogue among ethnic groups. Accordingly, the demand for a proper form to carry out psychological studies concerning culture and ethnicity can thus be conceived in terms of the following question: can a study of ethnic and cultural psychology be both an action, engaged itself in the activity or process toward culture and ethnicity and, at the same time, going beyond the trap of cultural relativism and answering the challenge of power issues?

It is in answering this question that I intend to propose in this paper a research framework called 'ethnic self-understanding', using the help of hermeneutical phenomenological thinking. While in most cases, we tend to understand human phenomena as though they were given with certainty and apart from ourselves, hermeneutical phenomenological thinking teaches us to first see how the human phenomena in question manifest themselves and how they are related to our inquiry. Therefore, to achieve my proposed framework, I will first start my articulation by considering myself as an example so as to show how researchers relate themselves to the potential research participants and the intended research phenomena. With this direction of thought, the research framework receives its own unique characteristic as an effort at ethnic self-understanding; that is, a reflexive understanding of the ethnic-cultural involvement to which both the researchers and the research participants belong. I will then discuss the primary phenomenon of investigation in ethnic self-understanding, that is, situatedness, as a way to understand culture and ethnicity. I will also sketch out a method of interpretation that coincides with my research framework and the characteristics of situatedness. In addition, in order to give this theoretical framework a sense of concreteness, I will provide an example that is derived from a study I conducted concerning the situatedness of people of Taiwanese descent living in America (Lee 1999, 2004). Finally, to conclude, I will briefly discuss the implications of this hermeneutical phenomenological approach in terms of it being a proper response to the challenges of the heterogeneity within ethnic groups and the dynamic nature of ethnicity, cultural relativism, and the understanding of research on ethnicity as social action.

A Hermeneutical Phenomenological Approach to Ethnic Self-Understanding

A Non-Objectifying Approach

Taking myself as an example, a Taiwanese researcher committed to the psychology of culture and ethnicity as related to Taiwan, the enterprise of ethnic cultural psychology points to a reflexive inquiry concerning the sociocultural grounds of people who recognize themselves as being of Taiwanese descent. If this ground is called ethnic and cultural, then ethnic culture is understood as a particular sociocultural involvement in which one understands oneself in terms of where and how one comes to be as such, and what and how one is going to be. My concerns about, and inquiries into the ethnic involvement to which I also belong can thus be seen as an effort at ethnic self-understanding.

According to this characteristic, however, I can neither step outside of my ethnic ground to inquire about it, nor can ethnicity be taken as an object and scrutinized analytically. That is to say, ethnicity is not a 'thing'. The ethnic involvement of people of Taiwanese descent does not bestow upon them a distinctive possession that comprises several 'components'. Additionally, ethnic involvement is not a container with clear boundaries in which I, or any other Taiwanese person, live. This understanding of the special nature of ethnicity should be taken as the starting point when considering a proper approach for studying it. To put ethnicity on any scale for direct measurement would inevitably result in the generation of a thing-like image of it; that is, an image with identifiable properties and boundaries, and that lacks its most primordial characteristic of constituting people's lives as such. Therefore, an inquiry into an ethnic and cultural involvement in terms of efforts at ethnic self-understanding calls for a special approach that should be *nonobjectifying*, in the sense that it does not turn ethnicity into an object based on the aim of grasping the knowledge or 'truth' of it.

It is in searching for a way to achieve a non-objectifying approach to culture and ethnicity that I find Heidegger's (1982a and 1982b) discussion of language to be a proper analogy for my concern. My reasons for adopting this analogy are several. First, Heidegger emphasizes the fact that we are already in language; that is, even when we raise questions about language, we cannot be separated from it. This emphasis on non-separateness corresponds with the demand of non-objectifying thinking. Second, instead of viewing language as the product of human beings, Heidegger points out that language is, rather, what gathers things together and opens up a region of relatedness for human dwelling. This idea of a region of human dwelling coincides with the characterization of ethnicity as a sociocultural involvement in which people understand themselves. Thus, Heidegger's approach to language can be an exemplar for that to ethnicity. And third, in Heidegger's point of view, people become speakers when they speak genuinely and creatively after they "are present and together with those with whom they speak, in whose neighborhood they dwell because it is what happens to concern them at the moment" (1982b: 120), and, furthermore, when they listen to the accompanying opening field of human possibilities. In other words, there is a close relationship between collective ethnic self-understanding and innovative discourse. Indeed, this characterization of human discourse is important to my project: since every ethnic self-understanding is carried out in human discourse, creating an innovative discourse as such is a concrete goal to pursue within a non-objectifying inquiry into our ethnic-cultural involvement.

The Call for an Ethnic Self-Understanding

To approach what we cannot grasp as an object, a unique form of access is required. With respect to this concern over access, Heidegger says:

"In order to be who we are, we human beings remain committed to and within the being of language, and can never step out of it and look at it from somewhere else. Thus we always see the nature of language only to the extent to which language itself has us in view, has appropriated us to itself" (1982b: 134).

Here, Heidegger suggests that, instead of taking language as an object under investigation, we the inquirers have to be 'appropriated' by what we intend to understand. This being-appropriated is a way "to let ourselves be properly concerned by the claim of language by entering into and submitting to it" (1982a: 57), and it happens "when we cannot find the right word for something that concerns us, carries us away, oppresses or encourages us" (1982a: 59). That is, when words are no longer available for what we face, we become appropriated and thus glimpse the nature of language as that which grants meaning to the encountered as such. Through this access, the epistemological status of subject and object undergoes a critical transformation: we the inquirers become what is 'grasped' and 'concerned' by the inquired.

Inspired by this special approach, I consider those untamed concerns of ethnic-cultural involvement as a starting point for ethnic self-understanding. In an ethnically diverse environment, there are always occasions wherein people find themselves in a conflictual situation that involves issues of themselves and others in regard to ethnicity. For example, are the people of Taiwanese descent Chinese or Taiwanese? Are those aboriginal peoples in Taiwan Taiwanese or Chinese? When living abroad, what does it mean to be a Taiwanese descendant in an ethnically diverse society such as America? What will be these people's pursuits in the future and how can they be achieved? When these questions arise, the ethnic-cultural involvement that those people root themselves in ceases to be taken-for-granted, becoming instead problematic, and calling them to make an inquiry into it. The power of appropriation is rooted in the fact that what is broken is precisely what people cannot detach themselves from, that is, the involvement they root themselves in. This approach to ethnic self-understanding is nonobjectifying in the sense that, at the very beginning, the inquirers are constituted by what calls for understanding rather than the reverse.

Innovative Understanding as Reconciliation

When a concernful conflict appears within our ethnic-cultural involvement and puts into question our understanding of who we are and how we are related to others, most of us would first encounter an experience of feeling stuck and uneasy. This uneasiness would urge us to put what we have experienced into words, to answer the questions that have arisen. However, we might at the same time discover that we are trapped in an unfamiliar situation in which we find ourselves unable to either act or grasp the proper words to speak. In most cases, we might just turn away so as to alleviate our sense of unease without recognition of what really concerns us.

And yet, how can we go beyond this feeling of being stuck due to the conflict in our ethnic-cultural involvement that is used to uphold our ongoing activities? In response to this question, Heidegger's notions of thinking, listening, and speaking within the experience of a loss of words can serve as a model for attaining understanding in a situation as such. For Heidegger, the breaking up of what is taken for granted is "the true step back on the way of thinking" (1982a: 108). Furthermore, thinking in this situation of questioning should be "a listening to the grant, the promise of what is to be put in question" (1982a: 71). Thinking as listening is an attempt to make sense of the troublesome by way of submitting ourselves to what is given. While language fades away and we are thrown into an unfamiliar status, a listening as sense-making should also be a creative relation-making; that is, to perceive and make a new form of relatedness among the scattered and conflictual events/experiences. With this new relatedness, there comes a new realm for seeing, speaking, and being. As we regain words to speak, we do not just fix some gaps in the old ground, because 'fixing' can only be applied to objects at our disposal. Instead, the speech constructively *articulates* things and events into a new region. Along with this innovative discourse, what was once obscure becomes visible again with new meanings.

In facing a concernful conflict in life that makes us stuck, the way to reconcile it lies not merely in analyzing and fixing the conflict, but in undertaking a sense-making process that lays bare the meanings of the conflict and envisions a new possibility to go beyond it. In a non-objectifying inquiry into our own ethnic-cultural involvement, understanding as reconciliation is, itself, an *innovative articulation* rather than a logical explanation. This approach is based on a capacity to perceive and construct new relatedness through what is dissimilar rather than to deduct from what has been known. Hence, referring again to people of Taiwanese descent as an example, if there is a discourse that can portray an ethnic group called Taiwanese, this discourse should not depend solely on various 'facts' or 'realities' based on the past. Instead, this discourse should also be able to envision a new understanding for this group of Taiwanese people. We can say that because the implicit conventional view about who we are and how we are related to each other is no longer sufficient for describing what we have been exposed to; we need to search for a new discourse so as to grant new meanings to the events in our lives, and correspondingly, to renew the understanding of ourselves together with that of others.

With the goal of achieving an innovative discourse that articulates a concernful conflict into a new understanding, the study of ethnicity inevitably points to a collective task of reconciliation. A discourse always involves speakers, listeners, and particular issues of concern, and is thus not a 'one-person' business. The people gathered to create an innovative understanding of ethnic concerns do not first have to be identified as belonging to the same historical heritage, and people sharing the same heritage do not necessarily have an interest in involving themselves in such a project. Essentially, the people participating in the understanding of a particular ethnic issue would be those who are concerned, or 'appropriated', by the conflictual issue occurring in their lives. A conflict manifests both the difference and the relatedness among people. It is with such a group of people, whose relatedness and difference are in question, that an inquiry into the very ground of ethnic-cultural involvement is necessary.

Inspired by Heidegger's discussion of language, the research action of ethnic self-understanding thus acquires several distinctive characteristics. First, it is nonobjectifying, for it demands that the inquirers first listen to what calls for understanding. Second, in the move from the concernful conflict to reconciliation, it aims at generating a new discourse about the researchers and the participants themselves and the world they are in. Third, since the way to go beyond the conflict is characterized as a regaining of discourse about the people themselves, this action of inquiry becomes a public gathering of speakers and listeners. The project of a non-objectifying ethnic self-understanding becomes, then, a collective action for innovatively building up a region for dwelling.

The above articulation, however, may also appear to be abstract and unusual due to its distinctive emphasis on the action dimension of research on culture and ethnicity. What does it mean to be in a broken upholding ground? What is 'a listening to the grant, the promise of what is to be put in question'? And what is an innovative discourse of such kind like? An example will be presented later in order to help readers resolve these questions. Next, however, let us continue with this line of thought a little further so as to work out the contours of the primary phenomenon of investigation and its correlative methodology in the present approach.

A Hermeneutical Phenomenological Characterization of Situatedness

Situatedness and Its Characteristic of Being a Phenomenological Phenomenon

After the forgoing discussion, one may wonder, what precisely is it that we call ethnic involvement? What is its nature such that the inquirer needs a non-objectifying approach and that his/her inquiry into it will result in an innovative discourse that can help to envision possibilities for action? How can this distinctive nature be characterized in terms of a hermeneutical phenomenological approach? And finally, what are the proper methods that will lead to the accomplishment of this unique pursuit?

In the present articulation, ethnicity is described as a particular sociocultural involvement in which one understands oneself in terms of where and how one comes to be as such and what and how one is going to be. To consider this characterization from a hermeneutical phenomenological perspective, we should begin with the activity of understanding. According to Heidegger's (1962) analysis of "Dasein", that is, the human kind of being, understanding is not just an ability to cognitively know, but rather it is the most primary, ongoing activity of human existence. Every move in our lives is a manifestation of what we understand. Furthermore, understanding as a mode of being is essentially temporal. That is, every move in our lives retains in itself the temporal dimensions of the past (taking up what we have been), the future (projecting what we are going to be), and the present (working on what we are now). As one moves around understandingly, the three temporal ecstases further manifest themselves as what Heidegger calls 'ecstatical horizons'. It is within the unity of the ecstatical horizons of temporality that one finds oneself situated alongside the entities that are understood. In Heidegger's description:

"We have defined Dasein's Being as 'care'. The ontological meaning of 'care' is temporality. We have shown that temporality constitutes the disclosedness of the 'there', and we have shown how it does so. In the disclosedness of the 'there' the world is disclosed along with it. The unity of significance¤that is, the ontological constitution of the world¤must then likewise be grounded in temporality. *The existential-temporal condition for the possibility of the world lies in the fact that temporality, as an ecstatical unity, has something like a horizon.* Ecstases are not simply raptures in which one gets carried away. Rather, there belongs to each ecstasis a 'whither' to which one is carried away. This 'whither' of the ecstasis we call the 'horizonal schema'" (1962: 416).

"Having its ground in the horizonal unity of ecstatical temporality, the world is transcendent. It must already have been ecstatically disclosed so that in terms of it entities within-the-world can be encountered" (1962: 417).

That is to say, as one encounters things in one way or another, one is already situated in a world whose essential structure is grounded in the horizonal unity of ecstatical temporality. The world is neither 'inside' the one who understands, nor is it a thing to be found among other entities within the world. In Heidegger's own words:

"Thus the significance-relationships which determine the structure of the world are not a network of forms which a worldless subject has laid over some kind of material. What is rather the case is that factual Dasein, understanding itself and its world ecstatically in the unity of the 'there', comes back from these horizons to the entities encountered within them. Coming back to these entities understandingly is the existential meaning of letting them be encountered by making them present; that is why we call them entities 'within-the-world'. The world is, as it were, already 'further outside' than any object can ever be" (1962: 417).

In Heidegger's ontological analysis of the human kind of being, therefore, the primary relationships among one who understands, the involvement in which one understands, and the things thus understood, are articulated.

It is by modeling this articulation of Heidegger that I have come to the conceptualization that ethnicity, as a particular sociocultural involvement, carries with itself the characteristics of 'the world'. And because this involvement is related to a person as a ground upon which he/she both is situated and understands, rather than as a personal possession or a physical setting, I call it 'situatedness'. Situatedness thus can be described as a sociocultural involvement wherein one is situated such that things appear in certain manners and, accordingly, one manages them in certain ways.

Situatedness, being constituted by the characteristic of temporal ecstases of the past, the future, and the present, should be understood accordingly as *a project of Being-in-the-world* rather than as the connections among certain factual settings that are ordinarily called 'situations'. That is to say, it is in one's comporting of oneself in one way or another that the things that one encounters and acts upon receive their meaning. Factual settings do not carry with themselves any fixed significance if they are not incorporated into a particular project of Being-in-the-world. The conceptualization of situatedness, therefore, should not be taken as an indication of a thing-like existence.

In hermeneutical phenomenological thinking, because of its nature of being *a source of meaning* for things that are encountered in our lives, situatedness must be treated according to the characteristic of a *phenomenological phenomenon*:

"What is it that phenomenology is to 'let us see'? What is it that must be called a 'phenomenon' in a distinctive sense? What is it that by its very essence is necessarily the theme whenever we exhibit something explicitly? Manifestly, it is something that proximally and for the most part does not show itself at all: it is something that lies hidden, in contrast to that which proximally and for the most part does show itself; but at the same time it is something that belongs to what thus shows itself, and it belongs to it so essentially as to constitute its meaning and its ground" (Heidegger 1962: 59).

"In the phenomenological conception of 'phenomenon' what one has in mind as that which shows itself is the Being of entities, its meaning, its modifications and derivatives" (Heidegger 1962: 60).

A phenomenological phenomenon indicates that which makes something seen as such but at the same does not show itself. Situatedness, as a project of Being-in-the-world, is precisely that from which we see things with their certain meaning and at the same time, that which remains hidden away from our awareness. This obscurity can be understood as the result of the process wherein we only see, for the most part, the meaning of the things and the action in our lives in terms of what they are up to but not the ground where they are from. According to this characteristic, the pursuit of situatedness can be considered as a pursuit of a phenomenological phenomenon. And therefore, as a kind of phenomenological phenomenon, situatedness can be disclosed through an interpretation of people's concrete actions and conversations regarding their particular concerns.

Interpretation and the Disclosure of Situatedness

For Heidegger, interpretation is not only the method to disclose the meaning of a phenomenological phenomenon; it is also a primary activity of human understanding. According to Heidegger's analysis:

"That which has been circumspectively taken apart with regard to its 'in-order-to', and taken apart as such—that which is *explicitly* understood—has the structure of *something as something* [...]. That which is disclosed in understanding—that which is understood—is already accessible in such a way that its 'as which' can be made to stand out explicitly. The 'as' makes up the structure of the explicitness of something that is understood. It constitutes that interpretation" (1962: 189).

"In interpreting, we do not, so to speak, throw a 'signification' over some naked thing which is present-at-hand, we do not stick a value on it; but when something within-the-world is encountered as such, the thing in question already has an involvement which is disclosed in our understanding of the world, and this involvement is one which gets laid out by the interpretation" (1962: 190).

Interpretation, as a primary activity of human understanding, is to see 'something as something', and at the same time, to lay out the involvement from which the encounter arises. In addition, in our everyday lives, what is thus understood and interpreted is, for the most part, expressed in discourse. This point about discourse should, however, be understood properly. That is, discourse does not express meaning in the sense that it indicates what is already there, as if the words are the representatives of

450

the properties of things. Rather, it expresses meaning by way of *articulating* it into the whole involvement. In his ontological analysis, Heidegger writes: "Discourse is the Articulation of intelligibility [...] that which gets articulated as such in discursive Articulation, we call the 'totality-of-significations'" (1962: 203-04) and "Discoursing or talking is the way in which we articulate 'significantly' the intelligibility of Being-in-the-world" (1962: 204). It is in language that the relatedness among things and people gets articulated and a whole involvement is thus given. In this sense, discourses are activities through which speakers display both the things they understand and interpret as well as the ways they understand and interpret in everyday encounters.

In accordance with this structure of interpretation as a primary activity of human understanding, *the materials to be interpreted* and *the interpretation of these materials* are defined. In terms of the materials, an interview with people with regard to their experiences in and with a particular concern is an exemplary vehicle for an interpretation that is expected to accomplish the disclosure of such people's situatedness. I make this statement because, together with the various topics explicitly discussed, the utterances in the interviews also implicitly carry with themselves the ways in which these experiences are understood and interpreted by the speakers. And these ways of understanding and interpreting, though given and yet latent in the utterances, constitute the 'intelligibility of Being-in-the-world' that belongs to the speakers, that is, the intelligibility of their situatedness. Accordingly, in terms of the interpretation of these materials, the task is to explicitly bring out the ways in and through which people understand and interpret their experience. When the research method of interpretation is to characterize the utterances of an interview discourse so as to delineate the situatedness given along with them, a research project of ethnic self-understanding is, then, the involvement both of where the researcher, as an interpreter, stands and where this research interpretation is enacted.

In this task of interpretation, the utterances, however, have to be transformed from being expressive articulations of meaning to being utterance 'entities' that are to be articulated in terms of the project of the disclosure of situatedness. Practically, this step of interpretation can be achieved by using recording devices so as to fix the speech event into a repeatable audio record that can then be transcribed into written form. This operation indeed alters the status of a conversational discourse from being an event to being a text. However, from a hermeneutical phenomenological perspective, this transition from event to text, contrary to being a deficiency in the method of interpretation, instead helps to make apparent the distinctive characteristic of the interpretation of situatedness as a kind of phenomenological phenomenon. That is, what is to be achieved in the method of interpretation is not knowledge that matches the factual settings mentioned or referred to in the discourse, but rather a description of certain *possible modes of being* revealed from the discourse/text. As Ricœur points out in his essay 'The Hermeneutical Function of Distanciation':

"My thesis here is that the abolition of a first-order reference, an abolition effected by fiction and poetry, is the condition of possibility for the freeing of a second-order reference, which reaches the world not only at the level of manipulable objects but at the level that Husserl designated by the expression *Lebenswelt* [life-world] and Heidegger by the expression *being-in-the-world*" (1991a: 85-86).

"If we can no longer define hermeneutics in terms of the search for the psychological intentions of another person which are concealed *behind* the text, and if we do not want to reduce interpretation to the dismantling of structures, then what remains to be interpreted? I shall say: to interpret is to explicate the type of being-in-the-world unfolded *in front* of the text.

Here we rejoin one of Heidegger's suggestions concerning the notion of *Verstehen*. Recall that, in Being and Time, the theory of 'understanding' is no longer tied to the understanding of others, but becomes a structure of being-in-the-world. More precisely, it is a structure that is explored after the examination of *Befindlichkeit* [state of mind]. The moment of 'understanding' corresponds dialectically to being in a situation: it is the projection of our ownmost possibilities at the very heart of the situations in which we find ourselves. I want to retain from this analysis the idea of 'the projection of our ownmost possibilities', applying it to the theory of the text. For what must be interpreted in a text is a *proposed world* that I could inhabit and wherein I could project one of my ownmost possibilities. That is what I call the world of the text, the world proper to *this* unique text" (1991a: 86).

And in the essay "The Model of the Text":

"To understand a text is at the same time to light up our own situation all the significations that make a *Welt* of our *Umwelt*. It is this enlarging of the *Umwelt* into the *Welt* that permits us to speak of the references *opened up* by the text—it would be better to say that the references *open up* the world. Here again the spirituality of discourse manifests itself through writing, which frees us from the visibility and limitation of situations by opening up a world for us, that is, new dimensions of our being-in-the-world.

452

In this sense, Heidegger rightly says—in his analysis of *Verstehen* in *Being and Time*—that what we understand first in a discourse is not another person but a project, that is, the outline of a new being-in-the-world. Only writing, in freeing itself not only from its author but from the narrowness of the dialogical situation, reveals this destination of discourse as projecting a world" (1991b: 149).

In other words, as a discourse is transcribed into written form, the distanciation from the original time and space of the speech event helps us to recognize that, in discourse, what we get acquainted with is neither others' internal psychic realities nor factual environmental settings. Rather, what is disclosed through the interpretation of discourse is precisely a possible mode of being, that is a project of Being-in-the-world. This characteristic of the interpretation of discourse, then, corresponds to situatedness since the latter is also understood as a project of Being-in-the-world.

The above extensive quotations also bring to view the recognition that the process of interpretation inevitably involves the interpreter's own project of Being-in-the-world. That is to say, unlike most of the research following the doctrine of positivism that always seeks to deny and avoid the 'subjective' influence of the researcher, a research adopting an interpretive approach recognizes that the participation of the researcher is required. This participation of the researcher, however, is not only a methodological choice; rather, it is a necessity grounded in the fundamental structure of the ways we live our lives. First, human discourse always involves speakers and listeners; that is, discourse carries with itself the interrelatedness between people. As Heidegger points out:

"In this 'something said', discourse communicates. [...] In this more general kind of communication, the Articulation of Being with one another understandingly is constituted. Through it a co-state-of-mind gets 'shared', and so does the understanding of Being-with. Communication is never anything like a conveying of experiences, such as opinions or wishes, from the interior of one subject into the interior of another. Dasein-with is already essentially manifest in a co-state-of-mind and a co-understanding. In discourse Being-with becomes 'explicitly' *shared*; that is to say, it is already, but it is unshared as something that has not been taken hold of and appropriated" (1962: 205).

With human discourse as the exemplary subject for interpretation, the project of disclosing situatedness is from the beginning a gathering of a group of people who communicate with each other with regard to their particular concern. In other words, the coexistence of the speakers and listeners in discourse points out that the situatedness given along with the discourse is always a *shared situatedness*. Inevitably, a research project as such is, in its nature, a reflexive disclosure of a sociocultural involvement in which both the researchers and the participants take part. And second, as an activity of a certain kind of understanding, the interpretation of situatedness is eventually carried out through a discursive articulation. This characteristic of the research result as a discourse also points to a gathering of the participants, the researchers, and those who are of a potential audience to the very discourse itself, and who are potential participants in pursuit of the disclosure of their own situatedness. The pursuit of situatedness in relation to ethnicity in terms of the interpretation of human discourse presents itself, then, as a project of ethnic self-understanding.

Given this characterization of situatedness as a kind of phenomenological phenomenon and the interpretation of discourse as the method for its disclosure, this research framework for culture and ethnicity appears to be a collective work that is directed towards a reflexive understanding of certain projects of Being-in-the-world. A pursuit as such, therefore, does not result in a kind of knowledge that is a *representation* of factual situations, that is, a kind of knowledge whose validation rests on its ability to match the 'facts'. Instead, the articulation of situatedness obtained through a hermeneutical phenomenological approach is itself a *presentation*, a manifestation of the possible modes of human existence within certain conditions. With regard to the goal of a particular study of ethnic self-understanding, then, the situatedness of people living with particular shared concerns is not about collecting things and events that have 'factually' happened to them; instead, the articulation of the situatedness, as a human possibility, of these people will become a reflexive, comprehensible *discourse* of their own sociocultural involvements, a discourse about themselves. The significance of presenting the situatedness as such lies in its service of opening up visions of how people live their own lives, and of making the limits and alternatives perceivable. This methodological framework is, then, also a framework for a reflexive construction of ethnic self-understanding.

People of Taiwanese Descent Living in America: An Example

The discussion so far has presented an articulation of situatedness—as people's cultural and ethnic involvement—and of the access to it, using the ontological analysis of the human kind of being, especially in its relationship to language, found in the works of Heidegger and Ricœur. To give this theoretical framework of cultural and ethnic study a sense of concreteness, it is better to have a completed study as an example. In accordance with the examples referred to in the preceding paragraphs, therefore, I will in the following section present materials from a study of mine that investigates the situatedness of people of Taiwanese descent living in America (Lee 1999, 2004). This example should demonstrate how an ethnic cultural involvement is presented as problematic, no longer upholding the ground for people's ongoing activities concerning their culture and ethnicity; how this situatedness is constituted in terms of people's concrete discourses in their lives; and what it means to obtain an innovative and integrative understanding of people's lives that will make the limits and alternatives perceivable.

The Strengths and Limitations of the Constituent Discourses of the Situatedness of People of Taiwanese Descent Living in America

As the approach of ethnic self-understanding suggests, the inquiry should begin with people's words about their ethnic and cultural involvement. For people living in America as Taiwanese descendants, it is common to say or hear words like: "American citizens have a lot of privileges all over the world because the American government is the strongest. It is good to have an American passport"; "We know that we have to work harder and harder and be cautious in order to have a better life in America"; "There are a lot of students from Taiwan who changed after they came to America. They became bad"; "There's a big difference between the East and West cultures. I feel that it is an advantage to be exposed to the two sides"; "People from Taiwan easily accept foreign cultures"; "American people might feel that the way they deal with things is the best because no one could do things better than them"; and "Sometimes I feel that, since I will go back to Taiwan, I may not have a serious friendship here". Although these statements are so familiar in their lives and all seem to be factual and reasonable, they are, however, in conflict with each other. That is, such people of Taiwanese descent feel at times that it is good to be in America, while sometimes they feel it is better to go back to Taiwan with an American passport. In addition, they sometimes feel good about their Taiwanese background while, at others, they feel it is troublesome to assert their Taiwanese identity. In a sense, these words, spoken so confidently, lead people to experience great ambivalence and confusion toward their own ethnic and cultural involvement. In most cases, what people do with such ambivalence and confusion is to just repeat words like: "It is good to be in America" and "It is good to have a Taiwanese background", even though they know that these words do not have the power to get them through what they are experiencing.

Although the lack of words indicates a kind of stuckness in the lives of people of Taiwanese descent living in America, nonetheless, it is precisely their ambivalence and confusion as such that the inquiry of ethnic self-understanding could begin with. Indeed, in order to listen 'to the grant, the promise of what is to be put in question', the inquirers with such concern should attend carefully to the words said. With an interpretative analysis (Lee 1999, 2004), the words people commonly say and hear to account for their Taiwanese and American lives present themselves as gathered into six different identifiable patterns and usages of language. These patterns and usages can be described as the following six discourses:

1. The discourse of advantages. This discourse accounts for people's involvement with America. It holds America as a more advantageous place than Taiwan for one's life in terms of education, job opportunities, average salary, and sociopolitical situation. This discourse also includes the view that moving to America has been a social trend in Taiwan.

2. The discourse of a precarious America. This discourse portrays America as a place of precariousness in terms of beginning life there with an illegal resident status—a common experience for foreign people who seek ways to stay in America—, the demands accompanying the opportunities provided in America, and the corruption of people in the face of life in America. This discourse of a precarious America also includes the view that one has to work hard and be conservative and cautious in order to stay out of trouble and achieve something.

3. The discourse of pride over possessing a Taiwanese background. This discourse accounts for the advantages of having such a background. It praises the advantages of the Taiwanese people's capacity for the Chinese language and of the opportunities and flexibility in having contact with different cultures in comparison with most Americans. The advantage of a Taiwanese background is also presented in terms of having good family discipline and the corresponding conservative behavior patterns.

4. The discourse of the power status between Americans and people with a different cultural background. It accounts for people's experience with Americans. This discourse provides a form of understanding for unfriendly treatment from Americans in terms of a kind of

Amero-centricism and racial discrimination. Nevertheless, this discourse of power status also includes the view that those Americans who are unfriendly are, in fact, inferior in terms of their educational level and their narrow view of people outside of America.

5. The discourse of memories of Taiwan. This discourse accounts for the preference to be with people from Taiwan. It holds Taiwan as the source of the close feeling one has while together with one's fellow people from Taiwan because everyone can share with each other memories and stories of life in Taiwan. An additional discourse of the promise to return to Taiwan is also commonly presented with this discourse of memories of Taiwan.

6. The discourse of self-naming by people from Taiwan. This discourse holds the expectation that people who bear the label Taiwanese while in America should both express distinctive concerns over Taiwan as well as assert a Taiwanese identity without being susceptible to any accompanying confusion or confrontation from Americans and Chinese.

The above discourses also lay bare several 'projects' that are commonly shared in the lives of Taiwanese descendants living in America. The reason I call them 'projects' is that they give people both specific directions to take when thinking about the things in their lives as well as specific reasons for the actions they are going to take. Each of these projects leads to a desired goal of theirs; for example, to have a wealthy and advanced life, to survive the challenges they face, to treasure their Taiwanese background, to ease unfriendly experiences with some Americans, to enjoy the companionship of their fellow people, and to assert a position for people from Taiwan in America. Therefore, people can be quite confident about living their lives in accordance with these projects. In addition, referring to the preceding conceptualization of situatedness, each of these projects indicates a particular aspect of the situatedness of Taiwanese descendants living in America.

While each of the projects seems to be just right for people of Taiwanese descent living in America, they may, however, have also found themselves frequently stuck in the middle of them, seeing no clear road to go through. Such limitations and weaknesses of these six discourses can be described in terms of: (1) the confusion and ambivalence that emerge amongst the discourses, such as the contradiction between the discourse of advantages of life in America and that of the precariousness of life in America; (2) the indecision that emerges between one's life direction derived from the discourse of memories of Taiwan and that derived from the discourse of the advantages of life in America; and (3) the inadequate nature of these discourses in terms of carrying people with a Taiwanese background into a realm of flourishing companionship with people in America, including both Taiwanese and Americans. This inadequacy is embedded in several of the discourses: the discourse of advantages, which creates comparison and differentiation among people from Taiwan in terms of the levels of their involvement with America, that is, citizenship, the Green Card, and the temporary residence permit such as a student visa; the discourses of pride over a Taiwanese background and of memories of Taiwan, both of which create differentiation between Taiwanese people and American people; the discourse of power status, which creates differentiation between Americans and people with a different cultural background; and the discourse of self-naming by people from Taiwan, which creates comparison and differentiation among people from Taiwan.

In sum, the language that people of Taiwanese descent use to describe their various projects of living in America appears to lack the words that can bond them together with certain groups of people. Furthermore, they also lose the sense of a grounded connection with either Taiwan or America because of their confused and ambivalent feelings toward both countries. While people of Taiwanese descent in America mostly think, talk, and do in accordance with these common projects in their lives, what such projects lead them to, however, is a proud but lonely figure, drifting in the world.

An Innovative Articulation of the Constituent Discourses as a Whole

While in most cases, studies concerning culture and ethnicity would likely stop at the above findings—regarding them as the invariable ethnic or cultural traits of this particular group of people—, the approach of ethnic self-understanding, goes further to articulate the intelligibility among the apparently contradictory projects of living. This act aims at regaining words for what is scattered. With this task, the situatedness of this particular group of people—to be brought out as an integrative whole—obtains the characteristic of that which upholds the various projects of living as such and yet, at the same time, remains hidden away from people's awareness; that is, the characteristic of being a phenomenological phenomenon. Accordingly, what has to be done next is to begin again an innovative sense-making process that can reveal the intelligibility of these projects/discourses. This step can be guided in terms of the following question: "What is the most appropriate image of Being-in-the-world and the description of it that can bring out the intelligibility of these projects/discourses?"

The primary image of Being-in-the-world that I have chosen in order to achieve this second layer of interpretation—since it grants a comprehension of those constituent discourses as a whole—is a particular force of *hunger* in the lives of people of Taiwanese descent living in America. That is to say, those projects are, in a sense, only facets of 'hunger', a hunger for any available advantages in terms of a better life.

Let us see how this hunger reveals itself as the dominant force in this particular group of people's lives. In contrast to the goal of having a wealthy and advanced life in America, the departure point for the pursuit of American advantages is, ironically, a kind of lack. What the people lack is what they want to obtain through their involvement with America; for example, a better education, better job opportunities, a better citizenship, and, in sum, a better life. In other words, the project of pursuing the advantages of living in America is also a project of taking in, of filling up the lack resulting from people's background from Taiwan. The image implied by this pursuit is, therefore, not just of an enriched person, but also of a person with a hunger for a better life.

Living on a track of 'taking in for hunger', people of Taiwanese descent hardly enjoy themselves. On the one hand, they always discover more advantageous opportunities, and thus put more demands on their own shoulders. On the other hand, they have to safeguard the gains that they have made so far. In a sense, their hard-working and conservative life style also reveals itself as being driven by a hunger for a secure, protected, and guaranteed life. While disturbing, unfriendly experiences with some Americans take them to a social position that is lower than that of Americans, people from Taiwan ease the feeling of being deprived by saying to themselves that we people from Taiwan possess more advantages than those Americans. Ironically, their Taiwanese background, which had been seen as being disadvantageous in comparison with the conditions of life in America, becomes a source of pride, which the project of taking in for hunger turns back to. Corresponding to this move back toward their Taiwanese background, people enjoy the status of being a Taiwanese native even though they are outside of their native place. Are there not many 'little Taipeis' in different American cities? In a sense, they have moved 'back' to Taiwan without even knowing it.

In a sense, because of this hunger for a better life, people have neither left Taiwan nor arrived in America. The America they come to is just 'the land of opportunities'. Few of them have ever stepped on America, the nation that needs devotion from its constituents in order to resolve its problems and keep growing. On the other hand, they never leave the Taiwan where they experience confusion and debate over which name they should call themselves. The lack of a clear language to account for themselves continues to hang over them, just as it does for their fellow people back in Taiwan. As a result, people have neither left life in Taiwan nor arrived in America; they situate themselves in a *magical realm* in which they are not in Taiwan but, magically, live in Taiwan, and they are in America but, magically, do not live in America. Ambivalence, loneliness, and ungroundedness become, thus, inevitable experiences for this group of people.

Although this discourse of 'being situated in a magical realm' helps to understand the pursuits and conflicts in the lives of people from Taiwan in America, the purpose of this discourse is not to hold this description as an invariable trait. Rather, the goal is to seek clarity about the ways people of Taiwanese descent live their lives in America, and, therefore, to make room for the growth of alternatives.

The Action and Emotionality Involved in the Discourse of Situatedness

The ways that people live their lives, which had been hidden under ambivalence and confusion, are now brought to light in terms of the approach of ethnic self-understanding. Because the understanding of such situatedness is not to be taken as factual reality but rather as an intelligible vision of how people have been, what also becomes clear is the recognition that people do live in America rather than in Taiwan; they do choose to rest there; and they do have rather than they lack. It also becomes clear that to say good-bye to the hunger does not mean to say good-bye to their Taiwanese heritage or their concerns about Taiwan. As a result, a realm of dwelling is opened up for people to try out alternatives to live in their neighborhood, their community, or even the society at large, in a way that belongs to people of Taiwanese descent; that is, a Taiwanese way. As an action toward culture and ethnicity, the approach of ethnic self-understanding itself belongs to the development and growth of culture and ethnicity.

One important point that should be noted here is that a discourse that draws people to a transparent comprehension of their own lives is always a discourse loaded with emotion. To elaborate a clear articulation of the strengths and limitations of people's taken-for-granted projects of living is itself a destruction of their familiarity with them. This destruction occurs because a scrutinizing look into these projects requires detaching themselves from them. And destroying old and familiar understandings of how they live their lives generates anxiety. Further, a renewed understanding also indicates a renunciation of familiar projects of living, and this understanding may lead to a sense of grief and loss. However, this renunciation may also be accompanied by a sense of relief because of the detachment from those familiar but broken projects of living.

Consequently, an integrative discourse of the situatedness of people of Taiwanese descent living in America is not only a presentation of comprehensible portraits of their projects of living, but the discourse itself has to deal with the emotionality involved so as to help people to be transparent to themselves in these projects. The practice of the present interpretive methodology thus presents itself as an action that brings people toward their culture and ethnicity.

Conclusion and Implications

In the present paper, I propose that ethnic cultural psychology is, in its essence, an action toward culture and ethnicity. Accordingly, I articulate an approach named 'ethnic self-understanding' as a theoretical and practical framework for this kind of inquiry with the help of hermeneutical phenomenological thinking. The other features that this approach includes are that it is: (1) nonobjectifying, for it does not treat culture and ethnicity as thing-like entities with distinctive properties that can be measured by numbers, either directly or indirectly; (2) interpretative, for it aims at disclosing 'the intelligibility of Being-in-the-world' through an interpretation of people's concrete actions and conversations regarding their particular concern; (3) reflexive, for it leads the research participants to see how they live their own lives, and makes the limits and alternatives perceivable; and (4) innovative, for it is also a move from concernful conflict to reconciliation within which people generate a new discourse about themselves and the world they are in.

In addition to the above distinctive characteristics, this hermeneutical phenomenological approach to ethnic cultural psychology can also be a proper response to the challenges in this area of studies: first, the heterogeneity within ethnic groups and the dynamic nature of ethnicity; second, the challenge of cultural relativism; and third, the understanding of research on ethnicity as a social action. A full discussion of these issues would not fit the purpose of this paper. But because I have put forth their significance, I will here briefly illuminate the challenges and the responses from the research framework of ethnic self-understanding.

In the framework of ethnic self-understanding, the heterogeneity within ethnic groups and the dynamic nature of ethnicity are no longer posited as being problematic. That is, rather than seeing heterogeneity as a deficiency in achieving generalizations about people with the same ethnic cultural background, this dimension is taken as the starting point for constructing an ethnic self-understanding. The results are to be articulated as a comprehensible discourse that shows a renewed understanding of the situatedness belonging to the particular group of people. The whole process of understanding in this approach is, therefore, in accordance with the dynamic nature of ethnicity.

The project of ethnic self-understanding responds to the challenge of cultural relativism by considering culture and ethnicity in terms of its non-objectifying approach. Here, culture is recognized as that which constitutes the way we live our lives. Nevertheless, the idea of culture as a 'blueprint', that is, as *pre-set* with certain contents and boundaries that determine the way we live our lives, misrepresents this constituent relationship of culture to our lives. That is to say, culture and ethnicity should not be taken as thing-like images, and their constituent character demands that we approach them in a way that does not objectify them. According to this understanding, the researcher must not assume either that people with different cultural backgrounds should be different, or that people with the same cultural background should be the same. Instead, as the differences between people emerge, regardless of whether they are intra- or interethnic groups, they are taken as the starting point for exploration rather than as problems to be resolved. In other words, ethnic self-understanding uncovers so as to go beyond the implicit ethnic-cultural involvement where ethnic conflicts can emerge. Hence, the awareness of cultural differences is the impetus for a renewed understanding of culture rather than the proof of cultural relativism.

The approach of ethnic self-understanding is, in its essence, a social action that points to an innovative construction of ethnicity that serves as preparation for a new mode of ethnic interaction in the larger societal context. Besides, this research action is not just for the researcher's interest, but, more importantly, for the people participating in the project. Furthermore, the characteristic of being a social action is actualized in terms of the presentation of the research results of ethnic self-understanding. It is prepared so as to introduce to the participants, and other audience members who share the same concerns, renewed visions of their ethnic situation. In other words, the knowledge produced in ethnic self-understanding is always purposive; that is, it is not objective nor universal, but closely connected to people's needs so as to benefit their lives. Because the research results are to be prepared for direct communication with the participants and other audience members, researchers should use language that is concrete and comprehensible to them rather than academic jargon. Such a manner of presenting the research results provides

462

the possibility for the understanding obtained through this research project to be 'co-owned' by both the researchers and the research participants.

References

Blauner, R. (1987). Colonized and Immigrant Minorities. In: R. Takaki (Ed.). From Different Shores: Perspectives on Race and Ethnicity in America (pp. 149-160). New York: Oxford University Press.

Darder, A. (1995). The Politics of Biculturalism: Culture and Difference in the Formation of Warriors for Gringostroika and The New Mestizas. In: A. Darder (Ed.). Culture and Difference (pp. 1-20). Westport, CT: Bergin/Garvey

Heidegger, M. (1962). Being and Time. New York: Harper & Row.

Heidegger, M. (1982a). The Nature of Language. In: On the Way to Language (pp. 57-108). New York: Harper & Row.

Heidegger, M. (1982b). The Way to Language. In: On the Way to Language (pp. 111-136). New York: Harper & Row.

Howard, G.S. (1991). Culture Tales: A Narrative Approach to Thinking, Cross-Cultural Psychology, and Psychotherapy. In: American Psychologist, 46 (3), 187-97.

Hughes, D./Seidman, E./Williams, N. (1993). Cultural Phenomena and the Research Enterprise: Toward a Culturally Anchored Methodology. In: American Journal of Community Psychology, 21, 687-703.

Lee, W.L. (1999). People of Taiwanese Descent Living in America: Constructing Ethnic Self-Understanding. Unpublished Doctoral dissertation, Duquesne University, Pittsburgh, PA.

Lee, W.L. (2004). People of Taiwanese Descent Living in America: A Discursive Approach. Manuscript submitted for publication.

Ratner, C. (1996). Activity as a Key Concept for Cultural Psychology. In: Culture & Psychology, 2, 407-34.

Ratner, C. (1999). Three Approaches to Cultural Psychology: A Critique. In: Cultural Dynamics, 11, 7-31.

Ratner, C. (2000). Outline of a Coherent, Comprehensive Concept of Culture. In: Cross-Cultural Psychology Bulletin, 34 (1 & 2), 5-11.

Ricœur, P. (1991a). The Hermeneutical Function of Distanciation. In: From Text to Action (pp. 75-88). Evanston, IL: Northwestern University Press.

Ricœur, P. (1991b). The Model of the Text: Meaningful Action Considered as a Text. In: From Text to Action (pp. 144-167). Evanston, IL: Northwestern University Press.

Sampson, E.E. (1993). Identity politics: Challenges to Psychology's Understanding. In: American Psychologist, 48 (12), 1219-1230.

Sasao, T./Sue, S. (1993). Toward a Culturally Anchored Ecological Framework of Research in Ethnic-Cultural Communities. In: American Journal of Community Psychology, 21, 705-727.

Sue, S. (1991). Ethnicity and Culture in Psychological Research and Practice. In: J.D. Goodchilds (Ed.). Psychological Perspectives on Human Diversity in America (pp. 47-85). Washington, DC: American Psychological Association.

Torres, R.D./Ngin, C. (1995). Racialized Boundaries, Class Relations, and Cultural Politics: The Asian-American and Latino Experience. In: A. Darder (Ed.). Culture and Difference (pp. 55-69). Westport, CT: Bergin & Garvey.

Van Dijk, T.A. (1993). Elite Discourse and Racism. Newbury Park, CA: Sage Publications.

Weinreich, P. (1988). The Operationalization of Ethnic Identity. In: J.W. Berry/R.C. Annis (Eds.). Ethnic Psychology: Research and Practice with Immigrants, Refugees, Native Peoples, Ethnic Groups and Sojourners (pp. 149-168). Berwyn, PA: Swets North America.

CULTURAL VALUES REGARDING CHILDREN AND FAMILY: THE CULTURAL MEANING OF PARENT-CHILD RELATIONSHIPS

GISELA TROMMSDORFF

Introduction

Culture is conceived here as a complex meaning system interrelated with ecological and socioeconomic conditions and individual development. Thus, culture is seen as constituting the relevant conditions for development by penetrating all spheres of economic, social, and individual processes, and at the same time being influenced by these processes. Culture provides constraints and resources that are part of individual development. Human development can therefore be seen as a product of culture, as affecting culture, and as being part of a cultural niche, thus fostering interrelations between culture and individual behaviour.

This view is influenced by theoretical assumptions of the influential Six Cultures Study by Whiting and Whiting (1975), the multilevel ecological approach by Bronfenbrenner (1977), the culture-ecological approach by Berry, Poortinga, Segall and Dasen (1992, 2002; Trommsdorff and Dasen 2001), the value approach (e.g., Hofstede 1980; in press), the developmental niche hypothesis (Super and Harkness 1997), and the developmental paths approach (Greenfield, Keller, Fuligni, and Maynard 2003; Rothbaum, Pott, Azuma, Miyake, and Weisz 2000) (for an overview see Trommsdorff, in press a, c).

These approaches have in common that it is necessary to 'peel the onion' of culture, and to take the complex characteristics of culture seriously when explaining individual development. One (and maybe the most difficult) problem lies in the task of theoretically bridging the context and the person. One promising step in this direction is the attempt to study the cultural meaning and its effect on individual behavior (Boesch 1991; Bruner 1990, 1996). Thereby, the cultural context and its psychological meaning are analysed with respect to their functions inside and

465

outside the psychological system of the individuals. The focus of this approach is on how culture and psyche 'make each other up'.

In the first section of this chapter, the theoretical framework is introduced. This is followed by a brief description of a complex socio-demographic problem, the description of an ongoing cross-cultural study, and some recent empirical results. In the concluding part, an outline for future research on the transmission of cultural meaning is presented.

Cultural and Individual Values as Different Levels of Analyses

There are many difficulties to be solved when studying the cultural meaning system empirically. The value theories are well known for their attempt to bridge the context and the person by introducing the concept of value orientations. The influential value theory by Hofstede (1980; 2001; in press) identifies global aspects of culture on the basis of general (and national) cultural values such as individualism and collectivism, power distance, uncertainty avoidance, masculinity/femininity, and time perspective (Hofstede 1980, 2001, in press). Hofstede's approach has created several misunderstandings and led to wrong conclusions, including the wrong assumption that individualism/collectivism represents the most important dimension and the other dimensions could be neglected, the assumption that these values constitute two opposite poles of one dimension, and the assumption that cultural and individual values overlap. The first assumption has been refuted by other approaches, such as the universalistic value theory by Shalom Schwartz (Schwartz 1992, 2004; Schwartz and Bilsky 1990) who demonstrated a multidimensional structure of a universal value system consisting of seven dimensions. Schwartz showed that cultures can be described by other than Hofstede's value dimensions. Also the assumption of a one-dimensionality of individualism/collectivism cannot be empirically validated and has been frequently criticized (e.g., Kagitcibasi 1996; Oyserman, Coon, and Kemmelmeier 2002). Furthermore, the assumption of an overlap between cultural and individual values cannot be accepted since cultural and individual values are related to different concepts and to different methodological approaches. Triandis (1995) has therefore differentiated between the cultural value of individualism and the individual value of ideocentrism on the one hand and cultural value of collectivism and the individual value of allocentrism on the other hand in order to specify the cultural and the individual level. This necessary differentiation precedes the empirical testing of the relations between the cultural context and the individual behavior.

Cultural values function on a different level than individual value orientations. A focus on whole cultural entities takes into account political institutions, religious orientations, socioeconomic, and socio-demographic conditions. A focus on the person takes into account the individual goals, beliefs, and behaviour. Accordingly, cultural values are part of a complex system of ecological, socio-economic, and demographic conditions. They may overlap with individual value orientations of certain populations from the same or even from other cultures; the degree of overlap may be an indicator for cultural heterogeneity and socio-cultural change.

The relation between cultural and individual values is of special interest in culture-psychological research. The interesting question is whether cultural values can be transformed into individual values, and how this process can be described. From a developmental psychological perspective, this question is dealt with by socialization theories (Grusec and Hastings, in press). One aspect of socialization is to prepare children to adopt cultural values and internalize them such that they can achieve optimal development in their specific cultural context. Such socialization is effective via several interconnected levels of transmission: the macro, the meso-, and the micro-levels (Bronfenbrenner 1977). The transmission of values through parent-child interactions is only one specific process. In developmental psychology, the impact of parental discipline as part of the transmission belt has been of significant interest in various studies (Grusec and Goodnow 1994). However, most of these studies were carried out in Western countries. They have neglected the cultural context and the respective cultural values and related meaning system, thus ignoring that a specific parenting style can have very different effects on child development (Chao and Tseng 2002; Rothbaum and Trommsdorff, in press; Trommsdorff 1995; Trommsdorff in press a, b, c; Trommsdorff and Kornadt 2003).

Cultural values constitute an essential part of the developmental niche; they organize the developmental path of the child and influence the belief system and value orientation of those individuals interacting with the developing child, the caretaker's child-rearing goals, beliefs, and practices, as well as the parent-child relationship, are especially important. Some of the caretaker's beliefs are related to more or less diffuse and general values, while other beliefs are more related to specific value orientations that guide individual and interpersonal behaviour.

On the other hand, *individual values* can affect cultural values on the basis of individual behaviour and related consequences for the primate and distal developmental contexts which, according to Bronfenbrenner (1977) have to be seen as an interrelated eco-system (e.g., the parent-child relation; family structure, educational and political system). Culture is based on social interactions in and outside the family, and cultural values are transmitted from one generation to the next by socialization processes. Therefore values of children and the family, as well as intergenerational relations, are important aspects of such interrelated processes.

It can be assumed that these values are part of the developmental niche and of conditions for individual development. These values can also be assumed to influence individual behaviour, such as giving birth to a child or not, whether and why children are valued, which values underlie child-rearing goals, practices, and parent-child relationships, and which values are transmitted by which means to the next generation. The respective values of children and the family will influence child-rearing practices, e.g., fostering certain value orientations and competences in the child, which in turn will influence the developmental niche and the related cultural values. Therefore, values of children and family are seen here as related to the general cultural context on the one hand, and to the individual socialization experiences including past and present parent-child relationships (see figure 1) on the other.

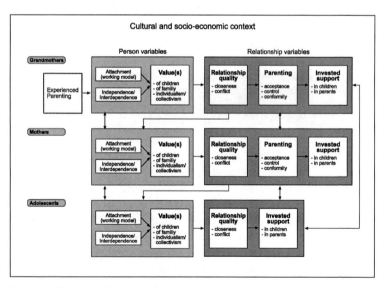

Figure 1: Parent-child relations in three generations

Accordingly, individual development, parent-child relationships, and culture are seen here as mutually related in a process in which specific values become prominent and influential for the person and for the cul-

468

tural meaning system. The cultural meaning system can be seen as filtering the transmission of values. The transmission of culture is a part of 'meaning making'. The cultural meaning system gives a certain meaning to certain values (e.g., individualism, independence, collectivism, interdependence) in such a way that their transmission and psychological function for development may differ among cultures.

One important condition for the transmission of cultural values to the next generation is the quality of the parent-child relationship, which again is assumed to be affected by the cultural context and the value of children and the family (Trommsdorff 2001, in press b, c) (see figure 1). In the following discussion on the relationship between culture and individual values, we will therefore focus on the parent-child relationship as a transmission belt for cultural values. This focus is of high relevance due to the ongoing dramatic socio-demographic changes all over the world.

In the following we will present some obvious reasons for intensifying the study of value of children and the family by including the parent-child relationship in different cultures. We will therefore first refer to the observations of significant socio-demographic changes and related problems for cultures and individual development.

Sociodemographic Changes

A dramatic demographic transition can presently be observed worldwide. These changes imply changes both in the context for individual development and in developmental outcomes, including individual value orientations. Increasing longevity and declining fertility underlie the explosion in the number of older people and the drastic decline of the birth rate in many countries. Recent statistics by the United Nations show that at least 9.3 billion people will populate the earth in the year 2050. This means an increase of more than 50% of the total population of today. Ninety-nine percent of the increase will occur in less developed countries. Only six countries share the responsibility for the increasing birth rate: The population increase in India is about 21%, in China about 12%, and in Pakistan, Nigeria, Bangladesh, and Indonesia the increase is about 5% in each. In general, the population in the third world will increase dramatically even if the birth rate in these countries decreases and the death rate due to AIDS is not taken into account. Otherwise, an increase to about 12 billion is to be expected.

In contrast, the demographic situation in the industrialized regions (altogether about 1.2 billion people) is quite different. A decrease in birth rate is presently confined to European countries and Japan. This decrease implies a decline of the total population in these countries 50 years from now: The United Nations estimates a decrease in population of the 15 countries of the European Union of about 10%; that means about 40 million people fewer than today will live in the EU. More dramatically, in Japan and in Germany the decline is about 14%, in Italy and Hungary about 25%, and in Russia, Georgia, and the Ukraine about 28 to 40%.

The general population growth and its effects on consumption of finite natural resources has recently been described as the most urgent problem for the global ecosystem (Bandura 2002). The combination of high fertility rates in poor countries, low fertility in some parts of the world, and increased global longevity contribute to risking ecologically sustainable development. Both physical and social ecology are endangered by factors accompanying population growth, such as mass migration to urban areas. This is a condition for the increase of slum settlements and related unemployment, poverty, and risky health conditions. These factors contribute to undermining socio-economic development and growth.

These demographic changes create a variety of problems. One resulting problem is how to feed and educate the increasing number of newborn children in those parts of the world which typically belong to impoverished countries, countries that need substantial economic and other support to fulfill these obligations. Another resulting problem is how to take care of the increasing number of elderly who face longevity and who often do not have the necessary financial, social, and emotional resources. In some societies the elderly can rely almost entirely on the family; in other countries, the social welfare system takes care of the medical and economic needs of the elderly. Thus, one can assume that different cultural contexts provide different answers to these demographic problems.

For more than a century, a change toward longevity has been observed all over the world. In 2005, 10% of the global population was 60 years and older. In the year 2050, the number will increase up to 22% worldwide (United Nations. Department of Economic and Social Affairs. Population Division, 2005). In Japan and Germany (also in the U.S. and Spain) over 15% of the population is above the age of 65. This fact of ageing societies is not confined to industrialized countries. In a short while, the number of people older than 60 years will increase in the developing countries from about 8% of the population to 20%. The age of sixty will be reached by 17% of the Indian population in the year 2025. In Japan, the average life expectancy is 86 years for women, and 77 years for men. The increase of the elderly population in the last decade has been 129% in Japan and 50 to 60% in other Western countries. To give an example, in Germany and in other European countries, one child is matched by two senior people. Increasing longevity is related to changes on different levels of societies, e.g., the European welfare systems is currently experiencing increasing problems because of expenses for health care and other services for aged people.

These demographic changes consist of shifts in population growth rates and in the age structure of populations (differential fertility: low in industrialized and high in developing countries), as well as increasing average worldwide longevity in less developed countries and greater increases in highly industrialized ones. These demographic changes are a result of both value changes and changes in economic and technological development. How these dramatic changes will affect individual development and value orientations is yet unclear. In the following I will discuss whether these demographic changes are related to cultural values and to values of children and family.

Cultural Differences in the Value of Children

The Original Value of Children Study

More than 30 years ago, socio-demographic research attempted to explain the increasing birth rate in many regions of the world; currently the question is how to explain the dramatic decline in fertility. More than 30 years ago, economists and demographers started a large international study on the "Value of Children" (VOC) (Arnold et al. 1975; Fawcett 1977). The main goal was to find out the reasons why young couples or parents want (or do not want) children. Thus, both the positive and negative value of children was of interest for the study. The original "Value of Children" (VOC) study was designed to explain to what degree economic factors were related to fertility.

The empirical results showed that parents mainly preferred economic, social, and emotional reasons as the value of children. The next question was whether and how far such values were related to the economic and social structure, and furthermore, whether these values predict fertility rates. The underlying hypothesis for the further study was that an economic and socio-normative value of children in contrast to an emotional value of children was related to high fertility and son preference. The results from different cultures are in line with this hypothesis. Results from the original VOC study have clearly demonstrated differences

471

among countries with higher and lower economic status with respect to the preference of emotional versus economic/social values of children (Arnold et al. 1975; Fawcett 1977).

Theoretical and Empirical Extensions of the VOC Study

Analysis of Psychological Variables.

The previously economic approach to fertility and family size had to be expanded to include psychological variables. The interest shifted to additional theoretically relevant variables such as family structure, individual values, and caretaking (Kagitcibasi 1982, 1996). Empirical results of these studies showed that in traditional cultures where agriculture is the normal economic basis as compared to urban and more modernized areas, fertility was high. In these cultures, the economic and social values of children prevailed; this included the expectation that children will be of economic utility and will help their aged parents in the future (children as old-age security). In contrast, in urban areas the emotional value of children was more preferred, and the fertility rate was relatively lower. In traditional agrarian regions, sons were preferred as part of the traditional value of children, and parenting was based more on strictness and control. The results from these studies were in line with the general assumption that economic conditions influence fertility. However, these studies go beyond the assumption of a simple unidirectional causality by including the value of children as a mediating variable (Kagitcibasi 1996).

Family Model Approach

In her theory on family models, Kagitcibasi (1996, 2005b) integrated findings from this and further studies to explain changes in the value of children and the family as being related to modernization. The author has suggested family models of independence and interdependence that differ with respect to the preference for emotional as compared to traditional (economic and social) values of children, family size, gender equality, and parenting. According to this theoretical approach, both family models undergo changes by accommodating each other's characteristics. The family model of interdependence is assumed to change by including aspects of the independent model while still remaining different with respect to the preference of relatedness as the basis for individual development; this is in contrast to the family model of independence where the preference for autonomy is the basis for individual development (for a review on the relation between relatedness and autonomy see Kagitcibasi 2005a).

472

A Social Change and Multigenerational Approach

Theoretical and empirical extensions of the original VOC study were introduced recently by a partial replication of the previous study, including some of the same countries in order to measure effects of economic, social, and value changes (Trommsdorff and Nauck 2005a, b). First results from this revised study on changes in values demonstrate the increased importance of the emotional value of children and decreased importance in the economic value of children in most countries over the last three decades (Makoshi and Trommsdorff 2002; Nauck 2000; Trommsdorff, Zheng, and Tardif 2002). However, the emotional value of children is still less and the economic value is more important in regions with low economic status (for the People's Republic of China, see Trommsdorff, Zheng, and Tardif 2002; for Turkey, see Kagitcibasi 1996; Kagitcibasi and Ataca 2005; for the Republic of Korea, see Kim, Park, Kwon, and Koo 2005; for several countries see Nauck 2005; Mayer and Trommsdorff 2005).

In the original Value of Children Study, the value of children was seen as the most important factor in explaining fertility. Other aspects such as intergenerational relationships were not taken into account. This is surprising since the quality of intergenerational relationships can be assumed to be associated to the value of children and the family, and also can be assumed to be of major importance for predicting the transmission of cultural values (see figure 1) (Trommsdorff 2001). Questions related to social change can be more precisely answered by studying intergenerational relationships. On the one hand, the quality of intergenerational relations can influence social change, e.g., by changing the role of the family and family solidarity. On the other hand, it can also be affected by socio-economic and demographic changes, including increasing longevity and a related gender gap in life expectancy, decreasing fertility, increasing postponement of first childbirth, decreasing family stability, and increasing diversity of family structure (due to divorce, single-parent families, second or third marriage, changing gender roles) (cf. Bengtson 2001; Trommsdorff and Nauck 2005 a, b; Zarit and Eggebeen 2002). However, increasing divorce rates, the increasing number of children living with stepfathers or stepmothers, or living in single-parent families have not negatively affected family solidarity in North America (Bengtson 2001).

One obvious psychologically relevant consequence of longevity on parent-child relationships in current affluent societies is the increase in joint lifetimes. Until the end of the 19th century, personal contact with grandparents in middle childhood was an exception. In Germany, mothers born in 1875 had a mean joint lifetime of 42 years with their children;

473

this has increased to almost 58 years for those born in 1940. The joint lifetime of grandparents and grandchildren has changed accordingly (Klein and Nauck 2005). Longevity means an extended lifetime for intergenerational relationships: ageing parents can expect to share an increasing number of years with their own parents and also with their children, far beyond their adolescence and even into their children's retirement. Due to increased longevity, intergenerational relationships can persist through an increasing number of years of the life span.

Different aspects of intergenerational relationships have to be taken into account when studying their associations with values in different cultures. Intergenerational relations can exist between grandparents and grandchildren, between adult children and their ageing parents, and between parents and their children. The relationship quality may be analyzed according to emotional closeness, solidarity between the generations, patterns of intergenerational exchanges and support, family eldercare, the continuity or discontinuity of intergenerational relations over time, and similarities and differences between the generations with respect to values (e.g., Bengtson and Robertson 1985; Cooney 1997; King and Elder 1997; Trommsdorff in press b, c; Zarrit and Eggeben 2002).

The Cross-Cultural Study on Value of Children and Intergenerational Relations

So far, there is little empirical evidence of the ongoing sociodemographic changes in different cultures and their associations with the value of children, the family, and parent-child relationships. Therefore, we initiated a large cross-cultural study (e.g., Nauck 2005; Trommsdorff 2001; Trommsdorff and Nauck 2005a; b). This study is a partial replication and extension of the original "Value of Children" study (Arnold and Fawcett 1975; Fawcett 1973).

Theoretical Frame and Research Goals

The present cross-cultural study aims to go beyond questions of fertility and takes into account cultural and individual values, family structure, parenting, and intergenerational relations; thereby it suggests a major theoretical revision of the former explanatory model (see reports on eight countries in Trommsdorff and Nauck 2005b). One question is whether ongoing socio-demographic changes (e.g., longevity and decline of high fertility rates) are related to value orientations and intergenerational relationships in different countries.

474

We have mentioned before that increasing longevity is a worldwide phenomenon that also includes developing countries. Due to the world-wide increase in longevity, parents and their children will, in general, share on average almost five decades as adults. However, the effects of an increasing length of overlapping lifetime on the quality of the parent-child relationships beyond childhood and adolescence and on intergenerational relations and cultural transmission are not yet known. Therefore, we are especially interested in studying this relationship over the lifespan in different cultures (Trommsdorff in press b, c).

One hypothesis is that the culture-specific structure of intergenerational relations, its components, and influential factors are associated with different cultural values, including the value of interdependence and filial piety as a basis for parent-child relations in East Asian cultures in contrast to the value of individualism and independence in Western cultures (see Chao 1994; Ho 1986; Rothbaum and Trommsdorff in press; Trommsdorff and Kornadt 2003). Cultural values (regarding the family and children) are assumed to be related to specific socialization experiences (including attachment and parenting) and the quality of the parent-child relationship over the lifespan (see figure 1).

The present study thus can be seen as a quasi experimental approach to the study of the cultural meaning system: most countries face the problem of dramatic socio-demographic changes. How they will cope with this problem depends on their respective cultural meaning systems, which affect the parent-child relationship and the transmission of values. In the following, we focus on individual values and on aspects of the parent-child relationship.

Individual Values (General and Specific)

Individualism (idiocentrism) in contrast to *collectivism* (allocentrism) is usually understood as encompassing a preference for self-assertion, more distant and detached social behaviour, autonomy, competition and conflict, egalitarian relationships, privacy and solitude, preference for temporary relationships, and low in-group versus out-group differentiation (Hofstede, in press; Triandis 1995). The differentiation between the *independent* in contrast to the *interdependent* self was introduced by Markus and Kitayama (1991). The independent self is usually understood as separate from the social context and as striving for autonomy and self-assurance; the interdependent self is usually understood as being closely related to members of the family and the in-group; accordingly, the individual experience is the self in relation to others. The model of the interdependent self is to fit in with others, to fulfil social obligations, and engage in harmonious interpersonal relationships. The interdependent self is related to high importance of family values (have good relationships with one's relatives, feel close with one's family members, feel responsible for family members' well-being) (Georgas et al. 2001). The values of individualism and independence, as compared to collectivism and interdependence, have different implications for developmental goals and outcomes (e.g., Greenfield et al. 2003; Rothbaum et al. 2000; Rothbaum and Trommsdorff in press).

Much research has been carried out to demonstrate differences in the preference of independence and interdependence as compared to collectivism and interdependence in North American (or European) as compared to Asian (or African) countries, with higher scores on individualism and independence in North American people. In contrast, research on the value of children is rare.

The *value of children* in the original Value of Children (VOC) model (Arnold et al. 1975) was conceptualized in terms of positive and negative values of children and the value in having a large or a small family. Positive values include emotional benefits, economic benefits and security, self-enrichment and development, identification with children, and family cohesiveness and continuity. Negative values include emotional and economic costs, restrictions or opportunity costs, physical demands, and family costs. The *emotional value of children* (emotional benefits and self-enrichment) has been studied in contrast to the economic and practical, social, or religious value of children as part of the model in order to predict fertility and family planning.

Parent-Child Relationship

At present, there is a lack of research integrating general or specific values assumptions with values of children and the family, and to also take into account the parent-child relationship in different cultures. Rothbaum, Pott et al. (2000) have suggested that different patterns of parent-child relationships in Western and non-Western countries (e.g., Japan and the U.S.) are related to different cultural models of an individualistic and a social orientation. These patterns are assumed to be based on different needs: the need for separation or closeness, for independence or interdependence, and for autonomy or relatedness.

The *individualistic pattern* is described by the value of 'generative tension', which is based on the concern to establish and maintain independence and to fulfill individual goals. Here, parent-child relations are characterized by independence and partnership, acceptance of conflicts, and negotiations of individual interests. The *social-oriented pattern* is characterized by the cultural value of 'symbiotic harmony', which is based on the concern to maintain interdependence by fulfilling one's du-

476

ties and obligations, and to meet social expectations. Therefore, children's obedience, filial piety, their compliance with their parents' expectations, their life-long duties, and obligations in honor of the parents, are highly valued. Such interdependent parent-child relationships are characterized by harmony, cooperation, and the obligation to 'reciprocate'. The authors are less interested in describing differences in the importance and strength than in differences in the *meaning and dynamics* of parent-child relationships.

This theoretical approach to parent-child relationships is empirically validated by several studies (for an overview see Trommsdorff, in press a, b, c). In Western countries, parent-child relationships are characterized by a need for independence which can be related to conflicts but also to mutual support. Support is usually related to an emotionally close relationship. In Asian countries, children's and parents' behavior is part of a stable relationship of mutual obligation, based on emotional interdependence as indicated by the concepts of *filial piety* and reciprocity (e.g., Kim, Kim, and Hurh 1991; Schwarz, Trommsdorff, Kim, and Park, in press; Wang and Hsueh 2000). Asian adolescents prefer values of deference, obligation and respect for their parent and family elders in contrast to their European and American peers (Ying, Coombs, and Lee 1999). The adult children feel obliged to their parents; they are aware of their parents' and especially their mothers' sacrifices. In line with the Confucian values of seniority and filial piety, aging parents have high ranking positions in the family and are often regarded as the 'honorable elders' (Palmore and Maeda 1985; Wang and Hsueh 2000). The *filial piety* is seen less as fulfilling a formal duty but rather as an emotional solidarity which is also related to the shared belief in ancestors and the continuity of the family. This family orientation is part of cultural transmission and continuity in most Asian cultures.

Samples

We included countries that differ in cultural values, socio-demographic variables (fertility and longevity), socio-economic conditions (industrialization, urbanization), religious orientation, and political system. For example, Germany, is a Western highly industrialized, democratic, individualistic country with declining fertility rates; Republic of Korea is a society in transition with rather stable and low fertility rates and Confucian value orientations; The People's Republic of China is a rapidly changing country with strong differences between urbanized and rural areas, a long history of Confucian value orientation and family structure, high population growth, presently advocating the one-child policy; Indonesia is a still traditional mainly agrarian country with Islamic religious background, high fertility, and a strong family orientation (for more extensive descriptions of the countries included in the VOC study see Trommsdorff and Nauck 2005a, b). So far, the countries included in our VOC study are Germany, France, Turkey, Israel, Palestine, Indonesia, Republic of Korea, The People's Republic of China, India, and South Africa. Some of these countries have participated in the original VOC study (Turkey, Indonesia, and the Republic of Korea). Data from those samples can be compared with the results from the original VOC study in order to assess social, economic, and value changes. In each country, we have chosen samples of three (biologically related) generations (belonging to one family: grandmothers, mothers, adolescents) (300 families in each country) plus a sample of young mothers with a preschool-child (300 in each country) (altogether 1000 persons in each country).

Procedures and Instruments

All participants were interviewed based on a standardized interview which was the result of pilot studies in cooperation with the team members from the different countries. We used instruments validated in various cultures for assessing general and specific value orientations (such as individualism, collectivism; independence, interdependence; family orientation; social-economic and emotional value of children), parenting (warmth and control), the quality of the intergenerational relations (attachment; communication quality, e.g., intimacy, conflict; and support, e.g., instrumental, emotional, and prospective future support given to the aging parents) (for a detailed description of the instruments see Schwarz, Chakkarath, Trommsdorff, Schwenk, and Nauck 2001).

Empirical Results of the Revised VOC and Intergenerational Relations Study

In the following we will focus on the cultural meaning system when reporting on first empirical results on the values and parent-child relationships. We will discuss the results within the theoretical framework of the cultural model of independence and interdependence (e.g., Markus and Kitayama 1991; Greenfield et al. 2003; Kagitcibasi 2005 a, b; Rothbaum et al. 2000; Rothbaum and Trommsdorff, in press; Trommsdorff in press, a, b, c).

Parent-Child Relationship

One aspect of the parent-child relationship is the quality of communication and the mutual subjective perception of the relationship quality. In one of our studies comparing German and Indonesian samples of grand-mothers and their adult daughters (mothers) we found that low self disclosure ('intimacy') of Indonesian mothers of adult daughters was related to their collectivistic value orientation (Schwarz and Trommsdorff, in press). This result is not surprising when taking into account that in a social-oriented culture like Indonesia, mutual understanding as part of the relationship quality is not necessarily based on verbal exchange of personal needs and wishes but rather on an empathic feeling with the other. Empathy is an essential part of the interdependent self and characteristic for the cultural model of interdependence (Markus and Kitayama 2001). The results from our study thus are in line with assumption that collectivistic values are associated with the preference for empathy in case of an interdependent parent-child relationship.

Value of Children

The cultural model of interdependence has consequences for another aspect of parent-child relationships, the value of children and the willingness of children to give support to their parents. Children's providing support to their aging parents (as part of old age security) is an important *economic value of children* in traditional agrarian countries as our own studies on the value of children (VOC) in different countries demonstrate (Nauck 2000; Mishra et al. 2005; Mayer and Trommsdorff 2005; Trommsdorff, Zheng, and Tardif 2002; Trommsdorff and Nauck 2005, a, b). This is in line with the previous studies on the value of children (Kagitcibasi 1982; 1996). With modernization, the economic-utilitarian value of children has declined; raising children has become more expensive, and old-age security is usually provided by social security and welfare systems. This has contributed to the decline of fertility.

However, is the economic value of children the only reason for giving birth to a child? As Kagitcibasi (1982; 1996) has pointed out there are other needs to be fulfilled when having a child such as *the emotional value of the child* which, however, is related to lower fertility (one does not need to have many children to experience emotional satisfaction). While the previous studies on the VOC have usually pointed out to the difference between the economic and the emotional value of children in traditional versus modernized countries, in our own cross-cultural studies it was obvious that the emotional value of children is generally important even in those countries where the social-economic value of children is high (Mayer and Trommsdorff 2005). The economic value of children is still high in traditional agrarian countries such as India, Indonesia, and South Africa; it is less important in China, Israel, Turkey, and the Republic of Korea; and it is nearly not important in Germany. In our further

479

analyses on the relations between the value of children and planned fertility of adolescents from different countries we found that we have to differentiate between predictions on the cultural and on the individual level. These results are based on multi-level analyses of individual and cultural effects on the planned number of children. On the cultural level, the economic value of children was positively related, and the emotional value of children was negatively related to planned fertility. However, on the individual level, the economic value of children was unrelated, and the emotional value of children was positively related to the planned number of children (Mayer and Trommsdorff 2005). The advantage of such multi-level analyses is to clarify differential effects on the cultural and the individual level. The empirical results stimulate the need to clarify whether the function of the emotional value of children differs in traditional and modernized cultures. Accordingly, the question of the cultural meaning of the value of children arises. It may well be that the emotional value of children is high (and of similar importance) in very different cultures but has different implications for fertility and possibly also for parent-child relationships.

Parent-Child Relationship

Therefore, we now have a brief look at some results of our study on the associations between the emotional value of the child and aspects of the parent-child relationship in different countries. In China where the economic value of the child is of medium high importance, and the one-child policy is practiced, adult daughters' emotional value of the child is significantly associated with a positive relationship to their parents (high intimacy or self-disclosure and high readiness for supporting old parents). In Indonesia, where the traditional economic value of the child is highly important, intimacy in the communication is unrelated but supporting aging parents is positively related to the emotional value of child. In Germany, were the economic value of the child is low and the emotional value of the child is high, the emotional value of the child is also significantly related to intimacy in communication (the same as in China) but not related to supporting aging parents (quite different from China and Indonesia) (Trommsdorff, unpublished data). These correlational results demonstrate different culture-specific patterns of associations between the emotional value of children and a relevant aspect of the parent-child relationship. The pattern of these results indicates that the function of the emotional value of the child for the parent-child relationship varies among cultures. This gives rise to the question whether these variations are in line with a culture-specific meaning of the value of children and parent-child relationships. In order to pursue this question, we will discuss some further results of our study.

Supporting Aging Parents

Giving support to aging parents can be seen as an important behavioral aspect of parent-child relationships (Trommsdorff, in press, b, c) and as an essential element of family solidarity which is especially relevant in societies with growing longevity and need for social security of the aging population (Bengtson, 2001). In line with our hypothesis, in our East Asian and Western samples, a high importance of family values was associated with more support-oriented intergenerational relationships (e.g., in Indonesia and in India as compared to Germany) (Albert, Trommsdorff, Mayer, and Schwarz 2005; Mishra, Mayer, Trommsdorff, Albert, and Schwarz 2005).

In further studies we tested whether other aspects of the parent-child relationship (self-disclosure in communication) are associated with giving emotional and instrumental support to aging parents. We found a clear pattern of positive associations in all cultures (Trommsdorff, unpublished data). At first sight, these results indicate cross-cultural similarities. However, we should be careful not to be mislead by this simple view. We have reason to assume that self-disclosure and support each have a different meaning in Western and East Asian cultures as indicated above. High self-disclosure may be related to support in Western cultures since this kind of communication usually indicates a positive relationship which in turn increases the altruistic prosocial motivation to give support. However, in East Asian cultures, high self-disclosure may rather indicate a low relationship quality since a high relationship quality in these cultures is characterized by empathy and refraining from the expression of own needs and wishes through self-disclosure (see above, Trommsdorff and Schwarz, in press). Giving support under such circumstances is based less on an altruistic prosocial motivation but rather on a normative prosocial motivation.

When looking at conflict as another aspect of the communication quality, no significant association with instrumental or emotional support occurs for the German sample however, a significantly positive association occurs for the Korean and the Indonesian samples. Taking into account the cultural meaning of conflict in parent-child relationships, these results are of special interest since they indicate that even though conflict is quite rare in Asian in contrast to the Western cultures, conflict does not undermine giving support to parents in Asian samples; also giving support to parents does not reduce potential conflict in the relationship. The life-long obligation to honor and support one's parents is a dominant norm which regulates parent-child relationships in case of being social-ized according to an interdependent cultural model.

This interpretation shows that cultural similarities in the pattern of results (associations) may hide culture-specificities in the underlying individual motivation. Therefore, further analyses are necessary to clarify whether or not culture-specific functional relations are underlying seemingly cultural similarities. Such further analyses may consist in taking into account other theoretically relevant variables which allow to clarify the cultural meaning of the results. Giving support to the parents can be based on different motivations. A differentiation between an altruistic and a norm-oriented motivation seems to be useful when studying the cultural meaning of the parent-child relationship and giving support to parents (Trommsdorff, a, c).

In the following we will ask whether different motivations for giving support are related to differences in the cultural meaning of 'reciprocity'. Reciprocity in Western theorizing is usually understood as the balanced give and take in interpersonal relationships. We doubt that this meaning of reciprocity is the same in non-Western cultures where the cultural model of interdependence prevails. Therefore our further analyses deal with the question whether the relationship quality is affected by the sub-jective perception of a balanced give and take between the adult daughter and the elderly mother, and whether cultural values play a role. A com-parison of German and Indonesian samples clearly showed that the Indo-nesian as compared to the German adult daughters do not mind to give more than they receive (Schwarz, Trommsdorff, Kim and Park, in press). Obviously, traditional values of filial piety and supporting one's parents is accepted as a life-long obligation in Indonesia. Thus, different cultural meanings of the communication quality and of reciprocity are to be taken into account when studying parent-child relationships over the life span.

Further results from Korean, Chinese and German samples of grandmothers and their adult daughters (mothers) confirm the hypothesis of the culture-specific meaning of parent-child relationships (Schwarz and Trommsdorff, in press). When the cultural model of interdependence prevails, the readiness to give support is high. This is independent of the support received in the parent-child relationship as can be shown from the results of the Korean and Chinese samples. In contrast, when the cul-tural model of independence prevails, the readiness for supporting one's aging parents depends on the 'rational' norm of reciprocity, that is the perceived balance of received and given support; this is the case for the German sample.

In these Asian countries, the value of filial piety underlie the child's life-long obligation to give (unconditional) support to the parents. Here, the readiness for support is not based on the rational norm of reciprocity with checking the balance of how much support one has received from the parents or how much support one has already given to the parents. Rather, the readiness to support one's parents is based on the deep-rooted feeling of life-long interdependence and of the obligation to give (unconditional) support to one's parents. Giving support in parent-child relationships in different countries is therefore based on different conceptions and cultural meanings of 'reciprocity'.

Past experience of non-balanced support in East Asian countries does not affect adult daughters' willingness to support their parents in contrast to German daughters; German adult daughters rather give support to their parents in line with the norm of reciprocity which is based on calculating the balance of give and take. German adult daughters also give (instrumental and emotional) support to their parents in case of favoring an interdependent self (Trommsdorff, unpublished data). These results are in line with the view that the cultural model of independence or interdependence can predict whether and why adult children support their aging parents.

Transmission of Values

As suggested in our model of intergenerational relations over the life span (Trommsdorff 2001; in press b, c), the relationship quality between mothers and adolescent children should influence the extent of transmission. According to the two-step model by Grusec and Goodnow (1994) (pointing out to the function of the accurate perception and acceptance of parental values by children) it was assumed here that intimacy in the relationship and perceived acceptance enhances the communication between adolescents and their mothers and thereby increases the accurate perception and the acceptance of maternal values. Therefore, we tested the (moderating) effects of the parent-child relationship on the transmission of values (general and domain-specific values like individualism/collectivism, value of family and interdependence) for a German sample of mothers and their adolescent children by regression analyses (Albert and Trommsdorff 2003, August). The results showed that all four value orientations of the adolescents were predicted by the value orientations of mothers. The prediction of individualism, however, was relatively weak, indicating a rather selective transmission of values. Mean values of mothers and adolescents on all scales differed indicating a relative as opposed to an absolute transmission. Apart from this, intimacy and felt acceptance by parents turned out to be successful transmission belts for values of collectivism and the value of the family, but not for individualism and interdependence. Furthermore, all aspects of the relationship quality had direct effects on the value orientations of the adolescents. These results support the assumption that the relationship quality has an important impact on the development of value orientations of adolescents beyond its role as a moderator.

In further studies, we tested the model of transmission of values in cross-cultural comparison by analyzing the role of controlling parenting for the transmission of various values in Germany and France, two individualistic countries with different values of the family and of children (Albert, Trommsdorff, and Sabatier 2005). In both countries, significant associations between the preference of collectivistic values and controlling parenting occurred; moreover, in France the value of the family and controlling parenting were significantly associated. Regression analyses showed that parental control explains the successful transmission of collectivistic values in the German sample and the successful transmission of family values in the French sample. These results indicate the culture-specific function of both, parenting (as one aspect of parent-child relationships) and value orientations for the transmission of values. This study also underlines the necessity to test the functional equivalence of aspects of parent-child relationships in different cultures in order to gain a better understanding of the respective cultural meaning systems.

Conclusion and Outlook

One major aim of this chapter was to analyse associations between values and parent-child relationships over the life-span by taking into account parenting and the transmission of values in different cultures. The presently ongoing study on "Value of Children and Intergenerational Relationships" will tell us more about cultural differences and similarities in the associations between values and parent-child relationships by taking into account the cultural meaning systems.

Culture has been understood here as a complex meaning system interrelated with socio-demographic, and economic conditions, and penetrating all spheres of economic, social, and individual processes. The cultural meaning system has been seen here as the basis for parent-child relationships which in turn is the basis for the transmission of cultural values. The transmission of cultural values is a part of 'meaning making'. Thus the cultural meaning system filters the transmission of values according to the general cultural model.

In certain cultures, the general cultural model of interdependence prevails while in other cultures the model of independence dominates. The related culture-specific values are partly internalized by caretakers and affect their values, beliefs, behavior, and their relationship with their children (Greenfield et al. 1993; Rothbaum and Morelli 2005; Schwarz, Schäfermeier, and Trommsdorff 2005; Trommsdorff 2001, in press a, b, c; Trommsdorff and Friedlmeier 2004; Trommsdorff and Kornadt 2003). The different means of socialization and transmission of culture in different cultural contexts with preference for the independent versus the interdependent model have been described on the basis of numerous empirical studies (e.g., Chao and Tseng 2002; Rothbaum and Trommsdorff in press; Rothbaum, Weisz et al. 2000; Stevenson and Zusho 2002; Trommsdorff and Kornadt 2003).

According to these general cultural models and the related culture-specific meaning systems, quite different qualities of intergenerational relationships develop which in turn affect the intergenerational cultural transmission. Our results have shown that the quality, and the function of the parent-child relationships can be more adequately described when taking into account the cultural meaning of the relationship, and the individual value orientations e.g., the value of the child and the family (Rothbaum, Weisz, Pott, Miyake, and Morelli 2000; Trommsdorff, in press b, c). For example, we have shown that communication, support, and reciprocity have a very different cultural meaning in East Asian as compared to Western countries, depending on the cultural model of independence and interdependence.

A shortcoming of our study certainly is that we are still too much speculating about the cultural meaning system without providing sufficient empirically tested evidence. Therefore, further research is needed to empirically assess the cultural meaning, e.g., by relating data from the cultural and the individual level. This can be methodologically solved by multi-level analyses including a larger number of cultures overcoming a shortcoming of most cross-cultural research with the focus on only a limited number of cultures. Further cross-cultural studies on the cultural meaning system should be carried out on both, the level of cultures and on the individual level, relating the cultural and the individual level in a systematic way. For example, the above mentioned socio-demographic changes on the country level point to a new role of grandparents and to corresponding effects on the parent-child relationship on the individual level in different generations.

Rapidly changing cultural contexts may be related to a reversal in the direction of the transmission of cultural values. Intergenerational relations will be of special interest for the study whether and how a transmission of cultural values takes place from the younger to the older generation, and how this affects the intergenerational relations and future socio-cultural change. Results from our studies actually point to more similarities among German grandparents and adolescent grandchildren than among grandparents and their adult children (Trommsdorff, Mayer, and Albert 2004). Adolescent children may initiate changes in the values, beliefs and behavior of their parents who in turn develop value orientations which become increasingly different from the value orientations of their elderly parents (grandparents). However, even such studies will be of little theoretical value when neglecting cultural factors.

Since a systematic study of intergenerational relationships in different cultures is still missing, we have started our project on the "Value of Children (VOC) and Intergenerational Relations" (Trommsdorff and Nauck, in press, a). This study will take into account possible socioeconomic, socio-demographic and cultural changes and overcome a shortcoming of most studies on parent-child relationships with the focus on adjacent generations. The present study thus can be seen as a quasi-experimental approach to the study of the cultural meaning system: Most countries face the problem of dramatic socio-demographic changes. How they will cope with this problem depends on their respective cultural meaning systems which affect the parent-child relationship and the transmission of values. Accordingly, the cultural meaning of parent-child relationships needs to be theoretically and empirically clarified in order to improve our understanding of developmental outcomes, including the transmission of values from a multi-generational and life-span developmental view.

The goal of the present chapter has been to point out that psychological research will systematically increase its theoretical contribution when taking into account the cultural meaning of the methods used and the empirical results. Our study has shown that the value of the child and the family and its associations with parent-child relationships can be better understood when taking into account their respective functional meaning in the cultural context.

References

Albert, I./Trommsdorff, G. (2003, August). Intergenerational Transmission of Family Values. Poster presented at the XIth European Conference on Developmental Psychology in Milan, Italy.

Albert, I./Trommsdorff, G./Mayer, B./Schwarz, B. (2005). Value of Children in Urban and Rural Indonesia: Socio-Demographic Indicators, Cultural Aspects and Empirical Findings. In: G. Trommsdorff/B. Nauck (Eds.). The Value of Children in Cross-Cultural Perspective. Case Studies from Eight Societies (pp. 171-207). Lengerich, Germany: Pabst Science.

Albert, I./Trommsdorff, G./Sabatier, C. (2005, July). Parenting and Intergenerational Transmission of Values in Germany and France. Paper presented at the 7th European Regional Congress of the International Association for Cross-Cultural Psychology 'New Scenarios for Cultural Interaction', San Sebastian, Spain.

Arnold, F./Bulatao, R.A./Buripakdi, C./Chung, B.J./Fawcett, J.T./ Iritani, T., et al. (1975). The Value of Children: A Cross-National Study, Vol. 1. Introduction and Comparative Analysis. Honolulu, HI: East-West Population Institute.

Arnold, F./Fawcett, J.T. (1975). The Value of Children, Vol. 3. Hawaii. Honolulu, HI: East-West Center.

Bandura, A. (2002). Environmental Sustainability by Sociocognitive Deceleration of Population Growth. In: P. Schmuch/W. Schultz (Eds.). The Psychology of Sustainable Development (pp. 209-238). Dordrecht, The Netherlands: Kluwer.

Bengtson, V.L. (2001). Beyond the Nuclear Family: The Increasing Importance of Multigenerational Bonds. In: Journal of Marriage & Family, 63, 1-16.

Bengtson, V.L./Robertson, J.F. (Eds.). (1985). Grandparenthood. Beverly Hills, CA: Sage Publications.

Berry, J. W./Poortinga, Y. H./Segall, M. H./Dasen, P. R. (1992). Cross-Cultural Psychology: Research and Applications. New York: Cambridge University Press.

Berry, J.W./Poortinga, Y.H./Segall, M.H./Dasen, P.R. (2002). Cross-Cultural Psychology: Research and Applications, Vol. 2. New York: Cambridge University Press.

Boesch, E.E. (1991). Symbolic Action Theory and Cultural Psychology. Heidelberg: Springer.

Bronfenbrenner, U. (1977). Toward an Experimental Ecology of Human Development. In: American Psychologist, 32, 513-531.

Bruner, J. S. (1990). Culture and Human Development: A New Look. In: Human Development, 33, 344-355.

Bruner, J.S. (1996). Acts of Meaning. Cambridge, MA.: Harvard University Press.

Chao, R.K. (1994). Beyond Parental Control and Authoritarian Parenting Style: Understanding Chinese Parenting Through the Cultural Notion of Training. In: Child Development, 65, 1111-1119.

Chao, R./Tseng, V. (2002). Parenting of Asians. In: M.H. Bornstein (Ed.). Handbook of Parenting, Vol. 4. Social Conditions and Applied parenting (2nd ed., pp. 59-93). Mahwah, NJ: Erlbaum.

Cooney, T.M. (1997). Parent-Child Relations Across Adulthood. In: S. Duck (Ed.). Handbook of Personal Relationships (2nd ed., pp. 451-468). Chichester, UK: Wiley.

Ehrlich, P.A./Ehrlich, A.H./Daily, G.C. (1995). The Stork and the Plow: The Equity Answer to the Human Dilemma. New York: Putnam's.

Fawcett, J.T. (1977). The Value and Cost of Children: Converging Theory and Research. In: L.T. Ruzicka (Ed.). The Economic and Social Supports for High Fertility (Vol. 2, pp. 91-114). Canberra, Australia: Department of Demography.

Fawcett, J.T. (Ed.). (1973). Psychological Perspectives on Population. New York: Basic Books.

Georgas, J./Bafiti, T./Poortinga, Y.H./Christakopoulou, S./Kagitcibasi, C./Kwak, K., et al. (2001). Functional Relationships in the Nuclear and Extended Family: A 16-Culture Study. In: International Journal of Psychology, 36, 289-300.

Greenfield, P. M./Keller, H./Fuligni, A. J./Maynard, A. (2003). Cultural Pathways Through Universal Development. In: Annual Review of Psychology, 54, 461-490.

Grusec, J.E./Goodnow, J.J. (1994). Impact of Parental Discipline Methods on the Child's Internalization of Values: A Reconceptualization of Current Points of View. In: Developmental Psychology, 30, 4-19.

Grusec, J.E./Hastings, P. (Eds.) (in press). The Handbook of Socialization. New York: The Guilford Press.

Ho, D.Y.F. (1986). Chinese Patterns of Socialization: A Critical Review. In: M.H. Bond (Ed.). The Psychology of the Chinese people. (pp. 1-37). Hong Kong: Oxford University Press.

Hofstede, G.H. (1980). Culture's Consequences: International Differences in Work-Related Values. Beverly Hills, CA: Sage.

Hofstede, G.H. (2001). Culture's Consequences: Comparing Values, Behaviors, Institutions and Organizations Across Nations (2nd ed.). Thousand Oaks, CA: Sage.

Hofstede, G.H. (in press). Der kulturelle Kontext psychologischer Prozesse [The Cultural Context of Psychological Processes]. In: G. Trommsdorff/H.-J. Kornadt (Eds.). Enzyklopädie der Psychologie: Themenbereich C. Theorie und Forschung: Serie VII. Kulturvergleichende Psychologie: Band 1. Theorien und Methoden in der kulturvergleichenden und kulturpsychologischen Forschung. Göttingen, Germany: Hogrefe.

Kagitcibasi, C. (1982). The Changing Value of Children in Turkey. Honolulu, HI: East-West Center.

Kagitcibasi, C. (1996). Family and Human Development Across Cultures: A View from the Other Side. Mahwah, NJ: Erlbaum.

Kagitcibasi, C. (2005a). Autonomy and Relatedness in Cultural Context: Implications for Self and Family. In: Journal of Cross-Cultural Psychology, 36, 403-422.

Kagitcibasi, C. (2005b). Modernization Does not mean Westernization: Emergence of a Different Pattern. In: W. Friedlmeier/P. Chakkarath/B. Schwarz (Eds.). Culture and Human Development. The Importance of Cross-Cultural Research for the Social Sciences (pp. 255-272). Hove, UK: Psychology Press.

Kagitcibasi, C./Ataca, B. (2005). Value of Children and Family Change: A Three Decade Portrait from Turkey. In: Applied Psychology: An International Review. Special Issue: Value of Children in Socio-Cultural Contexts, 54(3), 317-337.

Kim, K.C./Kim, S./Hurh, W.M. (1991). Filial Piety and Intergenerational Relationship in Korean Immigrant Families. In: International Journal of Aging and Human Development, 33, 233-245.

Kim, U./Park, Y.-S./Kwon, Y.-E./Koo, J. (2005). Values of Children, Parent-Child Relationships, and Social Change in Korea: Indigenous, Cultural, and Psychological Analysis. In: Applied Psychology: An International Review. Special Issue: Value of Children in Socio-Cultural Contexts, 54 (3), 338-354.

King, V./Elder, G.H. (1997). The Legacy of Grandparenting: Childhood Experiences with Grandparents and Current Involvement with Grandchildren. In: Journal of Marriage & Family, 59, 848.

Klein, T./Nauck, B. (2005). Families in Germany. In: B.N. Adams/J. Trost (Eds.). Handbook of World Families (pp. 283-312). Thousand Oaks, CA: Sage.

Makoshi, N./Trommsdorff, G. (2002). Value of Children and Mother-Child Relationships in Japan: Comparisons with Germany. In: U. Teichler/G. Trommsdorff (Eds.). Challenges of the 21st Century in Japan and Germany (pp. 109-124). Lengerich, Germany: Pabst Science.

Markus, H.R./Kitayama, S. (1991). Culture and the Self: Implications for Cognition, Emotion, and Motivation. In: Psychological Review, 98, 224-253.

Mayer, B./Trommsdorff, G. (2005, July). Adolescents' Values and Future Orientation. Multi-Level Analyses from 11 Cultures in the Value-of-Children Study. Paper presented at the 7th European Regional Congress of the International Association for Cross-Cultural Psychology 'New Scenarios for Cultural Interaction', San Sebastian, Spain.

Mishra, R.C./Mayer, B./Trommsdorff, G./Albert, I.,/Schwarz, B. (2005). The Value of Children in Urban and Rural India: Cultural

Background and Empirical Results. In: G. Trommsdorff/B. Nauck (Eds.). The Value of Children in Cross-Cultural Perspective. Case Studies from Eight Societies (pp. 143-170). Lengerich, Germany: Pabst Science.

Nauck, B. (2000). Social Capital and Intergenerational Transmission of Cultural Capital within a Regional Context. In: J. Bynner/R.K. Silbereisen (Eds.). Adversity and Challenge in Life in the New Germany and in England (pp. 212-238). Houndmills, UK: Macmillan.

Nauck, B. (2005). Changing Value of Children: An Action Theory of Fertility Behavior and Intergenerational Relationships in Cross-Cultural Comparison. In: W. Friedlmeier/P. Chakkarath/B. Schwarz (Eds.). Culture and Human Development. The Importance of Cross-Cultural Research for the Social Sciences (pp. 183-202). Hove, UK: Psychology Press.

Oyserman, D./Coon, H.M./Kemmelmeier, M. (2002). Rethinking Individualism and Collectivism: Evaluation of Theoretical Assumptions and Meta-Analyses. In: Psychological Bulletin, 128, 3-72.

Palmore, E.B./Maeda, D. (1985). The Honorable Elders Revisited (Otoshiyori saikô). Durham, NC: Duke University Press.

Rothbaum, F./Morelli, G. (2005). Attachment and Culture: Bridging Relativism and Universalism. In: W. Friedlmeier/P. Chakkarath/B. Schwarz (Eds.). Culture and Human Development. The Importance of Cross-Cultural Research for the Social Sciences (pp. 99-123). Hove, UK: Psychology Press.

Rothbaum, F./Pott, M./Azuma, H./Miyake, K./Weisz, J. (2000). The Development of Close Relationships in Japan and the United States: Paths of Symbiotic Harmony and Generative Tension. In: Child Development, 71, 1121-1142.

Rothbaum, F./Trommsdorff, G. (in press). Do Roots and Wings Complement or Oppose one Another? The Socialization of Relatedness and Autonomy in Cultural Context. In: J. E. Grusec/P. Hastings (Eds.). The Handbook of Socialization. New York: The Guilford Press.

Rothbaum, F./Weisz, J./Pott, M./Miyake, K./Morelli, G. (2000). Attachment and Culture: Security in the United States and Japan. In: American Psychologist, 55, 1093-1104.

Schwartz, S.H. (1992). Universals in the Content and Structure of Values: Theoretical Advances and Empirical Tests in 20 Countries. In: M.P. Zanna (Ed.). Advances in Experimental Social Psychology (Vol. 25, pp. 1-65). San Diego, CA: Academic Press.

Schwartz, S.H. (2004). Mapping and Interpreting Cultural Differences Around the World. In: H. Vinken/J. Soeters/P. Ester (Eds.). Comparing Cultures: Dimensions of Culture in a Comparative Perspective (pp. 43-73). Leiden, The Netherlands: Brill Academic Publishers.

Schwartz, S.H./Bilsky, W. (1990). Toward a Theory of the Universal Content and Structure of Values: Extensions and Cross-Cultural Replications. In: Journal of Personality & Social Psychology, 58, 878-891.

Schwarz, B./Chakkarath, P./Trommsdorff, G./Schwenk, O./Nauck, B. (2001). Report on Selected Instruments of the Value of Children (Main study). Unpublished manuscript, University of Konstanz, Konstanz, Germany.

Schwarz, B./Schäfermeier, E./Trommsdorff, G. (2005). The Relationships Between Value Orientation, Child-Rearing Goals, and Child-Rearing Behavior: A Comparison of Korean and German Mothers. In: W. Friedlmeier/P. Chakkarath/B. Schwarz (Eds.). Culture and Human Development: The Importance of Cross-Cultural Research to the Social Sciences (pp. 203-230). Hove, UK: Psychology Press.

Schwarz, B./Trommsdorff, G. (in press). Reciprocity in Intergenerational Support: A Comparison of Korean, Chinese, and German Adult Daughters. Current Sociology.

Schwarz, B./Trommsdorff, G./Kim, U./Park, Y.-S. (in press). Intergenerational Support: A Comparison of Women from the Republic of Korea and Germany. In: Current Sociology.

Stevenson, H.W./Zusho, A. (2002). Adolescence in China and Japan: Adapting to a Changing Environment. In: B.B. Brown, R.W. Larson/T. S. Saraswathi (Eds.). The World's Youth: Adolescence in Eight Regions of the Globe (pp. 141-170). Cambridge, MA: Cambridge University Press.

Super, C.M./Harkness, S. (1997). The Cultural Structuring of Child Development. In: J.W. Berry/P.R. Dasen/T.S. Saraswathi (Eds.). Handbook of Cross-Cultural Psychology, Vol. 2. Basic Processes and Human Development (2nd ed., pp. 1-39). Boston: Allyn & Bacon.

Triandis, H.C. (1995). Individualism & Collectivism. Boulder, CO: Westview Press.

Trommsdorff, G. (2001). Eltern-Kind-Beziehungen aus kulturvergleichender Sicht [Parent-Child Relations from a Cross-Cultural Perspective]. In: S. Walper/R. Pekrun (Eds.). Familie und Entwicklung: Aktuelle Perspektiven der Familienpsychologie (pp. 36-62). Göttingen, Germany: Hogrefe.

Trommsdorff, G. (in press a). Entwicklung im kulturellen Kontext [Development in a Cross-Cultural Context]. In: G. Trommsdorff/H.-J.

Kornadt (Eds.). Enzyklopädie der Psychologie: Themenbereich C. Theorie und Forschung: Serie VII. Kulturvergleichende Psychologie: Band 2. Kulturelle Determinanten des Erlebens und Verhaltens. Göttingen, Germany: Hogrefe.

Trommsdorff, G. (in press b). Intergenerational Relations and Cultural Transmission. In: U. Schönpflug (Ed.). Perspectives on Cultural Transmission. Oxford, UK: Oxford University Press.

Trommsdorff, G. (in press c). Parent-Child Relations Over the Life-Span. A Cross-Cultural Perspective. In: K.H. Rubin/O.B. Chung (Eds.). Parenting Beliefs, Behaviors, and Parent-Child Relations. A Cross-Cultural Perspective. New York: Psychology Press.

Trommsdorff, G./Dasen, P.R. (2001). Cross-Cultural Study of Education. In: N.J. Smelser/P.B. Baltes (Eds.). International Encyclopedia of the Social and Behavioral Sciences (pp. 3003-3007). Oxford, UK: Elsevier.

Trommsdorff, G./Friedlmeier, W. (2004). Zum Verhältnis zwischen Kultur und Individuum aus der Perspektive der kulturvergleichenden Psychologie [The Relation Between Culture and Individual from the Perspective of Cross-Cultural Psychology]. In: A. Assmann, U. Gaier/G. Trommsdorff (Eds.). Positionen der Kulturanthropologie (pp. 358-386). Frankfurt a. M., Germany: Suhrkamp.

Trommsdorff, G./Kornadt, H.-J. (2003). Parent-Child Relations in Cross-Cultural Perspective. In: L. Kuczynski (Ed.). Handbook of Dynamics in Parent-Child Relations (pp. 271-306). Thousand Oaks, CA: Sage.

Trommsdorff, G./Mayer, B./Albert, I. (2004). Dimensions of Culture in Intra-Cultural Comparisons: Individualism/Collectivism and Family-Related Values in Three Generations. In: H. Vinken/J. Soeters/P. Ester (Eds.). Comparing Cultures: Dimensions of Culture in a Comparative Perspective (pp. 157-184). Leiden, The Netherlands: Brill Academic Publishers.

Trommsdorff, G./Nauck, B. (2005a). Parenting and Social Demographics. Manuscript submitted for Parenting: Science and Practice.

Trommsdorff, G./Nauck, B. (Eds.). (2005b). The Value of Children in Cross-Cultural Perspective. Case Studies from Eight Societies. Lengerich, Germany: Pabst Sciences.

Trommsdorff, G./Schwarz, B. (in press). The "Intergenerational Stake Hypothesis" in Indonesia and Germany: Adult Daughters' and their Mothers' Perception of their Relationship. Current Sociology.

Trommsdorff, G./Zheng, G./Tardif, T. (2002). Value of Children and Intergenerational Relations in Cultural Context. In: P. Boski/F.J.R. van de Vijver/A.M. Chodynicka (Eds.). New Directions in Cross-

Cultural Psychology. Selected papers from the Fifteenth International Conference of the International Association for Cross-Cultural Psychology (pp. 581-601). Warszawa, Poland: Polish Psychological Association.

United Nations. Department of Economic and Social Affairs. Population Division. (2005). World Population Prospect, the 2004 Revision: Highlights. (ESP/P/WP/.193). New York: United Nations.

Valsiner, J. (Ed.). (1988). Parental Cognition and Adult-Child Interaction. Stamford, CT: Ablex Publishing.

Wang, Q./Hsueh, Y. (2000). Parent-Child Interdependence in Chinese families: Change and Continuity. In: C. Violato/E. Oddone-Paolucci/M. Genuis (Eds.). The Changing Family and Child Development (pp. 60-69). Aldershot, UK: Ashgate.

Whiting, B.B./Whiting, J.W.M. (1975). Children of Six Cultures: A Psycho-Cultural Analysis. Cambridge, MA: Harvard University Press.

Ying, Y.W./Coombs, M./Lee, P.A. (1999). Family Intergenerational Relationship of Asian American Adolescents. In: Cultural Diversity and Ethnic Minority Psychology, 5, 350-363.

Zarit, S.H./Eggebeen, D.J. (2002). Parent-Child Relationships in Adulthood and Later Years. In: M.H. Bornstein (Ed.). Handbook of Parenting, Vol. 5. Practical Issues in Parenting (2nd ed., pp. 135-161). Mahwah, NJ: Erlbaum.

DEVELOPMENT AS ENCULTURATION AND ACTIVE FORMATION REVISITED

Culture in Developmental Psychology

Cultural contexts form human development and they are, in turn, shaped and modulated by subjects in development. Therefore, it is hardly surprising that the concept of culture plays such an important theoretical, methodological, and empirical role in developmental psychology (in a large body of work, these are some exemplary publications: Berry, Dasen and Saraswathi [1997], Friedlmeier, Chakkarath and Schwarz [2005], the special issue of Human Development, 45, 4 [2002], Keller and Eckensberger [1998], Lonner, Dinnel, Hayes and Sattler [2002, Units 11 and 12], Oerter [2002], Rogoff [2003], Saraswathi [2003], Stigler, Shweder and Herdt [1990], Trommsdorff [2003], Valsiner [2000]).

The nexus of culture and development comes into focus from rather different perspectives and is approached with heterogeneous (in part complementary, in part contradictory) targets in mind. There are at least six areas of scholarly interest that can be identified in this context and that I would like to recall at this point: enculturation from a phylogenetic perspective; enculturation from an ontogenetic perspective; development as acculturation; developmental processes from a cross-cultural perspective; culturally specific developmental processes; development of "high-cultural" forms of action, experience, and thought.

In each of these areas it is necessary to concentrate on the explanation and clarification of the dialectical interrelation between development, subjects, and culture. And they are all likely to profit in one way or another from action-theoretical models, without which these interrelationships cannot be analyzed. In the following essay, I will develop an action-theoretical proposal that will explicate development as enculturation and active formation. This proposal will not only enable us to ask important questions concerning an action and cultural psychology of ontogenesis, but will also allow us to further work on them in theoretically constructive and profitable ways.

In a first step, I will discuss work that has been conducted in developmental psychology and that paid particular attention to intentional action. I will mainly deal with recent revisions of a "strong" model of intentional action. I will then bring into play substantial extensions of an action-theoretical idiom, concentrating on "spelling out" this idiom for the purpose of a culturally reflexive developmental psychology. Taking the developmental psychology of the construction of historical meaning as an example, I will demonstrate how such a spelling out operates, thus exposing the potential of an actional paradigm of development *beyond* a model of merely intentional action. Following this line of argument, I will close by introducing suggestions for an ontogenetic reconstruction of rule-governed action.

The Actional Paradigm of Development

Its rich tradition in psychology notwithstanding, the action theory approach to psychology, as represented for example by Jean Piaget's genetic structuralism, Lev S. Vygotsky's sociohistorical approach to psychology, Alexej N. Leontiev's activity theory, and George Herbert Mead's social psychology, was marginalized for many decades. This situation did not change until the cognitive turn when psychology as the study of action became an attractive enterprise. Commonly, the publication of Miller, Galanter, and Pribram (1960) is acknowledged as the starting point of this turn; in the German-speaking context, the works of Groeben and Scheele (1977) as well as Werbik (1978) are of particular significance.[1]

With a slight delay, action-theoretical thought also entered the realm of developmental psychology. This was brought about by the formula of children and youth, or more generally, of individuals as the "producers" of their own development, a formula that was as influential as it was bold and daring (Lerner 1982, Lerner and Busch-Rossnagel 1981). Other, similarly short formulas for the action-theoretical program were provided

---

1 Even decidedly psychologically oriented action theories profit from the relevant discourses of neighboring disciplines, most of all, but not exclusively from analytical philosophy (cf. Greve [1994] and Straub [1999a: 7-162]), which is why it always pays to look at multi-, inter-, and transdisciplinary publications (Hans Lenk's four-volume Handlungstheorien Interdisziplinär [1978-84] is still of great significance; for a view of more recent debates see the anthology edited by Straub and Werbik [1999]).

by Silbereisen, who talked about "self-development through action", and Hurrelmann, who considers "the subject that recognizes and actively works through problems" the starting point of his theory (quoted in Fend 2001: 209). Located at the center of this program is a concept of action that strictly binds it to means, purposes, and goals: human subjects intend to achieve a certain goal, believe that they can only achieve it if they engage in specific actions, and hence, become active and do whatever they deem necessary to do. This constitutes the core of the Aristotelian practical syllogism which, of course, can be complicated in many different ways.

One of the problems of this "early" version of the actional paradigm was that, to a certain extent, it suggested an omnipotent subject. Descriptions and explanations of actions that did not require recourse to intentionality, i.e., actions that are constituted or governed by rules, slipped the attention of many studies, to say nothing of the challenges and temptations constituted by the body and the unconscious, by the contingency, situatedness, and creativity of actions, and the unavailable aspects of our existence and development. In hindsight, this stage of disciplinary development may be considered an (understandable) overreaction to the behavioristic elimination of the intentional. But those days are definitely past. Even the arbiters of an actional paradigm of development relinquished the idea that a "strong" concept of intentional action can serve as a guiding principle. In this context, it is worthwhile to look more closely into a more recent conceptual proposal.

In addition to (comparatively short) comments on the polyvalence of action and on action constituted and governed by rules, Brandtstädter (2001; see also Kölbl 2003) mainly discusses intentional action. He differentiates between pre-, peri-, and contraintentional aspects of action (see also Brandtstädter and Greve 1999). These aspects allow a theoretical model of intentional action that is more adequate to the life-world (*Lebenswelt*).

Preintentional aspects: These aspects concern psychic processes such as emotions, which "[entail] intentional attitudes without being intentionally produced themselves" (Brandtstädter 2001: 132). Brandtstädter continues: "Strictly speaking, the intention to produce a certain idea already implies this very idea (as G.Ch. Lichtenberg aptly observed in his aphorisms, 'some people *get* an idea while others are *struck* by it [...] One does not say, I gave myself to an idea [...]'). Paradoxically, it is exactly those mental states in which we essentially experience ourselves as a person—our beliefs, insights, and creative ideas—whose *Aktualgenese* we cannot steer intentionally" (ibid.: 133).

Periintentional aspects: These aspects describe motivations for action that are focused on intentional consequences, fully accepting the occurrence of expected side effects. "Self-damaging effects can be easily included in intentional actions as periintentional elements. [...] This is particularly well-illustrated in a phenomenon such as *self-handicapping* [...]. A student who takes time off and embarks on a trip instead of preparing for an upcoming exam reduces his or her chances of passing the exam but can easily justify a failure, while a possible success under those self-produced difficult circumstances may count as a sign of special competence. That which is accepted as a side effect of one's own actions may contain a set of motivations that one doesn't even admit to oneself or which are not explicitly conscious" (ibid.: 130).

Contraintentional aspects: These aspects of action evolve from the opacity of action contexts in which we may conduct an action that produces effects that are diametrically opposed to our intentions. "Gavrilo Princip [the assassin of the Archduke of Austria, C.K.] pulls the trigger. The result, or rather, a complex bundle of results whose individual folds cannot be easily differentiated from each other is World War I" (ibid.: 126).

With this model, Brandtstädter modifies the "original" action perspective. It involves, if you will, a decentralization of the actor, which feeds into the Freudian sentence of the Ego who is not the master in his own house (for an overview of the history as well as of the state of the art of the actional paradigm of developmental psychology see Brandtstädter [1998] and Brandtstädter and Lerner [1999]). As important and as interesting as these modifications of the intentional action model are, we do not have to stop here but can go further.

Action and Cultural Psychology of Ontogenesis

The proposal outlined above is of special interest because—in terms of an actional paradigm of *development*—it investigates the ontogenesis of a complex concept of intentional action. This is done in two ways: On the one hand, the model reconstructs the ontogenesis of the ability to engage in intentional action. On the other hand, development is analyzed as the result of intentional action. Brandtstädter (2001: Ch. 1) aptly describes this project as an "action psychology of ontogenesis". The action-theoretically oriented, explanative work of the scientist is as much part of this project as the ontogenetic reconstructions of descriptions and explanations of actions provided by the examinees themselves. In addition, this action psychology of ontogenesis is fashioned as a psychology covering the entire life-span. The author systematizes knowledge that already exists in the field of developmental psychology; and he presents the results of his own theoretical modelings and empirical investigations. He covers a wide theoretical range: drawing for example on Piaget, Brandtstädter reconstructs the trajectories of intentional action during childhood; he underlines the emergence of the category of the future during adolescence as a central constituent of intentional self-development; and with great detail he introduces a model for the description and explanation of "securing personal continuity and identity during the course of one's life" (ibid.: Ch. 6), whose descriptive and explanative value is of particular pertinence for the analysis of adulthood and old age. This model of assimilation, accommodation, and immunization describes and explains processes of eliminating discrepancies between actual and desired trajectories of development, and of shielding one's own self-esteem and self-continuity against evidence that is discrepant with one's self-image.

There are two more things that need to be pointed out here.

1. In accordance with other authors (Boesch 1991, Eckensberger 1991), Brandtstädter understands the triad of development, action, and culture as being in a state of close, mutually constitutive interdependence (see also Brandtstädter 1997): Culture creates possibilities *and* limits for action and development. Here, development is conceptualized as both the condition of action and the result of the subject's active interventions. After all, culture is not static but a product of collective action, and hence, always subject to change. Therefore, development is always enculturation: the developing subject can only survive in a given culture by appropriating cultural constraints and affordances.

2. Given the interdependence of development, action, and culture, it seems obvious that development can be explicated as active formation through recourse to cultural factors. And that is what Brandtstädter does (2001, 2006); he is also interested in "subpersonal mechanisms" as explanative factors (Brandtstädter 2001: 134). In what follows, cultural (i.e., extra-, trans-, or interpersonal) factors will come into prominence as instruments of explanation.

An action *and cultural psychology* of ontogenesis can be enriched by means of recent extensions of the action-theoretical idiom, as has been done from the perspective of phenomenology (Waldenfels 1999), sociology/social philosophy (Joas 1996), and most significantly from the perspective of cultural psychology (Straub 1999a). In light of these extensions, other types of action move into the center of scholarly interests and supplement investigations into intentional action, thus further complicating previous conceptualizations of action. I am particularly thinking of action governed and constituted by rules and regulated by norms, but also of action as and in history/stories (for a detailed view of this, see Straub 1999a: 56-162, who I will discuss in more detail below[2]; see also Straub 1999b; 2001a: 153pp; 2005a; Boesch and Straub 2006). These types and models of action each require descriptions and explanations of their own, and can neither be reduced to an intentionalist nor to a covering-law model of explanation.

A number of examples and annotations will illustrate what is meant by these different types of action: playing chess is an action constituted by rules, stopping at a red light is governed by rules, greeting an acquaintance is regulated by norms. To describe and explain an action *as* a story means to describe its development in time. Playing chess, stopping at a red light, and greeting an acquaintance are actions that can be told as stories with a beginning, a middle, and an end. To act *in* history/stories means that a certain type of action can only be understood in the context of other stories or of history, i.e., in the context of a specific historical context. The example mentioned above of Gavrilo Princip pulling the trigger may serve as an example of a type of action which, with the help of the extended model, could not only be described and explained from the perspective of contraintentionality and of the "complex bundle of results whose individual folds cannot be easily differentiated from each other", it would also make it possible to address the question of *how the pulling of the trigger came about*. Answering this question would involve a narrative description and explanation in which the "personal" story of the assassin as well as the larger historical context unfold, constituting a relationship between the two. Of course, this model is also of use for less spectacular, but, from a psychological perspective, equally interesting actions and occurrences. Think, for example, of the narrative reconstruction of a failed exam, of being committed to a psychiatric ward, the loss of a close relative, the extension of a couple's dyad upon the birth of a child, an "identity crisis", the transition to retirement, etc., etc. (all these experiences are framed by stories covering the time before and after).[3] It is important to note that stories enable the processing of contingency. In the act of narration, events that could have happened *in one way or another*, or, in other words, were contingent, are integrated into an intelligible structure, thus becoming understandable. Such events are not pro-

---

2   I am not concerned with a complete "import" of a complex argument of one or several works but rather with a selective discussion of major analytic results and their application in another context.

3   The last examples on the list indicate that the narrative model is also of interest for "classic" problems in developmental psychology.

duced intentionally—they are occurrences, no matter whether they are bad or good.

In the current context, the differentiation of the concept of action is of special interest because it now seems possible to apply what Brandtstädter developed for intentional action to other types of action as well—i.e., a cultural and action psychology of ontogenesis. However, the analysis would no longer be limited to the psychological structure of intentional action and its "interconnection" with development, but could be extended not only to the structure of action regulated by norms, governed by rules, and constituted by rules, but also to action as and in history/stories, as well as to the effect these aspects have on the developing subject. It is also important to pay attention here to the explanative strategies of the scientist as well as to the ontogenetic reconstructions of the descriptions and explanations of actions provided by the examinees. Basically, this allows us to follow Brandtstädter and systematize the existing knowledge of developmental psychology, to develop additional theoretical models, and to conduct corresponding empirical investigations. Taking the developmental psychology of the construction of historical meaning as an example, I will sketch out the effectiveness of the narrative model in a cultural and action psychology of ontogenesis. In doing so, I wish to contribute to the project of correcting the "undynamic and ahistoric image" of action analysis in psychology (Brandtstädter 2001: 122). This will include a few brief comments on the ontogenesis of rule-governed action.

Example: The Developmental Psychology of the Construction of Historical Meaning

All modes of constructing historical meaning share a common function: in more or less complex ways they relate the collectively significant past to the present and the future. As a function of the narrative model discussed here, this relationality will be understood as "acts of meaning" (Bruner 1990).[4] Historical narrative, historically mediated processes of identity formation, and historical thinking count as modes of constructing historical meaning (which, albeit not logically disjunct, are nevertheless accentually different from each other).

Just as mathematical and logical thinking, as well as moral judgment, are not only subjects of mathematics, logic, and moral philosophy, respectively, but are also investigated from psychological and genetic perspectives, processes of constructing historical meaning are not only of interest for the discipline of history but also for (developmental) psy-

---

4 Unlike German, English makes it possible to speak about "doing history".

chology (for theoretical foundations, methodological considerations, surveys of the current state of research, and for empirical analyses, see Billmann-Mahecha and Hausen 2005; Kölbl 2004a, 2004b, 2005; Kölbl and Straub 2001, 2003; Straub 2001b, 2005a, 2005b).

How can we now identify aspects of a developmental psychology of the construction of historical meaning that will make possible its employment in the project of an action and cultural psychology of ontogenesis?[5]

Methodological approach: Conducting open interviews that evoke telling historical narratives is one method for producing empirically sound and well-founded evidence of the development of the construction of historical meaning. Arthur Danto's (1980: 371p.) schematization of narrative explanation provides a loose frame for conducting interviews (see also Kölbl 2004a: 208pp.). This well-known schematization appears thus:

(A) x is F at t_1
(B) H happens with x at t_2
(C) x is G at t_3

In this formula, (A) and (C) function as the explanandum, and (B) as the explanans. In other words, this opens up a temporal frame that is marked by an origin and an end point and in which something—x—is different at time t_3 than at time t_1. In order to explain how and why x at t_1 is F but at t_3 is G, it becomes necessary to tell a story that explains the change by referring to one or several events at t_2. Following this framework, interviewees can be asked to first name and describe in some detail historical events, eras, figures, etc. (A). In a next step, they are asked whether the phenomena are of any relevance today, i.e., do they still exist (C)? And finally: How can we explain that something is the way it is today, whereas it used to be different in the past? This last question is supposed to generate a historical narrative in which (B) comes to the fore.

Genetic epistemology/Theory of mind: The method sketched above is one, but not the only approach that promises insights into the development of basic structures of the construction of historical meaning. The comparative analysis of historical narratives of adolescents allows for a formulation of a developmental hypothesis concerning the following issues (ibid.: 280-352): 1. differentiations of the concepts of time and his-

---

5   Of course there are other research areas in psychology that are indebted to a narrative model of action and that can be classified as part of an action and cultural psychology of ontogenesis. Most prominently, this is true for biography research which, in turn, is closely connected with a developmental psychology of the construction of historical meaning.

tory; 2. categories concerning the order of history; 3. concepts of historical development; 4. forms and foundations to explain the validity of historical statements; 5. modes of historical understanding and explanation.
If successfully applied, the ontogenetic reconstruction of the basic structures of the construction of historical meaning represented by these short
formulas opens up a view onto the constituents of a developing "theory
of history". Such a "theory of history" provides a frame of reference for
children and adolescents and helps them to describe and explain the actions of individual and collective actors. They do so by *narrating*, i.e., by
utilizing the narrative model of action and explanation (in whatever ru-
dimentary form). The ontogenetic elaboration of specific (cognitive)
conditions for the application of modes of constructing historical meaning can be seen as a genetic and epistemological venture which, in its
focus on actions of individual and collective historical actors, finds an
ally in the "theory of mind" approach.

Historically mediated identity formation: The construction of historical meaning is not just a matter of "theoretical and historiographical"
operations; it is also of a more personal concern for individuals (ibid.:
266-280). This is particularly true when someone is "entangled in history", as Wilhelm Schapp (1976) would formulate it, i.e., when an individual explicitly, or more often implicitly identifies with certain historical groups. Historically mediated processes of identity formation can be
studied in group discussions during which older German adolescents, for
example, present different but structurally similar narratives that demonstrate to what degree and how strongly their historically mediated identity was formed by the history of Nazi Germany. (Very often, children
and younger adolescents use "humanity" as a central reference point of
their historically mediated identity formation.) In these stories, a class
trip to Normandy or a visit to the concentration camp in Auschwitz unfold as narratives, which express an action in stories, with history providing the reference point. Yet these stories are, in turn, also embedded in
history: a class trip to Normandy may signify something different to the
persons involved, depending on whether the trip is made 40, 50, or 60
years after the end of World War II.

Explanative strategies: If, as just described, empirical material is collected and analyzed with an explanative intention, the researcher, for two
reasons, cannot help but take recourse to a narrative action model as
well:

1. Oftentimes, the stories presented by the subjects become significant and explicable only in relation to the larger history (a phenomenon
hinted at at the end of the previous section). The form and genesis of basic structures of the construction of historical meaning discussed above

in the section on "Genetic epistemology/Theory of mind" can also be understood better through recourse to history. It allows for the reconstruction of the individual development of such structures as an appropriation of a specifically modern, scientific form of constructing historical meaning. If, in addition to mobilizing these "macrosystemic" aspects that are linked to the historically evolved constitution of a society and refer to meaningful systems of signs, knowledge, and interpretation, it is also possible to uncover and display "microsystemic" processes of mediation in families, schools, and peer groups, then the conditions for a complex explanation, in which culture and psychology intersect, are fulfilled. Such an explanation focuses on exactly those aspects that are also addressed in the "latest" actional paradigm of development. However, a stronger focus on these aspects seems useful and promising because extra-, trans- and interpersonal "mechanisms", or, more precisely, processes of mediation "generate" development. However, the results of these mediations do not simply imprint themselves on the subject, but the subject appropriates them by way of creatively transforming what is culturally supplied.

2. The action expressed by the examinees as and in history/stories does not simply catch the researcher's eye. Rather, it requires interpretative work because such action becomes explicable only in the course of reconstructing constructions. If these reconstructions are successful, then they are intersubjectively understandable and become themselves transparent stories of stories, i.e., the action as and in history/stories is, as it were, "retold" by the researcher. Such "retellings" inevitably take a first-person perspective as their point of origin but must also transcend this very perspective. Otherwise they are deadlocked in paraphrase and will be devoid of any "explanative surplus". Ideally, such a surplus occurs if comparative analyses (see Straub 1999a: 201-326) are conducted by way of minimal and maximal contrasts on different levels (age, type of school, cultural background), and the collective systems of signs, knowledge, and interpretation mentioned above as well as the trans-, extra, and interpersonal processes of mediation can be linked with the explanandum in a meaningful way.

The construction of historical meaning and self-referentiality: With regard to the development of intentional action, Brandtstädter speaks of a "'self-referentiality' of ontogenesis" (2001: 207). How does "self-referentiality" come into play in the narrative model? Or put differently: Is there a feedback relationship between the (narratively) acting subject and his or her own development in the action as and in history/stories model? This question can be answered in the positive, for after all, we are always active creators of (hi)stories.[6] The developed ability to act as and in history/stories enables us to participate in the complex network of history/stories in which we are willy-nilly entangled, thereby, not only changing the network but also ourselves *and others*.[7] In this context it is necessary to not only acknowledge a way of dealing with oneself grounded in "instrumental" reason, but also something that might be called "narrative intelligence" (see Straub 2005a: 71-81, who develops this concept by drawing on Paul Ricœur and Jerome Bruner). Based on such "instrumental" reason, the subject becomes the object of its own intentional, active interventions. In contrast, a form of intelligence that can be called narrative makes it possible to "calculate" the "invasion" of contingency in the subject's development and, hence, the (partial) inaccessibility and impossibility to plan development. Yet as pointed out above, contingency can be worked on and modified in such a way that it assumes meaning and significance through narrative structure. "Narrative compels a reconception and a revision of structures of experiences and expectation. It reorganizes existing symbolic systems. From a psychological point of view, this is, in all essential aspects, a creative act. Narrative manages contingency; it adapts disruptions in order to be able to preserve an endangered orientation, or even restore a lost one. Narrative restitutes the order ruptured by change; it reconstructs it, creating a new order that assimilates this particular experience of novelty or surprise" (ibid.: 73). Or simply: "Narrative creates understanding" (ibid.). Narrative creates understanding in such a way that the position of actively producing one's own development (which suggests something like an image of the human subject as *homo faber*) needs to be complemented by something that Western philosophy described as a state of imperturbability or composure (*Gelassenheit*). Such a state does not imply a renunciation of an active formation of one's own development, but indicates an awareness of the possibility of the failure of such formative processes without falling into the trap of terror and hopelessness. Narrative also creates understanding in that it rehabilitates a sense of possibility: "Specifically historical consciousness and historical action exploit a space of potentiality first disclosed by the reflexive presentation of 'history'. In its 'posi-

---

6   It is important to note that the options to create one's own (hi)story are unevenly distributed within society. Moreover, the concept of development as active creation and formation—whether it is intentional action, action as and in history/stories or rule-governed action (which will be discussed in more detail below)—appears to be a thoroughly modern idea, which cannot at all lay claim to universal validity.

7   And others—the emphasis is necessary in view of an actional paradigm of development that tends to speak about individuals as the producers of their own development, thus running the risk of losing sight of the (more or less) significant social others.

tive' tendency, it looks for opportunities for freedom of action that are only first created by a specific kind of temporalization of reality" (ibid: 75).

Applied to our example of a developmental psychology of the construction of historical meaning, this suggests that the developing subject uses past collective experiences and aspects of a collectively significant past to develop certain expectations which, in turn, guide future actions in history/stories. Narrative symbolizations of past experiences are of consequence for present and future actions, and these actions, in turn, open or close developmental paths. This is true even when one mistrusts the dictum of "history as teacher". It makes a difference whether, for example, adolescents, drawing on the history of Nazi Germany, define their historically mediated identities as the descendants of a "nation of perpetrators" or whether they "take responsibility for the past" without constructing a continuity of collective guilt, whether they are indifferent to Germany's Nazi past or whether they, more or less openly, identify with some aspects of National Socialism.

Example: Rule-Governed Action—Jean Piaget's Children Playing Marbles

Finally, I will provide another example in support of my thesis that it is necessary and possible to extend the action and cultural psychology of ontogenesis, namely with regard to rule-governed action. Following Brandtstädter, who draws on classic works in developmental psychology for his ontogenetic reconstruction of intentional action, I will base my argument on Jean Piaget's study *Le jugement moral chez l'enfant* (*The Moral Judgment of the Child*), first published in 1932.[8] As is commonly known, Piaget was not only concerned with the moral judgment of the child in the strict sense of the word, but also with the development of a sense of rules and regulations as well as the practice that follows from them. This is exactly why his study becomes interesting in the current context. His reconstructions are based on the example of children playing marbles.

With regard to a practice of rules, Piaget develops the following stages (1983: 38p.): 1. In the first, purely motoric and individual stage, the child develops ritual schemata. Since, however, the play in this stage remains individual, Piaget speaks of *motoric rules*. 2. In the second stage the child receives external rules and imitates the example of others. This is either done alone or with others. Yet because the child does not at-

---

8   Quotations will be translated from the German edition "Das moralische Urteil beim Kinde" (1983).

tempt to enter a competition with others, this stage can be called *egocentric*. Even playing with others, the child remains self-centered. 3. During the third stage, the child *begins to cooperate* with others. By now children are interested in standardizing and controlling rules. However, these rules are still subject to great variation. 4. In the fourth stage, *rules are codified*. From now on, all participants are familiar with the entire body of rules and regulations governing the game of marbles, including all kinds of possible and impossible variations.

For the development of a sense of rules and regulations Piaget identifies three stages, basically covering the evolution from heteronomy to autonomy. The key difference between a lower and a higher developed sense of rules lies in the idea of rules as "sacrosanct", "immutable", and "everlasting" versus a firm belief in rules as mutable and negotiable. The latter approach is noteworthy insofar as it marks a point of convergence of a sense of rules with a *modern* sense of history (see Kölbl 2005): something is different today than it was yesterday, and it can change yet again in the future. The rules of the game of marbles are always subject to contingency. You can play the game one way or another. Or, as Piaget demonstrates in one of the interviews he conducted: "'And what about you, could you come up with a new rule?'—'*Oh yes ...(he thinks) we could play with our feet.*'—'Would that be right?'—'*I don't know, I just said that.*' —'And if you showed it to the others, do you think it would work then?'—'*That would work. Someone else wants to try it, too. Others don't, good heavens!* [...]'—'And if everyone would play like you?'—'*Then it would be a rule just like any other rule*'" (Piaget 1983: 85p.).This convergence indicates that in both cases the appropriation of important structural characteristics of modern societies—mutability and negotiability, contingency—is crucial for development.

If one accepts that rule-governed action essentially depends on a sense of mutability and negotiability as well as on cooperation and collective codification of rules, then it stands to reason that this type of action also involves a self-referentiality of ontogenesis. Once a sense and a practice of rules are in place, the narrower and the wider contexts in which rules that shape one's own development are operative (in peer groups and groups of friends, in the family and in partnerships, in schools and on the job), can be actively formed. One way to do so is through negotiations, with negotiations being (at least partially) subject to rules. Again, it is necessary to note that the possibilities for participating in these formative processes are unevenly distributed.

Piaget's ontogenetic reconstructions no doubt reach their limits where the concern is no longer with explicit rules that govern our actions but with implicit rules that cannot easily become a subject of discourse, are not easily mutable and negotiable, and cannot be codified in a more or less egalitarian process. Such implicit rules are by no means less important for our actions than explicit rules, and from a psychological perspective, they constitute the more interesting and often more burning issues for those involved[9] (for an instructive discussion of the role of implicit or procedural knowledge in the context of a "post-cognitivistic" psychology, see Zielke 2004).

At this point, I want to mention that there are valuable, empirical studies on the structure of a sense and a practice of such implicit rules that are subject to experience. Drawing on the research program on "Subjective Theories" and on biographical interviews conducted with students and managers who spent a longer term in Taiwan, Weidemann (2001, 2004) analyzed how and under which circumstances her research partners developed an adequate, rule-governed practice as well as an understanding of the concept of "face" that is so central in many Asian cultures and operates implicitly. She also investigated how and to what extent the ability or inability to understand this concept shaped the further development of the interviewees. Studies like Weidemann's, which do not have to be restricted to foreign culture contexts or groups of adults, promise important new insights for an action and cultural psychology of ontogenesis that includes the discussion of rule-governed action.

Conclusion

This essay has been concerned with an extension of an action and cultural psychology of ontogenesis to include types of action beyond the model of intentionality as well as beyond a model that is qualified or "opened up" by emphasizing pre-, peri-, and contraintentional aspects of action. The models of action as and in history/stories and of rule-governed action served as illustrations. The discussion of action as and in history/stories elaborated the thesis in a more detailed manner, using a developmental psychology of the construction of historical meaning as an example. In particular, I made reference to the following levels: methodological approach, genetic epistemology/theory of mind, historically mediated identity formation, and explanative strategies as well as the construction of historical meaning and self-referentiality. For rule-governed action I provided suggestions based on Piaget's classic work on

---

9   This is particularly relevant in practical psychology: the skills of therapists, counselors, mediators, and trainers manifest themselves in situations when perceived or real violations of rules that guide actions are not out in the open but need to be reconstructed in a more or less tedious process.

the moral judgment of the child. If this article has uncovered unused potentials of a culturally reflexive developmental psychology, it has served its modest purpose.

References

Berry, J.W./Dasen, P.R./Saraswathi, T.S. (Eds.) (1997). Handbook of Cross-Cultural Psychology. Volume 2: Basic Processes and Human Development. Boston, London, Toronto, Sydney, Tokyo, Singapore: Allyn and Bacon.

Billmann-Mahecha, E./Hausen, M. (2005). Empirical Psychological Approaches to the Historical Consciousness of Children. In: J. Straub (Ed.). Narration, Identity, and Historical Consciousness (pp. 163-186). New York, Oxford: Berghahn.

Boesch, E.E. (1991). Symbolic Action Theory and Cultural Psychology. Berlin, Heidelberg, New York: Springer.

Boesch, E.E./Straub, J. (2006). Kulturpsychologie. Prinzipien, Orientierungen, Konzeptionen. In: H.-J. Kornadt/G. Trommsdorff (Eds.). Enzyklopädie der Psychologie, Themenbereich C. Theorie und Forschung. Serie VII: Kulturvergleichende Psychologie. Band 1: Theorien und Methoden kulturvergleichender Psychologie. Göttingen: Hogrefe (in press).

Brandtstädter, J. (1997). Action, Culture and Development: Points of Convergence. In: Culture & Psychology, 3, 335-352.

Brandtstädter, J. (1998). Action Perspectives on Human Development. In: R.M. Lerner (Ed.). Handbook of Child Psychology. Volume 1: Theoretical Models of Human Development (pp. 807-863). New York: John Wiley & Sons.

Brandtstädter, J. (2001). Entwicklung—Intentionalität—Handeln. Stuttgart: Kohlhammer.

Brandtstädter, J. (2006). Agency in Developmental Settings of Modernity: The Dialectics of Commitment and Disengagement. In: Handlung, Kultur, Interpretation. Zeitschrift für Sozial- und Kulturwissenschaften, 15 (in press).

Brandtstädter, J./Greve, W. (1999). Intentionale und nichtintentionale Aspekte des Handelns. In: J. Straub/H. Werbik (Eds.). Handlungstheorie. Begriff und Erklärung des Handelns im interdisziplinären Diskurs (pp. 185-212). Frankfurt/M.: Campus.

Brandtstädter, J./Lerner, R.M. (Eds.) (1999). Action and Self-Development. Theory and Research through the Life-Span. Thousand Oaks, CA: Sage.

Bruner, J. (1990). Acts of meaning. Cambridge, MA: Harvard University Press.

Danto, A.C. (1980 [1965]). Analytische Philosophie der Geschichte. Frankfurt/M.: Suhrkamp.

Eckensberger, L.H. (1991). On the Difficulties to Culturalize Psychology. Lecture at the "Symposium in Honour of Ernst E. Boesch, The Cultural Environment in Psychology", October 21st-24th, 1991. Saarbrücken: unpublished manuscript.

Fend, H. (2001). Entwicklungspsychologie des Jugendalters. Ein Lehrbuch für pädagogische und psychologische Berufe. Opladen: Leske + Budrich.

Friedlmeier, W./Chakkarath, P./Schwarz, B. (Eds.) (2005). Culture and Human Development. The Importance of Cross-Cultural Research to the Social Sciences. Hove: Psychology Press.

Greve, W. (1994). Handlungsklärung. Die psychologische Erklärung menschlichen Handelns. Bern: Huber.

Groeben, N./Scheele, B. (1977). Argumente für eine Psychologie des reflexiven Subjekts. Darmstadt: Steinkopff.

Human Development (2002). How can we Study Cultural Aspects of Human Development? 45, 4.

Joas, H. (1996 [1992]). The Creativity of Action. Chicago, Ill.: The University of Chicago Press.

Keller, H./Eckensberger, L.H. (1998). Kultur und Entwicklung. In: H. Keller (Ed.). Lehrbuch Entwicklungspsychologie (pp. 57-96). Bern, Göttingen, Toronto, Seattle: Hogrefe.

Kölbl, C. (2003). Das aktionale Entwicklungsparadigma jenseits subjektseitiger Allmachtsansprüche. Review essay on: J. Brandtstädter. Entwicklung—Intentionalität—Handeln. In: Handlung, Kultur, Interpretation. Zeitschrift für Sozial- und Kulturwissenschaften, 12, 181-189.

Kölbl, C. (2004a). Geschichtsbewußtsein im Jugendalter. Grundzüge einer Entwicklungspsychologie historischer Sinnbildung. Bielefeld: transcript.

Kölbl, C. (2004b). Zum Aufbau der historischen Welt bei Kindern. In: Journal für Psychologie, 12, 25-49.

Kölbl, C. (2005). Moral im Geschichtsbewusstsein. Theoretische Überlegungen und empirische Befunde als mögliche Anknüpfungspunkte für den Geschichtsunterricht in der Sekundarstufe I. In: D. Horster/ J. Oelkers (Eds.). Pädagogik und Ethik (pp. 235-257). Wiesbaden: VS Verlag für Sozialwissenschaften.

Kölbl, C./Straub, J. (2001). Historical Consciousness in Youth. Theoretical and Exemplary Empirical Analyses [118 paragraphs]. In: Fo-

510

rum Qualitative Sozialforschung / Forum: Qualitative Social Research [On-line Journal], 2 (3). Available at: http://www. qualitative-research.net/ fqs/fqs-eng.htm.

Kölbl, C./Straub, Jürgen (2003). Geschichtsbewusstsein als psychologischer Begriff. In: Journal für Psychologie, 11, 75-102.

Lenk, H. (1978-1984). Handlungstheorien interdisziplinär. Bände 1-4. München: Fink.

Lerner, R.M. (1982). Children and Adolescents as Producers of their own Development. In: Developmental Review, 2, 342-370.

Lerner, R.M./Busch-Rossnagel, N.A. (Eds.) (1981). Individuals as Producers of their Development: A Life-Span Perspective. New York: Academic Press.

Lonner, W.J./Dinnel, D.L./Hayes, S.A./Sattler, D.N. (Eds.) (2002). Online Readings in Psychology and Culture. Unit 11: Culture and Human Development: Infancy, Childhood and Adolescence. Unit 12: Culture and Development: Adulthood and Old Age. Center for Cross-Cultural Research. Western Washington University, Bellingham, Washington, U.S.A. Available at: www.ac.wwu.edu/~culture/readings.htm.

Miller, G.A./Galanter, E./Pribram, K.H. (1960). Plans and the Structure of Behavior. New York: Holt, Rinehart and Winston.

Oerter, R. (2002). Kultur, Ökologie und Entwicklung. In: R. Oerter/L. Montada (Eds.). Entwicklungspsychologie (pp. 72-104). Beltz, PVU: Weinheim.

Piaget, J. (1983 [1932]). Das moralische Urteil beim Kinde. Stuttgart: Klett-Cotta.

Rogoff, B. (2003). The Cultural Nature of Human Development. New York: Oxford University Press.

Saraswathi, T.S. (Ed.) (2003). Cross-Cultural Perspectives in Human Development. Theory, Research, and Applications. New Delhi: Sage.

Schapp, W. (1976 [1953]). In Geschichten verstrickt. Zum Sein von Mensch und Ding. Wiesbaden: Heymann.

Stigler, J.W./Shweder, R.A./Herdt, Gilbert (Eds.) (1990). Cultural Psychology. Essays on Comparative Human Development. Cambridge: Cambridge University Press.

Straub, J. (1999a). Handlung, Interpretation, Kritik. Grundzüge einer textwissenschaftlichen Handlungs- und Kulturpsychologie. Berlin, New York: de Gruyter.

Straub, J. (1999b). Narrative Handlungerklärungen im Licht einer pragmatisch-epistemischen Erklärungstheorie. In: J. Straub/H. Werbik

(Eds.). Handlungstheorie. Begriff und Erklärung des Handelns im interdisziplinären Diskurs (pp. 261-283). Frankfurt/M.: Campus.

Straub, J. (2001a). Psychologie und Kultur, Psychologie als Kulturwissenschaft. In: H. Appelsmeyer/E. Billmann-Mahecha (Eds.). Kulturwissenschaft. Felder einer prozeßorientierten wissenschaftlichen Praxis (pp. 125-167). Weilerswist: Velbrück.

Straub, J. (2001b). Temporale Orientierung und narrative Kompetenz. Zeit- und erzähltheoretische Grundlagen einer narrativen Psychologie biographischer und historischer Sinnbildung. In: J. Rüsen (Ed.). Geschichtsbewußtsein. Psychologische Grundlagen, Entwicklungskonzepte, empirische Befunde (pp. 15-44). Köln, Weimar, Wien: Böhlau.

Straub, J. (2005a): Telling Stories, Making History: Towards a Narrative Psychology of the Historical Construction of Meaning. In: J. Straub (Ed.). Narration, Identity, and Historical Consciousness (pp. 44-98). New York, Oxford: Berghahn.

Straub, J. (Ed.) (2005b): Narration, Identity, and Historical Consciousness. New York, Oxford: Berghahn.

Straub, J./Werbik, H. (Eds.) (1999). Handlungstheorie. Begriff und Erklärung des Handelns im interdisziplinären Diskurs. Frankfurt/M.: Campus.

Trommsdorff, G. (2003). Kulturvergleichende Entwicklungspsychologie. In: A. Thomas (Ed.). Kulturvergleichende Psychologie. Ein Lehrbuch (pp. 139-179). 2nd ed. Göttingen, Bern, Toronto, Seattle: Hogrefe.

Valsiner, J. (2000). Culture and Human Development. An Introduction. London, Thousand Oaks, New Delhi: Sage.

Waldenfels, B. (1999). Symbolik, Kreativität und Responsivität. Grundzüge einer Phänomenologie des Handelns. In: J. Straub/H. Werbik (Eds.). Handlungstheorie. Begriff und Erklärung des Handelns im interdisziplinären Diskurs (pp. 243-260). Frankfurt/M.: Campus.

Weidemann, D. (2001). Learning about 'Face'—'Subjective Theories' as a Construct in Analysing Intercultural Learning Processes of Germans in Taiwan. In: Forum Qualitative Sozialforschung / Forum: Qualitative Social Research [On-line Journal], 2(3). Available at: http://www.qualitative-research.net/fqs-texte/3-01/3-01weidemann-e.htm.

Weidemann, D. (2004). Interkulturelles Lernen. Erfahrungen mit dem chinesischen "Gesicht": Deutsche in Taiwan. Bielefeld: transcript.

Werbik, H. (1978). Handlungstheorien. Stuttgart: Kohlhammer.

Zielke, B. (2004). Kognition und soziale Praxis. Der soziale Konstruktionismus und die Perspektiven einer postkognitivistischen Psychologie. Bielefeld: transcript.

AUTHORS

Jacob A. v. Belzen graduated in social sciences, history, philosophy and sciences of religion. He is a professor of psychology at the University of Amsterdam, the Netherlands. Cultural psychology, mental health issues, psychohistory are among his research interests, as well as history and foundations of psychology and psychiatry. belzen@hum.uva.nl

Ernest E. Boesch is emeritus professor of psychology, University of the Saar, Saarbrücken, Germany. His former positions include the directorship of the UNESCO International Institute for Child Study in Bangkok, Thailand. Main areas of work and interest: cultural psychology and symbolic action theory.

Pierre R. Dasen is a professor of anthropology of education and cross-cultural psychology at the Faculty of Psychology and Education, University of Geneva, Switzerland. His research topics have included visual perception, the development of sensory-motor intelligence, the causes and effects of malnutrition, the development of concrete operations as a function of eco-cultural variables and daily activities, definitions of intelligence, number systems, and spatial orientation. His current interests are everyday cognition, informal education and parental ethnotheories. pierre.dasen@pse.unige.ch

Maria Lucia Duarte Pereira is a professor of social science in nursing and public health at the State University of Ceará, Fortaleza, Brazil. She is currently working on cross-cultural issues of infection and contagion, AIDS, and public health. mlduarte2fortalnet.com.br

Kenneth J. Gergen is Mustin professor of psychology at Swarthmore College, Pennsylvania, USA. Gergen's general research topics are social construction of knowledge, relational theory of action, therapy research, technology and society, and psychology and its historical context. kgergen1@swarthmore.edu

Rom Harré is distinguished research professor at the Department of Psychology, Georgetown University, Washington D. C., USA. Current research includes further work in positioning theory, the foundation of cognitive science, and semantic aspects of psychology of music. harre@georgetown.edu

Hede Helfrich-Hölter is a professor of psychology at the Faculty of Psychology, University of Hildesheim, Germany. Her general research topics are apperception and cognition as well as human reliability and mistakes and the comparison of culture. helfrich@rz.uni-hildesheim.de

Gustav Jahoda is emeritus professor at the Department of Psychology, University of Strathclyde, Glasgow, Scotland. His fields of research are the influence of culture on cognition and perception, social aspects of cognitive development, race and racism, culture theory in psychology and anthropology as well as history of psychology and anthropology. g.jahoda@strath.ac.uk

Carlos Kölbl is a researcher and lecturer at the Institute of Pedagogical Psychology, University of Hannover, Germany. His research interests include the ontogenesis of historical consciousness, sociohistorical psychology, intercultural topics in contexts of education, professional biographies of teachers, and qualitative methods.
koelbl@erz.uni-hannover.de

Hans-Dieter König is apl. professor at the Department of Sociology and Psychoanalytical Social Psychology, University of Frankfurt am Main, Germany. His fields of research are psychoanalysis and depth-hermeneutics, particularly in the context of cultural analysis.
mail@hd-koenig.de

Nicole Kronberger is assistant professor at the Department of Education and Psychology, University of Linz, Austria. Her research focus is on morality, public understanding of science (biotechnology), gender issues, and qualitative methodology. nicole.kronberger@jku.at

Wei-Lun Lee is associate professor at the Department of Clinical and Counselling Psychology, National Dong Hwa University, Taiwan. His areas of specialization include: phenomenological psychology, existential psychotherapy, psychological assessment in a life-world approach, and the development of an indigenized clinical psychology.
wllee@mail.ndhu.edu.tw

Ulrike Popp-Baier is a professor of psychology of religion at Utrecht University, the Netherlands, and associate professor of psychology at the University of Amsterdam, the Netherlands. Her research topics include theoretical psychology of religion and empirical research in religious studies. upopp@theo.uu.nl

Tatsuya Sato is associate professor at the Department of Psychology, Ritsumeikan University, Japan. His general interests are the history, theory and methodology of psychology. He is also interested in social and cultural aspects of human development. satot@lt.ritsumei.ac.jp

Robert Serpell is vice chancellor of the University of Zambia and former professor of applied developmental psychology at the University of Maryland, Baltimore County, USA. His research topics are developmental and cross-cultural psychology. serpell@umbc.edu

Patricia Simon works with the Department of Psychology, University of Regensburg, Germany. Her research interests are the psychology of cultural comparison and intercultural psychology as well as social psychology, especially the research about small groups. She is further interested in organizational psychology and methods of social psychology. patricia.simon@psychologie.uni-regensburg.de

Jürgen Straub is a professor at the Institute of Media Communication and Intercultural Communication, Chemnitz University of Technology, Germany. His fields of research include cultural psychology, intercultural communication and competence, violence in modern societies, action theory, identity, (personal and collective) memory, historical consciousness, narrative psychology, long-term psychosocial and cultural effects of the Shoah, migration research, and theory, methodology, and methods of qualitative social research. juergen.straub@phil.tu-chemnitz.de

Gisela Trommsdorff is a professor at the Department of Developmental Psychology and Cultural Comparison, University of Konstanz, Germany. Her general research topics are "Value-of-Children Studies" concerning the generational behaviors and relations between parents and their children. Besides she does research on the functions of emotions in development, and the process of pro-social actions. Further research activities include the cultural comparison of the conditions of socialisation during the development of pro-social and anti-social motivation. gisela.trommsdorff@uni-konstanz.de

José Valencia is a professor at the Department of Social Psychology and Methodology, University of the Basque Country, San Sebastián, Spain. His expertise is on the social psychology of language and culture, group and inter-group processes, political psychology, and social representation. pspvagaj@ss.ehu.es

Jaan Valsiner is a professor at the Department of Psychology, Clark University, Worcester, USA. His general interests include cultural organization of mental and affective processes in human development across the whole life-span. He is also interested in psychology's history as a resource of ideas for the contemporary advancement of the discipline, and in theoretical models of human development. jvalsiner@clarku.edu

Wolfgang Wagner is a professor at the Department of Social and Economic Psychology, University of Linz, Austria. His research interests are: Socially shared and distributed cognition, science and technology in society (STS), e.g. biotechnology, cultural psychology, cultural change, social representation and social construction, social cognitive science, discourse theory and media communication, evolutionary social psychology. w.wagner@jku.at

Jürg Wassmann is a professor of social anthropology and director of the Institute of Social Anthropology, University of Heidelberg, Germany. Wassmann's general research topics are cognitive anthropology, conceptions of person, space and time, with a regional focus on Oceania. juerg.wassmann@urz.uni-heidelberg.de

Doris Weidemann is a researcher and lecturer at the Institute of Media Communication and Intercultural Communication, Chemnitz University of Technology, Germany. Her research interests include the psychology of Chinese-German interactions, challenges of transnational research collaboration, and effects of international sojourns on families. doris.weidemann@phil.tu-chemnitz.de

Barbara Zielke is a researcher and lecturer in psychology, University of Erlangen-Nürnberg, Germany. Her general research topics are psychology and sociology of knowledge, psychology of the self, social constructionist psychology and qualitative methods; her current research is on intercultural communication in psychotherapy and counselling. barbara.zielke@phil.uni-erlangen.de